A HANDBOOK
on
LEVITICUS

The Handbooks in the **UBS Handbook Series** are in-depth commentaries providing valuable exegetical, historical, cultural, and linguistic information on the books of the Bible. They are prepared primarily to assist practicing Bible translators as they carry out the important task of putting God's Word into the many languages spoken in the world today. The text is discussed verse by verse and is accompanied by running text in at least one modern English translation.

Over the years church leaders and Bible readers have found the UBS Handbooks to be useful for their own study of the Scriptures. Many of the issues Bible translators must address when trying to communicate the Bible's message to modern readers are the ones Bible students must address when approaching the Bible text as part of their own private study and devotions.

The Handbooks will continue to be prepared primarily for translators, but we are confident that they will be useful to a wider audience, helping all who use them to gain a better understanding of the Bible message.

Helps for Translators

UBS Handbook Series:

A Handbook on . . .

Leviticus
the Book of Joshua
the Book of Ruth
the Book of Job
the Book of Psalms
Lamentations
the Book of Amos
the Books of Obadiah and Micah
the Book of Jonah
the Books of Nahum, Habakkuk,
    and Zephaniah
the Gospel of Matthew
the Gospel of Mark
the Gospel of Luke
the Gospel of John

the Acts of the Apostles
Paul's Letter to the Romans
Paul's First Letter to the Corinthi-
    ans
Paul's Letter to the Galatians
Paul's Letter to the Ephesians
Paul's Letter to the Philippians
Paul's Letters to the Colossians
    and to Philemon
Paul's Letters to the Thessalonians
the Letter to the Hebrews
the First Letter from Peter
the Letter from Jude and the
    Second Letter from Peter
the Letters of John
the Revelation to John

Guides:

A Translator's Guide to . . .

Selections from the First Five
    Books of the Old Testament
Selected Psalms
the Gospel of Mark
the Gospel of Luke
Paul's Second Letter to the Corin-
    thians

Paul's Letters to Timothy and to
    Titus
the Letters to James, Peter, and
    Jude
the Revelation to John

Technical Helps:

Old Testament Quotations in the
    New Testament
Short Bible Reference System
New Testament Index
The Theory and Practice of Trans-
    lation
Bible Index

Fauna and Flora of the Bible
Marginal Notes for the Old Testa-
    ment
Marginal Notes for the New Testa-
    ment
The Practice of Translating

A HANDBOOK ON

Leviticus

by René Péter-Contesse
and John Ellington

UBS Handbook Series

United Bible Societies
New York

Books in the series of **Helps for Translators** may be ordered from a national Bible Society, or from either of the following centers:

United Bible Societies
European Production Fund
W-7000 Stuttgart 80
Postfach 81 03 40
Germany

United Bible Societies
1865 Broadway
New York, New York 10023
U.S.A.

L.C. Cataloging-in-Publication Data

Péter-Contesse, René
  [Manuel du traducteur pour le livre du Lévitique. English]
  A handbook on Leviticus / by René Péter-Contesse and John Ellington.
      p.   cm. — (UBS handbook series) (UBS helps for translators)
  Includes bibliographical references and index.
  ISBN 0-8267-0110-8 : $9.95
  1. Bible. O.T. Leviticus—Translating. I. Ellington, John.
II. Title. III. Title: Leviticus. IV. Series. V. Series: UBS helps for translators.
[BS1255.5.P4713 1992]
222´.13077—dc20

92-20509
CIP

ABS-1992-300-1,050-EB-1-104588

Contents

Preface vii

Abbreviations Used in This Volume ix

Introduction: Translating Leviticus 1

I. Laws about sacrifices and offerings
   A. Instructions for the people
      Chapter 1 9
      Chapter 2 25
      Chapter 3 36
      Chapter 4 45
      Chapter 5 62

   B. Instructions for the priests
      Chapter 6 75
      Chapter 7 90

II. The responsibility of the priestly family
   A. Rules about ordaining priests and offering sacrifices
      Chapter 8 108
      Chapter 9 128

   B. Specific regulations concerning priests
      Chapter 10 140

III. Laws about ritual cleanness and uncleanness
      Chapter 11 155
      Chapter 12 176
      Chapter 13 181
      Chapter 14 206
      Chapter 15 228

IV. The Day of Atonement
      Chapter 16 240

CONTENTS

V. Holiness in life and worship
  A. Laws concerning holiness
    Chapter 17 262
    Chapter 18 270
    Chapter 19 283
    Chapter 20 301
    Chapter 21 314
    Chapter 22 326

  B. Laws about feasts, the tent, and the land
    Chapter 23 341
    Chapter 24 361
    Chapter 25 372

  C. Blessings and punishment
    Chapter 26 401

VI. Laws about gifts to the LORD
    Chapter 27 424

Bibliography 441

Glossary 445

Index 453

Diagrams and Outlines

Outline of Leviticus 2-3
Probable Arrangement of the Tent of the LORD's Presence 8
Division between "Holy" and "Common," "Clean" and "Unclean" 148
The Years of Rest and of Restoration 376

Illustrations

An Artist's Idea of the Tent of the LORD's Presence 7
An Altar with "Horns" 49
The Turban and Breastpiece 113
A Priest at the Altar of Incense 248

Lists

The Sacrifices in Leviticus 5
Names of Unclean Birds 162-163
Names of Clean Insects 165
Names of Unclean Animals 167-168

Preface

Several commentaries in the Helps for Translators series have already been translated into French from the English originals. This time, however, we have been able to reverse the procedure. The original version, *Manuel du traducteur pour le livre du Lévitique,* was published in 1985 with René Péter-Contesse as author. John Ellington has now adapted the material for the English version. It was not possible to make a direct translation, since many of the explanations and suggestions had to be rearranged and restated; not only does the Revised Standard Version (RSV) base of discussion present a different set of problems, but the sample texts from other English versions require their own kind of explanation. Yet the basic work was done by Péter-Contesse as the first author, and Ellington therefore could move through much of the same material in a more efficient manner than if he were the only author.

Leviticus deals with a vocabulary that touches much of the culture and the worship life of the community of Israel. Some translators may find it useful, therefore, to make Leviticus one of the first books they translate as they begin to deal with the Old Testament. The discourse structures encountered in a code of law are somewhat less complex than those of prophecy or of narrative, and therefore this Handbook does not display longer sections of text. Translators may refer to modern versions in languages they deal with, as they look for examples of paragraph division and other discourse markers. After a preliminary discussion of larger units of discourse, the individual short passages are then displayed in boldface and are discussed in detail. RSV serves as a base of discussion through which the authors explain the features and meaning of the ancient Hebrew text. The Today's English Version (TEV) then serves as the first of several models for demonstrating possible ways of expressing a functional equivalent of the Hebrew in the language of the translator. In the comments, words quoted from the RSV text under discussion are identified by underlined boldface, while words quoted from TEV are boldface and enclosed in quotation marks. Quotations from other versions are within quotation marks, as are quotations from RSV and TEV that are not from the verse being discussed.

Many translators possess the British edition of TEV. Handbooks are regularly based on the American edition as the original. However, in a number of places the British use of weights and measures according to the metric system will be important for determining local equivalents, and so both versions are shown in the biblical text, with the British metric equivalents marked off by square brackets.

The texts of the New Revised Standard Version and the Revised English Bible were available for consideration only during the last stages of the preparation of this Handbook. It was therefore no longer possible to make appropriate references to these two very useful versions, much to our regret.

This Handbook follows the tradition of the series by concentrating on exegetical matters that are of prime importance for translators, and it attempts to indicate possible solutions for translational problems that may arise because of language or culture. In this respect the Handbook attempts to deal with the full range of information important to translators. However, the authors do not attempt to provide help that other theologians and scholars may be seeking but which is not directly useful for the task of translating. It is assumed that such information is available elsewhere.

A limited Bibliography is included for the benefit of those who are interested in further study. Furthermore, a Glossary is provided that explains technical terms according to their usage in this volume. The translator may find it useful to read through the Glossary in order to become aware of the specialized way in which certain terms are used. An Index gives the location by page number of some of the important words and subjects discussed in the Handbook, especially where the Handbook provides the translator with help in rendering these concepts into the receptor language.

A special word of thanks goes to several groups of translators in the Africa region who worked through all or part of the draft for this Handbook and returned comments that were vital for making the material more suitable and useful for translators. The leaders of these groups include: The Rev. Don Slager; the Rev. Theodore Leidenfrost; Miss Barbara Runkel; and Mr. Phil Logan.

The editor of Helps for Translators is happy to receive comments from translators and others who use these books, so that future volumes may benefit and may better serve the needs of the readers.

Abbreviations Used in This Volume

General Abbreviations, Bible Texts, Versions, and Other Works Cited
(For details see Bibliography)

AT	American Translation	Mft	Moffatt
FFB	*Fauna and Flora of the Bible*	NAB	New American Bible
FRCL	French Common Language version	NASB	New American Standard Bible
GECL	German Common Language version	NEB	New English Bible
		NIV	New International Version
HOTTP	Hebrew Old Testament Text Project	NJB	New Jerusalem Bible
		NJV	New Jewish Version
JB	Jerusalem Bible	RSV	Revised Standard Version
KJV	King James Version	TEV	Today's English Version
LB	Living Bible	TOB	*Traduction œcuménique de la Bible*

Books of the Bible

Gen	Genesis	Psa	Psalms
Exo	Exodus	Pro	Proverbs
Lev	Leviticus	Isa	Isaiah
Num	Numbers	Jer	Jeremiah
Deut	Deuteronomy	Ezek	Ezekiel
Josh	Joshua	Hos	Hosea
1,2 Sam	1,2 Samuel	Matt	Matthew
1,2 Kgs	1,2 Kings	Rom	Romans
1,2 Chr	1,2 Chronicles	Gal	Galatians
Neh	Nehemiah	Heb	Hebrews

Translating Leviticus

Many modern readers feel ill at ease with the book of Leviticus. They think it is too difficult for the average person. It seems to be out of date and lacking in any real spiritual significance. The various rituals and regulations found in this book seem to have little to do with our modern situation. But this fear is unfounded. We often fear the unknown, and Leviticus is feared at least in part because it is not known. Yet as we grow more familiar with this book, we begin to feel more comfortable with it. Leviticus is like some people whom we may not like when we first meet them, but we find that the better we get to know them, the more we like them. Underneath the hard, external appearance we find a warm and lovable person.

Although the average lay person and even some pastors may keep their distance from the book of Leviticus, a Bible translator cannot avoid it unless he is to produce an incomplete Bible. Leviticus is not only unavoidable, it is essential to a proper understanding of other parts of Scripture. For example, the Letter to the Hebrews is very difficult to understand without the background of Leviticus. And we should not forget that when Christ summarized the Law in Matthew 22, he quoted Leviticus as containing the second most important commandment (Lev 19.18). This book also provides a foundation for the understanding of forgiveness (4.20,26,31,35, and others) and holiness (19.2,20,26, and others).

It is true, however, that there are many passages in this book that require a great deal of study, perseverance, reflection, and prayer before they can be properly understood and translated. Since some people involved in translating the Bible around the world have had little opportunity for advanced theological training, this volume is designed to help them with the difficult but important task of translating Leviticus. By using this Handbook it is hoped that they will be able to translate in such a way that the average reader or hearer will easily understand the meaning of this book. The book of Leviticus comes from a strange and ancient culture that is very different from those into which the Scriptures are being translated around the world today. Yet it has a message for people living today.

1. The Content of the Book

Leviticus is a legal document. Its ultimate authority is seen as God himself. In fact, fully 85% of the book is composed of orders from the Lord transmitted almost exclusively to Moses—for himself, for the priests, or for all the people of Israel. The rest is made up essentially of narrative chapters (8–10) and the thirty-seven occurrences of the formula "The LORD said to . . . ," which introduces the actual commands of the Lord.

The major sections of this book are: the commands of the Lord concerning sacrifice rituals (chapters 1–7); instructions about the priesthood (chapters 8–10); rules of purity (chapters 11–16); the behavior that is to be characteristic of a people

1

consecrated to a holy God (the so-called "Holiness Code" in chapters 17–26); and various vows and offerings (chapter 27). Some modern versions (such as the New Jerusalem Bible) provide two different levels of section headings to reflect more accurately the structure of the book. Major headings are placed at the beginning of chapters 1, 8, 11, and 17 in New English Bible (NEB), New American Bible (NAB), New Jerusalem Bible (NJB), and the American Translation (AT). NAB and AT also place a major heading at the beginning of chapter 27 to indicate that this supplementary chapter is not an integral part of the laws related to holiness in chapters 17–26.

The book contains a great deal of repetition, but it is highly organized. One way to outline the book is as follows:

I. Laws about sacrifices and offerings
    A. Instructions for the people

Sacrifices burned whole	1.1-17
Grain offerings	2.1-16
Fellowship offerings	3.1-17
Offerings for unintentional sins	4.1-5.13
Repayment offerings	5.14-6.7

    B. Instructions for the priests

Sacrifices burned whole	6.8-13
Grain offerings	6.14-23
Offerings for unintentional sins	6.24-30
Repayment offerings	7.1-10
Fellowship offerings	7.11-36
Summary of laws about sacrifices	7.37-38

II. The responsibility of the priestly family
    A. Rules about ordaining priests and offering sacrifices

The ceremony of ordination	8.1-36
The offering of sacrifices	9.1-24

    B. Specific regulations concerning priests

Two priests commit an unholy act	10.1-7
Strong drink forbidden to priests	10.8-11
What to do with food given to the priests	10.12-20

III. Laws about ritual cleanness and uncleanness

Animals that may be eaten	11.1-47
The purification of women after childbirth	12.1-8
Laws concerning skin diseases	13.1-46
Laws concerning mildew	13.47-59
Purification after having skin diseases	14.1-32
Mildew in houses	14.33-57
Unclean bodily discharges	15.1-33

IV. The Day of Atonement
    The ritual for the Day of Atonement   16.1-19
    The scapegoat   16.20-28
    Observing the Day of Atonement   16.29-34

V. Holiness in life and worship
    A. Laws concerning holiness
      The sacredness of blood   17.1-16
      Forbidden sexual practices   18.1-30
      Laws of holiness and justice   19.1-37
      Penalties for disobedience   20.1-27
      The holiness of the priests   21.1-24
      The holiness of the offerings   22.1-33

    B. Laws about feasts, the tent, and the land
      The calendar of religious festivals   23.1-4
      The Passover and unleavened bread   23.5-14
      The Harvest Festival   23.15-22
      The New Year Festival   23.23-25
      The Day of Atonement   23.26-32
      The Festival of Shelters   23.33-44
      The proper care of the lamps   24.1-4
      The bread offered to God   24.5-9
      Respect for the name of God   24.10-23
      The Rest Year   25.1-7
      The Year of Restoration   25.8-17
      The problem of the Seventh Year   25.18-22
      The restoration of property   25.23-34
      Loans to the poor   25.35-38
      The release of slaves   25.39-55

    C. Blessings and punishment
      Blessings for obedience   26.1-13
      Punishment for disobedience   26.14-39
      Hope for the future   26.40-46

VI. Laws about gifts to the LORD   27.1-34

2. Authorship

Some scholars consider that Moses himself is the author of every word of Leviticus, as of all the rest of the Pentateuch (Genesis–Deuteronomy), with the possible exception of the account of his own death in Deuteronomy 34. Other exegetes think that the final editing of this work dates from a much later period, following the exile of the people of Israel to Babylon. According to these scholars the book is not necessarily the work of a single author, but probably of a group of authors from the priestly class. They would have gathered together and presented the oldest elements, sometimes very old, in a single coherent whole.

Regardless of what theory of authorship is held, this has very little influence on the problems of translation in Leviticus. Therefore it will not be helpful to discuss the subject in greater detail.

3. **The text and the ancient versions**

The original document of what we now call the book of Leviticus is not available today. Scholars have to work with a copy of the original which is called the Masoretic text. This text was compiled between the seventh and tenth centuries after Christ. It is the primary source on which most modern translations are based. In this Handbook it will be referred to as "the Hebrew text" or simply "the Hebrew."

In addition to the Masoretic text, there exists another Hebrew document known as the Samaritan Pentateuch, which dates from the third century before Christ. And the ancient Greek translation (called the Septuagint) was made some time before the Christian era, much earlier than the Masoretic text existed. Sometimes scholars have judged that it is better to translate one of these documents rather than the Masoretic text.

The Dead Sea Scrolls, which were discovered in a cave at Qumran in 1949, contain only four small fragments of parchment from Leviticus which date from before the Christian era. In their own way they confirm the good state of the Masoretic text. These fragments contain only 112 letters—less than 40 words—but there is only one significant variant. This has to do with spelling and so has no effect on the meaning of the text.

4. **Language and style**

When reading the Book of Leviticus, one must expect a literary style which is different from that of the well-known narratives of the Bible, that of the prophets, or that of poetry like the psalms. The reason for this is that the type of literature required in legal texts demands precise forms, clear expressions, and a rather technical vocabulary. The concern for precision in the smallest detail sometimes results in a great deal of repetition and a rather heavy style. Such repetition, however, does not necessarily exclude a certain kind of stylistic beauty and grandeur.

The vocabulary of this book is not quite so impoverished as it is sometimes supposed. It is rich in certain specialized areas (such as the zoological vocabulary of chapter 11). And if in certain cases the writer avoids the use of synonymous terms, it is not because of a poverty of vocabulary, but because synonyms might slightly change the intended meaning.

In the matter of style as in all other aspects of the work of translation, the translator of Leviticus must take care not to be guided by a concern to reproduce the external form of the original text. Rather, the translator must find out what kind of style is used in legal and judicial texts in the language of the translation (if indeed such texts exist) and then be able to adapt the biblical text to the receptor language norms.

An important aspect of the technical vocabulary of Leviticus is the terminology used to refer to the various kinds of sacrifices in the first seven chapters. The summary table presented below is provided to give the translator an overall picture of the different sacrifices from the very beginning. Translators may wish to refer to this table from time to time, especially as they translate the first seven chapters.

The Sacrifices in Leviticus

NAME OF SACRIFICE	REF	OBJECT OFFERED	INSTRUCTIONS	PURPOSE
1. burnt offering (RSV) (whole) burnt offering (TEV)	1.1-17 6.8-13	male without defects (ritually clean)	completely burned	to gain God's favor
2. cereal offering (RSV) grain offering (TEV)	2.1-16 6.14-23	salted unleavened cakes or grain	part burned for God; rest left for priests	to give thanks and to secure God's favor
3. peace offering (RSV) fellowship offering (TEV)	3.1-17 22.18-30 7.11-36	male or female animal without defects (ritually clean)	fat burned; rest for priest and worshiper	to give thanks to God and have fellowship with him
a. as a thank offering	7.11-15			
b. in fulfillment of a vow or spontaneously	7.16-19a			
further instructions	7.19b-27			
special gift	7.28-31			
special contribution	7.32-34			
4. sin offering (RSV/TEV)	4.1-5.13 6.24-30	priest or congregation: bull ruler: ram individual: female goat lamb doves/pigeons meal offering	fat burned for God; rest left for priests	purification from sin
5. guilt offering (RSV) repayment offering (TEV)	5.14-6.7 7.1-10	ram without defects	fat burned for God; rest left for priests	to relieve guilt of misappropriation or loss

These five types of offerings listed above constitute the main sacrifices in the book of Leviticus and in the religious life of the people of Israel. There are, however, two more related expressions in this book that should be given special attention here. The words "wave offering" (23.15) or "waved as a wave offering" are used more than a dozen times in Leviticus. However, it probably was not a separate kind of offering. It is more likely that it had to do with a particular gesture associated with sacrifices that required something extra. Both TEV and NEB place the emphasis on the special nature of the sacrifice and not on the gesture itself.

The second expression that deserves some attention here is "offering(s) by fire" (2.3; RSV). It appears more than forty times in this book, but it is always used in the context of one of the five kinds of sacrifices listed above. It is usually taken as a simple description of the means by which the offering is made, because it is thought to be associated with the Hebrew word for "fire." But there are some commentators that see a connection with the word for "food" in a language closely related to Hebrew. So TEV and NEB render it "food offering." In any case, it is not a separate kind of sacrifice but a term that is used with one of the five main types.

5. The message

The "tent of meeting" or "Tent of the LORD's presence" was the sanctuary of the people of Israel during the crossing of the desert. It is mentioned more than forty times in the Book of Leviticus. This is no accident; the writer wants to explain to the Israelites the proper use of this "tent" so that it may truly be a place of "meeting" between God and his people. This does not mean that God is imagined as physically present in this structure; but it is there that he offers to human beings the opportunity to enter into a relationship of communion with him.

This relationship, however, is neither individual nor direct. Leviticus allows us to discover the fundamental role played by the priest in Israelite society: the priest was an intermediary in the God–man and man–God relationship. He was in fact the essential and unique intermediary at the time when there were neither kings nor prophets. Only the priest could enter into the tent of the LORD's presence; only he could approach the altar to present the sacrifices that human beings made to God; only he could perform certain rites and pronounce the promises of pardon, or determine the state of purity or impurity of people, animals, and things, or insure the proper teaching of moral and religious rules. Without the priest the relationship between God and human beings is broken.

In the New Testament the writer of the Letter to the Hebrews gives the title of "high priest" to Jesus (see, for example, Heb 9.11-12,25-28; 10.19-22). In this way he shows his belief that Leviticus proclaimed in advance that Jesus would be this essential and unique intermediary through whom God would provide pardon and life for all human beings.

Leviticus has many laws, regulations, and commandments which are often surprising to the modern reader. Yet the writer uses these to remind believers in all times and everywhere that communion with the true God is a vital necessity for all people.

6. The Title of the Book

Following their usual practice, the Jews designated this book by its first Hebrew word, *wayiqra*, which means "and he [the LORD] called." The ancient Greek version, the Septuagint, named it *levitikon*, meaning "book of the priests" (since the priests were the descendants of Levi). This title passed first into the Latin (Vulgate *Leviticus*) and from there into numerous modern languages in one form or another. In certain other languages, such as German, and in some English versions, the first five books of the Bible are called "The Five Books of Moses," and Leviticus is therefore designated as "The Third Book of Moses."

If in the language of the translation the book is already known under a name derived from "Leviticus," it is possible to retain this name, although it is preferable to provide a more meaningful title. If it is known as "The Third Book of Moses," it will definitely be necessary to complete this designation by adding something like "the book of the priests" (as was done in the recent common language German translation). But it is better to replace it completely with the more meaningful title. If the book is not well known, it is certainly recommended to supply a better equivalent such as "The book of the priests" rather than a borrowed name derived from "Leviticus." And in certain cases it may even be essential, in order to avoid any misunderstanding, to make it more explicit with something like "The book of the Israelite (or Hebrew) priests." Translators may also consider "The book about the duties of priests" or "The book about sacrifices."

7. The Tent of the LORD's Presence

Since the tent of meeting, or Tent of the LORD's Presence is so important in this book, the diagram on the following page may be helpful to the translator in understanding its arrangement. In some cases a similar diagram may also be included in the receptor language translation as a help for readers. For greater detail, see Exodus 25–30.

It should be noted that scholars are not in complete agreement as to the exact location and details of every part of the Tent of the LORD's Presence. What is presented here is not intended to be taken as definitive but is a probable arrangement designed to help the translator get a mental picture of the relative positions of the different articles in the Tent.

AN ARTIST'S IDEA OF THE TENT OF THE LORD'S PRESENCE

Probable Arrangement of

THE TENT OF MEETING
or
THE TENT OF THE LORD'S PRESENCE

North Wall

```
W                                              E
E                                              N
S          [T]              B                  T
T     M                                        R
  [C]  [I]  H        S                         A
W                                              N
A          [L]                                 C
L                                              E
L                                    A
```

South Wall

C A M P

		RSV	REFERENCES	TEV
M	=	most holy place; holy place within the veil	Lev 16.2	Most Holy Place
H	=	holy place	Exo 23.33	Holy Place
C	=	Ark (of the Covenant)	Lev 16.2	Covenant Box
I	=	altar to burn incense on	4.7	incense-altar
L	=	lampstand	24.4	lampstand
T	=	table(of shewbread)	24.6	table (for the bread offered to God)
B	=	laver	8.11	basin
S	=	altar (of sacrifice)	1.5	altar (of sacrifice)
A	=	place for ashes	1.16	place where the ashes are put

Chapter 1

Although Today's English Version (TEV) has only one level of headings throughout the book of Leviticus, other translations such as the New English Bible (NEB) place major headings at the beginning of chapters 1, 8, 11, and 17 (see introductory remarks on The Content of the Book, pages 1-2). Since the first seven chapters of Leviticus deal with the offerings and sacrifices that are a part of the Israelite religion, it may be appropriate to place a major heading at the beginning of chapter 1. In this case NEB may serve as a model: "Laws concerning offerings and sacrifices." The New American Bible (NAB) has "Ritual of Sacrifices," while the New Jerusalem Bible (NJB) has virtually the same title, "The Ritual of Sacrifice."

TEV Section Heading: **"Sacrifices Burned Whole"**

Another possible model for the section heading here may be "Sacrifices of whole animals by fire." Some languages may require that a complete sentence be used in section headings. If this is the case, it may be necessary to say something like "Israel offers whole burnt sacrifices to God" or something similar.

The technical term "holocaust," found in the Jerusalem Bible (JB) and NAB, is a transcription of the Greek word used for this type of sacrifice. It means "completely burned" and is a descriptive Greek translation of the corresponding Hebrew word meaning "that which goes up" (on the altar, or in smoke toward God). It is worth noting that NJB translates more meaningfully than JB "The burnt offering." In this sacrifice the entire animal except the skin (see 7.8) is burned on the altar in honor of God. The NEB uses the term "whole-offering," which places the emphasis on the fact that the entire animal is offered to God. Most other English translations prefer "burnt offering," which describes what happens to the animal. Both represent an aspect of the meaning of the word. The TEV title attempts to retain both elements.

The use of the singular or plural in the title is somewhat dependent on the linguistic habits of the receptor language. If the use of the plural will indicate several different types of whole burnt sacrifices, then it is probably better to use the singular. Leviticus 1 simply describes three ways of proceeding, depending on whether the animal is a bull (3-9), a sheep or goat (10-13), or a bird (14-17).

In some languages it may be necessary to say "things burnt" or "gifts burnt," and sometimes adding "for God" or "by means of which God is worshiped," in order to express the religious nature of the act. The terms "sacrifice" and "offering" should, if possible, be distinguished in the receptor language. In the Bible "sacrifice" involves the killing of an animal or bird, while "offering" pertains to giving something to God—usually some kind of food (like grain) or drink (like wine).

1.1   RSV   TEV

The LORD called Moses, and spoke to him from the tent of meeting, saying,	**The LORD called to Moses from the Tent of the LORD's presence and gave him the following rules**

Verses 1-2 introduce chapters 1–3, or perhaps the entire section on offerings and sacrifices, chapters 1–7.

LORD: in order to translate the proper name of God from the Hebrew, RSV and TEV have adopted the solution chosen by numerous other English translations (NEB, NAB, New International Version [NIV], New American Standard Bible [NASB], and even King James Verson [KJV] in 1611). The word "LORD" with all capital letters is used when the Hebrew has *YHWH*, but "Lord" is used when the original has *Adonay*, meaning "Master," "Lord," or "Sovereign." In this verse the name of God is written with four consonants, *YHWH*. Its pronunciation in ancient times is uncertain, but was probably *Yahweh* or *Yahwoh*. Many centuries before the Christian era, this name was considered to have such special power that the Jews avoided pronouncing it (in technical terms, this is referred to as a "positive taboo"; see *Theory and Practice of Translation*, pages 82-83). Instead, they pronounced the Hebrew title meaning "Lord."

Some translations simply transcribe the Hebrew name *YHWH* as "Yahweh" (NJB), and others use the artificial form "Jehovah" (KJV in a few cases and American Standard Version consistently). The form "Jehovah" is based on a pronunciation that was first introduced in 1520 by Galatinus and was not the pronunciation of the ancient Jews. The transliteration of this form should therefore be avoided. There is, however, some merit in transliterating *YHWH*, since it is a proper noun. Other translators have made an effort to "translate" the supposed meaning of this name by "the Eternal" (Moffatt [Mft] and several French versions); but such renderings only replace a personal name by an impersonal abstraction. In some cultures there may be a personal name for God distinct from the generic term for "god" but quite similar in usage to the biblical term used here. In such cases it may be wise to adopt this name as the equivalent for *YHWH*. This possibility has often been overlooked in past translations of the Bible. But even though the commonly used name in the receptor language is not an exact equivalent of *YHWH*, it may be wise to use it in translation and give a full explanation of the biblical name in the glossary.

In some languages today it is also legitimate to add, if necessary, a possessive form such as "my LORD" or "their LORD" (according to the context), although this was never done with the personal name in Hebrew. For a more complete discussion of the divine name and other terms for God, see the April 1984 issue of *The Bible Translator.*

Called ... spoke ... saying ... : these three verbs are very similar in meaning. The Hebrew word translated **saying** in RSV often serves in Hebrew simply to mark the beginning of a quotation. So the use of quotation marks in the receptor language may adequately represent this word. But many languages have a similar word that can be used to introduce a quotation. Note that TEV has reduced this to two verbal expressions: **"called"** and **"gave ... rules."** In Hebrew the subject of the verb **called** is not made explicit. It is only in the second clause, "the LORD spoke," that **the LORD** is clearly given as the subject. Although the first verb does not have an expressed subject, it is obvious that it could only be the Lord himself. Most languages will probably require that the subject be stated with the first verb, as in the English versions. The meaning of the verb "call" is probably to "summon" or "call for attention."

From: in some languages it may be necessary to indicate the position of Moses relative to the tent at the time when the Lord called him. Since this verse is connected with the end of the book of Exodus, where the cloud covered the Tent of the Lord's Presence so that Moses could not go in (Exo 40.35), it is most probable that he was standing at or near the entrance when he was called, and that the voice of the Lord came from within the Tent.

The tent of meeting: a literal translation like that of RSV does not adequately convey the full meaning of this expression. It is the portable sanctuary of the people of Israel, described in Exodus 25-30, and in which God meets with Moses to communicate to him the divine will (see Exo 33.7-11). This tent was considered a very special place where God revealed himself to his people (Exo 29.42-46). The TEV rendering, "**Tent of the LORD's presence**," highlights these facts and provides a better model for most languages. In some languages one may say "the tent where God lives" (although one must not give the impression that he is restricted to the tent), or "the tent where the LORD is," or "the place where the LORD appears."

In some languages the word **tent** itself presents problems. It has to be translated "a temporary (or, portable) shelter" or "a house made of skins."

Saying: note that TEV supplies implicit information by translating here "**gave him the following rules.**" This may be a good model to follow in the receptor language, although the word "**rules**" may be better rendered "instructions" or "laws."

1.2	RSV	TEV

RSV	TEV
"Speak to the people of Israel and say to them, When any man of you brings an offering to the LORD, you shall bring your offering of cattle from the herd or from the flock.	for the Israelites to observe when they offer their sacrifices. When anyone offers an animal sacrifice, it may be one of his cattle or one of his sheep or goats.

It will be noted that the structures of RSV and TEV in this verse differ considerably. In Hebrew the direct discourse begins at the beginning of verse 2, as in RSV. In many languages it is not good to have a direct quotation (verse 2b) within another direct quotation (verse 2a). TEV has adopted the solution of not marking anything at all as a direct quotation. The equivalent of the RSV direct quotation is preceded in verse 1 by the words "gave him the following rules" in TEV. At this point the translator should take into account what is most natural in the receptor language, either maintaining the direct discourse in verse 2a or shifting to indirect discourse.

RSV includes within direct quotes certain information found in the introductory statement in TEV. TEV, on the other hand, leaves implicit the fact that sacrifices are made **to the LORD**, which the more literal RSV makes explicit. If the translation uses direct speech for the rules, it may seem unnatural for the Lord to refer to himself, in "sacrifices to Yahweh," and it may be better to follow TEV as model. Translators should consider the requirements of their own language with regard to the arrangement of this verse and translate the meaning as naturally as possible. It should also be noted that this problem appears frequently throughout the book of Leviticus (compare, for example, the first verse in chapters 4, 11, 12, 15, 17, 18, and elsewhere).

Speak to the people of Israel, and say to them: in most languages such repetition is unnecessary after the three similar verbs in the previous verse. It should be adequate to say simply "say to the people of Israel."

When . . . : in the first five chapters of Leviticus, there are two different words that may be translated "when" or "if." The Hebrew word *ki,* normally translated "when," is found here and in 2.1,4; 5.1,3,4,5,15; 6.1,4. The Hebrew word *'im,* usually rendered "if," occurs in this chapter in verses 3, 10, and 14, as well as at 2.5,7; 3.1, 6,12; 4.3,13,27,32; 5.5,11,17. These two words seem to be used almost interchangeably, but they serve as markers indicating paragraph breaks in the discourse. For example, the chapter begins by defining the general case, using the Hebrew conjunction *ki,* and then three subordinate cases introduced by *'im* (verses 3-9, 10-13, and 14-17), as indicated by Wenham. It is probably best to follow the example of TEV, using "when" at the beginning of each section and "if" to introduce the paragraphs within the section, unless the receptor language has a better way of marking such features of discourse.

Brings an offering: the noun and the verb have the same root, literally "offer an offering." TEV has **"offer their sacrifices."** In Numbers and Ezekiel as well as Leviticus, the Hebrew word for offering is a very general term used to designate anything given as a sacrifice to God. In Nehemiah 10.35 and 13.31 it is even used of nonsacrificial offerings made to God. In this context it should normally be translated by a very generic term in the receptor language rather than using terminology for a specific kind of sacrifice. Whatever term is chosen must cover both animals and plant products that may be burned or given to the priests.

Any man of you: this may be better translated in many languages as **"anyone"** or "a person." This will leave implicit the words **of you**, meaning "among you [Israelites]."

Offering of cattle from the herd or from the flock: literally, "offering from the animals from the herd or from the flock." To translators who do not speak English as their first language, RSV may give the impression that the offering only includes cattle. The word **herd** is usually used to refer to larger animals such as cattle or oxen. On the other hand, **flock** normally refers to smaller animals such as sheep or goats. And the word translated **cattle** in RSV is actually a very generic word that can refer to domestic animals of any kind. By translating "one of his cattle or one of his sheep or goats," TEV has made explicit the fact that the larger animals are cattle and the smaller animals refer to sheep or goats. Naturalness in the receptor language should be the determining factor in deciding whether to translate using more specific terms such as cattle, sheep, and goats, or more generic expressions such as "larger animals and smaller animals." While the terms **herd** and **flock** do not appear in *Fauna and Flora of the Bible* (FFB), the animals included in these groups are discussed. On "cattle," see pages 62-63; on "sheep," see pages 75-76; on "goat," see pages 36-38.

1.3 RSV TEV

"If his offering is a burnt offering from the herd, he shall offer a male without blemish; he shall offer it at the door of the tent of meeting, that he may be accepted before the LORD;	If he is offering one of his cattle as a burnt offering, he must bring a bull without any defects. He must present it at the entrance of the Tent of the LORD's presence so that the LORD will accept him.

Verses 3-9 describe the whole burnt offering of an animal taken from the group of larger animals referred to in verse 2.

If his offering is a burnt offering: this expression is similar to 3.1, **If a man's offering is a sacrifice of peace offering . . .** . In both cases the first term is the general one for anything offered to God, and the second is the more specific expression. The word translated **burnt offering** here has already been discussed under the heading for this section.

From the herd: TEV has **"one of his cattle."** This is parallel to "from the flock" (TEV "one of his sheep or goats") in verse 10 and "of birds" in verse 14. In each case the topic of the paragraph is introduced. If natural, the beginning of these three paragraphs should be made parallel in the receptor language in order to highlight the discourse structure of this chapter.

A male: in English the word **"bull"** contains the idea of maleness as well as a member of the group called cattle. The translator should use whatever conveys this idea naturally in the receptor language.

Without blemish: any kind of physical defect such as blindness, skin disease, or paralysis automatically excluded an animal from being offered in sacrifice to the LORD. The details of this requirement are given in 22.17-25. What is needed in this verse is a simple term that would include any kind of deformity. Some languages may have to say "that is not spoiled in the least," or "that has not the slightest flaw," or simply "flawless."

He shall offer it: this does not refer to the act of killing the animal, as a literal translation may imply, but to bringing it near to the LORD for use as a sacrifice. TEV **"present it"** is a good model.

At the door of the tent of meeting: the term **door** may be understood as referring either to the large entrance way leading into the court, or to the entrance way of the tent itself. In either case, it may not be appropriate to use the word "door" since this would give the idea of some kind of wooden or metal object used to close an entrance way. In this context the word probably refers to the opening or entrance way to the "Tent of the Lord's presence" and was near the altar of sacrifices on the outside of the Tent (see Exo 40.6-7,29-30). In some languages this may be expressed by a word meaning "mouth," "hole," or "opening."

That he may be accepted before the LORD: literally "for his/its favor before the LORD." Grammatically the Hebrew possessive may refer to the animal ("in order that *it* might be accepted"), as in NJB and NIV, or to the one who is offering the animal ("in order that *he* might be accepted"). The usage of this kind of expression elsewhere in the Old Testament leads many scholars to the latter meaning, which corresponds to what is found in RSV and TEV (see especially 19.5; 22.19,29; and 23.11, where the meaning is unambiguous). But the overall meaning of the passage is not radically changed if one accepts the other possibility. The person offering the sacrifice is accepted only if the sacrifice itself is acceptable. Compare the New Jewish Version (NJV) rendering: "for acceptance in his behalf before the LORD." A person who is "accepted" by the LORD in this context is one who is allowed to participate in this act of worship. He recognizes his unworthiness and his need to placate God. He is therefore considered "good enough" or "worthy" to offer the sacrifice.

It should be noted that here and throughout this passage, when the word **LORD** occurs, the translation will depend on the decision made about direct versus indirect discourse at the beginning of the chapter. If the translators have made this a direct quotation as in NIV, for example, most languages will require that the LORD speak of himself in the first person rather than the third person. So this verse will then read "before me" or "before me, the LORD." And verse 9 will then end with the words "pleasing to me" rather than "pleasing to the LORD." Since the passage that may be translated as a direct quotation is very long, it is easy to forget this modification. But translators should pay attention each time the word **LORD** appears, and ask themselves whether it is part of a passage where God himself is speaking. If it is unnatural in the language for a person to speak of himself in the third person, then the proper changes must be made in the translation.

1.4   RSV   TEV

he shall lay his hand upon the head of the burnt offering, and it shall be accepted for him to make atonement for him.

The man shall put his hand on its head, and it will be accepted as a sacrifice to take away his sins.

He shall lay his hand upon the head: by means of this gesture the person offering the sacrifice identifies himself as the one who is offering the animal, and in a sense he offers himself to God through the sacrificial animal. This gesture is important when a larger animal is offered to the LORD, since there may be several persons who physically bring the animal to the altar (compare verses 10 and 14, where this gesture is not mentioned in connection with a smaller animal or a bird). In those languages where it is necessary to specify which hand is laid on the head of the animal, this should be the right hand.

By using the noun "**man**" in place of the pronoun **he**, TEV makes it clear that it is the person offering the sacrifice and not the priest who places his hand on the head of the animal.

Upon the head of the burnt offering: the reference is clearly to the head of the animal which is brought as a burnt offering, but the gesture is made before it is actually burned.

It shall be accepted: this passive expression will have to be rendered actively in many languages. Since the implied subject is God, it may be translated "God will accept it . . . ." Note that in the previous verse this verb is taken to refer to the person offering the sacrifice, but in this case it seems to refer to the animal that is "regarded as good" by the LORD.

To make atonement for him: the Hebrew verb translated by this phrase appears often in the ritual of sacrifices offered to obtain forgiveness from God. The original meaning of the root word in Hebrew seems to have been "cover" or possibly "wipe off," but this meaning may have been lost. The idea of "atonement" is found nearly fifty times in Leviticus. It may signify either the means of undoing ritual defilement or the resultant reconciliation with God, who has been offended by a violation of his laws (or possibly both ideas may have been involved). The basic idea seems to be that of restoring harmony or putting things back in proper order. In this context it seems to indicate a particular ritual gesture on the part of the priest, who is charged to announce to the faithful that their sins have been forgiven (see 4.20). God is the one who pardons, and as a sign of forgiveness he accepts the animal sacrifice. In some languages it may be preferable to give a clearer statement by saying "Then the LORD will accept his offering and will pardon his sins." In other languages the word "pardon" or "forgive" has been rendered by such idiomatic expressions as "turn his back on sin," "heal the neck," or "God has spat on the ground for us."

1.5 RSV	TEV
Then he shall kill the bull before the LORD; and Aaron's sons the priests shall present the blood, and throw the blood round about against the altar that is at the door of the tent of meeting.	**He shall kill the bull there, and the Aaronite priests shall present the blood to the LORD and then throw it against all four sides of the altar located at the entrance of the Tent.**

He shall kill: literally "he shall slaughter." While the general term **kill** is used by both TEV and RSV, other translations seek to capture the special meaning of this word by using such terms as "slaughter" (NEB, NJV, NIV, and NJB) or "immolate" (JB). According to ancient Jewish custom, it was the lay person who offered the sacrifice that actually cut the throat of the animal. But in the ancient Greek translation rendering of this verse, and in 2 Chronicles 29.22-24, this rite is reserved for the priests. In Ezekiel 44.11 and 2 Chronicles 35.6 it is the responsibility of the Levites.

The bull: literally "a son of the herd." See verse 2 on "herd" and "flock." In expressions of this type the Hebrew word that usually means "son" or "child" expresses the idea of membership in a group. Compare the very frequent Old Testament expression "children of Israel," which means simply "Israelites," or the expression "son of a prophet," indicating membership in a group of prophets (see, for example, 1 Kings 20.35 and Amos 7.14). The idea of youth (translated "young bull" in NIV) is not an essential component of the meaning here. What is important in this context is that a male animal of the category of larger animals must be sacrificed.

Before the LORD: in this context the expression **before the LORD** refers to a particular place which is made clear in 17.3-5. In TEV the adverb **"there"** simply refers to "at the entrance of the Tent of the LORD's presence" in verse 3. A literal translation as in RSV runs the risk of hiding from the reader the implied reference to the location at the entrance to the Tent. In some languages this may be translated "there in my presence," if direct discourse is being used. It should be noted that the aspect of physical location is of less importance than the fact of the presence of the LORD.

Aaron's sons, the priests: the expression "sons of Aaron" may be understood in its more literal sense as referring to Nadab, Abihu, Eleazar, and Ithamar, the four sons born of Aaron's wife Elisheba (see Exo 6.23; Lev 10.1,6). Or it may refer more generally to "members of the group of Aaron's descendants" (see the explanation above on "son of the herd"). It is very likely that the more general meaning is to be understood here. In some languages it may be necessary to say "priests in the order of Aaron" or "Aaron's descendants who serve as priests." This expression also occurs in verses 8 and 11 of this chapter as well as in 2.2; 3.2; 7.35; 13.2; and 21.1. The plural "priests" occurs without mention of Aaron in 6.29; 7.6; 16.33; and 22.15. All other occurrences of the word (about 175 of them in Leviticus) are singular in form. In some cases there is no obvious reason for the selection of the plural form, but usually it appears where more general statements are being made.

The term **priest** may present special difficulties in some languages. The Levitical priests were representatives of the people, and thus their position involved great responsibility as well as honor and certain privileges. The primary duty of the priest was to serve as an intermediary between the LORD and his people. The means by which this was done was sacrifice. Thus in some languages this word has been translated "sacrificer" or "intermediary." But care should be taken to avoid negative connotations of a word like "sacrificer." If it evokes ideas of pagan sacrifice quite different from those of the people of Israel, then another term should be sought; for example, "one who offers gifts to God (for the people)."

Present the blood: the expression "**to the LORD**" is added in TEV because it is implied in the original. The Hebrew verb may be understood in the more technical sense of making a ritual presentation, or in the general sense of "take" or "bring." Probably this was a separate ritual act done before the blood was thrown on the altar. In some languages one may have to say "hold the blood up before the LORD" or something similar.

Throw the blood . . . : this is different from placing the blood on the corners of the altar (4.25). In this case the priest caught the blood in a container as it flowed from the arteries of the animal. According to later Jewish tradition it was then tossed against the northeast corner in order to cover the north and east sides. Next he threw the remainder against the opposite corner to cover the other two sides so that all four sides were covered. The use of the verb "sprinkle" (as in the KJV, NASB, and NIV) is probably somewhat off the mark. But if **throw** implies indiscriminate or accidental scattering of the blood in the receptor language, it will be necessary to find a verb meaning "deliberately pour out."

Round about: the word translated **round about** may be understood in the sense of "in the general vicinity" (as in Exo 7.24), but in this context it almost certainly has reference to the four sides of the altar. See the comments in the previous paragraph, which explains how this was done.

Altar that is at the door of the tent of meeting: the Hebrew word for **altar** comes from the verb "to slaughter." Eventually, however, it took on a more general meaning that included any place where any kind of sacrifice was offered to God. There are two altars related to the Tent of the LORD's presence: (1) the altar of sacrifice, which stood directly in front of the entrance to the Tent (Exo 27.1-8; 38.1-7), and (2) the altar of incense, which was inside the Tent just in front of the

"Holy of Holies." Some languages require completely different words for these two objects. In this verse it is clearly the altar of sacrifice that the writer has in mind. In some cases a descriptive phrase may be required: "the place where offerings are given to God" or "the table where sacrifices are burned for God."

1.6	RSV	TEV

And he shall flay the burnt offering and cut it into pieces;

Then he shall skin the animal and cut it up,

He: the reference here is to the lay person who is making the offering and not to the priests mentioned in verse 5, since that would require a plural subject.

Flay the burnt offering: the reference is clearly to the bull which has not yet been burned, so TEV says **"the animal."** It also has the common language **"skin"** in place of the technical term **flay**. But in other languages it will be clearer to say "remove the skin of the animal" or "take away the skin from the animal."

Cut it into pieces: the animal is simply cut into quarters, with the head and the suet (or fat) as separate pieces, so the translation should not give the impression that it is carved into many small pieces as if preparing to cook it for eating. Since it would be difficult to place the entire bull on the altar, it was a matter of practical necessity to cut it into manageable parts, but it was not necessary to cut it into small pieces.

The actions of verses 6 and 7 are probably simultaneous so that it is also possible to translate "While the man skins the animal . . . the priests light the fire . . . ."

1.7	RSV	TEV

and the sons of Aaron the priest shall put fire on the altar, and lay wood in order upon the fire;

and the priests shall arrange firewood on the altar and light it.

The sons of Aaron the priest: or "the sons of the priest named Aaron." Some Hebrew manuscripts and several ancient versions have the plural "sons of Aaron, the priests," but the singular "priest" is recommended by the committee for the Hebrew Old Testament Text Project (HOTTP). Nevertheless the meaning of the expression is not essentially different. Throughout this chapter there is an unusual alternation between the expression "the sons of Aaron, the priests" (found in verses 5, 8, and 11) and "the sons of Aaron, the priest" with the final word in the singular instead of the plural (here and in verses 9, 12, 13, and 15). But it is unnecessary to maintain this singular/plural distinction in translation. In most cases it is also pointless to repeat the expression **Aaron's sons** every time priests are mentioned.

Put fire on the altar, and lay the wood upon the fire: the TEV has seen fit to reorder these two verbs ("arrange . . . and light . . ."), probably because it seems more logical (and less dangerous!) to arrange the wood before lighting the fire. But it is possible that the priest(s) placed hot coals on the altar of sacrifice and then put wood on top of them.

1.8   RSV   TEV

and Aaron's sons the priests shall lay the pieces, the head, and the fat, in order upon the wood that is on the fire that is upon the altar.	They shall put on the fire the pieces of the animal, including the head and the fat.

Note that the TEV rendering is recast so that the various elements in t h e sentence are ordered differently. In order to give more prominence to the "**head**" and the "**fat**" which are focused on in the Hebrew, another possible structure for this verse can be "The head and the fat, along with the other parts of the animal, must be put in order on the fire by the priests" or "They [the priests] must put the head and the fat together with the other pieces of the animal on the fire."

Aaron's sons the priests: the repetition of the entire formula (see verses 5 and 7) is unnecessary and stylistically unacceptable in many languages. The pronoun "**they**," as in TEV, is sufficient to convey the meaning.

Upon the wood that is on the fire upon the altar: TEV avoids this awkward and possibly misleading construction by mentioning only the essential element "**fire**" and leaving the rest implicit. It may be wise to do something like this in many other languages. The word translated **fire** may be rendered "burning coals" in many cases.

Lay the pieces . . . in order: this is the same Hebrew verb that is translated "arrange" in the previous verse. It seems to indicate that the priests could not be satisfied with simply piling wood or pieces of meat in bulk on the altar; they had to be arranged in the proper manner, although we do not know precisely how this was done.

1.9   RSV   TEV

but its entrails and its legs he shall wash with water. And the priest shall burn the whole on the altar, as a burnt offering, an offering by fire, a pleasing odor to the LORD.	The man must wash the internal organs and the hind legs, and the officiating priest will burn the whole sacrifice on the altar. The odor of this food offering is pleasing to the LORD.

Its entrails: it was necessary to wash the stomach and intestines, because their contents were in the process of being digested and could not be a part of what was offered on the altar. The expression "**the internal organs**" in TEV is probably too general here, although this meaning fits the context much better in 4.12. Most versions retain the word **entrails** here. In some languages it will be necessary to translate "intestines."

Its legs: the Hebrew word here has been variously understood as referring to "**hind legs**" (as in TEV), "shins" (NEB and NJB), or simply **legs** (RSV and JB). What is clear is that these parts, like the internal organs, were most likely to be unclean, both ritually and in fact. They must therefore be washed.

He: according to TEV, the washing is the responsibility of the person bringing the sacrifice, while the priest is charged with the actual burning. However, the

Hebrew text is ambiguous and can be interpreted to mean that the priest performs this task as a part of his duties. It is probably best to follow TEV, which renders the pronoun **he** as "**The man**" and shifts the subject to the beginning of the sentence to make it more natural English. But in some languages it may be possible to use a passive or indefinite form which does not clearly define the subject: "The internal organs and hind legs must be washed, and then . . . ."

Wash with water: in most languages it is redundant to add the words "with water" since this is already implied in the verb "to wash."

The priest: some Septuagint manuscripts have the plural "priests," as in the preceding verse. However, the singular is recommended here.

Burn: the corresponding Hebrew verb is a technical term used in the language of sacrifice. It evokes the idea of smoke going up from the altar toward heaven. See the discussion under the section heading for this section.

As a burnt offering, an offering by fire: these words translate two Hebrew technical terms that are simply put together in this verse. The first term is discussed under the title of this section, "Sacrifices Burnt Whole" or "holocaust." The precise meaning of the second term is not known, but it is similar to the word for "fire" and has sometimes been translated "an offering by fire." It is used of whole burnt offerings and of fellowship offerings alike (see chapter 3). Both TEV and NEB take it to refer to "a food offering." This may be taken, then, not as a separate sacrifice, but as another way of referring to the burnt offering already mentioned. See the discussion of the different types of sacrifice in the introduction, "Translating Leviticus," page 5.

A pleasing odor to the LORD: this is a dynamic rendering of another technical term which is placed alongside the two preceding words. The phrase may be literally translated "aroma appeasing to the LORD." However, it is unnecessary to think of appeasement in the sense that God, angered by the sins of the people, had to be appeased by sacrifices. This expression is, in fact, used almost always of the whole burnt offerings (chapter 1), of the grain offerings (chapter 2) and of the fellowship offerings (chapter 3), but only once of a sacrifice in order to obtain God's pardon (4.31). It is possible therefore to translate this expression as "It is a whole burnt sacrifice with a pleasant odor which the LORD accepts gladly" or "in which the LORD takes pleasure and which he accepts."

1.10 RSV TEV

RSV	TEV
"If his gift for a burnt offering is from the flock, from the sheep or goats, he shall offer a male without blemish;	If the man is offering one of his sheep or goats, it must be a male without any defects.

Verses 10-13 describe the sacrifice of the whole burnt offering of a smaller animal. Since these verses repeat the text of verses 3-9 almost word for word, in the following section it is necessary only to point out the significant differences that exist.

From the sheep or goats: in this verse the expression **from the flock** (see verse 2) is made explicit in the Hebrew text, so that it is quite clear that the **flock** refers to **sheep or goats**. In some languages it may be necessary to use terms that imply maleness from the beginning of this section. The NEB, for example, uses the word "rams" instead of "sheep." On the identity of these animals, see the references to FFB in verse 2 above. There is no indication in the text as to why one would offer on of these smaller animals rather than the larger one, but presumably this depended upon a person's possessions and what one was able to bring as a sacrifice.

In the Hebrew text of verses 10-13, there is no equivalent of the phrase found in verse 4, "The man shall put his hand on its head," but this gesture is added in the Septuagint. The absence of any mention of the gesture does not necessarily indicate that it was omitted in the sacrifice of sheep or goats. It is possible that the author simply decided not to repeat all the mechanical details of the ritual. But in the case of the offering of a bird (verse 15), the reason for the omission is probably different. In any case, the translator is well advised not to follow the Septuagint in adding the gesture here, since it is not in the Hebrew text at this point.

1.11   RSV   TEV

and he shall kill it on the north side of the altar before the LORD, and Aaron's sons the priests shall throw its blood against the altar round about.

He shall kill it on the north side of the altar, and the priests shall throw its blood on all four sides of the altar.

This verse corresponds to verse 5 above, but gives added information not found in the section on cattle sacrifice. The ritual slaughter of the animal takes place **on the north side of the altar**, which corresponds to the instructions given in Ezekiel 40.38-43. In the sanctuary of the desert, as later in the ideal Temple of Ezekiel and in Herod's Temple, the altar seems to have been placed right in front of the main entrance, which was situated on the east. In the Temple of Solomon it was shifted to the right, which would be on the north. The slaughter **on the north side of the altar** therefore was performed with a certain measure of discretion behind the altar (compare Ezek 40.38-39, where the slaughter took place in a room off the northern entrance). In the translation of this verse it is essential to take into account the system of directions in the receptor language, and particularly the viewpoint of the writer, which may be the sanctuary in this case. In some cases it may be preferable to translate "on the north side of the altar of sacrifice, which is located in front of the Tent of the LORD's presence."

Directions are particularly difficult to express in some languages. The rising and setting of the sun often provide terms for east and west and an orientation for other directions. North becomes "to the right when facing the setting sun" and south is "to the left when facing the setting sun." But such expressions are often quite awkward to fit into a context such as this, where the orientation for "right" and "left" is based on the altar and not the sun. Other languages take their bearings from the direction of a river, so that "north" is the equivalent of "up river" and "south" is "down river." Great care should be taken in seeking to render directions according to the common usage in the receptor language, and checking with the average reader or hearer is essential.

Before the LORD: this is left implicit in TEV, but naturalness in the receptor language should determine whether it is included in the translation.

Throw its blood: see verse 5.

1.12   RSV   TEV

| And he shall cut it into pieces, with its head and its fat, and the priest shall lay them in order upon the wood that is on the fire upon the altar; | After the man cuts it up, the officiating priest shall put on the fire all the parts, including the head and the fat. |

Compare with verses 6 and 8.

He: the reference of this pronoun is made clearer by the use of the noun "the man" in TEV. Something similar should probably be done in a number of other languages.

1.13   RSV   TEV

| but the entrails and the legs he shall wash with water. And the priest shall offer the whole, and burn it on the altar; it is a burnt offering, an offering by fire, a pleasing odor to the LORD. | The man must wash the internal organs and the hind legs, and the priest will present the sacrifice to the LORD and burn all of it on the altar. The smell of this food offering is pleasing to the LORD. |

Compare with verse 9.

1.14   RSV   TEV

| "If his offering to the LORD is a burnt offering of birds, then he shall bring his offering of turtledoves or of young pigeons. | If the man is offering a bird as a burnt offering, it must be a dove or a pigeon. |

Verses 14-17 describe the whole burnt offering of a bird. This paragraph is not constructed like the two preceding ones. According to some scholars this is because the ritual described here was added some time after the other two were instituted. This ritual may have been adopted because some of the people who wanted to offer sacrifices were too poor to afford the larger animals.

His offering of turtledoves or of young pigeons: only these two kinds of birds could be offered by the Israelites as sacrifices. Other birds were considered unfit to be presented to the LORD. In Hebrew the two words are plural in form and are used in such a way as to indicate that one would be permitted to offer a single bird. The use of the plural in RSV, NEB, and other versions gives the impression that the offering must consist of more than one bird. While the bird (singular) is chosen from among the various acceptable kinds of "birds," TEV and NJB convey the meaning more clearly by using the singular forms in translation.

In some languages "doves" are considered wild while "pigeons" are domesticated. But in those languages which do not distinguish between "doves" and "pigeons," one may say "a pigeon of one kind or another" or "any kind of pigeon" or perhaps "a pigeon or a smaller pigeon," since the size of the bird is the distinctive feature in this context.

Young pigeons: literally, "sons of pigeons." As explained in verse 5, the words "sons of . . ." do not necessarily refer to youth but to membership in a group. The addition of the word **young** in RSV is therefore not a good model to follow, nor is "a young pigeon" in NIV.

The phrase in verse 4, "The man shall put his hand on its head," has no equivalent in verses 14-17 (compare also verse 10), but the reason for its absence is probably different in this case. If the offering were a bull, a ram, or a goat, it may have been brought to the altar by more than one person. So it would be necessary that the one actually offering the sacrifice should identify himself as the owner by placing his hand on the head of the victim. But in this case the person offering the dove or pigeon would bring it in his own hands. So it would be pointless to add an extra gesture to indicate that the offering was his.

1.15   RSV   TEV

And the priest shall bring it to the altar and wring off its head, and burn it on the altar; and its blood shall be drained out on the side of the altar;

The priest shall present it at the altar, wring its neck, and burn its head on the altar. Its blood shall be drained out against the side of the altar.

The priest: the priest presides over the entire ritual; there is no apparent division of labor between the lay person and the priest, as in the case where a larger animal is offered. In this verse the priest seems to be the implied subject of all four verbs.

Wring off its head: the meaning of the Hebrew verb in this verse is uncertain. It is found only twice in the Old Testament (see 5.8). It is generally thought that it implies the idea of squeezing or pinching off the head with the fingernail. Apparently the Hebrew verb implies the idea of a complete break or separation in this verse, since the priest must burn the head on the altar. In some languages it may be more natural to say something like "twist off at the neck." But in 5.8 it is explicitly stated that this gesture must be made "without pulling off its head." The context of verse 15 puts more weight on the fact that the head is detached from the body than on the way in which it is actually done.

Burn it: this refers to the head (see TEV) and not the entire bird. Compare verse 9.

Its blood shall be drained out: the verb used here is different from the one found in verses 5 and 11 regarding larger animals, and it should be translated differently here. The body of the bird was squeezed against the side of the altar, since there would not have been enough blood to perform the complete ritual described earlier. Mft translates "squeezed out." Although HOTTP recommends the passive reading at this point, many languages will have to translate the meaning actively and make the priest the subject of the verb. NAB does so with "and [the priest shall] squeeze out its blood . . . ."

1.16 RSV TEV

and he shall take away its crop with the feathers, and cast it beside the altar on the east side, in the place for ashes;

He shall remove the crop and its contents and throw them away on the east side of the altar where the ashes are put.

In order to show the sequence of events more clearly, it may be better to begin this verse with "Then . . . ."

Take away its crop: that part of the bird which serves as a receptacle for food and where the process of digestion begins must be removed, just as the stomach and intestines of the larger animals had to be removed (see verses 9 and 13). Here it is the most visible and most easily accessible part of the digestive apparatus of the bird that is eliminated.

With the feathers: the Hebrew word here has been understood in two very different senses: some translations (RSV, NJB, and NAB) have followed the ancient Greek and Latin translations and rendered it **feathers**; others (TEV, NEB, and NJV) follow the interpretation of the Targum and the Syriac translation and understand it as referring to the contents of the crop. The parallelism with verses 9 and 13 seems to favor this second interpretation.

Cast it beside the altar: the context clearly indicates that these parts were tossed aside as worthless rubbish. The ashes and rubbish thrown away in this manner were raked out just before dawn and eventually thrown into the Kidron valley.

On the east side: literally "on the side of the altar, on the east." But such a construction will be awkward in many languages. What is important here is that it is on the side of the altar that was farthest from the sanctuary where the ashes were deposited before removing them completely from the camp (see 4.12). These ashes are what remains after the burning of the sacrifices. The direction **east** (as in verse 11) should be expressed according to the receptor language system; for example, "on the side where the sun rises." Or in some cases it may be better to simply say "on the side of the altar away from the sanctuary" or "in front of the altar on the right side."

The place for ashes: there is no indication that there was a special container for the ashes. Rather it was probably an area on the east side of the altar where waste materials were piled up. The word for **ashes** comes from a root that means "fat." If the receptor language has a special word for ashes containing fatty material, it will be appropriate here. Some languages say "the place where they [indefinite] pile the ashes."

1.17   RSV   TEV

he shall tear it by its wings, but shall
not divide it asunder. And the priest
shall burn it on the altar, upon the
wood that is on the fire; it is a burnt
offering, an offering by fire, a pleasing odor to the LORD.

He shall take hold of its wings and
tear its body open, without tearing
the wings off, and then burn it whole
on the altar. The smell of this food
offering is pleasing to the LORD.

Here again it may be a good idea to show the continuity of the actions by
introducing the verse with "Then . . . ."

Tear it by its wings, but shall not divide it asunder: the unexpressed object
of the verb **divide** (or "sever") is very likely the two parts of the bird, rather than
its wings. The action of taking apart was probably done with the bare hands (using
the fingernails), and not with an instrument, as Jewish tradition states and as is
explicitly indicated in the Latin Vulgate.

Burn it: here we have the same conclusion as found at the end of verses 9 and
13. So the translation adopted here should be identical with the one used at the end
of the previous two paragraphs.

Chapter 2

TEV Section Heading: **"Grain Offerings"**

The section heading used here should probably be parallel in structure to the one at the beginning of chapters 1, 3, and 4, as well as at 5.14. If complete sentences are required in such cases, the translators may try "Israel offers grain sacrifices to the LORD" or "Grain offerings that the LORD expects of the people of Israel."

The Hebrew expression "an offering of grain" has been drawn from verse 1 (in RSV "cereal offering") and used as a title for this entire section. It consists of two words, the first of which is *qorban*, familiar to many Bible readers from Mark 7.11. It is the same general term found in Leviticus 1.3 and is used for all kinds of offerings. The second term, *minchah*, has two meanings: the first is a very general one which includes a wide variety of sacrifices and in some cases is even used of a simple gift from an inferior to a superior (for example, Gen 32.13; Judges 3.15; 2 Kgs 8.8). But it is also used in a more technical religious sense in those passages dealing with sacrifice in Exodus, Leviticus, Numbers, and Ezekiel. In those contexts it specifically refers to nonanimal sacrifices (grain, flour, or oil) made to God. It is this second meaning that is intended here.

2.1

RSV	TEV
"When any one brings a cereal offering as an offering to the LORD, his offering shall be of fine flour; he shall pour oil upon it, and put frankincense on it,	When anyone presents an offering of grain to the LORD, he must first grind it into flour. He must put olive oil and incense on it

Verses 1-3 bring together general information with regard to this type of offering.

When . . . : see the discussion of "when" and "if" at 1.2.

Any one: literally "a soul." The word is probably best translated "a person" in this context.

Cereal offering: the term used here is a general one for any offering of grain, but the remainder of the verse and the following paragraph describes one of the ways the grain was to be treated in order to make it acceptable as an offering to the LORD. Verses 4-10 describe another kind of offering using the same materials prepared differently, and verses 11-13 give still another possibility. In those languages which have no generic word for "grain," a serious translation problem may arise. The general term refers to the seed of cultivated cereal grasses including wheat, barley, millet, and sorghum. In some cases translators are forced to resort to something like "small seeds" with an explanation in a footnote or glossary entry.

To the LORD: if direct discourse is being used as in RSV, NIV, and many other versions, this should probably be translated "to me" in most languages.

Fine flour: in Hebrew there are two words that refer to ground grain. The first, which is used here, represents a kind of semolina or coarser wheat flour. It is a product that is less finely ground than the material referred to by the second word (found in Num 5.15, for example). However, the first type was considered a more sumptuous kind of flour (made from wheat), used primarily in ritual offerings. The second type, on the other hand, was just ordinary flour (made from barley or wheat) and was rarely used in offerings to God. In translation the primary focus should not be on the fineness of the grinding, but on the high quality of this particular kind of flour as opposed to the commonness of the other type. If the translator has trouble finding corresponding terminology, it is possible to use an ordinary word for the common flour or meal (or "coarse meal, or flour") and the same word qualified by "best" or "finest" for the more luxurious product (compare NJV "choice flour").

Oil: the term used here is a very general one which, in other contexts, may mean "fat." But here it refers to **oil**, and for all practical purposes the people of Israel knew only olive oil. This is made explicit in TEV. In those languages where olive trees are unknown, it is possible to use a more general term referring to vegetable oil, but excluding animal fat in this context.

Frankincense: a resin, or gummy substance which comes from a tree or shrub (see FFB, pages 121-122, and Zohary, page 197). It was dried and in some cases reduced to a powder. This substance was often used in rituals of antiquity, because it produces a pleasant odor when burned. It was a very expensive product because it was usually imported from the southeastern coast of the Arabian peninsula, through the intermediary of Arabia. Normally it was used only in ritual ceremonies. To give a meaningful rendering of this term, some translators have had to resort to expressions like "something that smells sweet when it is burned" or "tree sap that smells like perfume when burned."

Pour . . . and put: TEV uses a single verb for what is done with the oil and the incense, but the Hebrew has two. In the receptor language it may be better to separate the two actions as in RSV: **pour** for the oil and **put** or "apply" with regard to the incense, since one is liquid and the other is in the form of a solid or a powder. Translators should be careful not to give the impression that the incense is mixed in with the flour. Rather it is given alongside or on top of it.

2.2 RSV	TEV
and bring it to Aaron's sons the priests. And he shall take from it a handful of the fine flour and oil, with all of its frankincense; and the priest shall burn this as its memorial portion upon the altar, an offering by fire, a pleasing odor to the LORD.	and bring it to the Aaronite priests. The officiating priest shall take a handful of the flour and oil and all of the incense and burn it on the altar as a token that it has all been offered to the LORD. The odor of this food offering is pleasing to the LORD.

Aaron's sons the priests: see the discussion under 1.5 and 1.7.

He: TEV translates the pronoun **he** by the phrase "**the officiating priest**" in order to make it clear that the reference is to the priest and not to the person making the offering. This model should probably be followed in many other languages.

Take from it a handful of the fine flour and oil: the actual quantity of flour and oil brought by the lay person is not made clear. And while the amount to be taken for burning by the priest is not precise, probably the term **handful** is to be taken as a reference to the amount an average person could scoop up with a single hand. This may be better translated in some languages as "dip his hand into the flour . . . and take some out to burn . . . ."

With all of its frankincense: the oil and flour are only partially used in the offering, and what remains is taken by the priests for food (see verse 3). Only the incense is totally offered to God.

Burn: see 1.9.

Altar: the altar of sacrifice and not the altar of incense (see comment under 1.5).

As its memorial portion: the RSV rendering is somewhat obscure. The term may indicate the fact that the sacrifice reminded God of the person who brought it to him. Mft has "as a reminder to the Eternal." Or it may mean "pledge" because the small part was representative of the whole. This is the meaning adopted by TEV, NAB, and NEB with the use of the word "**token**." In other languages this may have to be expressed as "something showing the LORD that the whole offering is his" or something similar.

The remaining flour and oil not burned in the offering could be eaten by the priests. According to Nehemiah 13.12 the tithes of grain, wine, and olive oil were stored within the Temple building.

2.3	RSV	TEV
	And what is left of the cereal offering shall be for Aaron and his sons; it is a most holy part of the offerings by fire to the LORD.	The rest of the grain offering belongs to the priests; it is very holy, since it is taken from the food offered to the LORD.

What is left of the cereal offering: the part of the grain offering (and of certain animal sacrifices) that was not burned was considered as belonging to the priestly class.

Aaron and his sons: although the wording is slightly different in this verse, the meaning is the same as "Aaron's sons the priests" (see 1.5, for example). It includes Aaron's descendants as well as his immediate sons. In this context it may be translated simply "the priests."

A most holy part: literally "holiest of holy ones," a construction often used in Hebrew to express the idea of the superlative. These same words are frequently used in the Old Testament with reference to a particular place—"the most holy place"— within the Tent of the LORD's presence and later in the Temple (see Exo 26.33; 1 Kgs 8.8). In this verse, however, this is not the case. In Leviticus it is used only to designate that which comes from offerings consecrated to God and can only be used for sacred purposes. In this case they were reserved for the priests and their families.

The preposition **of** which links **a most holy part** with **the offerings by fire** should not be translated literally. Here it has the meaning "selected from." TEV makes the meaning clearer by showing the causal relationship: **"since it is taken from the food offered to the LORD."**

The translation of the word **holy** is particularly difficult in some languages. It is used throughout the Old Testament to qualify more than fifty different nouns. In most cases the primary component of meaning is "set apart from ordinary use" or "dedicated to God." The idea of moral purity is a secondary component in some contexts, but this is clearly not the case here. The RSV addition of **part** is not recommended. The TEV rendering **"it is very holy"** is better, but in the receptor language it may be necessary to say something like "it is strictly set apart from ordinary use," or ". . . for God's purposes," or ". . . for them [the priests] alone." Translators should try to avoid using terms meaning physically "clean" or "white" to express the idea of holiness. Some languages have a word for ritual purity which may be adequate if it is accompanied by a proper explanation in the glossary giving details of the Jewish system.

Offerings by fire: see 1.9.

2.4   RSV   TEV

"When you bring a cereal of-fering baked in the oven as an offer-ing, it shall be unleavened cakes of fine flour mixed with oil, or unleav-ened wafers spread with oil.

If the offering is bread baked in an oven, it must be made without yeast. It may be thick loaves made of flour mixed with olive oil or thin cakes brushed with olive oil.

Verses 4-8a concern three (or perhaps four) ways of preparing and presenting the grain offering: two kinds of bread baked in an oven (verse 4); bread cooked on a griddle (verses 5-6); and bread cooked in a pan (verse 7). The unity of these verses is marked in Hebrew by the fact that the second person singular pronoun is used throughout the section, whereas the second person plural appears in verses 11-12. This is not evident in English translations, since the singular and plural pronouns are identical. If the use of the second person singular pronoun in the receptor language is taken as referring to one individual, then it is probably better to use the plural or some kind of impersonal construction—such as "someone"—throughout.

Baked in the oven: the **oven** was either a kind of hole dug in the earth or a hollow round object made of baked clay and placed on the ground. A fire is made under this object, and when it is well heated, the dough is inserted through the top opening and placed against the inner walls in order to cook it. Some languages may have to say something like "cooked in a hot enclosure" or "made into bread by a hot box." Note that the use of a loanword may imply a modern electric or gas oven and should be avoided.

Cakes . . . wafers: scholars are not certain as to the exact makeup and means of preparation of these kinds of bread. The first was probably a circular loaf placed on a stick (compare 26.26). In most languages the use of the term for **cakes** will be quite misleading if used for either term. The second term indicates something more like a kind of flat biscuit which is still eaten in the Near East today. The translator should use two rather general terms, but it is important that they designate kinds of bread that are made without yeast. In most cultures there is a way to distinguish between thicker, loaf-type bread and a flatter bread like a biscuit. Possible models are "thick bread and flat bread" or "soft bread and hard bread."

Mixed with oil: more accurately "kneaded in oil." If the translator wants to keep the verb "knead," it is better to make the direct object "flour" (compare verse 5) rather than **cakes**.

Unleavened: in translating the idea **unleavened** or **"without yeast,"** some languages have had to say something like "lacking that which causes it [bread] to rise."

Spread with oil: or "brushed," "smeared," "coated" with oil.

2.5

RSV	TEV
And if your offering is a cereal offering baked on a griddle, it shall be of fine flour unleavened, mixed with oil;	If the offering is bread cooked on a griddle, it is to be made of flour mixed with olive oil but without yeast.

Baked on a griddle: a thick plate made of pottery (and later of metal) with small depressions similar to a modern waffle iron. In some languages one may have to say "a flat cooking pan" or "a flat iron for baking." This object was placed on three stones between which a fire was built. The dough was then put on the surface of the pan or disk and cooked.

Fine flour: see verse 1.

Mixed with oil: see verse 4.

2.6

RSV	TEV
you shall break it in pieces, and pour oil on it; it is a cereal offering.	Crumble it up and pour the oil on it when you present it as an offering.

You shall break it in pieces: the future tense here has an imperative meaning. The exact significance of this part of the ritual is uncertain, but perhaps it is intended to correspond to 1.6, where the animal sacrifice is cut into pieces. It may be possible in some languages to leave the subject impersonal, but otherwise the subject pronoun **you** may be rendered "the person making the offering."

Pour oil on it: in some cases it may be wise to say something like "pour more oil on it" in order to make it clear that this is the second time oil is used in this ritual.

It is a cereal offering: this information may seem unnecessary or repetitious in some languages. But the intention of the writer was probably to mark the end of the paragraph on grain offerings of this type. It may be translated as a kind of summary statement: "This is the way a person offers this kind of grain offering."

2.7 RSV	TEV
And if your offering is a cereal offering cooked in a pan, it shall be made of fine flour with oil.	**If the offering is bread cooked in a pan, it is to be made of flour and olive oil.**

It will be advisable in many languages to restructure the first part of this verse to say something like "if the offering you bring is bread cooked in a pan" or "if what you offer is pan-baked bread" or "if your grain offering is one made into bread in a pan . . . ."

Cooked in a pan: a metal disk, slightly rounded or bent upward at the edges, something like a frying pan. In some cases an instrument was made so that it could serve as a pan when held one way and a griddle (verse 5) when turned over.

It shall be made: an impersonal passive form such as this is often used in giving instructions. In the previous verses (4-6) as well as in the beginning of this verse the pronouns are second person singular. But both the second person singular and the passive forms are used for giving directions of a general nature. In some receptor languages an impersonal third person (singular or plural) may be used, but others may retain the second person singular or use a second person plural everywhere—including those places where the source text has the impersonal passive. The most important question the translators must ask themselves is "How do we normally speak when giving general instructions?" The same forms should then be used in this context.

This verse does not explicitly state that the bread is prepared without yeast (is unleavened), but verse 11 leaves no doubt that this is the case. So this information should probably be supplied, if there is any danger that the reader might think that yeast would be used in this case.

2.8 RSV	TEV
And you shall bring the cereal offering that is made of these things to the LORD; and when it is presented to the priest, he shall bring it to the altar.	**Bring it as an offering to the LORD and present it to the priest, who will take it to the altar.**

TEV has restructured and shortened this verse considerably. The future tense at the beginning of this verse becomes an imperative. The qualifying word **cereal** is omitted because it is unnecessary in the larger context. Similarly, **made of these things** has been left implicit. Finally the temporal clause starting with **when . . .** has also been made into an imperative to make a more natural-sounding sentence. The final independent clause of RSV becomes a relative clause in the dynamic rendering. While the meaning remains the same and flows much more naturally in TEV, some may feel that this structure tends to downplay the role of the priest in bringing the offering to the altar.

Made of these things: this may be understood in two different ways. It may be taken to refer only to the last-mentioned kind of grain sacrifice and meaning "made in this way" or **made of these things** (that is, the way or the materials described in verse 7). If this interpretation is adopted, this verse would be a continuation of the paragraph started in verse 7, as in RSV, TEV, NEB, and many other versions. Although this interpretation is probably best, some scholars understand it to refer to any of the three ways mentioned in the preceding verses. NJV, for example, translates "made in any of these ways" and makes this a new paragraph. American Translation (AT) and NAB read the same but without making a new paragraph. This solution is also adopted by certain other versions. Mft begins the verse "all these cereal offerings . . . ."

The preparation and cooking would have been done at home, and then the finished product was brought to the Tent of the LORD's presence for the ceremonial offering. There is a change from second person singular to third person singular in the second part of this verse in the original, and this corresponds with the change of place from the home of the offerer to the Tent.

To the LORD: some translations have rendered this phrase "to the sanctuary," since that is where the LORD was thought to be present in a special way (see 1.5). And it should be remembered that in many languages it is necessary to say "to me" when direct discourse is being used.

Presented to the priest: that which is offered to God could not be presented directly by the lay person. It was necessary to have the priest as an intermediary in making this presentation.

2.9   RSV   TEV

And the priest shall take from the   The priest will take part of it as a
cereal offering its memorial portion   token that is has all been offered to
and burn this on the altar, an offer- the LORD, and he will burn it on the
ing by fire, a pleasing odor to the   altar. The odor of this food offering
LORD.   is pleasing to the LORD.

This verse is similar to the last part of verse 2 above, but the following slight differences are important and should be noted by the translator: (1) This verse has the additional clause **shall take from the cereal offering . . . and**. (2) The words **its memorial portion** are a complement of the verb **take from** in this additional phrase rather than of the verb "to burn" as in verse 2b. The receptor language translation should reflect these differences.

2.10   RSV   TEV

And what is left of the cereal offering The rest of the offering belongs to
shall be for Aaron and his sons; it is   the priests; it is very holy, since it is
a most holy part of the offerings by   taken from the food offered to the
fire to the LORD.   LORD.

This verse is identical with verse 3 above and should be translated in the same way, unless there is something in the immediate context that requires slightly different wording in the receptor language.

2.11   RSV   TEV

"No cereal offering which you bring to the LORD shall be made with leaven; for you shall burn no leaven nor any honey as an offering by fire to the LORD.

None of the grain offerings which you present to the LORD may be made with yeast; you must never use yeast or honey in food offered to the LORD.

Verses 11-16 present a somewhat disjointed text in which subjects introduced are tied together by an association of ideas instead of being handled in a logical, systematic way. Grammatically there is a switch from the second person plural (in verses 11-12) to the second person singular (in verses 13-15). Because of the nature of modern English, this shift is not seen in our translations, but in KJV it is apparent in the use of "ye" for the plural and "thou/thy" for the singular. This kind of shift is common in Old Testament texts and is thought by some scholars to reflect different source documents. However, what is important in translation is to decide whether or not the persons referred to by these pronouns are the same or different. Since they are thought to be the same, the translation must reflect that fact and avoid confusing the reader. Some languages will use the singular throughout while others will have the plural. Naturalness in the receptor language will determine the translator's choice.

No cereal offering . . . shall be made with leaven: the word for **leaven** ("**yeast**") here is not the same as in verse 4 above. The previous verse has a word meaning "bread made without yeast." In this verse two other words are used. The first literally means "that which is sour" (a very similar word is used in Hebrew for "vinegar"), and the second is the name of the product (yeast) that causes things to ferment or to become sour. The first term is translated in NEB as "anything that ferments," which brings out the general nature of the word in Hebrew. The second term is then specifically translated **leaven**. After understanding the ideas involved, translators should simply translate them as naturally as possible in their language.

Honey: this word is used both of honey from bees and a kind of concentrated fruit syrup made from raisins or dates. In the context of this chapter on grain offerings, the second meaning is preferred by some scholars, but most simply translate it **honey**. Honey and yeast are to be understood here as two separate items and not as a mixture. However, they are mentioned together probably because they both involve fermentation. Some languages distinguish between honey found in the forest and that which is bought in stores. In this context the term for natural wild honey is clearly more appropriate.

The point of forbidding the offering of yeast and honey was that they could not be burned. Things that ferment, like the blood of the animals offered in sacrifice (see 17.11), were thought to have a life of their own and were therefore excluded from those items that could be offered by fire to God.

2.12   RSV   TEV

As an offering of first fruits you may bring them to the LORD, but they shall not be offered on the altar for a pleasing odor.	An offering of the first grain that you harvest each year shall be brought to the LORD, but it is not to be burned on the altar.

This verse is in contrast with the preceding one because it does not involve burning. Therefore it may be well to introduce it with a conjunction like "However" or "But."

You may bring them: as in RSV, many versions interpret this verb as giving permission rather than actually requiring that the first fruits be brought to the LORD. Others, however, see it as a strict requirement. In addition to TEV and a number of French versions, the following English renderings should be noted: "you shall bring them" (NASB) and "you shall present them" (NEB). It is also worthy of note that while the English version of JB and NJB have "you may offer them," both the 1955 and the 1973 French version of the *Bible de Jérusalem* have "you shall offer them." In many languages the passive of TEV will not be a possible solution. If this is the case, probably an expression indicating permission as in RSV is best.

Them: this pronoun seems to refer to the grain offerings made with yeast or honey mentioned in verse 11. They are acceptable as first fruits but are not to be burned on the altar.

First fruits: the first fruits were regularly offered by the people of Israel at their yearly harvest festival which is sometimes known as the Festival of Weeks (Lev 23.15-22). The first grain harvested, like the first born animal or child, was thought to belong particularly to the LORD. The word used here is not the same as in verse 14. In this case it means simply "beginning" but refers to grain in this context. In other contexts it is used to refer to wine, oil, and honey as well as to grain (2 Chr 31.5). In these cases they seem not to have been burned, even partially, on the altar. Probably they were simply given to the priests to be presented to God before they ate them.

For a pleasing odor: because this is repetitious and is a part of what is being negated, TEV has seen fit to omit it. Other languages may also prefer to leave this information implicit.

2.13   RSV   TEV

You shall season all your cereal offerings with salt; you shall not let the salt of the covenant with your God be lacking from your cereal offering; with all your offerings you shall offer salt.	Put salt on every grain offering, because salt represents the covenant between you and God. (You must put salt on all your offerings.)

Season . . . with salt: the origin and meaning of this custom of putting salt on offerings to God is not certain. But it was an ancient ritual practice in other groups as well as among the Jews. Salt was used to symbolize consecration and making something permanent. The basic idea probably came from the fact that salt was used to conserve food (in contrast with the fermentation brought about by honey and yeast). A "covenant of salt" meant a permanent agreement (see Num 18.19 and 2 Chr 13.5) which could not be broken or modified. TEV has made explicit the fact that putting salt on offerings made to God **"represents the covenant."** An even more explicit translation may say something like "because salt is a sign of the permanent covenant which God (or, I) made with you" or "since salt is a sign that the covenant which God (or, I) made with you will last forever."

Covenant: the concept of covenant is central to the thought of the Old Testament. The term has to do with a compact or formal agreement between two parties. Each party commits himself to undertake certain things on behalf of the other. And this commitment was sealed by an oath. The word used here originally had to do with "binding" or an "obligation."

You shall not let the salt of the covenant with your God be lacking from your cereal offering: this is a redundant and rather awkward way of saying the same thing as the first clause of this verse, but with the addition of the expression **the salt of the covenant with your God**. The two are reduced to one and translated simply at the beginning of the verse in TEV as **"put salt on every grain offering."** But in some languages the repetition may be acceptable. In fact, it may serve to emphasize the importance of the statement. The expression **the salt of the covenant with your God** will need to be clarified so that the reader understands that **salt** represents the mutual commitment between God and his people Israel. Some languages may say "do not leave the salt out of your offerings to God because the salt should remind you of your agreement with God."

With all your offerings: the final statement becomes a parenthetical one in TEV. This sets it off as a more general requirement than has been given up to this point. Translators should make it clear that the requirement is not limited to grain offerings, but that all offerings are to be accompanied by salt. In some languages a good model may be "Indeed, you must put salt on all your offerings."

2.14 RSV	TEV
"If you offer a cereal offering of first fruits to the LORD, you shall offer for the cereal offering of your first fruits crushed new grain from fresh ears, parched with fire.	When you bring to the LORD an offering of the first grain harvested, offer roasted grain or ground meal.

The words of this verse are reordered in TEV so that **cereal** is represented by "grain" later on in the verse, and the expressions **cereal offering** and **first fruits** are not repeated as in RSV. This produces a shorter and clearer sentence that should probably be followed in other dynamic translations.

First fruits: this is the more technical term for the first grain gathered at the beginning of the harvest period. But the meaning is essentially the same as the word translated **"first fruits"** in verse 12.

Crushed new grain from fresh ears, parched with fire: the text is difficult and may be understood in two different ways. TEV and NJB give the impression that there were two possible kinds of offerings—either roasted grain or ground meal. RSV and most other versions seem to indicate that only one kind of offering was involved—meal from fresh grain that is first roasted and then ground or pounded. Either interpretation is acceptable.

2.15   RSV   TEV

And you shall put oil upon it, and lay   **Add olive oil and put incense on it.**
frankincense on it; it is a cereal of-
fering.

This verse is essentially the same as 1b above. However, the subject in this case is second person singular in keeping with the section beginning at verse 13. In verse 1, however, it is third person singular and refers to "anyone."

Note that the final clause, **it is a cereal offering**, has been omitted by TEV as being redundant. But in many languages such repetition may be quite natural and should be retained.

2.16   RSV   TEV

And the priest shall burn as its me-   **The priest will burn that part of the**
morial portion part of the crushed   **meal and oil that is to serve as a**
grain and of the oil with all of its   **token, and also all the incense, as a**
frankincense; it is an offering by fire   **food offering to the LORD.**
to the LORD.

Memorial portion: this is probably to be understood in the sense of a "token" or "reminder." See verse 2 above.

Frankincense: see verse 1.

An offering by fire: see 1.9.

35

Chapter 3

TEV Section Heading: "**Fellowship Offerings.**"

In keeping with previous section headings, it may be necessary to say something like "Israel (offers) sacrifices to God to restore fellowship" or some other complete sentence taking into account the information given in the following paragraph.

A third type of sacrifice is described in this chapter. It has been given a wide variety of names in different versions of the Bible. RSV and some other English versions have called it a "peace offering," while TEV (and NIV) used the term "Fellowship Offering." In NJB it is called "The Communion Sacrifice." The animal sacrificed is divided into three parts: the first is burned for God on the altar (verses 3-5), the second goes to the priest (see 7.31-36), and the third is eaten in a community meal by the worshiper, his family, and—in some cases—other invited guests (see 7.15-21). The idea of fellowship or "communion" (compare NJB) is therefore central to this ritual. It involves communion with God as well as fellowship with other human beings. It is possible in some languages to translate "shared offering" as in NEB. In others, it may be necessary to use a more descriptive phrase such as "the sacrifice performed together with a common meal" or "the sacrifice followed by a meal together."

Chapter 3 is made up of two main sections: the first is devoted to the sacrifice of a larger animal (verses 1-5), and the second concerns a smaller animal (verses 6-16a). This second section is subdivided into two paragraphs dealing with the offering of a sheep (verses 7-11) or a goat (verses 12-16a). Verses 16b-17 provide the conclusion in the form of two general rules.

3.1   RSV   TEV

"If a man's offering is a sacri-   When anyone offers one of his
fice of peace offering, if he offers an   cattle as a fellowship offering, it is to
animal from the herd, male or female,   be a bull or a cow without any de-
he shall offer it without blemish be-   fects.
fore the LORD.

The structure of RSV, roughly following the Hebrew (which actually has four "ifs"), is awkward because of the repetition of the word **if**. The first **If** is similar to the one in 1.3 marking the contrast between the whole burnt offering of chapter 1 and the fellowship offering in this chapter. It is better translated in many languages as "when," since it is assumed that the sacrifice will be made. The second **if** corresponds to the one in 3.6, which contrasts the offering of a larger animal with the presentation of a smaller animal. In most cases it will be wise to do something like

TEV at this point and say "When a person offers . . ." or "In the case that someone offers . . . ." Another possibility is to use **If** in the first case but omit it in the second: "If the offering is to restore fellowship and the animal brought is a bull or a cow, then it must be without any defect at all . . . ."

Notice also that the RSV rendering of this verse contains two occurrences of both the noun **offering** and the verb **offer**. The reproduction of the form of RSV in this verse will probably be considered quite unnatural in most languages. In most cases this repetition can easily be reduced as in TEV.

From the herd: the TEV rendering, "**a bull or a cow**," contains both the idea of **herd** and **male or female**. On the meaning of **herd** see 1.2.

Without blemish: see 1.3 as well as the text of 22.17-25.

Before the Lord: this part has been left implicit in TEV, and it may be more natural to do so in some other languages. See also 1.3.

3.2	RSV	TEV
	And he shall lay his hand upon the head of his offering and kill it at the door of the tent of meeting; and Aaron's sons the priests shall throw the blood against the altar round about;	The man shall put his hand on the head of the animal and kill it at the entrance of the Tent of the LORD'S presence. The Aaronite priests shall throw the blood against all four sides of the altar

He: the pronoun is better translated by the noun "The man" in order to avoid any confusion. Otherwise it might be understood that the priest is to place his hand on the head of the animal. See 1.4.

Upon the head of his offering: that is, on the head of the animal which he has brought. See 1.4.

Kill: or better, "slaughter" or "cut the throat." See 1.5.

At the door of the tent of meeting: that is, somewhere near the altar. Compare 1.5. See also the diagram of the Tent of the LORD's Presence on the last page of the introduction, "Translating Leviticus."

Aaron's sons the priests: see 1.5. In some languages it may be advisable to leave implicit the mention of Aaron's sons at this point and say simply "the priests."

Round about: see 1.5,11.

3.3	RSV	TEV
	And from the sacrifice of the peace offering, as an offering by fire to the LORD, he shall offer the fat covering the entrails and all the fat that is on the entrails,	and present the following parts of the animal as a food offering to the LORD: all the fat on the internal organs,

He: again this pronoun refers to the lay person offering the sacrifice and not to the priest. This should be clear to both the reader and the hearer.

TEV adds the words **"the following parts"** to introduce the list which begins in this verse and continues in verse 4. This kind of addition may be helpful in other languages. Compare also verse 9.

The peace offering: these words are left implicit in TEV since they have already been mentioned in the Section Heading and in the first verse of this chapter. This also serves to reduce the redundancy found in RSV.

An offering by fire: the term is translated as **"food offering"** by TEV and NEB. See 1.9 as well as the table "The Sacrifices in Leviticus," with its discussion, in the introduction, "Translating Leviticus."

The fat covering the entrails and all the fat that is on the entrails: the fat is considered the choicest part of the animal (see Gen 45.18; Psa 63.5) and was therefore to be offered to the Lord. A literal translation, following the wording of RSV, seems unnecessarily repetitious in many languages and may be shortened as in TEV without losing any of the meaning.

Entrails: the stomach and intestines as in 1.9. The TEV rendering **"the internal organs"** is probably too general and should be avoided.

3.4 RSV	TEV
and the two kidneys with the fat that is on them at the loins, and the appendage of the liver which he shall take away with the kidneys.	the kidneys and the fat on them, and the best part of the liver.

The two kidneys: in some languages it is unnecessary and even surprising to use the number **two** in this context, since this is implicit in the word **kidneys**. It may be common knowledge in the receptor language that an animal normally has two kidneys. In other languages it may be advisable to say "both kidneys" in order to make it clear that not just one is used.

At the loins: this may also be considered redundant in some languages since the location of the kidneys will also be well known. This refers to that part of the body on either side of the backbone between the ribs and the hipbone. NEB renders this expression "beside the haunches."

The appendage of the liver: among certain neighboring tribes of the Israelites, the liver was used in divination rites. Possibly this is why Jewish legislation required that it be burned. But it is also true that, like the fat, this particular part of the liver referred to as the **appendage** was considered a delicacy and was therefore appropriate to be set aside for God. In many languages it is best to render it as "the choicest part of the liver," since that will probably communicate the meaning better than the name of a particular part of the organ.

Which he shall take away with the kidneys: this phrase provides additional information which may be left implicit in some languages because it is repetitious. The verb **take away** in RSV is misleading. The meaning is "remove" (NEB).

3.5   RSV   TEV

Then Aaron's sons shall burn it on the altar upon the burnt offering, which is upon the wood on the fire; it is an offering by fire, a pleasing odor to the LORD.	The priests shall burn all this on the altar along with the burnt offerings. The odor of this food offering is pleasing to the LORD.

Aaron's sons: for the sake of clarity and naturalness, it may be better to say simply "**The priests**" as in TEV. See 1.5,7,8.

It: the singular pronoun in RSV reflects a singular in the original, but the Hebrew pronoun clearly refers to all the items listed in verses 3-4. The translation should therefore reflect this fact. NJV has "these," and NAB, like TEV, translates "**all this**."

Upon the burnt offering: the preposition **upon** is misleading. It should be translated "with" (NJV and NAB), "**along with**" (TEV), or "in addition to" (NJB). These were to be burned along with the offerings presented to God each morning. Compare Exodus 29.38-42.

Which is upon the wood on the fire: this information has been left implicit in TEV. This may also be done in many other languages, since "**burnt offerings**" implies wood and fire. See 1.8.

An offering by fire: or "**food offering**" as in TEV and NEB; see 1.9 and the introductory discussion.

Pleasing odor . . . : see 1.9.

3.6   RSV   TEV

"If his offering for a sacrifice of peace offering to the LORD is an animal from the flock, male or female, he shall offer it without blemish.	If a sheep or goat is used as a fellowship offering, it may be male or female, but it must be without any defects.

Verses 6-11 describe the sacrifice of a sheep as a fellowship offering and therefore constitute a separate paragraph. Verse 6 deals with the smaller animals, but it corresponds to verse 1 above, where the instructions concern the larger animals offered in sacrifice.

From the flock: the expression used here implies a sheep or a goat, and this has been made explicit in TEV. See 1.2,10.

Without blemish: see 1.3; 3.1. In some languages it may be necessary to make it clear that these words are intended to qualify the animal brought as a sacrifice rather than the worshiper who offers it.

To the LORD: this has been left implicit in TEV, since the act of making an offering in this context implies God as the object of worship. But in some languages it will serve to provide emphasis as to the special character of the offering.

3.7 RSV TEV

If he offers a lamb for his offering, then he shall offer it before the LORD,

If a man offers a sheep,

He: as in verse 2 above, the pronoun refers to the person bringing the sacrificial animal. In order to avoid possible confusion between the worshiper and the priest, it may be better to use the noun "the man."

Lamb: although the word used here is traditionally translated **lamb**, indicating a young sheep, the age of the animal is very likely not significant here. Both TEV and NJV render it "**sheep**." NEB has "ram," but this is not advisable, since the information given in verse 6 makes it clear that the animal could be male or female.

Then he shall offer it before the LORD: this information may be left implicit in many languages. Its repetition seems to add nothing to the meaning.

3.8 RSV TEV

laying his hand upon the head of his offering and killing it before the tent of meeting; and Aaron's sons shall throw its blood against the altar round about.

he shall put his hand on its head and kill it in front of the Tent. The priests shall throw its blood against all four sides of the altar

This verse (with reference to smaller animals) corresponds to verse 2 above, where the sacrifice of a larger animal is in view. With the exception of a few minor stylistic variations, it is identical to the earlier verse and should be translated similarly. This verse, however, says **before the tent of meeting**, while verse 2 has "at the door of the tent of meeting." This distinction, though admittedly a relatively insignificant one, should probably be maintained in translation, unless it is stylistically awkward in the receptor language or implies a different location. Also, it should be noted that where verse 2 has "the blood," this verse has **its blood**.

3.9 RSV TEV

Then from the sacrifice of the peace offering as an offering by fire to the LORD he shall offer its fat, the fat tail entire, taking it away close by the back bone, and the fat that covers the entrails, and all the fat that is on the entrails,

and present the following parts of the animal as a food offering to the LORD: the fat, the entire fat tail cut off near the backbone, all the fat covering the internal organs,

Then from the sacrifice of the peace offering: the wording of RSV reflects the Hebrew but may be somewhat confusing. Some have translated "Since it is a fellowship offering, these parts must be given as a food offering to the LORD: . . ." or "He shall present part of the fellowship offering as a food offering to the LORD

. . . ." NIV begins this verse: "From the fellowship offering he is to bring a sacrifice . . . ." Compare verse 3.

An offering by fire: see verse 5 above.

The fat tail entire: the tail of the kind of sheep raised in Palestine may have contained as much as seven or more kilograms of fat and was considered a delicacy. While this kind of information is important in understanding the text, it cannot be included in the text of the translation. It may therefore be wise to give such information in a cultural footnote. See FFB, page 75.

Cut off near the backbone: the word for **backbone** used in this verse is found only here in all the Old Testament. Probably it referred to a specific place on the spinal column of the animal. Such precision is important in a text of this kind and, as far as possible, translators should choose an equivalent technical term in their own language. If this proves to be impossible, a natural descriptive phrase should be used. For example, "at the very end of the spinal column (or, backbone)" or in some cases "the entire tail" may imply cutting off at this particular point. In other languages the same idea can be conveyed by speaking of the "very beginning of the tail."

On the translation of **entrails** as "**internal organs**" in TEV, see 1.9

3.10   RSV   TEV

and the two kidneys with the fat that   the kidneys and the fat on them, and
is on them at the loins, and the ap-   the best part of the liver.
pendage of the liver which he shall
take away with the kidneys.

This verse is word-for-word the same as verse 4 above and should normally be translated identically, unless there are discourse considerations in the larger context that require some modification.

3.11   RSV   TEV

And the priest shall burn it on the   The officiating priest shall burn all
altar as food offered by fire to the   this on the altar as a food offering to
LORD.   the LORD.

Verse 11 repeats the information given in verse 5 but in a slightly different form. While this verse has **the priest** in singular form, verse 5 has "Aaron's sons" in the plural. In this verse the expression "one of the priests" may be used.

The most significant difference between verses 5 and 11 consists in the use of the word **food** (here and in verse 16a) along with the Hebrew term corresponding to **offered by fire** (see 1.9), translated together as "**a food offering**" in TEV. In 21.22 the word rendered **food** here is translated "bread" in RSV but refers to all that is not eaten by the lay persons; in other words, both the part offered to God as well as the part reserved for the priest(s). Perhaps it was under the influence of this understanding of the word that it came to be used here, even though God does not actually "eat" this food. The translator must avoid using a term that would give the impression that God actually partakes of the meal. See 1.9 and the remarks on the expression "offered by fire" in the introduction, "Translating Leviticus," following the table of "Sacrifices in Leviticus."

As in verse 5 above, the pronoun **it** refers to all the items mentioned in the previous verses. So it is probably better translated "**all this**," as in TEV.

3.12   RSV   TEV

  "If his offering is a goat, then   If a man offers a goat,
he shall offer it before the LORD,

If his offering . . . : see verse 7.

A goat: the vocabulary choices of some languages may make it impossible for the translator to use a single word at this point. Two separate words may be required to make explicit the fact that the goat may be male or female. This is clearly implied in the larger context (verse 6).

Before the LORD: this phrase is again left implicit in TEV (see 1.3).

3.13-15   RSV   TEV

13 and lay his hand upon its head,   13 he shall put his hand on its head
and kill it before the tent of meeting;   and kill it in front of the Tent. The
and the sons of Aaron shall throw its   priests shall throw its blood against
blood against the altar round about.   all four sides of the altar 14 and
14 Then he shall offer from it, as his   present the following parts as a
offering for an offering by fire to the   food-offering to the LORD: all the fat
LORD, the fat covering the entrails,   on the internal organs, 15 the kid-
and all the fat that is on the entrails, neys and the fat on them, and the
15 and the two kidneys with the fat   best part of the liver.
that is on them at the loins, and the
appendage of the liver which he
shall take away with the kidneys.

Verses 13-15 repeat in a very similar way the ideas presented in verses 8-10. However, there is no mention here of the tail (found in verse 9). This was left out here because it concerns only the sheep. Other minor variations between these verses and verses 8-10 above have to do with the pronouns instead of full nouns, but naturalness in the receptor language should determine which of these is used.

3.16 RSV TEV

And the priest shall burn them on the altar as food offered by fire for a pleasing odor. All fat is the LORD's.

The priest shall burn all this on the altar as a food offering pleasing to the LORD. All the fat belongs to the LORD.

The first part of verse 16 corresponds to verse 11. The expression **for a pleasing odor** (compare 1.9 and 3.5) is then added.

Them: this corresponds in meaning to the pronoun "it" in verses 5 and 11. It refers to the totality of those items mentioned in the previous verses.

As food offered by fire: see verse 9 as well as 1.9.

All fat is the LORD's: this is a concluding statement summing up an important aspect of chapter 3. It is a general rule that may have to be expressed more explicitly by saying something like "All the fat of the sacrificial animals belongs to the LORD as a special offering." Some versions, such as *Traduction œcumenique de la Bible* (TOB,) set it off as a separate paragraph. Compare also the French common language version (FRCL), which makes this phrase the beginning of a new paragraph that includes verse 17 as well.

3.17 RSV TEV

It shall be a perpetual statute throughout your generations, in all your dwelling places, that you eat neither fat nor blood."

No Israelite may eat any fat or any blood; this is a rule to be kept forever by all Israelites wherever they live.

Verse 17 develops further the concluding statement at the end of the previous verse. It emphasizes the absolute character of the prohibition against the eating of fat or blood.

A perpetual statute throughout your generations: this phrase occurs seventeen times in Leviticus. It indicates a rule that is to be observed by all Israelites for all time. The rule forbidding the eating of blood or fat was to apply not only to the Israelites living at that time, but also to all future generations. This expression must be translated in such a way as to include both. It may be rendered "This regulation is to last for all time . . ." (Mft), or "This is a rule for all time from generation to generation . . ." (NEB), or "This is a permanent law for all your descendants."

In all your dwelling places: it has been suggested that the emphasis here is not on the individual houses in which Israelites dwell, but on the fact that this rule is to apply in whatever country they may live. If they were living outside the Promised Land they could not offer sacrifices, but they would still have to abstain from eating blood or fat. However, it is more likely that these words mean "anywhere in Palestine" (compare Ezek 6.6,14). Some possible models of translation are: "all over the country" (Mft); "wherever you may live" (NJB); "wherever you live" (NIV and NEB). TEV has "**wherever they live**," with the focus on future generations.

Neither fat nor blood: in some languages it may be necessary to specify "the blood or any fatty parts (of the animals)." This is especially true in those languages where there is no distinction between animal fat and vegetable oil, since the consumption of vegetable oil is not forbidden. The mention of blood, the symbol of life (see 17.10-14), completes the picture.

It may be more natural to reverse the order of the two propositions in this verse, as has been done by TEV. That is, the rule against eating fat or blood may be stated first and then followed by the requirements regarding time and place.

Chapter 4

Section Heading: "**Offerings for Unintentional Sins.**"

The TEV section heading is fuller than the actual name given in the text for this fourth kind of sacrifice. The term used in the text (verse 3) is simply "sin offering." The context of this chapter, however, makes it quite clear that unintentional sins are meant. The word used here is the same as the Hebrew word usually translated simply as "sin" in English, but it has two other meanings. It may refer to the sacrifice offered to God to obtain pardon, as in verse 3 (RSV). TEV simply translates "for his sin" in verse 3, but in 4.13 and 4.32 it appears as "sin-offering." In other contexts it is used to refer to the animal offered in such a sacrifice (verse 25). In those languages that require complete sentences as headings, one might try "The priest (offers) sacrifices to God when people sin without meaning to," or "Israel seeks pardon for careless sins," or "Israel makes offerings to God for unintentional sins," or "Offerings to be made when people sin accidentally."

The animal that is sacrificed is divided into two parts: the fat parts are burned on the altar for God; all the rest is to be burned outside the camp (6.30) except in those cases where the meat is given to the priests (6.24-29).

The section about the sacrifice to obtain pardon includes six paragraphs, following the introduction in the first two verses.

1. 4.3-12:	the ritual required when a high priest commits sin.
2. 4.13-21:	the ritual required when the whole community sins.
3. 4.22-26:	the ritual required when a ruler commits sin.
4. 4.27-35:	the ritual required when an ordinary lay person commits sin.
5. 5.1-6:	some concrete examples of unintentional sin.
6. 5.7-13:	a softening of the law's requirements with regard to the poor.

Paragraphs 4 and 6 are further subdivided into two parts each. These subdivisions will be discussed at the beginning of these sections.

4.1-2   RSV   TEV

1 And the LORD said to Moses,
2 "Say to the people of Israel, If any
one sins unwittingly in any of the
things   which   the   LORD   has

1 The LORD commanded Moses
2 to tell the people of Israel that
anyone who sinned and broke any of
the LORD's commands without in-

45

**commanded not to be done, and
does any one of them,**

**tending to, would have to observe
the following rules.**

Verses 1 and 2 serve as an introduction to the entire section from 4.1 through 5.13.

And the LORD said to Moses: literally "And the LORD spoke to Moses saying." In this verse there are two different words meaning "speak" and "say." In most languages this is considered repetitious, and one of the words is omitted as in RSV. If, however, such an introductory formula is natural in the receptor language, then it should be used in translation. TEV has rendered it even more dynamically with **"The LORD commanded Moses to tell . . . ,"** because verse 2 begins with another verb with the same meaning. This formula is repeated more than thirty times with minor variations throughout the book of Leviticus. Compare 1.1.

Say: the same as the first verb in verse 1, but imperative in form. In RSV this begins a direct quotation of what the LORD said to Moses, but in TEV the entire section is translated as an indirect quotation. The usual practice of the receptor language should determine whether direct or indirect discourse is to be used here. It is very important to make proper adjustments in the text if indirect discourse is chosen. Similarly, if direct discourse is used, it may sound unnatural in many languages to have the LORD speaking of himself in the third person. It would be more natural to say "I, the LORD" or simply "I."

People of Israel: literally "sons of Israel." This could also be translated simply "Israelites." But it should be determined whether or not the receptor language distinguishes between "Israelites" (the people of ancient Israel) and "Israelis" (citizens of the modern State of Israel founded in 1948).

Any one: the traditional translation of the word used here is "a soul" (see KJV). But it actually has a wide variety of meanings throughout Scripture and may be translated according to its context as "person," "self," "soul," "life," "breath," "throat," or "corpse." Each occurrence of the word must be translated according to the particular context in which it is found. In this context it clearly means "person," which may be translated as "someone," "anyone," or "any person."

Sins: the primary meaning of the Hebrew word used for "sin" here is not a moral one, as if breaking a specific commandment of the Law. It conveys rather the idea of breaking a relationship. At the heart of its meaning is the notion of "missing the mark," or "failure to attain something," or "to be out of harmony with someone," or "not to be in a normal and right relationship with someone." In this case, it is God that has been harmed.

Unwittingly: that is, involuntarily or unintentionally. The word comes from a root which means "to wander" or "to get lost." Both NAB and NEB translate "inadvertently," while Mft speaks of "sinning unawares." The problem of unintentional sin versus deliberate sin is treated in more detail in Numbers 15.30-36.

Which the LORD has commanded not to be done: taken literally, this would seem to refer to prohibitions or the commandments that are formulated negatively (such as "Do not commit murder" or "Do not steal"), in opposition to those commandments framed in positive terms (such as "Respect your father and your mother . . . "). But the idea may be a disregard for any of the LORD's commandments. However, most versions retain the negative meaning: "does what is forbidden" (NIV) or "does anything prohibited . . . " (NEB).

In TEV the words **"would have to observe the following rules"** have been added. This idea is implied in the text and serves to introduce the rather long section dealing with the various cases that are described in the following verses. A similar phrase may be necessary in a number of other languages.

4.3   RSV   TEV

if it is the anointed priest who sins,
thus bringing guilt on the people,
then let him offer for the sin which
he has committed a young bull without blemish to the LORD for a sin-
offering.

If it is the High Priest who sins
and so brings guilt on the people, he
shall present a young bull without
any defects and sacrifice it to the
LORD for his sin.

If it is . . . : these words are also used in verses 13, 22, and 27. They serve to set apart the four different cases described in these paragraphs.

The anointed priest: on the word **priest** see 1.5. On the idea of "anointing" see 8.10. According to 6.22, 8.12, and 16.32, it is without question the "**High Priest**" who receives the anointing with oil, which indicates his special consecration, although there are other texts (7.35-36 and 10.7) which seem to indicate that all the priests were so anointed. In this verse it is best to translate explicitly "**the High Priest**," since the Hebrew has the definite article **the** before **anointed priest**.

Thus bringing guilt on the people: or "thereby causing all the people to be guilty of sin." Another way of saying this might be "transmitting guilt to everyone in the community" or "thereby making the people also become guilty" (NAB). The High Priest, the intermediary between God and the people, is not considered a mere private individual whose affairs concern only himself. He is, rather, a public person whose actions affect all those he represents before God.

For the sin which he has committed: literally, "the sin which he has sinned." The noun and the verb have the same root. In some languages this repetition of information may be omitted as stylistically unacceptable, even though it seems to add emphasis in the original. In TEV it has been shortened to "**for his sin**" and has been placed at the end of the sentence in accordance with natural English usage. If the noun is used here, it should be noted that the collective singular is unnatural in some languages and should be translated by a plural, that is, "sins."

A young bull: literally "a (young) bull, a son of the herd." The idea of youth is not essential to the meaning of the word and has been omitted in some translations (NJV and NASB), but most versions retain it. On the identity of this animal, see FFB, pages 62-63. And for the expression "son of the herd," see the discussion under 1.5. This expression is usually omitted as redundant in most languages.

Without blemish: see 1.3 and the text of 22.17-25.

For a sin offering: see the discussion of this expression under the section heading for this chapter.

4.4   RSV   TEV

He shall bring the bull to the door of
the tent of meeting before the LORD,

He shall bring the bull to the entrance of the Tent, put his hand on

and lay his hand on the head of the bull, and kill the bull before the LORD.	its head, and kill it there in the LORD's presence.

The beginning of this ritual is very similar to the one for the Whole Burnt Offering; see 1.3-5.

To the door of the tent of meeting before the LORD: if the priest is at the entrance to the Tent, it is implied that he is in the presence of the LORD. For this reason the words **before the LORD** may be left implicit in some languages. This is especially true since the same phrase is again repeated at the end of this verse. If, however, the use of repetition for emphasis is natural in the receptor language, then it should be retained.

Lay his hand on the head of the bull: see 1.4.

Kill: or better "slaughter." See 1.5.

Before the LORD: see above.

4.5   RSV   TEV

And the anointed priest shall take some of the blood of the bull and bring it to the tent of meeting;	Then the High Priest shall take some of the bull's blood and carry it into the Tent.

The anointed priest: if the reference is clear, this may be translated by the pronoun "he" referring back to verse 3. Otherwise it may be best to specify again using the full noun phrase "**the High Priest**" as in TEV.

Shall take some of the blood of the bull: only a part of the blood is taken to the Tent of the LORD's presence. In some languages it is required to state how the blood is carried to the Tent. In such cases it may be necessary to use the name of a specific kind of container (for example, "in a bowl"), but it should be kept as generic as possible, since the original does not specify the kind of container.

To the tent of meeting: see 6.30; 10.18; 16.27.

4.6   RSV   TEV

and the priest shall dip his finger in the blood and sprinkle part of the blood seven times before the LORD in front of the veil of the sanctuary.	He shall dip his finger in the blood and sprinkle it in front of the sacred curtain seven times.

His finger: if the receptor language has no general word for finger, it may be necessary to indicate which finger was used. In such a case it is probably better to specify the index finger of the right hand.

Sprinkle: this is not the same verb as in 1.5,11; 3.2,8,13, which has also sometimes been mistakenly translated "sprinkle." In this verse the idea is indeed sprinkling and may be translated "cause to spatter."

Seven times: the number seven represents completeness or fullness and was considered sacred in the ancient Near East. For this reason it was thought to be especially effective in such rituals. A footnote explaining this detail may be advisable in some languages.

Before the LORD: although this phrase is left implicit in TEV, it is significant because the LORD was thought to be symbolically present especially in the Most Holy Place where the Covenant Box was kept. In many receptor languages it will be better to make these words explicit.

In front of: that is, on the east side of the curtain dividing the Holy Place and the Most Holy Place, or the side facing the High Priest as he stood inside the Holy Place but outside the Most Holy Place, where he entered only once a year (see chapter 1—especially verse 34—and the arrangement of the Tent in the diagram on page 8). In some languages the meaning may be more clearly rendered "just outside the Most Holy Place" instead of **in front of the veil of the sanctuary**.

The veil of the sanctuary: Exodus 26.33 provides a description of this object. It has been translated **"the sacred curtain"** (TEV), "the sacred veil" (NEB), and "the curtain of the inner sanctuary" (Mft). In some languages there may be no specific term for curtain, so it may be necessary to translate the "holy cloth" (that separates the Holy Place from the Most Holy Place). On the word **"sacred"** or "holy," see 2.3.

4.7   RSV   TEV

And the priest shall put some of the blood on the horns of the altar of fragrant incense before the LORD which is in the tent of meeting, and the rest of the blood of the bull he shall pour out at the base of the altar of burnt offering which is at the door of the tent of meeting.

Then he shall put some of the blood on the projections at the corners of the incense altar in the Tent. He shall pour out the rest of the blood at the base of the altar used for burning sacrifices, which is at the entrance of the Tent.

The horns of the altar: while the Hebrew term is the same as the one used to refer to the horns of animals (cattle or oxen, for example), it is not necessary to retain this image in translation. In some languages this may be the natural thing to do, but in others it will probably be preferable to use a word like **"projections"** (TEV), or "knobs" (Mft), or "protruding corners." Some scholars maintain that the horns were intended to represent the animals sacrificed, but others feel that they originally functioned as points on which cooking utensils rested (see 1 Sam 2.14).

The altar of fragrant incense: the writer carefully distinguishes the incense altar from the altar of sacrifice which is at the entrance to the Tent of the LORD's presence (see diagram on page 8 and the discussion under 1.5). On the terms for **incense**, see 2.1.

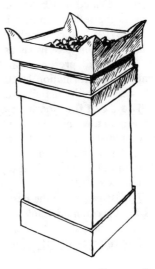

AN ALTAR WITH "HORNS"

Before the LORD: the phrase is again repeated for emphasis, and unless the repetition is considered awkward, it should probably also be repeated in the receptor language.

Pour out: this is the ordinary word for pouring; it is not the same as "tossing" (in 1.5,11; 3.2 and elsewhere) or "sprinkling" (in 4.6 above).

At the base of the altar: elsewhere the word translated **base** means "foundation" (Micah 1.6; Psa 137.7) or "beginning." Here it refers to the bottom part of the altar. It may be equally well translated "at the foundation of the altar." NJB has "at the foot of the altar . . . ."

Altar of burnt offering: this is the altar of sacrifice, as opposed to the altar of incense mentioned above.

4.8-10   RSV   TEV

8 And all the fat of the bull of the sin offering he shall take from it, the fat that covers the entrails and all the fat that is on the entrails, 9 and the two kidneys with the fat that is on them at the loins, and the appendage of the liver which he shall take away with the kidneys 10 (just as these are taken from the ox of the sacrifice of the peace offerings), and the priest shall burn them upon the altar of burnt offering.

8 From this bull he shall take all the fat, the fat on the internal organs, 9 the kidneys and the fat on them, and the best part of the liver. 10 The priest shall take this fat and burn it on the altar used for the burnt offerings, just as he does with the fat from the animal killed for the fellowship offering.

As indicated in 10a, these verses describe a ritual which corresponds to what is done in the fellowship offering described in 3.3-4. Translators should make sure that verse 10a refers to what precedes and not to what follows. One dynamic translation of this passage is as follows: "these are the same parts as those taken from the animal presented in the fellowship offering." Another has shifted the parenthetical information in 10a to verse 8, beginning this section with the words "Just as he did with the bull given as a fellowship offering, he shall take the fat . . . ."

The ox of the sacrifice of the peace offerings: the word translated **ox** by RSV refers to any animal of the bovine species (FFB, page 62) whether young or old, male or female. In order to clarify the meaning of the first preposition **of** in this phrase, it may be better to translate "the ox [bull] offered to God as a peace [fellowship] offering." It is also possible to translate by a more general term such as **"animal"** (see TEV).

The priest: since the person referred to here is still the High Priest (see verses 3 and 5), it is often advisable to make this clear in translation. The word **priest** may be wrongly understood to mean any one of the priests.

The altar of burnt offering: or the altar of sacrifice. See verse 7.

4.11-12   RSV   TEV

11 But the skin of the bull and all its flesh, with its head, its legs, its entrails, and its dung, 12 the whole bull he shall carry forth outside the camp to a clean place, where the ashes are poured out, and shall burn it on a fire of wood; where the ashes are poured out it shall be burned.

11 But he shall take its skin, all its flesh, its head, its legs, and its internal organs, including the intestines, 12 carry it all outside the camp to the ritually clean place where the ashes are poured out, and there he shall burn it on a wood fire.

But: this may be seen as marking the contrast between what is done with the other parts of the animal in verses 8-10 and the parts mentioned here, so the transition word **But** is used in most versions. However, in some languages this word may be misleading. Since a sequence of events is being described, some translators have preferred to introduce this verse with a word like "Then," or "Next," or something similar. Or it may be omitted as in NJB, NAB, AT, and Mft.

Verses 11 and 12 constitute a long and rather complex sentence in both RSV and TEV. Translators may consider breaking them down into two shorter and simpler sentences in the receptor language.

In RSV, which reflects the Hebrew, there is no verb in verse 11; it appears at the beginning of verse 12 after **the whole bull**. In many languages it will be necessary to restructure these two verses so that the verb is shifted forward and the ideas flow more naturally. This, of course, will require the combined numbering of the two verses as 11-12.

He shall carry: it is very unlikely that the High Priest actually performed this action himself. A more literal translation may say "he causes to go out." AT and JB have rendered this idea by a passive expression "[the bull] must be carried out(side)." In other languages where the passive is not a valid option, it may be possible to say something like "he shall cause (or send, or command) someone to carry it all out . . . " or "they [indefinite] shall carry it out." Note that NJB has "he will then have carried out."

The whole bull: since the preceding verse has stated that certain fatty parts have already been burned on the altar, it may be misleading to translate literally **the whole bull**. "All the rest of the bull," or "all the remaining parts of the animal," or something similar, may be more appropriate.

Its entrails, and its dung: (compare Exo 29.14) the term rendered **entrails** in RSV has been understood by some scholars as referring rather to the heart and lungs, and the one translated **dung** to mean "**intestines**." Others think that the first word refers to the intestines and the second to fecal matter (as in RSV). If the latter is accepted as correct, care should be taken to translate in such a way as to indicate that the fecal matter was still contained in the intestines of the animal at the time of its death, rather than material already excreted from the body before death. However, the interpretation of TEV is probably better in this context; but compare 1.9.

A clean place: the reference here is not just to a place that has been thoroughly sterilized, but to one that has been reserved for this special ritual purpose. In some cases it may be possible to add a qualifying term as in TEV "**the**

ritually clean place," or "the ceremonially pure place," but in other languages the word sometimes translated "taboo" may be appropriate to qualify the place.

It shall be burned: if the receptor language cannot use a passive form here, it is advisable to use an impersonal form such as "they shall burn it," or make the High Priest the subject of a causative verb and say "he shall cause it to burn," or perhaps better, "he shall command that they burn it."

In the case of this sacrifice, no part of the animal offered is eaten by the priest(s). This conforms to the rule explicitly stated with regard to grain offerings in 6.16 and is equally valid for the other offerings made by the priests.

It should be noted that the recurring phrase which is repeated in verse 20b, 26b, 31b, 35b, as well as in 5.10b, 13a, 16b, 18b, and 6.7 ("the priest shall make atonement for them [or, him]") does not appear at the end of this paragraph. Since the sacrifice is offered for the High Priest himself, it is hard to see how he could perform this ritual gesture on himself. For details on this ritual see verse 20.

4.13   RSV   TEV

"If the whole congregation of Israel commits a sin unwittingly and the thing is hidden from the eyes of the assembly, and they do any one of the things which the LORD has commanded not to be done and are guilty;

If it is the whole community of Israel that sins and becomes guilty of breaking one of the LORD's commands without intending to,

If . . . : marking the beginning of a new topic within the overall subject of offerings for unintentional sins (see verse 3). If the receptor language uses several levels of headings, it will be appropriate to place one at the beginning of this verse. It may read "The sacrifice for the whole community." Compare NJB. It may be advisable in some languages to introduce this hypothetical situation with something like "Suppose a person commits . . . " or "Let us say that someone sins . . . ." This kind of structure will make it possible to have shorter sentences that will be more easily understood in the material that follows.

The whole congregation of Israel: since the High Priest was a part of the community, this case is very similar to the preceding one, and the rituals are almost identical.

Commits a sin: see verses 2 and 3.

Unwittingly: see verse 2.

Congregation . . . assembly: two different words are used for the same sociopolitical reality which is the people of Israel. The first word seems to have a more marked religious connotation than the second. In translation it is unnecessary to search for two different terms, since this might lead the reader to think that two separate realities are being discussed. The use of this abstract collective noun (**congregation** or **assembly**) as the subject of verbs like "to sin" and in some cases "to not know" may present difficulties in some languages. In such cases it may be better to use an expression like "all the people of Israel" as the subject.

And the thing is hidden from the eyes of the assembly: it is difficult to imagine how the whole community could be guilty of a sin of which they were all unaware. If this were the case, it would never be known. While it is possible that the LORD might reveal it to them, there may have been some one or some few persons in the group that would be aware of the sin. In this case it may be better to translate "and *most* of the people [group or assembly] are unaware of it." The passive formulation **is hidden** may also be misleading in some languages. Other ways of rendering this idea may be "even though the community is unaware of the matter" (NIV) or "some wrong which escapes the notice of the people" (Mft).

And are guilty: the idea of guilt may be difficult to express in some languages. In this context the words **are guilty** may have to be translated in some languages as "bear responsibility" or "deserve punishment."

4.14　　　　　RSV　　　　　　　　　　　　　　TEV

when the sin which they have committed becomes known, the assembly shall offer a young bull for a sin offering and bring it before the tent of meeting;	then as soon as the sin becomes known, the community shall bring a young bull as a sin offering. They shall bring it to the Tent of the LORD's presence;

When the sin . . . becomes known: the passive idea is again better translated in many languages by an expression like "when they discover [or realize] that they have been sinning," or "when they become aware of their sin," or "when someone calls attention to the sin." But it would almost certainly be someone within the group, not from outside, that would call attention to it.

The assembly: or "the people [of Israel]."

Young bull: this is exactly the same expression used in 4.3, so it should be translated in the same way here.

A sin offering: while the subject of this chapter has been the sin offering from the beginning, this is the first use of the technical term in the text itself. It is probably the easiest of the different names of sacrifices to translate. In most cases it is adequate to say "an offering for unintentional sin," but some may prefer "an offering to seek forgiveness." See the discussion of the section heading at 4.1.

The end of verse 14 picks up the same information that is found in verses 3b-4a, except that the words "without blemish" are left implicit as in Hebrew. Receptor language usage should determine whether or not they need to be made explicit here.

4.15　　　　　RSV　　　　　　　　　　　　　　TEV

and the elders of the congregation shall lay their hands upon the head of the bull before the LORD, and the bull shall be killed before the LORD.	the leaders of the community shall put their hands on its head, and it shall be killed there.

Compare this verse with 4b.

The elders: in ancient times, as in many cultures today, age was thought to be a guarantee of wisdom. Consequently older persons were entrusted with greater responsibility within the community. In translation the accent should probably be placed on the position of leadership and authority these people held and not on the number of years they had lived. If in the receptor language these two ideas are synonymous as in ancient Israel, then **elders** will be a good translation. Otherwise it may be better to follow the TEV model and translate something like "**leaders**."

Lay their hands: see 1.4. The use of the plural **hands** follows the Hebrew and is used because there were several persons involved. But the parallels with verses 4, 24, 29, and 33 seem to indicate that each elder or leader placed only one hand on the head of the animal. Every language has its own way of clarifying such nuances. It is up to the translator to decide what is the most natural way of expressing this meaning.

Shall be killed: the RSV rendering is passive in form, but literally the text has only a third person masculine singular. It says simply "he must kill (or, slaughter)." Some ancient versions have the plural "They must kill," but the singular seems to fit better here. In those languages where the passive is not possible and an agent must be named, it is probably best to say "one of them [the elders] shall kill." The expression "someone shall kill" is too vague and might give the impression that the person performing this action is from outside the group of Israelite leaders. Some have suggested that it was the High Priest who killed the animal, but this is unlikely since in the other paragraphs it is always the one who lays his hand on the head of the animal who then slaughters it. The High Priest appears in the ritual only in the following verse.

Before the LORD: see verse 4.

4.16-19   RSV   TEV

16 Then the anointed priest shall bring some of the blood of the bull to the tent of meeting, 17 and the priest shall dip his finger in the blood and sprinkle it seven times before the LORD in front of the veil. 18 And he shall put some of the blood on the horns of the altar which is in the tent of meeting before the LORD; and the rest of the blood he shall pour out at the base of the altar of burnt offering which is at the door of the tent of meeting. 19 And all its fat he shall take from it and burn upon the altar.

16 The High Priest shall take some of the bull's blood into the Tent, 17 dip his finger in it, and sprinkle it in front of the curtain seven times. 18 He shall put some of the blood on the projections at the corners of the incense altar inside the Tent and pour out the rest of it at the base of the altar used for burning sacrifices, which is at the entrance of the Tent. 19 Then he shall take all its fat and burn it on the altar.

These verses repeat, in a somewhat simplified form, the same basic content found in verses 5-10. Translators should carefully compare their rendering of these

verses with 5-10 in order to assure that both the similarities and the minor differences between the two are reproduced in translation.

4.20   RSV   TEV

Thus shall he do with the bull; as he did with the bull of the sin offering, so shall he do with this; and the priest shall make atonement for them, and they shall be forgiven.	**He shall do the same thing with this bull as he does with the bull for the sin offering, and in this way he shall make the sacrifice for the people's sin, and they will be forgiven.**

Thus shall he do with the bull; as he did with the bull of the sin offering, so shall he do with this: the wording in RSV is rather awkward and should probably, in most languages, be restructured along the lines of TEV. The idea is "he [the High Priest] shall proceed with this bull in exactly the same way as he did with the bull offered for his own sin." NAB reads "doing with this bullock just as he did with the other sin offering bullock . . . ."

And the priest shall make atonement for them, and they shall be forgiven: this formula is repeated in slightly different forms in each of the different cases of unintentional sin, except in the case of the High Priest himself (see 4.26b, 31b, 35b; 5.6b, 10b, 13b, 16b, 18b; 6.7). The translation should make clear that **them** refers to the people of Israel. But beyond this the expression has been understood in two different ways:

(1) It is interpreted as being a summary of the ritual described in the preceding verses. See, for example, TEV, NEB, NIV, and other versions "**in this way . . . .**" But if this is the case, it is difficult to see why such an affirmation is not made at the end of the paragraph regarding the sin of the High Priest (see verse 12).

(2) The second interpretation is that this constitutes the continuation and conclusion of the ritual. That is, the High Priest adds to what has already happened, by a word or a gesture (or both) confirming explicitly the validity of what has taken place. In this case it is easy to understand why the affirmation is absent from verse 12. If this second interpretation is followed, the last half of this verse might begin with "And then the priest shall . . . ." Or, following JB, "When the priest has performed the rite of atonement over the people, they will be forgiven." See also TOB and NJV.

The final expression **be forgiven** in either case is passive and must be changed to active form in some languages. While the agent is not expressed, it is clearly God who will forgive the people. So it may be necessary to say "and God will forgive them" or "they obtain God's forgiveness."

4.21   RSV   TEV

And he shall carry forth the bull outside the camp, and burn it as he burned the first bull; it is the sin offering for the assembly.	**Then he shall take the bull outside the camp and burn it, just as he burns the bull offered for his own sin. This is an offering to take away the sin of the community.**

The first part of this verse corresponds to verse 12 above.

And: the transition word here should indicate a continuation in the sequence of events. "Then" in TEV (as well as NIV) is a good model. Both NAB and Mft restructure and use the word "also." It might also be possible in some languages to say something like "Next . . . " or "Afterward . . . " at the beginning of the verse.

He shall carry forth: as in verse 12, it may be better to say "he shall have [the bull] carried out . . . " or "they shall carry . . . ," since more than likely the High Priest did not do the work himself. Compare NJB, which reads "he will then have the bull carried out of the camp."

The first bull: NEB reads "the other bull." The reference is to the bull **"offered for his own sin,"** as it is clearly stated in TEV. In most languages this kind of explicit statement will be necessary, since many readers may otherwise fail to make the connection with verses 3-12.

It is the sin offering for the assembly: this summary statement has no parallel at the end of the other paragraphs in this section. In place of the word **assembly**, it may be more natural to say "all the people" in some languages.

4.22   RSV   TEV

"When a ruler sins, doing unwittingly any one of all the things
which the LORD his God has commanded not to be done, and is
guilty,

If it is a ruler who sins and becomes guilty of breaking one of the
LORD's commands without intending
to,

If several levels of headings are being used, verse 22 begins a new paragraph that may be titled "The sacrifice for a ruler (of the community)." Compare JB or NJB.

This verse is almost the same as verses 3 and 13 above, except that this section has a different subject.

When . . . : the Hebrew word used here is different from the one introducing the previous paragraph (verse 13) and the following paragraph (verse 27), but this variation is probably only stylistic.

A ruler: here we are concerned not with a religious leader like the High Priest, but a civil ruler. NJV has "chieftain"; Mft reads "chief"; NAB has "a prince." NJB and NIV translate simply "a leader," while NEB has "a man of standing." In the context of Israel his authority was limited, and his sin did not bring guilt on others as was the case with the High Priest (in verse 3). Nevertheless, because of his position of leadership, his responsibility was greater than that of an ordinary person (compare verse 27).

The LORD his God: in some languages the use of the possessive pronoun in this expression presents serious problems. The receptor language rendering should avoid the impression that God somehow belongs to the ruler, or that the ruler is the only one who worships God. The expression may indicate that the ruler himself was also subject to higher authority, namely God's. In some cases it may even be necessary to omit the pronoun altogether if the wrong meaning is communicated by its presence in the text.

4.23　　　　RSV　　　　　　　　　　TEV

if the sin which he has committed is made known to him, he shall bring as his offering a goat, a male without blemish,	then as soon as the sin is called to his attention, he shall bring as his offering a male goat without any defects.

If the sin . . . is made known to him: see verse 14.

A goat, a male: if the receptor language has a single word that contains the idea of maleness as well as the idea of **goat**, then it should be used here. The choice of the animal is related to the status of the person who had sinned. A male goat was considered of less value than a bull (see verse 3) but more valuable than a female goat (see verse 28).

Without blemish: see 1.3 and 22.17-25.

In some languages translators may feel that it is necessary to add the implicit information which states the purpose of the sacrifice, "to obtain the forgiveness of God" (FRCL).

4.24　　　　RSV　　　　　　　　　　TEV

and shall lay his hand upon the head of the goat, and kill it in the place where they kill the burnt offering before the LORD; it is a sin offering.	He shall put his hand on its head and kill it on the north side of the altar, where the animals for the burnt offerings are killed. This is an offering to take away sin.

He: the pronoun here refers to the ruler or leader who has committed the sin and has brought the animal as a sacrifice.

Shall lay his hand upon the head: see 1.4 and 4.15.

Kill: or "slaughter." See 1.5.

In the place where they kill the burnt offering: this detail in the ritual does not appear in verses 4 or 15. However, this does not seem to imply that the slaughter of the male goat is performed in a different place from the slaughter of the bull in the two preceding cases. Consequently TEV fills out the implied information by adding "**on the north side of the altar.**"

4.25　　　　RSV　　　　　　　　　　TEV

Then the priest shall take some of the blood of the sin offering with his finger and put it on the horns of the altar of burnt offerings and pour out the rest of its blood at the base of the altar of burnt offering.	The priest shall dip his finger in the blood of the animal, put it on the projections at the corners of the altar, and pour out the rest of it at the base of the altar.

The priest: the reference here is not to the High Priest, but to whichever of the ordinary priests that happened to be on duty at the time (compare verses 3-10, 16).

His finger: the wording here is slightly different in verse 6 above, but the meaning does not seem to be significantly affected.

The horns of the altar: see verse 7.

The altar of the burnt offering: see verse 7. Since this altar was situated on the outside of the sanctuary, the blood was not taken into the sanctuary as was done in the two preceding cases (see also 10.18).

4.26

RSV	TEV
And all its fat he shall burn on the altar, like the fat of the sacrifice of peace offerings; so the priest shall make atonement for him for his sin, and he shall be forgiven.	Then he shall burn all of its fat on the altar, just as he burns the fat of the animals killed for the fellowship offerings. In this way the priest shall offer the sacrifice for the sin of the ruler, and he will be forgiven.

He shall burn . . . : see verses 8-10.

Peace offerings: see 3.12-16.

Make atonement . . . : see verse 20.

So: compare verse 20b.

For him for his sin: this is awkward and repetitious. TEV "**for the sin of the ruler**" will be much clearer and more natural.

4.27

RSV	TEV
"If any one of the common people sins unwittingly in doing any one of the things which the LORD has commanded not to be done, and is guilty,	If it is one of the common people who sins and becomes guilty of breaking one of the LORD's commands without intending to,

Since this verse begins a new paragraph, a subtitle will be appropriate here in those translations using more than one level of heading. A suggested title is "The sacrifice for a common person."

Any one of the common people: literally "a soul of the people of the land." That is, any member of the community of Israel not included among the priests or leaders already mentioned (compare verse 22). On the word "soul," see verse 2.

See verses 3, 13, and 22 for comments on the other elements of this verse.

4.28 RSV TEV

when the sin which he has committed is made known to him he shall
bring for his offering a goat, a female
without blemish, for his sin which he
has committed.

then as soon as the sin is called to
his attention, he shall bring as his
offering a female goat without any
defects.

When the sin . . . is made known: see verse 14.
A goat, a female: compare verse 23 above.
Without blemish: see 1.3 and 22.17-25.

In this verse, as in verse 23, some translations have made explicit the fact that
the offering is made "to obtain forgiveness from God." At the same time it may be
advisable to leave implicit the expression **which he has committed**, which is
repeated twice in the more literal versions.

4.29-30 RSV TEV

29 And he shall lay his hand on the
head of the sin offering, and kill the
sin offering in the place of burnt
offering. 30 And the priest shall take
some of its blood with his finger and
put it on the horns of the altar of
burnt offering, and pour out the rest
of its blood at the base of the altar.

29 He shall put his hand on its head
and kill it on the north side of the
altar, where the animals for the burnt
offerings are killed. 30 The priest
shall dip his finger in the blood of
the animal, put it on the projections
at the corners of the altar, and pour
out the rest of it at the base of the
altar.

These two verses repeat almost word-for-word verses 24 and 25. But careful
comparison should be made in order to reflect any differences that will be natural
in the receptor language. For example, the words "it is a sin offering" found at the
end of verse 24 are omitted here.

4.31 RSV TEV

And all its fat he shall remove, as the
fat is removed from the peace offerings, and the priest shall burn it
upon the altar for a pleasing odor to
the LORD; and the priest shall make
atonement for him, and he shall be
forgiven.

Then he shall remove all its fat, just
as the fat is removed from the animals killed for the fellowship offerings, and he shall burn it on the altar
as an odor pleasing to the LORD. In
this way the priest shall offer the
sacrifice for the man's sin, and he
will be forgiven.

He shall remove . . . : see 3.3-4. Grammatically the pronoun **he** may refer to
the guilty person or to the priest. The specific mention of the priest later in the verse

may indicate that the subject of the previous verb **remove** is the person offering the sacrifice. If the receptor language requires that the subject of this verb be made explicit, it is probably best to make it the offerer of the sacrifice. Compare 1.6 and 3.3, where the offerer seems to be the one who performs such actions.

For a pleasing odor to the Lord: see 1.9.

And the priest shall make atonement . . . : see verse 20 above.

4.32   RSV   TEV

"If he brings a lamb as his of-   If a man brings a sheep as a sin
fering for a sin offering, he shall   offering, it must be a female without
bring a female without blemish,   any defects.

He brings . . . : the subject of the sentence here is the guilty person. This should be made clear in translation.

A lamb: the term used in Hebrew in this verse refers to an animal of the sheep species without reference to age or sex (see FFB, pages 75-76). The fact that it is a female is made clear later in the verse.

Without blemish: see 1.3 and 22.17-25.

As in verses 23 and 28, it may be a good idea to make explicit the fact that the sacrifice is made "to obtain forgiveness from God for unintentional sins."

4.33-35   RSV   TEV

33 and lay his hand upon the head   33 He shall put his hand on its head
of the sin offering, and kill it for a sin   and kill it on the north side of the
offering in the place where they kill   altar, where the animals for the burnt
the burnt offering. 34 Then the priest   offerings are killed. 34 The priest
shall take some of the blood of the   shall dip his finger in the blood of
sin offering with his finger and put it the animal, put it on the projections
on the horns of the altar of burnt   at the corners of the altar, and pour
offering, and pour out the rest of its   out the rest of it at the base of the
blood at the base of the altar. 35   altar. 35 Then he shall remove all its
And all its fat he shall remove as the   fat, just as the fat is removed from
fat of the lamb is removed from the   the sheep killed for the fellowship
sacrifice of peace offerings, and the   offerings, and he shall burn it on the
priest shall burn it on the altar, upon altar along with the food offerings
the offerings by fire to the Lord; and   given to the Lord. In this way the
the priest shall make atonement for   priest shall offer the sacrifice for the
him for the sin which he has commit-   man's sin, and he will be forgiven.
ted, and he shall be forgiven.

These verses repeat almost word-for-word verses 29-31. The most significant difference is the explicit mention of "**sheep**" near the beginning of verse 35. In the offering of a sheep, the tail is counted as a part of the fat (see 3.9).

Another minor difference is the absence of the phrase "for a pleasing odor to the LORD" (verse 31), which is replaced by **upon the offerings by fire to the** LORD. On this latter expression, see 1.9.

Chapter 5

TEV Section Heading: "**Cases Requiring Sin Offerings**."

On the terminology for "**Sin Offerings**," see the first subheading at the beginning of chapter 4.

Verses 1-13 of this chapter provide the reader with several concrete examples where sacrifice is required because a person has unintentionally committed a sin. Alternative section headings may therefore be something like "Examples from everyday life" or "Some people who must bring sin offerings." NAB entitles this section "For special cases," but it is better to see these as examples rather than special cases. FRCL has "Some concrete examples" (compare also TOB). NJB offers the following heading to guide the reader: "Some cases of sacrifice for sin."

In each of the first four verses of this chapter a specific example is given to illustrate the kinds of sins committed by an ordinary person that require a sin offering. Different languages have various ways of introducing such hypothetical cases. One may say "Suppose that . . ." or "An example: . . . ." Or the whole section may begin with an introductory statement similar to the one in TEV: "Sin offerings are required in the following cases." This actually takes the words "any of these [cases]" from verse 4 and translates them dynamically at the beginning of the section. Both JB and NJB, for example, begin this chapter with the words "If someone sins in any of these following cases: . . . ."

5.1   RSV   TEV

"If any one sins in that he hears a public adjuration to testify and though he is a witness, whether he has seen or come to know the matter, yet does not speak, he shall bear his iniquity.

Sin offerings are required in the following cases.

If someone is officially summoned to give evidence in court and does not give information about something he has seen or heard, he must suffer the consequences.

If . . . : it is equally possible to begin with "For example . . ." or "Suppose that . . . ." See the introductory paragraph above.

If any one sins: literally, "And a soul (person), if she sins." This formula is used with slight variations to introduce each of the four examples in verses 1-4. The mention of "sin" is left implicit in TEV because the context makes it clear that these are cases where "**sin offerings are required**." If this word must be made explicit in the receptor language, this may be done by saying something like "If a person commits sin by not giving information when called to give evidence . . . ."

Hears a public adjuration: the term translated **public adjuration** may refer to a court case in a more restricted legal sense, or more generally to any public palaver where a person would be solemnly charged to tell others what he had seen or heard. NIV, for example, has "public charge." But the courtroom setting seems preferable, as in TEV. After a witness had been called into court, the judge pronounced a curse on him if he should lie or fail to give important information. This was a formal, official way of requiring a person to tell what he had seen or heard about a particular case. It is very similar to the modern practice of requiring a person to swear that he will tell the truth in a court of law.

Yet does not speak: that is, the person fails to testify in court what he knows about the case in spite of the fact that he has been required to do so by the judge.

He shall bear his iniquity: this frequently-used expression usually emphasizes a person's guilt and the fact that he must suffer the consequences and be punished. Most languages have expressions that communicate easily the idea of "suffering the consequences of one's actions." Some say "he must bear the weight of his deed" or "he will not escape the punishment for what he has done." Others have still more idiomatic ways of rendering this idea. What is important is that the meaning be conveyed as naturally as possible.

This verse seems out of place to some scholars because it says nothing about the sin being committed unintentionally (in contrast with the cases mentioned in verses 2-4). But the translator should simply translate the text as it stands. When the text was compiled, there was apparently some connection between this sin and the others that follow.

5.2   RSV   TEV

Or if any one touches an unclean thing, whether the carcass of an unclean beast or a carcass of unclean cattle or a carcass of unclean swarming things, and it is hidden from him, and he has become unclean, he shall be guilty.

If someone unintentionally touches anything ritually unclean, such as a dead animal, he is unclean and guilty as soon as he realizes what he has done.

Or: this marks the introduction of the second example. In some languages it may be better to say "Or, to take another example . . ." or simply "Another case: . . . ."

Unclean thing: in Leviticus the term **unclean** or "impure" is extremely important. It does not have to do primarily with physical cleanliness but is basically a religious idea (see chapters 11–15). But this ritual uncleanness may be transmitted by physical contact or in some cases simply by sight. The general term **an unclean thing** is clarified by specific examples in the text. It may be (1) **the carcass of an unclean beast**, that is, a dead animal that is wild, (2) **a carcass of unclean cattle**, that is, a dead animal that is tame (domesticated) or (3) **a carcass of unclean swarming things**, that is, the body of an animal classed by the Jews as "swarmers" (mouse, weasel, lizard or other reptile, and perhaps also insects). Because of the diversity of this last group, it is difficult to translate in most languages. NIV has

translated accurately but awkwardly "unclean creatures that move along the ground."
AT, NEB, and Mft apparently understand the term as being limited to "reptiles." And
TEV has avoided the problem by grouping all the categories together under the
heading "**a dead animal**," although this may be considered too general in some
languages.

And it is hidden from him: most scholars take this to mean that the dead body
is touched accidentally or unintentionally. But NEB interprets it to mean that the
person performing this action conceals it from others, "and it is concealed by him
although he is aware of it." This interpretation, however, is unlikely and very few
versions follow it. It is better to translate "without being aware of it at the time"
(Mft). Compare 4.13.

5.3   RSV   TEV

Or if he touches human uncleanness, of whatever sort the uncleanness may be with which one becomes unclean, and it is hidden from him, when he comes to know it he shall be guilty.	If someone unintentionally touches anything of human origin that is unclean, whatever it may be, he is guilty as soon as he realizes what he has done.

Or: introducing another example (see verse 2). The receptor language may have
a different way of introducing one of a series of examples.

He: the translation should avoid giving the impression that the same person is
involved here as in the previous verse. This is simply another case which may involve
an entirely different person. It may be helpful to translate "**someone**" as in TEV or
even "someone else" in certain languages.

Human uncleanness: the various kinds of things that were considered **human
uncleanness** by the people of Israel are described in considerable detail in Leviticus
12–15. To translate the term in this context, it is probably best to say something like
"anything unclean that comes from another person." But it may be advisable to
include a cross reference to chapters 12–15 in a footnote.

And it is hidden from him: see verse 2.

When he comes to know it: while the person may be guilty before God as
soon as the action is committed, this verse focuses attention on that person's
awareness of his guilt. Compare 4.13.

5.4   RSV   TEV

Or if any one utters with his lips a rash oath to do evil or to do good, any sort of rash oath that men swear, and it is hidden from him, when he comes to know it he shall in any of these be guilty.	If someone makes a careless vow, no matter what it is about, he is guilty as soon as he realizes what he has done.

Or: introducing the fourth example of an unintentional sin (see verse 2).

With his lips: these words may be left implicit in most languages. Both the verb (utter) and the noun (oath) that follows would clearly imply that the lips or mouth were used in speaking and therefore in committing the sin.

A rash oath: the word **oath** implies taking God as witness when making a promise and indicating a willingness to accept divine punishment in case the promise is not fulfilled. Each language has its own way of talking about these kinds of serious promises before God; for example, "to raise the hand and swear," or "to say what cannot be withdrawn," or simply "to say in the presence (eyes) of God." The addition of the qualifying word **rash** (thoughtless or careless) complicates the translation in some languages. It indicates that the promise is made without thinking seriously about what it means. In some cases it may be necessary to use two verbal expressions such as "promise before God, but fail to consider the meaning (or, seriousness) of the matter."

To do evil or to do good: whether the purpose is good or bad, it is a serious matter to make an oath without thinking.

Any sort of rash oath that men swear: this information is repetitious, but it is added for emphasis. The habits of the receptor language with regard to repetition for emphasis will determine whether or not it should be repeated in translation.

And it is hidden from him: see verse 2.

In any of these: the last two words in the Hebrew text do not fit very well with the preceding word (translated literally "he shall be guilty"). The meaning of these words seems to be that the person will be considered guilty "in either case" (NEB); that is, whether the original purpose of the vow was for good or evil. However, TEV and a number of other versions have left these words out, possibly because they are considered to have been picked up from the following verse and mistakenly placed here (see TOB note).

5.5-6   RSV   TEV

5 When a man is guilty in any of these, he shall confess the sin he has committed, 6 and he shall bring his guilt offering to the LORD for the sin which he has committed, a female from the flock, a lamb or a goat, for a sin offering; and the priest shall make atonement for him for his sin.

5 When a person is guilty, he must confess the sin, 6 and as the penalty for his sin he must bring to the LORD a female sheep or goat as an offering. The priest shall offer the sacrifice for the man's sin.

Following the four examples given in the previous verses (1-4), the text now moves to an account of the ceremony required. Some languages may require some special transitional device to indicate this shift from the examples to the ritual. Most English versions simply begin a new paragraph with "When . . ." or "Whenever . . . ." But NJV sets off the entire first four verses by means of special indentation.

The ceremony itself consists of three parts:
1. a solemn public confession of the sin committed (verse 5);
2. the offering of the victim (verse 6a; a more detailed description of the ritual is given in 4.27-35);
3. the ritual gesture of forgiveness (verse 6b; see 4.20).

He shall confess: the sacrifice is valid only when there is a sincere confession. This involved a public acknowledgment of wrongdoing before the entire community. In some languages it will be necessary to add the word "publicly" in order to make the meaning of the verb clear. Otherwise a private confession might be envisioned. In some languages this idea will have to be rendered by an expression such as "admit in the eyes of (other) people that he did wrong" or "accept before others that he sinned."

The sin which he has committed: (in verse 6) literally "the sin he sinned" as in 4.3. This expression is not the same as the one translated very similarly in verse 5, but the meaning is the same. Both may easily be left implicit in a number of languages, but it should be made clear that the reference is to one of the unintentional sins mentioned previously.

From the flock: see 1.2.

His guilt offering . . . for a sin offering . . . : the mention of the **guilt offering** in this verse causes a great deal of confusion. The word used here is the same as the technical term for the guilt or repayment offering discussed in verses 14-16, but in this case it is not to be taken in its technical sense. Rather it is used to mean "as his penalty" (see TEV, NEB, NIV, and NJV).

And the priest shall make atonement for him for his sin: see 4.20.

At the end of this verse, one Hebrew text called the Samaritan Pentateuch adds the words "and he shall be forgiven," as in 4.20, 26, 31, and 35, as well as in verses 11, 13, 16, and 19 of this chapter. These words are added here by NEB, but very few other versions seem to find this addition necessary. It may be, however, that the TEV rendering "**for the man's sin**" is not strong enough.

5.7	RSV	TEV

"But if he cannot afford a lamb, then he shall bring, as his guilt offering to the Lord for the sin which he has committed, two turtledoves or two young pigeons, one for a sin offering and the other for a burnt offering.	If a man cannot afford a sheep or a goat, he shall bring to the Lord as the payment for his sin two doves or two pigeons, one for a sin offering and the other for a burnt offering.

The final part of this section (7-13) deals with the question of those members of the community who may not have sufficient means to offer a sheep or a goat. It shows that the forgiveness of God is not absolutely bound to the type of victim offered. The sacrifice is a symbolic expression of the request for forgiveness and the desire for reconciliation, as well as the need for restitution involving the life of a sacrificial animal.

But: the Hebrew conjunction here is a very common one and does not necessarily have to be translated explicitly in every instance. The translators of RSV (as well as NEB) apparently felt the need of a transition word here to mark the contrast between those who could afford the usual sacrificial animal and those who could not. NAB has "however." But many translations (including TEV, NIV, NJB, and AT) move directly to the case of the person who cannot afford a sheep or a goat without any transition word. They do, however, begin a new paragraph at this point.

If he cannot afford: literally, "if his hand does not reach the amount of . . . ." In some languages this idea will be expressed quite differently. It may be necessary to say "if he does not have enough wealth (or, possessions)" or perhaps simply "if he cannot get a sheep or a goat."

A lamb: that is, "**a sheep or a goat**." See 3.7.

Two turtledoves or two young pigeons: see 1.14.

As his guilt offering: as in verse 6 above, this is another nontechnical use of the same word that is also used for the "guilt offering" later in this chapter. Here it means "what he is required to bring," "as his penalty," or "as his punishment," as in the preceding verse.

One for a sin offering and the other for a burnt offering: in addition to bringing a bird for a **sin offering** to replace the sheep or goat mentioned in verse 7, a second bird is required as a whole burnt offering. This is perhaps to acknowledge God's gracious provision for those of lesser means.

5.8   RSV   TEV

He shall bring them to the priest, who shall offer first the one for the sin offering; he shall wring its head from its neck, but shall not sever it,

He shall bring them to the priest, who will first offer the bird for the sin offering. He will break its neck without pulling off its head

First: the **sin offering** retains the place of primary importance in the ritual.

Wring its head from its neck: see 1.15.

But shall not sever it: compare 1.17. According to the wording of RSV, this seems to contradict the preceding statement, but Jewish tradition reconciles the two acts by saying that the priest must avoid breaking the esophagus and the trachea while breaking the neck bones.

5.9   RSV   TEV

and he shall sprinkle some of the blood of the sin offering on the side of the altar, while the rest of the blood shall be drained out at the base of the altar; it is a sin offering.

and sprinkle some of its blood against the side of the altar. The rest of the blood will be drained out at the base of the altar. This is an offering to take away sin.

He shall sprinkle: see 4.6, 17.

The rest of the blood shall be drained out: some languages will require an active formulation of this passive idea with the agent being specified. In this case the agent is the priest. In some languages this will be rendered "the priest must drain out the blood . . . ." Compare 1.15.

The base of the altar: see 4.7.

Sin offering: in some languages it may be necessary to make explicit the fact that the sin referred to here is unintentional.

5.10   RSV   TEV

Then he shall offer the second for a burnt offering according to the ordinance; and the priest shall make atonement for him for the sin which he has committed, and he shall be forgiven.	Then he shall offer the second bird as a burnt offering, according to the regulations. In this way the priest shall offer the sacrifice for the man's sin, and he will be forgiven.

Then: the transition word here should indicate that the next step in a series of events is taking place.

The second: clearly meaning "the second bird." But in some languages it will be better to translate "the other bird."

According to the ordinance: the root meaning of the word used here is "judgment, verdict." But here it simply means according to the "rules" or "directions" given for normal whole burnt offerings.

And the priest shall make atonement . . . : see 4.20.

5.11   RSV   TEV

"But if he cannot afford two turtledoves or two young pigeons, then he shall bring, as his offering for the sin which he has committed, a tenth of an ephah of fine flour for a sin offering; he shall put no oil upon it, and shall put no frankincense on it, for it is a sin offering.	If a man cannot afford two doves or two pigeons, he shall bring two pounds [one kilogram] of flour as a sin offering. He shall not put any olive oil or any incense on it, because it is a sin offering, not a grain offering.

But: as at the beginning of verse 7, it may not be necessary to use such a strong transition word in translation. Naturalness in the receptor language should be the determining factor.

If he cannot afford . . . : the expression is slightly different from the beginning of verse 7, because the word "amount" does not appear here. And the verb translated **afford** is also different in this verse. The identical wording of verses 7 and 11 in both RSV and TEV is misleading. In view of the differences between the introductory words in the Hebrew of these verses, it is quite possible to translate here "if he does not have . . . ." TOB, for example, begins verse 11 with "If someone does not have in hand . . . ," and FRCL translates "If a person does not have at his disposition . . . ."

This second paragraph (5.11-13) probably does not represent a further reduction of the offering in favor of the extremely poor, as it has sometimes been interpreted. It seems rather to be a practical matter. In fact, the value of the flour required was probably not much less than that of two doves or two pigeons. But while everyone had a certain reserve of flour at home, not everyone was able to provide the birds required for the sacrifice. Consequently the translator should avoid any rendering that follows the first-mentioned interpretation (for example, "If he cannot afford even two doves or two pigeons . . ." as in Mft). The words may just as easily be translated "or if he does not have . . . ."

A tenth of an ephah of fine flour: the translation of terms of measurement such as **ephah** in TEV is given in pounds in the American version but in kilograms in the British version. The metric system will be shown in square brackets where it differs from the American version of TEV. The translator, of course, should select the system in common use in the area where the receptor language is spoken, and not translate both forms.

The meaning of the term **ephah** is very uncertain. Estimates of the value of this dry measure in modern versions range from 20 pounds (10 kilograms) in TEV to 30 kilograms in FRCL. A tenth of an ephah could therefore be from one to three kilograms. While the exact value of this measurement is uncertain, it is important that the term be translated consistently. Other references where the ephah is mentioned in Leviticus are 6.20; 14.10,21; 23.13,17; and 24.5. It also occurs in 19.36, but not as an exact measurement. Translators working with languages that do not use the metric system should look for the closest natural equivalent in their own culture, especially in those cases where flour is measured by weight rather than volume. It is better to provide the reader with a meaningful equivalent rather than transliterating or being overly concerned about the precise value of this uncertain term. A footnote explaining its uncertainty is acceptable if it is deemed necessary in the receptor language.

Fine flour: see the discussion of the two kinds of flour under 2.1. The word used here is the one for "choice flour" (NJV).

No oil . . . no frankincense: this is in contrast with 2.1, where olive oil and incense are mixed with the flour given as a grain offering. TEV makes the contrast more explicit by adding ". . . **not a grain offering**."

5.12　　　RSV　　　　　　　　　　　　TEV

And he shall bring it to the priest, and the priest shall take a handful of it as its memorial portion and burn this on the altar, upon the offerings by fire to the LORD; it is a sin offering.

He shall bring it to the priest, who will take a handful of it as a token that it has all been offered to the LORD, and he will burn it on the altar as a food offering. It is an offering to take away sin.

He: this, of course, refers to the man mentioned in verse 11.

The priest shall take a handful of it: in this verse (as opposed to 2.2) the role of the priest is made explicit. In 2.2 the subject of "take a handful" is unclear, but here there can be no doubt that it is the priest.

As its memorial portion: see 2.2.

Upon the offerings by fire: see 1.13 and the remarks on this expression in "Translating Leviticus" (page 5).

5.13	RSV	TEV
	Thus the priest shall make atonement for him for the sin which he has committed in any one of these things, and he shall be forgiven. And the remainder shall be for the priest, as in the cereal offering."	In this way the priest shall offer the sacrifice for the man's sin, and he will be forgiven. The rest of the flour belongs to the priest, just as in the case of a grain offering.

Thus: or "**In this way**" (NIV as well as TEV); or "By doing these things." This element may be shifted toward the end of the sentence in some languages so that the translation reads something like "The priest shall make atonement for him . . . in this way (or, when he does these things)."

In any one of these things: that is, all the cases mentioned in verses 1-4. This may be rendered "for whichever of these sins he is guilty" (NJV) or "in any of the above cases" (NAB). This is left implicit in TEV and NIV.

The priest shall make atonement . . . : see 4.20.

The remainder: this word is not in the original text. Literally, the Hebrew reads "it will be for the priest as a grain offering." The ancient Greek and Latin translations, however, assume that something has dropped out of the original text and therefore add the word "**rest**" or **remainder**. Most modern English translations follow these ancient versions. But if the text is not changed, it yields a perfectly acceptable meaning (See HOTTP, page 167). This meaning is contained in the NJB rendering "In this case, the priest has the same rights as for the cereal offering." See also TOB and NJV. Furthermore, none of the other paragraphs in the section on the sacrifices to obtain God's forgiveness deal with the question of what belongs to the priest(s). This subject is treated in 6.17-23.

TEV Section Heading: "**Repayment Offerings**."

The term "**Repayment Offering**" is a descriptive translation of the Hebrew word which has at its root the meaning "guilt." For this reason it is often translated "guilt offering" as in RSV and most other English versions. However, the explanation given in this section clearly shows that restitution or repayment is of central importance in this type of offering.

The difference between the "repayment offering" and the "sin offering" in the previous section is not altogether clear, especially with regard to which kinds of sins require one or the other sacrifice. It is offered whenever God or a neighbor has been wronged. The two main differences, which seem to be primarily on the level of the ritual, are as follows:

a) the payment of some kind of reparation or compensation to the one who has been harmed by the sin;

b) the offering of a ram (a male animal) by the guilty person (compare 4.28, 32).

5.14   RSV   TEV

    The LORD said to Moses,   **The LORD gave the following regulations to Moses.**

Said to Moses: since this introduces a new section, it is legitimate to render the verb **said** in the manner of TEV. The context shows that the Lord's communication with Moses had to do with giving regulations. See 4.1.

5.15   RSV   TEV

"If any one commits a breach of faith and sins unwittingly in any of the holy things of the LORD, he shall bring, as his guilt offering to the LORD, a ram without blemish out of the flock, valued by you in shekels of silver, according to the shekel of the sanctuary; it is a guilt offering.

If anyone sins unintentionally by failing to hand over the payments that are sacred to the LORD, he shall bring as his repayment offering to the LORD a male sheep or goat without any defects. Its value is to be determined according to the official standard.

    Any one: see verse 1.

    Unwittingly: see 4.2.

    Commits a breach of faith: literally, "frauds a fraud." The noun and the verb have the same root. This is a rather emphatic addition to **sins unwittingly** and should probably be retained in translation, unless the receptor language has strong reasons for leaving it implicit. But care should be taken not to give the impression that two separate and distinct acts are intended. This expression conveys the idea of an affront to authority (in most cases, the authority of God himself who is wronged either directly or indirectly by an affront to the priests or Levites). Taking the two expressions together, some languages may prefer to translate "sins unintentionally by not paying . . . ," or "commits a sin by failing to pay . . . ," or "sins by breaking his promise to pay . . . ."

    In any of the holy things of the LORD: this expression includes the following: 1. the offerings of the first grain harvested (2.14; 23.9-14); 2. the first-born animals (27.26-27); 3. the tithe (27.30-33; Deut 14.22-29); 4. offerings promised in a vow (27.1-25; Num 30.1-16); and 5. things unconditionally dedicated to God (27.28-29; Num 18.14). All these constitute the income of the priests and the Levites (22.1-16; Num 18.8-24). It may be translated "the payments that are sacred to the LORD," or "the things that are due only to God," or "the revenue that belongs to the LORD." Another way of wording the overall expression **sins unwittingly in any of the holy things of the LORD** may be "to prove himself unfaithful by neglecting to give the

LORD what belongs to him" or "to neglect one's obligations to the LORD without realizing it."

Ram: a male sheep. See FFB, page 75.

Without blemish: see 1.3 and 22.17-25.

Out of the flock: see 1.2.

Valued by you: literally, "of your value (evaluation)." But other uses of the expression seem to indicate that the possessive "your" had in fact lost any personal meaning, and that the idea is simply "value." So the words **by you** may be omitted in translation as has been done by TEV, NIV, NJB, and others. This expression is used very frequently in the final chapter of Leviticus.

In shekels of silver: the value of the ram is to be measured in terms of the silver coins of the time which were called **shekels**. But there is no indication in the text as to how many shekels the ram should be worth. Some scholars have assumed that the number has dropped out of the text, since elsewhere the term "shekel" occurs with a specific number. The ancient Latin Vulgate has "two shekels" (see NAB), but most versions take this simply as an indication that the value is to be set in money and not paid in kind. If this interpretation is correct, then there was no intent of setting a specific amount. NJV has "convertible into payment in silver." Another model might be FRCL: "a certain number of pieces of silver." Transliteration of the term **shekel** should be avoided if at all possible, since it would be meaningless in the receptor language. If used, the term should certainly be explained in the glossary.

According to the shekel of the sanctuary: the **shekel** is either a standard weight or a coin heavier than the one ordinarily used at the time. The way this phrase is worded seems to presuppose the existence of at least two different systems of weight, one for the sanctuary and another for ordinary commercial transactions. But the relationship between the two systems is unknown. The significance of this phrase is to insist that the system of the sanctuary be used in determining the value of the ram. TEV takes the whole expression **valued by you in shekels of silver according to the shekel of the sanctuary** to mean "Its [the ram's] **value is to be determined according to the official standard**." But it is probably better to add to this ". . . of the sanctuary" for the sake of clarity. Also, the religious component may have been significant in that some degree of consistency would have been used in such measures.

A guilt offering: this is the first technical use of the term which causes confusion in verses 6 and 7, where it is used in its nontechnical sense. The actual ritual of this sacrifice is not described here. In 7.7 the writer seems to indicate that it is quite similar to that of the sin offering. The rendering of TEV, "**repayment offering**," is therefore better, since compensation had to be made. NJB speaks of "the sacrifice of reparation."

5.16   RSV   TEV

He shall also make restitution for what he has done amiss in the holy thing, and shall add a fifth to it and give it to the priest; and the priest	He must make the payments he has failed to hand over and must pay an additional twenty percent. He shall give it to the priest, and the priest

shall make atonement for him with the ram of the guilt offering, and he shall be forgiven.	shall offer the animal as a sacrifice for the man's sin, and he will be forgiven.

Also: TEV omits this word, but it may be important to include it in the receptor language in order to make clear the two aspects of the ritual.

Make restitution: the idea of restitution in English is perhaps too strong for the Hebrew word found here (compare 6.5). The text does not indicate whether the repayment plus the additional interest should be made in kind or in money.

Shall add a fifth to it: fractions such as this are often difficult to express in some languages. Some have to say something like "one part in five" or "one piece taken from every five pieces." TEV prefers to convert the fraction into a percentage, and this may be helpful to some translators. The whole phrase may be reworded as follows: "He is obligated to give to the priest all that he owes him and add a fifth (or, twenty percent) more" or "He must pay the priest what he failed to pay and add to it a fine of a fifth (or, twenty percent)."

The priest shall make atonement . . . : see 4.20.

With the ram of the guilt offering: this detail indicates the means by which the atonement takes place. While it is not found in other instances of the atonement (forgiveness) formula, it emphasizes the necessity of the sacrifice and implies therefore that the repayment with interest is not adequate by itself to accomplish the ritual of forgiveness.

5.17	RSV	TEV

"If any one sins, doing any of the things which the LORD has commanded not to be done, though he does not know it, yet he is guilty and shall bear his iniquity.	If anyone sins unintentionally by breaking any of the LORD's commands, he is guilty and must pay the penalty.

The case cited in this verse is different from that of verses 14-16, in that the former has to do specifically with a person appropriating for his own use something that had been previously consecrated to the Lord. These verses (17-19) concern the more general case of committing any forbidden act.

Sins: see 4.2, 3.

Doing any of the things which the LORD has commanded not to be done: see 4.2.

Though he does not know it: although the wording is different, this has essentially the same meaning as "unwittingly" in 4.2 and elsewhere. Some translators, however, may prefer to maintain a distinction between these two expressions.

Shall bear his iniquity: see verse 1.

RSV	TEV
He shall bring to the priest a ram without blemish out of the flock, valued by you at the price for a guilt offering, and the priest shall make atonement for him for the error which he committed unwittingly, and he shall be forgiven.	He must bring to the priest as a repayment offering a male sheep or goat without any defects. Its value is to be determined according to the official standard. The priest shall offer the sacrifice for the man's sin, and he will be forgiven.

The first part of verse 18 presents a condensed version of the essential content of verses 15b and 16a. The only real difference is in the absence of any mention of repayment with interest. However, this does not necessarily mean that there was no repayment with interest in this case. Verse 18b, on the other hand, develops further the thought of 16b, emphasizing especially the unintentional nature of the sin committed (**which he committed unwittingly**). This detail is omitted in TEV but should be retained in the receptor language if possible.

Guilt offering: or, "**repayment offering**" as in TEV, since compensation had to be paid. See verse 15 and compare also verse 7.

RSV	TEV
It is a guilt offering; he is guilty before the LORD."	It is a repayment offering for the sin he committed against the LORD.

At first sight the situation described in verses 17-19 seems very similar to the sin offerings mentioned in 4.27-35, except with regard to the animal to be offered (here a ram instead of a female sheep or goat). The similarity probably comes from the fact that the writer here has in mind direct affronts to the authority and honor of the LORD himself (for example, disobedience to the commandments of Exo 20.3-7), and that in such cases there can be no possibility of making restitution or paying interest (see verse 18b). The emphasis on the involuntary nature of the sin (verse 18b) is also better understood from this point of view. The second proposition in this verse focuses on (a) the offering itself and (b) the person presenting the offering. It is because of the person's guilt that a guilt offering is required.

The expression **guilty before the LORD** is probably the key to the interpretation of verses 17-19 (direct affront on the LORD), because it is parallel to "a breach of faith" in verse 15 (an indirect affront).

The Hebrew Bible continues Leviticus 5.20-26 at this point, while most English versions follow the tradition of referring to those verses as 6.1-7. Further comments about the two numbering systems are provided at the beginning of chapter 6.

Chapter 6

NOTE: the verses numbered 1-7 of chapter 6 in most English versions are a part of chapter 5 in the Hebrew Old Testament and in a number of versions in other languages. Translators consulting commentaries based on the Hebrew, or consulting translations in other languages (as well as NAB and NJV in English), should remember that the verse numbering is different. In this Handbook numbers for the references according to the Hebrew system are included in square brackets below the regular references to RSV and TEV.

ENGLISH 6.1-7	=	HEBREW 5.20-26
ENGLISH 6.8-30	=	HEBREW 6.1-23

While the commentary in this handbook is based on the English system, the numbering to be used in the new translation should follow the Hebrew unless there is already a strong tradition established in favor of the English system in the area where the receptor language is spoken. In such cases it may be possible to follow the example of NJB and indicate both numbering systems.

The content of 6.1-7 (in English) is a continuation of the section on repayment offerings, so this is not a logical point for a chapter division. However, it is a new point and should be marked by a paragraph break as in TEV. Verses 2-7 are parallel to 5.15-19 above. They concern the social and legal offenses against other members of the community, in contrast with violations of the sacrificial system in the preceding verses. But these are also considered serious in that sins against one's fellow Israelite were regarded as an offense against the LORD of Israel.

6.1[a]　　　　RSV

[5.20]

　　The LORD said to Moses,

[a] 5.20 in Heb

TEV

　　The LORD gave the following regulations to Moses.

Said to Moses: see 4.1 and 5.14.

6.2　　　　RSV

[5.21]

"If any one sins and commits a breach of faith against the LORD by deceiving his neighbor in a matter of

TEV

An offering is to be made if anyone sins against the LORD by refusing to return what a fellow Israelite has left

deposit or security, or through robbery, or if he has oppressed his neighbor

as a deposit or by stealing something from him or by cheating him

As in 4.13, it may be necessary in some languages to introduce this hypothetical situation with words like "Suppose that a person commits . . ." (see FRCL), or "Let us say that a person sins . . . ," or "Another example might be . . . ." Such an introduction will permit the translator to complete the sentence at the end of verse 2. Unless this or some other device is used, the sentence beginning at verse 2 might continue to the end of verse 5, and this would constitute a sentence much too long and complicated for the average reader.

Any one: see 5.1.

A breach of faith: see 5.14.

Deceiving: this term conveys the idea "to act unfaithfully," or "to prove to be untrustworthy," or "to show oneself to be untruthful (unreliable)," but in some languages it may be acceptable to say simply "to deceive."

Neighbor: this word does not mean simply one who lives nearby; rather it refers to any other member of the Israelite community. One may say "fellow" (NJV), **"fellow Israelite"** (TEV), "fellow countryman" (NEB and NJB), or simply "another Israelite" to avoid misunderstanding. But care should be taken to avoid the choice of a word that is limited to one's own family, clan, or tribe. And the wording should not be such that the reader will understand that it is acceptable to deceive foreigners.

The text gives several ways in which one person might act unfaithfully toward another, but the list is not necessarily exhaustive. For this reason, some translators have felt it necessary to add the words "for example" or "in cases like this: . . ." to introduce the four cases cited.

In a matter of deposit or security: the Latin Vulgate treats these two as a single sin and this is the interpretation followed by TEV. Although the distinction between these two is uncertain, most versions retain them as separate matters. In both cases there seems to be a violation of trust placed in the guilty party, who has been asked to watch over something for another person. Instead of taking care of it as expected, he has used it for his own purposes. Therefore if the receptor language has two well-known terms in this area of meaning, they can be used. But if not, a single term will be enough.

Through robbery: this is a matter of outright theft which can be easily translated in most languages, although it is important to note that the word used here implies the use of force.

If he has oppressed his neighbor: the verb **oppressed** may be misleading. The idea here is one of gaining something that belongs to another person by means other than outright theft. It usually involves trickery of some kind. NAB comes very close to the meaning with "otherwise retaining his neighbor's goods unjustly," although this is a bit heavy and will be difficult to reproduce in many languages. Mft translates "by taking advantage of his neighbor." NJV has "or by defrauding his fellow" (5.21, following the Hebrew numbering system).

6.3   RSV   TEV
[5.22]

or has found what was lost and lied about it, swearing falsely—in any of

or by lying about something that has been lost and swearing that he did

all the things which men do and sin   not find it.
therein,

Swearing falsely—In any of all the things which men do and sin therein:
this seems to be a summary statement, but RSV takes the **swearing falsely** as being
in apposition with **lied about it**. Others, such as NEB, take it as a part of the
summary statement that follows and so translates "and swears a false oath in regard
to any sin of this sort that he commits" (see also NJV at 5.22). This interpretation is
followed by TEV and seems preferable.

6.4-5	RSV	TEV
[5.23-24]		

4 when one has sinned and become guilty, he shall restore what he took by robbery, or what he got by oppression, or the deposit which was committed to him, or the lost thing which he found, 5 or anything about which he has sworn falsely; he shall restore it in full, and shall add a fifth to it, and give it to him to whom it belongs, on the day of his guilt offering.

4-5 When a man sins in any of these ways, he must repay whatever he got by dishonest means. On the day he is found guilty, he must repay the owner in full, plus an additional 20 percent.

What he took by robbery . . . : instead of repeating the entire list of ways a
person may cheat his fellow Israelite, TEV has summarized with the words "**whatever
he got by dishonest means.**" If repetition of this type in the receptor language is
unnatural, the same kind of summary statement may be made. Otherwise, the
repetition is quite acceptable.

Become guilty: that is, when the guilt becomes known. The person would, of
course, be guilty in the eyes of God all along. For this reason some translators may
prefer to render this expression as "and his guilt becomes known" or something
similar. NJB has "and so becomes answerable," while NAB translates (at 5.23) "since
he has incurred guilt . . . ." Compare also 4.13,22,27; 5.2-4,19.

In addition to summarizing the various kinds of dishonesty, TEV has also recast
other elements in this verse. While the idea of being found **guilty** is given early in
verse 4 in RSV (reflecting the Hebrew structure), TEV has transposed it toward the
end of what is verse 5 in RSV and combined it with the statement sometimes
translated **on the day of his guilt offering** (see the discussion below). Since
elements of verses 4 and 5 cannot be neatly separated, TEV simply renumbers these
two verses together as 4-5.

He shall restore: here, as distinct from 5.16 (see the comments at that point),
the Hebrew verb implies the actual restitution of the object taken, and not just the
payment of compensation.

And shall add a fifth to it: see 5.16.

On the day of his guilt offering: this may be understood rather to mean "on
the day of his guilt"; that is, "as soon as he admits his guilt" or as in TEV "**on the
day he is found guilty.**" This was the understanding of the Septuagint. But it is

probably better to understand it as meaning "on the day when he brings his guilt (repayment) offering."

6.6   RSV   TEV
[5.25]

And he shall bring to the priest his guilt offering to the LORD, a ram without blemish out of the flock, valued by you at the price for a guilt offering;

He shall bring to the priest as his repayment offering to the LORD a male sheep or goat without any defects. Its value is to be determined according to the official standard.

Compare 5.15. Here the Hebrew text mentions **the priest** explicitly as the person to whom the **ram** must be brought. This information could have been left implicit as in 5.15 (see HOTTP), but for some reason the writer decided to make it explicit. It should therefore be made explicit in the receptor language unless there are compelling reasons to do otherwise.

A ram . . . out of the flock: while the word translated **flock** in RSV may in certain contexts refer to goats as well as to sheep, the term translated **ram** makes it quite clear that only sheep can be understood here. The TEV rendering is therefore not recommended.

6.7   RSV   TEV
[5.26]

and the priest shall make atonement for him before the LORD, and he shall be forgiven for any of the things which one may do and thereby become guilty."

The priest shall offer the sacrifice for the man's sin, and he will be forgiven.

Compare 4.20.

For any of the things which one may do and thereby become guilty: this is slightly different from the wording at the end of verse 3, but the meaning is essentially the same. These words may be left implicit as in TEV, if their repetition is awkward in the receptor language.

NOTE: as mentioned earlier chapter 6 begins at this point in the Hebrew text (followed by NAB and NJV in English). Consequently there is a difference of seven between the numbers in NAB and NJV, and the numbers in the other English versions.

The final part of the section on the "Laws about sacrifices and offerings" (6.8–7.38) contains a number of special regulations concerning priests (6.8–7.21) and lay people (7.22-36) with regard to the various offerings discussed in chapters 1–5. The last two verses (7.37-38) constitute the conclusion of this section and at the same time function as a general conclusion to the first seven chapters of Leviticus.

TEV Section Heading: **"Sacrifices Burned Whole"**

A more detailed title such as "Rules for the priests concerning the whole burnt offering" or "How the priests must perform the whole burnt offering" may also be considered. This section deals with the various kinds of sacrifices viewed from the point of view of the rights and duties of the priests. Ideas are not necessarily presented in the same order as in chapters 1–5.

6.8-9^b RSV   TEV
[6.1-2]

8 The LORD said to Moses,   8 The LORD commanded Moses
9 "Command Aaron and his sons,   9 to give Aaron and his sons the
saying, This is the law of the burnt   following regulations for burnt offer-
offering. The burnt offering shall be   ings. A burnt offering is to be left on
on the hearth upon the altar all night   the altar all night long, and the fire is
until the morning, and the fire of the   to be kept burning.
altar shall be kept burning on it.

^{b} Ch 6.1 in Heb

Said to Moses: see 4.1.

The decision about whether to use direct discourse (as in RSV) or indirect discourse (as in TEV) should be made on the basis of naturalness and clarity in the receptor language. See the discussion under 4.1.

The law: while this term is singular in form, the meaning is clearly plural, since it speaks of the totality of the various rules concerning the burnt offerings. In many languages it would be unnatural to use a singular here because the context clearly shows that many different regulations are under discussion. The use of the singular might give the impression that reference is being made only to the second half of verse 9 instead of the whole paragraph.

The hearth: this word occurs only here in the entire Old Testament. It is closely related to the verb "to burn" and may be translated "a place of burning." It is not the same word in Hebrew as is used in Ezekiel 43.15, 16, but many commentators assume that it refers to the same object, that is, to the plate or top of the altar on which sacrifices were normally placed. If the translation says "on the altar," then this word is left implicit. However, it is also possible that the word means "burning mass" and is so understood by the ancient Greek version and followed by NJB and TOB ("brazier") and by Mft ("firewood"). Compare also NJV at 6.2, "where it is burned."

All night until the morning: the words **until the morning** will be considered redundant and may be omitted in many languages, since this is clearly implied in **all night**.

Shall be kept burning: or "must not be allowed to go out," or "should not be extinguished."

6.10   RSV   TEV
[6.3]

And the priest shall put on his linen   Then the priest, wearing his linen
garment, and put his linen breeches   robe and linen shorts, shall remove
upon his body, and he shall take up   the greasy ashes left on the altar
the ashes to which the fire has con-   and put them at the side of the altar.
sumed the burnt offering on the
altar, and put them beside the altar.

And: the transition word in RSV is very weak. The rendering in the receptor language should make it clear that what is described in this verse takes place the day after the events mentioned in the previous verse. It may be possible to say "**Then**" (as in TEV, NEB, NIV, and others), but in some cases it may be necessary to say "the next day" or "on the following morning."

Linen: a white cloth material made from the fibers of flax (see FFB, pages 119-121) and known for its strength and coolness. In those areas where flax is unknown, one may have to use a more generic expression such as "fine white cloth." Or it may be necessary to settle for an approximation in the text and add an explanatory footnote.

Garment: an outer garment corresponding most closely to a "robe" or a "cloak."

Breeches: an undergarment for the lower body. Mft and NEB translate "drawers," while TEV has "**shorts**." NIV is close to the meaning, although more removed from common language, when it renders the word "undergarments." The closest natural equivalent in the receptor language should be used.

Upon his body: this information may be left implicit in many languages. But NIV retains this to emphasize the fact that the clothing in question is immediately "next to his body."

The ashes: TEV "**greasy ashes**." See 1.16.

In some languages it may be more natural to mention the actions of the priest first and then add "In order to do this, he [the priest] must wear the proper clothing: a linen robe and linen shorts." It should also be noted that in some languages it will be more natural to mention the underclothing first and then the outer clothing. But in others the reverse will be more natural.

6.11   RSV   TEV
[6.4]

Then he shall put off his garments,   Then he shall change his clothes
and put on other garments, and   and take the ashes outside the camp
carry forth the ashes outside the   to a ritually clean place.
camp to a clean place.

Put off his garments, and put on other garments: languages have a wide variety of ways of expressing the idea of "changing clothes." Translators should look for the most natural equivalent rather than following the form of the RSV too closely. The clothing removed is the priestly clothing described in verse 10. But no details are given in the text as to the nature of the **other garments** that are put on. Probably these were the priest's ordinary clothes worn when he was not performing his priestly duties.

A clean place: see 4.12.

6.12   RSV   TEV
[6.5]

The fire on the altar shall be kept   The fire on the altar must be kept
burning on it, it shall not go out; the   burning and never allowed to go out.
priest shall burn wood on it every   Every morning the priest shall put
morning, and he shall lay the burnt   firewood on it, arrange the burnt
offering in order upon it, and shall   offering on it, and burn the fat of the
burn on it the fat of the peace offer-   fellowship offering.
ings.

Kept burning: see verse 9.

It shall not go out conveys the same meaning as **kept burning** but makes the
statement more emphatic. In some languages the two may have to be combined, but
the emphasis should be retained where possible.

Shall burn wood on it: the priest must add new firewood every morning in
order to be able to perform his other duties at the altar. NEB translates "have fresh
firewood burning thereon." And NJV reads "feed wood to it," while NIV has ". . . is
to add firewood."

The fat: see 3.3-5.

6.13   RSV   TEV
[6.6]

Fire shall be kept burning upon the   The fire must always be kept burning
altar continually; it shall not go out.   on the altar and never allowed to go
                                             out.

This verse repeats almost word for word the beginning of verse 12 with the
addition of **continually** to add further emphasis.

TEV Section Heading: **"Grain Offerings"**

See comments on section heading for chapter 2.

6.14   RSV   TEV
[6.7]

"And this is the law of the cere-   The following are the regula-
al offering. The sons of Aaron shall   tions for grain offerings. An Aaronite
offer it before the LORD, in front of   priest shall present the grain offering
the altar.   to the LORD in front of the altar.

The law: see verse 9. In some languages it may be advisable to qualify the noun
law or **"regulations"** by a word like "additional" or "special."

The sons of Aaron: actually only one of the **sons of Aaron**, that is, a single priest is involved on any given occasion. NJB has "one of the descendants of Aaron," while TEV has "**an Aaronite priest.**"

In front of the altar: translators must be careful not to give the impression that this indicates the physical location of the LORD. In some languages it may be better to recast the whole sentence and say something like "the priest must approach the altar to present the grain offering to the LORD."

6.15   RSV   TEV
[6.8]

And one shall take from it a handful of the fine flour of the cereal offering with its oil and all the frankincense which is on the cereal offering, and burn this as its memorial portion on the altar, a pleasing odor to the LORD.	Then he shall take a handful of the flour and oil, and the incense on it, and burn it on the altar as a token that all of it has been offered to the LORD. The odor of this offering is pleasing to the LORD.

One: the Hebrew text has only the pronoun "he," but the reference is clearly to "one of the priests." NIV translates simply "the priest." TEV has related "**he**" to "An Aaronite priest" in the previous verse.

A handful: in some languages it may be more natural to say something like "shall fill his hand with fine flour taken from the cereal offering" or "shall remove from the cereal offering some fine flour with his cupped hand."

On the technical terms in this verse, see 1.9 and 2.1,2.

6.16-17   RSV   TEV
[6.9-10]

16 And the rest of it Aaron and his sons shall eat; it shall be eaten unleavened in a holy place; in the court of the tent of meeting they shall eat it. 17 It shall not be baked with leaven. I have given it as their portion of my offerings by fire; it is a thing most holy, like the sin offering and the guilt offering.	16-17 The priests shall eat the rest of it. It shall be made into bread baked without yeast and eaten in a holy place, the courtyard of the Tent of the LORD's presence. The LORD has given it to the priests as their part of the food offerings. It is very holy, like the sin offerings and the repayment offerings.

Compare 2.3,10.

Aaron and his sons: that is, only the priests.

Unleavened . . . leaven: see 2.11.

In a holy place; in the court of the tent of meeting: the two expressions refer to the same place. The second clarifies the meaning of the first. In some languages this relationship may need to be explicitly marked by adding something like "that is to say . . . ." On **holy**, see 2.3; compare also "a clean place" in verse 11.

The tent of meeting: see 1.1.

I have given it as their portion of my offerings by fire: the unexpected use of the first person singular pronouns, **I** and **my**, is problematic for translators. These pronouns clearly refer to the LORD and not to Moses, who communicated the commands of the LORD to Aaron and his sons (verse 9). In most languages the use of first person pronouns in this context will be totally out of place and very likely will be misunderstood by most readers. TEV has wisely transformed **I** to "**The LORD.**" Another possible alternative is to change this sentence from indirect to direct discourse and introduce the quotation with the words "The LORD says . . . ."

On the expression **offerings by fire**, see 1.9 and the discussion on page 5 in "Translating Leviticus."

It is a thing most holy, like . . . : here the grain offerings as a whole (not just the part given to the priests) are likened to the sin offerings (4.1–5.13) and repayment offerings (5.14–6.7) in that they are all very holy, that is, fully and completely dedicated to God. This, of course, does not imply that the other offerings not mentioned here are not holy. It simply focuses on these three.

6.18   RSV   TEV
[6.11]

Every male among the children of Aaron may eat of it, as decreed for ever throughout your generations, from the LORD's offerings by fire; whoever touches them shall become holy."

For all time to come any of the male descendants of Aaron may eat it as their continuing share of the food offered to the LORD. Anyone else who touches a food offering will be harmed by the power of its holiness.

Every male among the children of Aaron: although there are cases where the female members of the priestly family may eat a part of what is brought as an offering to God (see 10.14; 22.12-13), this is not to happen in the case under consideration. The intent of the text is to limit those sharing in the food to the male members of the priestly family. It may be translated "**the male descendants of Aaron**" (TEV), or "any male descendant of Aaron" (Mft), or possibly "any male member of the priestly family."

As decreed forever throughout your generations: it may be necessary in some cases to shift this information to the beginning of the sentence as in TEV. The word rendered **forever** in RSV has the meaning "regular" or "continual" in a context such as this. And the term **decreed** is actually a singular noun which in Leviticus and Ezekiel carries the meaning "portion" or "share." Therefore the rendering of TEV is more accurate: "**their continuing share.**"

From the LORD's offering by fire: see 1.9.

Whoever: the Hebrew word thus translated may also mean "whatever" (compare verse 27) and is so translated in NIV. Possibly both human beings and nonhumans were intended by the writer. In any case, the male members of the priestly family are not included since they were specifically given permission to eat. For this reason it may be better to translate "**Anyone else . . .**" as in TEV or "anyone who is not a priest." In some languages a contrastive conjunction like "but" may also be required.

Shall become holy: this verse highlights the fact that the word frequently translated **holy** does not have as its primary meaning the ethical and moral connotations often attributed to it. The central meaning has to do with being "set aside for a particular purpose" or "withheld (or, excluded) from ordinary use." In other contexts this implies being consecrated to God. But here it has more the idea of being unfit for ordinary human use. The meaning approaches that of "taboo" in some cultures. AT and Mft, in fact, translate here "shall be(come) taboo." TEV seeks to render this same idea more dynamically with **"will be harmed by the power of its holiness."** Another modern version translates "will experience unfortunate consequences." Care should be taken in this context not to translate in such a way as to give the impression that anyone or anything touching a food offering would suddenly change in moral character or receive any other positive benefit. What happens here is clearly negative. Some writers even suggest that the real meaning is that any person other than the male descendants of Aaron who touch the offering must die. Some other ways of rendering this idea are "will suffer from his act," or "will find misfortune," or "will experience dire consequences." The term used for **holy** will certainly need to be explained in detail in the glossary.

6.19 [6.12]	RSV	TEV
	The LORD said to Moses,	**The LORD gave Moses the following regulations**

The paragraph which is made up of verses 19-23 deals with the ceremony of consecration of the priests (compare 8.26 and 9.4) and seems to interrupt the more general instructions of the rest of the section. It has no parallel in chapters 1–5 and is omitted from the Septuagint. In 7.37 these ordination sacrifices are cited after the sin offering and the repayment offering, but in this passage they are dealt with before the others (see 6.24–7.7). This may be explained in the present context by the fact that only grain offerings are mentioned in these regulations. Therefore this paragraph seems to fit more naturally after 6.14-18, which deals with grain offerings. However, it is important that a new paragraph be started here.

Said to Moses: see 4.1.

6.20 [6.13]	RSV	TEV
	"This is the offering which Aaron and his sons shall offer to the LORD on the day when he is anointed: a tenth of an ephah of fine flour as a regular cereal offering, half of it in the morning and half in the evening.	**for the ordination of an Aaronite priest. On the day he is ordained, he shall present as an offering to the LORD two pounds [one kilogram] of flour (the same amount as the daily grain offering), half in the morning and half in the evening.**

Aaron and his sons: see 1.7 and 2.3. The singular pronoun which follows indicates clearly that the reference is to any one of the Aaronite priests.

On the day when ... : this may also mean "as soon as he is anointed" (compare the expression "on the day of his guilt offering" in verse 5). But most versions take it to mean "on the day of his ordination." NEB omits this part of the verse, indicating in a footnote that the text without these words is more probable. There are, however, few other versions that agree.

He is anointed: the verb used here actually means "to have oil poured on." Oil was poured on the head of a person in a special ritual to indicate that he had been chosen for a particular work in God's service. The king, the high priest, and perhaps all the priests during a certain period of Old Testament history were anointed for service in this way. The term may be translated **"ordained"** or "consecrated," since these terms correspond most closely to the ancient rite. But in some languages such technical words do not exist, and it will be more natural to retain the image of the ritual. For example, "he becomes a priest by having oil poured on his head." In some cases it will be essential to add a cultural note.

A tenth of an ephah: the exact equivalent of this measurement is uncertain. It is thought to be the equivalent of about two pounds or one kilogram. See 5.11.

Fine flour: see 2.1.

Regular: the work here carries the idea of "continually." This explains the rendering **"daily"** found in Mft as well as TEV.

Morning . . . evening . . . : that is, at the time of the regular sacrifices made each day (see Exo 29.38-42).

6.21 [6.14]	RSV	TEV
	It shall be made with oil on a griddle; you shall bring it well mixed, in baked*c* pieces like a cereal offering, and offer it for a pleasing odor to the LORD.	It is to be mixed with oil and cooked on a griddle and then crumbled and presented as a grain offering, an odor pleasing to the LORD.

c Meaning of Heb is uncertain

The structure of this verse in Hebrew is unusual, and the meaning of some words is uncertain. This has given rise to a number of very different interpretations.

It shall be made: this may also be understood in the active sense, "You shall make." And in those languages where passive forms are difficult or impossible, it must be changed to an active construction in any case. The subject should then be the same as in the second part of the verse, **you shall bring**, referring to the priest.

With oil on a griddle: on **oil** see 2.1; and on **griddle** see 2.5.

Well mixed: the structure of the Hebrew is such that these words can go with "It shall be made (prepared, cooked)" (as TEV, NJB, AT interpret) or with **you shall bring** (interpretation of RSV, NIV, NJV). Logically, it seems to fit better with the preparation of the offering rather than with its presentation.

In baked pieces: the word translated **baked** in RSV and some other English versions is difficult and uncertain. A number of other translations and commentaries have understood the word to mean "broken" or **"crumbled"** (TEV, NEB, NIV, NAB, AT, and Mft). Still others, following the Septuagint, see it as referring to a kind of pastry (JB, TOB). Translators should probably look for an equivalent to the idea of breaking or crumbling into small pieces. But it may be advisable to add a footnote explaining the uncertainty concerning this term and the different possible translations of it.

A pleasing odor to the LORD: see 1.9.

6.22
[6.15]

RSV	TEV
The priest from among Aaron's sons, who is anointed to succeed him, shall offer it to the LORD as decreed for ever; the whole of it shall be burned.	For all time to come this offering is to be made by every descendant of Aaron who is serving as High Priest. It shall be completely burned as a sacrifice to the LORD.

The priest from among Aaron's sons, who is anointed to succeed him: this picks up what has already been said less clearly in the two preceding verses. It emphasizes the fact that the person serving as High Priest (who must be a male descendant of Aaron) is to offer this sacrifice, that is, to actually carry out the ritual of burning the grain on the altar.

As decreed for ever: as in verse 18, it may be more logical in some languages to place this information at the beginning of the sentence.

To the LORD: this expression may be understood as going with the verb "to offer," which precedes it, as in RSV. Or it may go with the following verb, "to burn (completely)," as in TEV. In some cases it may be possible to combine the two with something like "This is an offering that must be burned completely for the LORD." But if a choice is forced, most scholars would recommend that it go with the verb "to burn."

6.23
[6.16]

RSV	TEV
Every cereal offering of a priest shall be wholly burned; it shall not be eaten."	No part of a grain offering that a priest makes may be eaten; all of it must be burned.

This verse develops and summarizes what is said at the end of verse 22. For this reason it may be desirable to insert some kind of transition word at the beginning of the verse. NJV introduces it with "So . . . ."

Cereal offering: see chapter 2.

Wholly burned: that is, burned completely for God. In some languages it will be wise to make explicit the fact that it is burned for God. Translators should be careful to avoid translating in such a way as to give the impression that the cereal offering is identical with the whole burnt offering.

In some languages it may be more natural to restructure as in TEV so that "not eaten" comes before "be burned."

TEV Section Heading: **"Sin Offerings"**

Compare the section heading for 4.1–5.13. A more complete heading here may be "Additional instructions concerning offerings for unintentional sins."

6.24-25   RSV   TEV
[6.17-18]

24 The LORD said to Moses, 25 "Say to Aaron and his sons, This is the law of the sin offering. In the place where the burnt offering is killed shall the sin offering be killed before the LORD; it is most holy.

24 The LORD commanded Moses 25 to give Aaron and his sons the following regulations for sin offerings. The animal for a sin offering shall be killed on the north side of the altar, where the animals for the burnt offerings are killed. This is a very holy offering.

Said to Moses: on the question of direct versus indirect discourse, see 4.1.

Aaron and his sons: see 1.5.

The law of the sin offering: or "the regulations concerning the sin offering." Compare verse 9.

The place where the burnt offering is killed: that is, the same place, the north side of the altar (see 1.11). It may be helpful to the reader if this information is made explicit.

Before the LORD: see 1.5.

It is most holy: this refers to the sin offering and not to the place or to the burnt offering. This often-repeated expression serves to emphasize the importance of this particular offering.

6.26   RSV   TEV
[6.19]

The priest who offers it for sin shall eat it; in a holy place it shall be eaten, in the court of the tent of meeting.

The priest who sacrifices the animal shall eat it in a holy place, the courtyard of the Tent of the LORD's presence.

The priest who offers it: the pronoun **it** refers to the animal that is sacrificed. One may also say "The priest who performs the ritual shall eat the animal that is sacrificed" or something similar.

Shall eat it . . . it shall be eaten: this repetition of the same idea in both active and passive forms may be unnatural in some languages. Where this is the case, or where passives do not exist, it is acceptable to translate the idea once. This rule does not require that a single priest eat the entire animal, as a rather superficial reading might seem to indicate. Verse 29 makes it clear that other members of the priestly family are also allowed to eat the meat. This verse simply emphasizes the fact that no person outside the priestly class should be allowed to eat it.

A holy place: a place that has been set aside for this specific purpose. The rest of the verse makes it clear that the reference is to the "**courtyard of the Tent of**

the LORD's presence." It is possible to translate the remainder of the verse "shall eat it in the courtyard of the Tent of the LORD's presence, the place that has been dedicated for this purpose."

6.27-28   RSV   TEV
[6.20-21]

27 Whatever[d] touches its flesh shall be holy; and when any of its blood is sprinkled on a garment, you shall wash that on which it was sprinkled in a holy place. 28 And the earthen vessel in which it is boiled shall be broken; but if it is boiled in a bronze vessel, that shall be scoured, and rinsed in water.

27 Anyone or anything that touches the flesh of the animal will be harmed by the power of its holiness. If any article of clothing is spattered with the animal's blood, it must be washed in a holy place. 28 Any clay pot in which the meat is boiled must be broken, and if a metal pot is used, it must be scrubbed and rinsed with water.

[d] Or *Whoever*

These two verses, which interrupt the logical progression from verse 26 to verse 29, develop the theme of the danger of contamination by contact with what is "holy."

Whatever: as in verse 18, the word may mean either **whatever** (RSV) or "whoever" (Mft), or both of these at the same time. TEV has taken the latter interpretation, and this is probably correct. Some languages, like Hebrew, may have a single word which refers to both humans and nonhumans.

Shall be holy: that is, shall suffer harmful consequences due to the effect of the positive taboo, since the meat was set aside for God and his special servants alone. See verse 18.

You shall wash: the subject is second person singular in Hebrew, but the person referred to is not clear. It may have a passive meaning as indicated in the TEV rendering. In those languages that do not have passives, the translator should look for an impersonal form such as "they [undetermined] shall wash . . ." or "someone shall wash . . . ."

That on which it was sprinkled: or "anything that has been stained by the blood" or "that has blood on it."

In a holy place: that is, in a special place set aside for this purpose. It was probably in the courtyard of the Tent of the LORD's presence, as in verse 26.

It may be better to restructure verse 28 so that each part begins with a conditional particle: "If it is washed in a clay pot . . . . But if it is washed in a bronze (or, metal) container . . . ."

The earthen vessel: a container made of clay. In ancient times pottery was made by shaping clay on a wheel and then baking the object in a kind of oven. If this kind of container were used for boiling the meat of the sacrifice, it could not be used for any further purpose and would have to be destroyed.

It is boiled: the pronoun **it** may be understood to refer to the article of clothing mentioned in verse 27, since in some cultures clothes are washed by boiling, and the referent is not clear in RSV. But the reference is almost certainly to the meat of the sacrifice. This should be made clear in the receptor language.

A bronze vessel: a container made of metal. Bronze is a mixture of copper and tin. In some cultures there may be no word for bronze, so it is advisable to use a more general term like **"metal."** What is important in this context is to distinguish clearly between those containers made of metal and those made of clay. Metal containers could be scoured and rinsed so that the "holiness" of the sacrifice they contained could be removed without destroying the container. This was not the case with a clay container. Note that all the accessories of the altar were made of bronze (Exo 38.3).

6.29 [6.22] RSV	TEV
Every male among the priests may eat of it; it is most holy.	Any male of the priestly families may eat this offering; it is very holy.

Every male among the priests may eat of it: this expresses the same idea as verse 18, but in a slightly different form.

It is most holy: see verse 17 and 2.3.

Following the parenthetical information in verses 27-28, this verse picks up and clarifies what is said in verse 26. The meat is not reserved exclusively for the officiating priest but may be eaten by other priests as well, and even by men excluded from the active priesthood because of some physical defect (see 21.22).

6.30 [6.23] RSV	TEV
But no sin offering shall be eaten from which any blood is brought into the tent of meeting to make atonement in the holy place; it shall be burned with fire.	But if any of the blood is brought into the Tent and used in the ritual to take away sin, the animal must not be eaten; it must be burned.

This verse alludes to 4.3-12 and 4.13-21. Only in these two cases a part of the blood was taken inside the Tent of the LORD's presence.

Shall be eaten: this passive construction may have to be rendered in some languages as "no person can eat . . ." or "all people must avoid eating . . . ."

Burned with fire: in many languages the words **with fire** will be considered redundant and unnecessary. Compare 4.11.

In some languages it may be more natural to reverse the order of the two verb phrases ". . . **must not be eaten**" and ". . . **must be burned**."

Chapter 7

This chapter is organized in various ways by different English versions. Verses 1-10 make up a single paragraph in RSV, AT, and NEB, but are broken at the beginning of verse 7 in most other translations (TEV, NJV, NIV, NAB, NJB). TOB makes the break at the end of verse 7.

Verses 11-18 constitute a single paragraph in RSV, but most other versions divide it at the end of verse 15, and some take verse 11 separately. While RSV makes a paragraph break at the end of verse 18 (along with NJV, NIV, and NJB [which takes verse 18 as a separate paragraph]), NEB breaks at the end of verse 19. And TEV as well as TOB make the break in the middle of verse 19.

Verses 22-27 are a single paragraph in RSV, TEV, NJV, and NIV, but two paragraphs in NEB and TOB—making the break at the end of verse 25. Similarly, verses 28-36 form a single paragraph in RSV, TEV, TOB, and NEB, but a break occurs after verse 34 in NJV, NIV, and NJB.

In view of the wide variety of paragraph division in this chapter by the different versions, translators are advised to adopt the system used in TEV. This will mean placing a section heading at verses 1 and 11 and making paragraph breaks at verses 7, 16, 19b, 22, 28, and 37. But it may also be advisable to add a new paragraph at verse 35, as in NIV, NJV, and NJB.

TEV Section Heading: **"Repayment Offerings."**

The paragraph 7.1-6 provides new information by comparison with 5.14-26, but nothing that is completely new when seen in the light of the first six chapters taken together. The ritual for the repayment offerings is presented here as essentially the same as that for the sin offering of a private individual (4.27-31). Verses 7-10 briefly describe the disposition of the sacred portions of the different types of sacrifice.

7.1 RSV	TEV
"This is the law of the guilt offering. It is most holy;	**The following are the regulations for repayment offerings, which are very holy.**

The law: better taken as a plural in many languages, since it refers to the complete set of rules. See 6.2.

The guilt offering: see 5.15.

It is most holy: see 2.3. Compare also 6.17, 25.

7.2   RSV   TEV

in the place where they kill the burnt offering they shall kill the guilt offering, and its blood shall be thrown on the altar round about.	The animal for this offering is to be killed on the north side of the altar, where the animals for the burnt offerings are killed, and its blood is to be thrown against all four sides of the altar.

In the place . . . : that is, on the north side of the altar. This is the same place where the animals for the burnt offerings are slaughtered. See 1.11. TEV makes this explicit, and such clarification may be desirable in other languages.

They kill . . . they shall kill: the subject in each case is indefinite. Many versions use a passive form here (NJV, NJB, NIV, as well as TEV). If the receptor language has no passive form and requires a definite subject with the active, "the priests" may be used. The verb **kill** actually means "slaughter," that is, to cut the throat of the animal.

The guilt offering: the animal brought as an offering.

Its blood shall be thrown on the altar round about: literally, "he shall throw . . . ." See 1.5, where the subject is plural, "Aaron's sons," rather than singular. Here RSV translates as a passive, but in those languages where passives are unnatural or nonexistent, one may continue with the indefinite third person plural subject.

7.3-4   RSV   TEV

3 And all its fat shall be offered, the fat tail, the fat that covers the entrails, 4 the two kidneys with the fat that is on them at the loins, and the appendage of the liver which he shall take away with the kidneys;	3 All of its fat shall be removed and offered on the altar: the fat tail, the fat covering the internal organs, 4 the kidneys and the fat on them, and the best part of the liver.

These two verses repeat information found in chapter 3. For detailed comment on each point see 3.3-4,9.

7.5   RSV   TEV

the priest shall burn them on the altar as an offering by fire to the LORD; it is a guilt offering.	The priest shall burn all the fat on the altar as a food offering to the LORD. It is a repayment offering.

Compare 1.9b.

7.6   RSV   TEV

Every male among the priests may   Any male of the priestly families may
eat of it; it shall be eaten in a holy   eat it, but it must be eaten in a holy
place; it is most holy.   place, because it is very holy.

Every male among the priests: see 6.22. The translation should avoid giving
the impression that there may have been females also among the priests. Both TEV
and NEB bring out the meaning more clearly by referring to "**the priestly families**"
rather than the actual priests.

May eat of it . . . it shall be eaten: see 6.26. And note that the pronoun **it**
refers to the remaining meat of the sacrificed animal.

7.7   RSV   TEV

The guilt offering is like the sin offer-   There is one regulation that
ing, there is one law for them; the   applies to both the sin offering and
priest who makes atonement with it   the repayment offering: the meat be-
shall have it.   longs to the priest who offers the
                                            sacrifice.

A new paragraph is required here because a new subject is introduced. What
follows in verse 7 deals with the sin offering and the repayment offering.

There is one law for them: in some languages this verse may require
restructuring so that **one law**, or "the same rule," is the subject of the sentence. If
so, TEV will serve as a good model. But ultimately, naturalness in the receptor
language will determine whether and how the restructuring is to be done.

It . . . it: the pronouns refer to the sacrificial animal in the first case and the
meat of the animal (see 6.26) in the second. Clarity in translation may require that
they both be made explicit.

In addition to the meat of the sacrifice mentioned in verse 7, the priest is also
to receive certain other items. For this reason verses 8-10 are inserted here in order
that all the various things that belong to the priests may be discussed together. Then
the final kind of sacrifice—the fellowship-offering—is taken up in verse 11. That is the
only case where a part of the offering goes back to the lay person.

7.8   RSV   TEV

And the priest who offers any man's   The skin of an animal offered as a
burnt offering shall have for himself   burnt offering belongs to the priest
the skin of the burnt offering which   who offers the sacrifice.
he has offered.

Note that the structure of this verse has been radically altered in TEV. Instead
of making the priest the subject of the sentence, he becomes the object of the verbal

expression "**belongs to.**" And the skin of the animal, which is the object of the verb **have** in RSV, becomes the subject of the sentence in TEV (see also NEB). Which solution should be adopted in the receptor language will be determined by deciding which structure is more natural sounding. But translators must not automatically follow the form of TEV simply because it is more dynamic in English.

And: in order to make the connection with the previous verse, one may use a stronger transition word. NAB has "Similarly . . . ." NJV renders it "So, too, ..." Another possibility is "Also . . . ."

Burnt offering: see 1.4 and the discussion under the section heading at the beginning of chapter 1.

Any man's burnt offering: some scholars see in this expression an indication that this regulation concerns only the whole burnt offering of a private individual. In this case "for someone" (NAB), or "for an individual," or "for one person" may be appropriate. While most English versions include this detail explicitly, it has been left implicit in TEV. In most languages it will probably be better to make it explicit.

The information given in this verse in unique in all the Old Testament. Nowhere else is any mention made of any part of the whole burnt offering being given to the priest (as a possession rather than as food to be eaten). It should be noted, however, that in 1.8-9 the skin is not specifically mentioned in the list of the parts that are burned on the altar, and that this is not something that can be eaten. Finally, it should be pointed out that the regulation is restricted to a certain kind of whole burnt offering: the expression **any man's burnt offering** seems to indicate a sacrifice given by a private individual and probably excludes the regular daily whole burnt offering, which was offered publicly and for the entire community. In that case it is possible that not even the skin belonged to the priest.

7.9   RSV   TEV

And every cereal offering baked in the oven and all that is prepared on a pan or a griddle shall belong to the priest who offers it.

Every grain offering that has been baked in an oven or prepared in a pan or on a griddle belongs to the priest who has offered it to God.

And: in some languages it may be wise to use a transition word such as "Likewise" at this point. This is another case where a part of an offering belongs to the priest who offers it.

Oven . . . pan . . . griddle: see 2.4-7.

Who offers it: the translation should not give the impression that the priest makes this offering for himself. Rather he presides over the ceremony in which another person has brought an offering. In some languages it may be necessary to say "the priest who offers it to God for another person."

7.10   RSV   TEV

And every cereal offering, mixed with oil or dry, shall be for all the sons of

But all uncooked grain offerings, whether mixed with oil or dry, belong

93

Aaron, one as well as another.   **to all the Aaronite priests and must be shared equally among them.**

This verse may be understood in one of two different ways: (a) It concerns a different case from the one dealt with in verse 9, the present case being related to uncooked grain offerings. Or (b) it concerns the same case as mentioned in verse 9, but adds new information regarding the distribution of the offering among the group of priests. It is recommended that the translator adopt the first interpretation and that, if necessary, the second be explained in a footnote, since some scholars consider it to be the more probable interpretation.

And: assuming that the first interpretation mentioned above is adopted, the transition word used here should probably show contrast with the previous verse since in that case the reference is to cooked grain offerings, while here uncooked grain offerings are involved. Both NJV and TEV introduce this verse with "**But**." It may also be advisable to add "**uncooked**" as in TEV, or say "But every other meal offering . . . ," as in NJV.

The sons of Aaron: see 1.7.

One as well as another: literally, "each equal with his brother." The meaning is clearly brought out in TEV "**and must be shared equally among them.**"

TEV Section Heading: "**Fellowship Offerings.**"

Compare chapter 3.

The following section deals with the lay person's eating of a part of the meat of the sacrifice as well as with the various kinds of "fellowship offerings."

7.11   RSV   TEV

"And this is the law of the sacrifice of peace offerings which one may offer to the LORD.   The following are the regulations for the fellowship offerings presented to the LORD.

This is the law: this is the same formula that is used in verse 1 to introduce the previous section. See also 6.2.

Peace offerings: see 3.1.

7.12   RSV   TEV

If he offers it for a thanksgiving, then he shall offer with the thank offering unleavened cakes mixed with oil, unleavened wafers spread with oil, and cakes of fine flour well mixed with oil.   If a man makes this offering as a thanksgiving to God, he shall present, together with the animal to be sacrificed, an offering of bread made without yeast: either thick loaves made of flour mixed with olive oil or thin cakes brushed with olive oil or cakes made of flour mixed with olive oil.

Verses 12-15 deal with the sacrifice made as "**a thanksgiving**." On the one hand, these verses develop certain aspects not mentioned in chapter 3 (such as grain offerings), and on the other hand, they deal with the lay person's eating his part of the sacrifice.

For a thanksgiving: or "in thanksgiving" (NAB), or "with praise" (NJB), or "as an expression of thankfulness" (NIV), or simply "because he is thankful [for something]." This focuses on the motivation behind the sacrifice. This particular fellowship offering is made to praise God because the worshiper wants to express his gratitude. It is mentioned in a number of Psalms (56.12; 100.2; 107.22) as well as in other Old Testament passages (Jer 17.26; Amos 4.5; 2 Chr 29.31; 33.16).

With the thank offering: that is, "in addition to the thank offering" (NEB) or "together with the sacrifice of thanksgiving" (NJV). In some cases it may be advisable to make this even more explicit with something like "in addition to the animal brought as a fellowship offering to express thanks to God . . . ."

Spread with oil . . . mixed with oil . . . : see 2.4.

Cakes . . . wafers . . . cakes: there were three types of unleavened bread to accompany the animal sacrifice: (1) The first were perforated loaves made with flour mixed with oil but without yeast. (2) The second are those mistakenly called **wafers**. These were a kind of thin round bread also made without yeast, but on which olive oil was spread. These were similar to biscuits or possibly pancakes. And (3) there is some question about exactly what is meant by the third kind of bread. It was apparently to be similar to the first, perhaps pierced or perforated, but there is no mention of its being made without yeast and no indication that it was actually baked. This has led some commentators to assume that it was merely a kind of dough made of choice flour and oil. However, TEV seems to understand the text to imply both the fact of being unleavened and of being baked. Since David shared such loaves with people (2 Sam 6.19), it seems best to assume they were baked. And although "unleavened" is not explicitly mentioned for the third type, the contrast with verse 13 probably indicates that they were made without yeast.

7.13	RSV	TEV
	With the sacrifice of his peace offerings for thanksgiving he shall bring his offering with cakes of leavened bread.	In addition, he shall offer loaves of bread baked with yeast.

With the sacrifice: meaning "in addition to" or "accompanying" the unleavened loaves, cakes, or wafers.

The sacrifice of his peace offering: this is left implicit in TEV but should probably be retained in many languages for the sake of clarity. Remember that what is called a **peace offering** in RSV is a "fellowship offering" in TEV.

For thanksgiving: see verse 12.

Cakes: or "**loaves**." See 2.4.

Leavened bread: that is, "**bread baked with yeast**." The earliest printings of TEV had "loaves of bread baked without yeast," but this was an error that has been corrected in subsequent printings. Translators should be certain that they are working with the latest edition of TEV or of any important reference volume used in translation.

7.14   RSV   TEV

And of such he shall offer one cake from each offering, as an offering to the LORD; it shall belong to the priest who throws the blood of the peace offerings.	He shall present one part of each kind of bread as a special contribution to the LORD; it belongs to the priest who takes the blood of the animal and throws it against the altar.

Of such . . . one cake from each offering: that is, one part of each of the three kinds of unleavened bread described in verse 12 and the leavened bread of verse 13. Compare NIV, which has "He is to bring one of each kind . . . ."

As an offering to the LORD: the term used here indicates something "lifted out of" the rest of the offering to be presented to God. In some versions this has been interpreted as something that was lifted up and waved up and down or from side to side (KJV "an heave offering"; Living Bible (LB) "by a gesture of waving it before the altar"). But the best available scholarship shows that it probably has nothing whatever to do with the act of waving. It is simply a special gift to the Lord which is eventually eaten by the officiating priest while the rest is consumed by the worshiper. NIV has simply "a contribution," while TEV has "**a special contribution.**"

The priest who throws the blood of the peace offerings: the officiating priest who performs the function described in 3.2. The use of the singular here—as opposed to the plural "priests" in 3.2—is due to the fact that the earlier passage is more general in nature, but does not imply that several priests are required in any particular ritual.

The direction of the action verb translated **throw** (or "sprinkle" in NIV) is not specified in the text, but in many languages this will have to be spelled out. TEV and NEB have made explicit the fact that it is the blood which is thrown "**against the altar**" (compare 3.2).

7.15   RSV   TEV

And the flesh of the sacrifice of his peace offerings for thanksgiving shall be eaten on the day of his offering; he shall not leave any of it until the morning.	The flesh of the animal must be eaten on the day it is sacrificed; none of it may be left until the next morning.

The flesh of the sacrifice: the **flesh**, or "meat," here refers to that part of the sacrifice left to the person making the offering, after certain (fatty) parts had been burned on the altar (see 3.3-5) and others had been given to the priests (7.28-36). This may need to be made explicit in some languages by saying something like "the meat left for the offerer of the sacrifice."

His peace offerings for thanksgiving: the pronoun **his** refers to the person offering the sacrifice (referred to as "one" in verse 11). **Peace offerings** is also a repetition of information found in verse 11, and **for thanksgiving** is repeated from verse 12. Since this verse is still a part of the same paragraph, some or all of this information may be left implicit in many languages.

Shall be eaten on the day of his offering; he shall not leave any of it until the morning: the same requirement is repeated in both positive and negative form at the end of the verse. In those languages where such repetition is undesirable, the meaning may be translated one time in either the positive or the negative form, but with added emphasis if possible. In some languages it will be convenient to drop the passive formulation in order to make the verse less repetitious.

This rule is similar to the requirement about the eating of the Passover lamb in Exodus 12.10.

7.16   RSV   TEV

But if the sacrifice of his offering is a votive offering or a freewill offering, it shall be eaten on the day that he offers his sacrifice, and on the morrow what remains of it shall be eaten, | If a man brings a fellowship offering as fulfillment of a vow or as his own freewill offering, not all of it has to be eaten on the day it is offered, but any that is left over may be eaten on the following day.

But: the contrastive word, **But**, is used here because the subject matter is slightly different in this paragraph. In contrast with fellowship offerings (peace offerings) given because the offerer is thankful (verses 12-15), here we are concerned with those brought as a freewill offering or in fulfillment of a vow. However, in some languages a word marking the transition to a new subject will be necessary, while in others the beginning of a new paragraph—as in TEV—will be sufficient to indicate the change in subject.

A votive offering . . . a freewill offering: these two types of offering always go together (see 22.18, 21, 23; 23.38), and the entire phrase may simply indicate "required or voluntary offerings." The first is the result of a vow or promise made, and the second is due to a spontaneous desire on the part of the worshiper. Some languages may find it more natural to mention voluntary offerings ("offerings from the heart") before those required by a vow or promise.

On the morrow what remains of it shall be eaten: this is different from the case described in 11-15, since in this case leftovers are permitted to be eaten the following day. The words **shall be eaten** may be interpreted as a strict obligation (compare AT and NAB "should be eaten"), but the sense is most probably that the remaining food **"may be eaten"** (NIV, NJB, as well as TEV). And, of course, some languages will have to transform this into an active form such as "they [indefinite] may eat."

7.17 RSV	TEV
but what remains of the flesh of the sacrifice on the third day shall be burned with fire.	**Any meat that still remains on the third day must be burned.**

The permission to eat meat even on the second day is surprising, because in a hot climate like that of the Near East meat spoils very quickly. Consequently it was strictly forbidden to eat any meat remaining on the third day. It had to be burned.

With fire: following the verb "to burn," this may be considered redundant in many languages because it follows the verb "to burn." If this is the case, it may be omitted in translation.

7.18 RSV	TEV
If any of the flesh of the sacrifice of his peace offering is eaten on the third day, he who offers it shall not be accepted, neither shall it be credited to him; it shall be an abomination, and he who eats of it shall bear his iniquity.	**If any of it is eaten on the third day, God will not accept the man's offering. The offering will not be counted to his credit but will be considered unclean, and whoever eats it will suffer the consequences.**

If any of the flesh . . . is eaten on the third day: this passive formulation will have to be made active in some languages: "If a person eats . . . on the third day."

He who offers it shall not be accepted: this is another passive form that may have to be rendered "God will not accept the person who offered the sacrifice . . . ." TEV interprets this to mean that "**the man's offering**" rather than the person himself is not accepted by God. The translations are almost equally divided as to whether the pronoun should be "it" (NIV and NJV) or "him" (see NJB and NEB). However, it is probably better to see it as referring to the person.

Neither shall it be credited to him: still another passive, but in this case the meaning is essentially the same as above, although here the subject is clearly the offering and not the person. It may be translated "He shall receive no credit for it," or "It will not be honored (or, recognized)," or "It will be counted as worthless."

An abomination: "**unclean**" or impure (see 5.2), but the word used here is even stronger. It comes from a root word meaning "corpse." The whole phrase **it shall be an abomination** is introduced by the conjunction "**but**" in TEV, and NAB has "rather." NIV, on the other hand, inserts "because." While the text has no overt marker of the relationship between this and the first part of the verse, the relationship is probably one of contrast. However, most versions have no transition word here.

Bear his iniquity: see 5.1,17.

7.19   RSV   TEV

"Flesh that touches any un-   If the meat comes into contact with
clean thing shall not be eaten; it   anything ritually unclean, it must not
shall be burned with fire. All who are   be eaten, but must be burned.
clean may eat flesh,   Anyone who is ritually clean
                                     may eat the meat,

RSV and a number of other English versions begin a new paragraph at the
beginning of this verse, but TEV takes the first part of this verse as belonging to the
previous paragraph (similarly FRCL and TOB). Some versions assume that the general
rules begin at verse 18 (see NJB). Translators are advised to follow the paragraphing
of TEV at this point.

Flesh: the word thus translated in RSV could theoretically refer either to the
meat of the peace offering mentioned in the previous verse or to meat in general.
However, it is almost certain that it refers more specifically to the meat offered to
the LORD. Therefore it may be advisable to translate "that meat" or "this meat,"
clearly referring back to verse 18. Mft renders the term "sacrificial flesh."

Unclean: that is, ritually unclean (see 5.2).

With fire: see verse 17.

All who are clean . . . : or "ritually clean" (see 5.2).

7.20   RSV   TEV

but the person who eats of the flesh   but if anyone who is not clean eats
of the sacrifice of the LORD's peace   it, he shall no longer be considered
offerings while an uncleanness is on   one of God's people.
him, that person shall be cut off from
his people.

Of the LORD's: that is, "that has been offered to the LORD."

While an uncleanness is on him: in contrast with the details given in verse
21, verse 20 probably involves a case of ritual impurity which comes about as a result
of some action performed or experienced by the individual himself: birth (see chapter
12), sickness (chapter 13), nocturnal emission, or menstruation (chapter 15). This has
been translated "[while] in a state of uncleanness" (Mft, NAB, and NJV) and "while
unclean" (NEB).

Shall be cut off from his people: although this formula is rather frequent in
the Old Testament, its exact meaning is not known with certainty. Some scholars see
in it a condemnation to death. But it is more likely that it involves the excommunication of the person from the social and religious community of Israel. Having all vital
links to his former human fellowship severed, the guilty party is left to the justice of
God himself (compare 20.6). Some languages may say "he will no longer be counted
one of the people of God," or "they [indefinite] will no longer consider him an
Israelite," or "he will be expelled from the community of God's people."

The Hebrew term translated **people** (see 4.3) is used in several different expressions having slightly different meanings ranging from a very broad "kin" to membership in a particular tribe or clan. If the receptor language has several different words to describe different degrees of kinship, it is probably best to use the most general term in this context. If there is any possibility that the reader or hearer will misunderstand **his people**, then it should be translated "the people of Israel," or perhaps "the nation of Israel."

7.21   RSV   TEV

And if any one touches an unclean   Also, if anyone eats the meat of this
thing, whether the uncleanness of   offering after he has touched any-
man or an unclean beast or any   thing ritually unclean, whether from a
unclean abomination, and then eats   man or an animal, he shall no longer
of the flesh of the sacrifice of the   be considered one of God's people.
LORD's peace offerings, that person
shall be cut off from his people."

This verse may need to be restructured in some languages in order to bring out the meaning more clearly. The structure of RSV, **if any one touches . . . and then eats . . .** , following the chronological order of the events, may be adequate for some languages, but others may prefer "If anyone eats . . . after having touched . . ." (compare Mft as well as TEV). Translators should consider both structures to determine which one is more natural in the receptor language.

Uncleanness of man or an unclean beast: perhaps better summed up as in TEV **"anything ritually unclean, whether from a man or an animal"** (which would also include the following phrase).

Or any unclean abomination: this is usually understood as meaning "any unclean, detestable thing." But some Hebrew manuscripts have a slight alteration of the word here that yields the meaning "reptile" (see Mft, NEB; compare also NAB "some loathsome crawling creature"). Although this is recommended in HOTTP, the majority of English translations have avoided this reading.

7.22-23   RSV   TEV

22 The LORD said to Moses,   22 The LORD gave Moses the
23 "Say to the people of Israel, You   following regulations 23 for the peo-
shall eat no fat, of ox, or sheep, or   ple of Israel. No fat of cattle, sheep,
goat.   or goats shall be eaten.

Said to Moses: see 4.1.

You shall eat no fat: the passive formulation of TEV will have to be avoided in many languages. In this case RSV will serve as a better model.

7.24 RSV TEV

The fat of an animal that dies of itself, and the fat of one that is torn by beasts, may be put to any other use, but on no account shall you eat it.	The fat of an animal that has died a natural death or has been killed by a wild animal must not be eaten, but it may be used for any other purpose.

That dies of itself: as in TEV, NEB and many other versions, the meaning here is "any animal that dies a natural death." This is in contrast with the following expression indicating violent death as a result of an encounter with a wild animal.

Torn by beasts: a literal translation of this phrase may be misleading, since it would leave open the possibility of an animal that survived an attack by a wild animal. The intent is surely "any animal that has been killed by a wild animal."

The structure of the last part of this verse may be strange if a literal translation is made into other languages. The phrase **any other use** anticipates the prohibition **on no account shall you eat it**. TEV has wisely shifted the prohibition forward but has perhaps lost some of its emphasis. It may be better to say "must in no case be eaten" or, where passive forms are not appropriate, "you must in no case eat . . . ." Another way of rendering the last part of this verse may be "people must never eat the fat of such an animal, but it may be used for other things."

7.25 RSV TEV

For every person who eats of the fat of an animal of which an offering by fire is made to the Lord shall be cut off from his people.	Anyone who eats the fat of an animal that may be offered as a food offering to the Lord will no longer be considered one of God's people.

This verse is a logical continuation of verse 23, following verse 24 which constitutes a kind of parenthetical statement.

An offering by fire: that is, "**a food offering**." See 1.9.

Cut off from his people: see verse 20.

7.26 RSV TEV

Moreover you shall eat no blood whatever, whether of fowl or of animal, in any of your dwellings.	No matter where the Israelites live, they must never use the blood of birds or animals for food.

In verse 3.17 passing mention is made of "blood" along with the fat that is not to be consumed. Verses 26 and 27 develop and clarify this prohibition. It will be further discussed and justified in 17.3-14.

Moreover: in addition to being somewhat archaic, the transition word used in RSV is too strong. The word in Hebrew at this point is the common conjunction that is often translated "and" or "but," but is frequently left untranslated. Some versions make a paragraph break at this point (NEB, NJB, and TOB) but have no transition word. Others (such as TEV) continue the same paragraph without any transition word.

You: the plural pronoun indicates that the people of Israel are being addressed directly and as a group. Note that the restructuring of TEV makes it necessary to transform the direct address to a kind of indirect address and change the pronoun to "**they**."

Fowl: that is, any kind of bird.

In any of your dwellings: see 3.17, where the Hebrew is the same in spite of the slightly different renderings in RSV. Here this information has been shifted forward in TEV and rendered "**No matter where the Israelites live . . . .**" However, in some languages such a rendering may give too much prominence to this element.

7.27   RSV   TEV

Whoever eats any blood, that person   Anyone who breaks this law will no
shall be cut off from his people."   longer be considered one of God's
                                             people.

Whoever eats any blood: a literal rendering as in RSV seems to indicate a more general rule than is intended here. In this context the idea is more specific and closer to the TEV translation "**Anyone who breaks this law.**"

Cut off from his people: see verse 25. In some languages it may be desirable to add a word to show the relationship between this case and the one mentioned in verse 25. For example, "will also (or, likewise) no longer be considered one of God's people." The addition of "likewise" or "similarly," or "in the same way," will indicate to the reader that the two cases are parallel.

7.28-29   RSV   TEV

28 The LORD said to Moses,   28 The LORD gave Moses the
29 "Say to the people of Israel, He   following regulations 29 for the peo-
that offers the sacrifice of his peace   ple of Israel. Whoever offers a fellow-
offerings to the LORD shall bring his   ship offering must bring part of it as
offering to the LORD; from the sacri-   a special gift to the LORD,
fice of his peace offerings

Said to Moses: see 4.1.

Say to the people of Israel: see 1.2.

Verses 29-36 deal with the parts of the sacrifice which the lay persons are required to give to the priest when they make the fellowship offering: the parts which the priest must burn on the altar for God as well as that which constitutes the salary of the priests themselves. The wording of RSV is repetitious and confusing and should be simplified in the receptor language.

His peace offering . . . his offering: the first of these two terms is the usual word of this type of offering, translated "**fellowship offering**" in TEV (see 3.1). The second is a technical term which literally means "that which is brought near," but in this context it indicates that part of the fellowship offering which is presented as a special gift to the Lord. In many languages it would be redundant to repeat the possessive pronoun **his** in this case.

From the sacrifice of his peace offerings: this phrase at the end of verse 29 actually goes with verse 30. But since it is a repetition, it may be omitted in translation.

7.30 RSV	TEV
he shall bring with his own hands the offerings by fire to the LORD; he shall bring the fat with the breast, that the breast may be waved as a wave offering before the LORD.	bringing it with his own hands as a food offering. He shall bring the fat of the animal with its breast and present it as a special gift to the LORD.

Bring with his own hands: the task of bringing this offering to the Lord could not be delegated to another person. In some languages it may be more natural to say something like "he himself must bring . . . ."

The offerings by fire: see 1.9 and discussion on page 5, in "Translating Leviticus."

The fat: in some languages the meaning will be clearer if the words "**of the animal**" are added here, as in TEV.

With the breast: literally, "over the breast." The preposition here has been interpreted in three different ways:

a) "the fat [which is] on the breast." This is the interpretation followed by NJB with "the fat adhering to the forequarters."

b) The preposition may be understood in a strictly locative sense: "he will bring the fatty parts [placing them] on the breast," but very few scholars accept this.

c) The preposition is taken in the sense of "along with" or "in addition to." This is the interpretation of the majority of English versions including both RSV and TEV.

The word translated **breast** in most versions has been rendered "forequarters" in the 1985 edition of the New Jerusalem Bible (NJB).

Waved as a wave offering: this is not a separate kind of offering. It is more likely that it had to do with a particular gesture associated with sacrifices that required something extra. Both TEV and NEB place the emphasis on the special nature of the sacrifice rather than on the gesture itself. It is probably best to translate here "**present it as a special gift**," as in TEV. This is similar to the problem discussed in verse 14, but the word used here is different.

7.31   RSV   TEV

The priest shall burn the fat on the altar, but the breast shall be for Aaron and his sons.	The priest shall burn the fat on the altar, but the breast shall belong to the priests.

It is especially important in this verse to note that the word **priest** in the beginning of the verse refers to the particular priest involved in the ceremony, while the expression **Aaron and his sons** refers to the entire priestly community (see 1.7). The second expression may be better rendered "the priestly clan" or something similar.

Burn: see 1.9.

7.32   RSV   TEV

And the right thigh you shall give to the priest as an offering from the sacrifice of your peace offerings;	The right hind leg of the animal shall be given as a special contribution

And: the force of this conjunction may be better rendered in many languages by saying something like "you shall also give to the priest . . . ," that is, in addition to the fat and the breast mentioned in verse 30.

The right thigh: some translations have understood this to refer to the shoulder rather than to the thigh (KJV), but it is almost certainly the upper joint of the animal's hind leg that is meant. Both TEV and NEB specify "**the right hind leg**." Situated near the organs of reproduction, this part was related to the mystery of life and was withdrawn from normal consumption. This was especially true for the right thigh, given the importance of the right side among the people of Israel. If the right does not have any special positive connotation in the receptor language, it may be advisable to include this information in a note.

7.33   RSV   TEV

he among the sons of Aaron who offers the blood of the peace offerings and the fat shall have the right thigh for a portion.	to the priest who offers the blood and the fat of the fellowship offering.

He among the sons of Aaron who offers the blood . . .: this long and awkward expression simply means "to the officiating priest," but since the blood and the fat are important here, it may be better to translate as in TEV, "**the priest who offers the blood and the fat**."

TEV makes one sentence of verses 32 and 33 by simplifying the structure and eliminating redundant elements. This should serve as a good model for many other languages.

7.34 RSV TEV

For the breast that is waved and the thigh that is offered I have taken from the people of Israel, out of the sacrifices of their peace offerings, and have given them to Aaron the priest and to his sons, as a perpetual due from the people of Israel.	The breast of the animal is a special gift, and the right hind leg is a special contribution that the LORD has taken from the people of Israel and given to the priests. This is what the people of Israel must give to the priests for all time to come.

That is waved: see verse 30.

That is offered: this word, similar in meaning to the one above, indicates the special character of the offering.

I have taken . . . and have given . . . : as in 6.17, the use of the first person singular pronoun here is surprising, and in most languages a literal translation would probably be confusing. In Hebrew this form emphasizes in a solemn manner the divine origin of these instructions. TEV brings this out by translating "**that the LORD has taken . . . and given . . . .**" It may be made a bit stronger by saying "the LORD himself . . . ." Compare 6.17.

To Aaron the priest and his sons: that is, to the descendants of Aaron, the priests (see 1.5).

As a perpetual due: as in Exodus 29.28, this expression indicates the permanent right of the priests. Compare also 6.18.

7.35 RSV TEV

This is the portion of Aaron and of his sons from the offerings made by fire to the LORD, consecrated to them on the day they were presented to serve as priests of the LORD;	This is the part of the food offered to the LORD that was given to Aaron and his sons on the day they were ordained as priests.

Verses 35-36 are somewhat ambiguous in Hebrew. Do they form a part of the direct discourse begun in verse 29 as indicated by the punctuation of RSV? Or are they rather a part of the conclusion to the section verses 28-34 (NJB, NAB and FRCL)? If indirect discourse is used throughout this section, there is less of a problem here. But it may be wise to begin a new paragraph at this point, if the latter interpretation is accepted. By not starting a new paragraph here, TEV seems to follow the first option.

The portion: this word may come from a verb "to measure" or "to distribute," but the use of a similar form which means "to anoint" in the following verse has lead some to believe that it is related to anointing. However, it is probably best simply to translate with a word meaning "share" (NAB and Mft), "allotment" or "due." NJV has "perquisites," while AT has the equally uncommon language "emolument." While this term refers to the immediately preceding context, it may also have a more general meaning alluding to the priestly part of sacrifices as a whole.

Of Aaron and of his sons: in view of the historical perspective of the text at this point, it is preferable to retain the form **of Aaron and of his sons** here, rather than to translate it simply as "priests," as in many other contexts.

The offerings made by fire: see 1.9.

Consecrated to them: there is no Hebrew equivalent for these words in RSV, so there is no reason why they should be translated.

On the day they were presented to serve as priests: literally, "on the day that he brought them forward to be priests to the LORD." On the expression **on the day**, see 6.5,20. This concluding verse (together with verse 36) is at the same time a transition to the next section of Leviticus, where the ordination or installation of the Aaronite priests is dealt with in detail (chapters 8–10). The expression may be translated "from the time they were installed (or, ordained) as priests." NJV has "once they have been inducted to serve the LORD as priests."

7.36   RSV   TEV

the LORD commanded this to be   On that day the LORD commanded
given them by the people of Israel,   the people of Israel to give them this
on the day that they were anointed;   part of the offering. It is a regulation
it is a perpetual due throughout their   that the people of Israel must obey
generations."   for all time to come.

This: this may be too vague or too restricted for many readers. "**This part of the offering**" (TEV) is much clearer. NEB has "these prescribed portions," which is probably better, since it uses the plural.

To be given: the passive may be transformed into an active form as in TEV.

On the day that they were anointed: literally, "on the day of his anointing them." This clause should probably be shifted to the head of the sentence and the redundancy omitted in many languages. TEV summarizes by simply saying "**On that day . . . .**"

A perpetual due: see verse 34.

Throughout their generations: see 3.17.

7.37   RSV   TEV

This is the law of the burnt   These, then, are the regulations
offering, of the cereal offering, of the   for the burnt offerings, the grain
sin offering, of the guilt offering, of   offerings, the sin offerings, the re-
the consecration, and of the peace   payment offerings, the ordination
offerings,   offerings, and the fellowship offer-
                                            ings.

While verses 35 and 36 serve as a minor conclusion to chapters 6 and 7, verses 37 and 38 provide at the same time a further conclusion to these chapters (see the use of **law** here and in 6.2,7,18, and so on) and also a major conclusion to the entire first section of Leviticus (chapters 1–7).

This is the law: this expression is the same as the beginning of verses 1 and 11, except that the definite article precedes **law**, and the conjunction is absent in this verse. The earlier verses have the conjunction but lack the definite article. In this context, however, it seems clear that we are dealing here with a summary statement. See also 6.2.

The burnt offering . . . the cereal offering . . . : each of the names of the first three kinds of sacrifices in this list is singular in form, but used in a collective sense. In many languages it will be necessary to make them all plural so that the collective meaning is clear. The translator should make certain that the names used in this summary statement correspond to the names given to each kind of offering in its own section and in the section headings.

Consecration: this word may be better translated "installation" (AT), "ordination" (NIV), or "investiture" (NJB). The same word is used elsewhere for the setting of a jewel (Exo 25.7, for example). It carries the idea of putting in place. And in this context where the plural form is used, it obviously has to do with the offerings associated with the priests' installation or ordination. For this reason several versions say explicitly "ordination offering" (NIV and NAB), "installation offerings" (NEB), or something similar.

7.38   RSV   TEV

which the LORD commanded Moses on Mount Sinai, on the day that he commanded the people of Israel to bring their offerings to the LORD, in the wilderness of Sinai.

There on Mount Sinai in the desert, the LORD gave these commands to Moses on the day he told the people of Israel to make their offerings.

Note that TEV has made a separate sentence of this verse, which is a relative clause in RSV and in Hebrew.

On Mount Sinai . . . in the wilderness of Sinai: these two phrases may be translated as one in order to eliminate the needless repetition of **Sinai**. The term **wilderness** should be translated in such a way as to indicate an uninhabited region.

Chapter 8

The second major section in Leviticus is made up of chapters 8–10. It deals with the consecration of the first priests, Aaron and his sons. Chapter 8 describes the actual ceremony of installation or ordination. Chapter 9 gives an account of the newly ordained priests taking up their posts. And chapter 10 provides some specific rules and regulations which the priests must respect as they perform their duties.

On the use of major section headings or different levels of headings, see the remarks in the introduction, "Translating Leviticus," pages 1-3, and under the first major heading (chapter 1).

TEV Section Heading: "**The Ordination of Aaron and His Sons.**"

In some languages it will be more natural to use a complete sentence as a heading. It may also be necessary to mention the word "ceremony" specifically. Translators may consider something like "Aaron and his sons are installed (or ordained, or consecrated)" or, where passive forms are not used, "Moses installs (or ordains, or consecrates) Aaron and his sons." However, it may be better to use the word "priests" in place of "Aaron and his sons" in the title, since the section deals with more than the narration of a historical event involving only Aaron and his four sons. It is at the same time a rite to be performed afterwards in the consecration of all priests and high priests. Some languages have even tried a more dynamic section heading like "How men become priests" or "Instructions about making people priests."

The instructions which God gave to Moses with regard to this ceremony are recorded in detail in Exodus 29.1-37. The ceremony in this chapter is made up of five main events:

1. Those men who are about to become priests are purified (verse 6).
2. Aaron (verse 7-9) and his four sons (verse 13) receive their priestly clothing.
3. Aaron is anointed with oil (verses 10a and 12; see also verse 30).
4. The required sacrifices are offered (verse 14-29).
5. The priests spend a week separated from others, symbolizing their "setting apart" (verses 31-36).

8.1-2	RSV	TEV

1 The LORD said to Moses, 2 "Take Aaron and his sons with him, and the garments, and the anointing oil, and the bull of the sin offering, and the two rams, and the

1 The LORD said to Moses, 2 "Take Aaron and his sons to the entrance of the Tent of my presence and bring the priestly garments, the anointing oil, the young bull for the

| basket of unleavened bread; | sin offering, the two rams, and the basket of unleavened bread. |

Said to Moses: see 4.1.

Take . . . : this single verb has seven different objects in Hebrew as reflected in RSV. In most languages this type of construction is too heavy, and it may be impossible to use the same verb with all the various objects mentioned in this verse (human beings, animals, and inanimate objects). TEV divides it into two parts and adds the verb "**bring.**" FRCL cuts it three ways and uses three different verbs. In some languages it may be necessary to reorder the objects and group the inanimate objects together (garments, oil, basket) instead of having them separated by the mention of the two rams. In addition the Hebrew verb does not necessarily imply that the subject (Moses) must personally perform the action of bringing the various items to the entrance of the Tent. So in some languages a causative or some other form may be used. For example, "Send Aaron and his sons . . ." or "Make Aaron and his sons go to the entrance . . . ." One may also consider using a verb like "call" or "convoke."

Note also that TEV has taken information from verse 3, "**to the entrance of the Tent of my presence,**" and shifted it forward for the sake of clarity. This may be advisable in a number of other languages.

With him: this simply indicates that Aaron and his sons are taken together at this point. These words may be left implicit in many languages.

The garments: the word "vestments," used in several English versions, implies that these were special garments for use in some sort of religious ceremony. But this is hardly common language. The definite article here implies that some specific articles of clothing are intended. The need for some clarification is seen in the fact that the ancient Greek version adds "his," and the Vulgate adds "their." But the reference is to the clothing of both Aaron and his sons (see Exo 28). In this case it may be better to say "**priestly garments**" (as in TEV) or "sacred clothing" rather than simply "the clothing."

The anointing oil: see Exodus 30.22-33.

The bull . . . and the two rams: see Exodus 29.1-3.

The sin offering: see 4.3-12.

The basket of unleavened bread: or "the basket containing bread without yeast." (See chapter 2, especially verse 11.)

8.3   RSV   TEV

| and assemble all the congregation at the door of the tent of meeting." | Then call the whole community together there." |

Assemble: Moses is to convoke, or summon, the entire group, or "all the people of Israel," for this ceremony. This public aspect of the ordination of the priests is not explicitly mentioned in Exodus 29.

At the door of the tent of meeting: on **door** see 1.3. Since this element has been shifted forward to the beginning of verse 2 in TEV, it is translated here by the adverb "**there.**"

8.4   RSV   TEV

And Moses did as the LORD com-   **Moses did as the LORD had**
manded him; and the congregation   **commanded, and when the commu-**
was assembled at the door of the   **nity had assembled,**
tent of meeting.

Moses did as the LORD commanded: the verb here may be better translated
in some languages by "Moses obeyed what the LORD had commanded him" or
"Moses followed the instructions which the LORD had given him."

And the congregation was assembled: what is the relationship between this
and the first part of the verse? Some versions take it to be an explanation of Moses'
obedience, and therefore they begin a new paragraph at the end of this verse (RSV,
NIV). Others make it a relative clause introducing the verses that follow (TEV, NJV,
NAB). It is probably best to follow the TEV solution and not begin a new paragraph
at the end of this verse.

At the door of the tent of meeting: in some cases it may be possible to leave
implicit the words **of meeting**, since the context makes it quite clear which tent is
intended. And in fact the entire phrase is left implicit in TEV, since it appears in the
previous verses.

8.5   RSV   TEV

And Moses said to the congre-   **he said to them, "What I am now**
gation, "This is the thing which the   **about to do is what the LORD has**
LORD has commanded to be done."   **commanded."**

Moses said: if the structure of TEV is followed at the end of verse 4, it is
possible to render the subject noun by a pronoun in this context, since it would
clearly refers to Moses.

The congregation: as in the case of Moses above, the noun **congregation**
may be translated by a pronoun referring to the people of Israel assembled. But
translators should be certain that the reference is clear.

This is the thing . . . : the **thing** referred to in this case may be unclear if
these words are translated literally. What Moses is talking about is the event that is
about to take place, or the actions he is about to perform. The meaning is much
more clearly conveyed by something like "The thing(s) I am going to do next" or
"What I am now about to do . . ." (TEV). It is also possible to avoid the use of a
direct quotation and say something like "He told them that he must fulfill the
LORD's orders." Compare NAB "Moses told them what the LORD had ordered to be
done."

8.6   RSV   TEV

And Moses brought Aaron and his   **Moses brought Aaron and his**
sons, and washed them with water.   **sons forward and had them take a**
ritual bath.

And: the transition word here may be very important in some languages. In order to make the connection with the previous verse, it is probably better to say "Then . . ." (NIV, NJV) or "Immediately . . . ." Mft has "Whereupon . . . ," which is not common language but indicates that some kind of transition word may be needed.

Brought: the verb here is often translated "brought forward" (as in TEV, NIV, NAB, NJV, and Mft). But NJB renders it more dynamically with "made Aaron and his sons come forward."

Washed them with water: the words **with water** may be redundant in many languages. Translators should also be careful not to give the impression that Moses washed his brother and his adult nephews the way a mother washes her baby. Rather he had them bathe themselves in the ritual manner required. Care should be taken not to translate by an expression that will evoke the idea of baptism ("to enter into the water" or "to be plunged into water"), but one must also avoid "**take a ritual bath**" if such an expression carries negative connotations because of association with indigenous practices. In seeking to avoid wrong meanings, it may be necessary to use a rather neutral translation such as "he had them wash themselves" or "he caused them to wash themselves."

Note that NAB supplies the word "first" ("he first washed them with water"), which is implied but not clearly stated in the source text.

Although the text itself is not altogether clear on this point, it is most probable that Aaron and his sons were not totally naked in the presence of the assembled community. If different words are used in the receptor language for a bath in which one is totally nude and one in which the person is partly covered, then the latter will be more appropriate here.

8.7 RSV	TEV
And he put on him the coat, and girded him with the girdle, and clothed him with the robe, and put the ephod upon him, and girded him with the skillfully woven band of the ephod, binding it to him therewith.	He put the shirt and the robe on Aaron and the sash around his waist. He put the ephod[a] on him and fastened it by putting its finely woven belt around his waist.
	[a] EPHOD: *See Word List.*

On him: it is probably better to specify "**on Aaron**" (TEV) in most languages in order to clarify the meaning.

The precise identification of the various articles of clothing listed in this verse is very difficult. In some cases the exact meaning is unknown. The translator should try to visualize the whole and then formulate it in such a way as to be meaningful to the readers. Footnotes may be necessary in order to emphasize the fact that the clothing mentioned here was special and reserved for the priests. The practice of transliterating the Hebrew terminology should be avoided if at all possible, but if no other solution can be found, a footnote or glossary explanation will definitely be required. For more details on the clothing of the priests, see Exodus 28.1-43 and 39.1-31.

The coat: in Exodus (28.4,39; 39.27) this garment is mentioned without any detailed description. In ordinary usage the Hebrew word refers to an everyday article of clothing worn by men and women alike and was probably a sort of "**shirt**." The RSV **coat** is misleading, since it was not an outer garment but one worn underneath other clothing and next to the body. It has often been translated "tunic" (NIV, NEB, NAB, NJB, NJV).

The girdle: (see Exo 28.4,39; 39.29) in modern English the word **girdle** is also misleading. This piece was a long embroidered sash that was wrapped around the midsection and served as a kind of belt. However, in addition to its purely functional use, it also seems to have had a symbolic meaning as a sign of the priesthood. Many English versions use the word "**sash**," but in some languages it may be necessary to say "the broad band." In any case, it should be carefully distinguished from the **skillfully woven band of the ephod**, or "**belt**," mentioned later in this verse.

The robe: this garment is described in Exodus 28.31-35 and 39.22-26. It was a kind of outer shirt consisting of a large piece of cloth with a hole cut for the head and with the edges around the hole sewn in order to prevent shredding. It probably reached down to the feet like the long flowing robe worn in the Middle East and parts of West Africa today.

The ephod: this term is a transliteration of the Hebrew and is by far the most difficult piece of the priestly clothing to translate. It is often mentioned in Exodus without ever being described in detail (Exo 25.7; 28.6; 29.5; 39.2-3). In the Old Testament this same word refers to at least three different items: (1) It was a kind of white linen undergarment worn by the priest on his lower body (see 1 Sam 2.18; 2 Sam 6.14,20; 1 Chr 15.27). (2) It was some sort of cultic object, like a statue, used in divination (Judges 17.5; 18.14,17; 1 Sam. 2.28; 21.9) or possibly a sack or some other kind of container used to hold such cultic objects (see TOB note on Judges 8.27). (3) But in the present case it seems to have been a kind of apron with shoulder straps and tied with the **skillfully woven band** probably behind the back (See Exo 28.6-7; 39.2-4). Almost all English versions transliterate, but AT has simply "the apron," and Mft translates "the sacred apron." In other languages it may be possible to say something like Mft's rendering or "the priestly apron."

The skillfully woven band: this band or belt seems to have been made with the same material as the **ephod** (Exo 28.8) and attached to its corners so that it could be tied. The use of the singular does not necessarily mean that there was only one. The term may have been used in a collective sense. According to an ancient Jewish interpretation, the word translated **skillfully** has no place here. The word simply means "girdle," or "waistband," or "**belt**." This idea is therefore omitted in NJB and NEB as well as in many non-English versions, and may also be left out of the receptor-language rendering. It is interesting to note, however, that NJV has "the decorated band."

8.8	RSV	TEV

And he placed the breastpiece on him, and in the breastpiece he put the Urim and the Thummim.	He put the breastpiece on him and put the Urim and Thummim[b] in it.

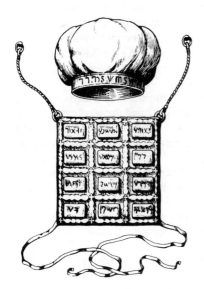

THE TURBAN AND BREASTPIECE

b URIM AND THUMMIM: *Two objects used by the priest to determine God's will; it is not known precisely how they were used.*

The breastpiece: this item is described in detail in Exodus 28.15-29 and 39.8-21. It is a square piece of material with pockets or pouches in which the Urim and the Thummim (see below) were placed. It may possibly be rendered "the sacred pouch" (Mft) or "the pockets over the heart."

On him: in some languages this may be too vague or may lead the reader to believe that the breastpiece is placed on top of his head. In such cases it is better to say "he placed the breastpiece on his chest" or "over his heart," or something similar.

The Urim and the Thummim: (see Exo 28.30) as the TEV footnote indicates, these two objects were somehow used by the priest to find out the will of God (see, for example, Num 27.21; 1 Sam 14.41; 28.6). In most versions the two words are simply transliterated, but Mft renders the meaning quite adequately with "the sacred lots." Other languages may have to say "the lots of God." In either case it is advisable to include a footnote explaining the meaning in greater detail.

8.9	RSV	TEV

And he set the turban upon his head, and on the turban, in front, he set the golden plate, the holy crown, as the LORD commanded Moses.

He placed the turban on his head, and on the front of it he put the gold ornament, the sacred sign of dedication, just as the LORD had commanded him.

He set: the verb is used twice in the verse at hand. This may be imitated if the style of the receptor language permits such repetition, and if the same verb is suitable for both actions. Otherwise the meaning may be conveyed quite naturally by structuring the verse in such a way as to translate this verb only once, or to use two separate verbs for the two different objects.

The turban: mentioned in Exodus 28.4,39; 39.28; Leviticus 16.4, but no detailed description is given. This headdress was a piece of material wrapped around the head, but it may have been wound permanently and taken on and off like a hat. In some languages there may be a very general word covering anything worn on the head. If such a term is used, it may be helpful to include a footnote explaining that such a headpiece symbolized the authority of the High Priest. In some languages the translation may be more detailed, such as "a covering made of cloth and wrapped around the head."

The golden plate: the word translated **plate** here may mean "blossom" or "flower" as in Numbers 17.8 (verse 23 in Hebrew), or "a shining thing." Used with the qualifying word **golden**, it is taken by many English versions in the sense of **plate**. FRCL, however, translates "a golden jewel in the form of a flower." NJB has simply "the golden flower." In any case, these words are in apposition with the expression that follows and are explained by these words.

The holy crown: this was clearly not a crown in the sense of a sign of royalty. The word translated **crown** may also mean "consecration," and the whole expression probably indicates that **the golden plate** was a symbol of the High Priest's dedication to God. It has been suggested that the meaning of this phrase may be rendered by an expression like "a sign showing that Aaron was given over to (or, consecrated to) God." Another possible model for translating these two expressions (**the golden plate, the holy crown**) may be "a golden object showing that he was dedicated to God."

As the LORD commanded Moses: it is most probable that this refers to all the actions mentioned above and not just to the last phrase.

8.10   RSV   TEV

      Then Moses took the anointing   Then Moses took the anointing
oil, and anointed the tabernacle and   oil and put it on the Tent of the
all that was in it, and consecrated   LORD's presence and everything that
them.   was in it, and in this way he dedi-
                                         cated it all to the LORD.

Anointed: see Exodus 30.22-33. Up to this point in Leviticus, only the priests have been anointed. Now this verb is applied to the Tent and all the various objects in it (see diagram at the end of the introduction, "Translating Leviticus"). In some languages a different word may be required for human beings and inanimate objects. But a general word like "put it [the oil] on . . ." may be preferable, and in some languages a verb like "sprinkle" (as in the following verse) may be necessary.

The tabernacle: in Leviticus the term ordinarily used is "tent of meeting," but here as well as in 15.31 and 17.4 we find a different word. In this case the root meaning is "the dwelling place." It is often used elsewhere in the Old Testament to refer to the place where God manifests his presence among human beings. Some commentators have supposed that this term is used to refer to the entire sanctuary area, including the courtyard. The translator may wish to use an expression like "the dwelling place of God" or "the place where God shows himself (or, meets with people)," but it is important not to give the impression that a place other than the "tent of meeting" or **Tent of the LORD's presence** is intended. Some scholars feel that the terms for "sanctuary," "tent of meeting," and "tabernacle" should be translated differently because they are thought to come from different traditions. (See Noel Osborn, 1990, "Tent or tabernacle? Translating two traditions," *The Bible Translator* 41 [April]:214-221.)

Consecrated them: the pronoun **them** refers to the Tent of the LORD's presence and everything it contained. In some cases it may be clearer to make explicit the fact that they are consecrated "**to the LORD**," as in TEV. The rendering **consecrated** here and in verses 11 and 12 is not based on the same Hebrew word as "consecrate" in RSV at 7.35. The parent noun of the verb here is related to the word for "holy" and is thus rendered "sanctify" in KJV. It indicates a state of belonging to the realm of the sacred, that is, to God himself. In some languages it may be rendered by a causative form, but in others it will have to be translated more dynamically in this context by something like "and in this way he showed that they belonged to the LORD."

8.11   RSV   TEV

And he sprinkled some of it on the altar seven times, and anointed the altar and all its utensils, and the laver and its base, to consecrate them.

He took some of the oil and sprinkled it seven times on the altar and its equipment and on the basin and its base, in order to dedicate them to the LORD.

The altar: if necessary the translator may make explicit the fact that it is the altar of sacrifice and not the incense altar that is referred to here.

Seven times: compare 4.6.

All its utensils: that is, those articles that were used on the altar. Since there are several different items listed in this verse that are to be sprinkled, some translators may wonder whether the action is to be performed individually or collectively. If the receptor language requires such a distinction, it is probably better to indicate a collective action rather than seven individual sprinklings of items.

The laver: a bronze basin stood "between the tent of meeting and the altar" (Exo 30.18). Later in the history of the people of Israel there were more basins (1 Kgs 7.27-39), and they were probably arranged differently.

To consecrate them: see verse 10.

8.12   RSV   TEV

And he poured some of the anointing oil on Aaron's head, and anointed him, to consecrate him.

He ordained Aaron by pouring some of the anointing oil on his head.

This verse may have to be restructured in some languages so that the idea of consecration or ordination is shifted forward and made the main verb of the sentence. And if the same verb is used of Aaron as of the objects in verses 10 and 11, it may be necessary to add "also" to the sentence. "He also consecrated Aaron . . ." or "He also showed that Aaron belonged (completely) to the LORD by pouring oil . . . ." The term translated **consecrate** here is the same as in the two previous verses.

115

8.13 RSV	TEV
And Moses brought Aaron's sons, and clothed them with coats, and girded them with girdles, and bound caps on them, as the LORD commanded Moses.	**Next, Moses brought the sons of Aaron forward and put shirts on them, put sashes around their waists, and tied caps on their heads, just as the LORD had commanded.**

And: the receptor language transition word will, in some cases, have to be stronger than in RSV. Some versions have "**Next**" (Mft, TEV); but most have "Then" (NJV, NIV, NEB, NAB). The translator should use whatever naturally shows the progression from one event to another.

Brought . . . : it may be better in some languages to use a causative form like "Moses caused the sons of Aaron to come forward" or ". . . told them to come forward." Compare verse 6.

Coats . . . girdles: see verse 7.

Bound caps on them: this is an additional article of priestly clothing which is mentioned but not described in detail in Exodus (28.40; 29.9). Exodus 39.28 indicates that they are made of linen, like Aaron's turban, but they are apparently a different type of head covering. The translator may use two different terms that are close in meaning, without indicating that Aaron and his sons wore the exact same kind of headpiece. But it is also possible to use a term here indicating a cap without a protruding brim, while translating **turban** in a way that shows that it was a piece of cloth wrapped around the head.

As the LORD commanded: as in verse 9 above, this refers to the whole of the preceding verse and not just to the final action.

8.14 RSV	TEV
Then he brought the bull of the sin offering; and Aaron and his sons laid their hands upon the head of the bull of the sin offering.	**Then Moses brought the young bull for the sin offering, and Aaron and his sons put their hands on its head.**

On verses 14-17, see Exodus 29.10-14.

Then: once again the transition word should indicate movement toward another step in a progression of events.

He: the pronoun refers to Moses, and this should be made clear in translation. Otherwise the reader may think that it refers to Aaron.

The bull of the sin offering: see 4.3-12.

Laid their hands upon the head of the bull: see 1.4. On the use of the singular or plural of "hand," see 4.15. The repetition of **the bull of the sin offering** may be considered unnecessary in many languages; TEV, for example, uses a simple pronoun.

8.15   RSV   TEV

And Moses killed it, and took the blood, and with his finger put it on the horns of the altar round about, and purified the altar, and poured out the blood at the base of the altar, and consecrated it, to make atonement for it.	Moses killed it and took some of the blood, and with his finger put it on the projections at the corners of the altar, in order to dedicate it. He then poured out the rest of the blood at the base of the altar. In this way he dedicated it and purified it.

Moses: the Hebrew has only the pronoun here. Literally the verse begins "he killed it and Moses took . . . ." This has led some commentators to believe that the first action was performed by Aaron. But the majority of the scholars feel that Moses is the subject of both verbs in spite of this unusual structure.

Killed it: or better, "slaughtered it" (see 1.5).

The blood: the ancient Greek version has "some of the blood." This is only logical, since the remainder of it is poured out at the base of the altar later in the verse. For this reason it will be wise in many languages to translate as in TEV, "**some of the blood**" and "**the rest of the blood**."

His finger: see 4.6.

The horns of the altar: the altar referred to is the altar of sacrifice (see verse 11). The word **horns** refers to the corners of the altar. See 4.7.

Purified . . . and consecrated . . . : it may be difficult in some languages to find two different verbs to express these two ideas. The first verb contains the rather negative idea of removing "sin" or eliminating the mundane character of the altar. The second verb is a more positive statement of the same idea and may be translated "set apart" or "given over to God." The root of this verb is the same as in verses 10-12. One translation sums up the purpose of this dedication by saying "In this way he consecrated the altar [of sacrifice] so that it might be suitable for ceremonies for the forgiveness of sins." Another possibility is "he removed all sin from the altar and dedicated it to God." To use the verb "**dedicate**" twice in succession, as in TEV, may give the wrong impression that two separate acts of dedication took place.

Poured out the blood: that is, the blood that remained after having used some of it on the corners of the altar.

To make atonement for it: this indicates the purpose of previous actions. It may be that some languages will require a different word for **atonement** here, since this involves an altar instead of people (compare 1.4 and 4.20). NJV has "cleansing the altar," and NJB has "performing the rite of expiation over it."

8.16   RSV   TEV

And he took all the fat that was on the entrails, and the appendage of the liver, and the two kidneys with their fat, and Moses burned them on the altar.	Moses took all the fat on the internal organs, the best part of the liver, and the kidneys with the fat on them, and burned it all on the altar.

This is essentially a repetition of what is found in 3.3-4 and 4.8-10a.

He: although some feel that the structure of the Hebrew requires us to understand Aaron as the implied subject, again the pronoun refers to Moses, and this should be made clear in the receptor language. The proper name is, in fact, used at the end of the verse, but it will be more helpful to the reader if it is shifted forward.

Burned them: see 1.9.

8.17   RSV   TEV

But the bull, and its skin, and its flesh, and its dung, he burned with fire outside the camp, as the LORD commanded Moses.	He took the rest of the bull, including its skin, flesh, and intestines, and burnt it outside the camp, just as the LORD had commanded.

But: in some languages it will be important to use a transition word here that shows the contrast between the parts of the animal that were burned as a sacrifice and those parts that had to be taken out of the camp. This has not been done in TEV.

The bull: that is, what remained of the bull after the fatty parts mentioned in the previous verse had been burned on the altar. Note that TEV has "**the rest of the bull.**"

Its dung: see 4.11.

Burned with fire: the addition of the words **with fire** will be considered redundant and will therefore be omitted in some languages. See 6.30.

8.18   RSV   TEV

Then he presented the ram of the burnt offering; and Aaron and his sons laid their hands on the head of the ram.	Next, Moses brought the ram for the burnt offering, and Aaron and his sons put their hands on its head.

On verses 18-21, see Exodus 29.15-18.

He: it will be better in many languages to supply the noun "**Moses**" as in TEV.

The ram: although the word used here is different, it refers to the same kind of animal as in 1.10-13. The word **ram** is another way of saying a male sheep. Compare also 8.2. This, of course, is the first of two rams, the second being mentioned in verse 22 below.

The burnt offering: see chapter 1.

Laid their hands: see 1.4 and 4.15.

On the head of the ram: compare verse 14.

8.19   RSV   TEV

And Moses killed it, and threw the blood upon the altar round about.	Moses killed it and threw the blood on all four sides of the altar.

Moses: as in verse 15 above, the text actually says "he killed it and Moses sprinkled . . . ." But most versions see Moses as the subject of both verbs (see the remarks on verse 15).

Killed it: see verse 15.

Threw the blood . . . round about: see 1.5.

8.20-21   RSV   TEV

20 And when the ram was cut into pieces, Moses burned the head and the pieces and the fat. 21 And when the entrails and the legs were washed with water, Moses burned the whole ram on the altar, as a burnt offering, a pleasing odor, an offering by fire to the LORD, as the LORD commanded Moses.

20-21 He cut the ram in pieces, washed the internal organs and the hind legs with water, and burned the head, the fat, and all the rest of the ram on the altar, just as the LORD had commanded. This burnt offering was a food offering, and its odor was pleasing to the LORD.

See 1.6-9.

Was cut: this passive formulation may be transformed to an active expression with Moses as the subject of the verb. But as in the previous verse, it is possible that Aaron is the implied subject here.

Entrails: see 1.9.

The legs: as in 1.9 and 7.32, this refers to the hind legs of the animal.

An offering by fire: that is, a food offering. See 1.9.

Note that TEV has restructured these two verses, making the end of the verse a kind of summary statement.

8.22   RSV   TEV

Then he presented the other ram, the ram of ordination; and Aaron and his sons laid their hands on the head of the ram.

Then Moses brought the second ram, which was for the ordination of priests, and Aaron and his sons put their hands on its head.

Verses 22-30 describe the third sacrifice offered as a part of the ceremony of ordination of Aaron and his sons (see Exo 29.19-28). The ritual is quite similar though not identical to the one prescribed in chapter 3 for the "peace offering" or "fellowship offering."

He: if the referent of the pronoun is in any doubt, it will be necessary to translate using the noun, "**Moses**," as in TEV.

The other ram, the ram of ordination: the first ram, mentioned in verse 18, was for the burnt offering; the second was specifically for the ceremony to ordain Aaron and his sons as priests. On the term **ordination**, see verse 7.37, where the same root word is translated "consecration" in RSV.

Laid their hands on the head of the ram: see 1.4; 4.15; and verse 18 above.

119

8.23

RSV	TEV
And Moses killed it, and took some of its blood and put it on the tip of Aaron's right ear and on the thumb of his right hand and on the great toe of his right foot.	Moses killed it and took some of the blood and put it on the lobe of Aaron's right ear, on the thumb of his right hand, and on the big toe of his right foot.

Killed it: that is, slaughtered it. See verse 15.

The tip of Aaron's right ear: the RSV use of the word **tip** is imprecise. The lower tip of the ear, or the lobe, is what is intended. Those languages that have no special word for earlobe may use expressions like "the bottom of the ear" or "the fat of the ear."

Right ear . . . right hand . . . right foot . . . : on the significance of the right side, see 7.32. The mention of the ear, the hand, and the foot was probably intended to represent the totality of the person.

8.24

RSV	TEV
And Aaron's sons were brought, and Moses put some of the blood on the tips of their right ears and on the thumbs of their right hands and on the great toes of their right feet; and Moses threw the blood upon the altar round about.	Then he brought Aaron's sons forward and put some of the blood on the lobes of their right ears, on the thumbs of their right hands, and on the big toes of their right feet. Moses then threw the rest of the blood on all four sides of the altar.

And: once again the transition word should show the progression from one event to another in the ordination ceremony. Words like "**Then**" or "Next" are probably better than simply **And**.

Aaron's sons were brought: literally, "**he brought Aaron's sons.**" This construction may have a passive meaning, but the passive formulation of RSV does not reflect the Hebrew text. The idea is clearly that Moses caused the sons of Aaron to come forward for this part of the ceremony. This will have to be made active in many languages. But translators should also avoid the misunderstandings inherent in TEV, "**he brought . . . forward,**" as seen in verse 13 above.

The blood: that is, the rest of the blood (see verse 15).

Threw the blood upon the altar round about: see 1.5; 3.2; and similar passages.

8.25

RSV	TEV
Then he took the fat, and the fat tail, and all the fat that was on the entrails, and the appendage of the	He took the fat, the fat tail, all the fat covering the internal organs, the best part of the liver, the kidneys

liver, and the two kidneys with their fat, and the right thigh;	with the fat on them, and the right hind leg.

See 3.9-10 and verse 16 for a very similar list of animal organs.

The fat: according to some commentators this is a general term covering all the parts detailed in the list that follows.

And the fat tail . . . : the coordinating conjunction here has the value of an adverb introducing the detailed list. In some languages it may be translated "namely," or "that is to say," or something similar. But some English versions have used punctuation to convey the idea: NAB has a colon after the word "fat," while NJV uses dashes to set off the definition. For comments on **the fat tail**, see 3.9 and 7.3.

Appendage of the liver: see 3.4.

The two kidneys: see 3.4.

The right thigh: while this is not found in chapter 3, it is mentioned in 7.32 as the part reserved for the officiating priest. Here the thigh of the hind leg is burned on the altar (verse 28), since it was forbidden to Moses, who was officiating but was not a priest. Aaron and his sons were not able to eat it because they were only in the process of becoming priests, and they were not officiating.

8.26 RSV TEV

and out of the basket of unleavened bread which was before the LORD he took one unleavened cake, and one cake of bread with oil, and one wafer, and placed them on the fat and on the right thigh;	Then he took one loaf of bread from the basket of unleavened bread dedicated to the LORD, one loaf made with oil, and one thin cake, and he put them on top of the fat and the right hind leg.

And: verses 25-27 make up one long sentence broken only by semicolons in RSV. TEV makes three sentences of this material and uses the transition word "**Then**" at this point in order to demonstrate the continuity of the narration.

The basket of unleavened bread: see verse 2.

Which was before the LORD: this is not intended to give a physical location, but to indicate that the basket of breads without yeast had been dedicated to the LORD. So in many languages it is preferable to translate "which had been dedicated to the LORD."

Cake . . . wafer: on the terminology for these baked goods, see 7.12-13 as well as chapter 2.

8.27 RSV TEV

and he put all these in the hands of Aaron and in the hands of his sons, and waved them as a wave offering before the LORD.	He put all of this food in the hands of Aaron and his sons, and they presented it as a special gift to the LORD.

All these: this apparently refers to both the baked goods mentioned in verse 26 and the fatty parts and hind leg of the animal in verse 25. NJB translates "he placed these [the breads] on the fat and the right thigh and put it all into Aaron's hands . . . ." This may provide a good model for some other languages.

In the hands: some translations insist on using the word "palms" in this verse (NJV), but this seems unnecessary and will be awkward or unnatural in many languages.

Waved them as a wave offering: see 7.30 on the question of a **wave offering** as opposed to "**a special gift**." But there is an additional problem here of determining the real subject of the verb. The Vulgate has "they," referring to Aaron and his sons, but the Hebrew has the third person singular pronoun, which seems to refer to Moses. This, however, is logically impossible. How could Moses perform any action with items that had already been placed in the hands of his brother and nephews? While TEV translates "**they**," other reliable versions use a kind of causative form retaining the third person singular pronoun. NAB, for example, has ". . . whom he had wave them as a wave offering" (similarly Mft and TOB). FRCL says "he told them to offer . . . ." The meaning seems to be that Moses was somehow the agent in causing the action to be performed, but that he did not actually perform it himself. In view of the fact that **wave offering** actually means "**a special gift**," it may be best to translate the idea "and he [Moses] made them [Aaron and sons] present this food as a special gift to the LORD."

8.28   RSV   TEV

Then Moses took them from their hands, and burned them on the altar with the burnt offering, as an ordination offering, a pleasing odor, an offering by fire to the LORD.	Then Moses took the food from them and burned it on the altar, on top of the burnt offering, as an ordination offering. This was a food offering, and its odor was pleasing to the LORD.

Took them: the pronoun refers to the fatty parts, the right hind thigh, and the different breads he had placed in their hands in the previous verse. In some languages it will be more natural to say "he took them back."

With: as in 3.5, it is probably more accurate to understand this as meaning **with** (RSV, NJV, NJB). However, other versions render the preposition "**on top of**" (TEV, NEB, NIV, Mft).

The burnt offering: see verses 18-21.

As an ordination offering: these words are taken in many translations as the beginning of a new sentence which constitutes a summary statement of what has already been described. NJV has "This was an ordination offering for a pleasing odor . . ." (see also NEB, NJB).

A pleasing odor: see 1.9.

8.29 RSV TEV

And Moses took the breast, and waved it for a wave offering before the LORD; it was Moses' portion of the ram of ordination, as the LORD commanded Moses.	Then Moses took the breast and presented it as a special gift to the LORD. It was Moses' part of the ordination ram. Moses did everything just as the LORD had commanded.

The breast: NJB translates "the forequarter," and this may be a good model for some languages where **breast** implies only the mammary gland. The idea is rather "chest" or "brisket." Although this part is normally reserved for Aaron and his sons (see 7.30-34), it is here given to Moses, since he was in charge of the ceremony.

Waved it for a wave offering: that is, "**presented it as a special gift**" (TEV). See verse 27 and 7.30.

8.30 RSV TEV

Then Moses took some of the anointing oil and of the blood which was on the altar, and sprinkled it upon Aaron and his garments, and also upon his sons and his sons' garments; so he consecrated Aaron and his garments, and his sons and his sons' garments with him.	Moses took some of the anointing oil and some of the blood that was on the altar and sprinkled them on Aaron and his sons and on their clothes. In this way he consecrated them and their clothes to the LORD.

Then: most English versions retain some sort of connecting word here, but TEV and NEB have left the transition implicit. Naturalness in the receptor language should be the determining factor in deciding how to handle this.

The anointing oil: since this verse does not otherwise mention anointing, some versions have preferred to translate here "the holy (or, sacred) oil" (FRCL).

The blood: see verse 24.

Note that the order of the sprinkling is different in TEV, where "**Aaron and his sons**" are mentioned together, and "**their clothes**" is a combined expression for both **garments**. Translators should consider which is the most logical and natural order in their own language.

On the altar: the location of the anointing oil is not specified here. Grammatically the phrase **which was on the altar** refers only to the blood. But the two liquids were mixed and then sprinkled on the priests and their clothing.

Sprinkled . . . .: this ritual established a special relationship between the priests (and their clothing) and the altar. From this point on only they were allowed to approach the altar and to present the sacrifices brought by the people of Israel. Only they could serve as intermediaries between God and the worshiping community.

It: referring to the mixture of the oil and blood. In some languages a plural pronoun may be required. In others it may be better to say more explicitly "the mixture," or simply "the oil and the blood."

So: this introduces a kind of summary statement. TEV has **"in this way."** But Mft and Wenham have "then . . . ," indicating more of a continuation of action.

He consecrated . . . : the verb used here comes from the root meaning "to set apart" or "to make holy." See 2.3. In some languages it may be better to translate "he set them apart with their clothing to serve God" or "he made them and their clothing special in the presence of God."

8.31   RSV   TEV

And Moses said to Aaron and   Moses said to Aaron and his
his sons, "Boil the flesh at the door   sons, "Take the meat to the entrance
of the tent of meeting, and there eat   of the Tent of the Lord's presence,
it and the bread that is in the basket   boil it, and eat it there with the bread
of ordination offerings, as I com-   that is in the basket of ordination
manded, saying, 'Aaron and his sons   offerings, just as the Lord command-
shall eat it';   ed.

And: some versions leave the transition implicit here (TEV, NEB). Both NIV and NJB have "then." Mft has "Moses further said . . . ." But since this is considered the last in a long series of events, the most imaginative transition is found in NAB, "Finally . . . ." This solution may well commend itself to those working in other languages.

Boil: this verb has a causative sense here, and some translators may prefer to say something like "Make (or, Cause) the meat to boil (in water) . . . ." In some languages logic may require that the meat be taken to the entrance of the Tent before mentioning the boiling (TEV). The Hebrew verb is a general term for "cooking" and does not actually indicate whether it is boiled, roasted, or fried. However, in most cases it is associated with some kind of container which would suggest boiling, and the majority of versions interpret it in this way. But it is also possible in some languages to use a more general term meaning simply "prepare for eating."

The flesh: this refers to the meat of the second ram (verse 22). In some cases it may be wise to make this information explicit in the receptor language, as in FRCL "the meat of the second ram."

As I commanded . . . : the following direct quotation (**'Aaron and his sons shall eat it'**) seems to emphasize the exclusiveness of the order. However, in many languages this emphasis may be better conveyed by means other than a direct quotation within another direct quotation. One may say, for example, "you alone are to eat it there . . . ."

The use of the first person pronoun, as in 6.17 and 7.34, may be confusing in many languages. In most cases it is clearer to revert to **"as the Lord commanded."**

Some scholars have proposed that the text may be understood in a passive sense, "I have been commanded" (as in verse 35 below), but this is rejected by HOTTP.

8.32   RSV   TEV

and what remains of the flesh and   **Burn up any meat or bread that is**
the bread you shall burn with fire.   **left over.**

Compare 7.15,17 and Exodus 29.34.

Note that TEV has reordered the elements of meaning in this short verse so that
it begins with an imperative verb. This may also be more natural in a number of
other languages.

Burn with fire: **with fire** will be considered redundant in many languages. See
6.30.

8.33   RSV   TEV

And you shall not go out from the   **You shall not leave the entrance of**
door of the tent of meeting for seven **the Tent for seven days, until your**
days, until the days of your ordina-   **ordination rites are completed.**
tion are completed, for it will take
seven days to ordain you.

You shall not go out: this may also be phrased in a more positive way: "you
must remain inside the Tent . . . ," or perhaps better, "you must remain near (or, at)
the entrance of the Tent."

For seven days: the number seven (see 4.6) represents totality and thus a
complete setting apart to the service of God. It is also a kind of probation period to
make sure that there are no obstacles to divine service. Such a period is a common
feature in rituals required to remove uncleanness (compare 14.8; 15.13,19,28).

Ordination . . . ordain: see verse 28 and 7.37.

The structure of a more literal rendering like RSV may be seen as awkward and
repetitious in some languages. If this is the case, the restructuring of TEV will be
helpful.

8.34   RSV   TEV

As has been done today, the LORD   **The LORD commanded us to do what**
has commanded to be done to make   **we have done today, in order to take**
atonement for you.   **away your sin.**

As has been done . . . : the Hebrew text of this verse may be interpreted in
several ways:
  a) These words may be considered a part of the previous verse and thus
     translated "for during seven days you will be ordained, as has been done
     today . . ." (see TOB).
  b) These words may be attached to what follows, but in a rather loose way, as
     a kind of comparison: **As has been done today, the LORD has**
     commanded . . . (RSV, AT).

c) They may be more strictly attached to the following, as an identification rather than a comparison: "What was done today followed the LORD's command . . ." (NEB). Similarly NJB says "Yahweh has ordered us to do as we have done today . . . ." This is the most frequently chosen option and should probably be followed.

Today: since a seven-day period is mentioned in the preceding verse and the following verse, the use of **today** may be confusing to some readers. The words used here may equally well be translated "at this time" or "now" (see Mft).

To make atonement for you: see 1.4; 4.20.

Note that once again TEV has ordered the various elements of meaning in a way that is quite different from that of RSV.

8.35

RSV	TEV
At the door of the tent of meeting you shall remain day and night for seven days, performing what the LORD has charged, lest you die; for so I am commanded."	You must stay at the entrance of the Tent day and night for seven days, doing what the LORD has commanded. If you don't, you will die. This is what the LORD has commanded me."

You shall remain: some commentators have seen in this a prohibition to entering all the way into the Tent. They are not yet fully priests and therefore cannot go into the holiest places, but they are no longer laymen and so should not go outside. While this may be true, the main point seems rather that they are not to leave the area of the sanctuary (compare verse 33).

Day and night: in some languages it is much more natural to reverse the order of these two words and say "night and day." What is important is that the expression indicate the totality of the twenty-four hour period.

Performing what the LORD has charged: literally, "you will observe the observance of the LORD." The verb and the noun have the same root. However, the meaning is clearly "executing (or, doing) what the LORD has required (or, demanded)." This is a very general statement, so the translator should avoid any expression that will communicate the idea of obedience to a particular commandment.

Lest you die: or "in order that you may not die." NAB renders this expression "Otherwise you shall die." NJB has "Do this and you will not incur death." The same meaning is conveyed more simply by TEV, **"If you don't, you will die."**

For so I am commanded: this may be transformed into a simple active statement such as "for this is what the LORD commanded me," or more dynamically, "for these are the orders I received from God."

8.36

RSV	TEV
And Aaron and his sons did all the things which the LORD commanded by Moses.	So Aaron and his sons did everything that the LORD had commanded through Moses.

And: in some translations (NJV, NEB, *Bible de la Pléiade*, Mft) this verse has been set apart as a new paragraph in order to emphasize its summary character. This may also be indicated by the use of a stronger transition word such as "So . . ." (TEV, NAB, NJB).

By Moses: literally, "by the hand of Moses." The idea of agency is difficult to express in some languages. A wide variety of expressions are used to convey this meaning. In this context one may try "with the mouth of Moses," or "by the lips of Moses," or "through the words of Moses."

Chapter 9

TEV Section Heading: "**Aaron Offers Sacrifices**."

The section heading proposed in TEV is rather weak, because it speaks only of Aaron and does not indicate the special character of the sacrifices that are offered. The particular sacrifices described in this chapter are important because they marked the beginning of the new priest's work. Other possible section headings for this chapter are "Aaron and his sons begin their work," or "Aaron and his sons begin to exercise their office," or "The priests assume their functions" (NJB), or "The priests begin their ministry," or "The first sacrifices offered by Aaron and his sons."

9.1	RSV	TEV

On the eighth day Moses called Aaron and his sons and the elders of Israel;	The day after the ordination rites were completed, Moses called Aaron and his sons and the leaders of Israel.

On the eighth day: on the day following the seven days of the ceremony of ordination described in chapter 8, the service was to continue and reach its climax as the newly ordained priests took office and began to perform their duties. Some commentators feel that the TEV rendering "**The day after . . .**" indicates too much of a break between the previous events and those described in the following verses. It may be possible to say "On the eighth day of the ceremony" or "Eight days after the beginning of the ceremony," since in most languages it is unwise to begin a new section and a new chapter without some connection with the previously described ceremony.

Called: the context seems to indicate the need for a verb that is a bit more solemn than simply "call." If there is a common language equivalent to "convoke" or "summon," or "formally invite" in the receptor language, it may be appropriate here.

The elders: a technical term referring to those having authority or holding positions of leadership. In most cultures around the world age is still associated with authority and wisdom. The Hebrew term actually means "the beards" or "the bearded ones." So a word indicating age and at the same time leadership may be used. However, in order to avoid indicating only age, it may be wise in some languages to say "respected leaders" or something similar.

9.2
RSV	TEV
and he said to Aaron, "Take a bull calf for a sin offering, and a ram for a burnt offering, both without blemish, and offer them before the LORD.	He said to Aaron, "Take a young bull and a ram without any defects and offer them to the LORD, the bull for a sin offering and the ram for a burnt offering.

Take: literally, "Take for yourself" (see NEB). But mention of self does not seem to have any special significance and is left implicit in most translations.

A bull calf: literally, "a calf, a son of the herd" (compare 1.5 where the word "calf" does not appear). The idea of youth (TEV **"young bull"**) is contained in this additional word and not in the expression "son of . . . ." The word used here is also different from 4.3, where there is no emphasis on the youth of the animal.

A sin offering: see 4.1–5.13.

A ram for a burnt offering: see 1.10-13.

Without blemish: see 1.3 and 22.17-25. The word **both** has been added in RSV to make it clear that this requirement applies to the bull as well as the ram. This may be necessary in a number of other languages.

Before the LORD: that is, to the LORD.

The TEV rendering has been recast in such a way as to indicate a bit more clearly which animal is used for which offering. This may be a helpful model to follow in some other languages.

9.3
RSV	TEV
And say to the people of Israel, 'Take a male goat for a sin offering, and a calf and a lamb, both a year old without blemish, for a burnt offering,	Then tell the people of Israel to take a male goat for a sin offering, a one-year-old calf, and a one-year-old lamb without any defects for a burnt offering,

The direct discourse within another direct quotation in this passage may be better translated by changing to indirect discourse in the embedded quotation, as in the TEV model.

And: a stronger transition word may be required in many languages in order to make clear the continuation of the instructions. A number of English versions have **"Then"** (TEV, NEB, NIV, NJB). Mft has "Also."

Say: literally, "speak saying." But the use of two words for the same action is considered redundant in most languages.

To the people of Israel: the Septuagint (which is the ancient Greek translation of the Old Testament) and one Hebrew version of the Pentateuch (the first five books of the Old Testament) have "to the elders of Israel" to harmonize with verse 1. (The elders were, of course, a part of the people of Israel.) This reading is adopted by NAB, but it is not mentioned in HOTTP and is not recommended.

A male goat: see 4.22-27; in 4.13-21 a bull is required to obtain forgiveness for the Israelite community.

A calf: this does not refer to the same "bull calf" mentioned in verse 2.

A lamb: see 3.7.

Both a year old: literally, "sons of a year." Each of the two animals must be approximately a year old. The receptor language translation should avoid giving the impression that the combined ages of the two animals is one year.

Without blemish: see 1.3 and 22.17-25.

9.4   RSV   TEV

and an ox and a ram for peace offerings, to sacrifice before the LORD, and a cereal offering mixed with oil; for today the LORD will appear to you.' "	and a bull and a ram for a fellowship offering. They are to sacrifice them to the LORD with the grain offering mixed with oil. They must do this because the LORD will appear to them today."

An ox: the Hebrew term indicates any member of "the herd," that is, of the larger animals, including oxen and cattle, either male or female. This corresponds to the information found in chapter 3. But given the context, which speaks only of male animals, the term "**bull**" is satisfactory here. In languages which have only a general term which does not specify the sex of the animal, this word will also be acceptable without providing any additional information.

Cereal offering: TEV "**grain offering**." See chapter 2.

The LORD will appear to you: the verb tense used in Hebrew indicates completed action and may be more literally rendered "for the LORD has been seen by you." But the ancient versions and most modern translations understand it to refer to an assured future event. The verb **appear** must be translated in some languages as "reveal himself" (NAB), "show himself," "present himself," "make himself known," or "cause people to see him," but in others a passive form "be seen" will be most natural.

9.5   RSV   TEV

And they brought what Moses commanded before the tent of meeting; and all the congregation drew near and stood before the LORD.	They brought to the front of the Tent everything that Moses had commanded, and the whole community assembled there to worship the LORD.

The Hebrew text leaves implicit the transmission of an order by Aaron which would fill a logical gap. In verse 3 Aaron is told to give certain instructions to the people of Israel, and verse 5 shows that this has been done. If the structure of the receptor language normally requires this intermediate step to be made explicit, it will be legitimate to include it in the translation. This may be done by adding at the end of verse 4, following the quotation, "and he did so," or "so he told them," or something similar. But this is recommended only where the receptor language will be unclear or unnatural without it.

They: the pronoun here is impersonal and indefinite. In some languages a passive may be more natural: "The things Moses ordered were taken to the front of the Tent . . . ."

Before the tent of meeting: the animals required were to be brought forward "**to the front of the Tent.**"

Tent of meeting: see 1.1.

All the congregation: this indicates the entire community and may be better translated in some languages as "all the Israelites" or "all the people of Israel."

Drew near and stood before the LORD: implicit in this statement is the purpose of approaching the LORD. It was in order to worship him. This information may have to be made explicit in some languages, as the TEV model indicates.

9.6	RSV	TEV

And Moses said, "This is the thing which the LORD commanded you to do; and the glory of the LORD will appear to you."	**Moses said, "The LORD has commanded you to do all this, so that the dazzling light of his presence can appear to you."**

The first part of this verse is almost identical to 8.5.

You: the pronoun here is plural and refers to the Israelites in general. The actual command, however, is fulfilled by Aaron on behalf of the entire community (verse 7).

And the glory . . . will appear: the connection between doing what the Lord commanded and the appearance of his glory is not very clear in RSV. The conjunction used may indicate a number of different relationships between the two actions— including mere coincidence. It will be better in most languages to use a stronger word or expression such as "in order that" or "**so that**" (see TEV, NEB, NJV, NIV, NJB). Translators may also consider "and as a result," "and afterward," or "and the glory of the LORD will then appear."

The glory of the LORD: this expression is often used today with very little understanding of its meaning. The root meaning has to do with "weight" or "heaviness," and by extension "importance" or "honor." It is most frequently used to describe an external appearance of prosperity (Isa 61.6; Psa 49.16), as of an Eastern king demonstrating his greatness. The **glory of the LORD** then is the dazzling splendor that accompanies his appearance. In many accounts of his appearance, extremely bright light is said to be seen. NJV speaks of "the Presence," while Mft has "splendour" (compare TEV "**the dazzling light of his presence**").

Will appear: in a number of languages it may be more natural to formulate the entire last part of the verse differently. The verb **will appear** may be rendered by a form with another agent, so that the entire expression may be rendered "so that you will be able to see the glory of the LORD's presence." Some have proposed "so that the LORD may show his splendor . . . to you" or "in order that you may see the dazzling light of the LORD's presence."

9.7 RSV	TEV
Then Moses said to Aaron, "Draw near to the altar, and offer your sin offering and your burnt offering, and make atonement for yourself and for the people; and bring the offering of the people, and make atonement for them; as the LORD has commanded."	Then he said to Aaron, "Go to the altar and offer the sin offering and the burnt offering to take away your sins and the sins of the people. Present this offering to take away the sins of the people, just as the LORD commanded."

Moses: TEV has the pronoun "**he**," but since the Lord has been mentioned in the previous verse, there may be some confusion on the part of the reader. Consequently the noun may be preferable in many languages.

Draw near to the altar: the perspective of the speaker (Moses) is very important in the translation of this verse. The use of the RSV expression, or the NEB "Come near," will imply in some languages that the speaker is already present and is requesting the other person to join him. This, however, is clearly not the case. It was forbidden that any person who was not a priest should approach the altar (Num 18.3). So the receptor language translation must not leave the impression that Moses is standing at the altar as he speaks. Verbs like "**Go to . . .**" or "Approach . . ." are preferable to "Come . . ." or **Draw near . . . .**

Your sin offering and your burnt offering: on these two types of offerings, see 4.3-12 and 1.4. The use of the possessive pronouns at this point in some languages will clearly indicate the ones who are offering the sacrifices. However, in other languages they may be confusing, since all sacrifices belong to God (or to whatever being they are offered to). TEV has simply omitted the pronouns. In certain other versions they are used but do not really make much sense. The pronouns translated **your** are singular in Hebrew, but the addition of **and for the people** indicates that there is more involved here than individual atonement. The solution to the problem may lie in the handling of the following phrase.

For the people: the Septuagint, followed by NEB, NAB, NJB, and Mft, has rather "for your household (family)." Then it is supposed that the next clause, where the words **of the people** appear, refers to another sacrifice for the entire community. Although HOTTP does not recommend this, it does have the advantage of giving some sense to the use of the pronouns in **your sin offering and your burnt offering**.

And: the conjunction introducing the final sentence of this verse will depend on how the above textual problem has been solved. If the Septuagint reading, "for your family," is adopted, a stronger transition will be needed. The four versions mentioned above as following the Septuagint all have "then."

9.8 RSV	TEV
So Aaron drew near to the altar, and killed the calf of the sin offering, which was for himself.	Aaron went to the altar and killed the young bull which was for his own sin offering.

So: the receptor language rendering should indicate that what is described in this verse is the logical consequence of what precedes. Many versions have "So," but one may also suggest "Therefore." This is based not on the Hebrew original, which has the common conjunction that may be translated in a wide variety of ways, but on the habits of the receptor language. The opening of a new paragraph may be considered an adequate transition in some cases.

Drew near: or "approached," or "**went to**," depending on how the verb is handled in the previous verse.

Killed: or "slaughtered" (see 1.5).

The calf: see verse 2.

9.9   RSV   TEV

| And the sons of Aaron presented the blood to him, and he dipped his finger in the blood and put it on the horns of the altar, and poured out the blood at the base of the altar; | His sons brought him the blood, and he dipped his finger in it, put some of it on the projections at the corners of the altar, and poured out the rest of it at the base of the altar. |

Presented: this was a formal, ritual presentation. The verb "**brought**" as in TEV may be too weak in some languages. If a common language equivalent to "present" is available, it is preferable to "bring."

The blood: in some languages it may be more natural and clearer to make explicit that this was "the blood of the [sacrificial] animal."

It: as has been seen elsewhere, this does not refer to all of the blood, since the remainder is said to have been poured out at the base of the altar. For this reason it may be better to follow the TEV model and say "**some of it**."

His finger: see 4.6. In a number of languages it will be unnecessary to use the pronoun **his**. This will be clearly understood and should be left implicit.

The horns of the altar: see 4.7.

Poured out the blood . . . : obviously this refers to the remainder of the blood after the previous actions. In some languages it may be a good idea to say "the rest of the blood" (compare 8.15,23-24).

9.10   RSV   TEV

| but the fat and the kidneys and the appendage of the liver from the sin offering he burned upon the altar, as the LORD commanded Moses. | Then he burned on the altar the fat, the kidneys, and the best part of the liver, just as the LORD had commanded Moses. |

The list of fatty parts given here is an abbreviated version of what is found in 4.8-9.

The sin offering: this clearly refers to the animal offered as a sacrifice, and the animal should be made explicit in some languages; or else **from the sin offering** may be left implicit, as in TEV.

9.11

RSV	TEV
The flesh and the skin he burned with fire outside the camp.	But he burned the meat and the skin outside the camp.

Compare 4.11-12, where a more detailed list is given.

Note that TEV introduces this verse with the conjunction "**But**," which highlights the contrast between what happens to the meat and the skin, as opposed to the fatty parts burned on the altar. It also reorders the elements in the sentence, so that the subject occurs at the beginning.

Burned with fire: as elsewhere, the words **with fire** will be considered redundant in many languages (see 6.30).

Outside the camp: see 4.12.

9.12

RSV	TEV
And he killed the burnt offering; and Aaron's sons delivered to him the blood, and he threw it on the altar round about.	He killed the animal which was for his own burnt offering. His sons brought him the blood, and he threw it on all four sides of the altar.

This verse and the two that follow describe the enactment of what is prescribed in 1.11-13. The detail of location found in chapter 1 is omitted in this verse. Also, in this case Aaron's sons present the blood to their father, who in turn throws it on the altar. It is the sons who perform this action in chapter 1. With the exception of the verb **delivered** (which corresponds more or less to "present" in 1.5), the terminology is the same as in chapter 1.

9.13

RSV	TEV
And they delivered the burnt offering to him, piece by piece, and the head; and he burned them upon the altar.	They handed him the head and the other pieces of the animal, and he burned them on the altar.

Compare 1.12.

Piece by piece, and the head: the structure of RSV at this point is awkward and needs restructuring. Since the head is one of the pieces of the animal, TEV has "**the head and the other pieces**." In some cases one may prefer "**and all the other pieces**."

9.14

RSV	TEV
And he washed the entrails and the legs, and burned them with the burnt offering on the altar.	Then he washed the internal organs and the hind legs and burned them

on the altar on top of the rest of the
burnt offering.

Compare 1.13.

And: a more imaginative translation of the Hebrew conjunction will be required
in most languages. The text indicates the next step in a series of events.

9.15 RSV TEV

Then he presented the people's
offering, and took the goat of the sin
offering which was for the people,
and killed it, and offered it for sin,
like the first sin offering.

After that, he presented the
people's offerings. He took the goat
that was to be offered for the people's sins, killed it, and offered it, as
he had done with his own sin offering.

Then: or "Afterwards," or "**After that**" (TEV), or "Next . . ." (NJV). NAB has
"Thereupon . . . ." Most versions also begin a new paragraph at this point.

He: it may be important is some languages to specify Aaron in place of the
pronoun in this case. This is especially true in those cases where this verse starts a
new paragraph.

The people's offering: TEV takes the first part of this verse as a separate
sentence and a kind of introduction to the section that follows. For this reason it has
the plural "**offerings**," which refers to the various offerings mentioned in the verses
that follow. However, most versions retain the singular **offering**, which then refers
only to the sin offering in this verse.

Like the first sin offering: this refers to the offering Aaron had previously
made for his own sin (see verse 8). In some cases one may say "as he had done with
the calf (or, bull)."

9.16 RSV TEV

And he presented the burnt offering,
and offered it according to the ordinance.

He also brought the animal for the
burnt offering and offered it according to the regulations.

Presented: since the offering was not actually burned at this point (see verse
24), it may be better to translate this verb "brought forward" (NJV and NJB).

The burnt offering: this is singular in form but may have a collective meaning
referring to the "calf" and the "lamb" mentioned in verse 3. It is thus interpreted by
FRCL and rendered "the two animals." But others use a singular form (as "**the
animal**" in TEV) and therefore seem to take it as referring to the "ram" mentioned
in verse 2. But since verse 12 indicates that Aaron's burnt offering has already been
killed, it seems more reasonable to take it as referring to the two animals ("a calf
and a lamb" of verse 2) designated as the burnt offering for the people. Following
TEV too closely at this point may therefore be misleading for other languages.

The ordinance: see 5.10.

9.17   RSV   TEV

And he presented the cereal offer-   He presented the grain offering and
ing, and filled his hand from it, and   took a handful of flour and burned it
burned it upon the altar, besides the   on the altar. (This was in addition to
burnt offering of the morning.   the daily burnt offering.)

Cereal offering: TEV "**grain offering**." See chapter 2.

Of the morning: this refers to the burnt offerings which were to be made every
morning and are described in greater detail in Exodus 29.38-46. Consequently it is
better translated "the morning's burnt offering" (NIV), "the daily burnt offering," or
"the burnt offering made every morning."

This whole verse may need to be restructured in a manner similar to the
following: "In addition to the regular morning burnt offering, he also presented the
grain offering, taking a handful of it and burning it on the altar." Note that TEV
indicates that this statement is a kind of commentary on the main subject by
enclosing it in parentheses.

9.18   RSV   TEV

He killed the ox also and the   He killed the bull and the ram as a
ram, the sacrifice of peace offerings   fellowship offering for the people.
for the people; and Aaron's sons   His sons brought him the blood, and
delivered to him the blood, which he   he threw it on all four sides of the
threw upon the altar round about,   altar.

While neither RSV nor TEV has translated the conjunction at the beginning of
this verse, the word "Finally" is used in NAB to show that this is the conclusion of
a series of events.

Killed: slaughtered. See 1.5.

The ox . . . and the ram: see verse 4.

Peace offering: TEV "**fellowship offering**." See chapter 3.

Delivered: see 12-14.

Threw upon the altar round about: see 1.5.

9.19   RSV   TEV

and the fat of the ox and of the ram,   Aaron put the fat parts of the bull
the fat tail, and that which covers the   and the ram
entrails, and the kidneys, and the
appendage of the liver;

This verse repeats the essential elements of 3.3-4 and 9.10, but can easily be translated in summary fashion as in TEV if the receptor language is averse to the repetition of such details.

There is a minor textual problem in this verse since the Septuagint has *"the fat* covering the entrails, and the *two* kidneys *with the fat upon them."* But these additions merely clarify the meaning of the Hebrew text. Consequently the problem has little bearing on a dynamic rendering.

9.20   RSV   TEV

and they put the fat upon the breasts, and he burned the fat upon the altar,	on top of the breasts of the animals and carried it all to the altar. He burned the fat on the altar

They put . . . : according to TEV (and NJB) it was Aaron who performed this action. Mft avoids the problem with the passive "were placed." The TEV reading requires a slight change in the Hebrew text and is not followed by the majority of scholars. HOTTP recommends the plural pronoun.

9.21   RSV   TEV

but the breasts and the right thigh Aaron waved for a wave offering before the LORD; as Moses commanded.	and presented the breasts and the right hind legs as the special gift to the LORD for the priests, as Moses had commanded.

Right thigh: see 7.32.

Waved for a wave offering: or "presented as a special gift"; see the comment on 8.22-28 as well as the remarks in the introduction, "Translating Leviticus," page 5.

As Moses commanded: by adding two words to the Hebrew text, some versions give a different meaning. NAB, for example, has "in keeping with the LORD's command to Moses," and NJB says "as Yahweh had ordered Moses," making the LORD the subject of the verb "command." But this is rejected by HOTTP and by the majority of English versions. (Compare 8.31.)

9.22   RSV   TEV

Then Aaron lifted up his hands toward the people and blessed them; and he came down from offering the sin offering and the burnt offering and the peace offerings.	When Aaron had finished all the sacrifices, he raised his hands over the people and blessed them, and then stepped down.

It may be necessary in many languages to restructure this verse in a way similar to the TEV rendering. Verses 22-24 constitute a kind of closing statement describing the conclusion to the first sacrifices for the community. The first word and the final clauses in RSV are translated in the beginning of the TEV rendering to set the stage for the final blessing: **"When Aaron had finished all the sacrifices . . . ."** This presumably refers to the sacrifices of the people as well as to Aaron's sacrifices.

Lifted up his hands: in many languages it is considered redundant and unnatural to say "his hands." The pronoun may be left implicit, as with "his finger" in verse 9. In the Jewish tradition the idea of lifting the hands was not necessarily associated with blessing, as it is in many Christian groups today. The Hebrew expression corresponds rather to a gesture of prayer or of an oath. In this verse the addition of **toward the people** shows the special character of the expression, which is clarified by what follows. The gesture was probably accompanied by words similar to those in Numbers 6.22-27, but this is not stated in the text and is not certain.

Blessed them: this idea is very difficult to translate in many languages since it is used in so many different ways in the Old Testament. It is quite possible that an entirely different word should be used, depending on whether the object is a thing, a person, or God himself. In this case the object of the blessing is "the people." So it may be translated "asked God to give them prosperity," or "wished them well" (although this may be too weak), or "asked for peace [in the sense of health, wisdom, prosperity, and general well-being] on them." Translators should carefully seek a term that is commonly understood and that gives the idea of conferring total well-being on persons.

Came down: in some languages it will be more natural to say "came back down," and in other cases it may be necessary to add "from the altar." In some languages it may be necessary to say "come down from the place where the altar was," in order to avoid giving the impression that Aaron was on top of the altar. The use of this verb seems to indicate that there was some sort of elevation in the tabernacle where sacrifice was made. And this was certainly the case later, in the Temple.

9.23   RSV   TEV

And Moses and Aaron went into the tent of meeting; and when they came out they blessed the people, and the glory of the LORD appeared to all the people.	Moses and Aaron went into the Tent of the LORD's presence, and when they came out, they blessed the people, and the dazzling light of the LORD's presence appeared to all the people.

For the first time Aaron enters **"the Tent of the LORD's presence."** With regard to Moses, see Exodus 40.35 and Leviticus 1.1. The writer does not indicate what Aaron and Moses do inside the Tent. We are simply reminded that this is the right of the priestly class.

They blessed the people: this additional blessing of the people by Aaron and Moses together is not explained. We do not know why it was necessary to bless them a second time or whether it included a gesture like the first. To emphasize the joint character of this blessing, it may be necessary in some languages to say something like "together they blessed the people" or something similar.

The glory of the LORD: see verse 6.

9.24   RSV   TEV

And fire came forth from before the LORD and consumed the burnt offering and the fat upon the altar; and when all the people saw it, they shouted, and fell on their faces.	Suddenly the LORD sent a fire, and it consumed the burnt offering and the fat parts on the altar. When the people saw it, they all shouted and bowed down with their faces to the ground.

And: while the Hebrew text has only the most common connecting word at the beginning of this verse, the content of what follows seems to indicate the need for a much stronger transition. TEV tries to capture the emotion that must have been present by using the word "**Suddenly . . . .**"

Fire came forth from before the LORD: this unusual expression was probably used to avoid saying directly "fire came from the LORD." TEV conveys the meaning with "**the LORD sent a fire.**" In some cases in the Old Testament, this word is used to refer to lightning (see Job 1.16, for example). The sending of fire to consume what was left on the altar was seen as a confirmation that the sacrifice was considered acceptable by God.

The fat upon the altar: some translators have found it necessary to state clearly the origin of these fatty parts, and have thus translated "the burnt offering and the fatty parts of the other sacrifices."

The people: or "the people of Israel," or "the Israelites." It may be wise to make this explicit in translation.

Shouted: this verb is often used in the context of ritual observances and seems to represent a liturgical practice rather than disorder or fear. However, the people could have shouted spontaneously.

Fell on their faces: this common biblical expression often causes amusement or misunderstanding when translated literally into other languages. It involved bowing in such a way that the face actually touched the ground. In the Old Testament this gesture was an indication of the most profound and deepest respect before a superior. In this case the superior is God himself. Some languages will have words with similar connotations, while others may have to resort to something like "bowed down in respect" or "prostrated themselves to show that they honored him (or, God)."

Chapter 10

This chapter is seen by many commentators as containing more specific regulations regarding the priests. The story of the two sons of Aaron is thought to be merely an example teaching that exact observance is required. Consequently the title given for verses 1-7 does not include the names of Nadab and Abihu in some versions (TOB and NJB). NEB has no title at all and thus implies that this is a continuation of the section begun at 8.1. The following two-level outline is proposed by NJB:

COMPLEMENTARY LEGISLATION	
a. A lesson in exact observance	verses 1-3
b. Removal of bodies	verses 4-5
c. Rules for priestly mourning	verses 6-7
d. Wine forbidden	verses 8-11
e. The priests' portion in offerings	verses 12-15
f. A special regulation concerning sacrifice for sin	verses 16-20

On the other hand, TEV divides the chapter into only two parts: the first, including a, b, and c above, is titled "The Sin of Nadab and Abihu" and is seen as a single story. The second comprises the rest of the chapter and is simply called "Rules for Priests." This simpler division into only two parts will probably be acceptable to most translators.

TEV Section Heading: **"The Sin of Nadab and Abihu."**

A more complete heading may be "Aaron's sons sin and suffer the consequences," or "The consequences of disobeying God's rules," or a more general statement like "When people sin, they suffer." FRCL gives the heading "Rules regarding mourning" without any reference to the names of the persons involved in the incident. But this may change the focus of the passage in some languages. FRCL adds parallel headings at verse 8 ("Rules regarding alcoholic drinks") and at verse 12 ("Rules regarding the meat of sacrifices").

10.1 RSV	TEV
Now Nadab and Abihu, the sons of Aaron, each took his censer,	Aaron's sons, Nadab and Abihu, each took his fire pan, put live

and put fire in it, and laid incense on it, and offered unholy fire before the LORD, such as he had not commanded them.	coals in it, added incense, and presented it to the LORD. But this fire was not holy, because the LORD had not commanded them to present it.

Now . . . : in some languages a transition word should be used here to indicate that a new subject is being taken up or that a new story is about to be told. In other languages the section heading and the beginning of a new paragraph will be adequate.

The sons of Aaron: according to Exodus 6.23 Aaron also had two other sons (also mentioned in verse 6 below). So the translation should not give the impression that these were his only sons. Some translators may prefer "two of Aaron's sons."

Censer: this object used in the priestly liturgy is mentioned more than twenty times in the Old Testament. It was probably a shallow metal container, most likely made of bronze, with a handle—something like a modern frying pan or a shovel used to transport coals or ashes. It comes from a root which means "to carry fire." Such a utensil was used for carrying live coals from the altar, but also to contain incense to be placed on the sacred fire. It is this second function that is in focus in this verse (see also Num 16.6). In some languages it may be advisable to state explicitly "the pans in which they burned incense."

Put fire in it: depending on the habits of the receptor language, one may have to say "burning coals" or "something burning," since **fire** by itself may be impossible.

Incense: the writer does not specify whether this is the incense described in Exodus 30.34-38 or some other type. In any case it was certainly a powdery substance (not a liquid) which gave off a pleasant odor when burned. (See comments on 2.1.)

Unholy fire: the Hebrew word translated **unholy** literally means "foreign," "alien," or "strange" (compare KJV). It was "unauthorized" (NIV and NJB), or "illicit" (NEB), or "unlawful" (JB). In Numbers 16 it was considered illegal for lay persons (people who were not priests) to make such offerings to the LORD. But this passage indicates that it may happen that even the sons of Aaron could perform actions that are not legally correct. The meaning is further explained in the following words, **"because the LORD had not commanded them to present it."** FRCL speaks of the use of "ordinary incense, not conforming to what had been prescribed."

Before the LORD: some commentators see in this expression a slight difference in meaning from **"to the LORD."** But most versions take the two as being essentially synonymous. Compare 1.3.

10.2 RSV TEV

And fire came forth from the presence of the LORD and devoured them, and they died before the LORD.	Suddenly the LORD sent fire, and it burned them to death there in the presence of the LORD.

And: the situation here is quite similar to the one described in 9.24. See comments on the transition word in that case. The renderings of NIV, "So," and NAB, "Therefore," emphasize the relationship between what happened in the previous verse. TEV's **"Suddenly"** focuses on the suddenness of the event.

Fire came forth: in some languages it is unnatural or impossible to translate this literally. The origin of the fire must be indicated. In such cases the TEV rendering "**the LORD sent fire**" may serve as a good model.

Devoured them, and they died: the sense of these two verbs is that the guilty parties were burned to death. In some languages the two verbs may be translated as one.

Before the LORD: in this context the meaning is "in the sight of the LORD" or "**in the presence of the LORD**" (TEV).

10.3

RSV	TEV
Then Moses said to Aaron, "This is what the LORD has said, 'I will show myself holy among those who are near me, and before all the people I will be glorified.' " And Aaron held his peace.	Then Moses said to Aaron, "This is what the LORD was speaking about when he said, 'All who serve me must respect my holiness; I will reveal my glory to my people.' "[c] But Aaron remained silent.

[c] I will reveal my glory to my people; *or* my people must honor me.

This is what the LORD has said: this expression does not simply introduce a quotation. Rather it emphasizes that what happened was a kind of fulfillment of these words of the LORD. In some languages it may be better to translate "What has happened confirms what the LORD said . . . ." NJB renders it "This is what Yahweh meant when he said . . . ." Another possibility may be to translate "This is what the LORD was warning (you) about when he said . . . ."

The quotation which follows is an example of Hebrew parallelism, and most modern versions set it off as such and translate the two passive forms, using a similar structure. TEV may not be a good model here, since the parallel structure is less evident.

I will show myself holy . . . : the source of this quotation is unknown, since it is not found anywhere else in the Old Testament. It may be understood in two different ways, depending on whether the Hebrew verbs are taken as reflexive or passive. 1. If it is understood as reflexive, the resulting translation will be similar to RSV or NIV: "among those who approach me I *will show myself* holy . . . ." 2. But if taken as a passive, the meaning will be like that in TEV or NEB: "among those who approach me I *must be treated as* holy . . . ." This second interpretation is also the one followed by the Greek Septuagint and by rabbinic tradition. It is therefore this interpretation, rather than the first, that is recommended.

Those who are near me: this is clearly a reference to the priestly class and may be translated directly as "those who serve me as priests" or simply "the priests" if necessary.

Before all the people: that is, to the whole community of Israel, or in this context, "to all my people."

I will be glorified: the verb used here has the same root as the noun "glory" considered in 9.6 and 23. In this context it means "to be recognized as having glory" or "to reveal glory." And in many languages it will be necessary to avoid the passive formulation of RSV. Some possible models are "all people will honor me as God," or "all people will give me glory," or ". . . will praise me."

And: to begin the last sentence of this verse, some versions prefer to omit any transition word. However, since the response of Aaron following Moses' remarks is not what may be expected, it is probably better to use a conjunction like "**But**" (TEV, NAB, AT).

Held his peace: the verb used here may be derived from two different roots: "remain silent" or "bemoan (lament)." Although the second possibility fits the context equally well, almost all versions prefer the first. In many languages it will be more natural to translate "But Aaron said nothing" (NAB, Mft) or "Aaron remained silent" (NIV, NJB). NEB is more vivid with "Aaron was dumbfounded" (following the Greek Septuagint).

10.4   RSV   TEV

And Moses called Mishael and Elzaphan, the sons of Uzziel the uncle of Aaron, and said to them, "Draw near, carry your brethren from before the sanctuary out of the camp."	**Moses called Mishael and Elzaphan, the sons of Uzziel, Aaron's uncle, and said to them, "Come here and carry your cousins' bodies away from the sacred Tent and put them outside the camp."**

The uncle of Aaron: this, of course, was Moses' uncle also. In some languages it may be more natural to refer to him in this way. In many languages it is essential to indicate which side of the family an uncle represents. The Hebrew word here designates the paternal uncle. But in some cases it may be necessary to say "Uzziel, the brother of Aaron's father." Elsewhere an uncle may be called "small father" or something similar.

Your brethren: the term **brethren** has a broader sense in Hebrew than "brothers" in some other languages. As in many parts of Africa, it is used of any member of the extended family. NJV has "kinsmen." In those languages where more precise designation is preferred, the term "**cousins**" may be used, as in TEV.

Since Nadab and Abihu are dead at this point, it may be preferable in the receptor language to state clearly "the bodies of your cousins" or "**your cousins' bodies**" (TEV) rather than simply "your cousins." And in some cases it may even be advisable to add "which are lying in front of the sanctuary." If this is done, it will almost certainly alter the rendering of the rest of this verse.

From before: the two prepositions used together here give the meaning "away from." There is no indication as to the precise location of Moses as he speaks, but presumably he was in or very near the Tent and next to the bodies of Nadab and Abihu.

The sanctuary: this is a synonym for the "Tent of the LORD's presence" and should be translated in such a way that the reader will know that it refers to the same object. See comments on "tent of meeting" and "tabernacle" at 8.10.

Out of the camp: see 4.12.

10.5   RSV   TEV

RSV	TEV
So they drew near, and carried them in their coats out of the camp, as Moses had said.	**So they came and took hold of the clothing on the corpses and carried them outside the camp, just as Moses had commanded.**

So: the transition word used here should indicate that the action described in the following words were the result of Moses' orders in the preceding verse. Most English versions have **So**, as in RSV.

Them: or "their bodies," as in the previous verse.

In their coats: this is ambiguous and may be understood as referring either to the coats of the bearers or to those of the dead men. It is scarcely logical to think that the bearers removed their own tunics to use them in the transportation of the cadavers. Some commentators see this as a confirmation that Nadab and Abihu had been ordained as priests (see 8.13). But the sense of this phrase seems to be that the bearers avoided direct contact with the dead bodies by grasping the clothing to carry their cousins' bodies outside the camp.

10.6   RSV   TEV

RSV	TEV
And Moses said to Aaron and to Eleazar and Ithamar, his sons, "Do not let the hair of your heads hang loose, and do not rend your clothes, lest you die, and lest wrath come upon all the congregation; but your brethren, the whole house of Israel, may bewail the burning which the LORD has kindled.	**Then Moses said to Aaron and to his sons Eleazar and Ithamar, "Do not leave your hair uncombed or tear your clothes to show that you are in mourning. If you do, you will die, and the LORD will be angry with the whole community. But all your fellow Israelites are allowed to mourn this death caused by the fire which the LORD sent.**

Because the priests were intermediaries between God and his people, they were required more than all others to avoid contact with death. This included both contact with dead bodies and with the whole mourning procedure. This verse lists three distinct funeral customs in which the priests were forbidden to participate. In some languages clarity will require that the whole verse be restructured and started with a summary statement as follows: "You must leave to all your fellow Israelites the task of mourning the dead. But you yourselves must not leave your hair uncombed . . . ." Choosing this structure will probably make it unnecessary to add "to show that you are in mourning" later in the verse.

And: the transition word here should indicate the continuation of the narrative.

And to . . . his sons: the TEV rendering here may be misunderstood as referring to Moses' sons. The translation should make it clear that the sons referred to are Aaron's (see Exo 6.23). Furthermore, it may be necessary to say something like "his other two sons" since the previous verses have already spoken of Nadab and

Abihu who were also sons of Aaron. A possible unambiguous model may be "And Moses said to Aaron and to Eleazar and Ithamar, Aaron's two remaining sons . . . ."

Do not let the hair of your heads hang loose: literally, "Do not neglect your heads." This may be understood as prohibiting the priests from leaving their heads uncovered (see NAB and NIV note), but most commentators prefer the interpretation followed in RSV and TEV. As a sign of mourning, ordinary Israelites often refused to take proper care of their hair. But this practice was forbidden to the priests. The words **of your heads** may be left implicit in most languages. The negative construction may have to be put positively in some languages, "Be sure to keep your hair orderly" or "Continue to pay attention to the combing of your hair."

And do not rend your clothes: the tearing of clothing was another common sign of mourning among the Israelites. In many places in the world the meaning of this gesture will not be understood. It should therefore be made clear in the receptor language by adding something like the phrase found in TEV: **"to show that you are in mourning"** or "as a sign that you are sad." If the introductory statement suggested at the end of the first paragraph under this verse is accepted, then this addition will probably be unnecessary here.

Lest you die: on the expression **lest** . . . see 8.35 (compare also verses 7 and 9).

Lest wrath come upon all the congregation: literally, "and he will be angry with all the community." The negation with the preceding verb "to die" also governs the verb "be angry." The entire construction is better restructured as a separate conditional sentence in many languages: "If you do this, you will die, and the LORD will be angry with the whole community."

The idea of anger, whether divine or human, is often expressed in very different ways in the languages of the world. Some ways of communicating this concept are "to feel hot toward someone," "to have a burning heart," "to have an angry stomach," or "to see anger."

Your brethren, the whole house of Israel: the term **brethren** is used here in its broadest sense (see comment on verse 4) and is explained by the phrase that follows. The word **house** refers to the tribe or nation that came from Israel (Jacob). Hence TEV **"your fellow Israelites."** Aaron and his sons were obviously a part of **the whole house of Israel**. NAB communicates this same fact by saying "the rest of the house of Israel."

Bewail: the word used here may be understood in the general sense "to cry" or in the sense of ritual lamentation. The latter meaning is more probable here. So it may be translated **"mourn,"** or in some languages simply "weep" or "cry over death."

The burning which the LORD has kindled: the noun and the verb used in this expression have the same root, but the whole phrase is used to represent the two men who were destroyed by fire. The people of Israel are therefore allowed to mourn for "those [men] whom the LORD destroyed by fire," or "those who died in the fire sent by the LORD," or "those punished by the fire of the LORD."

10.7   RSV   TEV

And do not go out from the door of the tent of meeting, lest you die; for the anointing oil of the LORD is upon you." And they did according to the word of Moses.	Do not leave the entrance of the Tent or you will die, because you have been consecrated by the anointing oil of the LORD." So they did as Moses said.

Do not go out . . . : the priests are directly forbidden to leave the entrance to the tent, but this is only a temporary order because of the ordination of the priests and the exercise of their functions. The translation should not give the impression that they were never permitted to leave the Tent of the LORD's presence. Some languages may have to say "Do not leave the entrance of the Tent during this time . . . ."

Lest you die: see verse 6 above. In this context it may be possible to translate "unless you want to die," or as a separate sentence, "If you do this, you will die."

For the anointing oil of the LORD is upon you: this literal rendering indicates the reason the priests are not to leave the Tent; it is because they have been set apart in the service of God by means of the oil that was poured on them in the ceremony of ordination. TEV makes this explicit by saying "**you have been consecrated . . . .**"

And: the transition word should indicate the logical result of Moses' prohibitions to Aaron and his two remaining sons. Many versions have "**So**" (TEV, NAB, NIV).

They: this refers to Aaron, Eleazar, and Ithamar. This may need to be made explicit in some languages, since the names of Aaron and his remaining sons are separated from the pronoun by a long and rather complex quotation that includes mention of another plural noun, the Israelites.

TEV Section Heading: "**Rules for Priests**."

See the comments at the beginning of this chapter with regard to the different ways of dividing it up. TEV provides a general heading for the rest of the chapter, which includes various kinds of rules.

10.8-9   RSV   TEV

8 And the LORD spoke to Aaron, saying, 9 "Drink no wine nor strong drink, you nor your sons with you, when you go into the tent of meeting lest you die; it shall be a statute for ever throughout your generations.	8 The LORD said to Aaron, 9 "You and your sons are not to enter the Tent of my presence after drinking wine or beer; if you do, you will die. This is a law to be kept by all your descendants.

The LORD spoke to Aaron, saying: the construction here is exactly the same as in 4.1, and it is used to begin many other paragraphs in this book. However, in those other cases only one verb is used in RSV. In most cases it will be more natural to use a single verb in this case also. But some languages naturally use such repetition to introduce a quotation.

Drink no wine nor strong drink: the restructuring of TEV makes it clearer that the priests are not necessarily forbidden alcoholic drinks in all circumstances, but that the restriction applied when they were about to go into the Tent. The word translated **wine** indicates a drink made from grapes, and the context makes it clear that fermentation is probably involved. The second term, rendered **strong drink** in RSV, actually refers to a fermented drink made from barley. The most common equivalent in many languages is "**beer**." But these two terms used together represent any alcoholic beverage, and the prohibition is not limited to two kinds. The translation should make it clear that a general rule is intended.

In some cases it may be better to restructure the entire verse 9 to say something like "No priest, whether you or your sons, shall enter the Tent of the LORD's presence after having drunk . . ." or "If you or your sons have drunk . . . , then you must not go into the Tent . . . ." The reason for this prohibition may be twofold: (a) the need to be sober and clear-thinking in order to distinguish between what is holy and what is common, between what is clean and unclean (see verse 10); but also (b) the need for separation of the Jewish priests from common Canaanite practices, since alcohol played an important role in Canaanite rites.

Lest you die: see verse 6.

It shall be a statute for ever: this gives the regulation a permanent value. See comments on 3.17b.

Throughout your generations: this includes the generation of Aaron and his sons as well as those who would come after them. Many languages will have to use a completely different expression such as "as long as your children continue to have grandchildren" or "as long as your family continue as priests."

10.10

RSV	TEV
You are to distinguish between the holy and the common, and between the unclean and the clean;	You must distinguish between what belongs to God and what is for general use, between what is ritually clean and what is unclean.

Some versions have found it necessary to repeat the prohibition of alcoholic drinks at the beginning of this verse to make clear the connection with the preceding verse. Or verse 10 may begin with the words "This is to be done in order that you may distinguish . . . ."

The holy and the common, . . . the unclean and the clean: the RSV rendering follows the order of the original literally. This kind of construction is commonly used in Hebrew and is called "chiasmus." It appears most often at the end of a discourse unit. The elements are positioned like a kind of cross: (holy . . . common . . . unclean . . . clean) A-B-B-A. However, in ordinary English and in many other languages, this kind of construction is not common. It is more logical to reverse the order of the last two elements so that the parallelism of the two groups can become more apparent: (holy . . . common . . . clean . . . unclean) A-B-A-B. This is what TEV has done. However, if the Hebrew-type structure is natural in the receptor language, it may be used in translation.

The basic meaning of the term **holy** is "that which belongs to God" or "especially dedicated to God," and the opposite is **common**, "that which is not holy," "that which is ordinary," or "that which is for everyday use." This meaning is clearly brought out in the TEV rendering of this verse. The terms **clean** and **unclean** refer to ritual appropriateness and not to physical cleanliness.

A very important question for translators is whether or not the two pairs of words are intended as synonyms or whether the writer had in mind two different kinds of distinctions that were to be made by the priests. Are the two words **holy** and **clean** identical? And similarly, do **common** and **unclean** refer to the same thing? In the New Testament the latter two appear to be synonymous (Acts 10.28), but in the Old Testament a very good case can be made that they are considered two different states. This is the only occurrence in Leviticus of the noun translated **common** (which occurs only six times elsewhere in the Old Testament). It is quite possible that it refers to anything that is not holy and would therefore cover things both **clean** and **unclean**. As the *Interpreter's Dictionary of the Bible* says, "in the Old Testament the common is ritually neutral and may be either clean or unclean" (Volume 1, page 663). The distinctions to be made by the priests could therefore be diagrammed as follows:

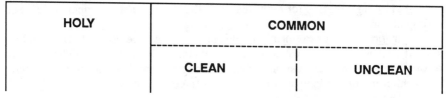

The practical implication for all this for the translator is that one should not attempt to convey the impression that the two pairs of words are intended as synonyms. Translators should avoid the meaning "between the holy and that which is not holy, that is to say, between the ritually clean and the ritually unclean." When the two pairs are separated by only a comma (as in TEV), this is at least one way of understanding the rendering. It would be better to say something like "between the holy and that which is not holy, as well as between the ritually clean and the ritually unclean." It will also be important to define these important terms in a glossary.

Note that the same two pairs of words occur in the same order in Ezekiel 22.26 and 44.23.

10.11　　　RSV　　　　　　　　　　　　　　　　TEV

and you are to teach the people of Israel all the statutes which the LORD has spoken to them by Moses."　　**You must teach the people of Israel all the laws which I have given to you through Moses."**

People of Israel: literally, "sons of Israel," but in most languages it will be more natural to translate **people of Israel** or "Israelites."

Statutes: the word here is a very general one for anything that is prescribed or decreed.

Which the LORD has spoken: since this is still a part of a direct quotation from God himself, TEV has replaced the noun **LORD** with the pronoun "**I**." This will also be necessary in most other languages, if direct discourse is being used.

To them: the use of the third person plural pronoun may give the impression that Aaron and his sons are not included among those to whom the laws were given. For this reason TEV uses the pronoun "**You**," which is intended to include the priests with the rest of the people of Israel. In some languages the translation will have to be even more explicit.

By Moses: literally, "by the hand of Moses." See 8.36.

10.12   RSV   TEV

And Moses said to Aaron and to Eleazar and Ithamar, his sons who were left, "Take the cereal offering that remains of the offerings by fire to the LORD, and eat it unleavened beside the altar, for it is most holy;

Moses said to Aaron and his two remaining sons, Eleazar and Ithamar, "Take the grain offering that is left over from the food offered to the LORD, make unleavened bread with it and eat it beside the altar, because this offering is very holy.

And: some languages will require a transition word like "Then." In others the beginning of a new paragraph will be sufficient to indicate that this is the continuation of the narrative. NJB and FRCL have a section heading at this point. NJB has "The priests' portion in offerings," and FRCL has "Rules concerning the meat of sacrifices."

His sons who were left: that is, the two surviving sons following the death of Nadab and Abihu. Some translators may prefer "his two sons who remained alive."

Cereal offering: TEV "**grain offering**." See 2.1.

The offerings by fire: see 1.9.

Eat it unleavened: TEV makes explicit the fact that the remaining grain is not eaten as such, but is first properly prepared according to the regulations in chapter 2. Then it is to be eaten by the priests.

Because . . . : in some cases it may be necessary to be more precise with something like "it is to be eaten by priests because it is a holy offering" or "you priests must eat it because it is very holy."

10.13   RSV   TEV

you shall eat it in a holy place, because it is your due and your sons' due, from the offerings by fire to the LORD; for so I am commanded.

Eat it in a holy place; it is the part that belongs to you and your sons from the food offered to the LORD. That is what the LORD commanded me.

You shall eat it in a holy place: in some languages it may be more natural to say something like "You must eat it only in a holy place," to emphasize that it may not be eaten anywhere else.

Your due and your sons' due: see 6.18. The word **due** may also be rendered "portion" or "right," or simply **"that belongs to you"** (TEV). It denotes something prescribed by law or custom and is therefore considered something that cannot be taken away.

Offerings by fire: see 1.9.

For so I am commanded: this passive expression is rendered more naturally **"That is what the LORD commanded me"** in TEV and should be handled similarly in many other languages (compare 8.9,13).

10.14 RSV	TEV
But the breast that is waved and the thigh that is offered you shall eat in any clean place, you and your sons and your daughters with you; for they are given as your due and your sons' due, from the sacrifices of the peace offerings of the people of Israel.	But you and your families may eat the breast and the hind leg that are presented as the special gift and the special contribution to the LORD for the priests. You may eat them in any ritually clean place. These offerings have been given to you and your children as the part that belongs to you from the fellowship offerings of the people of Israel.

But: this marks the contrast between the requirements for the leftover grain offering in the previous verse and the fellowship offering here.

That is waved: see 7.30.

In any clean place: the Septuagint has "holy" instead of **clean** here. But this is incorrect, since the text intentionally makes a difference. The grain offering was to be eaten only by the priests and therefore in a "holy" place (beside the altar); but the fellowship offering could be eaten by the entire family of the priest, including the daughters, and therefore could not be in the Holy Place, but could be in any place that was ritually clean. In languages where the word for **holy** is the same as the word for **clean**, special care should be taken to insure that the idea of any ritually clean place is conveyed here. The technical term used for "the Holy Place" should be avoided.

Your sons and your daughters: TEV translates this simply as **"your children,"** but in some languages this may not be adequate to emphasize the fact that **daughters** as well as **sons** were permitted to eat of this offering. It may be better to say "your sons and also your daughters," or "your female children as well as the males," or "the women in the priestly family as well as the men." There is no indication elsewhere in the Old Testament that Aaron had any daughters, but there is no proof that he did not. However, this regulation is intended as a general one that is applied to the descendants of Aaron as well as to the immediate situation.

Peace offerings: TEV **"fellowship offerings."** See 3.1.

10.15   RSV   TEV

The thigh that is offered and the   They shall bring the hind leg and the
breast that is waved they shall bring   breast at the time the fat is present-
with the offerings by fire of the fat, to   ed as a food offering to the LORD.
wave for a wave offering before the   These parts belong to you and your
LORD, and it shall be yours, and your   children forever, just as the LORD
sons' with you, as a due for ever; as   commanded."
the LORD has commanded."

This verse is a single sentence in RSV but should probably be broken down into
at least two sentences in the receptor language. It may also be necessary to reorder
the elements of this verse in certain languages. Some restructuring has been done by
TEV, and this may serve as a model. The basic information of this verse has already
been given in the preceding passage. The only really new element is the mention of
the permanent nature of these rules, which is brought out by the words **as a due
forever** (see 6.11).

The thigh: see 7.32.

That is waved . . . wave for a wave offering: see 7.30.

Offerings by fire: see 1.9.

And your sons: the context seems to indicate that the word translated **sons**
here is to be taken in its more general sense, meaning **"children."**

10.16   RSV   TEV

Now Moses diligently inquired   Moses asked about the goat for
about the goat of the sin offering,   the sin offering and learned that it
and behold, it was burned! And he   had already been burned. This made
was angry with Eleazar and Ithamar,   him angry at Eleazar and Ithamar,
the sons of Aaron who were left,   and he demanded,
saying,

Verses 16-20 in Hebrew present a number of different types of problems: the
text itself is unclear, and there are significant differences when compared with other
passages describing this ritual. But it is essential that the translator understands that
no one should attempt to harmonize this passage with others dealing with the same
subject. The text must be translated as it stands.

Now . . . : some versions take the first part of this sentence as a relative clause
and begin with "When Moses asked . . ." (NIV, Mft, AT). Others have "Then Moses
asked . . ." (NJV; compare also NJB). The translator should simply seek the most
natural means of moving on to the account of a new event and use it here.

Diligently inquired: the verb used here seems to indicate that an investigation
has taken place by means of questioning or by inward reflection. It has been variously
translated "inquired" (NIV, NAB, NJV), "made a careful search for" (Mft and AT), and
"made a searching inquiry" (NEB). There is no indication exactly whom Moses may
have interrogated, and as the Mft and AT rendering indicates, the verb may mean that
he actually looked for the goat. But most versions translate **inquired** or some other

verb indicating the asking of questions. In those languages that require an object for the verb "to ask," the translator will probably have to say "asked several people" or "asked someone."

Behold: this interjection appears in two other places in this paragraph (verses 18 and 19) but nowhere else in Leviticus. It usually calls attention to some fact on which action is required or on which some conclusion is based. It is impossible to translate in many languages, but the meaning is approximated with the use of an exclamation point at the end of the sentence (NJV, AT, and Mft). Other languages may have particles of a similar nature that convey this idea. However, they may be placed in a different position in the sentence.

It was burned: it may be clearer in some cases to say "the meat of the animal had already been burned." And where the passive must be avoided, "someone had burned the meat."

The sons of Aaron who were left: this information is redundant (see verse 12) and may be omitted if the repetition is unnatural in the receptor language.

Saying: the verb "to say" is rather weak in this context. What follows is a question, which at least requires the verb "to ask." But given the strong emotion expressed in the question, it may be more appropriate to use a verb like "**demanded,**" as in TEV.

10.17 RSV	TEV
"Why have you not eaten the sin offering in the place of the sanctuary, since it is a thing most holy and has been given to you that you may bear the iniquity of the congregation, to make atonement for them before the LORD?	"Why didn't you eat the sin offering in a sacred place? It is very holy, and the LORD has given it to you in order to take away the sin of the community.

In the place of the sanctuary: care should be taken here not to translate in such a way as to confuse the reader or give the impression that the Holy Place is intended here (Exo 26.33). This expression, which is also found in 14.13, means "in the vicinity of the sanctuary" or "in the area of the Sacred Tent" (but not inside the Tent), or more generally, "in a sacred place." See the details given in 6.26.

A thing most holy: the word **thing** may be too general in many languages. One may say "it is very holy food" or something similar.

It . . . has been given to you: this passive form may have to be transformed to an active in some languages. The TEV rendering "**the LORD has given it to you**" will serve as a good model.

That you may bear the iniquity of the congregation: literally, "to bear (or, take away) the guilt of the community." Some commentators wish to retain the meaning "bear" and attach this idea to the fact of eating the meat of the victim on whose head the hands were placed (4.15); thus the animal became the "bearer" of the sins of the community. By eating the meat of this animal, the priests took upon themselves the sin of the community. But this interpretation is highly improbable. (See, for example, the treatment of the scapegoat in 16.10,21-22, which is not actually eaten, but is sent away into the desert.) It is much better to follow TEV and most other modern translations (compare NJV "remove"), since the purpose was to get rid of the sin.

Make atonement for them: see 4.20. Note that TEV translates in a single expression (**"take away the sin of the community"**) the ideas contained in both **bear the iniquity** and **make atonement**.

10.18   RSV   TEV

Behold, its blood was not brought into the inner part of the sanctuary. You certainly ought to have eaten it in the sanctuary, as I commanded."	Since its blood was not brought into the sacred Tent, you should have eaten the sacrifice there, as I commanded."

Behold: see verse 16.

Its blood: it may be clearer to say "the blood of the animal" or "the blood of the animal that was sacrificed."

The inner part of the sanctuary: the inner part of the sanctuary area was the actual tent.

Certainly is used here to translate a common Hebrew construction made up of two forms of the same verbal root (literally, "eating you do eat"). This construction is used for strong emphasis (compare Gen 3.4). Some languages may have similar constructions to add emphasis; otherwise, some emphatic particle or other construction may be used.

Eaten it: the pronoun **it** refers to the sacrificial animal and not to the **blood**, as one might possibly imagine on reading RSV.

In the sanctuary: the term **sanctuary** is used in a very broad sense here. It refers to the whole area where the Tent of the LORD's presence was put up and not just to the Tent itself. These words may be translated by an adverb such as "there," depending on how the preceding context has been handled.

As I commanded: the verb **commanded** may require an object in some languages. If this is the case, it is probably best to say "as I commanded you." Some versions (NEB, NAB) alter the text slightly to read as a passive verb, "as I was commanded," but this seems unnecessary and should be avoided in the receptor language. HOTTP recommends that the text not be altered in this fashion.

10.19   RSV   TEV

And Aaron said to Moses, "Behold, today they have offered their sin offering and their burnt offering before the LORD; and yet such things as these have befallen me! If I had eaten the sin offering today, would it have been acceptable in the sight of the LORD?"	Aaron answered, "If I had eaten the sin offering today, would the LORD have approved? The people presented their sin offering to the LORD today, and they brought their burnt offering, but still these terrible things have happened to me."

This entire verse has been considerably restructured in TEV, and the questions have been shifted forward. This may be a helpful model to follow in the receptor language.

Said: since the quotation that follows is in answer to a question, it will be better in many languages to introduce it with a verb like "**answered**" or "responded."

Behold: see verse 16.

They: the pronoun may refer to the people who presented their sin offering before the LORD, or to the sons of Aaron (the priests). Both are true in a sense. The people brought their offerings to the priests, who in turn offered them to the LORD. Since the ultimate source of the offering was the people, it is probably better to make them the subject, if the receptor language requires that it be made explicit. In some languages a passive form may be used, and in others an impersonal, undefined **they** will be acceptable.

Such things as these have befallen me: the text does not make explicit the fact that Aaron is speaking of "bad things" or "misfortune" happening to him, but the context makes it clear. In most languages it will be clearer to the average reader if this is made explicit in the receptor language. Compare TEV "**terrible things.**" Both Mft and NAB use the word "misfortune." NJB has "these disasters." If the meaning of **such things as these** will be unclear in the receptor language, it may be necessary to state more explicitly "the death of my two sons."

Would it have been acceptable in the sight of the LORD: literally, "would he be pleased in the eyes of the LORD." But this is awkward, since the pronoun "he" refers to the Lord. The essential meaning is, however, clear: "would the LORD have approved?" or "would the LORD be pleased?"

10.20   RSV   TEV

RSV	TEV
And when Moses heard that, he was content.	**When Moses heard this, he was satisfied.**

Some early printings of TEV omitted the number 20, but the content of this verse was included with verse 19.

Heard that: that is, when he heard the explanation of Aaron. In some languages it may be good to make this explicit with "heard Aaron's words" or "heard the explanation of Aaron."

He was content: literally, "and it was good in his eyes." (Compare "good in the eyes of the LORD" in verse 19, where the same verb is used). If it can be done naturally in the receptor language, it may be good to translate this expression and the one in verse 19 in a similar way. For example, "would that have pleased the LORD?" in verse 19, and "he was pleased" in this verse. NJV uses the word "approved" in both cases. In some languages the verb translating the idea of being pleased, satisfied, or content will require an object. In such cases it may be necessary to say "pleased with what he heard" or something similar.

Chapter 11

The third major section of Leviticus is made up of chapters 11-16 (or 11-15, depending on how chapter 16 is considered). This section comes immediately after the installation of the priests and is made up primarily of examples of how to preserve the distinction between "what belongs to God and what is for general use." If two or more levels of section headings are being used in the receptor language, this part may be titled "Laws concerning purity" or "The things that are pure and those that are not pure," since purity and impurity constitute the unifying theme of the entire section. (See the discussion of the major sections of Leviticus in the introduction, "Translating Leviticus.")

Chapter 11 deals with the problem of impurity connected with certain kinds of birds and animals. Chapter 12 treats the laws of purification of women related to the birth of a child. In chapters 13 and 14 the writer handles a number of cases which the ancient Jews regarded as similar: human skin diseases, mildew on clothing, and ildew on the walls of houses. Chapter 15 is concerned with problems of impurity related to the genital organs and various bodily functions. Finally chapter 16 describes the ceremony of the "Day of Atonement." (Some scholars consider this chapter to be a separate section or a transition to the following one.)

TEV Section Heading: **"Animals That May Be Eaten."**

A more explicit title is "Animals that Israelites may eat and those that they may not eat" (see German Common Language version [GECL]). Others have suggested "Animals that are pure and impure" or "Laws about pure and impure animals" as possible titles, since this would highlight the unifying theme of the whole section. Since the section deals with birds and insects as well as four-legged animals, it may be necessary in some languages to find a more general term like "creatures," or to use two or more different words. This will depend on how the receptor language views the various creatures described in this chapter.

In keeping with the careful organization of Leviticus, this chapter is divided into two parts: verses 1-23 and 24-47. Some versions have added a section heading at verse 24. The first part is further subdivided into four paragraphs:

    a. verses 2-8   land animals
    b. verses 9-12   creatures of the sea
    c. verses 13-19   birds
    d. verses 20-23   insects

Note also the parallel passage in Deuteronomy 14.3-21.

11.1-2   RSV   TEV

1 And the LORD said to Moses and Aaron, 2 "Say to the people of Israel, These are the living things which you may eat among all the beasts that are on the earth.

1 The Lord gave Moses and Aaron the following regulations 2 for the people of Israel. You may eat any land animal

Said to Moses and Aaron: here both Moses and Aaron are addressed, but the construction is the same as in 4.1 and 10.8 (see comments on those verses).

Say to the people of Israel . . . : literally, "to the sons of Israel." On the question of direct versus indirect discourse, see comments on 1.2 and 4.1.

The living things: there are two different words for "animals" in this verse. The first one, used here, has the basic meaning of "anything having life," since the root on which the word is built is "life." It is thus a very general term referring to all kinds of creatures.

Beasts that are on the earth: the second word originally had the idea of "dumb animals," but the idea of dumbness is not essential in this context. When used together with the phrase that follows, the reference is to "land animals" as opposed to the various groups mentioned in the subsequent verses (creatures of the sea, birds, and insects). Although the receptor language may not divide created beings into categories that correspond exactly to these, an attempt should be made to reflect the world view of the ancient Jews. This phrase may be translated in some languages as "animals that live on dry ground" or "animals that walk on the earth."

In 5.2 the same two words for animals found in this verse are used to distinguish domestic animals and wild animals. But in this case the first is very general and the second refers to one of the four categories mentioned in this chapter. It is not necessary to translate the same here as in chapter 5. Note that TEV translates **living things** and **beasts** by the one word "**animal**."

You may eat: in some languages the permissive idea of the verb here is difficult to translate. It is not as strong as "you shall eat" (KJV), yet "you are able to eat" may give the wrong impression in some cases. Perhaps one may say "you have permission to eat," or a more radical restructuring may be necessary, yielding something like "It is not forbidden you to eat . . . ." Mft translates "you are allowed to eat."

Many English versions put a colon at the end of this verse to show that it introduces a list (NEB, NIV, NAB, NJV, NJB). TEV simply makes verse 3 a continuation of the sentence begun in the middle of this verse.

11.3   RSV   TEV

Whatever parts the hoof and is cloven-footed and chews the cud, among the animals, you may eat.

that has divided hoofs and that also chews the cud,

Whatever parts the hoof and is cloven-footed: **parts the hoof** is misleading, since it appears to be synonymous with **cloven-footed**. A literal rendering is "which possess hoofs and which have a split (or, division) in the hoof." According to some commentators, the twofold specification in Hebrew is intended, first, to separate animals with hoofs from those without, and secondly, to distinguish those with divided hoofs (like a cow) from those with undivided hoofs (like a horse). But the two may be summarized in a single statement, since those animals having divided hoofs obviously have hoofs. Well-known technical terms will be available to translators in some languages, while others will have to use descriptive phrases such as "with two-part feet" or "having feet that are separated."

Chews the cud: literally, "brings up the cud." This refers to the habit of certain animals that have two or more stomachs and that bring food back up from the first stomach into the mouth to be chewed again. Although the ancient Jews were probably not familiar with the details of this complex physiological happening, they were certainly able to observe that some animals "brought their food back up" to be chewed again. The most obvious, visible aspect of this process is the rechewing of the food. Some languages may have technical terms that are widely understood and may be used in translating this idea. In others it will be necessary to resort to a descriptive phrase such as "who eat their food a second time" or "who bring their food up to be chewed again."

Among the animals, you may eat: in many languages this constitutes unnecessary repetition of information found in the previous verse. TEV, for example, omits it entirely.

11.4-6 RSV TEV

4 Nevertheless among those that chew the cud or part the hoof, you shall not eat these: The camel, because it chews the cud but does not part the hoof, is unclean to you. 5 And the rock badger, because it chews the cud but does not part the hoof, is unclean to you. 6 And the hare, because it chews the cud but does not part the hoof, is unclean to you.

4-6 but you must not eat camels, rock badgers, or rabbits. These must be considered unclean; they chew the cud, but do not have divided hoofs.

Nevertheless: the transition word is important here. It marks a sharp contrast between what may be eaten (verse 3) and what must not be eaten (verses 4-6). AT and NJV have "However," while NAB and TEV have "**but**." NIV attempts to mark the contrast by beginning a new paragraph at this point, but a good translation of the transition word will probably be better in most languages.

You shall not eat: used with the negation, this verb form takes the character of a strong prohibition (compare verse 2), which is made clearer in TEV, "**you must not eat**."

The camel: the use of the singular to represent the entire class of animals is common in Hebrew but unnatural and unacceptable in many other languages. It will give the wrong impression if used in translation.

Since camels are unknown in many parts of the world, a borrowed word may have to be used and explained in a footnote or glossary. It is also advisable to use illustrations in order to help the reader. Technically, the word used here refers to a "dromedary," which has only one hump on its back and is somewhat smaller than a camel. But in ordinary English the term "camel" is used for both the dromedary and the camel. If the receptor language distinguishes between the two, then the word for dromedary should be used (see FFB, pages 13-14).

The animal referred to in English as **rock badger** (see FFB, pages 69-70) is a small grass-eating animal found in the Near East and North Africa. It is about the size of a rabbit and normally lives in groups in rocky terrain. Neither the badger nor the **hare** actually chew the cud as cows do, but by the way their jaws move they give the appearance of doing so, and for this reason they are excluded from the edible animals. On the other hand, some writers have suggested that the word usually translated **hare** is really some other animal that actually does "chew the cud." But this not taken seriously by Old Testament scholars.

There were several species of **hare** (FFB, pages 39-40) or "**rabbits**" in Palestine. They are members of the rodent family and have ears that are longer than those of other rodents.

The three animals mentioned here do not constitute a complete list but merely serve as examples. For this reason, in some languages it may be advisable to add "for example" at the most natural place in verses 4-6.

Is unclean to you: this expression is found in verses 5 and 6 in RSV but is rendered only once in TEV. The passive construction of TEV leaves implicit the words **to you**. But this may be translated as in NEB, "you shall regard it as unclean."

Verses 4-6 contain a great deal of repetition which may be eliminated in languages where such style is considered heavy or awkward. TEV provides a good model for reducing the repetition.

11.7

RSV	TEV
And the swine, because it parts the hoof and is cloven-footed but does not chew the cud, is unclean to you.	Do not eat pigs. They must be considered unclean; they have divided hoofs, but do not chew the cud.

Swine: the Hebrew term used here refers to the wild pig (see FFB, pages 80-81), since domesticated pigs as we know them today are a relatively recent development resulting from genetic selection and crossbreeding. This animal is singled out perhaps because swine were considered especially offensive and to be avoided at all cost. It is the prime example (but not the only one) of an animal to be avoided because, although it has a divided hoof, it does not chew the cud. Note that this is just the opposite of the category forbidden in verses 4-6. In some languages one may wish to say "although they have divided hoofs, they do not chew the cud" or "in spite of the fact that they have divided hoofs . . . ."

Is unclean to you: see verses 5-6 above.

11.8   RSV   TEV

Of their flesh you shall not eat, and their carcasses you shall not touch; they are unclean to you.

Do not eat these animals or even touch their dead bodies; they are unclean.

The beginning of this verse repeats part of the prohibition already stated in verse 4. This is probably done for emphasis. If the receptor language uses such repetition for emphasis, it should be retained as in both RSV and TEV. But it may be omitted in cases where such repetition is contrary to the style of the receptor language or where it is used for other purposes.

You shall not . . . : see comments on verse 4.

Their flesh: the pronoun here refers to all the animals that were forbidden in the previous verses, not just to the pigs of the previous verse.

Their carcasses you shall not touch: this is additional information in this context (although it has its parallel in 5.2). The supplementary character of this prohibition is highlighted in TEV by the addition of "**even.**" A similar form may be used in other languages to perform the same function.

To you: this element is again left implicit in TEV because readers will automatically assume this information without its being stated. But it may be retained in many languages. NEB has restructured this part of the verse to say "you shall regard them as unclean." Compare verses 5, 6, and 7 above.

11.9   RSV   TEV

"These you may eat, of all that are in the waters. Everything in the waters that has fins and scales, whether in the seas or in the rivers, you may eat.

You may eat any kind of fish that has fins and scales,

Verses 9-12 deal with creatures of the sea, and so a new paragraph should begin here. The structure of the first sentence is awkward and may be reformulated in a way that is natural in the receptor language. The structure may be parallel to verse 2b, where the land animals are first introduced. For example, "These are the sea creatures that you are allowed to eat . . . ." It may also be necessary to eliminate some of the redundant material such as the second occurrence of **in the waters** or of **you may eat**. The phrase **whether in the seas or in the rivers** is left implicit in this verse in TEV, and its second occurrence (in the following verse) is summarized as "living in the water," perhaps in order not to exclude oceans and lakes.

Fins and scales: these two characteristics were essential for a sea creature to be considered acceptable by the Jews. In cultures where such terminology is lacking, **fins** may be rendered by "flapping things" or "things which cause to move," or in some cases "wings," "arms," or "hands." **Scales** may be "things which cover the skin" in some languages.

11.10 RSV	TEV

| But anything in the seas or the rivers that has not fins and scales, of the swarming creatures in the waters and of the living creatures that are in the waters, is an abomination to you. | but anything living in the water that does not have fins and scales must not be eaten. |

But: again it is necessary to mark the contrast between what may be eaten and what is forbidden (see verse 4).

The threefold repetition of **in the waters** in addition to **in the seas or the rivers** will certainly be too awkward to be included in most receptor languages. TEV provides a good model for reducing the redundancy while retaining the meaning.

That has not fins and scales: presumably the prohibition would include sea creatures lacking either fins or scales. So in some languages it may be more appropriate to translate the conjunction **and** as "or."

Swarming creatures . . . living creatures: the creatures that live in the water are divided into two groups: "swarming things" and "others." The first term is used in 5.2 and 7.21, but the contexts in those two cases are different since the creatures do not necessarily live in water. The fundamental meaning seems to be "that which cannot be numbered," either because of their small size or their great number. So it is used here to designate small sea creatures, but in verse 20 it refers to "insects," and in verse 29 to "creepers" or small animals (such as rats, mice, moles, and lizards). The second term is used here to refer to larger sea creatures. NEB translates "small creatures in shoals and larger creatures," while NJB has "all the small water creatures and all the living things found there."

An abomination: this corresponds to the statement in the above verses, "they are unclean to you," but it is even stronger. The main component of meaning in this word is the idea of aversion or disgust. The unacceptable water creatures were to be held in contempt by the faithful Jew and were not to be touched. The TEV translation **"must not be eaten"** is a bit weak. Translators may consider "should be strictly avoided" or "must be seen as disgusting." NJB says "you will regard as detestable," while NAB has "are loathsome for you."

11.11 RSV	TEV

| They shall remain an abomination to you; of their flesh you shall not eat, and their carcasses you shall have in abomination. | Such creatures must be considered unclean. You must not eat them or even touch their dead bodies. |

This verse is essentially a repetition of verse 8, but with the addition of the idea of **abomination** (two times) from verse 10. Again the TEV rendering, **"must be considered unclean,"** is not as strong as is desired. For the last part of the verse, some versions may say "Abstain from eating them and avoid all contact with their dead bodies."

11.12 RSV	TEV
Everything in the waters that has not fins and scales is an abomination to you.	You must not eat anything that lives in the water and does not have fins and scales.

This verse is almost identical with the beginning of verse 10 without adding any new information. It may be legitimate in some languages to restructure verses 10-12 as a whole and eliminate the redundancy.

11.13-19 RSV	TEV
13 "And these you shall have in abomination among the birds, they shall not be eaten, they are an abomination: the eagle, the vulture, the osprey, 14 the kite, the falcon according to its kind, 15 every raven according to its kind, 16 the ostrich, the nighthawk, the sea gull, the hawk according to its kind, 17 the owl, the cormorant, the ibis, 18 the water hen, the pelican, the carrion vulture, 19 the stork, the heron according to its kind, the hoopoe, and the bat.	13-19 You must not eat any of the following birds: eagles, owls, hawks, falcons; buzzards, vultures, crows; ostriches; seagulls, storks, herons, pelicans, cormorants;[x] hoopoes; or bats.

[x] *The identification of some of the birds in verses 13-19 is uncertain.*

These verses deal with the third category of creatures which the Hebrews considered "birds." The terminology used in that day does not correspond exactly to that which is known in the modern world and may also be at variance with other views of what constitutes a "bird." For example, in many languages the **bat** mentioned in verse 19 cannot be called a "bird." The list is made up of no less than twenty species, which leads many commentators to believe that it was intended to be exhaustive (the parallel list in Deut 14.12-18 has twenty-one names). Ten of these names appear only here and in the Deuteronomy 14 list, but nowhere else in the Old Testament. Five others are found in only one additional case outside the two lists. For this reason it is extremely difficult to identify with any degree of certainty all the species involved. Even the ancient versions such as Greek and Latin demonstrate considerable differences in their translation of these names.

In Hebrew all the names on the list are given in singular form (compare RSV), but TEV has taken into account the fact that they are collective nouns and has made them plural in translation.

Since this is the beginning of the third group discussed in this chapter, a new paragraph should be started here. It may be well in many languages to use the same kind of introductory sentence as in verses 2b and 9. The passive formulation **shall not be eaten** may be rendered "You must not eat . . . ."

The repetition of the idea **they are an abomination** (compare verse 10) is significant because it appears for emphasis. Unless these repetitions are unacceptably awkward in the receptor language, it will be well to retain them in translation.

Many of the names on this list are followed by the expression **according to its kind** (compare Gen 1), which seems to indicate that the species in question is divided into two or more subgroups. In one case (verse 15) the name is preceded by the word "all" or "any" (**every raven** in RSV), but this does not really change the meaning. So it has been omitted in TEV.

The table below is intended to help the translator move quickly through this difficult passage. The Hebrew words are given in order to facilitate reference in FFB. References to this book are given in the third column: the first number(s) refer to the pages and those in parentheses refer to the item where several words are listed under a single heading. The RSV rendering is found in the fourth column. The final column gives alternative renderings and indicates in parentheses the version or versions in which they are found. It will be obvious that the more alternative renderings that are given, the more uncertain the identification of the bird.

VERSE	HEBREW	FFB Ref.	RSV	OTHER VERSIONS
13	*nesher*	84(1)	eagle	griffon-vulture (NEB) tawny vulture (JB)
	peres	84(3)	vulture	black vulture (NEB) griffon (JB)
	'ozniyah	84(5)	osprey	black vulture (NJV) bearded vulture (NEB)
14	*da'ah*	84(2);40(3)	kite	red kite (NIV) buzzards (TEV)
	'ayyah	40(2)	falcon	black kite (NIV) buzzard (JB)
15	*'orebh*	67-68	raven	crow (NEB, TEV)
16	*bath hayya'anah*	61(1)	ostrich	desert owl (NEB) horned owl (NIV)
	tachmas	61(2)	nighthawk	short-eared owl (NEB) screech owl (NIV, JB) owls (TEV)
	shachaph	61(3)	seagull	long-eared owl (NEB) gull (NIV)
	nets	40(1)	hawk	
17	*kos*	51	owl	little owl (NJV, NIV) tawny owl (NEB) horned owl (JB)
	shalak	18	cormorant	fisher owl (NEB)
	yanshuf	24-25	ibis	great owl (NJV, NIV) screech owl (NEB) barn owl (JB)

18	tinshemeth	61(7)	water hen	white owl (NJV, NIV)
				little owl (NEB)
				ibis (JB)
	qa'ath	61(8);65	pelican	horned owl (NEB)
				desert owl (NIV)
	racham	84(4)	carrion vulture	bustard (NJV)
				osprey (NEB, NIV)
				white vulture (JB)
19	chasidah	78	stork	
	'anafah	41	heron	cormorant (NEB)
	dukifath	42	hoopoe	
	'atallef	7-8	bat	

The second word in verse 18 is usually translated **pelican** because of the ancient Greek and Latin renderings, but some commentators find this unconvincing in the light of the fact that this same bird is mentioned in Isaiah 34.11, Zephaniah 2.14, and Psalm 102.7 as one living in the desert or in ruins. Perhaps the renderings of NIV or NEB are more likely.

In some languages it may be necessary to translate several terms by a single word in the receptor language. For example, there may be only one word for the various kinds of owls mentioned in the list. Translators may then have to say "the different kinds of owls" or something similar. In other languages there may be no word for certain of the birds in the list. If this is the case, it may be necessary to resort to a borrowing which is explained in a footnote or glossary entry. And although the final term in the list may not be considered a bird in the receptor language, it must be remembered that it was apparently included in this category in ancient Jewish thinking. So it should be a part of the bird list in this passage and not be placed in a special category. Even though the receptor-language classification of birds may be entirely different from the Old Testament system, the translator must respect what is found in the text. But an explanatory footnote will certainly be acceptable.

11.20   RSV   TEV

"All winged insects that go upon all fours are an abomination to you.   **All winged insects are** unclean,

The word translated **insects** here is the same as "swarming creatures" in verse 10 and "swarming things" in verse 29. But with the word **winged** or "flying" added, it is clear that the reference is to insects with wings.

That go upon all fours: this expression is surprising, since the ancient Jews almost certainly knew that winged insects had six legs. The expression was probably used in a nonliteral sense, meaning "to crawl," and was used of any flying creature with more than two legs, to distinguish the insects from other flying creatures such as the birds just mentioned in the previous verses. TEV has avoided the problem altogether, and other modern versions have omitted the number "four." FRCL, for example, has "insects which have wings and legs." In other languages the idea may possibly be rendered "with more than two legs."

Abomination: see verses 10 and 11.

11.21	RSV	TEV

Yet among the winged insects that go on all fours you may eat those which have legs above their feet, with which to leap on the earth.	**except those that hop.**

This constitutes an exception to the rule set down in the previous verse. While it is a complete sentence repeating many of the elements of verse 20, the full meaning is captured in the four words found in TEV. If a completely new sentence is used in the receptor language, it will be very important to introduce it with a transition word that clearly indicates that this is an exception. For example, **Yet** as in RSV, "But" (NJV and NAB), "However" (Mft, AT, and NIV), or "Nevertheless."

Which have legs above their feet: the word translated **legs** is a special term which comes from the root "to bow down" and means "jointed legs" or "bending legs." The idea is that they have the kind of legs that permit them to jump or hop. This is made quite clear by the words that follow. Some languages may say "except those insects that have the kind of legs that enable them to hop" or "those that are able to bounce because of their legs."

The traditional written Hebrew text actually reads "which have no legs," but the ancient Jewish experts in sacred literature (the Masoretes) recommended in the margin of their copies that what should actually be read is "which have legs." And virtually all modern scholars agree that this is the correct meaning to be translated.

11.22	RSV	TEV

Of them you may eat: the locust according to its kind, the bald locust according to its kind, the cricket according to its kind, and the grasshopper according to its kind.	**You may eat locusts, crickets, or grasshoppers.**

In some languages it may be more appropriate to begin this verse with something like "Therefore you may eat . . ." or "Here, then, are the ones you may eat: . . . ." The repetition of the phrase **according to its kind**, as in verses 13-19, may be dropped or left implicit. Although the Hebrew lists four different kinds of insects here, RSV and TEV have reduced this to three. The various kinds of locusts and grasshoppers of the Old Testament are discussed in FFB, pages 53-54. The wide variety of ways in which these terms have been understood can be seen in the chart below:

RSV	NEB	NJV	NIV	TEV
locust	great locust	locust	locust	locusts
bald locust	long-headed locust	bald locust	katydid	
cricket	green locust	cricket	cricket	crickets
grasshopper	desert locust	grasshopper	grasshopper	grasshoppers

The problem is dealt with in NJB by borrowing certain Hebrew terms: "the various kinds of *solham* locust, *hargol* locust and *hagab* locust." But this is not a satisfactory solution in a common language translation. An attempt should be made to find well-known words that correspond more or less to the biblical ideas. If the correspondence is not exact, an explanation may be offered in a footnote. In languages where there are very few words for this type of insect, a more general statement like "the various kinds of crickets and grasshoppers" may be required. It may even be necessary in some languages to say simply "all kinds of grasshoppers," but this is not advised unless it is impossible to do otherwise.

11.23　　　RSV　　　　　　　　　　　　　TEV

But all other winged insects which have four feet are an abomination to you.

But all other small things that have wings and also crawl must be considered unclean.

Although the wording is not identical with verse 20, this verse repeats the same basic information. Because the information shows contrast at this point in the text, it is important to introduce it this time by a transition word such as **But**, marking contrast with the previous verse.

11.24-25　　　RSV　　　　　　　　　　　　TEV

24 "And by these you shall become unclean; whoever touches their carcass shall be unclean until the evening, 25 and whoever carries any part of their carcass shall wash his clothes and be unclean until the evening.

24-28 Whoever touches the dead bodies of the following animals will be unclean until evening: all animals with hoofs, unless their hoofs are divided and they chew the cud, and all four-footed animals with paws. Whoever carries their dead bodies must wash his clothes, but he will still be unclean until evening.

Some commentators and translations consider verses 24-25 a part of the preceding paragraph (NEB, for example). But this is not satisfactory, since verses 1-23 deal with the permission to eat and prohibition against eating certain animals, while beginning with verse 24 the text is concerned with the question of impurity which comes as a result of physical contact with dead bodies. The words **their carcass** in verses 24 and 25 therefore do not refer back to the insects mentioned in the preceding verses; rather they look forward to the mention of the animals in verses 26-28.

Whoever: the word may also mean "whatever" (compare 6.18 and 27), but it is generally agreed that in this context it refers to any person in the community. It may therefore be translated "anyone" or "everyone," depending on the receptor language habits when forming a general prohibition such as this.

Unclean: see 5.2.

Touches . . . carries: in this context the two verbs used seem to refer to involuntary and voluntary contact with the dead bodies. In some cases a person may have to remove a dead animal from the camp for the protection of the group as a whole, even if it made him unclean.

Unclean until the evening: that is, in a state preventing him from participating in the ritual activities of the community. This condition continues until the setting of the sun. In some languages "until the sun goes down (or, disappears)" or "until the end of the day" is the most natural translation of the phrase **until the evening**. But translators must remember that for the Jews the day ended with the setting of the sun. The translation should not give the impression that the state of impurity continues until midnight or until the following morning.

Wash his clothes: this is a literal washing of the clothing in water, but the reason behind it was based more on ritual than on physical cleanliness. However, a literal washing does not exclude the possibility that ritual cleansing was also involved.

11.26-28   RSV   TEV

26 Every animal which parts the hoof but is not cloven-footed or does not chew the cud is unclean to you; every one who touches them shall be unclean. 27 And all that go on their paws, among the animals that go on all fours, are unclean to you; whoever touches their carcass shall be unclean until the evening, 28 and he who carries their carcass shall wash his clothes and be unclean until the evening; they are unclean to you.

[See the previous section for the TEV text and the discussion below on restructuring.]

In order to avoid the repetition of several different redundant phrases, TEV has restructured verses 24-28. RSV, on the other hand, represents a much more literal rendering of the Hebrew. If a radical restructuring such as in TEV is undertaken in the receptor language, it should be done on the basis of that language's requirements and not just as a literal rendering of TEV. A careful check should be made to be sure that all the components of meaning appear in the restructured version.

If the restructuring is less radical than in TEV, verse 26 should probably begin by repeating or rephrasing the words at the beginning of verse 24: "By these [animals] you shall become unclean" or "These are the animals that make people unclean . . . ."

Which parts the hoof . . . : see verse 3. Here two distinct categories of animals are involved: those which are **not cloven-hoofed** (such as horses and donkeys) and those which do not **chew the cud** (such as pigs). The text does not intend to speak of two characteristics of a single group of animals but of two separate categories. The translation should make this clear. Note that verse 3 has "cloven-footed," while here the term is "cloven-hoofed." However, the same term can be used in translation for both expressions.

That go on their paws: literally, "that walk on their palms." The distinction seems to be between those animals that walk on the flat of their feet (like dogs and cats), and those that have a hollow in their hoofs and whose feet therefore do not completely touch the ground when walking. Some versions make this clearer by using an expression like "flat paws" (NEB). JB translated "on the flat of their foot," but the revision of NJB has "on the flat of their paws." Perhaps the use of the word "**paws**" by itself, as in TEV, will be adequate to convey this meaning in some languages.

Among the animals that go on all fours: literally, ". . . that walk on fours." In some languages this may be redundant, coming after the words **that go on their paws**.

11.29-30   RSV   TEV

29 "And these are unclean to you among the swarming things that swarm upon the earth: the weasel, the mouse, the great lizard according to its kind, 30 the gecko, the land crocodile, the lizard, the sand lizard, and the chameleon.

29-30 Moles, rats, mice, and lizards must be considered unclean.

This verse includes a list of eight names of animals that are in some cases difficult to identify. The reference table below shows how they have been translated in certain English versions, and the column following the RSV reference indicates the page reference in FFB. It will be noted that a number of these terms are discussed on page 52 of FFB because they are closely related.

RSV	FFB Ref	NEB	NJV	NIV
weasel	55	mole-rat	mole	weasel
mouse	57	jerboa	mouse	rat
great lizard	52	thorn-tailed lizard	great lizard	great lizard
gecko	34-35	gecko	gecko	gecko
land crocodile	52	sand-gecko	land crocodile	monitor lizard
lizard	52	wall-gecko	lizard	wall lizard

sand lizard	52	great lizard	sand lizard	skink
chameleon	15	chameleon	chameleon	chameleon

NJB again transliterates several of these difficult terms ("the various kinds of lizards: gecko, *koah*, *letaah*, chameleon and *tinshamet*"), which is not very helpful to the common language translator or to the average Bible reader.

Even if these animals were easily identified, they are not always easy to translate into the languages of the world. It may be necessary to summarize as in TEV, using general and well-known terms that cover the intention of the writer, rather than trying to find an exact equivalent for each one. In some languages these animals may not be seen as significantly different from the other four-footed animals already mentioned, but for the people of Israel they are in a different category called **swarming things**. The list is probably intended to be representative of the whole group.

As in the list of birds (13-19), the singular form is used in its collective sense and will have to be translated as a plural in many languages.

11.31   RSV   TEV

These are unclean to you among all that swarm; whoever touches them when they are dead shall be unclean until the evening.

Whoever touches them or their dead bodies will be unclean until evening.

See verses 10 and 29. Compare also 5.2.

These are unclean to you: this may equally well be translated "You are to consider these unclean . . ." or "you must regard as disgusting . . ." (NJB).

Whoever: see verse 24.

11.32   RSV   TEV

And anything upon which any of them falls when they are dead shall be unclean, whether it is an article of wood or a garment or a skin or a sack, any vessel that is used for any purpose; it must be put into water, and it shall be unclean until the evening; then it shall be clean.

And if their dead bodies fall on anything, it will be unclean. This applies to any article of wood, cloth, leather, or sacking, no matter what it is used for. It shall be dipped in water, but it will remain unclean until evening.

The first part of this verse may have to be restructured so that it is more natural in the receptor language. One way to do this may be to follow TEV. Another possibility is to say "If any of them dies and falls on anything . . ." or "If, after having died, they fall . . . ." Presumably death occurs before the fall and is not caused by it.

An article of . . .: or "any object" (NJB), or "anything" (NEB). In some languages it may be necessary to say "a thing made of . . . ."

Of the four kinds of material, **wood** and **skin** are probably easier to translate, although **wood** may be the same as the word for "tree," and **skin** may have to be specified as "animal skin" to distinguish it from human skin or the bark of a tree. The word for "**cloth**" refers to something worn as a garment or used to cover an object. In the receptor language it may be a borrowed term or a relatively recently coined word. The fourth term is the same one that is used for "sackcloth" in other contexts. Here it refers to a coarse material made of goat or camel hair, or of flax, hemp, or cotton. It is distinguished from ordinary cloth by its coarseness and its use as a kind of sack. So one may have to say simply "coarse cloth" or "cloth used for sacks."

Put into water: in this context the verb probably refers to the washing of the object, but it must be remembered that ritual rather than physical cleanness is of primary importance. The TEV rendering "**dipped into the water**" (also NJV) is more precise than RSV **put . . .** , which seems to imply that the object remains in the water. In some languages it may be better to translate "washed" (Knox and FRCL) or "immersed" (NJB).

11.33   RSV   TEV

And if any of them falls into any earthen vessel, all that is in it shall be unclean, and you shall break it.

And if their bodies fall into a clay pot, everything that is in it shall be unclean, and you must break the pot.

In contrast with the objects mentioned in the previous verse, an **earthen vessel** into which an unclean animal falls is considered impossible to be purified and must therefore be destroyed. The words may be rendered "a container made of clay" in some languages. The term **earthen** implies the molding and baking of the clay, and many languages have special terms for such containers that may be used here.

11.34   RSV   TEV

Any food in it which may be eaten, upon which water may come, shall be unclean; and all drink which may be drunk from every such vessel shall be unclean.

Any food which could normally be eaten, but on which water from such a pot has been poured, will be unclean, and anything drinkable in such a pot is unclean.

Many elements in this verse have been left implicit in Hebrew. So it is not easy to understand. RSV translates more or less literally and fails to make explicit the relationship between this verse and its immediate context. Such a translation gives the impression of a very general statement which probably does not correspond to the intention of the original. The TEV rendering is a much better model at this point.

In it: these words are not found in the Hebrew text, and their inclusion here complicates the meaning.

Which may be eaten: this is a description of any food that is "edible" (see NJB) or acceptable for eating under normal circumstances within the regulations of

169

the Jewish community. Some may prefer to translate it using the negative form "which is not forbidden to eat."

Upon which water may come: this gives the impression that the writer meant any water at all, but the context indicates that it was water from the pot mentioned in verse 33 that the writer had in mind. This will have to be made explicit in most functionally equivalent translations. And the words **may come** will have to be rendered "has been poured." Where passive forms are not possible, one may say "has touched," "has fallen," or "has made contact." On the other hand, some commentators do not accept this interpretation. They feel that it means "any edible food that is prepared with water." And JB translates "even though it has been steeped in water." But the majority of modern scholarship supports the translation "any food which comes into contact with water out of such a pot."

Which may be drunk: this is parallel to the idea of "edible" food above. Similarly, it may be translated in some languages "which is acceptable (or, permitted) to drink" or "which is not forbidden to drink." NJB has "any drinkable liquid."

From every such vessel: that is, any container that has become contaminated by contact with the unclean. The container may be made of clay (verse 33) or of wood or skin (verse 32). In some languages the wording may be "any container, whatever material it is made of."

This verse does not explain what is to be done with such a container; but the rules given previously (verses 32-33) regarding purification or destruction apply here.

11.35   RSV   TEV

And everything upon which any part of their carcass falls shall be unclean; whether oven or stove, it shall be broken in pieces; they are unclean, and shall be unclean to you.

Anything on which the dead bodies fall is unclean; a clay stove or oven shall be broken,

Oven: see 2.4 for a description of such an oven. While the adjective "**clay**" may possibly be understood as describing only the stove in TEV, it is intended to qualify both the oven and the stove. It should also be noted that, while this adjective is added by TEV, it is not in the original Hebrew, and according to some experts it is both unnecessary and inaccurate.

Stove: the Hebrew word found here does not occur anywhere else in the Old Testament, and its meaning is uncertain. It probably refers to a kind of portable hearth supporting two cooking pots. However, the uncertainty of its meaning is clearly seen in the variety of renderings found in English versions. In addition to **stove** without any further qualification, we also find "ranges for pots" (KJV), "chafing pots" (Mft), "fire pot" (AT), "jar-stand" (NAB), "cooking pot" (NIV), and "**clay stove**" (TEV).

It shall be broken in pieces: the future tense is used here to indicate something which must be done. The passive form will have to be translated by an active form in some languages: "They [indefinite] must destroy it" or "You must destroy it."

11.36 RSV TEV

Nevertheless a spring or a cistern holding water shall be clean; but whatever touches their carcass shall be unclean.

but a spring or a cistern remains clean, although anything else that touches their dead bodies is unclean.

Nevertheless: there is contrast between the objects mentioned here, which remain clean, and those above, which are ritually unclean. The transition word used at the beginning of this verse should indicate this contrast.

A spring or a cistern: the first word refers to a natural spring of fresh water. The second is a pit hollowed out of a solid rock for the purpose of storing drinking water (see Jer 2.13). They may be as large as six meters square and six meters deep. And they were normally to be kept covered (Exo 21.33). The expression **a cistern holding water** may be translated "a hollowed place in a rock for storing water" or something similar.

The Hebrew text, followed by RSV, leaves implicit the idea "if a dead body falls on them," but this may have to be made explicit in translation.

Whatever: as in verse 24 and 6.18,27, this term may mean either "whatever" or "whoever." In this case it is translated "whoever" by NAB. NJB and NIV have "anyone," and AT has "he who . . . ." FRCL interprets it as "whoever removes the body . . . ." On the side of RSV and TEV, Mft has "anything used to lift out the dead body . . . ," which is more explicit. The meaning may well be a combination of these two: "anyone or anything involved in removing the dead body."

11.37 RSV TEV

And if any part of their carcass falls upon any seed for sowing that is to be sown, it is clean;

If one of them falls on seed that is going to be planted, the seed remains clean.

Any part of their carcass: most versions interpret this to mean "any one of their dead bodies." There is no special emphasis here on a part of a carcass.

Seed for sowing that is to be sown: this awkward English expression is a reflection of the Hebrew form. The meaning, however, is "any seed that is set aside to be planted." Other renderings are "seed grain to be sown" (NJV) and "seed intended for growing" (NEB).

11.38 RSV TEV

but if water is put on the seed and any part of their carcass falls on it, it is unclean to you.

But if the seed is soaking in water and one of them falls on it, the seed is unclean.

But: showing the contrast with the actual seed mentioned in the previous verse.

If water is put on the seed: the soaking of the seed in water is seen by some commentators as preparation for planting, but others see it as preparing the seed to be eaten (see FRCL). If the receptor language permits, it is probably best not to make too much explicit here, since we are not certain about the intention of the writer. In most cases it should be possible to translate "**soaking in water**" without indicating the purpose of this action.

11.39 RSV	TEV
"And if any animal of which you may eat dies, he who touches its carcass shall be unclean until the evening,	If any animal that may be eaten dies, anyone who touches it will be unclean until evening.

Verses 39-40 repeat the content of 24-25 and clarify their meaning.

Any animal of which you may eat: this refers to any animal that the Jewish people were permitted to eat by their dietary laws. Again, it may be necessary to say "any animal not forbidden to you under ordinary circumstances." Compare verse 34.

11.40 RSV	TEV
and he who eats of its carcass shall wash his clothes and be unclean until the evening; he also who carries the carcass shall wash his clothes and be unclean until the evening.	And if anyone eats any part of the animal, he must wash his clothes, but he will still be unclean until evening; anyone who carries the dead body must wash his clothes, but he will still be unclean until evening.

Who eats of its carcass: some may wish to translate "who eats any meat from the [dead] animal." This detail is unnecessary in the rest of the paragraph, because unclean animals are dealt with for the most part.

Shall wash his clothes: see verse 25.

11.41 RSV	TEV
"Every swarming thing that swarms upon the earth is an abomination; it shall not be eaten.	You must not eat any of the small animals that move on the ground,

Every swarming thing that swarms upon the earth: this includes snakes and centipedes as well as small four-footed animals like rats, mice, and moles (compare verse 29). This prohibition comes last, perhaps because there was little likelihood that people would be tempted to eat such animals. But in order to make the regulations complete, it was seen as necessary. Greater detail is provided in the following verse.

11.42   RSV   TEV

Whatever goes on its belly, and   whether they crawl, or walk on four
whatever goes on all fours, or what-   legs, or have many legs.
ever has many feet, all the swarming
things that swarm upon the earth,
you shall not eat; for they are an
abomination.

     Whatever goes on its belly: this same expression is used in Genesis 3.14; it
refers to creatures without legs, such as snakes and other reptiles which are not
mentioned elsewhere in this chapter.
     Whatever goes on all fours: this is probably intended to correspond with the
list given in 29-30.
     Whatever has many feet: this includes insects without wings which are not
mentioned elsewhere in this chapter, as well as the millipedes and centipedes.
     In translating these three categories, it is probably best to try to use general
terms, since too much would be left out if the translator tried to list the types of
creatures intended. One may say something like "those that slide along the ground,
those that run on four legs, and those that go along on many legs." One may possibly
want to add ". . . like snakes . . . like lizards . . . like centipedes" in some languages.

11.43   RSV   TEV

You shall not make yourselves abo-   Do not make yourselves unclean by
minable with any swarming thing that   eating any of these.
swarms; and you shall not defile
yourselves with them, lest you become unclean.

     The parallel structure of this verse is common in Hebrew. The words **make
yourselves abominable** are parallel to **defile yourselves**. And the pronoun **them**
in the second part corresponds to **any swarming thing that swarms** in the first. If
the repetition of the same idea using two different sets of words is unnatural in the
receptor language, then it will be acceptable to translate the meaning once. TEV
makes explicit that the uncleanness comes to a person as a result of eating these
unclean animals.

11.44   RSV   TEV

For I am the LORD your God; conse-   I am the LORD your God, and you
crate yourselves therefore, and be   must keep yourselves holy, because
holy, for I am holy. You shall not   I am holy.
defile yourselves with any swarming
thing that crawls upon the earth.

Verses 44-45 are the concluding remarks of the LORD in this part of Leviticus. These words summarize the historical and theological basis for the idea of purity and holiness among the Israelites. The first word in verse 44 is an important transition word, adding force to the affirmation that follows, while at the same time indicating a relationship to the preceding paragraphs. Most English versions have **For**, but some omit it altogether.

It must be emphasized that the idea of holiness in Hebrew has more to do with being "set apart" or "designated as special" than with moral purity. When the God of Israel says **I am holy**, he affirms that he is perfect in every sense and therefore completely different (or "set apart") from every human being and all of creation. When he requires of his people that they **be holy**, he invites them not so much to strive toward moral perfection, but to establish communion with him. He demands that they put aside all obstacles to that relationship—especially impurity or uncleanness. The translator usually tries to use the same word for what God is like and what he requires of his people. But in some cases it may be necessary to resort to the use of two different words or expressions in order to retain the meaning. For example, "I, the LORD your God, am holy, and this is why you must also live as people who are pure and who belong to me alone." One may also consider "I, the LORD your God, am completely different from all others (or, from everything else); and you too must live as a people that are completely different and who belong to me."

11.45   RSV   TEV

For I am the LORD who brought you up out of the land of Egypt, to be your God; you shall therefore be holy, for I am holy."	I am the LORD who brought you out of Egypt so that I could be your God. You must be holy, because I am holy.

The same transition word as in the beginning of verse 44 is found here. In this case it ties the requirement of holiness to the historical fact of the Israelites' deliverance from slavery in Egypt. When **the land of Egypt** was mentioned, all Israelites surely thought of slavery. But since this is not the case with many readers of the Bible today, it may be necessary to make this explicit in translation by saying something like "who freed you from slavery in Egypt" or "who delivered you from slavery and brought you out of the land of Egypt."

11.46   RSV   TEV

This is the law pertaining to beast and bird and every living creature that moves through the waters and every creature that swarms upon the earth,	This, then, is the law about animals and birds, about everything that lives in the water, and everything that moves on the ground.

Verses 46-47 are not a part of the words of the LORD. They are a kind of editorial statement by the writer, given to summarize the main points of the chapter. Similar summary statements are found at the end of each section in the third part of Leviticus (see 12.7b; 13.59; 14.32,54-57; 15.32-33). Mft translates "Such is the law . . . ," while NJV has "These are the instructions . . . ."

The law: in many languages the collective nature of this word is best shown by translating it as a plural, "These, then, are the laws." See 6.9.

That moves through the water: see verse 10-12.

That swarms upon the earth: see verses 44.

11.47 RSV	TEV
to make a distinction between the unclean and the clean and between the living creature that may be eaten and the living creature that may not be eaten.	You must be careful to distinguish between what is ritually clean and unclean, between animals that may be eaten and those that may not.

TEV provides one way of understanding the purpose clause at the beginning of this verse. NAB follows the same interpretation with "that you may distinguish . . ." (likewise Mft). NIV has "You must distinguish . . . ." However, another way of understanding the text is to see the implied subject as the "laws" mentioned in the previous verse. The translation will then read "These laws help you to distinguish between what is ritually clean and unclean . . ." (See FRCL). Similarly, NJB has "Its [the law's] purpose is to separate the clean and the unclean . . . ." But the essential meaning is not really different. These laws enable the people of Israel to make the important distinction between what is clean and unclean.

Chapter 12

According to the way of thinking of the ancient Israelites, the birth of a child caused a state of uncleanness for two reasons: first, it was related to sexuality and was therefore considered mysterious; and secondly, it involved a loss of blood. There is no indication that the event of childbirth was somehow immoral.

Some translations entitle this section something like "Purification after childbirth," without any indication that it is the woman who is considered unclean. But it is best to indicate in the title that it is the mother and not the child who is considered unclean. Other possible titles may include "After a child is born the mother is unclean" or "The uncleanness of a woman after bearing a child."

12.1-2 RSV TEV

1 The LORD said to Moses, 2 "Say to the people of Israel, If a woman conceives, and bears a male child, then she shall be unclean seven days; as at the time of her menstruation, she shall be unclean.

1 The LORD gave Moses the following regulations 2 for the people of Israel. For seven days after a woman gives birth to a son, she is ritually unclean, as she is during her monthly period.

Said to Moses: see 4.1.

Say to the people . . . : see 1.2.

If a woman conceives, and bears a male child: the Hebrew language often uses expressions like this, putting together two verbs where the first one indicates the beginning of a process and the second one describes the main action. This type of construction is not normal in many languages, since the first verb is implied by the second. A woman cannot give birth unless she has first conceived. So the verb "conceive" may be left implicit in many languages. The verb translated **bears** literally means "brings forth seed." Since each language has its own way of referring to childbirth, the translator must look for the most natural way of expressing this idea to a group of readers or hearers composed of men, women, and children.

In some languages it will be much more natural to say "**a son**," as in TEV, in place of **a male child**, but in others the expression may be just like RSV. The Hebrew actually only says "a male," leaving the word "child" implicit.

Seven days: since the number seven has special significance (see 4.6), some translators may wish to retain it in translation, but in some cases it may be necessary to say "a week," because that is much more natural.

As: this word indicates a comparison between the uncleanness of the woman at childbirth with the uncleanness at the time of her monthly period of menstruation. The similarity involves both the amount of time required and the consequences of the woman's uncleanness.

At the time of her menstruation: literally, "in the days of her separation for her weakness." The experience described here is common to women in every culture all over the world. But the way of talking about it varies widely from one language to another, because it is a very private matter. Some of the ways that this idea is expressed in other cultures are "to cause blood to flow," "to see blood," "to see the moon," "to have the sickness of women," and "to be avoided." The translator must be sure that the words chosen in the receptor language are natural, understandable, and suitable to the context of regulations concerning cleanness and uncleanness.

12.3   RSV   TEV

And on the eighth day the flesh of his foreskin shall be circumcised.

On the eighth day, the child shall be circumcised.

On the eighth day: in some languages it will be necessary to say "Eight days later," or "Eight days after the child is born," or "When the child is one week old."

The flesh of his foreskin shall be circumcised: the pronoun **his** obviously refers to the male child. But in languages where masculine and feminine pronouns are not distinguished, it may be wise to say "**the child**," as in TEV. In some cultures female circumcision is practiced, and this verse may be misunderstood.

As in the case of menstruation, there are also many very different ways of speaking of circumcision. Some examples are "to cut the child," "to make the mark," "to cause [the child] to undergo the ceremony," and "to remove the foreskin." But in some cultures the practice of circumcision may be unknown. In such cases the translator should attempt to find a descriptive expression that will not be shocking when read in public. But in some cases this may prove to be almost impossible, and it may be necessary to resort to a borrowed word, transliteration, or some special expression that will have to be explained in a glossary.

12.4   RSV   TEV

Then she shall continue for thirty-three days in the blood of her purifying; she shall not touch any hallowed thing, nor come into the sanctuary, until the days of her purifying are completed.

Then it will be thirty-three more days until she is ritually clean from her loss of blood; she must not touch anything that is holy or enter the sacred Tent until the time of her purification is completed.

In addition to the seven days already mentioned, the woman was to wait an additional thirty-three days to be certain that the discharge was completely over. The total of forty days constituted a sacred number for the Israelites at that time. During these forty days the woman was considered "taboo." Two things were specifically forbidden to her in this passage: to touch anything holy, and to enter the holy environment of the Tent of the Lord's Presence. These prohibitions show the ritual character of her impurity. A good model for the first part of this verse is NEB, which has "The woman shall wait for thirty-three [more] days because her blood requires purification . . . ." Mft has "and for thirty-three days further she shall stay at home, while the blood flows, till she is purified."

Come into the sanctuary: since women were probably not allowed to enter the sanctuary, some have rendered this expression "go to the sanctuary" (NJB and FRCL). This apparently assumes that the women went only to the entrance of the Tent. Verse 6 seems to confirm this assumption when it says "at the door of the tent."

12.5

RSV	TEV
But if she bears a female child, then she shall be unclean two weeks, as in her menstruation; and she shall continue in the blood of her purifying for sixty-six days.	For fourteen days after a woman gives birth to a daughter, she is ritually unclean, as she is during her monthly period. Then it will be sixty-six more days until she is ritually clean from her loss of blood.

This verse corresponds to verse 2b and 4, where the birth of a male child is considered.

But: since there is a contrast between what happens after the birth of a son and the birth of a daughter, it is a good idea to include a transition word in the receptor language at this point. Several versions begin a new paragraph at this point to indicate that a different subject is being considered (TEV, FRCL, and NJB).

A female child: literally, "a female." In many languages it will be more natural to use a term meaning "**daughter**," as in TEV.

Two weeks: this is the plural form of the same word translated in verse 2 as "seven days" or "a week." The birth of a daughter required the doubling of the time period.

As in her menstruation: (see verse 2) here the comparison cannot be with the length of time, but only on the consequences of her uncleanness. For this reason it may be better to restructure as follows: "she is unclean as during her monthly period, but for twice as long (or, for two weeks, or, for fourteen days)."

For sixty-six days: this period is also twice as long as required after the birth of a son. Since it is in addition to the fourteen days already mentioned, it may be better to say "**sixty-six more days**," as in TEV.

12.6

RSV	TEV
"And when the days of her purifying are completed, whether for a son or for a daughter, she shall bring to the priest at the door of the	When the time of her purification is completed, whether for a son or daughter, she shall bring to the priest at the entrance of the Tent of

tent of meeting a lamb a year old for a burnt offering, and a young pigeon or a turtledove for a sin offering,	the LORD's presence a one-year-old lamb for a burnt offering and a pigeon or a dove for a sin offering.

This verse and the first part of verse 7 constitute a single sentence in RSV, but it should be divided into two or three separate sentences in most languages. A single sentence is retained in the TEV translation of this verse, but FRCL divides it further. After stating that the woman must "go to meet the priest at the tent of meeting," there is a full stop. The second sentence begins: "She shall bring him . . . ." This may serve as a helpful model in restructuring other languages.

The days of her purifying: in some languages the possessive pronoun will be unnecessary, since it will be clear that the "period of purification" refers to her purification. In other languages a translator may have to say "the required number of days," or even "those thirty-three or sixty-six days," instead of simply **the days**.

For a son or a daughter: in some languages it may be clearer to say "after the birth of a son or a daughter."

The tent of meeting: see the discussion at 1.1 and the diagram in the introduction. While there were women who "served at the entrance of the Tent of the Lord's Presence" (Exo 38.8), they were probably not allowed to enter. However, their presence at the entrance both here and in Exodus 38 implies that they were permitted into the courtyard.

For a burnt offering: see 1.3 and the discussion under the section heading at the beginning of chapter 1.

A young pigeon: the age of the pigeon is not important here. See 1.14.

For a sin offering: see 4.14.

12.7 RSV TEV

and he shall offer it before the LORD, and make atonement for her; then she shall be clean from the flow of her blood. This is the law for her who bears a child, either male or female.	The priest shall present her offering to the LORD and perform the ritual to take away her impurity, and she will be ritually clean. This, then, is what a woman must do after giving birth.

He: in English this clearly refers to the priest, but in those languages that do not distinguish between masculine and feminine pronouns, it will be especially important to put the noun **"priest"** in place of the pronoun, in order to avoid confusion.

It: this pronoun refers to the two types of offerings brought by the woman (see verse 6). NAB and NIV have "them." Many translators will prefer to spell this out more clearly. In addition one may consider also "her offerings" (compare TEV).

Make atonement for her: the Hebrew verb used here usually means "to take away sin," but in this case it is not a question of "sin" in the usual sense of the word. (Compare 8.15, "to take away the sin of the altar.") Here it is a matter of removing ritual impurity. This is made clear in the TEV rendering.

From the flow of her blood: this is left implicit in TEV, and the same may be done in some other languages if the repetition at this point is seen as unnatural or unnecessary.

This is the law: compare 6.9,14,25. One may also say "This is what is required" or "**This, then, is what a woman must do . . .** " (TEV). Some versions set this off as a separate paragraph to highlight its summary character (FRCL).

Either male or female: this information is considered redundant in TEV, since the regulation is general and includes the birth of any child.

12.8 RSV	TEV
And if she cannot afford a lamb, then she shall take two turtledoves or two young pigeons, one for a burnt offering and the other for a sin offering; and the priest shall make atonement for her, and she shall be clean."	If the woman cannot afford a lamb, she shall bring two doves or two pigeons, one for a burnt offering and the other for a sin offering, and the priest shall perform the ritual to take away her impurity, and she will be ritually clean.

This verse is seen by some commentators as an addition to the original text, and that it may fit better before the concluding summary in 7b. But it is better to translate the text as it stands. What is important is that this is a concession to the poor woman who cannot afford to bring a lamb.

Compare this verse with 5.7-13.

If she cannot afford a lamb: literally, "If her hand find not the price of a lamb." In a number of languages the English verb "to afford" has to be expressed in ways much more like the Hebrew. One may say "if she does not have enough money for a lamb" or "if she lacks what is necessary for a lamb" or even "if she is to poor to bring a lamb."

Two young pigeons: see 5.7. Again, the age of the birds is not important here. For the rest of this verse, see 7a.

Chapter 13

Chapters 13—14 deal with ritual uncleanness which comes as a result of skin diseases, or as a result of mildew appearing on clothing or on the walls of a house. The Hebrew uses the same term for these problems, which are seen as very different in most cultures today. The word used has been traditionally translated "leprosy" in most English versions. But in fact, even when referring to human skin disease, the Hebrew word does not exactly correspond to what we call "leprosy" today. It is rather a very general term that perhaps includes ringworm, psoriasis, leucoderma, as well as "Hansen's disease" (the modern medical terminology used to refer to what is commonly called "leprosy" today). One physician who is very familiar with the problem is even more certain that our traditional rendering of this word is incorrect. He says that the term appears to refer to "a group of skin conditions, which today we cannot diagnose definitely." But he goes on to say that "we can state quite definitely that at the time when the Old Testament literature was created, leprosy simply did not exist in that part of the world." (*The Bible Translator*, April 1980, Vol 31, No 2, pages 208 and 209.)

The misunderstanding seems to arise because the word was poorly translated from Hebrew into the Greek of the Septuagint. Modern translators should be well aware of these facts. And yet in some modern versions (including the French and German common language translations), the word "leprosy" is still used because the alternative is considered "too heavy" or "too awkward." TEV, on the other hand, has totally avoided the terms "leprosy" and "leper." If at all possible, this example should be followed in the receptor language, since the use of the word "leprosy" is both unfair to persons suffering from Hansen's disease today and an inaccurate representation of the biblical term. But in those cases where this is for some reason judged impossible, it will be essential to include a detailed explanation in a footnote or preferably in a glossary entry, since the term occurs so frequently throughout the Bible.

Chapters 13 and 14 of Leviticus are divided into four subsections, with the third subsection being further subdivided:

1.	13.1-46	Human skin diseases
2.	13.47-59	Mildew on clothing, and its purification
3.	14.1-32	The purification of persons with skin diseases
	a. 1-20	General regulations
	b. 21-32	The case of the poor
4.	14.33-57	Mildew in houses, and their purification

The decisions of the priest with regard to persons or objects affected by this problem are not medical (sick or healed), but rather they are religious and ritual (unclean or clean). That which is "unclean" is excluded from the life of the community and its ritual practices (see 13.4b), and the "clean" is acceptable to the community and its rituals.

TEV Section Heading: **"Laws concerning Skin Diseases."**

While most versions give a single section heading to the whole of verses 1-46, NEB entitles verses 1-17 "The Malignant Skin Disease," and then has "Various Other Skin Diseases" at verse 18. NJB further divides this section in great detail, which may be more than necessary in most languages:

    a. Swellings, scabs, discolorations (1-8)
    b. Cases of dormant skin disease (9-17)
    c. Ulcers (18-23)
    d. Burns (24-28)
    e. Diseases of the scalp and chin (29-37)
    f. Rash (38-39)
    g. Loss of hair (40-44)

In its main title, NJB emphasizes that it is human skin diseases that are involved. And NIV focuses on a slightly different aspect, with "Regulations about Infectious Skin Diseases." It may be a good idea to include both of these ideas in the receptor language section heading. For example, "Rules about people who have skin diseases that may infect others."

13.1-2	RSV	TEV

1 The LORD said to Moses and Aaron, 2 "When a man has on the skin of his body a swelling or an eruption or a spot, and it turns into a leprous disease on the skin of his body, then he shall be brought to Aaron the priest or to one of his sons the priests.

1 The LORD gave Moses and Aaron these regulations. 2 If anyone has a sore on his skin or a boil or an inflammation which could develop into a dreaded skin disease, he shall be brought to the Aaronite priest.

Said to Moses and Aaron: this is the same expression translated in RSV by two verbs in 10.8, where only Aaron is the object, and by one verb in 11.1 and most other occurrences. See also 4.1.

A swelling: the meaning of this word is disputed by scholars. Some insist that it cannot mean **swelling** (Snaith page 70), but it is so translated by RSV, AT, NJV, NIV, and NJB. On the other hand, NAB has "scab," NEB has "discoloration," and TEV has simply "**a sore**." A more general term as in TEV is probably best.

An eruption: this may mean either a single eruption, as a "**boil**" (TEV) or "pustule" (NEB, NAB), or possibly more numerous eruptions in the same general area of the skin, which would be translated "a rash" (NJV, NIV).

A spot: the RSV rendering is too vague. The term refers to a "shining spot" (JB), "a white spot" (Mft), or a "bright spot" (NIV) because it is inflamed. A better rendering is therefore **"an inflammation"** (TEV and NEB) or an "inflamed spot" (AT).

And it turns into: this phrase indicates that the disease on that part of the skin could possibly become more serious. Hence it is translated "may develop into . . ." (NEB), "may become . . . ," or **"could develop into . . ."** (NJB and TEV).

A leprous disease: literally, "a mark of leprosy." See the discussion of the issue of "leprosy" at the beginning of this chapter. Similar to the TEV rendering seen above, NEB has "a malignant skin disease," and NIV has "an infectious skin disease" in this verse. Any of these is preferable to using the receptor language word for "leprosy."

He shall be brought: in place of this passive construction, some languages may have to say "they [indefinite] must bring him" or "someone must take him to the priest."

To Aaron the priest or to one of his sons the priests: see 1.5. This long expression simply means one of the priests from the family of Aaron. The wording of NEB may be helpful to some translators: "either to Aaron or to one of his sons." The word translated **sons** may also be understood to mean "descendants."

13.3 RSV TEV

RSV	TEV
and the priest shall examine the diseased spot on the skin of his body; and if the hair in the diseased spot has turned white and the disease appears to be deeper than the skin of his body, it is a leprous disease; when the priest has examined him he shall pronounce him unclean.	The priest shall examine the sore, and if the hairs in it have turned white and the sore appears to be deeper than the surrounding skin, it is a dreaded skin disease, and the priest shall pronounce the person unclean.

The diseased spot: this term corresponds to the word literally translated "mark" in verse 2 above. It seems to refer to the area on the person's body where any kind of difficulty may have been detected. One may translate "the place where the problem is" or "the sick part of the skin."

Hair: the translation should not give the impression of a single hair, but of many. The idea here is collective.

The disease appears to be deeper than the skin of his body: literally, "the appearance of the sore deeper than the skin of the flesh." The words **of his body**, or "of his flesh" are unnecessary in most languages, since it would be understood when "skin" or "his skin" are used. The idea here is that there is a depression in the skin. The affected area is **"deeper than the surrounding skin"** (TEV). NJB has "if the disease bites into the skin."

It is a leprous disease: this part of the sentence may be better introduced by a word like "then" in some languages. It is the logical result of the "if" clause which it follows.

When the priest has examined him: the Hebrew repeats the same verb as in the beginning of the verse, but this does not mean that a second examination takes place. It is better in some languages to omit this second occurrence, or to say "when the examination has been completed," or "when the priest finishes examining him," or, as suggested by FRCL, "immediately after the examination."

He shall pronounce him unclean: is this a ritual pronouncement made only to the sick person or a formal declaration to the whole community? The latter is more likely. The person is declared unfit to participate in the rituals of the community, and all are warned to have no contact with him. It is even possible to translate "he shall be regarded as unclean" or "the whole community must see him as unclean."

13.4 RSV	TEV
But if the spot is white in the skin of his body, and appears no deeper than the skin, and the hair in it has not turned white, the priest shall shut up the diseased person for seven days;	But if the sore is white and does not appear to be deeper than the skin around it and the hairs have not turned white, the priest shall isolate the person for seven days.

The two conditions stated here are different by comparison with the previous verse: the affected area is not deeper than the skin around it, and the hair has not turned white. But since there is still some doubt about the person's condition, a seven-day period of isolation is required. The person is to be **shut up** alone in a building for seven days. The expression **for seven days** is common in such rituals (see 8.33) and may be retained instead of "for a week" (see 12.2).

13.5 RSV	TEV
and the priest shall examine him on the seventh day, and if in his eyes the disease is checked and the disease has not spread in the skin, then the priest shall shut him up seven days more;	The priest shall examine him again on the seventh day, and if in his opinion the sore looks the same and has not spread, he shall isolate him for another seven days.

Examine: since this is, in effect, a reexamination, some languages will require the use of an expression like "examine again" or "examine a second time" in this verse.

In his eyes: that is, in his judgment, or as TEV has it, "**if in his opinion.**"

Is checked: the word **checked** here means "unchanged" (Mft). TEV has "**looks the same,**" implying that it appears as it had seven days earlier. It has not improved, but neither has it become worse. Some other possibilities conveying the same idea may be "remains as it was" (NEB), "is unchanged" (NIV), or "persists" (NJB). This has practically the same meaning as the phrase that follows, **and . . . has not spread**. The latter is merely a negative way of saying the same thing. So in some languages the two phrases may be translated by a single expression.

Seven days more: an additional period of seven days' isolation is required of the sick person. See comments on verse 4.

13.6 RSV	TEV
and the priest shall examine him again on the seventh day, and if the diseased spot is dim and the disease has not spread in the skin, then the priest shall pronounce him clean; it is only an eruption; and he shall wash his clothes, and be clean.	The priest shall examine him again on the seventh day, and if the sore has faded and has not spread, he shall pronounce him ritually clean; it is only a sore. The person shall wash his clothes and be ritually clean.

Examine him again on the seventh day: or, "seven days later the priest shall examine him a third time," since this is actually the third examination. Or this verse may begin with "At the end of this second period [of isolation]."

Dim: or "**faded**" in TEV, NEB, NIV, and NJV. This seems to indicate that the area is getting better and that the inflammation has virtually disappeared.

Pronounce him clean: see the opposite in verse 3.

It is only an eruption: the priest is convinced that the skin problem is not a serious one——not of the type that is greatly feared and must be considered unclean. He therefore requires only that the person **wash his clothes** (see 11.25), and he will again be allowed into the fellowship of the community.

The relationship between **pronounce him clean** and **be clean** in this verse is confusing, but in all probability the washing of the clothing simply completes the process already begun. Some may wish to translate the latter "he will be completely clean" or "his cleansing will be finished."

13.7 RSV	TEV
But if the eruption spreads in the skin, after he has shown himself to the priest for his cleansing, he shall appear again before the priest;	But if the sore spreads after the priest has examined him and pronounced him clean, he must appear before the priest again.

Verses 7-8 deal with the case where the priest's diagnosis is in error, or where the disease begins to spread after the third examination.

In some languages it may be more natural to reverse the order of the first two clauses and say something like "If after he has shown himself to the priest for his cleansing, the eruption spreads . . ." or "After he has shown himself to the priest . . . it may happen that the eruption spreads. . . . If this happens . . . ."

He shall appear again before the priest: there are many other ways of stating this same fact: "he must return to the priest to be reexamined," or "he must go back for another examination," or "he must present himself to the priest so that he can look at him again." However, in the light of the passive in verse 2, it may be better to translate "he must be brought back" or "they [indefinite] (or, someone) must bring him back."

13.8   RSV   TEV

and the priest shall make an exami-   The priest will examine him again,
nation, and if the eruption has   and if it has spread, he shall pro-
spread in the skin, then the priest   nounce him unclean; it is a dreaded
shall pronounce him unclean; it is   skin disease.
leprosy.

The priest shall make an examination: the form used here differs slightly from what is found in the beginning of verses 5 and 6, where object pronouns occur with the verb, "examine him." In this case there is no object pronoun, but it is understood that the same person is the object of the examination. So this may have to be made clear in the receptor language.

If the eruption has spread: NEB has "if it continues to spread." Mft says "if the eruption still spreads." The idea of "spreading" may mean either that the infected area became larger or that the infection appeared on other parts of the body. But here probably both are intended.

It is leprosy: similar to the TEV reading, NEB has "it is a malignant skin disease," and NIV "it is an infectious disease." See comments on the term "leprosy" in the introduction to this chapter.

13.9   RSV   TEV

"When a man is afflicted with   If anyone has a dreaded skin
leprosy, he shall be brought to the   disease, he shall be brought to the
priest;   priest,

This verse repeats the essential content of verse 2. The passive form, **he shall be brought**, may be rendered "someone must bring him."

13.10   RSV   TEV

and the priest shall make an exami-   who will examine him. If there is a
nation, and if there is a white swell-   white sore on his skin which turns
ing in the skin, which has turned the   the hairs white and is full of pus,
hair white, and there is quick raw
flesh in the swelling,

TEV has joined this verse more closely to the previous one. This may be a helpful model for some other translations to follow.

A white swelling: the term used here is the same as in verse 2, but it is now qualified by the adjective meaning **white** (see verse 3).

Quick raw flesh: the word **quick** in this context means "alive" and therefore sensitive to touch. Many versions translate as in RSV. But others take the whole expression to mean "an ulceration" (NEB), "an ulcer" (NJB), or "a patch of discolored skin" (NJV). TEV renders it more dynamically "full of pus," but this may be going too far.

13.11 RSV TEV

| it is a chronic leprosy in the skin of his body, and the priest shall pronounce him unclean; he shall not shut him up, for he is unclean. | it is a chronic skin disease. The priest shall pronounce him unclean; there is no need to isolate him, because he is obviously unclean. |

A chronic leprosy: that is, it is a skin disease that is seen as permanent, deep-rooted, or well established. NJB translates "a dormant skin disease," but this also implies that it has not gone away. In some languages one may have to say "it is a disease of the skin that will not go away" or "an advanced stage of the skin disease."

Pronounce him unclean: see verse 8.

He shall not shut him up: compare verses 4 and 5. It is not necessary to close this person up for observation and reexamination seven days later. It has already been determined that he definitely has a dreaded skin disease and must be more permanently isolated from the community. Some languages may say "it is useless to close him up," "there is no reason to shut him up," "closing him up [for later observation] serves no purpose," or "he [the priest] is not required to shut him up for seven days."

He is unclean: both TEV and NJB add "**obviously**," since this is the clear intent in this context.

13.12-13 RSV TEV

| 12 And if the leprosy breaks out in the skin, so that the leprosy covers all the skin of the diseased person from head to foot, so far as the priest can see, 13 then the priest shall make an examination, and if the leprosy has covered all his body, he shall pronounce him clean of the disease; it has all turned white, and he is clean. | 12 If the skin disease spreads and covers the person from head to foot, 13 the priest shall examine him again. If he finds that it actually has covered the whole body, he shall pronounce the person ritually clean. If his whole skin has turned white, he is ritually clean. |

And: it may be better here to use a transition word like "But" (NJB), "However," or perhaps an expression like "On the other hand." The case described in verses 12 and 13 contrasts with what was seen in the previous verse.

Breaks out in the skin: literally, "breaking out it breaks out" or "spreading it spreads." The Hebrew expression is one that uses two forms of the same verb stem for emphasis. Some languages have similar constructions that may be used here, but others will have to resort to adverbs which produce expressions like "really spreads" or "breaks out very much," or a stronger verb like "flourishes" or "runs rampant." The words "break out" may be misleading in some languages, since the idea is not the eruption of an open sore, but extending over a wide area.

From head to foot: this expression indicates the entire body. Other languages may have different ways of saying the same thing, such as "from top to bottom" or some other expression. And in some cases it may even be necessary to add the expression "the whole body" for the sake of clarity.

So far as the priest can see: the priest can only see those parts of the body that are not covered. This is why he must further examine the person to determine whether the parts of the body covered by clothing are also affected by the disease.

Make an examination: in this case it may be better to translate "examine him carefully" or "do a detailed examination [on the person]." TEV adds the word "**again**" here, since the person has already been examined once in verse 10.

It has all turned white: when the disease spreads over the entire surface of the body, it is an indication that it has run its course. White scabs form and eventually fall off.

Shall pronounce him clean: although this condition is also called "leprosy" in many versions, it is a skin condition that is not considered serious and does not require separation from the community. The person is pronounced **clean**, since his symptoms are different. It is the priest who decides whether a skin problem is serious enough to require isolation.

13.14-16

RSV	TEV
14 But when raw flesh appears on him, he shall be unclean. 15 And the priest shall examine the raw flesh, and pronounce him unclean; raw flesh is unclean, for it is leprosy. 16 But if the raw flesh turns again and is changed to white, then he shall come to the priest,	14 But from the moment an open sore appears, he is unclean. 15 The priest shall examine him again, and if he sees an open sore, he shall pronounce him unclean. An open sore means a dreaded skin disease, and the person is unclean. 16 But when the sore heals and becomes white again, the person shall go to the priest,

But: in contrast with the person who is pronounced "clean" in the previous verse, this case is considered **unclean**. The transition word should therefore indicate this contrast.

The primary distinguishing characteristic is the presence of **raw flesh** (see verse 10), which is mentioned four times in these verses. This expression is used of an open sore where the flesh is no longer covered by skin, but exposed and therefore sensitive. This is taken as a sign of a serious disease that must be regarded as making the person unclean.

If the raw flesh turns again: the verb translated "turn" really indicates "healing" in this context and should be so translated in most languages. However, in others a verb like "to change" may be appropriate to represent the idea of healing and will also be closer to the Hebrew.

13.17 RSV	TEV
and the priest shall examine him, and if the disease has turned white, then the priest shall pronounce the diseased person clean; he is clean.	**who will examine him again. If the sore has turned white, he is ritually clean, and the priest shall pronounce him clean.**

And the priest: TEV translates here, as in verse 10, with a relative pronoun which clearly refers to the priest. This provides a more natural structure in English and avoids needless repetition. A similar construction may be used in many other languages.

The disease: this is the same word that is translated "spot" in verse 3. It refers to the affected area on the skin.

He is clean: in some languages this phrase fits better before the pronouncement of the priest, as in TEV. The statement of the priest can come only after the fact. So it is more logical to state the fact first.

13.18 RSV	TEV
"And when there is in the skin of one's body a boil that has healed,	**If anyone has a boil that has healed**

Verses 18-44 deal with other possible causes of skin diseases. The first paragraph in this section (18-23) concerns boils.

A boil: the word used here is the same as found in Exodus 9.9-11 to describe one of the plagues in Egypt. It results from the infection of a skin gland, which becomes inflamed. It often contains pus. In the case cited here, the infection has subsided and the boil had apparently been healed.

13.19 RSV	TEV
and in the place of the boil there comes a white swelling or a reddish-white spot, then it shall be shown to the priest;	**and if afterward a white swelling or a reddish-white spot appears where the boil was, he shall go to the priest.**

Swelling . . . spot: while TEV has "**spot**" here, the same word seems to be translated "inflammation" in verse 2 above.

Reddish-white: this may be difficult to express in some languages. Translators should investigate the terms used in the receptor language to describe the kind of color change that takes place when a person has a boil.

It shall be shown to the priest: the passive construction in RSV must be made active in some languages. But the formulation of TEV leaves implicit the fact that the affected area must be shown to the priest. In some cases it will be appropriate to use two verbs, "he must go to the priest and show him the spot."

13.20 RSV	TEV
and the priest shall make an examination, and if it appears deeper than the skin and its hair has turned white, then the priest shall pronounce him unclean; it is the disease of leprosy, it has broken out in the boil.	The priest shall examine him, and if the spot seems to be deeper than the surrounding skin and the hairs in it have turned white, he shall pronounce him unclean. It is a dreaded skin disease that has started in the boil.

Make an examination: literally, "the priest shall examine." While no object is expressed in Hebrew, it is understood that the priest will examine either the person or the affected area of the skin. Since both are true, the translator should choose the one that is most natural in the receptor language.

It has broken out in the boil: that is, it has spread from the boil. Or, perhaps better, "it has spread from the place where the boil was." This is the same verb as in verse 12. See the discussion at that point.

13.21 RSV	TEV
But if the priest examines it, and the hair on it is not white and it is not deeper than the skin, but is dim, then the priest shall shut him up seven days;	But if the priest examines it and finds that the hairs in it have not turned white and that it is not deeper than the surrounding skin, but is light in color, the priest shall isolate him for seven days.

If the priest examines it: the wording of both RSV and TEV can give the impression that the priest may or may not do an examination, but that would be wrong. Therefore many modern versions make it clear that the conditional **if** refers to the findings of the priest and not to the examination itself. NEB and JB have "But if the priest on examination finds that . . . ." NJB reorders the same words, "But if on examination the priest finds . . . ." And NIV has "But if, when the priest examines it, there is no white hair . . ." (compare verses 3 and 26).

The hair: this is the collective use of the singular **hair**, but it should be translated by a plural in those languages where this is more natural.

Dim: the word here comes from the same Hebrew root as found in verse 6, where it is translated in the same way in RSV. Some versions use the word "faded" (NJV, NEB, and others), while NAB has "is already dying out." It seems to indicate that the condition does not appear too serious but should be watched for a time. For this reason the person is isolated for seven days.

13.22 RSV	TEV
and if it spreads in the skin, then the priest shall pronounce him unclean; it is diseased.	If the spot spreads, the priest shall pronounce him unclean; he is diseased.

The temporal relationship between verses 21 and 22 may be spelled out if the receptor language requires it. This verse may begin with "Afterwards," or "Then," or something similar.

It is diseased: literally, "it is a mark." The pronoun actually refers to the affected area of the skin, but the dynamic rendering of TEV makes the person the subject. Some versions follow a slightly different Hebrew text so that the translation reads "it is a malignant (or, contagious) skin disease" (NEB, NJB). This reading is not recommended by HOTTP. But what is rejected on textual grounds may be included as implicit information in a functionally equivalent translation.

13.23 RSV	TEV
But if the spot remains in one place and does not spread, it is the scar of the boil; and the priest shall pronounce him clean.	But if it remains unchanged and does not spread, it is only the scar left from the boil, and the priest shall pronounce him ritually clean.

Remains in one place: literally, "stays in its place." That is, if the problem remains confined to the area where it was first discovered. This has practically the same meaning as the phrase that follows: **and does not spread**. So in some languages the two may be translated by a single expression.

Shall pronounce him clean: see verse 6.

13.24 RSV	TEV
"Or, when the body has a burn on its skin and the raw flesh of the burn becomes a spot, reddish-white or white,	In the case of a person who has been burned, if the raw flesh becomes white or reddish-white,

Verses 24-28 make up the second paragraph in this section, and they deal with burns.

When the body has a burn on its skin: this construction is awkward in English. The translators should try to find the most natural way of speaking of a person who has injured his or her skin through contact with fire.

Raw flesh: see verse 10.

Reddish-white or white: this word order reflects the Hebrew but is unnatural in English. TEV has reversed the order of these two elements, because good English style seems to require the mention of the better-known color before the mixture of red and white. Many other languages will require the same kind of order.

13.25   RSV   TEV

the priest shall examine it, and if the hair in the spot has turned white and it appears deeper than the skin, then it is leprosy; it has broken out in the burn, and the priest shall pronounce him unclean; it is a leprous disease.

the priest shall examine him. If the hairs in the spot have turned white and it appears deeper than the surrounding skin, it is a dreaded skin disease that has started in the burn, and the priest shall pronounce him unclean.

Compare this verse with verse 3.

Broken out in: or "spread from." See verses 12 and 20.

In the burn: in some languages it may be more natural to say "in the place where he had been burned" or "in the place where the fire touched."

It is a leprous disease: the repetition of this information a second time in the same verse is judged unnecessary in TEV, and this will also be the case in many other languages.

13.26   RSV   TEV

But if the priest examines it, and the hair in the spot is not white and it is no deeper than the skin, but is dim, the priest shall shut him up seven days,

But if the hairs in it have not turned white and it is not deeper than the surrounding skin, but is light in color, the priest shall isolate him for seven days.

This contrasts with verse 25 and is almost identical with verse 21.

13.27   RSV   TEV

and the priest shall examine him the seventh day; if it is spreading in the skin, then the priest shall pronounce him unclean; it is a leprous disease.

The priest shall examine him again on the seventh day, and if it is spreading, it is a dreaded skin disease, and the priest shall pronounce him unclean.

This verse presents the case of a reexamination with negative results after seven days of isolation. There is no equivalent to it at the beginning of the chapter, but all the elements of meaning are discussed elsewhere. See verses 8 and 22.

13.28   RSV   TEV

But if the spot remains in one place and does not spread in the skin, but is dim, it is a swelling from the burn, and the priest shall pronounce him

But if the spot remains unchanged and does not spread and is light in color, it is not a dreaded skin disease. The priest shall pronounce him

clean; for it is the scar of the burn.   ritually clean, because it is only a
                                                scar from the burn.

The counterpart of verse 27 above. Compare verses 6 and 23.

13.29   RSV   TEV

"When a man or woman has a   When a man or a woman has a
disease on the head or the beard,   sore on the head or the chin,

Verses 29-37 concern sores on the chin under the hair of the beard and on top
of the head.
   A disease on the . . . beard: many English versions prefer to use the term
"chin" in place of **beard** (TEV, NEB, NJB and others). NAB has "on the cheek." The
word used may mean either "**chin**" or **beard**, but in this context it seems to refer
to a disease on the skin underneath the hair on the chin. Since women are
specifically mentioned in this verse, it is probably better to use the word for "**chin**"
in those languages where the hair on the chin of a woman would not be considered
a **beard**. The expression "in the beard" is used by NJV. The exact expression will
depend on how the receptor language normally speaks of such skin problems.

13.30   RSV   TEV

the priest shall examine the disease;   the priest shall examine it. If it seems
and if it appears deeper than the   to be deeper than the surrounding
skin, and the hair in it is yellow and   skin and the hairs in it are yellowish
thin, then the priest shall pronounce   and thin, it is a dreaded skin dis-
him unclean; it is an itch, a leprosy   ease, and he shall pronounce the
of the head or the beard.   person unclean.

   Deeper than the skin: see verse 3.
   Yellow and thin: NAB translates "fine yellow hair," and NEB "hair [that] is
yellow and sparse." The word translated **thin** may also mean "small," or in some
cases "withered." But here it is probably better to think in terms of an area where
there are less hairs and where the hairs are yellow.
   It is an itch: the word used here literally means "a tearing off," something so
annoying that the person who has it cannot keep his hands off it. Various attempts
have been made to identify this with skin diseases known today. Here is a sampling
of what modern versions have done with the word: "a scurf" (NEB); "a scall" (NJV
and NAB); "tinea" (JB); "ringworm" (AT, Mft, and almost all French versions). Only
NIV goes along with the general term **itch** in RSV. Translators should probably use
their own equivalent of "ringworm," or a more general expression as in TEV.

13.31   RSV   TEV

And if the priest examines the itching disease, and it appears no deeper than the skin and there is no black hair in it, then the priest shall shut up the person with the itching disease for seven days,	If, when the priest examines him, the sore does not appear to be deeper than the surrounding skin, but there are still no healthy hairs in it, he shall isolate him for seven days.

See the discussion under verse 21 regarding the conditional form of this sentence. It is interesting to note that in this case TEV makes it clear that the "**If**" applies to the condition of the sore and not to the examination itself.

If: see verse 21.

No black hair in it: the Hebrew clearly has **black hair** (but see verse 30). NEB and NJB have "yellow hair," following the Septuagint. HOTTP recommends "black hairs." But TEV avoids the problem by translating "**no healthy hairs**." Perhaps the receptor language can try something like "no normal hairs."

Shut up . . . for seven days: see comments under verse 4.

13.32-33   RSV   TEV

32 and on the seventh day the priest shall examine the disease; and if the itch has not spread, and there is in it no yellow hair, and the itch appears to be no deeper than the skin, 33 then he shall shave himself, but the itch he shall not shave; and the priest shall shut up the person with the itching disease for seven days more;	32 The priest shall examine the sore again on the seventh day, and if it has not spread and there are no yellowish hairs in it and it does not seem to be deeper than the surrounding skin, 33 the person shall shave the head except the area around the sore. The priest shall then isolate him for another seven days.

Verse 32 is very similar to verse 5.

He shall shave himself: literally, "he must be shaved," but the passive cannot be translated into all languages. The pronoun refers to the sick person rather than to the priest and this should be made clear in the receptor language. NAB and Mft translate "the man," while AT has "the person," and NJB "the sick person."

As the text stands it may give the impression that only the beard is to be shaved. But the intention is surely that the area around the affected part is to be shaved, whether it is on the head or in the beard. TEV provides a good model to follow at this point (assuming that "**head**" includes the chin as well as the top of the head). Wenham translates "he must shave himself except for the severely infected area."

Seven days more: see verse 4.

13.34   RSV   TEV

and on the seventh day the priest   On the seventh day the priest shall
shall examine the itch, and if the itch   again examine the sore, and if it has
has not spread in the skin and it   not spread and does not seem to be
appears to be no deeper than the   deeper than the surrounding skin, he
skin, then the priest shall pronounce   shall pronounce him ritually clean.
him clean; and he shall wash his   The person shall wash his clothes,
clothes, and be clean.   and he will be clean.

Compare verse 6.

Examine: better, "reexamine" or "examine again."

Wash his clothes: see 11.25.

13.35   RSV   TEV

But if the itch spreads in the skin   But if the sore spreads after he has
after his cleansing,   been pronounced clean,

Compare verses 7.

His cleansing: this refers to the pronouncement by the priest that the sick
person was clean. The passive formulation of TEV will have to be made active in
some languages: "after the priest has pronounced him clean."

13.36   RSV   TEV

then the priest shall examine him,   the priest shall examine him again. If
and if the itch has spread in the skin,   the sore has spread, he need not
the priest need not seek for the yel-   look for yellowish hairs; the person
low hair; he is unclean.   is obviously unclean.

Compare verse 8.

Yellow hair: see verse 30.

13.37   RSV   TEV

But if in his eyes the itch is checked,   But if in the priest's opinion the sore
and black hair has grown in it, the   has not spread and healthy hairs are
itch is healed, he is clean; and the   growing in it, the sore has healed,
priest shall pronounce him clean.   and the priest shall pronounce him
                                           ritually clean.

This is the opposite of verses 35-36. Compare verse 23.

In his eyes: that is, "in the judgment of the priest." See verse 5.

The itch is checked: literally, "the itch remains." NASB has "the scale has remained." But the intent is almost certainly that the disease has not changed but has remained as it was. Some languages may say "the itch did not get worse" or "the skin has not changed."

Black hair: see verse 31.

13.38   RSV   TEV

"When a man or a woman has spots on the skin of the body, white spots,

When a man or a woman has white spots on the skin,

Verses 38-39 have to do with harmless skin conditions.

White spots: literally, "spots-spots white ones." The word translated **spots** is the same as the one found in verse 2, but here it is reduplicated. It has been translated "streaked with white discolorations" (NJV); "inflamed patches on the skin" (NEB); "spotted with white blotches" (NAB); "shiny spots" (JB); "inflamed spots" (AT); "bright spots, bright white spots" (Mft).

On the skin of the body: in many languages the words **of the body** will be unnecessary, since they are implied in the word **skin** (see TEV).

13.39   RSV   TEV

the priest shall make an examination, and if the spots on the skin of the body are of a dull white, it is tetter that has broken out in the skin; he is clean.

the priest shall examine that person. If the spots are dull white, it is only a blemish that has broken out on the skin; the person is ritually clean.

A dull white: literally, "dull ones, white ones." The term rendered **dull** here is the same as translated "dim" in verse 21.

A tetter: the Hebrew word used here comes from a root which means "to shine." It appears only here in all the Old Testament and seems to indicate some kind of harmless eruption on the skin. The word found in RSV and many other English versions is not well known. The meaning is closer to TEV, **"only a blemish,"** or NIV "a harmless rash." FRCL proposes "the problem which has developed is not serious . . . ."

Broken out: compare verses 12, 20, and 25.

13.40-41   RSV   TEV

40 "If a man's hair has fallen from his head, he is bald but he is clean. 41 And if a man's hair has fallen from his forehead and temples,

40-41 If a man loses his hair at the back or the front of his head, this does not make him unclean.

**he has baldness of the forehead but
he is clean.**

Verses 40-44 deal with baldness in men. Note that verses 40 and 41 are combined in TEV and in GECL, since essentially the same thing is said of two slightly different types of baldness.

If a man's hair has fallen: literally, "And a man, when his head loses its hair." In contrast with verse 38 above, women are not mentioned. Languages may have many different ways of describing what happens in baldness. Some may speak of "losing hair" (as in Hebrew and in TEV), or of hair "falling out" or "disappearing," or of the head being "polished" or "bare," or some other expression. Whatever is natural in the receptor language should determine the translation of the verb here.

From his head: this obviously refers to the crown or top of the head and should be translated in such a way that it contrasts with the terms in verse 41.

From his forehead and temples: literally, "from the front of his head." This contrasts with a bald spot on the top of the head and is characterized by the loss of hair in the front.

Baldness of the forehead: the Hebrew had a special word for this type of baldness as opposed to the baldness on the top of the head. It is related to the verb meaning "to be high" and is always used in contrast with the baldness of the top of the head. Compare the English expression "to have a high forehead."

13.42	RSV	TEV
	But if there is on the bald head or the bald forehead a reddish-white diseased spot, it is leprosy breaking out on his bald head or his bald forehead.	But if a reddish-white spot appears on the bald spot, it is a dreaded skin disease.

But: contrary to the case of normal baldness, this verse introduces the idea of baldness due to disease, which was thought to make the person unclean. The transition word should indicate this contrast.

On the bald head or the bald forehead: since both types of baldness are being discussed here, it may not be necessary in some languages to distinguish them and mention each one explicitly. The use of **"the bald spot"** in TEV covers both cases. In some languages one may say "the place where there is no hair" or "the place where the hair has fallen out."

A reddish-white diseased spot: same expression as in verse 24.

Leprosy: see verse 2 and the introduction to this chapter.

Breaking out . . . . : see verse 12. The repetition of the location of the baldness may be omitted if it would be awkward in the receptor language.

13.43   RSV   TEV

Then the priest shall examine him, and if the diseased swelling is reddish-white on his bald head or on his bald forehead, like the appearance of leprosy in the skin of the body,	The priest shall examine him, and if there is a reddish-white sore,

Then: the transition word thus translated in RSV is the common conjunction that is usually translated "and." It may easily be left untranslated here.

On his bald head or on his bald forehead: these words are again repeated in Hebrew but may be summarized in translation with "the bald part" or "the place where the hair has been lost." Or it may simply be left implicit, as in TEV.

Like the appearance of leprosy: see verse 2 and the introduction to this chapter on the word translated **leprosy**. The meaning of the whole phrase seems to be "similar to the disease on other parts of the skin [other than in the hair]" (see NAB).

13.44   RSV   TEV

he is a leprous man, he is unclean; the priest must pronounce him unclean; his disease is on his head.	the priest shall pronounce him unclean, because of the dreaded skin disease on his head.

This verse may be seen as containing four different clauses. The first two may be related as follows: "Since he has a dreaded skin disease, he is unclean" or "this man is unclean because he has a dreaded skin disease." The relationship between the third and fourth sentence is also one of cause and effect: "The priest must pronounce the man unclean because of the disease on his head." The words **"because of"** do not appear in RSV, but something similar should probably be found in most dynamic translations. In addition to TEV, the following versions also clearly indicate this causal relationship: NIV, AT, and NAB.

13.45   RSV   TEV

"The leper who has the disease shall wear torn clothes and let the hair of his head hang loose, and he shall cover his upper lip and cry, 'Unclean, unclean.'	A person who has a dreaded skin disease must wear torn clothes, leave his hair uncombed, cover the lower part of his face, and call out, "Unclean, unclean!"

Verses 45-46 describe the behavior required of the person who has been declared unclean by the priest.

The leper: that is, the diseased person. The term "leprosy" has already been dealt with at the beginning of this chapter. But it should be stressed here that the word **leper** in particular is to be avoided, since it marks out individuals as outcasts from society and has a particularly devastating effect on their lives.

Wear torn clothes: see 10.6. The tearing of clothing is a traditional way of showing that a person is in mourning. Since the person with the dreaded skin disease is considered almost dead, he is required to mourn. In some translations this may be explained in a footnote (as in FRCL), but in others it may be possible to say "wear torn clothes to show his sadness" or something similar.

Let the hair of his head hang loose: see 10.6. The words **of his head** are unnecessary in most languages since they would be implied in **hair**. Some scholars understand this to mean "his head shall be left bare" (NJV), but this is unlikely. Most experts follow the interpretation "to leave the hair uncared for." This may be translated in some languages as "must not comb his hair."

Cover his upper lip: the word translated **upper lip** has been understood by some as referring to a "moustache" (NASB, AT, Mft), while others translate as RSV (NEB, NJV, JB). But the meaning seems to be the entire lower part of the face (see TEV, NIV). In some languages translators will be required to indicate what is used to cover the lower part of the face. In those cases, the hand is probably the most logical thing to be used.

Unclean, unclean: in many languages it will be wise to use a complete sentence to translate these words: "Unclean, I am unclean," or "I am unclean, I am unclean," or "Look out, I am unclean." This was to serve as a warning to any other members of the community who might accidentally approach the diseased person.

13.46 RSV TEV

He shall remain unclean as long as he has the disease; he is unclean; he shall dwell alone in a habitation outside the camp.

He remains unclean as long as he has the disease, and he must live outside the camp, away from others.

Remain unclean . . . is unclean: the repetition may be unnecessary in many languages.

He shall dwell alone: in many languages it will be helpful to the reader to indicate the relationship between this phrase and the one before it. FRCL proposes "this is why he must live alone." Or one may use a transition word like "therefore" or "so." It may also be helpful to make it clearer what **alone** means by saying something like "apart from the rest of the community" or "away from normal (or, healthy) people." The emphasis is not on complete separation from all others, since people with this condition were permitted to live with each other, but they had to be away from the rest of the community (see 2 Kgs 7.3-10).

TEV Section Heading: **"Laws concerning Mildew."**

The term rendered "mildew" here is identical with the one rendered "leprosy" earlier in this chapter. This is reflected in the NAB heading "Leprosy of Clothes." But the term "leprosy" is clearly to be avoided here. Some other possible headings for this section are "Rules about contaminated clothing" or "Uncleanness in clothes and skins" (NEB).

13.47

RSV	TEV
"When there is a leprous disease in a garment, whether a woolen or a linen garment,	When there is mildew[d] on clothing, whether wool or linen,

[d] MILDEW: *The Hebrew word for "dreaded skin disease" and "mildew" is the same.*

In Hebrew the word for **garment** or **"clothing"** occurs three times in this short verse. But even the usually literal RSV has reduced this to two. And in many languages the sentence may be structured in such a way as to use the word only once without losing any of the meaning (as in TEV).

Leprous disease in a garment: the RSV translation demonstrates the error of the traditional translation. Articles of clothing cannot possibly have "leprosy" in any modern sense of the word. The ancient Israelites obviously saw some kind of relationship between skin diseases in human beings and a growth on nonhuman objects like clothing and the walls of houses (see 14.33-53). But in most languages around the world today, no such relationship exists. If we are to translate naturally, a totally different word will be required in this context. TEV, NEB, and NIV all have **"mildew."** In the receptor language it may be necessary to resort to a longer phrase such as "a growth caused by a fungus" or simply "a growth of foreign matter." Some languages apparently use the same word for "mildew" on cloth and for "rust" on metal.

13.48

RSV	TEV
in warp or woof of linen or wool, or in a skin or in anything made of skin,	or on any piece of linen or wool cloth or on leather or anything made of leather,

In warp or woof: this is the meaning that the words of the text have taken in modern Hebrew. But in the text of Leviticus, such a meaning is unlikely. People familiar with weaving will be aware that this expression is used to speak of the threads of yarn that go in different directions. But it is hardly possible that this is the meaning here. It is difficult to see how the threads going in one direction could be affected by the mildew without affecting those running at right angles to them. Nor would the requirement that the affected part be torn out make sense (verse 56), because the whole garment would be destroyed. While the interpretation is far from certain, the meaning of these words is probably "any woven or knitted material," as in AT, NAB, and NIV, as well as TOB in French. TEV has reduced this to **"any piece,"** but such reduction should probably be avoided in the receptor language, if possible.

Linen: see 6.10.

Wool: the soft wavy undercoat of hairy animals such as sheep is used in the Middle East to weave a fabric from which clothing is made. In some languages one may have to translate **linen or wool** as "cloth made from the fibers of a plant or from the hair of a sheep."

A skin . . . made of skin: some languages will have a special word for "leather" and "leather materials," but many will use the same word as for "the skin of an animal."

13.49 RSV TEV

if the disease shows greenish or reddish in the garment, whether in warp or woof or in skin or in anything made of skin, it is a leprous disease and shall be shown to the priest.

if it is greenish or reddish, it is a spreading mildew and must be shown to the priest.

The disease: that is, the contaminated or affected spot.

Whether in warp or woof: see verse 48. But it may be possible to leave these words implicit in the receptor language. In the same way the words **skin** and **anything made of skin** may also be left implicit, as in TEV.

Greenish: sometimes translators have to render this color term by means of a comparison, using grass, or copper, or some other object that is well known in the culture.

Shall be shown to the priest: those languages without passive forms will have to reword this phrase to say something like "the owner must show it to the priest" or "someone must ask the priest to examine it."

13.50 RSV TEV

And the priest shall examine the disease, and shut up that which has the disease for seven days;

The priest shall examine it and put the object away for seven days.

Shut up: this is the same expression as it used in verse 4 and elsewhere in this chapter, but since the context is different here, the verb may also be different. When speaking of things rather than persons, some languages may say "put away," "put aside," "isolated," "hidden," or "separated."

That which has the disease: some languages may prefer "the thing which has the spot" or simply "the object" [referred to earlier].

For seven days: see verse 4.

13.51 RSV TEV

then he shall examine the disease on the seventh day. If the disease has spread in the garment, in warp or woof, or in the skin, whatever be the

He shall examine it again on the seventh day, and if the mildew has spread, the object is unclean.

use of the skin, the disease is a
malignant leprosy; it is unclean.

Some translators may prefer to restructure the beginning of this verse by saying "Seven days later, the priest must reexamine the object." It may also be necessary to leave implicit the list of different kinds of objects that is repeated from the previous verses. Compare TEV.

Whatever be the use of the skin: this parenthetical information is intended to make it clear that such skin would have to be pronounced unclean regardless of the purpose for which the skin had been previously used. In some cases one may prefer to put this in parentheses. TEV has simply left it implicit, but it may be better to make it explicit in the receptor language.

A malignant leprosy: this seems to mean a persistent type of mildew. It may be translated "an incurable condition" or "a destructive mildew" (NIV), or "a rotting mould" (NEB).

13.52   RSV   TEV

And he shall burn the garment, whether diseased in warp or woof, woolen or linen, or anything of skin, for it is a malignant leprosy; it shall be burned in the fire.

The priest shall burn it, because it is a spreading mildew which must be destroyed by fire.

He: the pronoun refers to the priest, and this should probably be made explicit in many languages.

A malignant leprosy: see verse 51.

It shall be burned in the fire: the words **in the fire** will be unnecessary in many languages, since they are implied by the verb "to burn." The passive formulation must become active in other languages, and the agent will have to be specified. Translators may consider "he must burn it" or "the priest must have it burned" or ". . . cause it to burn."

13.53   RSV   TEV

"And if the priest examines, and the disease has not spread in the garment in warp or woof or in anything of skin,

But if, when he examines it, the priest finds that the mildew has not spread on the object,

And: since this verse involves the contrary of the case introduced in verse 51, it should begin with a transition word marking contrast, such as "**But**," "However," or something similar. See also verses 21 and 26.

If the priest examines: as in verses 21 and 31, the conditional **if** goes with the findings of the priest and not with the examination. The RSV rendering reflects the Hebrew text of this verse, which provides no object for the verb. But the implied object is clearly the infection (compare verses 21 and 31). In English as well as many other languages, it is unnatural for the verb "examine" to stand without an object. This is why TEV has "**when he examines it.**" In some cases it may be necessary to indicate which examination is involved, by saying "when he examines it on the seventh day."

13.54   RSV   TEV

| then the priest shall command that they wash the thing in which is the disease, and he shall shut it up seven days more; | he shall order that it be washed and put away for another seven days. |

The priest: in some cases it may be more natural and equally understandable to use the pronoun here.

Command that they wash the thing: in some languages a causative form will be more natural: "he must cause it to be washed." See comments on 11.25 with regard to "washing."

Shut it up seven days more: this is the same expression as at the end of verse 4, but since the context speaks of things rather than persons, a different expression may be used.

13.55   RSV   TEV

| and the priest shall examine the diseased thing after it has been washed. And if the diseased spot has not changed color, though the disease has not spread, it is unclean; you shall burn it in the fire, whether the leprous spot is on the back or on the front. | Then he shall examine it, and if the mildew has not changed color, even though it has not spread, it is still unclean; you must burn the object, whether the rot is on the front or the back. |

Examine: this is actually a reexamination, since it was already examined in verses 50 and 51 (compare verse 34). In some languages the beginning of the verse may be restructured to say "As soon as it has been washed, he must look at it again. If the mildew has not changed . . . ."

Has not changed in color: it will be clearer in some languages to say "If it is still greenish or reddish" (verse 49).

You shall burn it in the fire: as in verse 52, **in the fire** may be omitted as redundant. But the construction of the other part is not the same. The pronoun **you** (singular) is used in this verse in place of "he" of verse 52. This pronoun may refer to the priest or to the owner of the object that is to be burned. JB takes it to mean the same as verse 52 and translates with the passive "It must be destroyed by fire." But NJB reverts to the more literal "you will burn it." But it is possible to say "the priest will cause it to be burned" (see verse 52). While most versions retain the second person pronoun, the referent is unclear in TEV and RSV alike. In verse 57,

TEV translates the same expression as referring to the owner of the object. This should also be done in this verse if using a passive (as in NAB, JB, and NJV) is not possible in the receptor language.

Leprous spot: the word translated "leprosy" elsewhere is not used here. This word in Hebrew literally means "a boring or eating out." The translation "**rot**" is good (TEV, NEB). Translators may also consider Mft's "it has eaten into the stuff."

On the back or on the front: the Hebrew uses the same two words that are used to describe the two types of baldness in verse 42. But here the context is very different. NEB translates "on the right side or the wrong"; NJV "on its inner side or on its outer side"; NIV "one side or the other"; NJB "through and through." In the context of clothing it seems to make more sense to speak of "inside and outside."

13.56	RSV	TEV
	"But if the priest examines, and the disease is dim after it is washed, he shall tear the spot out of the garment or the skin or the warp or woof;	But if, when the priest examines it again, the mildew has faded, he shall tear it out of the clothing or leather.

This is the counterpart of the previous verse. It should be introduced in such a way as to show contrast.

If: see the comments on verse 21 and 31.

The disease: that is, the affected area or spot.

Dim: see verse 6.

He shall tear . . . : this is in contrast with the complete destruction of the object in verse 55. For this reason one may wish to say something like "he only has to tear it out" or "he must limit himself to tearing out the affected area."

13.57	RSV	TEV
	then if it appears again in the garment, in warp or woof, or in anything of skin, it is spreading; you shall burn with fire that in which is the disease.	Then, if the mildew reappears, it is spreading again, and the owner shall burn the object.

It: the pronoun refers to the mildew (or the "greenish or reddish spot"), and this should probably be made clear in most languages.

It is spreading: the word used here comes from the same root as the verb rendered "to break out" in verses 12, 20, and 25 and may be translated in a similar manner in the receptor language.

You shall burn with fire: compare verse 55. In this case TEV rightly takes the second person singular pronoun to refer to the owner of the object.

13.58 RSV TEV

But the garment, warp or woof, or anything of skin from which the disease departs when you have washed it, shall then be washed a second time, and be clean."

If he washes the object and the spot disappears, he shall wash it again, and it will be ritually clean.

Warp or woof: yet another repetition that may be considered unnatural and unnecessary. It may be left implicit.

From which the disease departs: NJV restructures the first part of this verse slightly and begins "If, however, the affection disappears . . . ." This may serve as a good model for other languages.

When you have washed it: TEV again takes the second person singular pronoun to refer to the owner of the object. But here the pronoun "**he**" is substituted.

13.59 RSV TEV

This is the law for a leprous disease in a garment of wool or linen, either in warp or woof, or in anything of skin, to decide whether it is clean or unclean.

This, then, is the law about mildew on clothing, whether it is wool or linen, or on linen or wool cloth or on anything made of leather; this is how the decision is made as to whether it is ritually clean or unclean.

This verse is a summary statement regarding the instructions about mildew on clothing. The word **law** should probably be translated as a plural in many languages, since there are a number of different regulations involved. NIV reads "These are the regulations," while NJV has "This is the procedure." See 6.8 and 11.46-47.

To decide whether it is clean or unclean: this element was omitted in earlier editions of TEV but is now included in "**this is how . . . unclean.**" It may be rendered in a separate sentence saying "These regulations allow you [Israelites] to determine whether these things are clean or unclean."

Chapter 14

TEV Section Heading: "**Purification after Having Skin Diseases**."

Some other possible headings may be "What must be done with people who have skin diseases" or "How to treat people with skin diseases." The discussion of the terms "leper" and "leprosy" at the beginning of chapter 13 is equally important to this chapter.

The first part of this chapter describes the rituals necessary for a person to be accepted again by other members of the community after having been cured of a dreaded skin disease.

14.1-2   RSV   TEV

1 The LORD said to Moses, 2 "This shall be the law of the leper for the day of his cleansing. He shall be brought to the priest;

1 The LORD gave Moses 2 the following regulations about the ritual purification of a person cured of a dreaded skin disease. On the day he is to be pronounced clean, he shall be brought to the priest,

Said to Moses: see 4.1.

The law: a collective singular which should probably be translated as a plural in most languages. See the comments on 6.8.

The day of his cleansing: while the actual process of being cured of the skin disease would take a long time, this phrase refers to the day when the priest declares that he is ritually clean and is no longer to be isolated. This comes at the end of the healing process.

He shall be brought to the priest: this apparently simple phrase is the cause of numerous difficulties for the translator. First, the exact meaning is questionable. While most versions go along with the interpretation of RSV and TEV, some feel that this does not present a logical progression of events. As long as the diseased person is not definitely cured, he should not be brought into the camp. And since the pronoun translated **he** may also be understood as referring to the problem rather than the person, the translation can be "When the matter has been brought to the attention of the priest . . . ," or "When it [the case] has been reported to the priest . . ." (NJV), or "His case must be brought to the priest . . ." (AT). In either case, it is probably better to consider this as a relative clause which is connected with the beginning of verse 3. Finally, the verb is passive in form and must be rendered actively in many languages. The subject should then be an indefinite "they" or "someone." When all of these problems have been considered, the recommended rendering will be something like "When someone reports the matter to the priest, he shall go out . . . ."

14.3 RSV TEV

and the priest shall go out of the camp, and the priest shall make an examination. Then, if the leprous disease is healed in the leper,

and the priest shall take him outside the camp and examine him. If the disease is healed,

Out of the camp: according to 13.46 the diseased person was required to live in a special place away from others in the community. The priest, therefore, had to go away from the place where healthy people lived and into the area of the diseased.

Shall make an examination: or, "shall look carefully at that person."

If the leprous disease is healed: in some languages one must say "If the person is healed" or "If the disease is gone." Compare 13.2.

14.4 RSV TEV

the priest shall command them to take for him who is to be cleansed two living clean birds and cedarwood and scarlet stuff and hyssop;

the priest shall order that two ritually clean birds be brought, along with a piece of cedar wood, a red cord, and a sprig of hyssop.

The priest shall command them: literally, "the priest shall command and he shall take . . . ." The RSV rendering actually follows a slightly different text which reads ". . . and they shall take . . . ." In either case, the identity of the person or persons referred to by this pronoun is uncertain. But it is clearly indefinite as in 8.31 and 9.21. The TEV rendering with a passive verb is not helpful to those languages where passives are not used. If an indefinite third person singular or plural pronoun can be used naturally in such a context in the receptor language, then it should be used here. Otherwise it may be necessary to say something like "the priest shall order someone to bring . . . ."

For him who is to be cleansed: TEV leaves this information implicit. But the text makes clear that these actions are to be performed by one or more unnamed individuals on behalf of the diseased person.

Two living clean birds: the two birds that are to be brought must meet two requirements: (1) they must still be alive when they are presented; and (2) they must not be from among those birds that were considered ritually unacceptable by the Jews (see 11.13-19). If the receptor language requires a distinction between large birds and small ones, the word for "small birds" should probably be used here. Note that TEV leaves implicit the fact that the birds must be alive when presented. However, it is probably advisable to make this explicit in the receptor language.

Cedarwood: see FFB, page 107. In many languages it will be necessary to know what quantity of wood or what size **"piece"** is intended. While we cannot be certain, probably it was a piece that could be carried in one hand of a single individual. In those languages where cedar trees are unknown, it may be necessary to use a more general expression like "a piece of wood with a strong smell" or something similar.

Scarlet stuff: the word translated **scarlet** here normally refers to "dark red cloth." The other word literally means the worm or insect (called "cochineal") which produces a dark red color used as a dye. In this context the entire expression is thought to refer to a kind of string (AT), thread (MFT), yarn (NIV, NAB), or cord (TEV) which was dark red in color. If the receptor language makes such distinctions naturally, the color should be stated as "dark red." Otherwise the closest natural equivalent will have to be considered adequate.

Hyssop: NEB and Mft render this word as "marjoram," but most versions retain the traditional rendering **hyssop**. See FFB, page 129-130. In some languages it will be necessary to say "a branch of hyssop," or "a stick of hyssop," or "a plant called hyssop." Where hyssop is unknown, it may be necessary to transliterate the word and give a full explanation in the glossary.

14.5   RSV   TEV

and the priest shall command them to kill one of the birds in an earthen vessel over running water.	Then the priest shall order that one of the birds be killed over a clay bowl containing fresh spring water.

And: in some languages it will probably be advisable to use a different transition word here. "**Then**" is used in NJB, NAB, and AT as well as TEV.

Shall command them: the problem here is identical with the one in verse 4 above. Although there is doubt about whether the pronoun in the original was singular or plural, there is no doubt that it is indefinite in meaning. See HOTTP, page 179.

In an earthen vessel: the preposition "in" is not to be taken literally. The translator should certainly be careful not to give the impression that the person killing the bird is inside the clay pot. The Hebrew preposition implies that the action is rather to be performed over the clay pot so that the blood of the bird falls into the pot and is mixed with the spring water.

Running water: literally, "living water." This refers to water from a spring rather than from a cistern or a well. Flowing water, which would have been considered fresh and clean, is what is called for in this ritual.

14.6   RSV   TEV

He shall take the living bird with the cedarwood and the scarlet stuff and the hyssop, and dip them and the living bird in the blood of the bird that was killed over the running water;	He shall take the other bird and dip it, together with the cedar wood, the red cord, and the hyssop, in the blood of the bird that was killed.

He: the pronoun here refers to the priest.

The living bird: it may be more natural to say "**the other bird**" in some languages, as in TEV. Others may say "the remaining bird, the live one." Special care should be taken to distinguish clearly between the live bird and the one that was killed, which is mentioned at the end of this verse.

With ... and ... and ...: this is translated "together with" by TEV and indicates that all these items were dipped simultaneously into the water. The translation should not give the impression of a series of dippings.

Over the running water: although the RSV translation is different here, the words are essentially the same as in the previous verse. The repetition of this information here may be unnecessary in some languages.

14.7 RSV	TEV
and he shall sprinkle it seven times upon him who is to be cleansed of leprosy; then he shall pronounce him clean, and shall let the living bird go into the open field.	He shall sprinkle the blood seven times on the person who is to be purified from his skin disease, and then he shall pronounce him clean. He shall let the live bird fly away over the open fields.

Seven times: see 4.6.

Upon him who is to be cleansed: it will be better to use a simpler and more natural expression in a number of languages. One may consider "the person who had been healed," or "the person who used to have the skin disease," or "the person about to be declared clean." But Wenham's suggestion, "who is being cleansed," may be better. It emphasizes the ongoing character of the process. This phrase is repeated in verses 7, 8, and 14. Compare the translation of the same expression in verse 4, where TEV leaves it implicit. Some other possible models are ". . . on the person needing cleansing" or ". . . on the person whose leprosy healed."

Into the open field: this expression simply means that the bird is allowed to go free and fly wherever it wishes. It does not imply that the priest attempts to guide the freed bird in any particular direction. In some languages it may be better to say simply "let the living [remaining] bird go free."

He shall pronounce him clean: this is actually only the first step in the process of purification. The following verses indicate that there are other steps necessary before the person is completely accepted by the community.

14.8 RSV	TEV
And he who is to be cleansed shall wash his clothes, and shave off all his hair, and bathe himself in water, and he shall be clean; and after that	The person shall wash his clothes, shave off all his hair, and take a bath; he will then be ritually clean. He may enter the camp, but he must

he shall come into the camp, but shall dwell outside his tent seven days.	live outside his tent for seven days.

He who is to be cleansed: this expression is identical with the one used in verses 4 and 7, but in this case an even shorter phrase may be used, since this is the third occurrence. It may also be confusing to the reader to use the words **to be cleansed** here, since this would seem to imply a still future event. He has, in fact, already been pronounced clean in verse 7.

Wash his clothes: see 11.25.

Shave off all his hair: this apparently refers to all the hair on his entire body, or at least on his whole head. In the following verse, where he is required to shave himself a second time, greater detail is given. In some languages it may be more natural to give this detail here and provide a briefer reference in verse 9. In such cases it is advisable to put the verse numbers 8 and 9 together and then give the content of the two verses.

Bathe himself in water: the use of the words **in water** with the verb "to bathe" will be considered repetitive and unnecessary in many languages. In others it may be necessary to say "wash his body" as opposed to **wash his clothes** above.

Shall come into the camp: that is, he shall join the normal, healthy members of the community with whom he had been forbidden contact while he was diseased (13.46).

Shall dwell outside his tent seven days: just as the newborn is required to wait seven days to be fully accepted as a part of the community, so the person healed of this skin disease must also wait seven days before he finds complete acceptance.

14.9 RSV	TEV
And on the seventh day he shall shave all his hair off his head; he shall shave off his beard and his eyebrows, all his hair. Then he shall wash his clothes, and bathe his body in water, and he shall be clean.	On the seventh day he shall again shave his head, his beard, his eyebrows, and all the rest of the hair on his body; he shall wash his clothes and take a bath, and then he will be ritually clean.

This verse repeats and amplifies the same expressions used in the previous verse. See the comments on the above verse. The important thing here is to make it clear in the receptor language that these rituals are to be performed a second time after the passage of the seven days mentioned at the end of verse 8.

He shall be clean: this is the completion of the second stage in the ritual of purification (compare verse 7). One may translate "he shall be completely clean" or "his ritual cleansing shall be finished."

14.10 RSV TEV

"And on the eighth day he shall take two male lambs without blemish, and one ewe lamb a year old without blemish, and a cereal offering of three tenths of an ephah of fine flour mixed with oil, and one log of oil.

On the eighth day he shall bring two male lambs and one female lamb a year old that are without any defects, five pounds [three kilograms] of flour mixed with olive oil, and half a pint [a third of a liter] of olive oil.

Verses 10-20 describe the part of the purification ritual which reestablishes the relationship between the formerly diseased person and God.

Two male lambs without blemish . . . : NEB follows a different Hebrew text and adds here "yearling," but this is not recommended by HOTTP. On the terms **lambs** and **ewe lamb**, see FFB, pages 75-76.

Without blemish: see 1.3 and 22.17-25.

Three tenths of an ephah: TEV has "**five pounds**" in the American edition, but the British edition has "three kilograms," and FRCL has "nine kilograms." The NJB footnote estimates that the amount is 13.5 liters, while the NIV footnote has 6.5 liters. The exact equivalent of this amount is obviously uncertain. Some commentators speculate that **three tenths** were necessary because there were three lambs, but the evidence for this is less than conclusive. The receptor language should translate as naturally as possible, using whatever measuring system is normally used of dry substances like flour. Compare 5.11 and 6.20 as well as Exodus 16.36 and Ruth 2.17.

Fine flour: see 2.1.

One log of oil: as usual, this refers to olive oil. The most natural term used in measuring liquids should be employed here. It should be the equivalent of about "a third of a liter" (British TEV) or "**half a pint**" (American TEV). The same amount is also used in verses 12, 15, 21, and 24.

14.11 RSV TEV

And the priest who cleanses him shall set the man who is to be cleansed and these things before the LORD, at the door of the tent of meeting.

The priest shall take the man and these offerings to the entrance of the Tent of the LORD's presence.

Who cleanses him . . . who is to be cleansed: the information in these two clauses may be left implicit in many languages. This will also simplify the structure of this otherwise complicated verse.

These things: the Hebrew has only the pronoun "them." But this clearly refers to the offerings mentioned in the previous verse. In many languages it will be better to use a more specific term than the word **things**. Compare "his offerings" (NIV and NEB) and "**these offerings**" (TEV).

The tent of meeting: see 1.1.

14.12   RSV   TEV

And the priest shall take one of the | Then the priest shall take one of the
male lambs, and offer it for a guilt | male lambs and together with the
offering, along with the log of oil, | half pint [one-third of a liter] of oil he
and wave them for a wave offering | shall offer it as a repayment offering.
before the LORD; | He shall present them as a special
| gift to the LORD for the priest.

And: translators should consider whether this is the most natural transition word to use in this context. NIV, NEB, Mft, and TEV have "**Then . . . .**"

Guilt offering: see 5.6.

He: the implied subject, "**the priest**," is supplied in TEV in place of the pronoun. However, the addition of "**for the priest**" at the end of the verse is unnatural and should probably read "for himself" or be left out altogether.

Wave them for a wave offering: see the discussion at 7.30.

14.13   RSV   TEV

and he shall kill the lamb in the place | He shall kill the lamb in the holy
where they kill the sin offering and | place where the animals for the sin
the burnt offering, in the holy place; | offerings and the burnt offerings are
for the guilt offering, like the sin | killed. He must do this because the
offering, belongs to the priest; it is | repayment offering, like the sin offer-
most holy. | ing, belongs to the priest and is very
| holy.

The structure of this verse is somewhat awkward in RSV. Translators should remember that their translations are to follow the natural structure of their own language and not imitate the structure of RSV or TEV.

Where they kill . . . : the most reliable Hebrew texts have "where he slaughters . . . ." But the pronoun is indefinite and has a passive meaning (see verses 4 and 5 above). On the translation of the verb **kill** as "slaughter," see 1.5.

Sin offering: see 4.14.

Burnt offering: see 1.3.

The holy place: this most probably does not refer to the "Holy Place" just outside the "Most Holy Place." It would be unthinkable that an animal should be slaughtered in the sanctuary itself. This expression probably refers to "that sacred place where animals are usually killed." JB renders the expression "that spot inside the sacred precincts where victims . . . are immolated." See the discussion at 6.26 and 10.17

For: TEV clarifies the meaning of this transition word, using the phrase "**He must do this because . . . .**" A similar clarification may be necessary in the receptor language.

It is most holy: see 2.3. As is frequently the case with the use of this phrase, it seems almost to be supplied later as an afterthought. However, it serves as an emphatic reminder of the special nature of the action described.

14.14 RSV	TEV
The priest shall take some of the blood of the guilt offering, and the priest shall put it on the tip of the right ear of him who is to be cleansed, and on the thumb of his right hand, and on the great toe of his right foot.	The priest shall take some of the blood of the lamb and put it on the lobe of the right ear, on the thumb of the right hand, and on the big toe of the right foot of the man who is to be declared ritually clean.

The subject, **the priest**, is given a second time in RSV, following the Hebrew. But this will probably be unnecessary and distracting in many languages. In fact, even some Hebrew texts substitute the pronoun for the second occurrence (see HOTTP, pages 180-181). For the rest of this verse, compare 8.23-24.

The guilt offering: that is, "the lamb."

Him who is to be cleansed: or some languages may require "of the person who is being cleansed," since the process has already begun. And in some cases this may be left implicit and simply rendered "the person." Compare verses 4, 7, and 8, where the same expression occurs. In view of the frequent repetition of the phrase in this passage, it may be left implicit in some languages.

His right hand . . . his right foot: the pronouns here still refer to the person being purified and not to the priest, as the RSV rendering may possibly be misunderstood. The translation should make this clear to all readers.

14.15 RSV	TEV
Then the priest shall take some of the log of oil, and pour it into the palm of his own left hand,	The priest shall take some of the olive oil and pour it in the palm of his own left hand,

Some of the log of oil: in most cases it will be unnecessary to repeat the name of the measure in this verse. This is especially true in light of the uncertainty of its equivalence. In most languages "some of the oil" or "**some of the olive oil**" should be adequate.

Into the palm of his own left hand: literally, "in the palm of the left [hand] of the priest," but such a rendering would very likely confuse the reader. What is important is for the reader to understand that it is indeed the left hand of the priest and not that of the person being purified. And this idea must be clearly conveyed in the most natural language possible.

14.16-17 RSV	TEV
16 and dip his right finger in the oil that is in his left hand, and sprinkle some oil with his finger seven times before the LORD. 17 And some of the	16 dip a finger of his right hand in it, and sprinkle some of it seven times there in the LORD's presence. 17 He shall take some of the oil that is in

oil that remains in his hand the priest shall put on the tip of the right ear of him who is to be cleansed, and on the thumb of his right hand, and on the great toe of his right foot, upon the blood of the guilt offering;	the palm of his hand and some of the blood of the lamb and put them on the lobe of the right ear, on the thumb of the right hand, and on the big toe of the right foot of the man who is to be declared ritually clean.

The TEV rendering of these two verses avoids some of the unnecessary repetition found in RSV and also seeks to simplify the structure.

His right finger: this probably refers to the index finger, but it could be any finger of the right hand. If the language requires the naming of a specific finger, it is probably best to use the index finger (the finger next to the thumb).

Seven times: see 4.6; 14.7.

14.18   RSV   TEV

and the rest of the oil that is in the priest's hand he shall put on the head of him who is to be cleansed. Then the priest shall make atonement for him before the LORD.	He shall put the rest of the oil that is in the palm of his hand on the man's head. In this way he shall perform the ritual of purification.

Him who is to be cleansed: or "the person who is being cleansed," or simply "the person." See verse 4, 7, 8, and 14.

The priest's hand: as in verse 15, **the priest** is specifically identified, but in many languages the pronoun will be adequate here.

Shall make atonement for him before the LORD: compare the TEV rendering, and see 12.7.

14.19   RSV   TEV

The priest shall offer the sin offering, to make atonement for him who is to be cleansed from his uncleanness. And afterward he shall kill the burnt offering;	Then the priest shall offer the sin offering and perform the ritual of purification. After that, he shall kill the animal for the burnt offering

The sin offering: see chapter 4. The animal sacrificed is the female lamb mentioned in verse 10. See especially 4.32-35.

The burnt offering: see chapter 1. The animal here is the second lamb mentioned in verse 10 (see 1.3).

14.20 RSV TEV

and the priest shall offer the burnt offering and the cereal offering on the altar. Thus the priest shall make atonement for him, and he shall be clean.	and offer it with the grain offering on the altar. In this way the priest shall perform the ritual of purification, and the man will be ritually clean.

Cereal offering: see chapter 2 as well as 14.10.

Shall offer . . . : TEV has **"and offer it with . . . ,"** showing that this is in addition to what has already been mentioned in the preceding verse. In some languages it may be more natural to say "shall also offer . . . ."

Shall make atonement for him: this is the third and final mention of the ritual of purification (see verses 18 and 19). In view of this, some translators have felt it necessary to add "once again" or "one last time" in this verse.

14.21 RSV TEV

But if he is poor and cannot afford so much, then he shall take one male lamb for a guilt offering to be waved, to make atonement for him, and a tenth of an ephah of fine flour mixed with oil for a cereal offering, and a log of oil;	If the man is poor and cannot afford any more, he shall bring for his purification only one male lamb as his repayment offering, a special gift to the LORD for the priest. He shall bring only two pounds [one kilogram] of flour mixed with olive oil for a grain offering and half a pint [a third of a liter] of olive oil.

As in 5.7 and 12.8, provision is made in the following verses for those who may be too poor to bring the required offering.

Cannot afford so much: literally, "his hand cannot reach." In many cases it will be clearer if this is translated "does not have the required offerings." NJB has "cannot afford all this," which clearly refers to the requirements in verse 10. TEV's **"any more"** seems to refer forward to the one lamb and the lesser amount of flour.

A tenth of an ephah: see verse 10 as well as 5.11.

14.22 RSV TEV

also two turtledoves or two young pigeons, such as he can afford; the one shall be a sin offering and the other a burnt offering.	He shall also bring two doves or two pigeons, one for the sin offering and one for the burnt offering.

Two turtledoves or two young pigeons: see 5.7 and 12.8.

Such as he can afford: literally, "which his hand can reach" (compare verse 21, where the negative of the same expression is used). Both NEB and Wenham translate "whichever he can afford," referring to the doves or pigeons only and not to all the items listed in the previous verse. This whole phrase has been left implicit in TEV, but it should probably not be omitted in translation unless there are good receptor language reasons for doing so.

14.23	RSV	TEV
	And on the eighth day he shall bring them for his cleansing to the priest, to the door of the tent of meeting, before the LORD;	On the eighth day of his purification he shall bring them to the priest at the entrance of the Tent.

Compare verses 10 and 11.

For his cleansing: in some languages it may be better to say "for the ritual of purification" or simply "of the ceremony." TEV leaves this information implicit.

14.24	RSV	TEV
	and the priest shall take the lamb of the guilt offering, and the log of oil, and the priest shall wave them for a wave offering before the LORD.	The priest shall take the lamb and the olive oil and present them as a special gift to the LORD for the priest.

Compare verse 12.

Note that TEV leaves implicit some information which is explicit in the original (**the log**). But it also makes explicit some information left implicit in the original ("**olive oil**"). Translators who are sensitive to the needs and understanding of their readers may do the same, but this does not mean blindly following TEV.

And the priest shall wave . . . : that is, "present as a special gift." Some Hebrew texts have the pronoun "he" in place of **the priest** here, but the meaning is the same. The final rendering should follow what is most natural in the receptor language. But in most cases the noun will probably be better than the pronoun. TEV again adds "**for the priest**" (see verse 12), which may be awkward and unnecessary in some languages.

14.25-29	RSV	TEV
	25 And he shall kill the lamb of the guilt offering; and the priest shall take some of the blood of the guilt offering, and put it on the tip of the right ear of him who is to be cleansed, and on the thumb of his right hand, and on the great toe of his right foot. 26 And the priest shall	25 He shall kill the lamb and take some of the blood and put it on the lobe of the man's right ear, on the thumb of his right hand, and on the big toe of his right foot. 26 The priest shall pour some of the oil into the palm of his own left hand 27 and with a finger of his right hand

pour some of the oil into the palm of his own left hand; 27 and shall sprinkle with his right finger some of the oil that is in his left hand seven times before the LORD; 28 and the priest shall put some of the oil that is in his hand on the tip of the right ear of him who is to be cleansed, and on the thumb of his right hand, and on the great toe of his right foot, in the place where the blood of the guilt offering was put; 29 and the rest of the oil that is in the priest's hand he shall put on the head of him who is to be cleansed, to make atonement for him before the LORD.

sprinkle some of it seven times there in the LORD's presence. 28 He shall put some of the oil on the same places he put the blood: on the lobe of the man's right ear, on the thumb of his right hand, and on the big toe of his right foot. 29 The rest of the oil that is in his palm he shall put on the man's head and in this way perform the ritual of purification.

Compare verses 13-18.

14.30   RSV   TEV

And he shall offer, of the turtledoves or young pigeons such as he can afford,

Then he shall offer one of the doves or pigeons

And: many languages will find a more appropriate transition word here. TEV, NIV, NJV, and NAB all have "**Then**" at the beginning of this verse.

He . . . he: the first pronoun denotes the priest, while the second refers to the person who is to be purified. In many cases it will be better to use the nouns rather than the pronouns in order to distinguish them.

Such as he can afford: see verse 22.

14.31   RSV   TEV

one^x for a sin offering and the other for a burnt offering, along with a cereal offering; and the priest shall make atonement before the LORD for him who is being cleansed.

as the sin offering and the other as the burnt offering with the grain offering. In this way the priest shall perform the ritual of purification.

^{x} Grk Syr: Heb *afford, ^{31} such as he can afford, one*

Compare verses 19-20.

In the Hebrew this verse begins with the same words found at the end of the previous verse: "such as he can afford." These words are omitted by both RSV and TEV but are included in NJV, JB, and NASB. But they may be omitted here on the grounds of translation principles if not for textual reasons.

And: the relationship between the two parts of this verse is made clearer by something like **"In this way . . ."** (NIV as well as TEV), or "Thus . . ." (NEB and NAB), or "so . . ." (Mft).

Shall make atonement: see 1.4; 4.20.

14.32   RSV   TEV

This is the law for him in whom is a   This is the law for the man who has
leprous disease, who cannot afford   a dreaded skin disease but who
the offerings for his cleansing."   cannot afford the normal offerings
                                              required for his purification.

This is the law: NJV translates "Such shall be the ritual . . . ," which seems to be closer to the intent of the writer. In the receptor language it may be advisable to use a plural such as "These are the regulations . . ." (NIV). Compare 6.2 and 11.46-47.

A leprous disease: see the comments at the beginning of chapter 13 regarding the terms **leprous**, "leper," and "leprosy."

Cannot afford: see the similar expressions in verses 21, 22, and 30.

TEV Section Heading: **"Mildew in Houses."**

This section deals with another form of what the ancient Jews thought of as "leprosy." But the "leprosy" found on the walls of a house is what modern English refers to as mildew. NJB entitles this section "Similar infections in houses" in an attempt to show the relationship with the other types of infections already discussed (on human skin and on cloth and leather). From the modern scientific point of view, mildew and skin disease have little in common, but they do both affect the surface of various objects.

14.33-35   RSV   TEV

33 The LORD said to Moses and   33 The LORD gave Moses and
Aaron, 34 "When you come into the   Aaron 34-35 the following regulations
land of Canaan, which I give you for   about houses affected by spreading
a possession, and I put a leprous   mildew. (These were to apply after
disease in a house in the land of   the people of Israel entered the land
your possession, 35 then he who   of Canaan, which the LORD was
owns the house shall come and tell   going to give them as their posses-
the priest, 'There seems to me to be   sion.) If someone finds that the LORD
some sort of disease in my house.'   has sent mildew on his house, then
                                        he must go and tell the priest about
                                        it.

Said to Moses and Aaron: see 4.1; 11.1; 13.1.

Notice that the structure of verse 34 in TEV differs greatly from that of RSV. Since this is the beginning of a new section, the main subject (mildew in houses) is given a more prominent place. The information about entering the land of Canaan is parenthetical and is treated as such in TEV. The receptor language translation should also keep in mind that the focus should be on the main subject, and that the other information should be treated as secondary. Languages have many different ways of showing that information is of secondary importance. It may be that a better way can be found instead of simply using parentheses like TEV.

The land . . . which I give you: several versions use a progressive tense, "which I am giving you" (NJB, AT, NAB, and NIV). Mft translates "which I assign you." In some languages a kind of immediate future tense may be more appropriate. But the tense will also depend on the structure of the sentence. Compare TEV "**was going to give them.**"

And I put . . . : some commentators feel that this may be better translated as the first part of a conditional sentence, "and if I put . . . ." This is followed by NEB, NAB, NJB, AT, and Mft. Here, too, the precise translation will depend on the structure of the whole verse.

A leprous disease: this is, of course, mildew or mold on the walls of the houses. See 13.2,47. Modern science defines mildew as a usually whitish growth found on the surface of various forms of organic matter and caused by a fungus. Because of a very superficial similarity with skin diseases, it was classified by the ancient Jews as "leprosy." It would, however, be an error to use the receptor-language word for "leprosy" in translation here instead of the common word for "mildew" in the language.

TEV avoids the repetition of the word **possession**, since this would be somewhat awkward in English.

Structurally this verse must be taken along with the previous one, since it represents the second part of the conditional ("If . . . , then . . .") sentence. TEV brings out the general nature of the instructions by beginning with "**If someone . . . .**"

RSV places a direct quotation within another quotation, but this presents some serious problems in certain languages. This can be avoided by an indirect statement similar to the one used in TEV. However, some commentators consider this to be an oversimplification. NEB gives a fuller but still indirect rendering: "shall . . . report to the priest that there appears to him to be a patch of infection in his house."

14.36	RSV	TEV
	Then the priest shall command that they empty the house before the priest goes to examine the disease, lest all that is in the house be declared unclean; and afterward the priest shall go in to see the house.	The priest shall order everything to be moved out of the house before he goes to examine the mildew; otherwise everything in the house will be declared unclean. Then he shall go to the house

The priest: the priest is specifically mentioned three times in this verse. In most languages it will be more natural to refer to him using the pronoun "he" in the last two cases.

Shall command that they empty the house: literally, "shall command and they [indefinite] shall empty the house." Some languages may be quite similar to the rather literal rendering of the Hebrew expression in RSV. The verb "to empty" will have to be rendered "take everything out . . ." in some cases.

Lest: TEV "**otherwise**." In some languages it may be necessary to begin a completely new sentence and say something like "If this is not done . . . ." Another way of handling this is to say "in order that nothing in the house will have to be declared unclean" (compare NIV and NJV).

Afterward: meaning "after the house has been emptied" or "as soon as the things of the house have been taken out."

14.37   RSV   TEV

And he shall examine the disease;   and examine the mildew. If there are
and if the disease is in the walls of   greenish or reddish spots that ap-
the house with greenish or reddish   pear to be eating into the wall,
spots, and if it appears to be deeper
than the surface,

The disease: literally, "the mark (or, spot)." The priest actually inspects the affected area of the house. In some languages it may be wise to say this directly.

And if: literally, "and behold!" as in KJV. But the obvious meaning is conditional.

Greenish or reddish: see 13.49.

Deeper than the surface: this corresponds to the depressions in the skin mentioned in 13.3. Here the idea may be expressed in a variety of ways. Mft has "below the surface of the plaster." NJB speaks of the walls of the house being "pitted." And TEV depicts the fungus as actively "**eating into the wall**."

14.38   RSV   TEV

then the priest shall go out of the   he shall leave the house and lock it
house to the door of the house, and   up for seven days.
shut up the house seven days.

Out of the house to the door of the house: in some languages this may give the impression that the door is detached from the house and somewhere in the courtyard. This is obviously to be avoided. The expression **shut up the house** clearly implies that the priest is at the door. The briefer rendering of TEV loses none of the meaning.

Seven days: the usual waiting period. See 4.6; 8.33.

14.39   RSV   TEV

**And the priest shall come again on   On the seventh day he shall return
the seventh day, and look; and if the   and examine it again. If the mildew
disease has spread in the walls of   has spread,
the house,**

And look: in many languages it will be more natural to say "**examine it
again**," as in TEV, or something similar to indicate that this is a second inspection.
Spread: other ways of expressing this idea may be "become bigger" or "moved
to other places."

14.40   RSV   TEV

**then the priest shall command that   he shall order that the stones on
they take out the stones in which is   which the mildew is found be re-
the disease and throw them into an   moved and thrown into some un-
unclean place outside the city;   clean place outside the city.**

Command that they take out the stones: literally, "command and they shall
take out . . . ," as in verse 36. The passive construction of TEV ("**be removed and
thrown**") is not helpful in languages that do not use passives. But since the identity
of those performing the action is unknown, some sort of indefinite construction will
have to be used. Compare verses 4 and 5.
An unclean place: that is, in a place especially designated for the disposal of
objects considered unclean or impure. Such a place would obviously have to be away
from the area where people lived, which is expressed in the text as **outside the city**.

14.41   RSV   TEV

**and he shall cause the inside of the   After that he must have all the inte-
house to be scraped round about,   rior walls scraped and the plaster
and the plaster that they scrape off   dumped in an unclean place outside
they shall pour into an unclean place   the city.
outside the city;**

And: a more vivid transition may be necessary in many languages. In addition
to TEV's "**After that . . . ,**" NEB, NJB, and NAB each have "then."
Cause . . . to be scraped: the causative form of the verb indicates that the
priest is responsible to see that the job is done, but he does not actually do it
himself. The passive of "scrape" must be made active in many languages: "he shall
cause that they [indefinite] scrape . . . ."
Round about: if translated literally into the receptor language, this term may
be too vague. The idea is that "**all the interior walls**" were to be scraped in order
to remove every trace of the mildew. Another way of saying this is "the inside of the
house must be thoroughly scraped on all sides."

Plaster: NIV "material"; NAB, AT, and Mft "mortar"; NEB "daub"; NJV "coating." But the word may also be translated "dry earth" or "dried mud." This would be an accurate description of the material used in Palestine and a quite natural translation in many languages of the world.

An unclean place: since this almost certainly was the same place mentioned in verse 40, some languages may require that this be indicated, either by using a definite article in this case, or by some other means such as "that place" or "the place outside the city." One should avoid giving the impression that there were two different places of this kind.

14.42   RSV   TEV

| then they shall take other stones and put them in the place of those stones, and he shall take other plaster and plaster the house. | Then other stones are to be used to replace the stones that were removed, and new plaster will be used to cover the walls. |

Those stones: that is, the stones that had been thrown into the unclean place.

He: the use of the singular pronoun in the last part of this verse has led some to suggest that the priest himself was required to put the new plaster (or mud) on the walls. But this is unlikely. This is probably another case of the third person singular pronoun being used to refer to some unknown person.

14.43   RSV   TEV

| "If the disease breaks out again in the house, after he has taken out the stones and scraped the house and plastered it, | If the mildew breaks out again in the house after the stones have been removed and the house has been scraped and plastered, |

Compare the similar cases of the recurrence of a similar problem in 13.7, 35-36,57.

Breaks out: see 13.12,20.

He: as in the previous verse, this pronoun does not refer to the priest, but is simply a way of saying "someone."

The stones: the reference may be made clearer by specifying "the affected stones," or "the damaged stones," or "the stones that had mildew on them."

Scraped the house and plastered it: in some languages it will be more natural to say "walls" or "walls of the house" instead of **house**.

14.44   RSV   TEV

| then the priest shall go and look; and if the disease has spread in the | the priest shall go and look. If it has spread, the house is unclean. |

**house, it is a malignant leprosy in
the house; it is unclean.**

Go: translated "come" in NJB, NJV, and NEB; "come in" in NASB. The point of
view of the writer within the receptor language will possibly require **go** rather than
"come" in most cases. The verb actually contains the idea of "going into" the house,
as in Mft ("enter") or AT ("go in").

Look: that is, make another inspection or examination. Some languages will
require "reexamine" or "examine again."

Is a malignant leprosy: on **leprosy** see the introduction to chapter 13. The
whole expression in this context means something like "it is fungus that cannot be
eliminated." NEB translates "it is a corrosive growth." NIV has "it is a destructive
mildew." Compare 13.51.

14.45 RSV	TEV
And he shall break down the house, its stones and timber and all the plaster of the house; and he shall carry them forth out of the city to an unclean place.	It must be torn down, and its stones, its wood, and all its plaster must be carried out of the city to an unclean place.

He shall break down the house: again, the third person singular pronoun is
impersonal and indefinite. It does not refer to the priest. The expression is translated
as a passive in NJB, NAB, NJV, NIV, NEB. In those languages without passives an
impersonal "they" may be the best rendering.

He shall carry . . . : or "it must be carried . . . ," or "they must carry . . . ." As
above, the subject is impersonal.

An unclean place: see verse 40. Compare also "a clean place" in 6.11.

14.46 RSV	TEV
Moreover he who enters the house while it is shut up shall be unclean until the evening;	Anyone who enters the house while it is locked up will be unclean until evening.

Moreover: this translates the same word that is usually rendered "and" in RSV.
Mft translates "Also . . . ." It simply indicates that, in addition to what has already
been stated, the following is also required.

He who enters: this is clearly a general statement and so must often be
translated "whoever goes in" or "**anyone who enters**," as in TEV.

While it is shut up: logic may require something like "during the time when
it was supposed to be closed up," since it would have to be opened in some way for
a person to enter. Another possibility is "during the days when the priest had
ordered it to be closed." Wenham translates "during the period it is officially shut
up." This refers to the week of quarantine mentioned in verse 38.

Until the evening: or "until sunset."

14.47

RSV	TEV
and he who lies down in the house shall wash his clothes; and he who eats in the house shall wash his clothes.	Anyone who lies down or eats in the house must wash his clothes.

This verse seems to be another general statement, although it may carry forward and amplify the thought of the previous verse. If this is the case, it should probably be introduced by something like "Furthermore" or "Also" in some languages.

The pronoun **he** should be translated in such a way as to convey the meaning "Whoever" or "**Anyone.**" Notice the way in which the structure has been simplified in TEV. This may serve as a good model in many other languages.

Wash his clothes: see 11.25.

14.48

RSV	TEV
"But if the priest comes and makes an examination, and the disease has not spread in the house after the house was plastered, then the priest shall pronounce the house clean, for the disease is healed.	If, when the priest comes to look, the mildew has not reappeared after the house has been replastered, he shall pronounce the house ritually clean, because the mildew has been completely removed.

But: this indicates contrast with the case where the mildew has spread (verses 44-47).

If the priest comes . . . : the conditional **if** does not refer to the coming of the priest but to the absence of mildew in the newly plastered house. The idea is "When the priest goes to examine the house, if the mildew has not spread, then . . . ."

14.49

RSV	TEV
And for the cleansing of the house he shall take two small birds, with cedarwood and scarlet stuff and hyssop,	To purify the house, he shall take two birds, some cedar wood, a red cord, and a sprig of hyssop.

On verses 49-53, compare verses 4-9 and 20 earlier in this chapter. Although less detail is given here, the ritual was probably the same.

He: this pronoun may be understood as an impersonal form, but it is more likely that it refers to the priest in this context.

Two small birds: the size of the birds is considered unimportant by most scholars. But if the receptor language requires a choice between small birds and larger ones, then it will be better to translate **small birds**. The word is the same as used in 14.4, although the qualifying words "clean" and "living" are not found in this context. However, these words are probably implied, since all the other elements are identical with those used in the ritual of purification for a person having had the dreaded skin disease in 14.4.

14.50 RSV TEV

and shall kill one of the birds in an earthen vessel over running water,

He shall kill one of the birds over a clay bowl containing fresh spring water.

Here it is the priest who kills the bird. Compare verse 5, where the priest commands others to perform the ritual killing of the bird. The same problems exist in this verse with regard to the exact positioning of the person performing the sacrifice, the bird, the clay pot, and the spring water. See the earlier discussion.

14.51 RSV TEV

and shall take the cedarwood and the hyssop and the scarlet stuff, along with the living bird, and dip them in the blood of the bird that was killed and in the running water, and sprinkle the house seven times.

Then he shall take the cedar wood, the hyssop, the red cord, and the live bird and shall dip them in the blood of the bird that was killed and in the fresh water. And he shall sprinkle the house seven times.

See verses 6 and 7a.

14.52 RSV TEV

Thus he shall cleanse the house with the blood of the bird, and with the running water, and with the living bird, and with the cedarwood and hyssop and scarlet stuff;

In this way he shall purify the house with the bird's blood, the fresh water, the live bird, the cedar wood, the hyssop, and the red cord.

This verse is a kind of summary of what has already been said in the previous verses. Perhaps the repetition is to emphasize the symbolic importance of the act. The verse may be introduced with something like "This, then, is how the priest is to purify the house . . . ."

14.53 RSV	TEV
and he shall let the living bird go out of the city into the open field; so he shall make atonement for the house, and it shall be clean."	Then he shall let the live bird fly away outside the city over the open fields. In this way he shall perform the ritual of purification for the house, and it will be ritually clean.

The first part of this verse is very similar to 7b, although the wording is slightly different. The last half of the verse corresponds to 20b.

14.54 RSV	TEV
This is the law for any leprous disease: for an itch,	These are the laws about dreaded skin diseases;

This is the law: again, a collective singular. Another way of translating is "These are the regulations (or, instructions)." See 6.2 and 11.46-47.

For any leprous disease: this is taken in RSV (and NJV) as a kind of title or cover term for all the various problems listed here and in the following verses. Other versions take it as the first term in the list. If it is taken as a cover term, a very general expression will be needed to include all of what follows. However, it is probably better to take it as the first word in the list.

14.55-56 RSV	TEV
55 for leprosy in a garment or in a house, 56 and for a swelling or an eruption or a spot,	55-56 sores, boils, or inflammations; and about mildew in clothes or houses.

TEV reorders the terms in the list and groups them logically so that all the human skin diseases come first. These are followed by the two types of mildew problems (in clothing and in houses).

Swelling: see 13.9-17.

An eruption or a spot: see 13.3-8.

14.57 RSV	TEV
to show when it is unclean and when it is clean. This is the law for leprosy.	These laws determine when something is unclean and when it is clean.

To show . . . : TEV takes the whole of verse 57 as belonging to a single sentence with **the law** as the subject. On the other hand, RSV and most other versions take the first part of this verse as the completion of the sentence begun in verse 54. This does not alter the meaning greatly, but it does make for a rather long and complicated sentence. The TEV rendering will be a better model for many languages.

Chapter 15

Section Heading: "**Unclean Bodily Discharges**."

One of the following headings may serve as a better model for some languages: "Discharges causing uncleanness" (NIV), "Personal uncleanness" (NAB), or "Sexual impurities" (NJB).

This chapter deals with ritual uncleanness related to human sexual organs. The first half of the chapter concerns men (verses 1-17), and the second part deals with women (verses 19-30). Verse 18 is a kind of bridge between the two sections, and verses 31-33 constitute a common conclusion. If a two-level system of section headings is being used, subheadings like "Impurities of men" and "Impurities of women" may be used at the appropriate places.

15.1-2	RSV	TEV

RSV	TEV
1 The LORD said to Moses and Aaron, 2 "Say to the people of Israel, When any man has a discharge from his body, his discharge is unclean.	1 The LORD gave Moses and Aaron the following regulations 2 for the people of Israel. When any man has a discharge from his penis, the discharge is unclean,

Said to Moses and Aaron: see 4.1.

Say to the people of Israel . . . : compare 1.2.

Discharge: this refers to an abnormal fluid that comes out of the male sexual organ as a result of some kind of sickness. Some versions make more explicit the fact that the discharge is the result of some kind of infection. This distinguishes it clearly from the discharge of semen discussed in verses 16 and 17. A good model for some languages may be FRCL, "When a man suffers from an infection of his sexual organs, the resulting discharge is unclean." Other translations have been more specific, suggesting that the disease in question is probably "gonorrhea."

From his body: literally, "out of his flesh," as in KJV. The word "flesh" or **body** (RSV) is nothing more than a polite way of referring to the male sexual organ in this context. Some English versions say "member" or "private parts." TEV puts it more bluntly. In other languages such frankness may be unacceptable. There will be a wide variety of ways of referring to the sexual organs without naming them directly. Whatever term is used, it should meet two requirements: (1) it should be clearly understood; and (2) it should be acceptable terminology in speaking to men and women together (or as nearly so as possible).

15.3 RSV TEV

And this is the law of his uncleanness for a discharge: whether his
body runs with his discharge, or his
body is stopped from discharge, it is
uncleanness in him.

whether the penis runs with it or is
stopped up by it.

The first sentence in this verse is essentially a repetition of information already
given in verse 2. Consequently it may be left implicit here, as has been done in TEV.

Body: literally, "flesh." This again refers to the male sexual organ, as in the
previous verse.

Runs: or "flows," or "drains." Depending on how the previous verse is
translated, it may be necessary to say "continues to flow" or something similar.

His body is stopped from discharge: one way of understanding this passage
is that the discharge caused by the infection may block the opening in the penis as
in TEV. But NEB interprets the last two verbs differently: "whether it [the discharge]
continues or has been stopped." This seems to answer the question as to whether or
not only a persistent discharge is to be regarded as unclean. But the interpretation
"stopped up" is more likely to be the correct one. In either case the person is said
to be unclean. This contrasts with verse 2, where only the discharge is said to be
unclean.

Both the Samaritan Pentateuch and the Greek Septuagint have a different and
longer text in this verse. This longer reading is reflected in very few English
translations. Translators are therefore advised to follow the Masoretic text, as do the
majority of English versions.

15.4 RSV TEV

Every bed on which he who has the
discharge lies shall be unclean; and
everything on which he sits shall be
unclean.

Any bed on which he sits or lies is
unclean.

The TEV rendering of this verse seems to indicate that a chair or any other
object on which such a person sat might be not considered unclean, since only beds
are mentioned. However, in view of the context and especially the phrase **everything
on which he sits**, it is certain that any such object would be regarded as unclean.
Compare the renderings of NAB, NJB, NJV, AT, and other versions. Translators should
be careful not to follow TEV too closely at this point, since the statement involves any
object on which the infected man may sit or lie.

15.5-6 RSV TEV

5 And any one who touches his bed
shall wash his clothes, and bathe

5 Anyone who touches his bed 6 or
sits on anything the man has sat on

himself in water, and be unclean until the evening. 6 And whoever sits on anything on which he who has the discharge has sat shall wash his clothes, and bathe himself in water, and be unclean until the evening.

must wash his clothes and take a bath, and he remains unclean until evening.

In view of the almost exact repetition of the last part of verses 5 and 6, TEV has wisely translated only once. The receptor language may or may not accept the kind of repetition found in RSV. But in English it is certainly more natural to list such requirements only once. These requirements are similar to those in other cases of uncleanness (see chapter 11).

15.7   RSV   TEV

And whoever touches the body of him who has the discharge shall wash his clothes, and bathe himself in water, and be unclean until the evening.

Anyone who touches the man with the discharge must wash his clothes and take a bath, and he remains unclean until evening.

The body: is this to be taken literally, or is it once again a polite way of referring to the sexual organ itself, as it is in verses 2 and 3 and later in verse 19? Some commentators consider it euphemistic, but most English versions take it more literally here. The context of verses 4-12 seems to suggest more general contact. Instead of **body**, some versions simply say "**the man**" (NIV as well as TEV).

Again, the same ritual is required as in verses 5 and 6, if such contact is made.

15.8   RSV   TEV

And if he who has the discharge spits on one who is clean, then he shall wash his clothes, and bathe himself in water, and be unclean until the evening.

If the man with the discharge spits on anyone who is ritually clean, that person must wash his clothes and take a bath, and he remains unclean until evening.

Spits on: this gesture is usually a sign of intense dislike or rejection (see Num 12.14; Deut 25.9; Matt 26.67; 27.30). In the first two passages mentioned, it involves "spitting in the face of someone," but here the action may be accidental or to show contempt. In either case, the person on whom the infected man spits is required to wash his clothing and his entire body.

He shall wash . . . : the pronoun refers to the man who has been spat on and not the man with the discharge. This should be made clear in the receptor language.

15.9   RSV   TEV

And any saddle on which he who   Any saddle or seat on which the man
has the discharge rides shall be   with the discharge sits is unclean.
unclean.

Saddle: in some languages there may be no such technical term. In any case, a more general statement such as "Everything on which the man sits when riding" (NEB) is probably better. The word may refer to a saddle, or a cloth or the seat of a chariot.

15.10   RSV   TEV

And whoever touches anything that   Anyone who touches anything on
was under him shall be unclean until   which the man sat is unclean until
the evening; and he who carries   evening. Anyone who carries any-
such a thing shall wash his clothes,   thing on which the man sat must
and bathe himself in water, and be   wash his clothes and take a bath,
unclean until the evening.   and he remains unclean until eve-
                                         ning.

Anything that was under him: or "anything on which the man sat," as in TEV.

15.11   RSV   TEV

Any one whom he that has the dis-   If a man who has a discharge
charge   touches   without   having   touches someone without first hav-
rinsed his hands in water shall wash   ing washed his hands, that person
his clothes, and bathe himself in   must wash his clothes and have a
water, and be unclean until the eve-   bath, and he remains unclean until
ning.   evening.

Without having rinsed his hands: in Hebrew the subject of this clause may be either the man with the discharge or the person he touches. Both TEV and NJV take it to refer to the man with the discharge. *La Sainte Bible: Nouvelle version Segond révisée* (Segond) understands it as referring to the other person. Logically, it is much more likely that it is the man with the discharge. This should be made clear in translation.

15.12   RSV   TEV

And the earthen vessel which he   Any clay pot that the man touches
who has the discharge touches shall   must be broken, and any wooden

be broken; and every vessel of wood shall be rinsed in water.	bowl that he touches must be washed.

The earthen vessel: a literal translation of the RSV text may give the impression that a particular object is involved, since the definite article is used. But there is no doubt that this is a more general rule which applies to all containers made of clay, "**Any clay pot.**"

Every vessel of wood: this refers to any container of any kind that is made of wood. Compare 11.32-33.

15.13   RSV   TEV

"And when he who has a discharge is cleansed of his discharge, then he shall count for himself seven days for his cleansing, and wash his clothes; and he shall bathe his body in running water, and shall be clean.	After the man is cured of his discharge, he must wait seven days and then wash his clothes and take a bath in fresh spring water, and he will be ritually clean.

Is cleansed: this refers to the physical healing of the diseased person, which is not the same as his ritual purification at the end of the verse. It may be translated "no longer has this discharge," or "gets well," or "is healed of his sickness," or something similar. NAB has "becomes free of his affliction."

Count for himself seven days: see 12.2. Compare also verse 19. In many languages it would be a mistake to translate the verb **count** literally. Similar to TEV, NAB has "shall wait seven days." And both NJB and AT translate "must allow seven days."

For his cleansing: that is, "to begin the purification ritual."

The person healed of such a discharge must go through the same ritual of purification as those who came in contact with him. However, it is specifically added that he must bathe in fresh spring water.

15.14   RSV   TEV

And on the eighth day he shall take two turtledoves or two young pigeons, and come before the LORD to the door of the tent of meeting, and give them to the priest;	On the eighth day he shall take two doves or two pigeons to the entrance of the Tent of the LORD's presence and give them to the priest.

On the eighth day: compare 12.3 and 14.10,20.
Two turtledoves or two young pigeons: see 1.14; 5.7; 12.8; and 14.22.
The door of the tent of meeting: see 1.1.

15.15   RSV   TEV

and the priest shall offer them, one for a sin offering and the other for a burnt offering; and the priest shall make atonement for him before the LORD **for his discharge.**	**The priest shall offer one of them as a sin offering and the other as a burnt offering. In this way he will perform the ritual of purification for the man.**

<u>**Sin offering**</u>: see chapter 4.

<u>**Burnt offering**</u>: see chapter 1.

<u>**And**</u>: as in 14.52, the connection between the two sentences here will be much clearer if a different kind of transition is used. TEV has "**In this way . . .**"; Mft has "so."

<u>**Make atonement for him**</u>: compare 12.7. See also 4.20.

15.16   RSV   TEV

"And if a man has an emission of semen, he shall bathe his whole body in water, and be unclean until the evening.	**When a man has an emission of semen, he must bathe his whole body, and he remains unclean until evening.**

<u>**An emission of semen**</u>: this is not an infectious disease as in verses 2-12. What is involved here is an involuntary act (as opposed to verse 18) in which the sperm of any male is emitted. Languages typically have very different ways of referring to such matters. The translation should be meaningful but should avoid shocking the reader or hearer unnecessarily.

<u>**His whole body**</u>: the context seems to indicate that the word **body** is probably to be taken in its more literal sense here rather than as a euphemism for the sexual organ. However, it is true that the expression used for bathing here differs somewhat from "bathe in water" used earlier in this chapter. This leads some commentators to believe that this is a euphemistic expression. The word translated **body** here is the same as the one rendered "flesh" in verse 7.

15.17   RSV   TEV

And every garment and every skin on which the semen comes shall be washed with water, and be unclean until the evening.	**Anything made of cloth or leather on which the semen falls must be washed, and it remains unclean until evening.**

<u>**Every garment and every skin**</u>: the TEV rendering is much more natural in English, but other languages may be closer to the original as reflected in RSV.

<u>**Comes**</u>: the verb may be rendered "**falls**" (TEV) or "comes in contact," but in other languages "touches" may be better.

Be washed with water: this will be considered redundant in many languages and can be reduced simply to "**washed**." See 1.9.

15.18   RSV   TEV

If a man lies with a woman and has an emission of semen, both of them shall bathe themselves in water, and be unclean until the evening.	After sexual intercourse both the man and the woman must take a bath, and they remain unclean until evening.

This verse constitutes a transition between 1-17, dealing with men, and 19-30, which deal with women. It should probably be printed as a separate paragraph, to indicate its transitional nature. However, if there are two section headings in this chapter, verse 18 should be considered a part of the first section rather than the second.

If a man lies with a woman: this is one of the usual ways of referring to the act of sexual intercourse without saying so directly. Some languages may say "If a man sleeps with a woman . . . ." Others use expressions like "to touch," or "to love," or simply "to be with a woman."

The translator should be careful not to give the impression that there is anything morally wrong with the sexual relations mentioned here. This verse concerns normal sexual relations between husband and wife, even though the regulation would also apply to other cases. The translation should also avoid suggesting that, when a couple engage in sexual relations, a sin has been committed.

If there are to be two section headings in this chapter, this will be the place for the second: "Sexual impurities in women" or "Rules about women." It should parallel the heading used at the beginning of the chapter, concerning men.

This section is further subdivided into the following sections: verses 19-24 concerning normal menstruation; 25-27 dealing with cases that are considered abnormal but are not infectious; and 28-30 regarding the problems of purification.

15.19   RSV   TEV

"When a woman has a discharge of blood which is her regular discharge from her body, she shall be in her impurity for seven days, and whoever touches her shall be unclean until the evening.	When a woman has her monthly period, she remains unclean for seven days. Anyone who touches her is unclean until evening.

A discharge of blood: the same root word is used here as in verses 3 and following regarding the man. But the addition of the word **blood** makes it clear that menstruation is involved. As in the case of most matters dealing with sex, languages have very different ways of talking about this natural and recurring event in the lives of women. One may use an expression like "to see the moon"; another may say "to have the women's sickness"; others may have expressions that are even less direct than these. But speakers of the language should have no doubt about the meaning.

From her body: literally, "from her flesh." See the discussion under verse 7. The context permits either **from her body** as in RSV, or "from her sexual organs." Naturalness in the receptor language should determine which one is used.

In her impurity: that is, she shall be considered impure or unclean. This expression has virtually the same meaning as **shall be unclean** used at the end of this verse with regard to those who touch such a woman.

For seven days: see 4.6; 8.33.

Until the evening: or "until the next sunset." See 11.24.

15.20   RSV   TEV

And everything upon which she lies   **Anything on which she sits or lies**
during her impurity shall be unclean;   **during her monthly period is un-**
everything also upon which she sits   **clean.**
shall be unclean.

This verse corresponds to verse 4 concerning men, but it is not a word-for-word repetition. (Compare also verse 26.) Note that TEV has restructured and simplified this verse.

During her impurity: that is, during her time of menstruation. See the discussion under "a discharge of blood" in the previous verse.

15.21-23   RSV   TEV

21 **And whoever touches her bed**   21-23 **Anyone who touches her bed**
shall wash his clothes, and bathe   **or anything on which she has sat**
himself in water, and be unclean until **must wash his clothes and take a**
the evening. 22 **And whoever**   **bath, and he remains unclean until**
touches anything upon which she   **evening.**
sits shall wash his clothes, and
bathe himself in water, and be un-
clean until the evening; 23 **whether it**
is the bed or anything upon which
she sits, when he touches it he shall
be unclean until the evening.

Verses 21 and 22 correspond to 5 and 6 earlier in this chapter. Again it will be noted that TEV has avoided needless repetition and thereby produces a much shorter rendering while retaining the same meaning. Verse 23 is a kind of summary of the two previous verses; it is similar to 10a, but it is not identical with it.

15.24 RSV	TEV
And if any man lies with her, and her impurity is on him, he shall be unclean seven days; and every bed on which he lies shall be unclean.	If a man has sexual intercourse with her during her period, he is contaminated by her impurity and remains unclean for seven days, and any bed on which he lies is unclean.

The more specific case dealt with in this verse merely states one of the applications of the general rule outlined in verses 19-23 above.

Lies with her: see verse 18. The rendering of FRCL makes it clear that what is involved here is sexual intercourse at the very beginning of the woman's menstrual period: "If, at the time when the man sleeps with her, the blood of her period flows (that is, starts to flow) . . . ." The wording of TEV "**during her period**" seems to imply a deliberate violation of the taboo against sexual intercourse at such a time, rather than an accident.

Her impurity is on him: according to ancient Jewish thought, the ritual impurity of the woman was contagious and transmissible. As a result of sexual contact with a woman in a state of impurity, the man also became impure. He, in turn, would cause any bed on which he lay to become unclean.

He shall be unclean: in some languages it will be more natural to say "he shall also be unclean." In addition, the word "also" may be added with reference to the bed at the end of the verse. In languages that do not distinguish between the masculine and feminine pronouns, it will be important to use the noun "man" to make it clear that the text is not talking about the woman in this instance.

Seven days: see 4.6; 8.33.

15.25 RSV	TEV
"If a woman has a discharge of blood for many days, not at the time of her impurity, or if she has a discharge beyond the time of her impurity, all the days of the discharge she shall continue in uncleanness; as in the days of her impurity, she shall be unclean.	If a woman has a flow of blood for several days outside her monthly period or if her flow continues beyond her regular period, she remains unclean as long as the flow continues, just as she is during her monthly period.

Not at the time of her impurity: a literal rendering of this phrase may be misleading. This becomes, in fact, a "time of impurity" for the woman, but it is at a time other than her regular menstrual period. Or, in a second hypothetical case, it may be the continuation of her regular period beyond the normal limits. Mft translates "a discharge lasting beyond the time of her period."

15.26 RSV TEV

Every bed on which she lies, all the days of her discharge, shall be to her as the bed of her impurity; and everything on which she sits shall be unclean, as in the uncleanness of her impurity.

Any bed on which she lies and anything on which she sits during this time is unclean.

Compare verses 4 and 20, where the meaning is virtually the same even though the form is slightly different.

15.27 RSV TEV

And whoever touches these things shall be unclean, and shall wash his clothes, and bathe himself in water, and be unclean until the evening.

Anyone who touches them is unclean and must wash his clothes and take a bath; he remains unclean until evening.

See verses 5-6 and 21-22.

These things: in some cases it may be better to specify once again "such a bed or such a seat" or "these things on which she has placed her body."

15.28 RSV TEV

But if she is cleansed of her discharge, she shall count for herself seven days, and after that she shall be clean.

After her flow stops, she must wait seven days, and then she will be ritually clean.

This verse presents the same basic procedure as for the male in verse 13 above. However, there is no mention here of washing the woman's clothing or of bathing (see the discussion on verse 13). Here it appears that the mere passage of time is sufficient to insure ritual cleansing.

15.29-30 RSV TEV

29 And on the eighth day she shall take two turtledoves or two young pigeons, and bring them to the priest, to the door of the tent of meeting. 30 And the priest shall offer one for a sin offering and the other for a burnt offering; and the priest

29 On the eighth day she shall take two doves or two pigeons to the priest at the entrance of the Tent of the LORD's presence. 30 The priest shall offer one of them as a sin offering and the other as a burnt offering, and in this way he will perform the

shall make atonement for her before the LORD for her unclean discharge.

ritual of purification for her.

See verses 14 and 15.

15.31   RSV   TEV

"Thus you shall keep the people of Israel separate from their uncleanness, lest they die in their uncleanness by defiling my tabernacle that is in their midst."

The LORD told Moses to warn the people of Israel about their uncleanness, so that they would not defile the Tent of his presence, which was in the middle of the camp. If they did, they would be killed.

Thus: some versions omit the transition word and merely begin a new paragraph. Mft begins "So . . . ," and NEB has "In this way . . . ." Natural receptor language style should be used, but in many languages this will almost certainly require some kind of transition word. In view of the context some languages may begin "As for you . . . ," referring to Moses and Aaron.

You: the pronoun here is plural and apparently refers to Moses and Aaron, picking up information made explicit in the first verse of this chapter. It may be useful to remind the readers and hearers again that this section is still a part of what the Lord told these two leaders.

Separate: the basic meaning of the verb used here is "to separate," as in RSV and NIV. But this has presented serious problems of interpretation. AT translates "to get rid of." And LB has "to cleanse." HOTTP recommends the text with the verb **separate** but gives no clues about how it is to be understood. One commentator has suggested that in this context it should be rendered "to observe strict rules in respect to ritual uncleanness." Compare TOB. The majority of modern English versions, however, follow a modification of the Hebrew text which has the verb "to warn against" (NEB, TEV, NJV, NJB, NAB). This is judged necessary in spite of the HOTTP recommendation to the contrary. FRCL, however, makes good sense of the traditional Hebrew text recommended by HOTTP, rendering it "You must ask the Israelites to keep their distance from the sanctuary when they are in an impure state . . . ."

Lest they die: TEV shifts this phrase to the end of the verse and clearly translates the meaning as a separate conditional sentence. This may be a helpful model for many other languages.

My tabernacle: if indirect discourse is used as in TEV, the pronoun **my** will have to become "his." Also, the word **tabernacle** is used here instead of the usual "Tent of the LORD's presence," but the meaning is the same. This is why TEV translates as it does. See comments at 8.10. Another way to translate this is "the place where I live among them."

In their midst: in the middle of their camp. This simply specifies more clearly the location of the Tent of the LORD's presence.

15.32   RSV   TEV

    This is the law for him who has   **These are the regulations about**
a discharge and for him who has an   **a man who has a discharge or an**
emission of semen, becoming un-   **emission of semen,**
clean thereby;

    This is the law: see 6.2. Compare also 11.46-47.
    Him: the pronoun used here refers to any man who has a discharge of semen.
In most languages it will be clearer to say "the man" or "any man."
    A discharge: see verses 2-15.
    An emission of semen: see verses 16-17.

15.33   RSV   TEV

also for her who is sick with her   **a woman during her monthly period,**
impurity; that is, for any one, male or **or a man who has sexual intercourse**
female, who has a discharge, and for **with a woman who is ritually unclean.**
the man who lies with a woman who
is unclean.

    Her: as with the masculine pronoun in the previous verse, this may be more
clearly translated by a noun phrase such as "any woman."
    Sick with her impurity: see verses 19-23. Compare also 12.2.
    Any one . . . who has a discharge: this element seems to be lacking in TEV.
But since verses 32 and 33 are to be taken together as a summary statement, it may
be said that the meaning of this statement is included in verse 32. If this is the case
in the receptor language, the two verse numbers should be combined.
    Male or female: after having said **any one**, it may be unnecessary in many
languages to say explicitly **male or female**.

Chapter 16

Chapter 16 constitutes a kind of transition between the previous sections (1-7, Sacrifices and Offerings; 8-10, Ordination; and 11-15, Purity and Impurity) and the so-called "Holiness Code" of chapters 17-26. The chapter begins with a reference to chapter 10 (16.1-2), which showed how priests who went into the presence of God in an improper manner could be put to death. This chapter, therefore, describes the proper way of performing the ritual in order to avoid a fate like that of those described in chapter 10. This ceremony took place every year on the tenth day of the seventh month (see 23.26-32) and involved a variety of sacrifices and a special ritual which was performed to ask God's pardon on the whole community of Israel. The Hebrew name for this celebration (*yom hakkippurim*) does not appear in chapter 16. It is known to us through 23.27-28 and Numbers 29.11. The first word, *yom,* means "day," and *hakkippurim* is the plural, with definite article, of *kippur,* meaning "atonement" or "expiation" and coming from the verb *kipper* (4.20), "to make atonement (or, expiation)" or "to cover." This celebration continues in the Jewish calendar of today and is called "Yom Kippur."

Following the introductory statement in verses 1-2, this chapter may be broken down into the following subsections:
1. Verses 2-5: The behavior and dress of the High Priest.
2. Verses 6-28: The ceremonial ritual.
   a. Verses 6-10: An overall view of the ritual.
   b. Verses 11-28: A detailed view of the ritual.
      (1) Verses 11-19: the sprinkling of blood.
      (2) Verses 20-22: the scapegoat.
      (3) Verses 23-28: the cleansing of participants.
3. Verses 29-31: Additional instructions.
4. Verses 32-34: Conditions for the repetition of the ritual.

Translators may encounter some special problems in this chapter because the sequence of events may not be altogether clear. In verse 3 Aaron appears with a bull and a ram for his own offerings. In verse 4 he takes a bath before putting on the priestly clothing, but probably laying the garments down in order before the ritual bath. The bull mentioned in verse 3 is slaughtered in verse 6 (in the overview of the ritual), but the ram for the burnt offering is not slaughtered until verse 24 (in the detailed description of the ritual).

TEV Section Heading: "**The Day of Atonement**."

Some other possible headings may be "'About the day of atonement," "The great day of forgiveness," or "The yearly removal of sins."

16.1 RSV TEV

The LORD spoke to Moses, after the death of the two sons of Aaron, when they drew near before the LORD and died;

The LORD spoke to Moses after the death of the two sons of Aaron who were killed when they offered unholy fire to the LORD.

Spoke to Moses: see 4.1. In some languages it may be better to restructure this verse in such a way as to place these words at the end instead of the beginning of the verse. The same information is in fact repeated at the beginning of verse 2.

The two sons of Aaron: the receptor language translation should avoid giving the impression that Aaron had only two sons. In some cases it may be better to say "two of the sons of Aaron, those who were killed . . . ."

When they drew near before the LORD: many versions follow the Hebrew text quite literally at this point (RSV, NIV, AT, NAB, TOB, *la Bible du rabbinat français*, Segond, Mft). NJV interprets it to mean "when they came too close to the LORD." Others, however, follow the ancient Greek translation and translate as in TEV, "when they offered illicit fire before the LORD" (NEB, FRCL, NJB). This reading may be justified on the basis of implicit information (see 10.1-2) which would have been well known to the original readers and hearers. HOTTP, however, recommends translating the Hebrew text as in RSV.

And died: the translation should not leave the reader wondering what the cause of death was. It was unquestionably the LORD who took their lives, because they approached him in an unacceptable manner.

16.2 RSV TEV

and the LORD said to Moses, "Tell Aaron your brother not to come at all times into the holy place within the veil, before the mercy seat which is upon the ark, lest he die; for I will appear in the cloud upon the mercy seat.

He said, "Tell your brother Aaron that only at the proper time is he to go behind the curtain into the Most Holy Place, because that is where I appear in a cloud above the lid on the Covenant Box. If he disobeys, he will be killed.

And the LORD said to Moses: this is a repetition of information found in the previous verse. There is no reason to repeat it in the translation, if doing so would be unnatural in the receptor language. "**He said**," as in TEV, may be perfectly adequate in many languages.

Aaron your brother: translators should consider whether it is more natural in their language to reverse the order and say "**your brother Aaron**" or to maintain the biblical order **Aaron your brother**.

Not to come at all times: the Hebrew is not agreed on by all scholars and may possibly mean "he must under no circumstances enter . . ." (AT). However, it is virtually certain that the intention of the writer was "may not enter . . . whenever he chooses" (NJB). Others have translated "he is not to come at will into the Shrine" (NJV) or "he must not venture into the sacred place . . . whenever he chooses" (Mft).

One commentator even suggests "not just any time" or "not at all except on the one special occasion." Compare TEV **"only at the proper time."**

The holy place: throughout this chapter it seems clear that this expression is referring either to **"the Most Holy Place"** behind the curtain (as in TEV) or perhaps to the "sanctuary area" in general (as in NIV). It does not refer to the Holy Place marked "H" on the map of the Tent of the Lord's Presence in the introduction. Since it is taken to mean the Most Holy Place, it is important to indicate that he does not enter with the animals, but only after having brought them as sacrifices.

Within the veil: or "on the other side of the sacred curtain," or "beyond the sacred hanging cloth" as one language has put it.

The mercy seat: the phrase **mercy seat** came into our English Bibles from Luther's translation. The Hebrew word comes from a root meaning "to cover," but this may be understood in two different ways. It may have to do with the "covering" or forgiving of sin, or simply mean a "covering" or **"lid"** on top of the Covenant Box. Possibly the writer had both of these ideas in mind. The Hebrew word is *kapporet* and is related to the word for "atonement" in *yom kippur* discussed at the beginning of the chapter. The actual item referred to was a slab of refined gold placed on top of the Covenant Box and used to support the two cherubim. JB translates "throne of mercy" (although NJB reverts to "mercy-seat"). NIV has "atonement cover." Many other versions have simply "cover" (NJV, FRCL, Mft, NEB). Most French versions have *propitiatoire* (compare AT "propitiatory"), which has led some to suggest the common language translation "place of forgiveness." Compare Exodus 25.10-22. All things considered, it is probably better to translate "lid" or "cover."

The ark: the traditional English rendering **ark** is a transliteration of the Latin, which means "chest" or "box." This is based on a Hebrew word that simply means "box"; yet this is no ordinary box. Although in the beginning it was a simple wooden chest, it was very special to the Jewish people because it was related to their covenant relationship to God. This is why TEV has added a qualifying term and translated **"Covenant Box."** Translators should be aware that it is only by historical accident that the word used of Noah's ark and the Ark of the Covenant are the same in English. No attempt should be made to render them identically in the receptor language.

Lest he die: as in 15.31, this has been shifted to the end of the verse in TEV and translated more clearly as a conditional sentence. This will probably be a good model for many other languages.

I will appear in the cloud: the tense of the verb is intended to indicate habitual action rather than some future appearance. Those languages which have a habitual verb form should probably use it here.

16.3   RSV   TEV

But thus shall Aaron come into the holy place: with a young bull for a sin offering and a ram for a burnt offering.	He may enter the Most Holy Place only after he has brought a young bull for a sin offering and a ram for a burnt offering."

But: in contrast with the prohibition stated in verse 2. But most English versions omit the conjunction here. Perhaps a better way to begin this verse is "Only in this way may Aaron enter . . ." (NAB) or "When Aaron enters the sanctuary, this is what he must do: . . ." (compare NEB).

The holy place: see verse 2 above. Compare also Exodus 26.33.

A young bull . . . a sin offering: see 4.3-12.

A ram . . . a burnt offering: see 1.10-13.

Another possible way of handling this verse is to put it in a negative form, saying something like "He must never enter the Most Holy Place without first having offered the sacrifices . . . ." But since this verse gives a kind of overview of the procedure discussed in further detail in the verses that follow, it is also possible to structure the receptor-language rendering of this verse according to one of these models: (a) "These are the rules governing the way Aaron will be allowed to enter the Most Holy Place: beforehand he must bring a young bull for a sin offering and a ram for a burnt offering." Or (b) "This is the only way that Aaron can (or, should) go into the Most Holy Place: he must first offer a young bull for a sin offering and a ram for a burnt offering before going in."

16.4 RSV	TEV
He shall put on the holy linen coat, and shall have the linen breeches on his body, be girded with the linen girdle, and wear the linen turban; these are the holy garments. He shall bathe his body in water, and then put them on.	Then the LORD gave the following instructions. Before Aaron goes into the Most Holy Place, he must take a bath and put on the priestly garments: the linen robe and shorts, the belt, and the turban.

The instructions given in this verse are to be fulfilled before going into the Most Holy Place. Many languages may require the same kind of adjustment as TEV has made, introducing these instructions and clearly indicating that these events take place before going into the Most Holy Place. Note that TEV also reminds the reader of the origin of these guidelines by adding **"Then the LORD gave the following instructions."** This is not a part of the Hebrew text but is clearly implied.

The sequence of events is not altogether clear in verses 3 and 4, but probably the change of clothing mentioned here takes place before the actual bringing of the bull and ram required in the previous verse.

Holy linen coat: the modern understanding of the word **coat** is not adequate here. This is a longer garment like a robe. It is made of **linen**. And this also presents translation problems in languages where this type of material is not known. It is made of the stalks of flax (see FFB, page 120), which were dried, split, and woven into cloth. The other articles of priestly clothing were also made of this same material. See 8.7.

Linen breeches: see 6.10

Linen girdle: see 8.7.

Linen turban: see 8.9.

While the text has the descriptive adjective **linen** with each of the four nouns, this repetition may be unnatural in some languages. In those cases it may be better to have a summary statement at the end of the list, indicating that "All these garments must be made of linen." Or this information may even be included in the summary statement at the end of the verse, saying "holy linen garments."

Holy garments: this expression is intended to summarize the above mentioned articles of clothing. Special care should be taken to avoid the meaning "clean clothes." On the term **holy**, see 2.3. Note that TEV has translated in this context **"priestly garments."**

Bathe his body in water: literally, "wash his flesh in water." The words **in water** will probably be unnecessary in many languages. And since the bathing must be done before putting on the priestly clothing, it may be better to state this first in the receptor language translation, as has been done in TEV.

16.5	RSV	TEV
	And he shall take from the congregation of the people of Israel two male goats for a sin offering, and one ram for a burnt offering.	The community of Israel shall give Aaron two male goats for a sin offering and a ram for a burnt offering.

He shall take: the translation of this verb should not give the impression of taking the animals by force or against the will of the Israelite community. The verb "receive" is used in both NJB and NAB, while "procure" is found in AT. TEV turns the sentence around, making the **people of Israel** the subject, and simply says **"shall give."**

Two goats: see 9.3-4.

For a sin offering: the following verses indicate that only one of these goats is actually offered as a sin offering. The other one is allowed to live but is chased out into the desert (verses 20-22). If the translator feels it necessary, this may be translated "two goats suitable (or, acceptable) for a sin offering" or "two goats that could be offered for sin."

Ram . . . burnt offering: see verse 3 and 1.10-13.

16.6	RSV	TEV
	"And Aaron shall offer the bull as a sin offering for himself, and shall make atonement for himself and for his house.	He shall offer a bull as a sacrifice to take away his own sins and those of his family.

Aaron: if the reference is sufficiently clear, this noun may be translated by the pronoun **"He,"** as in TEV.

For himself: the first occurrence of these two words is taken by NJV as belonging to the preceding part of the verse: "his own bull."

Shall make atonement: see 4.20.

His house: this clearly refers to the family, or household, of Aaron and not to any building or dwelling place. In some languages it may be preferable to say "the people living in his house," **"his family,"** or "his people."

16.7	RSV	TEV

Then he shall take the two goats, and set them before the LORD at the door of the tent of meeting;	Then he shall take the two goats to the entrance of the Tent of the LORD's presence.	

Take . . . set . . . : TEV combines the translation of these two verbs as one. In other languages it may be more suitable to use a verb like "bring" or "present."
At the door of the tent of meeting: see 1.3.

16.8	RSV	TEV

and Aaron shall cast lots upon the two goats, one lot for the LORD and the other lot for Azazel.	There he shall draw lots, using two stones, one marked "for the LORD" and the other "for Azazel."[e]	

[e] AZAZEL: *The meaning of this Hebrew word is unknown; it may be the name of a desert demon.*

Aaron: instead of repeating the name of Aaron here, TEV has used the pronoun **"he"** for the sake of naturalness. But it then picks up the full noun in the following verse.

Shall cast lots upon the two goats: the root word from which **cast lots** comes is "stones." Probably two objects made of stone or some other material were placed in some kind of container. One of the objects would have had the words "for the LORD" or simply "LORD" written on it. The other object would have been designated "for Azazel" or "Azazel." This container would have been shaken in front of one of the two goats, and the first of the two objects that fell out of the container would indicate the destiny of that goat. If it said "for the LORD," that goat would have been sacrificed; if it said "for Azazel" then the other goat would have become the sacrificial animal and that goat would be set free. Translators need not describe the details of this method of drawing lots (especially since it is only an educated guess), but they should say in the most natural way possible that the fate of the two goats was decided in an arbitrary way. It was taken out of the realm of human decision-making. In some cases an explanatory footnote may be desired. One should avoid evoking ideas of sorcery in the translation. Also, particular care should be taken in the translation of the preposition rendered **upon** in RSV. One should not give the impression that the stones were thrown on top of the goats.

Azazel: this term has presented difficulties to translators for many centuries. There are three possible interpretations for the meaning of this term:

(1) It may mean "the goat that departs" (that is, a scapegoat), as in KJV, NASB, NIV, and LB.
(2) It may refer to "the place where the animal is dispatched" or "the Precipice," followed only by NEB.
(3) It may be considered the proper name of a demon inhabiting the desert (that is, **Azazel**). This is the meaning accepted by RSV, TEV, NAB, NJB, AT, *Bible de la Pléiade*, NJV, Segond, TOB, and Mft. This is not only the most popular interpretation but it is also the most likely. In the context of this verse it is probably better not to specify "the goat-demon called Azazel," but this can be explained in a footnote or included in the translation at verse 10, where it is next mentioned. The term is also used in verse 26.

16.9	RSV	TEV

And Aaron shall present the goat on which the lot fell for the LORD, and offer it as a sin offering;

Aaron shall sacrifice the goat chosen by lot for the LORD and offer it as a sin offering.

Shall present: in some languages the corresponding verb requires an object indicating to whom the goat is presented. In this case it may be stated explicitly that the goat is offered "to the LORD."

The goat on which the lot fell for the LORD: depending on the translation of the previous verse, this may be restructured to say something like "the goat chosen to be sacrificed" or "the animal designated for the LORD."

Sin offering: see the discussion of this term under the section heading at the beginning of chapter 4 as well as 4.14.

16.10	RSV	TEV

but the goat on which the lot fell for Azazel shall be presented alive before the LORD to make atonement over it, that it may be sent away into the wilderness to Azazel.

The goat chosen for Azazel shall be presented alive to the LORD and sent off into the desert to Azazel, in order to take away the sins of the people.

But: this indicates a contrast between the fate of the second goat as compared with the first one. Although this is omitted in TEV, such a transition word may be very important in some languages.

The goat on which the lot fell for Azazel: this should be structured in a way similar to the corresponding phrase in verse 9. Or the model of TEV, using the verb "**chosen**," may be followed in some languages.

Presented alive before the LORD: this goat is not to be killed but is to be made to stand before the LORD alive.

To make atonement over it: Mft reads "perform expiatory rites over it," and AT shows even more clearly the relationship between these words and what follows:

"that atonement may be made through it by sending it off to Azazel in the desert."
The restructuring of TEV also brings out this same kind of relationship.

Sent away into the wilderness: this is similar to the setting free of one of the
two birds in 14.7 and 14.53. The primary meaning of the word **wilderness** is
"uninhabited region." Compare 7.38. See also verses 21 and 22, where the same
word is used.

16.11   RSV   TEV

    "Aaron shall present the bull as   When Aaron sacrifices the bull
a sin offering for himself, and shall   as the sin offering for himself and
make atonement for himself and for   his family,
his house; he shall kill the bull as a
sin offering for himself.

As stated earlier, the subsection including verses 11-28 provides a more detailed
view of the ceremony which is briefly described in verses 6-10. Some translators may
wish to add a section heading here along the lines of NEB "The ceremonies of the
day of atonement," or possibly "How to make sacrifices for the day of atonement."

The first part of this verse repeats word-for-word the description in verse 6
above. But since the context is different, it is not necessarily required that the
translation be identical here. Naturalness in the receptor language should determine
whether or not there is any difference.

The wording of RSV is awkward and repetitious, since it follows the Hebrew
very closely. This verse actually sets the stage for the following one. This is why TEV
has made it a relative clause, "**When . . . ,**" indicating that this is not a second
sacrifice, but that the single event is being further described. Translators should be
careful not to give the impression that the same bull is sacrificed a second time or
that another bull is sacrificed. This is simply a more detailed description of the same
event.

And for his house: that is, for his family. See verse 6.

16.12   RSV   TEV

And he shall take a censer full of   he shall take a fire pan full of burn-
coals of fire from the altar before the ing coals from the altar and two
Lord, and two handfuls of sweet   handfuls of fine incense and bring
incense beaten small; and he shall   them into the Most Holy Place.
bring it within the veil

    Censer: see 10.1.

    Altar: see 1.5. The altar mentioned here is the "incense altar" located in the
sanctuary (see Exo 40.5).

    Two handfuls: it may be more natural to say "his hands full" or "a double
handful."

Sweet incense: since the word **sweet** often refers to taste in many languages, it may be better to say "sweet-smelling," "pleasant-smelling," or "fragrant."

Beaten small: this refers to incense that has been finely ground and is very powdery. It was made from a compound of spices and tree resins mixed together by expert perfumers (see Exo 30.34-38). The whole expression is translated "powdered fragrant incense" by NEB.

He shall bring it: the pronoun **it** refers to both the censer filled with burning coals and the incense. In some languages it may be clearer to say "these things," or even "the fire pan and the incense."

Within the veil: this clearly refers to the same place as in verses 2 and 3. TEV has translated the meaning clearly: "**into the Most Holy Place.**"

A PRIEST AT THE ALTAR OF INCENSE

16.13   RSV   TEV

and put the incense on the fire before the LORD, that the cloud of the
incense may cover the mercy seat
which is upon the testimony, lest he
die;

There in the LORD's presence he
shall put the incense on the fire, and
the smoke of the incense will hide
the lid of the Covenant Box so that
he will not see it and die.

Before the LORD: the action is more clearly situated in TEV by shifting these words to the beginning of the sentence. This serves to identify the expression "within the veil" of verse 12 as the place where the LORD is present.

On the fire: or, "on the (burning) coals."

The cloud of incense: the **cloud** here is thick smoke which prevents a person from seeing clearly. It is reminiscent of the smoke in Exodus 19.9, in which the LORD is at the same time hidden and revealed.

Cover: in this context the most important element of meaning is "to conceal" or "to hide," as is brought out in TEV.

Mercy seat: see verse 2.

The testimony: the context clearly shows that the Ark, or "**Covenant Box**," is intended here. In order to avoid confusing the reader, it is probably best to translate using the same terminology as in verse 2.

Lest he die: this expression already seen in verse 2 may be rendered "so that he will not die because of seeing it," or something similar. This will show more clearly the relationship between death and the hiding or covering of the lid of the box. In some languages it may be advisable to translate the pronoun **he** by the noun "Aaron," in order to make sure that the readers understand who is involved.

16.14	RSV	TEV
	and he shall take some of the blood of the bull, and sprinkle it with his finger on the front of the mercy seat, and before the mercy seat he shall sprinkle the blood with his finger seven times.	He shall take some of the bull's blood and with his finger sprinkle it on the front of the lid and then sprinkle some of it seven times in front of the Covenant Box.

On the front of . . . before: some commentators take these two prepositional phrases to be synonymous expressions describing a single action. Others see them as separate actions. One commentator (Keil) indicates that **on the front** means "not upon the top of the *capporeth* [mercy seat], but merely upon or up against the front of it." Several reliable modern versions, however, translate the first of these two expressions as "on the east side of" or "eastward" (NJV, NEB, AT, NJB, TOB, and Mft). The Israelites faced eastward when talking about directions, so the east side would be **the front of the mercy seat** and would be the same as **before** it. A good model for the two expressions in many languages is therefore "on the sunrise [east] side of the Covenant Box, that is, in front of it." The action was probably a scattering or sprinkling of the blood in the air immediately in front of the Covenant Box, with some of the blood falling on the front part of the box itself and some on the ground in front of it.

Seven times: see 4.6.

16.15	RSV	TEV
	"Then he shall kill the goat of the sin offering which is for the people, and bring its blood within the veil, and do with its blood as he did with the blood of the bull, sprinkling	After that, he shall kill the goat for the sin offering for the people, bring its blood into the Most Holy Place, and sprinkle it on the lid and then in front of the Covenant Box, as

**it upon the mercy seat and before   he did with the bull's blood.
the mercy seat;**

Then: or "Afterwards," or "Next . . . ," indicating the continuation of a sequence of events.

The goat of the sin offering: that is, the goat provided as a sin offering. Some may translate "the goat which had been brought as a sin offering."

Upon . . . before: the prepositions present the same problem as in verse 14. So the solution here should be similar to the one adopted in the previous verse. The use of the simple preposition "**on**" by TEV in this verse appears to be inconsistent with the expression "on the front of the lid" in the previous verse.

16.16   RSV   TEV

thus he shall make atonement for the holy place, because of the uncleannesses of the people of Israel, and because of their transgressions, all their sins; and so he shall do for the tent of meeting, which abides with them in the midst of their uncleannesses.	In this way he will perform the ritual to purify the Most Holy Place from the uncleanness of the people of Israel and from all their sins. He must do this to the Tent, because it stands in the middle of the camp, which is ritually unclean.

Thus: some languages may begin this verse by saying "This is what he must do to purify . . . ."

Make atonement: the verb here is more often used of making atonement for people, but note that in 8.15 atonement is also made for the altar. It may be necessary in some languages to use a different verb here, since it is a place that is involved and not a person. However, the context makes it quite clear that it is the sin of the people of Israel that makes the **holy place** unclean and in need of atonement.

The holy place: as in verses 2 and 3, the reference is certainly to the Most Holy Place, and this should be made clear in the translation.

Uncleannesses . . . transgressions . . . sins: the first two Hebrew words are almost synonymous in this context. It may be possible to translate the first in terms of failure to do what is right, and the second as actively doing what is wrong. However, it is unnecessary to strain for two separate terms if this becomes difficult in the receptor language. The idea is to include all possible forms of "sin."

The tent of meeting: see 1.1. Some translators may feel it necessary to say "the rest of the Tent of the LORD's presence," because the ritual had already been performed for the Most Holy Place, which is a part of the Tent.

In the midst of their uncleannesses: or "in the middle of the camp where they live unclean lives," or "surrounded by the uncleanness of the camp." There seems to be no special significance in the use of the plural **uncleannesses** here, and so it is translated by a singular form in many modern versions.

16.17   RSV   TEV

There shall be no man in the tent of   From the time Aaron enters the Most
meeting when he enters to make   Holy Place to perform the ritual of
atonement in the holy place until he   purification until he comes out, there
comes out and has made atonement   must be no one in the Tent. When he
for himself and for his house and for   has performed the ritual for himself,
all the assembly of Israel.   his family, and the whole community,

No man: this, of course, includes both men and women. It will probably be
better translated "**no one**" or "no person."

Until he comes out: this information is shifted forward in TEV and phrased in
a different way by saying "**From the time Aaron enters the Most Holy Place . . . ,**"
implying that the prohibition continues until he leaves. Note also that with regard to
the pronoun **he**, the reference is to Aaron, and this should probably be made explicit
in most languages.

The holy place: see verses 2, 3 as well as 6.16 and 26.

House: meaning "household" or "family," as in verses 6 and 11.

All the assembly of Israel: that is, the entire community of the Israelites.
Compare 4.13.

16.18   RSV   TEV

Then he shall go out to the altar   he must then go out to the altar for
which is before the LORD and make   burnt offerings and purify it. He must
atonement for it, and shall take some   take some of the bull's blood and
of the blood of the bull and of the   some of the goat's blood and put it
blood of the goat, and put it on the   all over the projections at the cor-
horns of the altar round about.   ners of the altar.

Then: or "Next," or "After that," once again indicating the continuation of a
sequence of events.

Go out to the altar: the Hebrew text may be understood in two different ways,
depending on whether the altar referred to is the altar of sacrifice, located at the
entrance to the Tent of the LORD's presence, or the altar of incense, which was
inside the first part of the tent. Jewish commentators generally prefer the second
interpretation, but modern Christian commentators are almost unanimous in their
support of the first. This means that Aaron goes "to the entrance of the Tent to the
altar of sacrifice." TEV makes this simpler and clearer by specifying "**the altar for
burnt offerings.**"

Which is before the LORD: this information, which serves to emphasize the
holiness of the altar, has been left implicit in TEV.

Make atonement for it: see 4.20 and 12.7.

Bull and . . . goat: see verses 11 and 15.

Horns of the altar: see 4.7.

And he shall sprinkle some of the blood upon it with his finger seven times, and cleanse it and hallow it from the uncleannesses of the people of Israel.	With his finger he must sprinkle some of the blood on the altar seven times. In this way he is to purify it from the sins of the people of Israel and make it holy.

Shall sprinkle . . . : compare verse 14.

His finger seven times: see 4.6.

Cleanse it: TEV adds **"In this way"** at the beginning of a new sentence in order to make clear that the ritual of purification is not a new and different act, but that it is actually performed by the sprinkling of blood on the altar.

Hallow it: this is the same verb that is often translated "sanctify" elsewhere. It may also be rendered "consecrate" or "make holy." FRCL has "restore its sacred character."

From the uncleannesses of the people of Israel: grammatically this phrase depends on the two preceding verbs, **cleanse** and **hallow** (as in RSV). TEV and NJV relate it more directly to the first of these verbs. The proximity of the sinful Israelites to the altar contaminated it little by little and made it necessary to have a ceremony to reestablish the proper state required for it to be used in relationship to God. As in verse 16, the plural **uncleannesses** seems to have no special significance.

TEV Section Heading: **"The Scapegoat."**

Other languages may not have such a short and simple term as exists in English. So translators may have to use a more descriptive phrase such as "The goat that takes away sins" or "The goat that bears sin."

"And when he has made an end of atoning for the holy place and the tent of meeting and the altar, he shall present the live goat;	When Aaron has finished performing the ritual to purify the Most Holy Place, the rest of the Tent of the LORD's presence, and the altar, he shall present to the LORD the live goat chosen for Azazel.[f]

[f] AZAZEL: *See 16.8.*

When he has made an end of atoning . . . : literally, "and he shall finish to atone . . . ." But this is to be taken as a relative clause setting the time for the presentation of the second goat mentioned in verses 7-10.

The holy place: see verses 2 and 16a.

The tent of meeting: this will have to be translated "the rest of the tent of meeting" in most cases. See verse 16b.

The altar: see verses 18-19.

Present: in many languages this verb requires an object. TEV makes explicit the fact that the animal is presented **"to the LORD."**

The live goat: see verses 8 and 10. TEV has taken implicit information found earlier in the chapter and made it explicit here by adding "**chosen for Azazel.**" Since this is some distance from the previous reference, it will be helpful in many languages to do something similar in the receptor language.

16.21 RSV	TEV
and Aaron shall lay both his hands upon the head of the live goat, and confess over him all the iniquities of the people of Israel, and all their transgressions, all their sins; and he shall put them upon the head of the goat, and send him away into the wilderness by the hand of a man who is in readiness.	He shall put both of his hands on the goat's head and confess over it all the evils, sins, and rebellions of the people of Israel, and so transfer them to the goat's head. Then the goat is to be driven off into the desert by a man appointed to do it.

Shall lay both his hands: in many languages it is unnecessary and even awkward to introduce the term **both** when the plural for **hands** is used. But in other cases it is possible to use the word for emphasis. Naturalness in the receptor language will determine what the translator does in this case. It should be remembered, however, that the usual practice was to put only one hand on the head of the sin offering (see 4.4). So some kind of emphasis is desirable if it can be done naturally in the language of translation.

The live goat: it may be unnecessary in some languages to repeat the word **live** if one says "that goat [already referred to in verse 20]" or simply "the goat," using the definite article.

Confess: if the usual term for this is a technical term which may have undesirable connotations, a similar term may be used, such as "recite," "admit," or "list." See 5.5.

Iniquities . . . transgressions . . . sins . . . : in the following verse these three terms are summarized with the single word "iniquities." They are practically synonymous here but should be translated as separate words if the receptor language has the resources to do so. See verse 16.

Put them upon the head of the goat: in some languages it may be better to omit the reference to the head of the animal, since it is the whole animal that goes away into the desert. But the more difficult problem is to understand how, or in what sense, the sins of the people can be transferred to the goat. It may be necessary to say something like "assigning them to the goat," or "passing them on to the goat," or "transmitting them to the goat." In some languages a careful choice of expression for **confess** may help clarify the idea of a transfer of guilt.

And send him away . . . : instead of the conjunction **and**, it may be more understandable if a stronger transition word such as "then" or "next" is used in this context. The verb used here has been understood to mean "**driven off**" (TEV) or "lead away" (compare AT). But the verb "to send" seems out of place here. According to Jewish tradition the goat is taken to the top of a high cliff or ledge and then pushed off in order that it might be killed. This would imply the presence of someone leading the animal up to the last moment.

By the hand of a man who is in readiness: specific reference to the hand is not necessary and may even be misleading in some languages. The point is that a particular person was designated in advance to be the one who would lead or drive the animal out into the desert. One may translate "by the person appointed (or, chosen) for the task."

16.22   RSV   TEV

The goat shall bear all their iniquities   The goat will carry all their sins away
upon him to a solitary land; and he   with him into some uninhabited land.
shall let the goat go in the wilder-
ness.

All their iniquities: or "the punishment for all their guilt" (see also verses 16 and 21).

To a solitary land: literally, "to a land of separation [or cutting]." The Hebrew word for "separation" or "cutting" used here is found nowhere else in the Old Testament, so its origin and exact meaning are uncertain. It has been understood in different ways by scholars. NJV translates "an inaccessible region"; NAB "an isolated region"; NJB "some desolate place." In this case it is synonymous with the word **wilderness**, which has as its main component of meaning the fact that no human beings live in the area. TEV has, in fact, shortened and combined the two parts of this verse into a single statement, taking **a solitary land** and **the wilderness** together.

He shall let the goat go: this provides added support for the argument that the animal is led away rather than driven from the camp. Both GECL and TEV have omitted this detail. Some versions take this last sentence as a temporal clause introducing the following verse. It is set off as a new paragraph in FRCL and translated "As soon as the goat has been sent into the desert . . . ."

16.23   RSV   TEV

   "Then Aaron shall come into   Then Aaron shall go into the
the tent of meeting, and shall put off   Tent, take off the priestly garments
the linen garments which he put on   that he had put on before entering
when he went into the holy place,   the Most Holy Place, and leave them
and shall leave them there;   there.

Then: see the remarks at the end of the previous verse.

Come into the tent: in many languages the verb **come** can only be used if the writer were himself inside the tent at the time of writing. In such cases it is much better to use the verb "to go," as in TEV, or "enter" (NEB and Mft). NJB emphasizes the fact that he is actually returning to the tent, by saying "Aaron will go back into the Tent . . . ."

Tent of meeting: see 1.1.

The linen garments: see verse 4 and 6.10.

The holy place: as elsewhere in this account, this refers to the Most Holy Place.

16.24   RSV   TEV

and he shall bathe his body in water   He must take a bath in a holy place
in a holy place, and put on his gar-   and put on his own clothes. After
ments, and come forth, and offer his   that, he shall go out and offer the
burnt offering and the burnt offering   burnt offering to remove his own
of the people, and make atonement   sins and those of the people.
for himself and for the people.

Bathe his body in water: literally, "bathe his flesh in water." The reference to water will be superfluous in many languages. And in others there may exist a verb like **bathe** which implies "to wash one's body." See verse 4.

A holy place: this is not the Holy Place as in verses 2 and 17 above, but rather a special place set aside for this purpose. Compare also 6.16.

His garments: some sort of adjustment may be necessary in order to avoid leaving the impression that it is the priestly clothing which is put back on. TEV has **"his own clothes."** AT and Mft have "his other clothes." Still others suggest "his usual (or, everyday) clothing." JB has "he is to put the vestments on again," but this is not recommended.

His burnt offering and the burnt offering of the people: FRCL proposes "the two burnt offerings." Given the context, this would lighten the otherwise heavy structure of the verse and lose nothing of the meaning. But it is important to make it clear that the priest's offering is separate from that of the people. For this reason TEV is not a good model at this point.

16.25   RSV   TEV

And the fat of the sin offering he   He shall burn on the altar the fat of
shall burn upon the altar.   the animal for the sin offering.

Some commentators have suggested that this verse is out of place and should follow verse 19 above (compare Mft). But translators are advised to deal with it here.

The fat: or "the fatty parts"; see 4.8-10.

The sin offering: this clearly refers to an animal, or perhaps animals. FRCL proposes the plural, since there were two that were offered, a bull in verse 3 and a goat in verse 5. The singular may give the impression that there was only one animal involved in this type of sacrifice.

16.26 RSV TEV

And he who lets the goat go to Azazel shall wash his clothes and bathe
his body in water, and afterward he
may come into the camp.

The man who drove the goat into the
desert to Azazel must wash his
clothes and take a bath before he
comes back into camp.

He who lets the goat go: or "the person who led [or drove] the goat . . . ."
Compare verse 21.

Wash his clothes: see 11.25.

Bathe his body in water: see verses 4 and 24 above.

And afterward he may come into the camp: in some languages it will be
better to make a new sentence and say something like "Only after doing these things
is he allowed to return to the camp." NEB has "not till then is he allowed to enter
the camp." It may also be possible in some languages to reorder the entire verse and
say something like "Before returning to camp, the man who led the goat into the
desert to Azazel is required to wash his clothes and take a bath." Or "before he is
allowed to rejoin the community, the one who took the goat to Azazel in the desert
must wash his clothes and his body."

16.27 RSV TEV

And the bull for the sin offering and
the goat for the sin offering, whose
blood was brought in to make
atonement in the holy place, shall be
carried forth outside the camp; their
skin and their flesh and their dung
shall be burned with fire.

The bull and the goat used for the
sin offering, whose blood was
brought into the Most Holy Place to
take away sin, shall be carried outside the camp and burned. Skin,
meat, and intestines shall all be
burned.

The structure of the first part of this verse may be simplified as in TEV.

The holy place: see 6.16,26 as well as verse 2 above.

Shall be carried: literally, "he shall carry." The passive of RSV may be
rendered actively as "the High Priest shall carry . . ." or "Aaron shall carry . . . ." Or
perhaps better, it may be translated by a causative expression like "he shall cause
someone to carry . . ." or "he must have it carried . . ." (see comments on 4.12).

Their dung: this is taken by TEV as referring to the intestines of the animals.
Several other versions take it to mean the contents of the intestines (NIV, NJB, NAB,
and NEB have "offal," while NASB says "refuse"). More than likely it referred to both
the intestines and their waste contents, since it is difficult to imagine the priests
separating the two in order to burn only the contents. The term used here is
therefore probably synonymous with the more explicit "entrails and . . . dung" in
4.11.

Shall be burned: literally, "they shall burn." This may be understood as an
impersonal or indefinite reference. But the reference is probably not to the High
Priest in this case; someone else or several other persons would take care of this
task. An indefinite "they" or "someone" will be adequate in most languages where

the passive is not possible. As in the expression above, this can also be rendered as a causative such as "he [the priest] must have someone burn . . . ."

With fire: as in 6.30, this will be considered redundant in many languages and may therefore be dropped.

16.28 RSV TEV

And he who burns them shall wash his clothes and bathe his body in water, and afterward he may come into the camp.

The one who burns them must wash his clothes and take a bath before he returns to camp.

He who burns them: this may also be made more explicit by saying "the person who burns the bull and the goat."

Wash his clothes: see 11.25.

Bathe his body in water: see verses 4, 24, 26, and 14.9.

Afterward . . . : see verse 26.

TEV Section Heading: "**Observing the Day of Atonement**."

NEB titles this section "A summarizing conclusion," while NAB has simply "The Fast." Several modern versions, including NJB, NIV, and FRCL, leave the section heading out at this point, considering the following paragraph a part of the previous section.

16.29 RSV TEV

"And it shall be a statute to you for ever that in the seventh month, on the tenth day of the month, you shall afflict yourselves, and shall do no work, either the native or the stranger who sojourns among you;

The following regulations are to be observed for all time to come. On the tenth day of the seventh month the Israelites and the foreigners living among them must fast and must not do any work.

A statute to you forever: this indicates that the set of rules given are to be considered permanent. See 3.17, where the same words are translated "a perpetual statute" in RSV. Compare also 10.9.

The seventh month, on the tenth day: translators should consider whether it is more natural in their own language to follow the RSV order (month, day) or the TEV order (day, month). In those languages where the seventh month will be understood as meaning July, something must be done to help the reader understand that the Jewish system was quite different from that of the receptor language. Probably the best way to do this is to prepare a table showing the different calendar systems used in the Old Testament, compared with the system or systems known to the reader. This should be included at the beginning or end of the translation and not

as a footnote to the text here. Both JB (page 477) and NJB (page 2076) have such a
table in their "Supplements" at the end of the book.

Afflict yourselves: literally, "afflict your souls." This is often taken to mean
"fasting," as in TEV, NJB, and TOB, but it may have been a more general self-denial
that included abstaining from all food, drink, sex, wearing sandals, and even bathing.
This interpretation is implied in the translations "deny yourselves" (NIV) and
"practice self-denial" (NJV). Many languages, however, do not allow such a general
statement without saying precisely what the person is to deny himself. It is probably
better to translate "**fast**" or "eat nothing," and if necessary a note may be added to
explain that the word may have a broader meaning. In those parts of the world where
Muslim influence is strong, translators must take special care to avoid the giving the
impression that "fasting" means only to abstain from food and drink during daylight
hours. Biblical fasting does not correspond to this Muslim concept. In some cases it
will be necessary to clarify this in a footnote or a glossary explanation, since there
may be only one word available in the language, but one that will almost certainly
convey the wrong idea.

Do no work: this requirement is generally associated with the Sabbath (see 23.3
and Exo 20.8-10) or with different feast days (Lev 23.7,21,25,28,35-36). As several of
these passages indicate, abstaining from work has a double goal: it allows for physical
rest, and it makes people available for serving God. The translator should be careful
to avoid an expression that will place the emphasis only on physical rest.

The native: this is a collective singular, but all the Israelites are obviously
intended. In some languages the word for **native** may be understood as a member
of one particular language group. This may be avoided by saying explicitly "you
Israelites" or something similar.

The stranger who sojourns among you: this is another collective singular
referring to any and all foreigners who happened to be among the people of Israel.
As in the case of **native** above, the word **stranger** may be understood as any person
who is not a member of the receptor-language group. If this is the case, it may be
necessary to say "any non-Israelites living among you" or "any other people (or,
tribes) living among you."

16.30   RSV   TEV

for on this day shall atonement be   On that day the ritual is to be per-
made for you, to cleanse you; from   formed to purify them from all their
all your sins you shall be clean be-   sins, so that they will be ritually
fore the LORD.   clean.

On this day: a literal translation of this expression may give the reader the
impression that the day referred to is the day on which he is reading the material, or
the day on which it was written. The reference, however, is clearly to the day of
atonement, which we are told in verse 29 was on the tenth day of the seventh month
in the Jewish calendar. It may be better to translate "on the appointed day" or
something similar. Or the verse may be more radically restructured to begin "That
is the day when atonement shall be made . . . ."

Shall atonement be made: this passive construction must be made active in some languages. The subject must then be "the High Priest." See 4.20.

You shall be clean before the LORD: this may also be translated "the LORD will make you [ritually] clean." See verse 2.

16.31   RSV   TEV

| It is a sabbath of solemn rest to you, and you shall afflict yourselves; it is a statute for ever. | That day is to be a very holy day, one on which they fast and do no work at all. These regulations are to be observed for all times to come. |

A sabbath of solemn rest: the term **sabbath** comes from the verb meaning "to abandon work" or "to rest." It is similar to the word for "seven," and it was on the seventh day that the LORD rested, following the work of creation. The basic meaning has to do with refraining from all work because of the special nature of the day. It is probably better in this context not to use a transliteration of the term but to translate dynamically, as in TEV. Some have even proposed "it shall be a day of complete rest, like the Sabbath." Compare 23.3.

Afflict yourselves: see verse 29.

A statute for ever: see verse 29. Compare also 3.17 and 10.9.

16.32   RSV   TEV

| And the priest who is anointed and consecrated as priest in his father's place shall make atonement, wearing the holy linen garments; | The High Priest, properly ordained and consecrated to succeed his father, is to perform the ritual of purification. He shall put on the priestly garments |

Is anointed and consecrated: literally "whom he (indefinite) anointed him and whose hand he (indefinite) has filled to be a priest." The passive forms of RSV may be translated actively with an impersonal subject, "they have (or, someone has) anointed and consecrated . . . ." This construction is, in fact, closer to the Hebrew. On the term "anoint," see 4.3. On the word "consecrate," see 7.35 and 8.10.

As priest: that is, as the High Priest.

In his father's place: or "to replace his father," or "as a successor to his father."

Make atonement: see 1.4.

Holy linen garments: literally, "the linen garments, the holy garments." The second expression in Hebrew emphasizes the fact that this clothing is reserved for a particular purpose. See verse 4.

16.33   RSV   TEV

he shall make atonement for the sanctuary, and he shall make atonement for the tent of meeting and for the altar, and he shall make atonement for the priests and for all the people of the assembly.	and perform the ritual to purify the Most Holy Place, the rest of the Tent of the LORD's presence, the altar, the priests, and all the people of the community.

Make atonement for the sanctuary . . . for the tent of meeting and for the altar: as seen in the literal rendering of RSV, the verb **make atonement** is repeated three times. But this repetition may be reduced as in TEV, if it is unnatural in the receptor language. Compare verse 16.

The sanctuary: this refers to the Most Holy Place. See verse 2.

The tent of meeting: or "the rest of the tent of meeting," since the Most Holy Place already mentioned was also a part of the Tent. See verse 16.

All the people of the assembly: the **assembly** or "**community**" refers to Israel. In some translations it may be advisable to make this explicit; for example, "all the people of Israel" or "the whole tribe of Israel."

16.34   RSV   TEV

And this shall be an everlasting statute for you, that atonement may be made for the people of Israel once in the year because of all their sins." And Moses did as the LORD commanded him.	These regulations are to be observed for all time to come. This ritual must be performed once a year to purify the people of Israel from all their sins. So Moses*g* did as the Lord had commanded.

g Moses: *or* Aaron.

Shall be: not at some distant future time, but "from now on."

An everlasting statute: although the noun is singular in form, it clearly refers to the entire set of rules. In some languages it will be much more natural to translate it as a plural. The qualifying word **everlasting** is intended to indicate permanence. Together they may be translated "permanent regulations" or "rules that will last forever."

That atonement may be made: this passive construction may be rendered actively with "the priests" as the subject.

Because of all their sins: or, "to cleanse them from all their sins."

And: in TEV this is translated "**So**" and is set apart as a separate paragraph which is intended to highlight the summary nature of this statement.

Moses: as the TEV footnote indicates, "Aaron" may be intended as the subject here. The text literally says "and he did just as the LORD had commanded Moses." The pronoun "he" may be understood to refer to Aaron rather than Moses (as in FRCL). NJB avoids the problem by using the passive form: "And as Yahweh ordered

Moses, so it was done" (similarly NIV, AT, and NAB). If the passive is not possible in the receptor language, translators may wish to make Aaron the subject in spite of the RSV base and the TEV model.

Chapter 17

Chapter 17 begins the last major section of Leviticus. This part is sometimes called the "Holiness Code." It groups together, under the theme of holiness, a variety of elements which distinguish the people of Israel from the other groups of people around them. The first chapter in this section speaks of the respect one should show to the blood of sacrificial animals. Chapters 18 and 20 deal in slightly different ways with the attitude of the believing Jew towards marriage. Chapter 19 shows how belief in God affects the social behavior of human beings. In chapters 21 and 22 there are a variety of regulations concerning the priests (21.1–22.16) and Israelites in general (22.17-33). Chapter 23 lists the various religious celebrations in Israel. In chapter 24 three rather diverse matters are dealt with. Chapter 25 presents the theme of the respect due to nature and the dignity of being human. Finally, chapter 26 is a sort of conclusion to this fourth major section of the book.

For the titles of the major sections of the book, see the remarks in the introduction and at the beginning of chapter 1. If more than one level of titles is being used, this section may be called "The holiness of Israel." If the translation of "holiness" presents a serious problem in the receptor language, one may try something like "What makes Israel different" or "Behavior which shows that Israel belongs to God."

TEV Section Heading: **"The Sacredness of Blood."**

Some other possible headings for this section are "Rules concerning the blood of sacrifices," "Eating blood forbidden" (NIV), or "The proper place of sacrifice" (NEB). This section heading serves for the entire chapter.

17.1-2	RSV	TEV

RSV	TEV
1 And the LORD said to Moses, 2 "Say to Aaron and his sons, and to all the people of Israel, This is the thing which the LORD has commanded.	1 The LORD commanded Moses 2 to give Aaron and his sons and all the people of Israel the following regulations.

Said to Moses: see 4.1.

Say: see 1.2. The structure of these two verses may be simplified according to the model provided by TEV, without losing any of the meaning. Three different levels of quotations may be too complex for many languages.

To Aaron and his sons: this can also be translated "to the priests," since this is clearly the meaning.

3 If any man of the house of Israel kills an ox or a lamb or a goat in the camp, or kills it outside the camp, 4 and does not bring it to the door of the tent of meeting, to offer it as a gift to the LORD before the tabernacle of the LORD, bloodguilt shall be imputed to that man; he has shed blood; and that man shall be cut off from among his people.

3-4 An Israelite who kills a cow or a sheep or a goat as an offering to the LORD anywhere except at the entrance of the Tent of the LORD's presence has broken the Law. He has shed blood and shall no longer be considered one of God's people.

In Hebrew, verses 3-5 constitute one long sentence, but this should be broken down into shorter and simpler sentences in the receptor language. Verses 3-4 together form one part of the law forbidding the killing of a sacrificial animal anywhere other than at the entrance of the Tent of the LORD's presence. HOTTP provides a long discussion of the textual problem in these two verses. The Greek Septuagint and the Hebrew of the Samaritan Pentateuch have a longer text which adds the words "to make it a burnt offering, or peace offerings or shared offerings, so as to be accepted, as a pleasing odor . . . ." These words come immediately after ". . . tent of meeting . . . ." This reading is recommended by HOTTP but is not adopted by any major modern version. Translators may therefore wish to follow the traditional text and, if necessary, add a simple footnote stating that the longer text exists.

Any man of the house of Israel: that is, any member of the tribe of Israel, or more simply "any Israelite."

Kills: this Hebrew verb, sometimes translated "slaughter" (Exo 29.16), suggests the usual mode of killing for sacrifice, which included cutting the throat of the animal to be offered and allowing its blood to drain out. In those cultures where this practice is customary, the translator should use the corresponding technical terms, provided they are well known. Where no such technical terms exist, a more generic formulation may be used.

An ox . . . a lamb . . . a goat . . . : see 7.23.

In the camp . . . outside the camp . . . : this entire construction is a rather awkward way of saying "any place other than at the entrance of the Tent."

Tabernacle: this term literally means "dwelling place" and is synonymous with the "tent of meeting," as in 8.10 and 15.31. The translation should therefore probably be the same, in order to avoid confusing the reader or hearer.

Bloodguilt shall be imputed to that man: This should probably be restructured in most languages. Some possibilities are "that man shall be considered guilty of spilling blood," or "they [indefinite] shall count that man guilty of shedding blood," or "they shall hold him responsible for pouring out blood."

Cut off from among his people: see 7.20. NJB translates here "that man will be outlawed from his people." Other possible translations are "he shall be isolated" or "his people shall have nothing more to do with him."

17.5   RSV   TEV

This is to the end that the people of Israel may bring their sacrifices which they slay in the open field, that they may bring them to the LORD, to the priest at the door of the tent of meeting, and slay them as sacrifices of peace offerings to the LORD;

The meaning of this command is that the people of Israel shall now bring to the LORD the animals which they used to kill in the open country. They shall now bring them to the priest at the entrance of the Tent and kill them as fellowship offerings.

This is to the end that ... : this expression is intended to indicate the purpose or meaning of the regulation. It may be more natural to say "The purpose of this rule is . . ." or "This rule exists so that . . . ."

Bring: TEV adds "**now**," since this is a new regulation. Or it may be better to say "from now on."

In the open field: that is, elsewhere than at the entrance to the Tent (compare verse 7).

Peace offerings: see chapter 3. The intention of the Israelite who killed an animal in the open country should have been to have meat to eat. Only in the "peace offering" does the owner of the animal receive a part of the meat. However, verse 7 seems to indicate that some were practicing an unacceptable kind of sacrifice which should be stopped.

17.6   RSV   TEV

and the priest shall sprinkle the blood on the altar of the LORD at the door of the tent of meeting, and burn the fat for a pleasing odor to the LORD.

The priest shall throw the blood against the sides of the altar at the entrance of the Tent and burn the fat to produce an odor that is pleasing to the LORD.

See 3.2-5.

The altar . . . at the door of the tent of meeting: this refers to the altar of sacrifice and not the incense altar.

17.7   RSV   TEV

So they shall no more slay their sacrifices for satyrs, after whom they play the harlot. This shall be a statute for ever to them throughout their generations.

The people of Israel must no longer be unfaithful to the LORD by killing their animals in the fields as sacrifices to the goat demons. The people of Israel must keep this regulation for all time to come.

They: the pronoun refers to the whole community of Israel; it will be better translated as a noun phrase in many languages; for example, "**The people of Israel**" (TEV).

Satyrs: the English word found in RSV, AT, NJB, and Mft suggests several meanings (including "a lecherous man"!), none of which is really appropriate here. The Hebrew word actually means "goats" and is so translated by at least three French translations. But it refers to something more than an ordinary goat. It is a kind of demonic being in the form of a goat. Therefore it is rendered "**goat demons**" by TEV, NJV, and NASB. KJV and NEB have simply "demons," but this leaves out a significant element. The NIV rendering "goat-idols" seems to imply something less lively than the context requires. The LB rendering "evil spirits" is inaccurate. Translators should consider "demons that look like goats" or something similar. Compare "Azazel" in 16.8,10,26, as well as Isaiah 13.21; 34.14.

Play the harlot: this is a common expression in the Old Testament to speak of unfaithfulness toward God. The LORD expects the undivided loyalty and complete love of his people (see Exo 20.4-6). A person who worships or makes sacrifices to another god while claiming loyalty to the LORD, is like a man committing adultery, who betrays his wife and is unfaithful to his promise. This is why the Old Testament uses this image so often. (See for example Exo 34.15-16 and the whole theme of the book of Hosea). This image has added significance in light of the fact that many pagan cults at the time practiced "temple prostitution" (see 19.29 and Hos 1.2). In many languages it will probably be better to drop the image and translate the meaning directly—something like "be unfaithful" or "deny your love." But in other languages it may be possible to retain the image and convey the meaning: "be unfaithful to the LORD, like a man cheating on his wife."

A statute for ever: see 3.17; 10.9; 16.29,31.

17.8 RSV	TEV
"And you shall say to them, Any man of the house of Israel, or of the strangers that sojourn among them, who offers a burnt offering or sacrifice,	Any Israelite or any foreigner living in the community who offers a burnt offering or any other sacrifice

In Hebrew verses 8 and 9 are worded in the same way as verses 3-4. They provide a resume of what has already been stated in the previous verses. But they also add two new bits of information: that the rule also applies to foreigners, and that it concerns burnt offerings as well.

And you shall say to them . . . : this is a repetition, or reminder, of what is said at the beginning (verses 1-2). It is quite possible to leave this information implicit, as has been done in TEV. But it may also be possible in some languages to use such a phrase to remind the reader that this is a continuation of what the LORD told Moses to communicate to the people of Israel.

Any man of the house of Israel: see verse 3.

Strangers that sojourn among them: here we are concerned with the category of foreigners or immigrants defined in 16.29.

Burnt offering: see chapter 1. Even if the desire to eat the meat of the animal (verse 5) is not the basic motivation, the slaughter of the animal may not take place just anywhere.

Sacrifice: TEV clarifies the meaning by adding "**any other sacrifice.**"

17.9 RSV	TEV
and does not bring it to the door of the tent of meeting, to sacrifice it to the LORD; that man shall be cut off from his people.	**as an offering to the LORD anywhere except at the entrance of the Tent shall no longer be considered one of God's people.**

Compare verse 4.

Cut off from his people: see verse 4 as well as 7.20.

17.10 RSV	TEV
"**If any man of the house of Israel or of the strangers that sojourn among them eats any blood, I will set my face against that person who eats blood, and will cut him off from among his people.**	**If any Israelite or any foreigner living in the community eats meat with blood still in it, the LORD will turn against him and no longer consider him one of his people.**

Any man of the house of Israel: see verse 3.

Strangers . . . : see verse 8. Compare also 16.29.

Eats any blood: it may be necessary to say "eats any meat from which the blood has not been drained" in many languages. Since blood is liquid, it cannot be "eaten" in many cultures. Mft's "tastes any blood" is probably too strong a statement. NJB makes the prohibition more general with "consumes blood."

I will set my face against: if the receptor language translation has chosen to use indirect rather than direct quotation, then the pronoun I should be translated "the LORD." The expression "set one's face against" may be translated in some languages as "turn one's back on" or "look away from" (see 20.3, 6; 26:17; Ezek 14.8; 15.7). The basic meaning is "to reject" or "to repudiate," implying hostile action.

Against that person who eats blood: since this expression has already been used at the beginning of this verse, it may be replaced by a pronoun here, "against him," or else simply "against that person."

Cut off . . . : in this context it is the LORD who is the subject of the verb (the pronoun I in the more literal rendering of RSV). The basic meaning of the verb is, however, essentially the same as in verses 4 and 9 as well as in 7.20, where it is passive in form. See the remarks at 7.20.

17.11 RSV TEV

For the life of the flesh is in the blood; and I have given it for you upon the altar to make atonement for your souls; for it is the blood that makes atonement, by reason of the life.	**The life of every living thing is in the blood, and that is why the LORD has commanded that all blood be poured out on the altar to take away the people's sins. Blood, which is life, takes away sins.**

The life of the flesh is in the blood: the word **flesh** is to be understood as referring to living beings in general, including humans, animals, birds, etc. NEB has "the life of a creature," and the TEV rendering "**every living thing**" is similar in meaning. NAB reads "every living body." In some languages one may say "everything that breathes."

I: if indirect speech is used, this pronoun must be translated once again by the noun "**the LORD**," as in TEV.

For your souls: or simply "for you," referring to all the people of Israel, not just the priests. This is why TEV has "**the people's sins.**"

Have given it for you upon the altar: the pronoun **it** refers to the blood. The verb **given** has the meaning of "appointed" (NEB). That is, God has arranged or ordered that blood be used as the means of taking away sins.

By reason of the life: the sense of this expression is that blood and life are equated. This does not differ from the meaning already expressed in the beginning of this verse, but it is added for emphasis and should be retained in the receptor language, unless the repetition of the same idea is stylistically unacceptable. In some translations the wording is even more explicit because the implied subject of the verb "take away sins" is the priest: "it is because blood carries life that the priest can use it in the ritual of pardoning sins." Others refer to the action of God rather than the priest as intermediary: "it is because blood is life that God can use it to pardon our sins."

17.12 RSV TEV

Therefore I have said to the people of Israel, No person among you shall eat blood, neither shall any stranger who sojourns among you eat blood.	**That is why the LORD has told the people of Israel that neither they nor any foreigner living among them shall eat any meat with blood still in it.**

I: again, the pronoun should be translated by the noun "**LORD**," if indirect speech is being used as in verses 10 and 11.

RSV has another direct quotation within the quotation of the words of the LORD. But this may be changed to indirect speech if it is more natural in the language. In that case translators should give attention to the necessary pronoun changes.

Eat blood: see verse 10.

17.13   RSV   TEV

Any man also of the people of Israel,   If any Israelite or any foreigner
or of the strangers that sojourn   living in the community catches an
among them, who takes in hunting   animal or a bird which is ritually
any beast or bird that may be eaten   clean, he must pour its blood out on
shall pour out its blood and cover it   the ground and cover it with dirt.
with dust.

Any man also of the people of Israel: literally, "and any man of the sons of
Israel." This expression is slightly different from the similar one in verses 3, 8, and
10 ("any man of the house of Israel"). But the meaning seems to be identical, so it
is unnecessary to search for a separate expression here.

Strangers: see verses 8, 10, and 16.29.

Who takes in hunting: this is a rather odd expression in the English of RSV.
But it simply means "who hunts." In some languages there may be completely
different words for hunting animals and hunting birds. If this is the case the logical
adjustments must be made, and the two verbs will appear in the receptor language
rendering. TEV's "catches" implies hunting.

That may be eaten: this refers to those animals and birds considered "clean"
according to chapter 11. If necessary the translator may want to say "an animal or
a bird which is ritually clean" (TEV). This is one way to avoid the passive form of
RSV.

Shall pour out its blood: in some languages it will be clearer to say "shall
pour the blood of the animal on the ground."

Cover it with dust: the Hebrew word here translated dust does not emphasize
the powdery nature of the material as the RSV rendering would lead us to believe.
It is rather a more general term for loose, dry earth. In 14.41-45 it is used three
times and translated "plaster." Here it is better to translate "earth" or "dirt."

17.14   RSV   TEV

"For the life of every creature is   The life of every living thing is in the
the blood of it,^e therefore I have said   blood, and that is why the LORD has
to the people of Israel, You shall not   told the people of Israel that they
eat the blood of any creature, for the   shall not eat any meat with blood still
life of every creature is its blood;   in it and that anyone who does so
whoever eats it shall be cut off.   will no longer be considered one of
                                       his people.

^e Grk Syr Compare Vg: Heb *for the life
of all flesh, its blood is in its life*

Although the wording is slightly different here, the meaning of the first phrase
in this verse is the same as verse 11, "the life of the flesh is in the blood." TEV has
therefore translated the two expressions identically. In RSV the same meaning is again
repeated later in the verse.

Therefore: both TEV and NIV have **"that is why . . . ."** The fact already stated explains why the LORD has forbidden the eating of meat from which the blood has not been drained.

I: to be changed to **"the LORD"** if indirect speech is used.

Eat the blood: see verse 10.

Be cut off: see 7.20 as well as verses 4, 9, and 10.

17.15	RSV	TEV

And every person that eats what dies of itself or what is torn by beasts, whether he is a native or a sojourner, shall wash his clothes, and bathe himself in water, and be unclean until the evening; then he shall be clean.	Any person, Israelite or foreigner, who eats meat from an animal that has died a natural death or has been killed by wild animals must wash his clothes, take a bath, and wait until evening before he is ritually clean.

What dies of itself or what is torn by beasts: literally, "a dead body or a torn [animal]." The first term refers to an animal that has died a natural death, and the second to one attacked and killed by another animal. In either case the blood of the dead animal would not have been properly drained, and so the meat could not be eaten.

Native or a sojourner: see 16.29, where the second term is different but the meaning is the same. In this context these terms actually qualify "any person" at the beginning of the verse. TEV and many other versions therefore shift them to a position earlier in the verse so that their function is clearer.

Wash his clothes: see 11.25.

Bathe himself in water: see 15.5.

Be unclean until the evening: see 15.24.

17.16	RSV	TEV

But if he does not wash them or bathe his flesh, he shall bear his iniquity."	If he does not, he must suffer the consequences.

But: marking the contrast between the person who does what is required and the one who fails to do so. NIV, NJV, and NJB also use this conjunction, but a number of English versions leave it untranslated.

Wash them or bathe his flesh: TEV has left this implicit. In other languages it may be better to say "if he does not do what is required" or something similar. Another possibility is to say more explicitly "if he fails to wash his clothes, or if he does not wash his body."

Bear his iniquity: although the precise consequences are not clearly stated here, the general meaning of this phrase is clear. The person failing to do what is prescribed must accept responsibility for his failure to act. Compare 5.1 and 7.18.

Chapter 18

TEV Section Heading: **"Forbidden Sexual Practices."**

Some other possible headings for this section are "The sanctity of sex" (NAB), or "Unlawful sexual relations" (NIV), or "Respect for marriage." This section describes various kinds of sexual relations that were practiced by some of the people who lived near the Israelites, but such practices were unacceptable for the people of God. There is a great deal of repetition of formulas forbidding these different acts. But this repetition is intentional and should be maintained in the receptor language if possible.

18.1-2   RSV   TEV

1 And the LORD said to Moses, 2 "Say to the people of Israel, I am the LORD your God.

1 The LORD told Moses 2 to say to the people of Israel, "I am the LORD your God.

Said to Moses: see 4.1.

Say to the people of Israel: while this may be changed to indirect speech, the actual words of the LORD affirming his identity should probably be retained as a direct quotation, as in TEV.

I am the LORD your God: this affirmation is often found at the beginning or the end of a list of commandments (see, for example, verse 30; 19.3,4,36; 20.24; Exo 20.2; Ezek 20.19); it is the basis on which the commandments are founded. Mft transposes it to the end of the previous section (at the end of chapter 17). But translators are advised to translate it here. It should be rendered in such a way as to give it prominence, rather than making it a part of some other phrase (compare 11.44).

18.3   RSV   TEV

You shall not do as they do in the land of Egypt, where you dwelt, and you shall not do as they do in the land of Canaan, to which I am bringing you. You shall not walk in their statutes.

Do not follow the practices of the people of Egypt, where you once lived, or of the people in the land of Canaan, where I am now taking you.

Literally, this verse reads "As the action [deeds] of the land of Egypt where you lived in it you must not do, and as the action of the land of Canaan where I am bringing you there, you must not do. And the practices of them you must not follow." The repetitive elements in this verse may be eliminated as in TEV, if they are stylistically unacceptable in the receptor language. The Israelites are forbidden to imitate what they had seen in the past (in Egypt) or what they would see in the future (in Canaan). The Egyptians practiced intermarriage of near relatives, which is forbidden in verse 6. And Canaan often symbolizes sexual perversion in the Old Testament (see verse 22 and Gen 19.4-9). Rather they are to follow the rules set down for them by the LORD himself.

Walk: as in many other passages of Scripture, this verb is used to speak of conduct or behavior in general. A literal rendering of RSV may be very misleading in many languages.

Statutes: in this context the word seems to refer more to the customs or practices of an alien culture than to any specific written law code. Hence the TEV rendering "**practices**" (also found in NIV and Mft). NAB reads "customs."

18.4	RSV	TEV
	You shall do my ordinances and keep my statutes and walk in them. I am the LORD your God.	Obey my laws and do what I command. I am the LORD your God.

You shall do . . . and keep: this is clearly not intended to have a simple future tense meaning. Rather it should be translated as an imperative.

Keep: care should be taken not to translate this verb in such a way as to give the impression of conserving or protecting a book containing laws. Instead, the meaning is to perform actively what God requires of his people.

Ordinances and . . . statutes: many languages have difficulty finding such synonyms for "law." TEV provides a good model in this context, with the verbal expression "**what I command.**"

Walk in them: or "live according to them." See verse 3.

18.5	RSV	TEV
	You shall therefore keep my statutes and my ordinances, by doing which a man shall live: I am the LORD.	Follow the practices and the laws that I give you; you will save your life by doing so. I am the LORD."

The beginning of this verse merely repeats in summary form the content of verse 4. The use of **therefore** in RSV serves to highlight the fact that this is a resumé of what goes before it.

By doing which a man shall live: literally, "which a man will do and he will live." The idea that obedience to God's commandments is a source of life is found throughout the Bible (see, for example, Ezek 18.9; Neh 9.29; Luke 10.28; Rom 10.5; Gal 3.12). The word **man** is not intended to focus on the maleness of the person involved; rather, it may be translated in some languages as "any person," or "the person who . . . ," or "whoever . . ." (NJB), depending on the particular structure adopted.

I am the LORD: compare verse 2.

18.6	RSV	TEV

"None of you shall approach any one near of kin to him to uncover nakedness. I am the LORD.	The LORD gave the following regulations. Do not have sexual intercourse with any of your relatives.

TEV shifts from direct to indirect discourse at the beginning of this verse. The nature of the material that follows will make this advisable in a number of languages. But others may wish to retain the direct discourse.

Approach . . . to uncover nakedness: this expression or one of the shorter forms, "uncover the nakedness of" and "approach," are used in almost every verse throughout the rest of this chapter. They simply mean "to have sexual intercourse" or "to commit a sex act." The LB rendering "marry" in verses 10, 11, 15, 17, and 18 is misleading and should be avoided. Since sex is a very private matter, the ways of talking about it are very different from one language to another. It is often spoken of in roundabout ways in expressions like "to hold closely," "to sleep with four feet," "to sleep warmly," or "to make love to." But the Hebrew expression here can also carry the idea of shame or disgrace associated with a sexual relationship that is unacceptable.

One near of kin: literally, "any of the flesh of his body." This expression is used of any close relation. This includes the extended family as well as the immediate family. In fact, the verses that follow list the various relations that are covered by this term. If necessary it will be legitimate in the receptor language to make it clear that the relatives in question are female, even though this is not explicitly stated in Hebrew.

I am the LORD: this is the third time (see verses 2 and 5) that these words are repeated. They are translated by TEV in a different form at the beginning of the verse in this context, since there is a shift to indirect discourse.

18.7	RSV	TEV

You shall not uncover the nakedness of your father, which is the nakedness of your mother; she is your mother, you shall not uncover her nakedness.	Do not disgrace your father by having intercourse with your mother. You must not disgrace your own mother.

In verse 7 and following, the pronouns in Hebrew are in the second person singular form rather than the second person plural as in verses 2-5. But since these are general prohibitions, it is quite acceptable to use the plural throughout in the language of translation.

Uncover the nakedness of your father, which is the nakedness of your mother: this long and awkward expression emphasizes the shamefulness of the act committed but also states the nature of the offense. The fact of having intercourse with the wife of one's own father (that is, the mother of the person committing the immoral act) was considered especially disgraceful. Both the character of the act and its shamefulness are brought out in a rendering like that of NAB "You shall not disgrace your father by having intercourse with your mother. Besides, she is your mother . . . ."

18.8

RSV	TEV
You shall not uncover the nakedness of your father's wife; it is your father's nakedness.	Do not disgrace your father by having intercourse with any of his other wives.

Your father's wife: this means any wife of the father other than the mother of the person spoken to here, since the matter of one's own mother has already been dealt with in the previous verse. Some languages have completely different words for "mother" and "stepmother." TEV translates the meaning clearly with "**any of his other wives**."

18.9

RSV	TEV
You shall not uncover the nakedness of your sister, the daughter of your father or the daughter of your mother, whether born at home or born abroad.	Do not have intercourse with your sister or your stepsister, whether or not she was brought up in the same house with you.

Uncover the nakedness: this expression is repeated more than twenty times in chapters 18 and 20. If such repetition is not natural in the receptor language, it is possible to omit it in some cases ("nor your sister . . . nor your granddaughter . . . nor your aunt . . ." and so forth), or a synonymous expression may be used. But if the repetition is acceptable, it should be retained.

The daughter of your father or the daughter of your mother: these words serve to further define what is meant by the term **sister**. In some languages **sister** can only mean a girl born of the same father and mother. If this is the case, it will be necessary to translate here in such a way that the following are included: (1) the person's full sister, that is, a girl born of both the same parents as the man involved; (2) the person's half-sister, that is, a girl born of the same father as the man but of a different mother, or a girl born of the same mother as the man, but of a different father. All three cases are covered here.

The relationship between the expression **the daughter of your mother** here and "your father's wife's daughter" in verse 11 is important and has been much debated by scholars. It is unlikely that the second expression is merely a repetition of the first. TEV has taken the words in this verse to mean "**stepsister**" (the daughter of one married to the man's own father) and in verse 11 as "half sister" (that is, a sister who has only one parent in common with the man). This appears to have the two reversed. Translators are therefore advised to convey the idea of half-sister in this verse and stepsister in verse 11 below.

Whether born at home or abroad: a number of English versions (RSV, NIV, NJV, and NJB) take the verb "to be born" in its literal sense. Others broaden the meaning to include the upbringing of the girl, with the birth being left implicit (TEV and NEB). The word translated **abroad** in RSV simply means anywhere other than in the home. It would be a mistake to translate simply "outside" as in NASB, giving the impression that it might have taken place just outside the house or in a nearby field. The term is meant to be much broader than this. Wenham translates "whether she belongs to local kindred or distant kindred," and this may provide a good model for some languages.

An example of disobedience to this commandment is found in 2 Samuel 13.1-14.

18.10   RSV   TEV

You shall not uncover the nakedness   **Do not have intercourse with your**
of your son's daughter or of your   **granddaughter; that would be a dis-**
daughter's daughter, for their naked-   **grace to you.**
ness is your own nakedness.

Your son's daughter or your daughter's daughter: in English, these expressions may be summed up with a single term **"granddaughter."** This may also be the case in many other languages. But in those cases where there exist different terms for a granddaughter born through a son and one born through a daughter, both terms should probably be used in the translation of this verse.

Their nakedness is your own nakedness: the meaning of this expression is uncertain, but probably it suggests something like "for that would ruin your own reputation," or "to do that would be dishonoring to you" (compare TEV, NEB, NIV), or "for that would be a disgrace to your own family" (NAB).

18.11   RSV   TEV

You shall not uncover the nakedness   **Do not have intercourse with a half**
of your father's wife's daughter,   **sister; she, too, is your sister.**
begotten by your father, since she is
your sister.

Some have seen this as a repetition of the prohibition found in verse 9, but this is unlikely. See the discussion under verse 9.

18.12-13   RSV   TEV

12 You shall not uncover the naked-   **12-13 Do not have intercourse with**
ness of your father's sister; she is   **an aunt, whether she is your** father's
your   father's   near   kinswoman.   **sister or your mother's sister.**
13 You shall not uncover the naked-
ness of your mother's sister, for she
is your mother's near kinswoman.

Verses 12 and 13 are parallel in structure and repeat a great deal of the same
information. The two may be translated together, and needless or unwanted
repetition may be eliminated, as in TEV.

Near kinswoman: literally, "the flesh of . . . ." This is the same word that is
used in verse 6 to describe any close relation.

18.14   RSV   TEV

You shall not uncover the nakedness   **Do not have intercourse** with your
of your father's brother, that is, you   **uncle's wife; she, too, is your aunt.**
shall not approach his wife; she is
your aunt.

In this verse the expression "to uncover the nakedness of" indicates "to
disgrace," and the verb "to approach" is a polite way of saying "to have sexual
intercourse with." (See Gen 20.4; Deut 22.14; Isa 8.3; Ezek 18.6) The whole verse
may be translated "Do not disgrace your uncle by having intercourse with his wife.
Remember that she is [also] your aunt." Of course some languages, like Hebrew,
have completely separate terms for "paternal aunt" and "maternal aunt." This is
clearly the "paternal aunt."

18.15   RSV   TEV

You shall not uncover the nakedness   **Do not have intercourse** with your
of your daughter-in-law; she is your   **daughter-in-law**
son's wife, you shall not uncover her
nakedness.

TEV avoids the repetition of the second half of this verse. This may be followed
in those languages where such repetition is annoying, but in others it may be
perfectly acceptable. The habits of the receptor language itself must determine which
model is followed.

18.16	RSV	TEV

You shall not uncover the nakedness of your brother's wife; she is your brother's nakedness. **or with your brother's wife.**

In order to avoid the monotony of the repeated use of the same verbal expression, TEV makes this a part of one sentence with the previous verse and allows one verb to serve in the place to two.

Brother's wife: some languages will have a special word rather than translating this literally. Mft renders this expression as "sister-in-law."

18.17	RSV	TEV

You shall not uncover the nakedness of a woman and of her daughter, and you shall not take her son's daughter or her daughter's daughter to uncover her nakedness; they are your^f near kinswomen; it is wickedness. **Do not have intercourse with the daughter or granddaughter of a woman with whom you have had intercourse; they may be related to you, and that would be incest.**

^f Grk: Heb lacks *your*

Another way of wording the first part of this verse is "If you have had intercourse with any woman, you must not also have intercourse with her daughter or her granddaughter." The idea is that by having intercourse with a woman, the man becomes her near relative. Therefore it would be unacceptable to have intercourse also with her child or her grandchild.

Take her son's daughter: the expression "to take a woman" is sometimes used to mean "marry," but in this context the emphasis is clearly on the actual sex act. Consequently it is taken as another synonym for "to have intercourse."

They are your near kinswomen: the textual problems in this part of the verse are considerable. The Hebrew literally has "they are flesh," which seems to indicate that they are related to each other. This is the text that seems to be followed by NJV, AT, and FRCL. A slight change in the final consonant makes the text read "they are your flesh," meaning **your near kinswomen**. This is the reading found in the ancient Greek translation and is followed by RSV, TEV, NJB, and Mft. Still other versions change the vowels to read "they are her flesh." Compare NIV "they are her close relatives," and NEB "they are her blood relations." This last interpretation is also accepted by NAB and TOB. In addition, it is the recommended reading of HOTTP and should probably be followed in the receptor language translation.

It is wickedness: this is a kind of summary statement emphasizing the evil of any such action. The term translated here as **wickedness** is a very general one which is also found in 19.29 and 20.14 and about twenty times in the rest of the Old Testament. It is used to describe any kind of morally unacceptable or detestable action. In verses 22 and 23 there are two other Hebrew terms which are also quite general in meaning. The first, translated as "an abomination" in RSV, is quite frequent in the Old Testament. The second is rarer and is translated "perversion." The precise difference between these three terms is very hard to distinguish, and in the context of this chapter, they may be seen as almost synonymous. If three synonymous terms are available in the receptor language, they should be used here and in verses 22 and 23. In any case, the translation of the three terms should be considered together.

18.18	RSV	TEV
	And you shall not take a woman as a rival wife to her sister, uncovering her nakedness while her sister is yet alive.	Do not take your wife's sister as one of your wives, as long as your wife is living.

Take: see verse 17. But the context here seems to indicate clearly that this refers to marriage and not simply the act of sexual intercourse.

A rival wife: while it was acceptable among the Israelites to have more than one wife, the relationship between the women had to be considered. They must not be sisters. In Hebrew, as in some other languages in the world today, for obvious reasons the word for cowife was the equivalent of **rival** (see, for example, 1 Sam 1.6).

18.19	RSV	TEV
	"You shall not approach a woman to uncover her nakedness while she is in her menstrual uncleanness.	Do not have intercourse with a woman during her monthly period, because she is ritually unclean.

Approach . . . to uncover her nakedness: another expression for sexual intercourse. See verse 6.

While she is in her menstrual uncleanness: literally, "in the time of her uncleanness," but this obviously refers to the ritual state of the woman due to her monthly period of menstruation.

18.20	RSV	TEV
	And you shall not lie carnally with your neighbor's wife, and defile yourself with her.	Do not have intercourse with another man's wife; that would make you ritually unclean.

Lie carnally with: literally, "give your spilling of semen to." This is yet another expression which, in the context of this chapter, refers to sexual intercourse outside of marriage. The expression used here is found only four times in the Old Testament (18.20,23; 20.15; Num 5.20).

Neighbor's wife: this obviously refers to the wives of other men in general and is not limited to those who live nearby. On the term "neighbor," see 5.21-22.

With her: these same words may mean "by it" (that is, by the whole affair) rather than **with her**. This is the meaning adopted by FRCL and TEV: "**that** (that is, the whole affair) **would make you ritually unclean**." This interpretation is also behind the NJB rendering: "you would become unclean by doing so."

18.21 RSV	TEV
You shall not give any of your children to devote them by fire to Molech, and so profane the name of your God: I am the LORD.	Do not hand over any of your children to be used in the worship of the god Molech, because that would bring disgrace on the name of God, the LORD.

The presence of verse 21 in the middle of this chapter dealing with forbidden sexual practices is surprising and seems out of place by some commentators. But a similar association of ideas is found in chapter 20 (verses 2-5 and 10-21). And even Mft, who freely transposes whole blocks of Old Testament text, retains this verse at this point in the text.

To devote them by fire: literally, "give them to be passed through [fire]." The word **fire** is not in the text here but is implied. In the ritual of the Canaanites, children were sacrificed by being made to pass through fire. Mft translates vividly "burned alive." This practice was condemned in 20.2-5 and in Deuteronomy 21.31 and 18.10. Nevertheless it was adopted by some Israelites (see 2 Kgs 16.3; 21.6; 23.10; Jer 7.31; 32.35; Ezek 16.21).

Molech: commentaries often mention the possibility that this word may be a common noun referring to a kind of human sacrifice instead of the proper name of a pagan god. But this interpretation is not found in any standard English translation. Most versions retain it as the name of a god to which sacrifices were offered. The word itself is said to have made Hebrew speakers think of two things: (1) the word for "king," which has the same consonants, and (2) the word for "shame," which has the same vowels. This information would suggest something like "the King of Shame." But it is probably best to retain the proper name and give the more detailed explanation in a footnote.

Profane: this carries the idea of "remove the sacred character of." To sacrifice children to a false deity is to act as if God is not the true God. It is to withdraw from him the respect and honor which he should rightly receive. When used of human beings the word is better translated "to disgrace" (compare 19.29), but here a stronger term like **profane** may be more appropriate.

The name: the name represents the person of God. To disgrace his name is to disgrace him. Most translations retain the word **name**, but it is also possible to translate in some languages "bring shame on me."

I am the LORD: see verse 2.

18.22   RSV   TEV

You shall not lie with a male as with   **No man is to have sexual** relations
a woman; it is an abomination.   **with another man; God hates that.**

You: this is obviously addressed to the males among the Israelites. Consequently the word **male** later in the verse is to be translated "**another man.**"

Lie with . . . as with a woman: the idea of sexual relations between two men
may be very difficult to express in some cultures, but the addition in Hebrew of the
words **as with a woman** indicates that it may have also been difficult for the
Israelites. The verb "to sleep with" is a more general term for sexual relations, and
the addition of the comparison with sleeping with a woman makes the meaning clear.

An abomination: see the discussion under "wickedness" in verse 17. TEV
renders this dynamically with the phrase "**God hates that.**"

18.23   RSV   TEV

And you shall not lie with any beast   **No man or woman is to have sexual**
and defile yourself with it, neither   **relations with an animal; that per-**
shall any woman give herself to a   **version makes you ritually unclean.**
beast to lie with it: it is perversion.

You: the pronoun at the beginning of the verse is again taken as being
addressed to men, but women are specifically included in the prohibition later in the
verse. This is why TEV has brought the two together and begins this verse "**No man
or woman . . . .**"

Lie with any beast: in some cultures people lie down with animals in order to
keep warm. So a literal translation of this expression would convey the wrong
meaning. The prohibition is against sexual relations and not simply lying down near
an animal.

Perversion: this is another very strong term indicating something that is to be
avoided at all cost. See verse 17.

18.24   RSV   TEV

  "**Do not defile yourselves by**   **Do not make yourselves un-**
any of these things, for by all these   **clean by any of these acts, for that is**
the nations I am casting out before   **how the pagans made themselves**
you defiled themselves;   **unclean, those pagans who lived in**
                                               the land before you and whom the
                                               LORD is driving out so that you can
                                               go in.

Defile yourselves: that is, make yourselves ritually unclean.

Any of these things: or, "by committing any of these forbidden acts," or "by
violating any of these sexual prohibitions" [in the previous verses].

The nations: this term may be translated "heathen" (NEB) or **"pagans"** (TEV). While it is literally rendered **nations**, it refers to those other nations who were not considered the people of God. Lists of these people are given in Genesis 15.19-21 and Deuteronomy 7.1. In this context it is possible to translate it as "those who are not my [the LORD's] people." The word is also used in 25.44; 26.33,38,45.

I: or "**the LORD**," if indirect discourse is being used.

Am casting out before you: this implies that these people had been living in the land previously and that they will be removed so that the people of Israel may go in.

18.25   RSV   TEV

and the land became defiled, so that   Their actions made the land unclean,
I punished its iniquity, and the land   and so the LORD is punishing the
vomited out its inhabitants.   land and making it reject the people
                                              who lived there.

The land became defiled: the unacceptable behavior of the people who lived in the land made the land itself unacceptable or ritually unclean in the sight of God.

Punished its iniquity: that is, the iniquity of the land. But it is the people who lived in the land who were ultimately responsible for the iniquity. So in some languages it may be necessary to say "I will punish the land because of the terrible sins committed by the people who lived there."

Vomited out its inhabitants: the verb used here is an image which suggests a violent rejection. In most languages, however, a literal rendering will be very unnatural. Some other possibilities are **"reject"** (TEV), "expel," "refuse," or "repudiate." The translation is further complicated by the fact that the word **land** is used as the subject of the verb. The ultimate agent is, however, the LORD himself. In some cases translators may have to say something like "I am rejecting them from the land." If the vivid image of the text is to be retained, one may even add ". . . as a person vomits up bad food."

I: or "the LORD," if indirect speech is being used.

18.26-27   RSV   TEV

26 But you shall keep my statutes   26-27 They did all these disgusting
and my ordinances and do none of   things and made the land unclean,
these abominations, either the native   but you must not do them. All of you,
or the stranger who sojourns among   whether Israelites or foreigners living
you 27 (for all of these abominations   with you, must keep the LORD's laws
the men of the land did, who were   and commands,
before you, so that the land became
defiled);

These two verses are combined and radically restructured in TEV. The information taken as parenthetical by RSV is shifted forward and given greater prominence. This may also serve as a good model in many other languages.

The men of the land: this means the former inhabitants of the land of Canaan. TEV simply uses the pronoun "**They,**" but it is probably wiser to make this more explicit. Some other alternatives are "the previous inhabitants" (NAB), "the local inhabitants" (Mft), "the people who lived in the country before you" (NJB).

Statutes and ordinances: see verse 4.

Abominations: see verses 17 and 22.

The native or the stranger . . . : see 17.15. Compare also 16.29.

18.28 RSV TEV

lest the land vomit you out, when you defile it, as it vomited out the nation that was before you.	**and then the land will not reject you, as it rejected the pagans who lived there before you.**

Lest . . . : this may have to be translated "If you do this, the land will reject you . . . ."

Vomit . . . vomited: that is, "**reject.**" See verse 25.

The nation: the traditional Hebrew text has the singular here. But other manuscripts have "nations," as translated in NIV, NAB, AT, and Mft. However, the singular is used collectively in Hebrew, so that it should be translated as a plural in many languages in any case. On the meaning of the word itself, see verse 24.

18.29 RSV TEV

For whoever shall do any of these abominations, the persons that do them shall be cut off from among their people.	**You know that whoever does any of these disgusting things will no longer be considered one of God's people.**

For: the word thus translated may also be rendered "Indeed" or "Because." NJB translates it "Yes, . . ." And TEV has "**You know that . . . .**" This introduces a kind of summary statement regarding the basic principles of sexual conduct.

Whoever . . . the persons . . . : these two expressions are identical in meaning and may therefore be translated once, as in TEV and some other modern versions. It may be rendered "anyone," "any person," or "everyone."

Any of these abominations: see verses 26-27.

Cut off from among their people: see 7.20; 17.4,9,10,14.

18.30 RSV TEV

So keep my charge never to practice any of these abominable customs	**And the LORD said, "Obey the commands I give and do not follow**

which were practiced before you, and never to defile yourselves by them: I am the LORD your God."	the practices of the people who lived in the land before you, and do not make yourselves unclean by doing any of these things. I am the LORD your God."

So . . . : this transition word is used in RSV to try to show the summary character of this concluding verse. TEV indicates the same thing by shifting back to direct discourse as at the beginning of the chapter.

Abominable customs: in some languages the idea of **customs** may be translated by using the habitual form of the verb "to do." This expression will then read something like "the awful (or, hated) things that they [habitually] do . . . ."

Practiced before you: that is, practiced by the people living in the land prior to your arrival there.

I am the LORD your God: see verse 2.

Chapter 19

TEV Section Heading: "**Laws of Holiness and Justice.**"

This chapter brings together a wide variety of commandments. It is difficult to see any reason for the order in which they appear in the text. Some of them are almost identical with the Ten Commandments, and others are more detailed regulations on a different level. This makes it necessary to provide a section heading that is very general in nature, as in TEV. Other suggestions for this section are "How to serve God properly" (compare FRCL), or "Moral and religious regulations" (NJB), or perhaps a better model for many languages, "Duties to God and neighbor" (NEB).

19.1-2 RSV	TEV
1 And the LORD said to Moses, 2 "Say to all the congregation of the people of Israel, You shall be holy; for I the LORD your God am holy.	1 The LORD told Moses 2 to say to the community of Israel, "Be holy, because I, the LORD your God, am holy.

Once again TEV avoids a direct quotation within another direct quotation by making the first one indirect. This will be a good model to follow in most languages.

Said to Moses: see 4.1.

Say . . . : see 1.2.

Be holy . . . : see 11.44-45.

19.3 RSV	TEV
Every one of you shall revere his mother and his father, and you shall keep my sabbaths: I am the LORD your God.	Each of you must respect his mother and his father, and must keep the Sabbath, as I have commanded. I am the LORD your God.

Every one of you: the text emphasizes the fact that this rule applies to every individual. Although there are some versions that do not underline this fact (NAB), it would probably be a mistake to omit this emphasis in the receptor language.

Revere: literally, "fear" as in KJV. But the meaning is "to show respect for." It is used most frequently with the deity as object, as in the expressions "fear the LORD" or "fear God." It is different from the word used in Exodus 20.12, which may be translated "honor," but the sense is virtually identical. Compare verse 14.

His mother and his father: this is not the usual order when the two parents are mentioned. So the writer must have changed the order intentionally. Therefore the unusual order should probably be maintained in translation, unless it is completely unnatural in the receptor language. The "holiness laws" show a particular concern for the mother by mentioning her first also in 20.19 and 21.2. If this is the natural order in the receptor language, it should be retained here.

Keep my sabbaths: it is a mistake to translate the verb literally in many languages. The idea is to obey the law concerning rest on the seventh day. The use of the plural **sabbaths** merely points up the habitual nature of the requirement. See Exodus 20.8-11. Some suggested renderings are "honor my Day of Rest," "observe the rules about the Day of Rest which I have ordained," or "do as I have commanded on the Day of Rest."

I am the LORD your God: this statement, or the shortened form "I am the LORD," is found 15 times in this chapter alone and many more times throughout the book of Leviticus. The repetition is a constant reminder of the basis of all laws and regulations. It should also be repeated in translation, unless it clearly violates the norms of the receptor language. See 11.44 and 18.2.

19.4   RSV   TEV

Do not turn to idols or make for yourselves molten gods: I am the LORD your God.

"Do not abandon me and worship idols; do not make gods of metal and worship them. I am the LORD your God.

Turn to: this implies turning away from the true and living God. TEV brings this out by translating "**abandon me and worship . . . .**"

Idols: this word comes from a root meaning worthless, inadequate, or nothingness. It is frequently used in the Old Testament to refer to the gods of other groups of people. The Israelites did not consider them of any value. A possible translation may be "worthless gods" or "good-for-nothing idols."

Molten gods: this refers to images made from metal that has been melted down and formed into particular objects, as opposed to those carved out of wood or stone. Exodus 20.4 and Leviticus 26.1 forbid carved images, but Deuteronomy 27.15 includes both.

I am the LORD your God: see verse 3.

19.5   RSV   TEV

"When you offer a sacrifice of peace offerings to the LORD, you shall offer it so that you may be accepted.

"When you kill an animal for a fellowship offering, keep the regulations that I have given you, and I will accept the offering.

Offer a sacrifice of peace offerings: since this offering involves the slaughtering of an animal (see chapter 3), it may be better to spell this out in the receptor language, as has been done in TEV.

To the LORD: this has been left implicit in TEV, since it is the LORD himself who is speaking, and it would be unnatural for him to refer to himself in the third person. In some languages one may wish to say explicitly ". . . to me."

So that you may be accepted: literally, "to be accepted for you." TEV changes this passive construction to an active form, making God the subject. Some versions interpret this to mean that the sacrifice is accepted, but others feel that the person offering the sacrifice is made acceptable. The meaning is probably "so that it [the sacrifice] may be accepted on your behalf" (NJV). See 1.3,4.

19.6-7   RSV   TEV

6 It shall be eaten the same day you offer it, or on the morrow; and anything left over until the third day shall be burned with fire. 7 If it is eaten at all on the third day, it is an abomination; it will not be accepted,	6 The meat must be eaten on the day the animal is killed or on the next day. Any meat left on the third day must be burned, 7 because it is ritually unclean, and if anyone eats it, I will not accept the offering.

See 7.16-18.

It: this, of course, refers to the meat of the animal offered as a fellowship offering.

Shall be eaten: instead of the passive form, some languages will require "someone must eat it . . ." or "people may eat it . . . ."

And: this conjunction may be better translated as "but" or "however" in many languages, since it marks the contrast between the period when the meat may be eaten and the time beyond that period—when it is forbidden to eat it.

An abomination: see 7.18 as well as 18.17,22,27.

19.8   RSV   TEV

and every one who eats it shall bear his iniquity, because he has profaned a holy thing of the LORD; and that person shall be cut off from his people.	Any one who eats it will be guilty of treating as ordinary what is dedicated to me, and he will no longer be considered one of my people.

Every one who eats it: there are some textual variations between "those who eat it" (plural) and "the one who eats it" (singular) here and in verses 12, 15, 27, and 33. But they are not important for translation, since the meaning is the same. HOTTP recommends "and whosoever eats it."

Bear his iniquity: in some cases the receptor language may require that this phrase be placed later in the verse in order to follow the chronological order of the events. See 5.1 and 17 as well as 7.18.

Profaned a holy thing: the words **a holy thing** are to be understood as something dedicated to God. To profane something is to treat it as if it were not sacred. The whole expression may be rendered "has shown his spite for what belongs to the LORD" or "has desecrated something the LORD considers sacred." Mft reads "has profaned the Eternal's sacred possession."

Of the LORD: reference to the LORD within a direct quote from God himself will be considered unnatural in many languages. TEV takes care of this by simply translating "**to me**."

Cut off from his people: see 7.20; 18.29.

19.9   RSV   TEV

"When you reap the harvest of your land, you shall not reap your field to its very border, neither shall you gather the gleanings after your harvest.

"When you harvest your fields, do not cut the grain at the edges of the fields, and do not go back to cut the heads of grain that were left.

In verses 9 and following the Hebrew shifts back and forth between the second person plural and the second person singular (compare KJV "ye . . . thou . . ."). There is no obvious reason for these shifts, so the plural should probably be used throughout in the receptor-language translation of this section.

When you reap the harvest . . . : this refers to a later time when Israel would be settled in the land of Canaan and have fields planted. If it is thought to be necessary, the translation may read "When you start to harvest what you have planted . . . ," or even "When you have settled in the land and begin harvesting your crops [grain] . . . ."

You shall not reap . . . border: literally, "do not finish reaping the edge (or, corner) of your field." This refers to the practice of being so meticulous that even the grain ordinarily overlooked is sought.

Gather the gleanings . . . : this can be rendered "go back over to pick up all that is left over." The two expressions together may be translated "you shall not be so careful that you reap absolutely everything" or "you must not take away every bit of the grain by harvesting carefully around the edges or by going over the whole field a second time."

19.10   RSV   TEV

And you shall not strip your vineyard bare, neither shall you gather the fallen grapes of your vineyard; you shall leave them for the poor and for the sojourner: I am the LORD your God.

Do not go back through your vineyard to gather the grapes that were missed or to pick up the grapes that have fallen; leave them for poor people and foreigners. I am the LORD your God.

Strip your vineyard bare: this is an additional prohibition which requires the same procedure regarding vineyards as for the grain fields in the previous verse. The person who is gathering must not be so selfish as to take absolutely every grape. On the word **vineyard**, see FFB, pages 188-192.

Leave them: the pronoun here probably refers to the grain in verse 9 as well as to the grapes in this verse. In many languages it will be good to make this explicit, since this provides the reason behind both prohibitions. Some may wish to say "leave some grain and some grapes . . . ."

Poor: in some languages it may be necessary to use a longer phrase—something like "the people who lack," or "those who have nothing," or "people with very little to eat."

Sojourner: or "those people who live among you but are not Israelites." See 17.15.

I am the LORD your God: see verse 3 and 11.44.

19.11	RSV	TEV

"You shall not steal, nor deal falsely, nor lie to one another.

"Do not steal or cheat or lie.

Steal: some commentators see this as having a more restricted meaning, having to do with the seizing of a person to make him a slave. But almost all versions take it as having a more general meaning. It is the same word as used in Exodus 20.15. The alternative may be dealt with in a footnote if necessary, stating that the word translated "steal" may mean "abduct," "kidnap," or "enslave."

Nor deal falsely with, nor lie: the two Hebrew verbs here are very similar in meaning. They serve to reinforce each other rather than to explain basic differences in meaning. So it is probably not a good idea to set them off as two separate and distinct laws, as is done in NIV.

To one another: literally, "a man to [against] his fellow." Compare 6.3, where the same word is translated "neighbor." TEV leaves the object implicit, but this may not be possible or desirable in many other languages. In some languages one may wish to say "compatriot" or "fellow citizen."

19.12	RSV	TEV

And you shall not swear by my name falsely, and so profane the name of your God: I am the LORD.

Do not make a promise in my name if you do not intend to keep it; that brings disgrace on my name. I am the LORD your God.

Compare 5.24; Exodus 20.7,16; Matthew 5.33.

You shall not swear by my name falsely: some others have proposed such translations as: "Do not use my name to give weight to a false promise," or "Do not use my name to swear anything that is not true," or "Make no vow [take no oath] in my name deceitfully." In some languages the verb corresponding to **swear** in English implies the use of the name of God without having to mention it specifically.

So: this indicates that the dishonor brought on God is the result of the act of making the false promise. This may be handled by making a separate statement such as "doing that would bring dishonor to me [my name]." Another suggestion is "showing in this way that you do not respect me."

Profane the name of your God: since this is a direct quotation, this phrase should be translated "profane my name," or "disgrace me," or "bring dishonor to me" in many languages. Since direct speech is being used, the expression **the name of your God** will have to be "**my name**" or simply "me." See 18.21.

I am the LORD: the text leaves implicit the words "your God," which are found in verses 3, 4, and elsewhere. In some translations they have been made explicit.

19.13   RSV   TEV

"You shall not oppress your neighbor or rob him. The wages of a hired servant shall not remain with you all night until the morning. | "Do not take advantage of anyone or rob him. Do not hold back the wages of someone you have hired, not even for one night.

Oppress: this verb, translated similarly in 6.2, carries the idea of exploitation or taking unfair advantage of another person. AT translates "defraud," while NJB has "exploit."

Neighbor: this word is used of a member of the same clan, of a fellow Israelite, or in the very general sense of any other person. In this context the most general meaning is probably intended. See 6.2 and 18.20.

Hired servant: any person who has agreed to do a particular job for a mutually acceptable price. One may wish to translate "a person you have hired for a particular job" or something similar.

Wages . . . shall not remain with you: a day laborer must be paid at sundown (compare Matthew 20.8).

All night until the morning: since this expression is redundant, it is probably unwise to translate it literally. There are many ways in which the meaning may be conveyed. For example, "after sundown," "overnight," "until the next day," or "through the night."

The entire second sentence of this verse may be restructured to read "If you agree with a worker on a particular job, do not refuse to pay him at the end of that day" or "If someone works for you, be sure to pay him before the day is finished."

19.14   RSV   TEV

You shall not curse the deaf or put a stumbling block before the blind, but you shall fear your God: I am the LORD. | Do not curse a deaf man or put something in front of a blind man so as to make him stumble over it. Obey me; I am the LORD your God.

Curse: or "insult" (NJV), or "treat . . . with contempt" (NEB). Even if the deaf person were unable to hear the curse, people thought that a curse had its own power to cause harm. And the deaf man would be unable to do anything to counteract it. This part of the book of Leviticus is especially concerned about people who were unable to take care of themselves.

The deaf: this may also be understood as "the dumb" (one who is unable to speak), as in JB. But most versions take it to mean a person who cannot hear. In actual fact, deaf people are generally unable to speak coherently, and some languages have a single word for "deaf and dumb" that will certainly be appropriate here.

A stumbling block: or "anything that could make a person stumble," or "any object that will make him fall down."

Fear your God: or "fear me," if direct discourse is being used. The verb **fear** may be translated "show respect for" in some contexts, but here the idea of "stand in awe of" is also a part of the meaning.

I am the LORD: see verse 12.

19.15　　　RSV　　　　　　　　　　　　　TEV

> "You shall do no injustice in judgment; you shall not be partial to the poor or defer to the great, but in righteousness shall you judge your neighbor.

> "Be honest and just when you make decisions in legal cases; do not show favoritism to the poor or fear the rich.

Do no injustice: literally, "Do not make a perversion of justice." The RSV rendering reflects the Hebrew, which has a negative formulation of this requirement. TEV has stated the same truth in a positive manner. The decision about which model to follow should be based on what is most natural in the receptor language.

In judgment: this term is used here in its stricter sense, meaning "legal rulings" or "in a court of law," rather than the general sense of an opinion expressed on any kind of subject.

Be partial to the poor: literally, "lift up the face of the poor." Some other languages have similar expressions for showing partiality or playing favorites, such as "to look at the face of . . ." or "treat with special care."

Defer to the great: the **great** in the context of this verse clearly refers to those who are the opposite of the poor, that is, **"the rich."** This is made explicit in NJV as well as TEV. Mft has "the powerful man" (similarly AT). NAB renders the same word "the mighty."

In righteousness shall you judge your neighbor: since this is a repetition of the same idea that is presented in negative form at the beginning of this verse, it may be left implicit at the end. On the word **neighbor**, see 6.2 and verse 13 above.

19.16　　　RSV　　　　　　　　　　　　　TEV

> You shall not go up and down as a slanderer among your people, and

> Do not spread lies about anyone, and when someone is on trial for his

you shall not stand forth against the | life, speak out if your testimony can
life^g of your neighbor: I am the LORD. | help him. I am the LORD.

^{g} Heb *blood*

Verse 16 still concerns the legal situation introduced in the previous verse.

Go up and down as a slanderer: more literally, "go about as a talebearer." NJV takes this to mean "deal basely with." But most commentators accept the traditional understanding, "to gossip" or "to spread lies."

Among your people: TEV takes this in the most general sense possible, as in the previous verse. But many modern versions interpret it with varying degrees of strictness: "your countrymen" (NJV) or "your own family" (NJB). NEB translates "your father's kin."

Stand forth against the life of your neighbor: literally, "stand upon [against] the blood of your neighbor." The exact meaning of this expression is uncertain. NJV translates rather obscurely, "Do not profit by the blood of your neighbor." But most commentators take it to mean that, whenever a person is in danger of losing his life as the result of a legal case, a witness should not fail to speak out. It is also possible that it means that a person should avoid giving false testimony that would result in the death sentence on a fellow Israelite, and this seems to be the meaning expressed in RSV. Translators are free to choose either interpretation, but RSV seems more likely.

| **19.17** | RSV | TEV |

"You shall not hate your brother in your heart, but you shall reason with your neighbor, lest you bear sin because of him. | "Do not bear a grudge against anyone, but settle your differences with him, so that you will not commit a sin because of him.^{h}

^{h} so . . . him; *or* so that you do not commit this sin against him.

It is grammatically possible to consider verse 17 as containing two completely separate commands, the first concerning the **brother** and the second concerning the **neighbor**. However, most modern dynamic translations (such as TEV, FRCL, and GECL) see in this verse two aspects of the same command. And both terms are to be taken in their broadest sense.

Hate . . . in your heart: the TEV rendering "**bear a grudge**" is the common-language equivalent of this expression. Other languages will have very different ways of expressing the idea of a deep and long-lasting hatred. Some languages say "continue to hate" or use the habitual form of the verb to hate. NEB has "nurse hatred."

Your neighbor: taken in TEV as the equivalent of **your brother** at the beginning of the verse. Compare 6.2 and verse 13 above.

Reason with: according to the majority of modern translations, the basic meaning of the verb here is "to rebuke" or "to admonish." FRCL translates "Do not hesitate to reprimand him." Mft has "warn him of his fault." And JB has "you must openly tell him . . . of his offense," while NJB reads "reprove [him] firmly." TEV, which takes this expression in the sense of "to reach agreement," is definitely in the minority.

Lest you bear sin because of him: this may also be understood to mean "so that you do not share in his guilt," if the previous verb is taken in the sense of "rebuke." So NIV and NEB.

19.18   RSV   TEV

You shall not take vengeance or bear any grudge against the sons of your own people, but you shall love your neighbor as yourself: I am the LORD.	Do not take revenge on anyone or continue to hate him, but love your neighbor as you love yourself. I am the LORD.

Take vengeance: this verb gives the idea of retaliating against someone who has committed a wrong. In some languages it may be rendered "Do not repay evil for evil" or something similar.

Bear any grudge against: NEB has "cherish anger towards." The idea is one of holding inside a feeling of dislike for another person over a long period of time without expressing the feeling. Some languages will have a single verb to convey this idea, but in others it will require a longer expression. There seems to be very little difference between this and the verb translated "hate" by RSV in verse 17.

The sons of your own people: this is yet another expression that should probably be taken in its most general sense, referring to fellow members of the Israelite community. Probably there is no difference in meaning between this and the word translated **neighbor** in the second part of the verse. On the use of "sons of . . . ," see 1.5.

You shall love your neighbor as yourself: as quoted in the New Testament (Matt 22.39; Rom 13.9; James 2.8), this is taken to mean "**as you love yourself**," but in this context some scholars have interpreted it to mean "as a man like yourself" (NEB) or "as one of your own" (AT). However, the more traditional understanding of this expression is probably the correct one.

19.19   RSV   TEV

"You shall keep my statutes. You shall not let your cattle breed with a different kind; you shall not sow your field with two kinds of seed; nor shall there come upon you a garment of cloth made of two kinds of stuff.	"Obey my commands. Do not crossbreed domestic animals. Do not plant two kinds of seed in the same field. Do not wear clothes made of two kinds of material.

You shall keep my statutes: this command points forward and thus begins a new paragraph or section in most modern versions. It stresses the importance of those rules which follow.

Keep . . . : see verse 3.

Cattle: the term is to be understood here in its most general sense, referring to all animals over which humans have control. Both TEV and NAB rightly translate **"domestic animals."**

Breed with: there will be a wide variety of ways of expressing the idea of mating animals. Some languages may use a causative form of the verb, meaning "cause to have intercourse" or "cause to meet together." Others may say something like "allow to come together" or "permit to produce offspring [with a different kind]."

Different kind: literally, "in two kinds." This word is found only here (three times) and in Deuteronomy 22.9. It is not the same as in Genesis 1, "after its own kind [species]." But it is, for all practical purposes, the opposite of the Genesis expression, and so may be translated in a similar manner but with a negative. For example, "not after its own kind" or "not of the same species."

Two kinds: the same word translated **a different kind** with regard to animals is used here with reference to seed and cloth material. This is not intended as a prohibition against mixing two varieties of the same kind of grain (as two types of corn), but rather against mixing two totally different grains.

Nor shall there come upon you: this is a roundabout way of saying "You must not wear . . ." or "Do not put on . . . ." In most cases the more direct statement will be better.

Stuff: this word is used only here and in Deuteronomy 22.11. In the later passage it is defined as "wool and linen together." This, then, is the source of the KJV rendering. Many languages will have difficulty in finding such a general word for **"material"** or **"fabric."** The word may also be understood in the sense of "thread" (NAB) or "yarn" (NEB). So it is possible to say "anything made of two different kinds of thread."

19.20 RSV	TEV
"If a man lies carnally with a woman who is a slave, betrothed to another man and not yet ransomed or given her freedom, an inquiry shall be held. They shall not be put to death, because she was not free;	If a slave girl is the recognized concubine of a man and she has not been paid for and freed, then if another man has sexual relations with her, they will be punished, but not[i] put to death, since she is a slave.

[i] they . . . not; *or* an investigation will be made but they will not be.

A man . . . another man . . . : in order to avoid confusion, it is best to distinguish clearly between the two or three men involved in this case. In the structure of RSV, the first **man** refers to a person who has relations with the slave girl. This could refer either to the owner of the slave or to a third party. An early

British edition of TEV takes it to mean the owner of the slave, but more recent editions agree with the American edition, which suggests that it is a different person—that is, neither the slave owner nor the fiancé. This interpretation seems more likely. The second man mentioned in the text (**another man**) clearly refers to the person to whom the slave girl has been promised. Note that TEV has restructured the verse to make the slave girl the subject of the first part of the verse. This may help to avoid some of the potential confusion. Another possible model may be the following:

> If any man has sexual relations with a slave girl who has been
> designated for another man, even though the other man has not paid
> the money, then the slave girl and the man who slept with her must
> be punished. But they don't have to be put to death, because the
> woman has not been set free.

This suggestion, and the TEV model, leave the slave owner in the background, and there is no need to mention him explicitly unless one follows the interpretation that makes him the one guilty of sleeping with the slave girl.

Lies carnally with a woman: literally, "lies with a woman with emission of semen." This is just another expression for having sexual intercourse with a woman, and may be translated as the other expressions used in chapter 18. See 18.20. Compare also 15.16-18.

Betrothed to another man: TEV shifts this part of the sentence forward to the beginning of the verse, for smoother English. This may be advisable in some other languages. The meaning in this context is "promised to," "assigned to," or "designated for."

Not yet ransomed: that is, the man has not yet paid the price necessary to make the slave girl his own.

An inquiry shall be held: the meaning of the Hebrew text at this point is very uncertain. The most likely meaning is "there shall be punishment." This is the interpretation followed by TEV, NIV, NAB, and NASB. But RSV, NEB, AT, and Mft follow the Greek Septuagint and translate **an inquiry shall be held**. It is also possible to understand the text as meaning "there shall be an indemnity" (NJV and TOB). Translators are, however, advised to follow the interpretation "there shall be punishment." But it is then necessary in some languages to decide who is to receive the punishment. Is it the woman only or the man only? Or is it both of the parties involved? More than likely both of them would have been punished. So one may translate "they shall be punished."

They shall not be put to death: JB is alone in following a different Hebrew text at this point, and translates "he is not to be put to death." But almost all other versions have the plural pronoun, and this should be followed in the receptor language. Even NJB abandons JB and reverts to this text.

19.21   RSV   TEV

RSV	TEV
but he shall bring a guilt offering for himself to the LORD, to the door of the tent of meeting, a ram for a guilt offering.	The man shall bring a ram to the entrance of the Tent of my presence as his repayment offering,

Note that TEV has reordered the wording of this verse. This structure may serve as a better model for some other languages.

He: it may be better to make this more explicit with something like "the man who has done this deed" or "the one who slept with the slave girl."

A guilt offering: see 5.20-25.

To the LORD: this has been left implicit in TEV.

A ram: see 5.15.

19.22   RSV   TEV

| And the priest shall make atonement for him with the ram of the guilt offering before the LORD for his sin which he has committed; and the sin which he has committed shall be forgiven him. | and with it the priest shall perform the ritual of purification to remove the man's sin, and God will forgive him. |

Compare 4.20 and 5.26.

His sin which he has committed: this phrase occurs twice in the text but may be translated once in the receptor language to avoid awkward repetition.

Shall be forgiven: this passive form may easily be rendered as an active, since God is clearly the subject.

19.23   RSV   TEV

| "When you come into the land and plant all kinds of trees for food, then you shall count their fruit as forbidden;[h] three years it shall be forbidden to you, it must not be eaten. | "When you come into the land of Canaan and plant any kind of fruit tree, consider the fruit ritually unclean for the first three years. During that time you must not eat it. |

[h] Heb *their uncircumcision*

Verses 23-25 describe the situation of a sedentary people involved in the cultivation of the land. Since Israel was still on the way to the promised land, it may be necessary in some languages to use the future tense in this paragraph in order to distinguish it from the rest of the chapter (where the imperative may have been used).

The land: it will be wise in many languages to make this more explicit by naming "**the land of Canaan**," as in TEV and FRCL.

Trees for food: one should be careful not to give the impression that the trees themselves are eaten for food. It is rather the fruit of the trees that will be eaten. Some may prefer to translate "trees which will bear fruit to be eaten" or something similar.

Three years: many trees require a period of several years before they begin to bear fruit. The three-year prohibition against eating their fruit began at the time that they started to produce, not from the time that they had been planted.

Forbidden: literally, "uncircumcised." Compare KJV. This is a rather curious use of the term normally used to describe non-Israelite people. But it serves here as a strong way of emphasizing that the fruit is to be completely avoided by the people of God for a period of three years. It is very unlikely that any modern language can use the same image to communicate the intended meaning naturally. It will be much wiser to translate **forbidden** as in RSV, or **"ritually unclean"** as in TEV.

It must not be eaten: this further clarifies the meaning of the above. But it will have to be transformed from a passive to an active sentence in many languages. The simplest way to do this is probably to say "You [Israelites] must not eat it."

19.24   RSV   TEV

And in the fourth year all their fruit shall be holy, an offering of praise to the LORD. | In the fourth year all the fruit shall be dedicated as an offering to show your gratitude to me,*j* the LORD.

j to show your gratitude to me; *or* in praise of me.

Holy: this may just as well be translated "a holy gift," "consecrated," **"dedicated,"** or "set aside as belonging to God."

An offering of praise: RSV has added **an offering of**, since the traditional Hebrew text has only "praise." But HOTTP recommends a slightly different Hebrew reading which is followed by NEB, "and this releases it for use." It is noteworthy, however, that the Revised English Bible reverts to a rendering of the more generally accepted text.

To the LORD: TEV rightly adjusts to the fact that this is direct discourse, and so translates **"to me, the LORD."**

19.25   RSV   TEV

But in the fifth year you may eat of their fruit, that they may yield more richly for you: I am the LORD your God. | But in the fifth year you may eat the fruit. If you do all this, your trees will bear more fruit. I am the LORD your God.

But: marking the contrast between what was forbidden up to this point and what is then permitted.

That they may yield more . . . . : it is not simply the eating of the fruit that will result in a greater yield in the future. It is rather adherence to the entire program, including abstaining from the fruit for four years. This should probably be made explicit in most languages, as in TEV **"If you do all this . . . ,"** or as in NIV "In this way your harvest will increase."

19.26   RSV   TEV

"You shall not eat any flesh   "Do not eat any meat with
with the blood in it. You shall not   blood still in it. Do not practice any
practice augury or witchcraft.   kind of magic.

You shall not eat any flesh with the blood in it: literally, "you shall not eat
upon the blood." The ancient Greek has "upon the mountains." But most modern
versions take it to mean the same thing as 17.12. Some commentators find this
strange in the context of witchcraft, but it is quite possible that "upon the blood"
refers to eating the sacrifice while standing on the ground where the blood had been
spilled. While certain French versions (FRCL and TOB) adopt this interpretation,
virtually all English versions follow the interpretation of RSV and TEV.

Practice augury: a Roman "augur" was an official who foretold the future as
a result of his observation of birds. But the English word **augury** has slightly changed
in meaning, and it is not well known today. The term used here actually refers to
divination, or the practice of foretelling the future, or discovering secret knowledge
by consulting spirits.

Witchcraft: sorcery, or the use of supernatural powers to control events.
Although TEV has translated the two terms together with "**any kind of magic**," it
will be quite easy in many languages to find two separate terms. But it is true that
the forbidding of the two should be all-inclusive, conveying the idea that all types of
magic are prohibited.

19.27   RSV   TEV

You shall not round off the hair on   Do not cut the hair on the sides of
your temples or mar the edges of   your head or trim your beard
your beard.

Round off the hair on your temples: literally, "do not round off the edge of
your head." It is usually translated something like "shave your temples." A complete
understanding of this prohibition and the following one is impossible for us today.
But they probably had to do with practices that were common in the pagan religions
of the people around the Israelites. These practices may have been linked with
mourning for the dead, as is made explicit in verse 28.

Since TEV makes verses 27 and 28 a single sentence, the connection with the
mourning practices in this verse is much clearer. Mft also combines these two verses
into one sentence. Such restructuring is almost essential to a proper understanding
of this passage. It is certainly erroneous to make a separate paragraph of verse 28,
as in NIV.

19.28   RSV   TEV

You shall not make any cuttings in   or tattoo yourselves or cut gashes in
your flesh on account of the dead or your body to mourn for the dead. I

tattoo any marks upon you: I am the **am the** LORD.
LORD.

TEV restructures this verse, placing the less severe practice of tattooing before the cutting of the flesh. But this may not be advisable (see below).

Make any cuttings in your flesh: the reference here is to the practice of making deep gashes in the skin while mourning the death of a relative. This was done to provide life blood for the spirit of the dead person rather than to express sorrow.

On account of the dead: as indicated above, this describes the purpose of all the actions in verse 27 as well as verse 28.

Tattoo any marks upon you: since this comes after the words "on account of the dead," some commentators do not see this as referring to a specific mourning rite. People frequently made some kind of mark on their skin to indicate that they were followers of a particular deity (see Gen 4.15; Ezek 9.4-6). But this custom that was so common among non-Israelites was forbidden to the people of God.

19.29	RSV	TEV

"Do not profane your daughter by making her a harlot, lest the land fall into harlotry and the land become full of wickedness.

"Do not disgrace your daughters by making them temple prostitutes;[k] if you do, you will turn to other gods and the land will be full of immorality.

[k] TEMPLE PROSTITUTES: *These women were found in Canaanite temples, where fertility gods were worshiped. It was believed that intercourse with these prostitutes assured fertile fields and herds.*

Profane: in this context this word clearly means "to disgrace." See verse 12, and compare also 18.21, where it is used of God.

Daughter: since the plural pronouns are being used throughout this section, it may be necessary to change the singular **daughter** to a plural, as in TEV.

A harlot: or "a religious prostitute." In some neighboring religions, people thought they were being pious by making their daughters participate in the cult of fertility. But such religious prostitution was not acceptable for the Israelites. In translation it is probably a good idea to bring out the religious nature of this prostitution, as is done in TEV. Compare 17.7.

Lest: this may be better translated "**if you do . . . ,**" as in TEV.

Fall into harlotry: this is translated by TEV as "**turn to other gods**," thus taking it as a figurative expression indicating unfaithfulness to God. See comments on a similar expression in 17.7.

Wickedness: see 18.17.

19.30   RSV   TEV

You shall keep my sabbaths and   Keep the Sabbath, and honor the
reverence my sanctuary: I am the   place where I am worshiped. I am
LORD.   the LORD.

    Keep my sabbaths: see verse 3.

    Reverence my sanctuary: perhaps the sanctuary had been used in the
practices forbidden in the previous verses. This says in a more positive way that
proper respect was to be shown to the Israelite place of worship.

19.31   RSV   TEV

    "Do not turn to mediums or   "Do not go for advice to people
wizards; do not seek them out, to be   who consult the spirits of the dead.
defiled by them: I am the LORD your   If you do, you will be ritually unclean.
God.   I am the LORD your God.

    Mediums or wizards: the second word literally means "those who have
knowledge." A common practice among the Canaanites was consulting the spirits of
the dead. This practice is strictly forbidden to the people of God. NEB translates "do
not resort to ghosts or spirits." See 1 Samuel 28.7-8. In a number of languages there
are specific technical terms for various categories of people who communicate with
the world of the dead. In those languages where this is the case, it is not advisable
to translate the more generic terms of TEV here. It will be much better to use two
well-known indigenous terms.

    Seek them out: or "go to them for advice," or "ask them to help you."

19.32   RSV   TEV

    "You shall rise up before the   "Show respect for old people
hoary head, and honor the face of an   and honor them. Reverently obey
old man, and you shall fear your   me; I am the LORD.
God: I am the LORD.

    Rise up before: getting up in the presence of an older person is one way of
showing respect. But the meaning here is more general and should be seen as
parallel with the second admonition which follows. Although most versions translate
this expression more or less literally, it will be better to follow the TEV model and
render it in more general terms.

    The hoary head: this is translated in NAB and NJV as "the aged." It refers to
any person who has gray hair. So it is the equivalent of **an old man** in the second
part of this verse.

    Honor the face: the **face** represents the person. It would be a mistake in most
languages to translate this literally. This is parallel to the expression **rise up before**.
It is just another way of saying "to show respect for." The first two parts of this verse

constitute a kind of parallelism that is very common in Hebrew. If the repetition of the same basic idea is distracting or confusing in the receptor language, the idea may be translated only once.

Fear your God: or "fear me" in direct discourse when the LORD himself is speaking; TEV "**Reverently obey me.**" See verse 14.

19.33　　RSV　　　　　　　　　　　　　　　　TEV

"When a stranger sojourns with you in your land, you shall not do him wrong.

"Do not mistreat foreigners who are living in your land.

The entire verse is recast in TEV to make the structure more natural in English. The same kind of restructuring may be helpful in other languages.

Stranger: see 16.29.

Do him wrong: the verb may be translated "**mistreat**," "oppress," "exploit," or "take unfair advantage of." In this context there seems to be the idea of a person in a position of power taking unfair advantage of one who is weak.

19.34　　RSV　　　　　　　　　　　　　　　　TEV

The stranger who sojourns with you shall be to you as the native among you, and you shall love him as yourself; for you were strangers in the land of Egypt: I am the LORD your God.

Treat them as you would a fellow Israelite, and love them as you love yourselves. Remember that you were once foreigners in the land of Egypt. I am the LORD your God.

Stranger: see verse 33.

As the native among you: in some languages one may say "as one of your own brothers (or, kinsmen)." See 16.29.

As yourself: see verse 18.

For . . . : this connecting word shows that what follows is one reason for obeying the command to love the strangers among the people of Israel. NEB translates the same word "because." TEV highlights this connection by beginning a new sentence with the words "**Remember that . . . .**"

In the land of Egypt: in order to impress the Israelites with what it is like to be a foreigner in a strange land, they are reminded of their own situation in Egypt in the past.

19.35　　RSV　　　　　　　　　　　　　　　　TEV

"You shall do no wrong in judgment, in measures of length or weight or quantity.

"Do not cheat anyone by using false measures of length, weight, or quantity.

Do no wrong in judgment: or "pervert justice" (NEB), "do no injustice" (AT). This phrase may be taken as a reference to justice in general or to legal cases specifically. But the whole verse clearly implies that all areas of life are included. Mft gives the following rendering: "You must never act dishonestly, in court or in commerce, as you use measures of length, weight, or capacity."

19.36 RSV	TEV

| You shall have just balances, just weights, a just ephah, and a just hin: I am the LORD your God, who brought you out of the land of Egypt. | Use honest scales, honest weights, and honest measures. I am the LORD your God, and I brought you out of Egypt. |

Just . . . : this adjective is repeated four times in this verse, but it would be unnatural to do so in many languages. TEV, translating it "**honest**," reduces it to three. In other languages once will be sufficient, but if the repetition does not violate the norms of the language, it serves to reinforce the idea.

Balances . . . weights: a balance is a device used by the ancient Jews to measure the weight of an object by balancing it against another object or set of objects having a known weight. It was possible to cheat a person either by tampering with the device itself or by falsifying the weights used (see Pro 11.1 and 16.11). Where such a system is unknown, the translation will have to be adapted to the system used in the receptor-language culture to measure weight.

Ephah . . . hin: the **ephah** (see 5.11) was a measure of capacity used for grain, and the **hin** (found also in 23.13) measured liquids. The terms are used here as general references to measurements and not for precise amounts. No useful purpose is served by transliterating these terms. The more general term "**measures**" is quite adequate in this context. Others may want to use a verbal expression like "when you measure grain or liquid."

19.37 RSV	TEV

| And you shall observe all my statutes and all my ordinances, and do them: I am the LORD." | Obey all my laws and commands. I am the LORD." |

Observe: in addition to "Obey" (TEV), this may also be translated "take seriously" or "not forget." This is the same word that is translated "keep" in the RSV rendering of 19.19.

I am the LORD: once again the basis for all these rules and regulations is made clear. It is the LORD himself who gives them, and it is he that acted mightily to deliver the Israelites from slavery in Egypt. See 18.2.

Chapter 20

TEV Section Heading: "**Penalties for Disobedience.**"

Some other versions have as headings "Punishments for sin" (NIV), "Penalties for various sins" (NAB), or simply "Penalties" (NJB).

The chapter may be divided into three main parts plus a conclusion:

Verses 1-8:   Improper worship
Verses 9-21:   Improper sexual relations
Verses 22-25:   Ritual uncleanness
Verses 26-27:   Conclusion

20.1-2   RSV   TEV

1 The LORD said to Moses,   1 The LORD told Moses 2 to say
2 "Say to the people of Israel, Any   to the people of Israel, "Any of you
man of the people of Israel, or of the or any foreigner living among you
strangers that sojourn in Israel, who   who gives any of his children to be
gives any of his children to Molech   used in the worship of the god Mo-
shall be put to death; the people of   lech shall be stoned to death by the
the land shall stone him with stones.   whole community.

Said to Moses: see 4.1.

Say . . . : see 1.2.

Any man of the people of Israel: since the phrase **people of Israel** is repeated here, it may be well to translate it by a pronoun, as has been done in TEV.

Strangers . . . : see 17.8. Compare 16.29.

Gives any of his children: see 18.21. Here the word **children** may be understood to refer to any descendants of a person; that is, their children, grandchildren, and so on. Although the scholars are divided on the subject, the verb "to give" in this context may imply the dedication of boys and girls to temple prostitution rather than to giving them to be burned as sacrifices. But since scholarly opinion is divided, it is best to use a more neutral term if one can be found.

To Molech: while some commentators understand **Molech** to be a technical term meaning "human sacrifice," it is probably better to take it as a proper name of a foreign deity. Compare Deuteronomy 18.10; 2 Kings 23.10; Ezekiel 20.31; as well as Leviticus 18.21.

Shall be put to death: this is a very emphatic construction in Hebrew which may be translated literally, "dying he shall die." The emphasis is retained in translations like "surely he shall be put to death" (KJV, NASB). Other English versions

301

underline the certainty of this punishment by using the auxiliary verb "must." Other languages may say something like "there is no doubt that he will be executed."

The people of the land: this means the whole people as a body, or "all the people." Compare 4.27.

Stone him with stones: literally, "stone him with the stone." This expression is a rather technical one, indicating the death penalty by means of throwing stones at the guilty party. It may be translated "shall kill him by throwing stones on him."

20.3   RSV   TEV

| I myself will set my face against that man, and will cut him off from among his people, because he has given one of his children to Molech, defiling my sanctuary and profaning my holy name. | If anyone gives one of his children to Molech and makes my sacred Tent unclean and disgraces my holy name, I will turn against him and will no longer consider him one of my people. |

It will be noticed that this verse has been restructured by TEV. The elements may also be arranged differently in the receptor language.

Set my face against: or "turn my back on," or "**turn against**." See 17.10.

Cut him off from among his people: on the expression **cut . . . off**, see 7.20. And note that **his people** may be translated "the people of Israel" if there is any possibility that this may be understood to mean that this person comes from a different group.

Because: the cause and effect relationship between giving a child to the foreign deity, Moloch, and being excommunicated from the people of God, is perhaps less clear in the structure of TEV. This relationship, however, should be clearly spelled out in the receptor language.

Molech: see verse 2 and 18.21.

My sanctuary: this may be understood as referring strictly to the Tent of the LORD's presence (as in TEV), or more generally to the whole area surrounding and including the Tent.

Profaning my holy name: see 19.8,12.

20.4   RSV   TEV

| And if the people of the land do at all hide their eyes from that man, when he gives one of his children to Molech, and do not put him to death, | But if the community ignores what he has done and does not put him to death, |

And: the transition word should mark the contrast between the case where the people of God act to stop such false worship and the situation where they pretend to be unaware of it. So conjunctions like "**But**" (TEV) or "However" are better than **And**. A number of versions omit the word altogether (NEB, NJB, NJV).

People of the land: see verse 2.

Hide their eyes from that man: literally, "closing, close their eyes." This is the same kind of construction as used with the verb "to die" in verse 2. It serves to emphasize the pretended ignorance of the people of God in the face of this serious evil. It may be translated "pretend not to know what that man is doing," or "close their eyes to what is happening," or some other expression commonly used in the receptor language to indicate willful inaction in response to something that is clearly wrong.

Molech: see verses 2, 3, and 18.21. Since this whole expression is repeated several times in this chapter, it is possible to translate here "when he does this terrible thing," or something similar, after the first few occurrences.

20.5 RSV TEV

then I will set my face against that man and against his family, and will cut them off from among their people, him and all who follow him in playing the harlot after Molech.	I myself will turn against the man and his whole family and against all who join him in being unfaithful to me and worshiping Molech. I will no longer consider them my people.

Set my face against . . . : see verse 3 and 17.10.

And against his family: other members of the family or clan are considered guilty because presumably they would have known about the evil practice but failed to act to stop it. The exact limits of the concept translated **family** are uncertain. But they may be defined in this context by the words **all who follow him** later in the verse.

Cut them off . . . : see verse 3 and 7.20.

Playing the harlot . . . : that is, being unfaithful to the LORD. On the figurative use of the image of prostitution, see 17.7.

20.6 RSV TEV

"If a person turns to mediums and wizards, playing the harlot after them, I will set my face against that person, and will cut him off from among his people.	"If anyone goes for advice to people who consult the spirits of the dead, I will turn against him and will no longer consider him one of my people.

Turns to: that is, enters into contact with, consults, or relies on for the purpose of contacting the dead. NEB translates "wantonly resorts to . . . ."

Mediums and wizards: see 19.31.

Playing the harlot: see verse 5 and 17.7.

Set my face against . . . : see verses 3, 5, and 17.10.

Cut him off . . . : see verse 3 and 7.20.

20.7	RSV	TEV

Consecrate yourselves therefore, and be holy; for I am the LORD your God.

Keep yourselves holy, because I am the LORD your God.

Consecrate yourselves . . . and be holy: these two verbs, **consecrate** and **be holy**, have the same root in Hebrew and express the same basic idea. For this reason they may be translated in some languages by a single verb. See 11.44. Given the difficulty in translating the concept of "holiness" in some languages, it may be possible in this context to say something like "Do not forget that you belong to me, and so live according to my will . . . ."

For: the transition word used here should indicate that the existence of the LORD and the fact that the Israelites belong to him should be the basis for their desire to become holy.

I am the LORD your God: see 18.2. The ancient Greek version as well as some Hebrew manuscripts have a variant reading here that may be translated "for I the LORD your God, am holy," as in verse 26 and 11.44-45. Although this is followed by NEB and NAB, it is not recommended by HOTTP and should probably not be used in the receptor-language translation.

20.8	RSV	TEV

Keep my statutes, and do them; I am the LORD who sanctify you.

Obey my laws, because I am the LORD and I make you holy."

Some commentators and translators take verse 8 as an introduction to the following section and therefore begin a new paragraph here (compare NJB, FRCL, and TOB). But most modern versions link it to the previous verse as a part of the conclusion to the first part of this chapter. Translators are advised not to set it off as a separate paragraph.

Keep . . . and do: the two verbs do not really mean different things but should be taken together to indicate "Be careful to put all my laws into practice" or "Follow all my laws completely." See 19.37.

I am the LORD who sanctify you: the pronoun **you** here is plural, indicating that the sanctification being talked about is not a private matter between individuals and God, but rather a concern of the whole community. The fact that this is a collective act may be brought out by translating "I make you a holy people" or something similar to this. On the idea of holiness, see 11.44.

20.9	RSV	TEV

For every one who curses his father or his mother shall be put to death; he has cursed his father or his mother, his blood is upon him.

The LORD gave the following regulations. Anyone who curses his father or his mother shall be put to death; he is responsible for his own death.

TEV adds at the beginning of this verse "**The LORD gave the following regulations**" in order to introduce the new paragraph and remind the reader that the ultimate origin of what follows is from God himself (see verse 1).

Curses . . . he has cursed . . . : the repetition of this verb may be eliminated as unnatural and awkward in many languages. But in others the repetition may be retained, and the whole verse may be restructured as follows: "If a man curses his father or his mother, he must be killed. He is responsible for his own death because he cursed his parents." On the meaning of the word "curse," see 19.14.

Shall be put to death: this is the same emphatic construction as used in verse 2. If the receptor language has no passive form, this may be translated "they [indefinite] must kill him."

His blood is upon him: it would be a mistake in many languages to translate this literally. This expression indicates that the person who committed the act is alone responsible for his own death. The blame cannot be shared with anyone else.

20.10   RSV   TEV

"If a man commits adultery with   If a man commits adultery with
the wife of[i] his neighbor, both the   the wife of a fellow Israelite, both he
adulterer and the adulteress shall be   and the woman shall be put to death.
put to death.

[i] Heb repeats *if a man commits adultery with the wife of*

The Hebrew text of the beginning of this verse literally reads "A man who commits adultery with the wife of another who commits adultery with the wife of his neighbor . . . ." The majority of modern English translations understand this to be an error made by someone copying a part of the manuscript twice over. Nevertheless, this text is recommended by HOTTP and is followed by NIV, NJV, NASB, and AT. The NJV rendering is typical of the way that sense is made of the longer text: "If a man commits adultery with a married woman, committing adultery with his neighbor's wife . . . ."

Commits adultery: the Hebrew verb thus translated has the meaning of "have sexual intercourse with someone other than one's marriage partner" or "be unfaithful to one's marriage promise." In other words, it is not just any unlawful sexual activity, but it always involves breaking the marriage covenant and violating the marriage relationship. In Hebrew thought a man committed adultery only when he slept with a married woman (another man's wife), but a woman was considered to have committed adultery if she slept with any person other than her husband. This specific case concerns the adultery of a male with the wife of another man. But in the end both the man and the woman were considered as having violated the law concerning adultery. See Exodus 20.14.

His neighbor: see 19.13 on the broader meaning of this word.

The adulterer and the adulteress: it may be more natural and simpler in some languages to say "both the man and the woman" or "the woman as well as the man involved in the act."

Shall be put to death: this is again the emphatic construction seen in verses 2, 4, and 9 above.

20.11   RSV   TEV

The man who lies with his father's wife has uncovered his father's nakedness; both of them shall be put to death, their blood is upon them.

A man who has intercourse with one of his father's wives disgraces his father, and both he and the woman shall be put to death. They are responsible for their own death.

Lies with: that is, "has sexual intercourse with." See 15.18. Compare also 18.8.

Has uncovered his father's nakedness: see 18.7.

Shall be put to death: again the emphatic construction seen in verses 2, 4, 9, and 10 above.

Their blood is upon them: in contrast with verse 9, where the singular **his** and **him** are found, the plural pronouns are used here. But the expression still emphasizes the responsibility of the persons involved.

20.12   RSV   TEV

If a man lies with his daughter-in-law, both of them shall be put to death; they have committed incest, their blood is upon them.

If a man has intercourse with his daughter-in-law, they shall both be put to death. They have committed incest and are responsible for their own death.

Lies with: see verse 11 and 15.18.

Daughter-in-law: compare 18.15.

Incest: this is the same word that is translated "perversion" in 18.23. It carries the idea of "confusion" or of something that is out of harmony with the normal order of creation. In view of the context it may be legitimately translated **incest** here. But in some languages a more general term equivalent to "perversion" may be used both here and in 18.23.

Their blood is upon them: see verse 11.

20.13   RSV   TEV

If a man lies with a male as with a woman, both of them have committed an abomination; they shall be put to death, their blood is upon them.

If a man has sexual relations with another man, they have done a disgusting thing, and both shall be put to death. They are responsible for their own death.

Lies with a male as with a woman: see 18.22.

An abomination: see 7.18; 11.10; 18.22.

They shall be put to death: this is the same emphatic construction as used in verses 2, 4, 9, 10, and elsewhere.

Their blood is upon them: indicating their personal responsibility as in verses 11 and 12 above. This constitutes a kind of summary statement which serves to emphasize the personal accountability.

20.14 RSV	TEV
If a man takes a wife and her mother also, it is wickedness; they shall be burned with fire, both he and they, that there may be no wickedness among you.	If a man marries a woman and her mother, all three shall be burned to death because of the disgraceful thing they have done; such a thing must not be permitted among you.

Takes: this is probably to be understood as meaning "**marries**" (NIV and NJV as well as TEV) or "takes as his wife." Wenham, however, suggests "cohabits with." See 18.17,18.

Wickedness: see 18.17.

Burned with fire: the redundancy may be reduced by omitting **with fire**. It may also be important in some languages to indicate clearly that the purpose of the burning is to put the guilty person to death (TEV "**burned to death**"). One should not give the impression that this is merely a painful means of corporal punishment. Some may prefer to say "they shall burn them alive" or "they shall kill them with fire." See 6.30.

They . . . both he and they: the pronouns here ultimately refer to all three parties involved in the affair: the man, his wife, and his mother-in-law.

20.15 RSV	TEV
If a man lies with a beast, he shall be put to death; and you shall kill the beast.	If a man has sexual relations with an animal, he and the animal shall be put to death.

Lies with a beast: that is, "has sexual intercourse with an animal." Compare 18.23a.

He shall be put to death: this is the same emphatic construction as used in previous verses in this chapter.

You: the pronoun here is singular but is used in an impersonal way, so that it is translated by a passive form in TEV. In those languages where this is not possible, some other means should be used to say that "someone" is to perform the action, without stating who that person should be.

20.16   RSV   TEV

If a woman approaches any beast and lies with it, you shall kill the woman and the beast; they shall be put to death, their blood is upon them.	If a woman tries to have sexual relations with an animal, she and the animal shall be put to death. They are responsible for their own death.

Approaches . . . and lies with: that is, enters into contact with an animal for the purpose of having sexual relations with it. See 18.6 and 15.18.

You: as in the previous verse, this is the impersonal use of the second person singular pronoun and may be translated by a passive or some other impersonal or indefinite form.

They shall be put to death: this is the same emphatic construction used in verses 2, 4, 9, 10, and so forth. Compare 19.20.

Their blood is upon them: see verse 11.

20.17   RSV   TEV

"If a man takes his sister, a daughter of his father or a daughter of his mother, and sees her nakedness, and she sees his nakedness, it is a shameful thing, and they shall be cut off in the sight of the children of their people; he has uncovered his sister's nakedness, he shall bear his iniquity.	If a man marries his sister or half sister, they shall be publicly disgraced and driven out of the community. He has had intercourse with his sister and must suffer the consequences.

Takes . . . : this is probably to be understood in the sense of "takes as a wife," or "**marries**," as in TEV and a number of other versions. See verse 14.

His sister, a daughter of his father or a daughter of his mother: see 18.9.

Sees her nakedness, and she sees his nakedness: or "they see each other naked" (NEB). But this may also be translated "and they live together as husband and wife." Compare Mft "he and she cohabit." This is not the same as the expression **uncover . . . nakedness** used later in this verse as well as in chapter 18 above.

A shameful thing: the idea of "shame" or "disgrace" is not usually difficult to express. But in some languages there may be a roundabout way of saying it, rather than using a single word.

They shall be cut off: see 7.20 and 17.10. The TEV rendering here is "driven out . . . ." This is more forceful than the TEV translation of the same expression elsewhere, but may perhaps be justified by the context.

In the sight of the children of their people: this highlights the public nature of the punishment. The word rendered **children of** is the same as that translated "son of" in 1.5 and elsewhere. It simply refers to members of a group—in this case the Israelite people.

Uncovered . . . nakedness: this is the same expression used so frequently in chapter 18. See, for example, 18.6.

He shall bear his iniquity: the Septuagint has "they shall bear . . . ," as in verses 11, 12, and 13, but this is not followed by any modern version consulted.

20.18   RSV   TEV

If a man lies with a woman having   If a man has intercourse with a
her sickness, and uncovers her na-   woman during her monthly period,
kedness, he has made naked her   both of them are to be driven out of
fountain, and she has uncovered the   the community, because they have
fountain of her blood; both of them   broken the regulations about ritual
shall be cut off from among their   uncleanness.
people.

Having her sickness: this is not the same expression as used in 18.19, but the meaning is identical, and so it may be translated the same.

He has made naked her fountain, and she has uncovered the fountain of her blood: the word **fountain** is used here to describe the menstrual flow of a woman during her monthly period. NJB and NIV speak of the "source" of her flow. NEB translates "exposed her discharge." TEV leaves this implicit, but the two expressions may be translated as a single phrase, "they have uncovered the place of her flow of blood." It would clearly be a mistake to translate this expression literally in most languages.

Cut off . . . : see verse 3 and 7.20.

20.19   RSV   TEV

You shall not uncover the nakedness   If a man has intercourse with
of your mother's sister or of your   his aunt, both of them must suffer
father's sister, for that is to make   the consequences for incest.
naked one's near kin; they shall bear
their iniquity.

Uncover the nakedness: see verse 17 and 18.6.

Your mother's sister or of your father's sister: in English it is easy to translate all this by the single word "**aunt**," but in other languages two separate terms must be used for maternal aunt and paternal aunt. However, in still other cases a more literal rendering will be appropriate.

For that is to make naked one's near kin: the word rendered **near kin** in RSV is literally "flesh." See 18.6. This entire expression may be left implicit, as in TEV.

They shall bear their iniquity: or "**suffer the consequences**." The word **iniquity** is the same term found in 5.1; 18.25; and elsewhere. In other contexts the meaning is more general, but the context here makes it possible to translate it "**incest**," as in TEV.

20.20	RSV	TEV

If a man lies with his uncle's wife, he has uncovered his uncle's naked- ness; they shall bear their sin, they shall die childless.

If a man has intercourse with his uncle's wife, he disgraces his uncle, and he and the woman will pay the penalty; neither one will have chil- dren.

<u>Lies with</u>: see verse 11 and 15.18.

<u>Uncle</u>: the word used in this verse designates the brother of one's father or a paternal uncle. See 10.4.

<u>Childless</u>: the root word here means "stripped," but it has traditionally been understood to mean "deprived of children." It is so translated in Genesis 15.2 to describe Abram. But in this context it is more likely that it means "stripped of posterity," indicating not only that the guilty parties would not bear any children, but also that any offspring that they already had (separately) would be taken from them. In Jeremiah 22.30 TEV translates the same word "lose his children." In this verse one may translate "they must die without leaving any descendants," or "they shall have no one to carry on the family name," or some similar expression. NEB renders it "they shall be proscribed . . . ." One commentator suggests "struck off the list."

20.21	RSV	TEV

If a man takes his brother's wife, it is impurity; he has uncovered his brother's nakedness, they shall be childless.

If a man takes his brother's wife, they will die childless. He has done a ritually unclean thing and has dis- graced his brother.

<u>Takes</u>: see verse 14 and 18.17,18.

Some have seen in this verse a contradiction of the law given in Deuteronomy 25.5, which allows the brother of a dead man to marry his brother's widow. But in this case the brother is still alive, and so this is a case of adultery. If necessary one may add the implicit information "while he [the brother] is still alive."

<u>Impurity</u>: this word indicates both ritual uncleanness and the idea of abhorrence, or of something to be avoided.

<u>Childless</u>: see verse 20.

20.22	RSV	TEV

"You shall therefore keep all my statutes and all my ordinances, and do them; that the land where I am bringing you to dwell may not vomit you out.

The LORD said, "Keep all my laws and commands, so that you will not be rejected by the land of Ca- naan, into which I am bringing you.

At the beginning of this verse, TEV again makes explicit what is implied throughout this section: the commandments given are from God. This kind of reminder is made necessary by the fact that readers do not always start from the beginning when reading Scripture.

The land where I am bringing you: "the land of Canaan" is obviously intended here, and this may be made explicit in translation if judged necessary.

Vomit you out: that is, reject you. See 18.28.

20.23   RSV   TEV

And you shall not walk in the customs of the nation which I am casting out before you; for they did all these things, and therefore I abhorred them.	Do not adopt the customs of people who live there; I am driving out those pagans so that you can enter the land. They have disgusted me with all their evil practices.

Walk in the customs: the verb "to walk" is frequently used in the Scriptures for "behavior" in general (see 18.3,4). To "walk in the custom" of another people means to behave as they do or to practice their way of living. Some may wish to translate "do not start living the way other people live."

The nation: as in 18.28, some versions have the plural here (NJB, NEB), but since the singular is probably used collectively, the meaning comes out the same.

20.24   RSV   TEV

But I have said to you, 'You shall inherit their land, and I will give it to you to possess, a land flowing with milk and honey.' I am the LORD your God, who have separated you from the peoples.	But I have promised you this rich and fertile land as your possession, and I will give it to you. I am the LORD your God, and I have set you apart from the other nations.

Inherit: there is no idea of the usual meaning of the English word "inheritance" here. The verb is better translated "take possession of," "take control of," or "take over from another."

A land flowing with milk and honey: this expression is well known in English but may be confusing in other languages. It is used four times in the book of Exodus (3.8,17; 13.5; and 33.3) to describe the land of Canaan, which God promised the people of Israel. It indicates abundance and fertility. Most English versions translate it literally, but James Mft comes closer to the meaning by making only a slight change of wording. His translation reads "abounding in milk and honey." In other languages one may say "where there is plenty of milk and honey," or more dynamically, "where there is plenty to eat and drink." TEV goes a step further with **"this rich and fertile land,"** but this is faithful to the meaning of the expression.

Separated you: this is the same root word as the one translated "make a distinction between" in the following verse. God has made his own people different from all others. He distinguished them from the surrounding groups of people. They are, therefore, "set apart from" all others (compare NJV).

The peoples: this is not the same term used in 18.24, but the meaning is essentially the same. This refers to the Canaanites and all other groups not considered a part of the people of God.

20.25 RSV	TEV
You shall therefore make a distinction between the clean beast and the unclean, and between the unclean bird and the clean; you shall not make yourselves abominable by beast or bird or by anything with which the ground teems, which I have set apart for you to hold unclean.	So then, you must make a clear distinction between animals and birds that are ritually clean and those that are not. Do not eat unclean animals or birds. I have declared them unclean, and eating them would make you unclean.

Therefore: this indicates that what follows is the result of the fact that God had set apart the Israelites and made them different from other peoples. Similarly, they are to differentiate between the ritually clean and unclean animals.

Make a distinction: the same root word as in the previous verse, but in this context it is reasonable to translate it "make a clear separation" (NEB) or "separate" (Mft). Other languages may use some form of the verb "divide."

Clean . . . and unclean: see 10.10.

Make yourselves abominable: this may be translated as a causative form in certain languages: "cause yourselves to be unacceptable to God" or "make yourselves to be defiled." The NAB rendering of this phrase is "be contaminated by . . . ."

Anything with which the ground teems: the expression found here is very similar to the one used in 11.44 and apparently refers to the creeping or swarming things mentioned several times in chapter 11. NEB has "anything that creeps on the ground." Translators are advised to avoid rendering the idea conveyed by LB with "though the land teem with them," as if this phrase qualifies the birds and animals already mentioned in this verse.

20.26 RSV	TEV
You shall be holy to me; for I the LORD am holy, and have separated you from the peoples, that you should be mine.	You shall be holy and belong only to me, because I am the LORD and I am holy. I have set you apart from the other nations so that you would belong to me alone.

Holy: see 11.44.

To me . . . be mine: both of these expressions emphasize the unique position of the Israelites as belonging only to God. Unless it violates the rule of naturalness in translation, it is probably good to repeat the idea as is done in TEV.

Separated: see verses 24 and 25 above.

The peoples: see verse 24.

20.27   RSV   TEV

"A man or a woman who is a medium or a wizard shall be put to death; they shall be stoned with stones, their blood shall be upon them."

"Any man or woman who consults the spirits of the dead shall be stoned to death; any person who does this is responsible for his own death."

Is a medium or a wizard: in 19.31 the prohibition is against seeking the advice of such a person, but this verse condemns the person who actually commits such practices.

They shall be stoned with stones: see verse 2. This passive construction may be rendered "you [plural] (or, someone) must kill them with stones," or something similar.

Their blood shall be upon them: see verses 9, 11, and others.

Chapter 21

Chapters 21–22 deal with a number of problems concerning the proper exercise of priestly functions. These two chapters may be divided up as follows:

1. Rules for the priests themselves   21.1–22.16
2. Rules about animals offered as sacrifices   22.17-30
3. A conclusion to these two chapters   22.31-33

Chapter 21 itself may be further subdivided into three paragraphs: verses 1-9 deal with all the priests. Verses 10-15 concern only the High Priest. And the final section (verses 16-24) has to do with deformities or diseases that make it impossible for a person to perform the functions of a priest.

TEV Section Heading: **"The Holiness of the Priests."**
The section heading in NEB is identical with that of TEV. NIV has "Rules for Priests." Some editions of RSV carry the section heading "The sanctity of the priesthood."

21.1	RSV	TEV

RSV	TEV
And the LORD said to Moses, "Speak to the priests, the sons of Aaron, and say to them that none of them shall defile himself for the dead among his people,	The LORD commanded Moses to tell the Aaronite priests, "No priest is to make himself ritually unclean by taking part in the funeral ceremonies when a relative dies,

The LORD said to Moses: here the formula introducing direct discourse is slightly different in Hebrew from the usual one (seen in 4.1 and at many other points throughout this book). Although the usual formula may perhaps be slightly more solemn, it is doubtful whether it will be possible or even desirable to try to indicate any difference in translation.

Speak . . . : as usual, RSV begins the direct quotation here and makes the following words an indirect quote, but TEV makes this a part of the indirect discourse and begins the direct quotation with the words that are actually to be spoken to the priests. Receptor language habits in this respect should determine which model is to be followed. But the TEV solution will probably be simpler in most languages.

The priests, the sons of Aaron: see 1.5.

None of them shall . . . : the Hebrew has the masculine singular third person pronoun here. But the use of this pronoun here clearly refers to "any of the priests," as almost all versions indicate.

Defile himself for the dead among his people: literally, "for a soul [person] he shall not make himself unclean among his kinsmen." But virtually all translations and commentators agree that the word for "soul" or "person" is to be understood in the sense of a person who has died. Any contact with a dead body was thought to make a person ritually unclean. See Numbers 19.

Regarding the word **people** or "kinsmen," see 7.20 and 19.16. This word is used four times in this chapter (here and in verses 4, 14, and 15) and in this context probably means "the tribe of Levi," all those who are a part of the priestly clan.

21.2	RSV	TEV
	except for his nearest of kin, his mother, his father, his son, his daughter, his brother,	unless it is his mother, father, son, daughter, brother,

Except: an exception is made to the general rule given in the previous verse. If the dead person is a member of the immediate family as defined here, then permission is granted to come in contact with the corpse. To express this idea, some languages will have to begin a new sentence and say something like "However, (or, But) if the dead person is . . . , then he may approach that person and make himself unclean." The last part of this sentence will, of course, be a part of verse 3 below.

His nearest of kin: literally, "his flesh" as in 18.12. In some languages this may be translated "his immediate family" or by a similar expression. But translators should be careful that the term used here is in keeping with the list that follows. Another possibility is to leave this general term implicit, since the persons involved are listed separately (compare TEV). Note that his wife is not specifically included in the list, but she may well be implied in **his nearest of kin** ("his flesh"), since the two are said to become "one flesh" (Gen 2.24).

His father: in some languages "the father that bore him" or "the father that engendered (or, sired) him," since the term **father** may have a broader meaning.

His mother: as above, some languages will require that this be translated "the mother that bore him."

His son, his daughter: these two terms may be translated by a single word in some languages. In others one must say "any children that he himself has begotten (or, borne)."

His brother: since the word **brother** may be understood in a very broad sense in many languages, this may have to be translated as "his brother borne by the same father and same mother." And if the word does not indicate the sex of the brother or sister, then it will also include the sister mentioned in verse 3. But at some point the translation should make it clear that a married sister is excluded from those whose body the priest is allowed to approach.

21.3   RSV   TEV

or his virgin sister (who is near to   or unmarried sister living in his
him because she has had no hus-   house.
band; for her he may defile himself).

Virgin sister: in this context the emphasis in the word translated **virgin** is not
so much on the sexual purity of the girl but on the fact that she has no husband to
take care of her in case of her death. It is translated "maiden sister" in NAB, and
"**unmarried sister**" in NIV as well as TEV.

Near to him: this phrase has been interpreted in various ways by the different
English versions. NEB takes it as going with the previous word and translates "full
sister." But most translations that do something other than a more or less literal
rendering seem to think it indicates a definite dependency on the priest in question.
TEV translates this dynamically with "**living in his house**," and NIV has "dependent
on him." AT has "still related to him" (compare NJB and Mft), because a married
sister would no longer be considered a part of the immediate family.

For her he may defile himself: while this refers specifically to the unmarried
sister, it is possible in translation to state that the priest is allowed to make himself
unclean for any of the relatives listed in verses 2 and 3. See comments on verse 2.

21.4   RSV   TEV

He shall not defile himself as a hus-   He shall not make himself unclean at
band among his people and so pro-   the death of those related to him by
fane himself.   marriage.[l]

                    [l] *Verse 4 in Hebrew is unclear.*

This verse is said to be the most difficult one in the entire book of Leviticus.
Any translation of these words must be considered a guess, because we really do not
know for sure what they mean. The RSV is a more or less literal rendering of the
Hebrew text, but its questionable meaning reflects the difficulties in this verse. Even
the ancient versions seem to have found this verse as difficult as modern scholars do.

The following interpretations have been given to these words:

1. The word translated **husband** may also be rendered "master," "chief," or
   "leader." The ancient Latin version follows this understanding of the word. LB
   has translated "For the priest is a leader among his people and he may not
   ceremonially defile himself as an ordinary person can." This interpretation has
   also been followed by a number of French translations, including FRCL, TOB,
   and Segond.

2. Some scholars think that a word meaning "married to" has dropped out of the text
   and must be restored. According to this school of thought, this word appeared
   in the original text preceding the word **husband**. Together the two words
   would mean "for one married to a husband." But the altered text is still subject
   to a variety of interpretations: NEB understands it to mean "nor shall he make
   himself unclean for any married woman among his father's kin . . . ." NAB reads

"but for a sister who has married out of his family, he shall not make himself unclean . . . ." And NJB has rendered this passage "but for a close female relation who is married, he will not make himself unclean." On the other hand, a number of modern versions take the expression in the more general sense **"related to him by marriage"** (NIV, TEV, NJV, AT, and GECL).

3. The ancient Greek version understood the questionable word to mean "suddenly" instead of **husband**. The text would then read "Among his kinsmen a priest must not suddenly make himself impure . . . ." This is the reading recommended by HOTTP, but it is not followed by any major modern version.

It is probably best to follow the second option, with the more general interpretation yielding **"related to him by marriage."** But whichever solution is adopted in the receptor language translation, it will be wise to include a footnote explaining the difficulties of the text and the other possible renderings.

Profane himself: see 18.21.

21.5   RSV   TEV

They shall not make tonsures upon   "No priest shall shave any part
their heads, nor shave off the edges   of his head or trim his beard or cut
of their beards, nor make any cut-   gashes on his body to show that he
tings in their flesh.   is in mourning.

They: the pronoun here refers to the priests. It may be wise to make this information more obvious in the receptor language translation, as does TEV.

Make tonsures upon their heads: this has nothing to do with natural baldness (as in chapter 13) but involves the intentional shaving of a part of the head to make a bald spot. This was done by some to mourn the dead. It is probably in error to say simply "shave their heads" as in NIV, since this may give the impression that the entire head is necessarily shaved. The expression indicates rather the shaving of a part of the head to make one part of it bald.

Shave off the edges of their beards: see 19.27.

Cuttings in their flesh: see 15.7 and 19.28.

As in 19.27-28, these acts were performed as a sign of mourning for the dead. TEV makes this implicit information explicit in translation by adding **"to show that he is in mourning."** This should probably be done in most other languages, since the purpose of these actions would otherwise be impossible for the reader to know.

21.6   RSV   TEV

They shall be holy to their God, and   He must be holy and must not dis-
not profane the name of their God;   grace my name. He offers food offer-
for they offer the offerings by fire to   ings to me, and he must be holy.
the LORD, the bread of their God;
therefore they shall be holy.

They: this still refers to the priests. But since TEV uses the singular expression "No priest . . ." in the previous verse, it also has the singular pronoun here.

Shall be: this is not a statement of something to take place at a future time; rather it is a present requirement of the priests. This is why TEV and other modern versions have "**must**."

Holy: see 6.9 and 11.44.

To their God . . . their God . . . the LORD: since it is God himself who is speaking, TEV has used the first person singular pronoun in place of the nouns **God** and **LORD**. In some languages the use of the pronoun **their** before **God** presents particular problems because it seems to be exclusive. However these words are rendered, translators should be careful not to give the impression that the LORD is God only of the priests involved.

Profane the name: one may also say "to dishonor," or "bring disgrace on," or "bring shame to." See 18.21.

The bread of their God: the word translated **bread** is to be understood in the more general sense of "**food**." See 3.11,16, where offerings made by fire are called "food offerings."

21.7   RSV   TEV

They shall not marry a harlot or a woman who has been defiled; neither shall they marry a woman divorced from her husband; for the priest is holy to his God.	A priest shall not marry a woman who has been a prostitute or a woman who is not a virgin or who is divorced; he is holy.

They: "**A priest**" in the singular in TEV, but the meaning is the same, since this is a general prohibition. The rules for priests concerning marriage are more strict than for the ordinary person.

Harlot: see 19.29.

A woman who has been defiled: this may be understood in two ways: (1) she may be a woman who has participated in cultic prostitution (see 19.29), and thus the phrase may be a further explanation of the word "**harlot**" used in this verse (as in NJV, NJB); or (2) she may simply be one who has been seduced or violated and therefore lost her virginity. TEV, NEB, AT, and NAB take it in this latter sense. The LB rendering "a woman of another tribe" is without justification and should be avoided in the receptor-language translation.

Divorced from her husband: the matter of divorce is dealt with in more detail in Deuteronomy 24.1-4. In some languages this idea is conveyed by expressions like "driven out" or "sent away" (which is very similar to the actual Hebrew word), or "refused," "rejected," or "returned to her parents."

21.8   RSV   TEV

You shall consecrate him, for he offers the bread of your God; he	The people must consider the priest holy, because he presents the food

shall be holy to you; for I the LORD, | offerings to me. I am the LORD; I am
who sanctify you, am holy. | holy and I make my people holy.

You: the pronoun here is singular in form, so some translators prefer to render it "Each Israelite . . ." (FRCL). But naturalness in the receptor language should be the determining factor in deciding whether to say "You people . . ." or "Each one of you . . . ." One commentator states that "the Israelites as a nation are addressed in the person of their chiefs" (that is, the priests).

Consecrate: the root word here is the same as for **holy** and **sanctify**. But the form used gives the idea of "regard as holy" (NIV) or "treat as holy" (NJV and NJB). RSV may give the wrong idea that a rite of consecration is involved, similar to ordination.

Bread: see verse 6.

Be holy . . . sanctify: the two verbs are closely related. The second is the causative form of the first. The verb **be holy** describes a state, while **sanctify** means "to make holy" or "cause to be holy." On the meaning of **holy**, see 2.3.

You: while the other cases of the pronoun in this verse are singular, the final occurrence of the English pronoun **you** corresponds to the second person plural in Hebrew. It clearly refers to the whole community of Israel. So TEV has rendered it "**my people**." Some versions follow a different text at this point and read "I . . . sanctify them" (NEB and AT). But this is not recommended.

21.9   RSV   TEV

And the daughter of any priest, if | If a priest's daughter becomes a
she profanes herself by playing the | prostitute, she disgraces her father;
harlot, profanes her father; she shall | she shall be burned to death.
be burned with fire.

Playing the harlot: this probably refers to cultic prostitution (see 19.29).

Profanes: see 19.29.

Burned with fire: that is, put to death by means of fire. See 6.30.

21.10   RSV   TEV

"The priest who is chief among | "The High Priest has had the
his brethren, upon whose head the | anointing oil poured on his head and
anointing oil is poured, and who has | has been consecrated to wear the
been consecrated to wear the gar- | priestly garments, so he must not
ments, shall not let the hair of his | leave his hair uncombed or tear his
head hang loose, nor rend his | clothes to show that he is in mourn-
clothes; | ing.

Verses 10-15 concern the private life of the High Priest. His position involves obligations and prohibitions that are even more strict than those for the ordinary priests. Verses 10-12 constitute a single sentence that is long and complex in RSV. It should be broken down into several shorter and simpler sentences.

The priest who is chief among his brethren: or "The priest greater than his brothers." But this has nothing to do with size or height. It is just another way of saying "**High Priest**." And in most languages it will be better to say this explicitly. See 8.12 with regard to his consecration.

Anointing oil is poured: on the practice of anointing, see 4.3 and 8.10. The passive construction here may be rendered actively by saying "on whose head they [indefinite] poured oil . . . ." In some cases the relationship between the pouring on of oil and the consecration may have to be spelled out more clearly. One way of doing this is to say "who has been consecrated by the pouring on of oil."

The garments: see 8.7-9. It may be helpful in many languages to supply the implied information and say "the sacred garments."

Let the hair . . . hang loose, nor rend his clothes: these were signs of mourning. See 10.6.

21.11-12   RSV   TEV

11 he shall not go in to any dead body, nor defile himself, even for his father or for his mother; 12 neither shall he go out of the sanctuary, nor profane the sanctuary of his God; for the consecration of the anointing oil of his God is upon him: I am the LORD.

11-12 He has been dedicated to me and is not to make himself ritually unclean nor is he to defile my sacred Tent by leaving it and entering a house where there is a dead person, even if it is his own father or mother.

Shall not go in to any dead body: this may be equally well translated "he must not approach any dead body" or "he must avoid contact with all dead bodies." The idea of going into a house (see TEV) is not necessarily implied. Compare NJB "he will not go near any corpse." (Similarly, NAB, AT, and Mft).

Even for his father or for his mother: this clearly shows that the requirements for the High Priest are more rigid than those for the ordinary priests. Compare verse 2. It is, of course, implied that if this is not done for the High Priest's own parents, it must certainly not be done for any of the other relatives mentioned in verses 2 and 3 above. It may be wise to say, as TEV has done, "**even if it is his own father or mother**."

Go out of the sanctuary: this does not mean that the High Priest was to remain in the holy place at all times, but only that he must not leave it for the purpose of taking part in a funeral. Compare 10.7.

21.13   RSV   TEV

And he shall take a wife in her virginity.

He shall marry a virgin,

Take a wife: marry a woman. See 18.17.

In her virginity: in some languages it may be better to say "He must marry only a woman who is still a virgin" or "He must take for his wife a woman who has never had sexual relations with another man." In some cases the word "**virgin**" may have to be translated by a longer expression meaning "who has never slept with a man" or "who has maintained her sexual purity."

21.14   RSV   TEV

A widow, or one divorced, or a woman who has been defiled, or a harlot, these he shall not marry; but he shall take to wife a virgin of his own people,	not a widow or a divorced woman or a woman who has been a prostitute. He shall marry only a virgin from his own clan.

Widow: or "a woman whose husband has died."

One divorced: or "a woman whose husband has rejected her (or, sent her away) . . ." or some similar expression.

Harlot: or "**prostitute**." See 17.7.

Take to wife: or "marry a woman."

A virgin: see verse 13.

Of his own people: meaning "from his own people" (NIV, NAB) or "from his father's kin" (NEB). Or some have proposed "of the priestly tribe (or, the tribe of Levi)." AT "of his own class" may be misleading, even though it is probably intended to mean the priestly class rather than social class.

21.15   RSV   TEV

that he may not profane his children among his people; for I am the LORD who sanctify him."	Otherwise, his children, who ought to be holy, will be ritually unclean. I am the LORD and I have set him apart as the High Priest."

That: this expresses the potential result of marrying someone other than the kind of person recommended. Marriage to an unacceptable woman can only produce unacceptable children. It will be possible in some languages to begin a new sentence with "If he does not obey this requirement, then . . . ." Note that TEV begins a new sentence with "**Otherwise . . . .**"

Sanctify: set apart. See verse 8.

Notice that the TEV rendering supplies implicit information at the end of this verse, since this is the conclusion of the paragraph on the requirements for the High Priest.

21.16-17   RSV   TEV

16 And the LORD said to Moses,   16 The LORD commanded Mo-
17 "Say to Aaron, None of your des-   ses 17 to tell Aaron, "None of your
cendants throughout their genera-   descendants who has any physical
tions who has a blemish may ap-   defects may present the food offer-
proach to offer the bread of his God.   ing to me. This applies for all time to
                                        come.

In those versions with two levels of section headings, a new subheading may be
introduced here. It is at this point that the subject of deformities in priests is begun.
The effect of this passage is to disqualify all abnormal descendants of Aaron from the
priesthood.

Said to Moses: see 4.1.

Say . . . : see 1.2.

Throughout their generations: this has been shifted to the end of verse 17
in TEV and translated as a separate sentence: "**This applies for all time to come.**"

A blemish: this word is used five times in the next seven verses. The RSV
rendering may be misleading. Most versions translate it "defect," but since the
context clearly defines it as a physical matter, TEV translates more clearly "**any
physical defects**." Mft has "is disfigured."

Bread: that is, "**food**." See verses 6 and 8 above.

21.18   RSV   TEV

For no one who has a blemish shall   No man with any physical defects
draw near, a man blind or lame, or   may make the offering: no one who
one who has a mutilated face or a   is blind, lame, disfigured, or de-
limb too long,   formed;

Blemish: see verse 17. This is further defined by what follows.

Draw near: this is the same word that is translated "approach" in the previous
verse, but here it has no object. In some languages it will be necessary to answer the
questions "Draw near to what?" and in some cases "For what purpose?" The obvious
answers are "draw near to me [God] to make offerings." In some languages it will
be acceptable to translate more simply "approach the altar."

Blind or lame: these two common physical deformities are usually not difficult
to translate. The term **lame**, however, may have to be rendered "crippled," or
"unable to move normally," or "physically disabled."

A mutilated face: the KJV rendering, "a flat nose," is not recommended. The
root word here is a verb meaning "to slit (or, pierce)" (usually of the nose, lip or
ear). Hence RSV **a mutilated face**, but the more general "**disfigured**" is better (NIV,
NJB, NASB, TEV). The rendering "a broken nose" (LB) is too restricted in meaning.
It is also possible to understand this word as meaning "stunted" or "dwarfed" (see
NEB and NJV), but the idea of disfigurement of the face or head is preferable. In
some languages this may have to be translated something like "having something
abnormal on the face" or "whose facial features have been spoiled."

A limb too long: the text does not literally speak of a **limb**. The word comes from a root meaning "to extend" or "to stretch." Hence, "to be too long." But again the more general sense of **"deformed"** is to be preferred. This idea may be rendered in some languages as "having something abnormal about his body" or "whose body is not like that of regular people."

21.19   RSV   TEV

or a man who has an injured foot or an injured hand,   **no one with a crippled hand or foot;**

An injured foot or an injured hand: some take this as a permanent deformity (NEB "a man deformed in foot or hand"), while others see it as a temporary problem (NJV "a broken leg or a broken arm"). The text may be understood in either way, but there is nothing that forces us to interpret it as something permanent.

21.20   RSV   TEV

or a hunchback, or a dwarf, or a man with a defect in his sight or an itching disease or scabs or crushed testicles;   **no one who is a hunchback or a dwarf; no one with any eye or skin disease; and no eunuch.**

A hunchback: a person with an abnormal bump on the back or shoulder.

A dwarf: the Hebrew adjective indicates something very thin or small (compare 13.30), and it usually has a negative connotation. It may be understood here either as an abnormally short person (**dwarf**) or as a person who is abnormally thin and sickly (NAB "weakly"). NEB has connected it with the eye problem which follows and has thus translated "a film [over his eye]." But this is not recommended. Most versions adopt the meaning **dwarf**.

A defect in his sight: literally, "a spot (or, defect) in his eye." Here again we are dealing with a word that is found only here in all the Old Testament, so we cannot be certain of its meaning. Probably the whole expression is to be taken as a general reference to any kind of eye disease.

An itching disease: the Hebrew text actually has two words for "festering or running sores" (NIV). Probably the two taken together are to be understood as referring to various kinds of skin diseases, or skin diseases in general.

Crushed testicles: this same defect prevented the ordinary Israelite from public worship (Deut 23.1). NAB translates "hernia," and both NJB and TEV render it more dynamically and perhaps inaccurately as **"eunuch."** However, to translate the idea into many languages, it will be necessary to say something very much like a more literal rendering of the text, "someone whose testicles have been damaged."

21.21   RSV   TEV

**no man of the descendants of Aaron   No descendant of Aaron the priest
the priest who has a blemish shall   who has any physical defects may
come near to offer the LORD's offer-   present the food offering to me.
ings by fire; since he has a blemish,
he shall not come near to offer the
bread of his God.**

This verse is a summary statement which states the same truth twice in slightly different words. TEV has reduced this to a single statement. Receptor language habits will determine whether it is more natural to follow the RSV or the TEV formulation.

Come near: the word used here is not the same as in verses 17 and 18 above, but the meaning is virtually identical.

The bread of his God: see verses 6 and 17.

21.22   RSV   TEV

**He may eat the bread of his God,   Such a man may eat the food offered
both of the most holy and of the holy   to me, both the holy food offering
things,   and the very holy food offering,**

He: or "a man [of the priestly family] with such a physical defect." Compare the beginning of the previous verse.

Bread: see verses 6 and 17.

Of the most holy and of the holy things: some commentators see the **holy things** as referring to the special gift mentioned in 7.34 and the **most holy . . . things** as being the priests' share of the grain offerings (6.17), the sin offerings (6.25-56), and the repayment offerings (7.6). While it is no doubt advisable to render these expressions in a rather general way, the word **things** is probably too vague, and something like TEV's **"food offered"** is better.

21.23   RSV   TEV

**but he shall not come near the veil   but because he has a physical de-
or approach the altar, because he   fect, he shall not come near the sa-
has a blemish, that he may not pro-   cred curtain or approach the altar.
fane my sanctuaries; for I am the   He must not profane these holy
LORD who sanctify them."   things, because I am the LORD and I
                                          make them holy."**

But: this word indicates the contrast between the permission to eat the food offerings and the denial of permission to perform the priestly functions associated with the actual offering of the food to God.

Come near to the veil: on this expression, see 4.6 and Exodus 26.31-35. In front of this curtain inside the Tent of the LORD's presence there was the table for the bread offered to God, the lampstand (Exo 26.35) and the incense altar (Exo 30.6). The expression **come near the veil**, then, means to go into the first part of the sanctuary to put the bread on the table, to light the lamps, and to burn the incense to God. These rites were reserved for those priests that were considered acceptable to the LORD, while those having any physical deformity were excluded. It is legitimate to translate less ambiguously as "must not go into the sanctuary."

Approach the altar: see verse 21.

Profane: see 18.21.

My sanctuaries: the use of the plural here is surprising and troubling to scholars. Some have suggested that it is evidence of a time when there were several shrines where the Israelites worshiped, but others see it as a reference to "my sanctuary and all its contents" (see TOB). This interpretation is essentially the one followed by NJB and NAB as well as TEV, and should be adopted in the receptor language. A literal rendering of **my sanctuaries** would be misleading, and the singular (as in NIV and LB) does not accurately reflect the text.

I am the LORD . . . : see verse 8 as well as 11.44.

Them: as it stands, the pronoun in RSV seems to refer to the word **sanctuaries**. But it is probably more likely that the reference here is to the priests. This interpretation is supported by the ancient versions. So it may have to be made explicit in some languages by saying "It is I, the LORD, who sanctify the priests" (compare FRCL). Whichever interpretation is adopted, the alternative should probably be indicated in a marginal note.

21.24	RSV	TEV

So Moses spoke to Aaron and to his sons and to all the people of Israel.	This, then, is what Moses said to Aaron, the sons of Aaron, and to all the people of Israel.

The RSV rendering of this verse may give the impression that Moses simply had a conversation with Aaron, his sons, and the people of Israel, without any indication of what they talked about. In fact, however, this verse is a kind of summary statement referring back to the words recorded in the previous verses. In some languages it may be wise to say something like "So Moses told all these things [referring back to the matters earlier in the chapter] to Aaron, his sons, and all the Israelites" or "So these are the things that Moses told Aaron and his sons and all the Israelites."

Chapter 22

Section Heading: **"The Holiness of the Offerings."**

NJB entitles this chapter "Holiness in consuming sacred food" and then divides it into three sections concerning the priests (1-9), lay people (10-16), and sacrificial animals (17-30). The concluding section (31-33) is a final exhortation. However, it is possible to use only one section heading for the entire chapter, which may be given a title like that of TEV or "Offerings that God accepts."

<u>22.1-2</u> RSV	TEV
1 And the LORD said to Moses, 2 "Tell Aaron and his sons to keep away from the holy things of the people of Israel, which they dedicate to me, so that they may not profane my holy name: I am the LORD.	1 The LORD commanded Moses 2 to tell Aaron and his sons, "You must not bring disgrace on my holy name, so treat with respect the sacred offerings that the people of Israel dedicate to me. I am the LORD.

Said to Moses: see 4.1.

Tell . . . : see 1.2.

Keep away from: a literal translation of this phrase will almost certainly be misunderstood by the average reader and create an unnecessary contradiction in the book of Leviticus. It is clearly indicated in other places in this book that the **holy things** are to be dealt with by the priests (see, for example, 14.13). How, then, is it possible that they should keep away from them or "be separated from" them (KJV)? There are three possible solutions to this problem, based on the interpretation of the verb used here: (1) Some scholars see it as meaning "consecrate" in this context. Hence NJB translates "They must be consecrated by the holy offerings . . . ." (2) Others feel that there is implied information that needs to be made explicit. Both FRCL and TOB (which usually sticks quite close to the Hebrew text) supply this information to make the text mean "Speak to Aaron and his sons about the cases where . . . they must keep away from the holy offerings . . . ." This, then, looks ahead to the cases mentioned in verse 3 and following. While this is clearly possible, the third solution must also be seriously considered. (3) A wide range of different translations, including NIV, NASB, NAB, AT, and NJV, agree with TEV that the meaning of the verb here is **"treat with respect,"** "be careful with," or "be scrupulous about." It should be noted, however, that this meaning of the Hebrew verb is not found in other contexts where the term occurs.

Dedicate: here and in the following verse, this verb is the same as the one translated "consecrate" in 8.10. The root meaning is "make holy."

Profane my holy name: see 18.21.

I am the LORD: see 19.3. Some versions (NJV, for example) take this as being in apposition with **my holy name**. But it is probably better to make it a separate statement, as in RSV and TEV.

22.3   RSV   TEV

Say to them, 'If any one of all your descendants throughout your generations approaches the holy things, which the people of Israel dedicate to the LORD, while he has an uncleanness, that person shall be cut off from my presence: I am the LORD.	If any of your descendants, while he is ritually unclean, comes near the sacred offerings which the people of Israel have dedicated to me, he can never again serve at the altar. This applies for all time to come. I am the LORD.

Say to them . . . : since the verb "tell" occurs in the previous verse, the repetition of this information may or may not be necessary, depending on the habits of the receptor language. Note that it has been omitted by TEV.

Of all your descendants: since the priesthood in Israel was hereditary, all the male descendants of Aaron made up the priestly class. It may be necessary in some languages to make it clear that only male descendants are intended here. Another way of saying this is "any man of the priestly family" or, as in NEB, "any man in your descent . . . ." NJV has "any man among your offspring."

Throughout your generations: in TEV this has been shifted toward the end of the verse and rendered dynamically as a separate sentence "**This applies for all time to come.**" Others have suggested that it may be translated simply "in the future" or "from now on."

Dedicate: see verse 2 above.

Approaches: this implies at least the possibility of actually touching the sacred offerings. If the receptor language verb specifically excludes the idea of physical contact, then it may be wise to translate "come near or touch."

To the LORD: more naturally in direct speech from the LORD himself, "dedicated to me, the LORD," or simply "to me."

While he has an uncleanness: this general term is explained in verses 4 and 5. The idea, of course, is that of ritual impurity (see 5.2 and 10.10). Note that in TEV this has been shifted to a more prominent position in the order of this verse.

Cut off from my presence: literally "cut off from before me." This is similar to the expression used in 7.20-21, but it is not identical. The meaning of this expression is clarified by another that is frequently used in the Old Testament, "to stand before someone" (see Deut 10.8, for example), which means "to serve someone." So the words "to be cut off from before someone" mean to be no longer allowed to serve that person. So TEV renders it "he can never again serve at the altar." Another possibility is to say "he will be relieved of his priestly duties." Mft says that such a person "shall be outlawed from my presence." It is not likely that the expression used here would indicate condemnation to death, as some commentators have supposed (see GECL).

22.4 RSV	TEV
None of the line of Aaron who is a leper or suffers a discharge may eat of the holy things until he is clean. Whoever touches anything that is unclean through contact with the dead or a man who has had an emission of semen,	"None of the descendants of Aaron who has a dreaded skin disease or a discharge may eat any of the sacred offerings until he is ritually clean. Any priest is unclean if he touches anything which is unclean through contact with a corpse or if he has an emission of semen

Compare 7.19b-21. There is all the more reason to forbid to the priests what is not allowed to the lay people.

None of the line of Aaron: the word translated **line** here has the same root as "descendant" in verse 3. This expression may equally well be translated "No priest . . ." or "No man in the priestly family . . . ."

Leper: better, "**who has a dreaded skin disease**," as in TEV. See 13.8 and the comments at the beginning of chapter 13.

Discharge: see 15.2.

An emission of semen: literally, "a discharge," but this word is used almost always of a discharge from the sexual organs. If the subject is a woman, it refers to the menstrual flow. But when the subject is a male, the reference is to seminal fluid. Some languages have very different ways of talking about this bodily function. One may say "pass the liquid of his manhood" or some other expression that is also far from the form of the source text. Compare 15.16-18.

The RSV rendering of the last part of this verse could easily give the impression that it is forbidden to touch anything that has been in contact with a dead body, or to touch a man who has had an emission of semen. In translation these words should be structured in such a way as to avoid such an impression. It should be clear that a priest becomes unclean either by touching an object that has touched a corpse or by having an emission of semen himself. There is no mention in this verse of touching another person who has had such an emission.

22.5 RSV	TEV
and whoever touches a creeping thing by which he may be made unclean or a man from whom he may take uncleanness, whatever his uncleanness may be—	or if he has touched an unclean animal or person.

A creeping thing: see 5.2 and 11.10, where the same word is translated "swarming things." Although NJB takes it in the more restricted sense of "reptile," here it should be taken as referring more generally to any unclean animal (whether dead or alive), since it stands in contrast with **man**. And it should be noted that in this context **man** is used in the sense of any human being—not just the male of the species. This is why it has been translated **"person"** in TEV and NIV, and "human being" in NEB and NJV.

Note also that TEV has restructured this verse and eliminated needless repetition.

22.6 RSV TEV

the person who touches any such shall be unclean until the evening and shall not eat of the holy things unless he has bathed his body in water.

Any priest who becomes unclean remains unclean until evening, and even then he may not eat any of the sacred offerings until he has taken a bath.

The person: literally "the soul" (see KJV). But the context clearly shows that the persons involved are members of the priestly family. TEV has made this explicit with "**Any priest**."

Any such: or "any thing of that kind," referring back to the previous verses. Since this is a kind of unnecessary repetition, TEV has chosen to leave it implicit here.

Shall not eat: translators should be careful not to use a future tense, since this is clearly a prohibition. It is better translated "is not allowed to eat" or "must not eat."

Bathed his body in water: in many languages it will be redundant to use the words **in water**, since that is implicit in the verb "to bathe." And in some cases there may be a single verb that conveys the idea "to wash the body." The word translated **body** here is actually "flesh," as in 15.7,16.

22.7 RSV TEV

When the sun is down he shall be clean; and afterward he may eat of the holy things, because such are his food.

After the sun sets he is clean, and then he may eat the sacred offerings, which are his food.

When the sun is down: this may either mean "at sunset," "when the sun goes down" (NJB, NEB) or "after sunset" (see TEV). Probably the most accurate rendering is that of NJV "As soon as the sun sets . . . ."

And afterward: or better, "only then . . . ," or "not until that time . . . ."

Because such are his food: this food comes from the offerings of the people of Israel and is the principal source of income for the priests. It does not belong to any priest personally but rather to the entire priestly family. In order to avoid giving the impression of personal ownership, it will be necessary in some languages to state more clearly "because this food belongs to the family of priests" or something similar.

22.8   RSV   TEV

That which dies of itself or is torn by beasts he shall not eat, defiling himself by it: I am the LORD.'

He shall not eat the meat of any animal that has died a natural death or has been killed by wild animals; it will make him unclean. I am the LORD.

The word order in this verse in the original, as reflected in RSV, may be very unnatural and require restructuring in many languages. Compare 7.24 and 17.15 on the expressions meaning "to die a natural death" and "to be killed by wild animals."

I am the LORD: see 18.2.

22.9   RSV   TEV

They shall therefore keep my charge, lest they bear sin for it and die thereby when they profane it: I am the LORD who sanctify them.

"All priests shall observe the regulations that I have given. Otherwise, they will become guilty and die, because they have disobeyed the sacred regulations. I am the LORD and I make them holy.

They: the Hebrew shifts from the singular to the plural pronoun at this point. This may be handled as in TEV by changing from "any priest" (verse 6) to "**All priests**" here.

My charge: this is a somewhat technical word referring to the ceremonial duties required of the priests and Levites. It may be translated by a longer phrase like "the things that I [the LORD] have told them to do" or "the instructions I have given them." Mft translates "observe my order of service."

Lest they bear sin: the expression **bear sin** really means to "be guilty" or "bear responsibility." In some languages it will be more natural to communicate the meaning of this whole phrase by beginning a new sentence as in TEV.

Profane: see 18.21.

22.10   RSV   TEV

"An outsider shall not eat of a holy thing. A sojourner of the priest's or a hired servant shall not eat of a holy thing;

"Only a member of a priestly family may eat any of the sacred offerings; no one else may eat them—not even someone staying with a priest or hired by him.

An outsider: the word here may be understood as "stranger" (KJV). But its basic meaning is "other" or "different." Here the meaning is certainly "one outside a priest's family" (NIV). Several versions, including NJV, render it "lay person." NEB says "no unqualified person." And TEV gives the same meaning in a more positive way, with **"Only a member of a priestly family . . . ."**

A sojourner of the priest's or a hired servant: that is, someone visiting in the home of the priest or a person hired by the priest to work for him. Other provisions had to be made for such persons who were not actually a part of the priestly family. The first word may be rendered "guest" or "someone who lives for a time with the priest." The second term may be translated "someone who is paid to do a task (or, to work) for the priest."

A holy thing: that is, the offerings given to God by the people of Israel.

22.11   RSV   TEV

but if a priest buys a slave as his property for money, the slave may eat of it; and those that are born in his house may eat of his food.	But a priest's slaves, bought with his own money or born in his home, may eat the food the priest receives.

But: marking contrast between the prohibition applying to the visitor and the hired person on the one hand, and the slave of the priest on the other hand.

Slave: the difference between a slave and a hired man (verse 10) is that a slave was considered legal property of a person and had no rights of his own. He received no wages, but his needs were taken care of by his master. Slaves could be purchased, but there were also slaves who were born of slave parents and therefore belonged to the master. The hired man, on the other hand, entered into a contract with a person to work for him and be paid for his work.

Provided that the meaning is fully retained, some of the repetition in this verse may be eliminated if it is unnatural in the receptor language.

22.12   RSV   TEV

If a priest's daughter is married to an outsider she shall not eat of the offering of the holy things.	A priest's daughter who marries someone who is not a priest may not eat any of the sacred offerings.

Outsider: as in verse 10, this refers to an Israelite layman who is not a member of the priestly class, rather than to a non-Israelite foreigner. Marriage to someone who was not a priest automatically excluded the daughter of the priest from those who could eat food that had been offered in sacrifice to God, even though she had previously been able to eat it.

22.13   RSV   TEV

But if a priest's daughter is a widow or divorced, and has no child, and returns to her father's house, as in her youth, she may eat of her fath-	But a widowed or divorced daughter who has no children and who has returned to live in her father's house as a dependent may eat the food her

331

er's food; yet no outsider shall eat of   father receives as a priest. Only a
it.   member of a priestly family may eat
    any of it.

But: contrasting the case of a daughter who is still living with her layman husband, and the situation in which death or divorce has separated her from her husband before she had any children. If such a woman returned to her father's house and submitted herself to his authority once again, she would again be permitted to eat the food provided for the priestly family. She was in effect reintegrated into the priestly family. This may have applied also to women who had had children who had died. The point is that she is childless at the time of her divorce or of her becoming a widow, and thus she has no one to care for her.

As in her youth: or "as she was before she got married," indicating her renewed dependence on her father.

Outsider: see verse 10. Here again TEV has rendered the idea more positively.

22.14	RSV	TEV

And if a man eats of a holy thing unwittingly, he shall add the fifth of its value to it, and give the holy thing to the priest. | "If any person who is not a member of a priestly family eats any of the sacred offerings without intending to, he must repay the priest its full value plus an additional 20 percent.

A man: it is implied that the man in question is also an "outsider," or one who is not permitted to eat food that was designated for the priestly family. This information should be made explicit, if it is not clear in the receptor language.

Unwittingly: that is, without realizing what he is doing, or without intentionally doing so. In some languages this will require a separate phrase saying "eats . . . but does not know what he is eating."

Add the fifth of its value: fractions and percentages alike present a particularly difficult problem in some languages. The meaning here is that the offerings eaten had to be replaced, and a supplementary offering was also to be given to the priest. In modern terms the additional amount would be the equivalent of twenty percent of the value of the item eaten. Both RSV and TEV speak of **value**, as if the repayment were monetary. But in fact it is not certain whether the guilty person was required to pay with money or in kind. FRCL leaves open the possibility of repayment in kind by translating "the equivalent of what he has taken with a supplement of a fifth." This may have to be expressed less precisely in some languages by something like "well over the original cost of the thing" or something similar. See 5.16.

Give the holy thing to the priest: obviously the man cannot give back to the priest something that he has already eaten. The idea here is that he should repay the priest for the thing eaten or replace it. On the idea of restitution in general, see 5.16. Here one may say "**he must repay the priest its full value . . .**" (TEV) or "he must make return to the priest the same amount as he has used [or eaten . . .]."

22.15 RSV TEV

The priests shall not profane the holy things of the people of Israel, which they offer to the Lord,

The priests shall not profane the sacred offerings

Verses 15 and 16 constitute a summary and conclusion to the section on which people could eat food offered in sacrifice (verses 1-16). TEV simplifies and restructures the two verses. This may be a good idea in a number of other languages.

The priests: RSV does not reflect the source text, which literally has only the pronoun "they." However, this obviously refers to the priests.

22.16 RSV TEV

and so cause them to bear iniquity and guilt, by eating their holy things: for I am the Lord who sanctify them."

by letting any unauthorized person eat them; this would bring guilt and punishment on such a person. I am the Lord and I make the offerings holy."

The meaning of this verse is unclear, since the identification of the referents of certain pronouns is not certain. A literal rendering of the text reads as follows: "and they (meaning, the priests) cause them (meaning, the Israelites) to bear the iniquity of the guilt offering, when they (priests, or Israelites?) eat their (the priests, or the Israelites in general?) holy things; for I am Yahweh who sanctifies them (the priests, Israelites, or holy things?)." The parentheses indicate just how difficult the pronouns are in this verse.

Cause them to bear iniquity and guilt, by eating: as indicated in the literal rendering above, it is not absolutely clear who does the eating. Most English versions either state explicitly that it is the nonpriests, or at least they imply this by the way the rendering is structured. In addition to TEV, which states explicitly "**any unauthorized person**," NEB has "men," and the Revised English Bible avoids charges of sexism by changing to "anyone." It should be noted, however, that several non-English versions, including FRCL and Segond, indicate or at least imply that it is the priests who eat the holy offerings, and that the fault lies in the fact that they do so in an impure state. This possibility may be given in a footnote, if this is thought to be necessary.

Their holy things: once again the pronoun is vague. The **holy things** may be seen as belonging to the Israelites who bring them, or to the priests who receive them. It is probably better to depict them as belonging to the Israelites, if the receptor language requires something explicit here.

Who sanctify them: see 21.15,23; 22.9. The pronoun **them** may refer to the priests or to the offerings, or possibly even to the Israelites in general. Most English versions indicate either implicitly or explicitly that it is the offerings that are sanctified (see NJB as well as TEV), but certain non-English versions indicate that the priests are the object of the verb. FRCL, for example, says "It is I who consecrate the priests to my service." Whichever solution is adopted, the receptor language should have a noun rather than an ambiguous pronoun here, and it should probably be consistent with what is done in 21.23.

RSV	TEV
17 And the LORD said to Moses, 18 "Say to Aaron and his sons and all the people of Israel, When any one of the house of Israel or of the sojourners in Israel presents his offering, whether in payment of a vow or as a freewill offering which is offered to the LORD as a burnt offering,	17 The LORD commanded Moses 18 to give Aaron and his sons and all the people of Israel the following regulations. When any Israelite or any foreigner living in Israel presents a burnt offering, whether as fulfillment of a vow or as a freewill offering, the animal must not have any defects.

Verses 17-30 deal with rules for deciding which animals may be chosen for making sacrifices. It is possible to include a new section heading at this point. NJB has simply "Sacrificial animals," while FRCL inserts the heading "Rules for choosing animals to sacrifice." In the case of FRCL, this section also includes the concluding exhortation in verses 31-33.

Said to Moses: this is the same verb as in 4.1 and many other passages in Leviticus. But in view of the context, and possibly also for stylistic variation, TEV has chosen to render it "**commanded**" here. The direct quotation of RSV is made indirect in TEV. See 2.1.

House of Israel: in many languages it will be unwise to translate this literally, since it is equivalent to the earlier expression "people of Israel" (literally, "sons of Israel").

Sojourners in Israel: this refers to foreigners living among the Israelites. See 16.29. HOTTP proposes a variant reading of the text that may be literally translated "any sojourner who sojourns in Israel." But this variation is of little significance in a dynamic-equivalent translation.

In payment of a vow or as a freewill offering: see 7.16.

A burnt offering: see chapter 1.

Note that TEV anticipates the expression **without blemish** in the following verse and introduces the idea here. It is then repeated in verse 19.

RSV	TEV
to be accepted you shall offer a male without blemish, of the bulls or the sheep or the goats.	To be accepted, it must be a male without any defects.

To be accepted: this passive expression will have to be rendered in some languages as active. Some suggestions are "If God is to accept the animal . . . ," "If you want God to accept your sacrifice . . . ," or, reordering the whole verse, "Unless the animal is a male without defects, the LORD will not accept it."

Without blemish: see 1.3. The following verses provide a list of the various "blemishes" or physical defects which exclude an animal from being offered as a sacrifice.

Of the bulls or the sheep or the goats: literally "among the herd (see 1.2), among the sheep or among the goats." On the latter two types of animals, see 1.10. In the present context this whole expression has been left implicit in TEV. However, it will probably be better in most languages to make it explicit. This information is expressed in TEV in the following verse as "any animal."

22.20 RSV	TEV
You shall not offer anything that has a blemish, for it will not be acceptable for you.	If you offer any animal that has any defects, the LORD will not accept it.

Compare Deuteronomy 17.1 and Malachi 1.8.

A literal rendering of the structure of this verse may sound odd in many languages. It is a general prohibition, but the consequence of violating the prohibition is given. One way to handle the structure is to say "You must not . . . . But if you do . . . ." or, as in TEV, "**If you offer . . . , the LORD . . . .**"

Anything: the word used here is very general, but the context requires "**any animal**," as in TEV. Mft has "any victim."

It will not be acceptable: or, in those languages where the passive is not appropriate, "**the LORD will not accept it**" (if indirect discourse is being used) and "I will not accept it" (where it is a part of direct discourse). Another suggestion is "it will not earn you my [God's] favor."

For you: this carries the idea of "on your behalf" but may be better left implicit in some languages.

22.21 RSV	TEV
And when any one offers a sacrifice of peace offerings to the LORD, to fulfil a vow or as a freewill offering, from the herd or from the flock, to be accepted it must be perfect; there shall be no blemish in it.	When anyone presents a fellowship offering to the LORD, whether as fulfillment of a vow or as a freewill offering, the animal must be without any defects if it is to be accepted.

This verse says essentially the same thing about the fellowship offering (peace offering) as is said in the previous verses about the whole burnt offering.

A sacrifice of peace offerings: that is, "a fellowship offering." See chapter 3.

To fulfill a vow: this is not the same expression as translated "in payment of a vow" in verse 18. The exact meaning of the Hebrew word translated **to fulfil** is uncertain. Some take it to mean "explicit" (NJV) or "special" (NEB, NASB, AT). But the majority of versions understand it as containing the idea of fulfillment (RSV and TEV).

From the herd or from the flock: see 1.2.

Perfect: the Hebrew word used here really means "complete, whole, sound, unimpaired." In this context it is the opposite of "defective" and is thus virtually synonymous with the expression that follows, **there shall be no blemish in it**. TEV renders the two expressions together as **"must be without any defects."**

22.22	RSV	TEV
	Animals blind or disabled or mutilated or having a discharge or an itch or scabs, you shall not offer to the LORD or make of them an offering by fire upon the altar to the LORD.	Do not offer to the LORD any animal that is blind or crippled or mutilated, or that has a running sore or a skin eruption or scabs. Do not offer any such animals on the altar as a food offering.

This verse lists six defects that make an animal unacceptable as a sacrifice. However, it is not easy to identify the meaning of each of these with certainty. Nor can we be sure whether the terms are intended as nouns or adjectives, but this has little effect on the actual translation. The prohibition is shifted to the beginning of the verse in TEV, in keeping with the more natural English structure.

Blind: this is the same word that is used of a blind person excluded from the active priesthood in 21.18.

Disabled: the root word here means "to break." In this context the translation may be "broken," "fractured," **"crippled,"** or "lame."

Mutilated: this comes from the root word meaning "to cut" and seems to indicate an animal that was so radically changed by having been cut that it was permanently deformed.

Having a discharge: this word occurs only here in the Old Testament. It is not the same word translated elsewhere in Leviticus as "discharge." It is taken by some English versions as meaning "with warts" (NIV). The same solution is adopted by a number of French versions, including FRCL and TOB. NJV as well as KJV have "a wen," meaning a cyst. But more than likely the word used here refers to some kind of a running sore (TEV, NEB, and NAB). Compare also NJB "ulcerous."

An itch: this refers to some kind of long-term skin disease and not a simple itching sensation. NAB translates "mange."

Scabs: NAB has "ringworm" here. This is some other kind or category of skin problem. Probably the last two terms should be understood together as referring to any permanent or long-term skin condition.

22.23 RSV TEV

A bull or a lamb which has a part too long or too short you may present for a freewill offering; but for a votive offering it cannot be accepted.	As a freewill offering you may offer an animal that is stunted or not perfectly formed, but it is not acceptable in fulfillment of a vow.

Note that this verse has been restructured in TEV. This may be a good model for other languages to follow.

A bull or a lamb: the first word used here is not restricted in meaning to the male of the species, but may also include females. NIV has "cow," and both TEV and Mft have the still more general word "**animal**" to cover both terms used here.

A part too long or too short: see 21.18. The first term indicates a limb that is overgrown or out of proper proportion. The meaning of the second term is uncertain. Both the Greek and Latin versions have "which have their tail cut off," but this seems far too limited. It probably carries the meaning of retarded or arrested growth of any body part. These two terms seem to refer to conditions due to birth defects rather than resulting from accidents as alluded to in the previous verse.

It cannot be accepted: see verse 20.

22.24 RSV TEV

Any animal which has its testicles bruised or crushed or torn or cut, you shall not offer to the LORD or sacrifice within your land;	Do not offer to the LORD any animal whose testicles have been crushed, cut, bruised, or torn off. This is not permitted in your land.

Bruised or crushed or torn or cut: any problem with organs that have to do with producing life would make an animal unfit to be used as a sacrifice. This included both accidental damage to the testicles and intentional castration. In some languages it may be necessary to say simply "damaged in any way" or "damaged in an accident or removed intentionally [by castration]."

You shall not offer . . . or sacrifice within your land: literally, "you must not offer to Yahweh and in your land you must not do." The last clause may be understood in two different ways: (a) it may be a way of insisting on what has just been said, by repeating the same idea in different words (RSV and TEV); or (b) the intention of the writer may have been to add another idea, namely, that castration as such must not be practiced in Israel. Thus FRCL begins a new sentence: "Do not perform such mutilations when you are in your land." Compare also NIV, NJV, and NJB.

Once again the structure of this verse has been altered in TEV in order to make the meaning clearer. However, the TEV rendering at the end of this verse may be ambiguous. To avoid misunderstanding, it may be better to translate "**This**" of TEV more explicitly as "To sacrifice such an animal . . . ."

22.25   RSV   TEV

neither shall you offer as the bread
of your God any such animals gotten
from a foreigner. Since there is a
blemish in them, because of their
mutilation, they will not be accepted
for you."

Do not offer as a food offering
any animal obtained from a foreigner. Such animals are considered
defective and are not acceptable.

The prohibition of sacrificing animals that have been castrated presupposes
their existence. There are two possible causes for the existence of such animals:
castration practiced by the Israelites (verse 24b), or castration practiced by foreigners
(it is the Canaanites that are in mind in verse 25).

The bread of your God: this clearly refers to any food offering. See 21.6,8.

Gotten from a foreigner: literally, "from the hand of a son of a foreigner."
The normal understanding of this expression is "any animal you have bought from
a foreigner [non-Israelite]." The word for **foreigner** here is different from the one
discussed in 10.1 and 16.29. The accent in this context is on the difference between
the Israelites and others, not on what they have in common in spite of their
differences (16.29). In this verse the word seems to refer specifically to the
Canaanites living in the land where the Israelites were going. The people of God
were to refrain from imitating the former inhabitants of the land and avoid being
influenced by them.

There is a blemish in them, because of their mutilation: this refers to the
Canaanite practice of castrating animals. It may be necessary to translate "they are
unfit for sacrificing because their owners have castrated them."

They will not be accepted: see verse 20. Compare 7.18; 19.7.

22.26-27   RSV   TEV

26 And the LORD said to Moses,
27 "When a bull or sheep or goat is
born, it shall remain seven days with
its mother; and from the eighth day
on it shall be acceptable as an offering by fire to the LORD.

26-27 When a calf or a lamb or
a kid is born, it must not be taken
from its mother for seven days, but
after that it is acceptable as a food
offering.

And the LORD said to Moses: in some languages it will be more natural to
say "And the LORD went on to say (or, also said)" or "The LORD continued . . . ,"
since this is actually a continuation of his words. In other languages it may be
unnecessary or undesirable to repeat this phrase at all. In TEV it is omitted as
redundant, since indirect discourse is being used.

A bull or sheep or goat: since these are newborn animals, words for newborns
should be used if they exist in the receptor language. Compare TEV.

It shall remain: the future tense has an imperative meaning, "it must remain."
Or stated negatively, "it must not be taken away."

From the eighth day on: in some languages it may be better to say "beginning on the eighth day" or "any time after the end of the seventh day . . . ."

It shall be acceptable: or "God will accept it." See verses 20 and 25.

An offering by fire: see 21.21 as well as 1.9.

22.28	RSV	TEV
	And whether the mother is a cow or a ewe, you shall not kill both her and her young in one day.	Do not sacrifice a cow and its calf or a sheep and its lamb or a goat and its kid on the same day.

Kill: or "slaughter" (see 17.3), but in this context the verb "**sacrifice**" may be better.

Ewe: the word used here may actually refer to a sheep or a goat. Hence the more accurate translation of TEV.

Note the restructuring of TEV. Terms for "mother cow" and "mother sheep" as well as "baby cow" and "baby sheep" should be used in this verse if they exist as separate terms in the receptor language.

22.29	RSV	TEV
	And when you sacrifice a sacrifice of thanksgiving to the LORD, you shall sacrifice it so that you may be accepted.	When you offer a sacrifice of thanksgiving to the LORD, follow the rules so that you will be accepted;

Sacrifice a sacrifice of thanksgiving: compare 7.12.

You shall sacrifice it: TEV has omitted the repetitious material and introduced what is implied in this phrase. One may also say "offer the sacrifice according to the rules . . . ."

So that you may be accepted: if it is necessary to avoid the passive construction, this may be translated "so that God will accept you" or, framed negatively, "in order that God will not reject you."

22.30	RSV	TEV
	It shall be eaten on the same day, you shall leave none of it until morning: I am the LORD.	eat it the same day and leave none of it until the next morning.

See 7.15.

It shall be eaten: the meaning is not future; it is rather to be understood as a requirement. If the passive is unacceptable, this may be translated "You must eat it."

Same day: that is, "the same day on which it was sacrificed."

I am the LORD: omitted in TEV, but partially translated in the following verse.
See 18.2.

22.31   RSV   TEV

"So you shall keep my com-   The LORD said, "Obey my commandments and do them: I am the   mands; I am the LORD.
LORD.

This is the beginning of the concluding exhortation to this chapter. This is
indicated in RSV by **So . . .** , which seems to be an attempt to translate contextually
the common Hebrew conjunction.

Keep . . . and do: the two verbs may be translated together in some languages,
as in TEV "**Obey**." Compare 18.4 and 19.37.

Commandments: in some languages it may be better to translate this by a
verbal expression: "what I command" or "what I have told you to do."

I am the LORD: see 18.2.

22.32   RSV   TEV

And you shall not profane my holy   Do not bring disgrace on my holy
name, but I will be hallowed among   name; all the people of Israel must
the people of Israel; I am the LORD   acknowledge me to be holy. I am the
who sanctify you,   LORD and I make you holy;

Profane my holy name: see 18.21.

I will be hallowed: again, the future tense indicates a requirement. This
expression can be translated "I must be acknowledged as holy." Where passives are
a problem, one may say "I want people to accept that I am holy" or "People must
acknowledge that I am holy." On the word **holy**, see 2.3.

Who sanctify you: see 20.8 and 21.8.

22.33   RSV   TEV

who brought you out of the land of   and I brought you out of Egypt to
Egypt to be your God: I am the   become your God. I am the LORD."
LORD."

Who brought you out of the land of Egypt: this relative clause, like the last
part of the previous verse, is made into an independent sentence in TEV. Compare
19.36.

To be your God: or "so that I may be your God," or "in order that I may
become your God." See 11.45.

I am the LORD: see 18.2.

Chapter 23

Section Heading: **"The Religious Festivals."**

This chapter may also be entitled "Celebrations in the life of the Israelites" or simply "Jewish holy days" (compare NAB). It deals with a number of religious festivals that were a part of the life of the people of Israel. These include the observance of the Sabbath (3-4), the Passover and the Festival of Unleavened Bread (5-14), the Harvest Festival (15-22), the New Year Festival (23-25), the Day of Atonement (26-32) and the Festival of Shelters (33-43). In those translations using two levels of section headings, each of these observances will constitute a subsection under the major heading. For a more detailed treatment of the festivals in Ancient Israel, see Roland de Vaux, *Ancient Israel*, Volume 2, pages 484-509. And on the problems of translating the names of these celebrations, see Daniel Arichea, "Translating Biblical Festivals," *The Bible Translator*, October 1981 (Vol. 32, No. 4), pages 413-423.

Note that there are parallel passages regarding these festivals in Numbers 28 and 29 that are generally more complete than the Leviticus record.

23.1-2

RSV	TEV
1 The LORD said to Moses, 2 "Say to the people of Israel, The appointed feasts of the LORD which you shall proclaim as holy convocations, my appointed feasts, are these.	1 The LORD gave Moses 2 the following regulations for the religious festivals, when the people of Israel are to gather for worship.

Said to Moses: see 4.1.

Say . . . : see 1.2.

Appointed feasts: the Hebrew word thus translated is used six times in this chapter. It is a technical term referring to special religious occasions in the Jewish tradition. In some languages there may be difficulty expressing the idea of "**religious.**" It may be necessary to translate "feasts for meeting God," or "celebrations in honor of God," or something similar. Some renderings in modern English versions are "fixed times" (NJV), "fixed festivals" (Mft), "appointed feasts" (NIV), and "solemn festivals" (NJB).

These sacred occasions are further defined by the words **as holy convocations** (or special gatherings). This expression is also used in eight other places in this chapter. The noun **convocations** (or gatherings, or assemblies) may easily be rendered by a verbal expression meaning "to come together" or "to assemble." And

341

the adjective **holy** has been translated in TEV by **"for worship."** The whole expression is taken as a temporal clause in TEV, **"when the people of Israel are to gather for worship,"** but most versions translate the idea contained in NJV, **"as sacred occasions."** In some languages one may have to express the idea of **"worship"** as "praying and learning about God."

The text of this verse contains both **the appointed feasts of the LORD** and **my appointed feasts**. The meaning of the two is, of course, identical, and the rendering will be determined by the choice of direct or indirect discourse. Note that TEV shortens and combines these two into one and makes the entire passage from verse 1 through 4 into an indirect quotation. The first person possessive pronoun **my** is to be retained only if this passage is translated as a direct quotation.

23.3 RSV	TEV
Six days shall work be done; but on the seventh day is a sabbath of solemn rest, a holy convocation; you shall do no work; it is a sabbath to the LORD in all your dwellings.	You have six days in which to do your work, but remember that the seventh day, the Sabbath, is a day of rest. On that day do not work, but gather for worship. The Sabbath belongs to the LORD, no matter where you live.

Compare Exodus 20.8-10.

Shall work be done: the meaning of this passive expression is well translated by "There are six days when you may work . . ." (NIV) or "You will work for six days" (NJB). This, in fact, corresponds to the rendering of the Greek Septuagint.

It is a sabbath of solemn rest: the words translated **sabbath** and **rest** have the same root in Hebrew, and the word for **seventh** is also very similar (see 16.31). The whole phrase seems to emphasize that the day must be set aside for religious observance, and that ordinary daily occupations were to be avoided. The latter expression, **a sabbath to the LORD**, serves to emphasize the sacred character of the day of rest. It belongs to the LORD.

Holy convocation: note that this is again rendered as the verbal expression "gather for worship" in TEV. Compare verse 2.

In all your dwellings: this phrase has been taken by some commentators as referring to settlements of Jews living outside the Promised Land, but it is more likely that it refers to the keeping of the sabbath in a very broad and general sense. Most modern versions translate it in this general sense: "wherever you live" (NEB, NIV, and NJB) or **"no matter where you live"** (TEV).

23.4 RSV	TEV
"These are the appointed feasts of the LORD, the holy convocations, which you shall proclaim at the time appointed for them.	Proclaim the following festivals at the appointed times.

This verse repeats the same information given in verse 2. Since one solemn occasion (the Sabbath) has already been dealt with in verse 3, it may be more natural in some languages to begin this verse with something like "these are the other festivals that you must proclaim . . ." (compare FRCL).

At the time appointed: others have understood this to mean "in their appointed order" (NEB). But the most widely accepted interpretation is "at their proper time" (NAB) or "each at its appointed time" (NJV).

TEV Section Heading: **"Passover and Unleavened Bread."**
On the translation of these two terms, see the discussion in the text below. Since these two festivals were celebrated together, it is possible to simplify the section heading by mentioning only the Passover, as in NAB.
Compare Numbers 28.16-25.

23.5 RSV	TEV
In the first month, on the fourteenth day of the month in the evening,*ʲ* is the LORD's passover.	The Passover, celebrated to honor the LORD, begins at sunset on the fourteenth day of the first month.

ʲ Heb *between the two evenings*

Note that the order of ideas in this verse has been completely changed in TEV. Such restructuring may be necessary in other languages.

The first month: this corresponds to the beginning of spring, and the month begins anywhere from the last half of March to the first half of April. (Hebrew months were determined by the moon, and so their calendar months constantly change with respect to our modern calendar.) Care must be taken in some languages to avoid giving the impression that this was the month of January. On the numbered months in the Old Testament, see 16.29. The fourteenth of this Jewish month occurred around the end of March or some time in April. (See also *The Bible Translator,* October 1978, Volume 29, Number 4, pages 409-413.) Many translators find it helpful to include a table of Old Testament calendar systems as a help for readers. Two good models for this are found in the NIV Study Bible at Exodus 12 and the NJB supplement on page 2076.

In the evening: literally, "between the two evenings," as indicated in the RSV footnote. Compare Exodus 16.12, where the same expression is translated by RSV as "at twilight." Some have taken this expression to mean "between dusk and dark" (NEB). However, in this context "beginning at twilight," "starting at sunset," or "towards evening" (Mft) is probably more appropriate.

Passover: this was the celebration where the Jews remembered their departure from Egypt (see Exo 12.1-14). This is the only place it is used in Leviticus. The term must be treated as a proper name, and it will be necessary to give a full explanation in the Glossary at the end of the translation. If the name of this celebration is already well known and understood in the receptor language culture, it may be used in the translation. Otherwise there are two possible approaches: (1) one may transliterate the Hebrew word *pesach* and depend on the glossary explanation and the teaching of Scripture to give the word meaning; or (2) an attempt may be made to translate the meaning. Although the precise meaning of the Hebrew word is uncertain, it probably comes from the root meaning "pass by," or "skip," or "spare." Translators may therefore attempt to capture at least a part of the meaning of the word by translating the idea of "deliverance" or "passing over." The latter may produce an expression that is too long and awkward for use in translation, but if a shortened form is found, it is preferable to a transliteration. In certain European languages there may be some confusion between the words for Easter and Passover. So borrowing the term for Passover from French or Spanish may result in a serious misunderstanding. If at all possible, transliteration should be avoided. (See TBT Volume 31, October 1980, pages 445-446.)

23.6   RSV   TEV

And on the fifteenth day of the same month is the feast of unleavened bread to the LORD; seven days you shall eat unleavened bread.	**On the fifteenth day the Festival of Unleavened Bread begins, and for seven days you must not eat any bread made with yeast.**

Since this celebration lasted for seven days, it is impossible in most languages to say that the fifteenth day is the feast of unleavened bread. **Is the feast** is therefore understood in the sense of "begins the feast" in Mft and Wenham as well as TEV. In some languages one may prefer to say "is the beginning of . . . ."

The feast of unleavened bread: on the translation of the idea of unleavened bread, see 2.4. This festival reflects an agricultural background and was celebrated at the beginning of the grain harvest. During this seven-day period the people ate unleavened bread and made an offering of the first fruits of their harvest. Compare also Exodus 12.15-20.

To the LORD: this phrase is left implicit in TEV. As in verse 3, it indicates the sacred character of the celebration.

You shall eat unleavened bread: this requirement excludes the eating of any other kind of bread. In some languages it will be better to state this negatively, as in TEV, or to say "the only bread you eat must be made without yeast."

23.7   RSV   TEV

On the first day you shall have a holy convocation; you shall do no laborious work.	**On the first of these days you shall gather for worship and do none of your daily work.**

The first day: that is, on the first day of the week of celebration, not the first day of the month or year. It is probably a good idea to make this explicit in translation; for example, **"On the first of these days"** (TEV).

A holy convocation: see verse 3.

Laborious work: there is an additional word qualifying **work** here that is not found in verse 3 above but does occur later in this chapter in verses 8, 21, 25, 35, and 36. Some see it as referring to especially difficult work: "hard work" (AT); "heavy work" (NJB); "field work" (Mft). On the other hand, some scholars take it to mean ordinary occupations: "regular work" (NIV); **"daily work"** (NEB and TEV); "work at your occupations" (NJV). Probably the latter is to be preferred. In this case some languages will have to say something like "the work that you usually do every day."

23.8	RSV	TEV
	But you shall present an offering by fire to the LORD seven days; on the seventh day is a holy convocation; you shall do no laborious work."	Offer your food offerings to the LORD for seven days. On the seventh day you shall again gather for worship, but you shall do none of your daily work.

But: the Hebrew word rendered thus is the common transition word that is often left untranslated. The strong conjunction marking contrast seems out of place in this context, so it is probably better to omit it here.

An offering by fire: see 1.9.

Holy convocation: see verse 3.

Laborious work: see verse 7.

23.9-10	RSV	TEV
	9 And the LORD said to Moses, 10 "Say to the people of Israel, When you come into the land which I give you and reap its harvest, you shall bring the sheaf of the first fruits of your harvest to the priest;	9-10 When you come into the land that the LORD is giving you and you harvest your grain, take the first sheaf to the priest.

And the LORD said to Moses, "Say to the people of Israel . . . : this is identical with verse 1 and 2a at the beginning of this chapter. Naturalness in the receptor language will determine whether or not these words need to be repeated here. The TEV translators decided it would be more natural in English to omit them. This version has also continued the indirect discourse rather than using direct discourse as in RSV.

Which I give you: when indirect discourse is used it will be necessary to change **I** to "the LORD." On the tense of the verb, see 14.34.

The sheaf of the first fruits of your harvest: compare Exodus 23.19; 34.26. In ancient cultures the first crops harvested and the firstborn animal of a flock were offered to the deity as a sign of thanksgiving. But it is unnecessary to create a special technical term like **first fruits**. The **"first sheaf"** is quite adequate. The word **sheaf** may present a problem in some cultures where the practice of tying grain into bundles is unknown. Some languages may have to say something like "the first bunch of grain you tie together." And in those cases where it is necessary to specify what kind of grain is involved, one may say "the first bundle of barley that you assemble."

23.11	RSV	TEV

23.11

RSV	TEV
and he shall wave the sheaf before the LORD, that you may find acceptance; on the morrow after the sabbath the priest shall wave it.	He shall present it as a special offering to the LORD, so that you may be accepted. The priest shall present it the day after the Sabbath.

Wave: the Hebrew verb seems to imply some kind of solemn gesture of presentation, but experts are not agreed on its exact nature. See 7.30.

Before the LORD: see 21.6.

That you may find acceptance: or "so that he [the LORD] will accept you." See 1.3.

On the morrow after the sabbath: this phrase presents serious exegetical problems, because scholars are not certain which **sabbath** is intended. It may be understood as the first day of the Festival of Unleavened Bread or as the seventh day. However, it is probably best to use the ordinary word for **sabbath** when translating this verse.

23.12

RSV	TEV
And on the day when you wave the sheaf, you shall offer a male lamb a year old without blemish as a burnt offering to the LORD.	On the day you present the offering of grain, also sacrifice as a burnt offering a one-year-old male lamb that has no defects.

You: the pronoun here contrasts with **he** (the priest) in the previous verse. For some commentators this is thought to mark a later revision of the text. It is plural in form and probably refers to the worshiping community as the priest acts on their behalf.

On the day when you wave the sheaf: or simply "on the same day," referring back to the day after the Sabbath mentioned in verse 11.

Without blemish: see 22.17-25.

Burnt offering: see chapter 1.

23.13

RSV	TEV
And the cereal offering with it shall be two tenths of an ephah of fine flour mixed with oil, to be offered by fire to the LORD, a pleasing odor; and the drink offering with it shall be of wine, a fourth of a hin.	With it you shall present four pounds [two kilograms] of flour mixed with olive oil as a food offering. The odor of this offering is pleasing to the LORD. You shall also present with it an offering of one quart [liter] of wine.

Two tenths of an ephah: probably about "two kilograms" (British TEV) or "four pounds" (American TEV). Compare 5.11.

Fine flour mixed with oil: see 2.1.

Offered by fire . . . a pleasing odor: see 1.9.

The drink offering: this term is also found in verses 18 and 37 of this chapter. A "libation" (NJV) is a liquid offering, usually wine, given to a deity. It is quite common in Middle Eastern cultures. In the case of the Jews, it was poured out at the base of the altar of sacrifice or on the ground. Compare Numbers 15.5 as well as Genesis 35.14.

A fourth of a hin: "**one quart**" or slightly more (American TEV), or about "one liter" (British TEV). See 19.36.

23.14 RSV	TEV
And you shall eat neither bread nor grain parched or fresh until this same day, until you have brought the offering of your God: it is a statute for ever throughout your generations in all your dwellings.	Do not eat any of the new grain, whether raw, roasted, or baked into bread, until you have brought this offering to God. This regulation is to be observed by all your descendants for all time to come.

Neither bread nor grain parched or fresh: TEV has reorganized the elements in this part of the verse, but all the meaning is present and it is quite natural.

The offering: this refers to the burnt offering (verse 12), which is also accompanied by a grain offering and a drink offering.

A statute for ever throughout your generations: see 3.17 and 10.9.

In all your dwellings: this is left implicit in the TEV rendering of this verse. See verse 3, where it is fully translated.

TEV Section Heading: "**The Harvest Festival.**"

Compare Numbers 28.26-31.

The text of Leviticus does not give the name of this festival, which actually has three different names (two in the Old Testament and one in the New Testament):

1. The feast of harvest (RSV) or The Harvest Festival (TEV): Exodus 23.16.

2. The feast of weeks (referring to the seven weeks mentioned in verse 15): Exodus 34.22; Numbers 28.26; and Deuteronomy 16.9-10. In order to avoid confusion, TEV also translates "Harvest Festival" in these passages.

3. Pentecost (that is, "the fiftieth day" in Greek; see verse 16). This was used because the festival in question was celebrated fifty days after the Feast of Unleavened Bread. See Acts 2.1; 20.16; 1 Corinthians 16.8.

It is probably not wise to retain the name "Feast of Weeks" in the receptor language translation. This places the emphasis on the period of time between the two festivals and not on the actual celebration. TEV uses "Harvest Festival" throughout the Old Testament, and GECL has "the Feast of Pentecost," which shows more clearly the ties with the New Testament. Whichever solution is followed, it is essential that this festival be fully explained in a glossary entry.

347

The Harvest festival, coming seven weeks or about fifty days after the beginning of the barley harvest (at the time of the Feast of Unleavened Bread), coincided with the final harvesting of the wheat crop.

23.15   RSV   TEV

"And you shall count from the morrow after the sabbath, from the day that you brought the sheaf of the wave offering; seven full weeks shall they be,	Count seven full weeks from the day after the Sabbath on which you bring your sheaf of grain to present to the LORD.

You shall count . . . : as is often the case, the future tense has an imperative meaning.

Sabbath: see verse 3 above as well as 16.31.

The sheaf: that is, the first fruits of the barley harvest mentioned in verse 10.

Wave offering: see 7.30.

23.16   RSV   TEV

counting fifty days to the morrow after the seventh sabbath; then you shall present a cereal offering of new grain to the LORD.	On the fiftieth day, the day after the seventh Sabbath, present to the LORD another new offering of grain.

Fifty days: according to the Hebrew way of calculating, the beginning and ending days of any given period are counted. Even if the receptor-language system is different, it is not recommended that this expression be modified to "forty-nine days" for mathematical reasons. This would probably only serve to confuse the issue.

A cereal offering of new grain: literally, "a new grain offering." The NEB rendering, "a grain offering from the new crop," seems to communicate the meaning more clearly than either RSV or TEV. TEV adds the word "**another**," because this offering of wheat mentioned here and in the following verse is distinct from the one of barley mentioned in the previous verses. Probably it is best to combine the ideas of TEV and NEB to say "another grain offering from the new crop [of wheat]."

23.17   RSV   TEV

You shall bring from your dwellings two loaves of bread to be waved, made of two tenths of an ephah; they shall be of fine flour, they shall be baked with leaven, as first fruits to the LORD.	Each family is to bring two loaves of bread and present them to the LORD as a special gift. Each loaf shall be made of four pounds [two kilograms] of flour baked with yeast and shall be presented to the LORD as an offering of the first grain to be harvested.

348

You shall bring from your dwellings: compare verse 14 and 3.17. The faithful were required to assemble in the sanctuary area from all over the land. So, each family unit had to bring the required offerings from their home. TEV seeks to highlight the nature of this offering as originating with "**each family.**" This is implied in the phrase **from your dwellings**, but it is probably better in most languages to make it more explicit.

To be waved: or "so that the priest may present them . . . ." See 7.30.

Two tenths of an ephah: see verse 13 and 5.11.

Fine flour: see 2.1.

Leaven: or "**yeast.**" See 2.11.

First fruits: see 2.12.

23.18   RSV   TEV

And you shall present with the bread seven lambs a year old without blemish, and one young bull, and two rams; they shall be a burnt offering to the LORD, with their cereal offering and their drink offerings, an offering by fire, a pleasing odor to the LORD.	And with the bread the community is to present seven one-year-old lambs, one bull, and two rams, none of which may have any defects. They shall be offered as a burnt offering to the LORD, along with a grain offering and a wine offering. The odor of this offering is pleasing to the LORD.

You: the pronoun here as well as in the following verse is plural in form and meaning, clearly referring to the Israelite "**community**" as a whole. It may be better to make this explicit in many languages.

With the bread: or perhaps better "in addition to the offering of bread."

Young bull: or simply "**bull.**" See 4.3.

Without blemish: in RSV this qualification seems to go only with the lambs, but actually it refers to all of the animals. This is why TEV has "**none of which may have any defects.**" See 1.3.

Burnt offering See chapter 1.

Cereal offering: see chapter 2.

Drink offering: see verse 13.

Offering by fire: see 1.9.

23.19   RSV   TEV

And you shall offer one male goat for a sin offering, and two male lambs a year old as a sacrifice of peace offerings.	Also offer one male goat as a sin offering and two one-year-old male lambs as a fellowship offering.

Sin offering: see chapter 4.

Peace offerings: or "**fellowship offering.**" See chapter 3.

23.20　　　　RSV　　　　　　　　　　　　　　TEV

And the priest shall wave them with the bread of the first fruits as a wave offering before the LORD, with the two lambs; they shall be holy to the LORD for the priest.	The priest shall present the bread with the two lambs as a special gift to the LORD for the priests. These offerings are holy.

Them: the pronoun here seems to refer back to the previous verse and also anticipates the mention of the two lambs later in this verse. The way in which the whole verse is restructured and simplified in TEV may serve as a helpful model in other languages.

First fruits: see 2.12.

Wave: or "**present . . . as a special gift.**" See 7.30.

Holy to the LORD for the priest: the structure of the last part of this verse in TEV has been altered, and the repetition of **to the LORD** has been omitted in order to make it sound more natural in English.

23.21　　　　RSV　　　　　　　　　　　　　　TEV

And you shall make proclamation on the same day; you shall hold a holy convocation; you shall do no laborious work: it is a statute for ever in all your dwellings throughout your generations.	On that day do none of your daily work, but gather for worship. Your descendants are to observe this regulation for all time to come, no matter where they live.

Make proclamation: the RSV rendering may be misleading. The idea here is better communicated by NJV "hold a celebration," or NJB "hold an assembly." It is practically synonymous with the expression **hold a holy convocation**, which follows.

Holy convocation: this is an assembly of people specifically for worship (see verse 3). It further defines the "celebration" mentioned in the previous phrase. Perhaps the two together may be translated something like "an announcement must be made and people must gather for worship."

Laborious work: see verses 7 and 8.

A statute for ever: see verse 14. Also 3.17 and 10.9.

In all your dwellings throughout your generations: compare verse 14, where the order of these two phrases is reversed. There seems to be no significance in the reversal of the order. Whichever is natural in the receptor language should be used here.

23.22　　　　RSV　　　　　　　　　　　　　　TEV

"And when you reap the harvest of your land, you shall not reap your field to its very border, nor shall you gather the gleanings after your	When you harvest your fields, do not cut the grain at the edges of the fields, and do not go back to cut the heads of grain that were left;

harvest; you shall leave them for the poor and for the stranger: I am the LORD your God."

leave them for poor people and foreigners. The LORD is your God.

This verse is almost identical with 19.9,10b.

TEV Section Heading: **"The New Year Festival."**

The two verses in this section deal with the festival held on the first day of the seventh month (of the year beginning in the springtime). This would mean that it was to take place in what we would call the fall of the year. Compare Numbers 29.1-6. In former times the people of Israel used a different calendar system, in which the year started in autumn (September or October), as is once again the case for Jewish people today. It was under the influence of other groups that during a certain period the people of Israel made the new year to begin in the spring. But this did not completely eliminate the habit of having a festival at the beginning of the autumn of the year. It was still a kind of "New Year's Festival." It is probably better not to give it such a name in the receptor-language translation, since this may result in confusion. NJB has the rather dull title "The First Day of the Seventh Month," while NIV speaks of the "Feast of Trumpets." The Cambridge Bible Commentary edition of NEB has "The Autumn Celebrations" as the title for the remainder of the chapter. Given the prominence of the trumpets in this festival, the NIV title may be best.

23.23-24 RSV	TEV
23 And the LORD said to Moses, 24 "Say to the people of Israel, In the seventh month, on the first day of the month, you shall observe a day of solemn rest, a memorial proclaimed with blast of trumpets, a holy convocation.	23-24 On the first day of the seventh month observe a special day of rest, and come together for worship when the trumpets sound.

And the LORD said to Moses, "Say to the people of Israel . . . : as in verses 9-10a this repetition from verses 1-2a may be unnecessary and awkward in the receptor language.

The seventh month: see 16.29.

A memorial proclaimed with blast of trumpets: literally, "a remembrance of acclamation," representing only two Hebrew words. These two words indicate the two special features of this festival: (1) it was to be a **memorial** or a day of "remembrance." Probably the original meaning of this word had to do with reminding God of the needs of his people, or to request that he remember their needs. (2) It was also a day of "acclamation." The same word is translated "a great shout" in Joshua 6.5. This ritual shout or perhaps the blowing of trumpets was to welcome in the new year. While the use of a musical instrument in making the loud noise is not essential to the meaning of the word, many modern translations see this as a reference to **trumpets** (NIV, NAB, AT, JB, Mft, and NASB, as well as RSV and

TEV). It is worthy of note, however, that NJB omits any reference to the use of trumpets. On the idea of a memorial acclamation, compare Numbers 10.1-10.

Holy convocation: see verse 3.

23.25   RSV   TEV

You shall do no laborious work; and   Present a food offering to the LORD
you shall present an offering by fire   and do none of your daily work.
to the LORD."

Laborious work: see verse 7.
An offering by fire: or "**a food offering.**" See 1.9.

TEV Section Heading: "**The Day of Atonement.**"

This important celebration is also described in chapter 16 as well as in Numbers 29.7-11. It may also bear the title "The great day of the forgiveness of sins" or something similar.

23.26-27   RSV   TEV

26 And the LORD said to Moses,   26-27 The tenth day of the sev-
27 "On the tenth day of this seventh   enth month is the day when the an-
month is the day of atonement; it   nual ritual is to be performed to take
shall be for you a time of holy convo-   away the sins of the people. On that
cation, and you shall afflict your-   day do not eat anything at all; come
selves and present an offering by   together for worship, and present a
fire to the LORD.   food offering to the LORD.

And the LORD said to Moses: as in verses 9-10a and 23-24a, this repetition may not be necessary in the receptor language.

The Hebrew text of verse 27 is introduced by an adverb which is often used to indicate contrast with what precedes ("but" or "however"). This is probably intended to contrast the festive nature of the acclamations of the first day of the seventh month with the more solemn and reserved celebration of the tenth day. Many translations omit the adverb altogether, but others have attempted to translate it: "Further, . . ." (NEB); "Mark, . . ." (NJV); "But . . ." (NJB).

Day of atonement: see chapter 16. Note that the focus is changed by the TEV rendering using the word "**ritual.**" This is not a good model, since the emphasis is on the fact of God's atonement and not on the performance of a rite.

A holy convocation: see verse 21.

Afflict yourselves: literally, "afflict your souls," but the meaning is "fast" ("refuse to eat") or "practice self-denial." See 16.29. *The Living Bible* translates this expression by "saddened by their sin" in this verse, "spend the day in repentance and sorrow" in verse 29, and "humble your souls and be filled with remorse." Each of these is somewhat off the mark of self-denial or fasting and should be avoided in translation.

An offering by fire: see verses 18 and 25 as well as 1.9.

23.28   RSV   TEV

And you shall do no work on this | Do no work on that day, because it
same day; for it is a day of atone- | is the day for performing the ritual to
ment, to make atonement for you | take away sin.
before the LORD your God.

Do no work: see verse 3. Compare also verse 7.

On this same day: in some languages it may be more natural to leave this information implicit.

It is a day of atonement: this may be considered as unnecessary repetition in some languages, since it has already been stated in the previous verse.

Before the LORD your God: these words have also been left implicit in TEV. But translators should determine for their own language whether it is more natural to omit them here.

23.29   RSV   TEV

For whoever is not afflicted on this | Anyone who eats anything on that
same day shall be cut off from his | day will no longer be considered one
people. | of God's people.

Whoever is not afflicted: that is, any person who does not fast or practice self-denial. TEV states the same thing without the use of the negative form: "**Anyone who eats anything . . . .**" See verse 27 above.

On this same day: as in the previous verse, it may be better in some languages to leave this information implicit.

Cut off from his people: the common expression for excommunication from the people of Israel. See 7.20.

23.30   RSV   TEV

And whoever does any work on this | And if anyone does any work on that
same day, that person I will destroy | day, the LORD himself will put him to
from among his people. | death.

I will destroy: if this is not a part of direct discourse, the pronoun I should be changed to the noun "**the LORD.**" The verb in this case means "to put to death," "eliminate," or more bluntly, "to kill." In some languages this may be too blunt, so a less shocking expression may be sought to express the same idea. But the meaning is clearly that the Lord will cause to die any person who dares to disobey the commandment to abstain from work during the Day of Atonement.

23.31	RSV	TEV

You shall do no work: it is a statute for ever throughout your generations in all your dwellings.

This regulation applies to all your descendants, no matter where they live.

You shall do no work: instead of repeating word-for-word the prohibition found in verse 28 and alluded to in verse 30, good style may require that it be phrased in a different way here. One may consider a general statement like "All work is forbidden" or "No work is allowed." TEV chooses to leave it implicit in this case.

It: the pronoun is translated **"This regulation"** in TEV and refers to the prohibition of work on the Sabbath, which is stated in verse 28 and repeated again at the beginning of this verse.

A statute for ever . . . : see 3.17 and 10.9.

23.32	RSV	TEV

It shall be to you a sabbath of solemn rest, and you shall afflict yourselves; on the ninth day of the month beginning at evening, from evening to evening shall you keep your sabbath."

From sunset on the ninth day of the month to sunset on the tenth observe this day as a special day of rest, during which nothing may be eaten.

It shall be to you a sabbath of solemn rest: this special day is likened to the regularly observed Sabbath. TEV attempts to convey the meaning with "**a special day of rest**," but others have proposed to make the comparison more explicit, saying "this shall be a rest day like the Sabbath." The expression **sabbath of solemn rest** is literally "sabbath of sabbathing," with the two words having the same root. Some versions see this as a kind of superlative indicating "complete rest" (NJV, NAB, AT, NJB, and Mft).

Afflict yourselves: see verse 27 and 16.29.

From evening to evening: in the Old Testament the day begins at sunset (compare Gen 1.5). Notice that TEV has radically restructured this verse and reduced some of the repetition to make it sound more natural in English.

TEV Section Heading: **"The Festival Of Shelters."**

Compare the parallel passage in Numbers 29.12-40.

The Hebrew name for this festival in Leviticus and, for example, in Deuteronomy 16.13 and 16 refers to temporary shelters made of leafy branches woven together (see Neh 8.15). The ancient Greek version translated it "tents," and the Latin has "tabernacles" (followed by KJV, JB, NEB, and NIV). But "booths" is preferred by NJV, NAB, NASB, AT, and Mft. This rendering or something similar is recommended (like "huts" or "shelters" in TEV and NJB).

23.33-34

RSV	TEV
33 And the LORD said to Moses, 34 "Say to the people of Israel, On the fifteenth day of this seventh month and for seven days is the feast of booths^k to the LORD.	33-34 The Festival of Shelters begins on the fifteenth day of the seventh month and continues for seven days.

^{k} Or *tabernacles*

And the LORD said to Moses, "Say to the people of Israel . . . : this may be left implicit. See comments on 9-10a and 23-24a.

The feast of booths: see the comments under the section heading with regard to the naming of this festival.

On the fifteenth day of this seventh month: it is probably better to say "Beginning on . . . ," since the festival actually lasts for seven days. With regard to the numbered month, see verse 5.

To the LORD: if direct discourse is being used, this should be changed to "in my honor" or something similar. This phrase is left implicit in TEV.

23.35

RSV	TEV
On the first day shall be a holy convocation; you shall do no laborious work.	On the first of these days come together for worship and do none of your daily work.

On the first day: the text implies the first of the seven days mentioned in the previous verse. For this reason TEV adds ". . . of these days."

Holy convocation: see verse 3.

Laborious work: see verse 7.

23.36

RSV	TEV
Seven days you shall present offerings by fire to the LORD; on the eighth day you shall hold a holy convocation and present an offering by fire to the LORD; it is a solemn assembly; you shall do no laborious work.	Each day for seven days you shall present a food offering. On the eighth day come together again for worship and present a food offering. It is a day for worship, and you shall do no work.

Offerings by fire: or "food offerings." See 1.9. The details of this ritual are given in Numbers 29.13-34.

You shall hold a holy convocation . . . : since this is the second gathering for worship during this festival, it may be better to say "have *another* gathering for worship" or "**come together *again* for worship**" as in TEV.

Laborious work: see verse 7.

23.37 RSV	TEV
"These are the appointed feasts of the LORD, which you shall proclaim as times of holy convocation, for presenting to the LORD offerings by fire, burnt offerings and cereal offerings, sacrifices and drink offerings, each on its proper day;	(37 These are the religious festivals on which you honor the LORD by gathering together for worship and presenting food offerings, burnt offerings, grain offerings, sacrifices, and wine offerings, as required day by day.

Verses 37 and 38 probably constitute the beginning of the conclusion to chapter 23 (which actually ends with verse 44). Some scholars take verses 39-43 as a later addition which interrupted the concluding paragraph. For this reason they have proposed shifting verses 37-38 and placing them between verse 43 and verse 44. However, it is probably best to leave them here, but set them off as a separate paragraph and put them in parentheses, as in TEV.

Appointed feasts: see verse 2.

Offerings by fire, burnt offerings and cereal offerings: see chapters 1-7.

Sacrifices: this is a very general term but probably refers to the fellowship offering or "peace offering" detailed in chapter 3. NEB translates "shared offering," and FRCL has "communion sacrifices."

Drink offerings: see verses 13 and 18.

Each on its proper day: literally, "the thing (or, affair) of the day for its day." That is, everything is to be done at the proper time required by the LORD.

23.38 RSV	TEV
besides the sabbaths of the LORD, and besides your gifts, and besides all your votive offerings, and besides all your freewill offerings, which you give to the LORD.	These festivals are in addition to the regular Sabbaths, and these offerings are in addition to your regular gifts, your offerings as fulfillment of vows, and your freewill offerings that you give to the LORD.)

Besides the sabbaths . . . : as indicated in the TEV rendering, this shows that the special annual festivals are in addition to the regular weekly celebrations of the people of Israel. It will be better in most languages to make this verse a separate sentence rather than attempting to follow RSV, which makes one sentence of the two verses. The fourfold repetition of **besides** may be quite unnatural in the receptor language. The meaning, however, is adequately conveyed by the single expression "**in addition to . . .** ," as in TEV, NAB, and Mft.

Votive offerings . . . freewill offerings: see 7.16 and 22.23.

23.39 RSV	TEV
"On the fifteenth day of the seventh month, when you have gathered in the produce of the land, you shall keep the feast of the LORD seven days; on the first day shall be a solemn rest, and on the eighth day shall be a solemn rest.	When you have harvested your fields, celebrate this festival for seven days, beginning on the fifteenth day of the seventh month. The first day shall be a special day of rest.

In Hebrew this verse is introduced by the same adverb discussed at the beginning of verse 27. Some see this as evidence that this section is a later addition. Most versions leave it untranslated, but NEB has "Further . . . ," NJV has "Mark . . . ," NJB "But . . . ," and NIV "So . . . ." NASB and AT take it as an adverb of time and translate it "On exactly . . . ." If the receptor language has some sort of particle that will somehow set this paragraph off as separate from the rest of the section, it should probably be used at the beginning of this verse.

On the fifteenth day . . . : or "**beginning on the fifteenth day . . . .**" See verse 34.

When you have gathered in the produce of the land: or "after you have brought in what the fields have produced . . . ," or "after having harvested the crops from the field . . . ."

Keep the feast: that is, celebrate the festival. Compare 19.3.

A solemn rest: compare verses 35-36.

Eighth day: in view of the mention of a seven-day period earlier, this may cause some confusion. In some languages it may be better to say "on the last day of the festival."

There seems to be an error at the end of this verse in TEV. RSV and all other versions consulted have a special rest day at the beginning and the end of the period. But TEV only has it on the first day. Possibly the mention of the seven-day period earlier in the verse is intended to cover this, but it does not do so adequately. This also affects the beginning of the following verse, which becomes ambiguous in TEV if both the first and eighth day are mentioned at the end of 39.

23.40 RSV	TEV
And you shall take on the first day the fruit of goodly trees, branches of palm trees, and boughs of leafy trees, and willows of the brook; and	On that day take some of the best fruit from your trees, take palm branches and limbs from leafy trees, and begin a religious festival to

you shall rejoice before the LORD honor the LORD your God.
your God seven days.

There is no indication in the text that the branches mentioned in this particular verse were to be used to build the "shelters" or "huts" involved in this festival. While this is not impossible, it is certainly improbable. It is more likely that the items mentioned here were carried in a joyous procession by the worshipers to express their gratitude toward God for the harvest.

The fruit of goodly trees: the exact meaning of the word translated **goodly** is uncertain. And the grammatical construction makes it possible to take it as qualifying either **fruit** or **trees**. Further, Jewish tradition has understood it as referring to citrus trees, and it is so translated by NEB. NJV simply transliterates "the product of *hadar* trees." But most versions retain a word meaning "beautiful," "majestic," or "fine." In addition to this problem, the word translated **fruit** may also be understood in a more general sense as referring to whatever the tree produces; hence "foliage" (NAB), "boughs" (AT), or "what the fine trees bear" (Mft). It is probably best to take the whole phrase as meaning something like "the fruit of citrus trees," as in NEB.

Branches of palm trees: this kind of tree is explained in FFB, pages 160-162.

Boughs of leafy trees: it is uncertain exactly what kind of tree is intended here, but it is possibly the myrtle tree (see FFB, pages 149-150, and Zohary, page 119).

Willows of the brook: this phrase presents a number of problems to the translator. First, the construction with **of** must be made clearer. Probably it should be translated "which grow beside [the brook, or water]." Secondly, there is some question as to what kind of tree is meant. While many versions translate **willows** (NJV, NEB, NASB, JB, TOB), it has also been identified as a poplar (so NIV and NAB). See the discussion under poplar in FFB, page 170, as well as Zohary, page 131. The fact that this is completely omitted in TEV further complicates the matter. But perhaps the best model to follow is that of NJB, "flowering shrubs from the river bank," or "bushes that grow by the water," or something similar.

23.41　　　RSV　　　　　　　　　　　　　　　　TEV

You shall keep it as a feast to the LORD seven days in the year; it is a statute for ever throughout your generations; you shall keep it in the seventh month.	Celebrate it for seven days. This regulation is to be kept by your descendants for all time to come.

There is a great deal of information in this verse that may be left implicit. Compare TEV.

A statute for ever . . . : see 3.17 and 10.9.

23.42 RSV TEV

You shall dwell in booths for seven days; all that are native in Israel shall dwell in booths,

All the people of Israel shall live in shelters for seven days,

You: the pronoun here is plural and refers to the whole community of Israel, and in meaning it is identical to **all that are native in Israel**. In many languages it will be advisable to clarify this identity by translating only once, "You Israelites" or "**All the people of Israel**" (TEV). The same meaning is repeated in two slightly different forms in this verse. If the receptor language rejects such parallelism, it is quite possible to translate the meaning only once, as has been done in TEV.

For seven days: in some languages it may be more natural to shift this to the beginning of the verse and say "During this week . . ." or something similar.

23.43 RSV TEV

that your generations may know that I made the people of Israel dwell in booths when I brought them out of the land of Egypt: I am the LORD your God."

so that your descendants may know that the LORD made the people of Israel live in simple shelters when he led them out of Egypt. He is the LORD your God.

That your generations may know: or "in order to remind your descendants . . . ," or perhaps "so that those who come after you may be aware . . . ."

I: if indirect discourse is being used, the occurrences of the pronoun will have to be changed, as in TEV.

The people of Israel: this may be more naturally translated in some languages as "their ancestors" in the context of this verse.

Booths: even those versions that translate the same word "tabernacles" in verse 34 and elsewhere are forced to use a simpler term here, since the context is considerably different. Some other renderings are "arbours" (NEB); "booths" (NIV); and "shelters" (JB). The idea is that of "temporary quarters." See the discussion under verse 34 as well as the section heading at verse 33.

23.44 RSV TEV

Thus Moses declared to the people of Israel the appointed feasts of the LORD.

So in this way Moses gave the people of Israel the regulations for observing the religious festivals to honor the LORD.

This verse constitutes a final conclusion to the chapter. But see the remarks on verses 38 and 39.

Thus: in some languages it may be better to begin "This is how Moses explained to the people of Israel . . . ."

The appointed feasts: see verse 2. But TEV makes this more explicit by adding "**the regulations for observing . . . .**" This may be helpful in many other languages.

Of the LORD: meaning "**to honor the LORD**," as in TEV.

Chapter 24

Chapter 24 is made up of three sections. The first two deal with matters related to the worship of the people of Israel, and the third has to do with legal questions, particularly regarding a man who cursed God. In some translations the first two are grouped together as a single section entitled something like "Rules about the lamps and the bread offered to God." TEV, however, separates verses 1-4 and verses 5-9 into two sections.

TEV Section Heading: **"Taking Care of the Lamps."**

In the heading for this passage, some English versions focus on the oil that is used in the lamps (RSV and NIV). However, it is probably better to look for a term that deals with the overall question of the way in which lamps in the LORD's presence were to be treated. The section may be entitled "Rules about lamps in the holy place," or "How to care for the lamps in God's presence," or something similar. Compare the parallel passages in Exodus 25.31-40 and 27.20-21.

24.1-2	RSV	TEV

RSV	TEV
1 The LORD said to Moses, 2 "Command the people of Israel to bring you pure oil from beaten olives for the lamp, that a light may be kept burning continually.	1 The LORD told Moses 2 to give the following orders to the people of Israel: Bring pure olive oil of the finest quality for the lamps in the Tent, so that a light might be kept burning regularly.

Said to Moses: see 4.1.

Command the people of Israel: in other contexts where a series of regulations is introduced, the verb used is simply "Say . . ." (as in 23.34 and elsewhere), but a stronger term is used in this verse. Also at this point the translator must once again decide whether to use direct (as in RSV) or indirect discourse (as in TEV). Naturalness in the receptor language should be the determining factor. It is even possible to have an additional level of quotation, since Moses tells the people what the LORD told him. But quotations within quotations are often a problem in languages that do not have a long history of written documents.

Pure oil from beaten olives: this indicates the purest and finest available olive oil, which results from pounding the olives in a mortar and then straining the liquid. The idea of purity may be expressed in some languages by the word "clear," which is very similar to the Hebrew. Compare 2.1 where the more general term for oil is used. On "olive," see FFB, pages 156-158. The whole phrase may be rendered "clear oil from olives that have been crushed."

The lamp . . . a light: the Hebrew has the singular forms **lamp** and **light** here, but the singular may possibly be taken in the collective sense, making it synonymous with "lamps" in verse 4. Porter, however, insists that this passage, together with Exodus 27.20-21 and other references, indicates the presence of a single lamp, separate from the lamps that were on the lampstand mentioned in verse 4 and following and that were described in Exodus 25.31-40 and 37.17-24. In this case, the distinction between the singular and plural (verse 4) should be maintained in the receptor language.

Continually: this may be translated "every evening" or "**regularly**," since the following verse makes it clear that they did not burn throughout the day. In some languages the habitual form of the verb may be adequate to translate the idea here.

24.3   RSV   TEV

Outside the veil of the testimony, in the tent of meeting, Aaron shall keep it in order from evening to morning before the LORD continually; it shall be a statute for ever throughout your generations.	Each evening Aaron shall light them and keep them burning until morning, there in the LORD's presence outside the curtain in front of the Covenant Box, which is in the Most Holy Place. This regulation is to be observed for all time to come.

The first part of this verse may be taken as going with the previous verse. NEB, for example, has "the lamp outside the veil . . . ." But most English versions begin a new sentence at the beginning of verse 3.

The veil of the testimony: compare 4.6. This refers to the curtain which separated the two parts of the Tent of the LORD's presence, that is, the Holy Place and the Most Holy Place (see Exo 26.31-35). On the word **testimony** referring to "**the Covenant Box**," see 16.13. Some languages may have to translate the whole expression by something like "the [hanging] cloth that conceals the Covenant Box" or "the cloth that divides the Tent of the LORD's presence."

The tent of meeting: see 1.1.

Keep it in order: the pronoun here refers to the "light (or, lamp)" in the previous verse. If a plural has been used in verse 2, then a plural pronoun will be required here. The verb has been understood in slightly different ways: TEV "**keep them burning**"; NIV "tend the lamps"; NJV "set them up"; NEB "keep in trim." But the basic idea is doing all that is necessary to assure that the lamps are burning at the proper time.

Before the LORD: or "before me" if direct discourse is being used.

Continually: see verse 2 above.

A statute for ever throughout your generations: this same expression is found in 7.36; 10.9; 23.41.

24.4   RSV   TEV

He shall keep the lamps in order upon the lampstand of pure gold before the LORD continually.	**Aaron shall take care of the lamps on the lampstand of pure gold and must see that they burn regularly in the LORD's presence.**

<u>He</u>: since the pronoun refers to Aaron, this has been made clear in TEV by the substitution of the noun for the pronoun. Other languages may find it necessary to make the same kind of adjustment.

<u>Keep the lamps in order</u>: this is exactly the same verb as used in the previous verse, but here TEV uses two verbal expressions that are more general in meaning: **"take care of . . . and see that they burn . . . ."** This makes explicit what is implied in the verb in this context. In contrast with verses 2-3 above, the word **lamps** here is plural. The context shows quite clearly that what is referred to in this case are the lamps **"on the lampstand."** This is probably something quite different from the single lamp mentioned earlier (verses 1-3) and should be clearly distinguished in the receptor language.

<u>Lampstand</u>: since there is no special word for lampstands in many cultures, this may have to be translated something like "lamp holder" or "thing on which lamps are placed." It should perhaps be emphasized that this object did not hold candles but oil lamps.

<u>Pure gold</u>: the text literally says "a pure lampstand" (so NJB and NJV), which possibly refers to the sacred character or ritual cleanness of the lampstand without reference to the material of which it is made. NEB, for example, has "the lampstand, ritually clean . . . ." But the majority of versions take it to mean "pure gold lampstand." If the **pure gold** interpretation is followed, the idea of "purity" in this case may have to be expressed as "containing no other things" or "made of nothing but [gold]." And the word for **gold** may have to be borrowed in some languages. If this is the case, it should be explained in the glossary.

<u>Continually</u>: see verse 2.

TEV Section Heading: **"The Bread Offered to God."**

This brief section may be given a more detailed title corresponding to the one recommended for the previous section: "Rules about the bread offered to God." Some translators have sought to reflect the idea of permanence in both of these sections by using "The permanent flame" for verses 1-4 and "The permanent offering" for verses 5-9.

24.5   RSV   TEV

"And you shall take fine flour, and bake twelve cakes of it; two tenths of an ephah shall be in each cake.	**Take twenty-four pounds of flour and bake twelve loaves of bread.**

This is a continuation of what the LORD says to Moses (see verse 1). If a section heading is placed before this verse, it may be advisable to repeat the formula "And the LORD also said to Moses . . . ."

You: the pronoun here is singular and presumably still refers to Moses. However, it may be that Moses would delegate this to Aaron or to one of the other priests.

Fine flour: see 2.1.

Cakes . . . cake: or rather "loaves of bread . . . bread." On the nature of this kind of bread, see 2.4.

Two tenths of an ephah . . . in each cake: compare 5.11; 14.10; 23.17. According to the restructured TEV each loaf would contain only about one kilogram or two pounds. But this is not consistent with the rendering of this same expression elsewhere. "Two kilograms (or, four pounds) shall be in each cake" would be more consistent. Or, if the TEV model is used, "Take twenty-four kilograms (or, fifty pounds) of flour."

24.6   RSV   TEV

And you shall set them in two rows,   Put the loaves in two rows, six in
six in a row, upon the table of pure   each row, on the table covered with
gold.   pure gold, which is in the LORD's
                                             presence.

You: see remarks on verse 5 above.

Two rows: the term used here is a general one for "arrangements" and may be understood as **rows** (as in most versions), or some other kind of arrangement such as "piles" (NAB, FRCL, TOB, and Mft) or "lots" (AT). The dimensions of the table were less than a meter long and a half meter wide according to Exodus 25.23, and so some have argued that it would have been impossible to make two rows of loaves of this size. Further, the order is given in verse 7 to sprinkle incense "on each arrangement." If the loaves had been arranged individually in rows, the writer would probably have said "on each loaf." The solution "two piles" is therefore probably to be preferred.

Table of pure gold: literally, "a pure table." The problem here is identical with the "pure lampstand" in verse 4. NEB translates "the table, ritually clean . . . ." The two problems should be solved in the same manner. If the **pure gold** solution is followed, it will be possible to say **"covered with pure gold"** (as in TEV) rather than "made of pure gold." Compare Exodus 25.24 and 31.8.

24.7   RSV   TEV

And you shall put pure frankincense   Put some pure incense on each row,
with each row, that it may go with the   as a token food offering to the LORD
bread as a memorial portion to be   to take the place of the bread.
offered by fire to the LORD.

Pure frankincense: on the adjective **pure**, see verse 2. On **frankincense**, see 2.1. The incense in this case was probably in solid form rather than liquid.

With each row: the text literally says "along the row [singular]." But the Syriac version has the plural, and most modern translations take it to mean **"on each row."**

Go with the bread: some experts take the corresponding Hebrew words to mean "along with the bread," while others think they mean "instead of the bread." TEV has **"to take the place of the bread."** And NJV has "for the bread." Mft reads "to serve as a reminder to the Eternal over the bread." Similarly NEB has "this shall be a token of the bread," and NIV reads "to represent the bread." Probably the idea of substitution is the best one to follow.

A memorial portion: see 2.2.

24.8   RSV   TEV

Every sabbath day Aaron shall set it   Every Sabbath, for all time to come,
in order before the LORD continually   the bread must be placed in the
on behalf of the people of Israel as a   presence of the LORD. This is Israel's
covenant for ever.   duty forever.

Aaron shall set it in order . . . : the Hebrew text does not have the name of Aaron here, but only the pronoun "he." Although it probably does refer to Aaron, most versions avoid the problem by using a passive form (see TEV). In those languages where it is impossible or unnatural to use a passive, it may be possible to find a less specific solution by saying "Someone must place the bread . . . ." But probably it is better to say "the priest" or to use the name of Aaron specifically.

Continually: better "regularly." See verse 2.

As a covenant forever: in this context the word translated **covenant** in RSV probably means simply "commitment" (NJV), or "agreement" (NAB), or "obligation." But it is qualified by the word meaning "perpetual" or "everlasting." It may be wise in many languages to make this a separate sentence as in TEV: **"This is Israel's duty forever."**

24.9   RSV   TEV

And it shall be for Aaron and his   The bread belongs to Aaron and his
sons, and they shall eat it in a holy   descendants, and they shall eat it in
place, since it is for him a most holy   a holy place, because this is a very
portion out of the offerings by fire to   holy part of the food offered to the
the LORD, a perpetual due."   LORD for the priests.

Compare 7.16-18.

It: this refers to the bread, or the loaves, which become the property of the priestly family (see 1.5). In some languages it may be better to say "This bread," making clear that the reference is to the previously mentioned bread.

Aaron and his sons: the word **sons** clearly means **"descendants"** in this context. The whole expression may be rendered "the family of the priests."

A holy place: see 6.9,19.

Since: or **"because."** This ties together the holiness of the bread with the fact that it must be eaten in a holy place. It is a cause-and-effect relationship.

For him: grammatically this refers back to Aaron, but the meaning is collective, "for them," that is, **"for the priests."**

It is . . . a most holy portion: literally, "[it is] the most holy of holy ones." On this expression see 2.3. The superlative idea is not fully communicated by TEV. NEB has rendered the phrase "it is the holiest of holy gifts." AT has "it is the most sacred part of the LORD's sacrifices."

Offerings by fire: see 1.9.

A perpetual due: see 6.11. This has been left implicit in TEV, since a similar meaning is contained in the previous verse.

TEV Section Heading: **"An Example of Just and Fair Punishment."**

Verses 10-23 contain a narrative (verses 10-14 and 23) which permits the introduction of a list of commandments about respect for God and neighbor (15-22). The TEV section heading concentrates on the story. But it is possible to provide a more general title. Other models for the title of this section are "The punishment of a man who cursed God" or "The penalty for blasphemy and murder." But perhaps a more general formulation such as "Rules concerning respect for God and his creatures" or "The law of retaliation" would be more appropriate. NEB has "Laws against Blasphemy and Assault."

24.10-11 RSV	TEV
10 Now an Israelite woman's son, whose father was an Egyptian, went out among the people of Israel; and the Israelite woman's son and a man of Israel quarreled in the camp, 11 and the Israelite woman's son blasphemed the Name, and cursed. And they brought him to Moses. His mother's name was Shelomith, the daughter of Dibri, of the tribe of Dan.	10-11 There was a man whose father was an Egyptian and whose mother was an Israelite named Shelomith, the daughter of Dibri from the tribe of Dan. There in the camp this man quarreled with an Israelite. During the quarrel he cursed the LORD, so they took him to Moses,

Now . . . : this transition word is used to indicate a break in the usual style of Leviticus, to begin a story. In other languages one may begin with "One day . . ." or "There was once a man . . ." (see TEV), to show that a different kind of material follows.

The Israelite woman's son: the second occurrence of this phrase is translated by NJV as "that half-Israelite." It is also possible to translate "this man" (NAB), or to use the simple pronoun "he" (NEB) if the reference is clear. This is also true of the third occurrence.

A man of Israel: in many languages it will not be adequate to translate "another Israelite," since there is an obvious contrast between the man who committed blasphemy and the other person with whom he quarreled. NEB translates the meaning accurately with "an Israelite of pure descent." In some languages it may be necessary to say "a man whose mother and father were Israelites."

Went out among the people of Israel: this may either mean that the man lived among the Israelites and left his tent, or that he lived outside the camp (compare Exo 12.38 and Num 11.4) and left his home to enter the camp. Some translators may prefer to leave this idea of "going out" implicit, since it is not certain which meaning is intended.

Blasphemed the Name, and cursed: the two verbs are very similar in meaning. On the word **cursed**, see 19.14 and 20.9. In some languages it may be necessary to translate the two by a single verb, using an adverb to reinforce the meaning. For example, "insulted terribly," "reviled," or "swore violently." Others translate "blasphemed with a curse" (NIV). The object of both verbs is **the Name**. Out of respect for God, the people of Israel often avoided using the name "YHWH" (see 1.1), especially with the verbs "blaspheme" or "curse." So they used the word **Name** to stand in the place of "YHWH." But in many languages it will be necessary to make it clear that God himself is intended. Some may wish to say "insulted God by using his name in a curse" or "swore against Yahweh (or, the LORD) with a curse."

They brought him to Moses: the subject pronoun here is indefinite. NJB renders this by a passive form: "He was taken to Moses." It may have to be translated in some languages as "Some people," or even "Some witnesses who heard it."

His mother's name was Shelomith ...: this background information concerning the man who committed blasphemy has been shifted forward in TEV (and NEB) to a more natural position in English, the place where the man's mother is first mentioned. In other languages it may be more natural to make a similar shift. But this will require the combining of verses so that 10-11 are listed together. Other versions maintain the order of the Hebrew text but place this information within parentheses as a kind of afterthought (see NIV).

24.12	RSV	TEV
	And they put him in custody, till the will of the LORD should be declared to them.	put him under guard, and waited for the LORD to tell them what to do with him.

They: this subject pronoun is again indefinite, as in verse 11. If it cannot be translated as a passive, the subject may be understood as being the same as in the previous verse, or as a different but equally unspecified group of persons. Some possible models are "Someone arrested him" or "People took him captive."

Put him in custody: this may have to be translated "arrested him and held him," or "assigned someone to guard him," or something similar.

Till the will of the LORD should be declared to them: this passive construction will have to be rendered actively in many languages. Some suggestions are "until the LORD should reveal his will to them" or "waited to find out what the LORD wanted them to do with him." Compare TEV.

24.13-14   RSV   TEV

RSV	TEV
13 And the LORD said to Moses, 14 "Bring out of the camp him who cursed; and let all who heard him lay their hands upon his head, and let all the congregation stone him.	13 The LORD said to Moses, 14 "Take that man out of the camp. Everyone who heard him curse shall put his hands on the man's head to testify that he is guilty, and then the whole community shall stone him to death.

And the LORD said to Moses: see 4.1. But in the context of this story, it may be better to say "Then the LORD said . . . ," in order to highlight the continuation of the story.

Him who cursed: this refers to the man whose father was Egyptian and whose mother was Israelite. He may be referred to in many different ways, depending on the habits of the receptor language, but it is important that the idea of cursing be maintained somewhere in this verse. TEV refers to him simply as **"that man"** but includes the crucial idea later in the verse with **"who heard him curse."** The Jewish law forbids blasphemy (see Exo 22.28, where "revile" translates the same word). This verse makes clear that the law applies to a half-Israelite as well as to full-blooded Israelites.

Lay their hands upon his head: see 16.21. In the Old Testament the laying on of hands usually indicates the transmission of holiness or of sin. Here it probably means that the man is responsible for his own death, and that those who stone him do not share in the responsibility simply because they heard the curse. They had become impure by hearing the curse, but the laying on of hands transmitted the sin back to the person who caused it. The TEV rendering, **"to testify that he is guilty,"** should probably be understood in the sense "to show that he [and not they] is the person who committed the sin."

All the congregation: that is, all those members of the Israelite community who were present at the time.

Stone him: or "kill him by throwing stones at him." See 20.2.

24.15   RSV   TEV

RSV	TEV
And say to the people of Israel, Whoever curses his God shall bear his sin.	Then tell the people of Israel that anyone who curses God must suffer the consequences

This begins the section (verses 15-22) that lists a number of more general commandments that Moses was to give the people of Israel. It may be wise to indicate clearly the break in the story by beginning with something like "Here, then, are the commandments that you [singular, referring to Moses] must communicate to the people of Israel: . . . ."

Curses his God: see verse 11 as well as 19.14 and 20.9.

Bear his sin: the Hebrew expression is similar to the one used in 5.1 and is identical in meaning: "bear the responsibility" or **"suffer the consequences."**

24.16 RSV TEV

He who blasphemes the name of the LORD shall be put to death; all the congregation shall stone him; the sojourner as well as the native, when he blasphemes the Name, shall be put to death.

and be put to death. Any Israelite or any foreigner living in Israel who curses the LORD shall be stoned to death by the whole community.

Blasphemes: this word and the one for "curse" in the previous verse refer to the same act (see verse 11). So it is possible to combine them in the translation, as has been done in TEV.

Put to death: see 20.2.

All the congregation shall stone him: see verse 14.

Sojourner: see 16.29. This leaves no doubt that foreigners and Israelites must be treated the same in this matter.

Blasphemes the Name: TEV has "**curses the LORD.**" See verse 11.

24.17 RSV TEV

He who kills a man shall be put to death.

"Anyone who commits murder shall be put to death,

Beginning with this verse the text moves beyond the specific case of the half-Israelite who cursed God. A series of more general rules are given concerning just punishment. In some languages it may be necessary to use some kind of device to indicate this transition. Mft, for example, begins with "Also . . . ." And most English versions set off verses 17-22 as a separate paragraph.

Kills: the Hebrew word used here has the root meaning of "hit" or "strike." But it is often extended to mean "strike a mortal blow." And in this context it seems to mean "commit murder," since there were some cases of accidental killing where the person was not punished by death. Compare Exodus 21.12-14.

Put to death: see 20.2.

24.18 RSV TEV

He who kills a beast shall make it good, life for life.

and anyone who kills an animal belonging to someone else must replace it. The principle is a life for a life.

Shall make it good: the Hebrew verb used here means "make restitution" (NJB, NAB, NJV) or "make amends." Specifically, the person who killed another person's animal had to replace it with a similar live animal.

369

Life for life: this may have to be translated more explicitly in some languages. Possible models in this context are "Only a life can replace another life" or "Only a live animal can replace the one whose life was taken away."

24.19	RSV	TEV

When a man causes a disfigurement in his neighbor, as he has done it shall be done to him,

"If anyone injures another person, whatever he has done shall be done to him.

When: in many languages it is difficult to distinguish between "when" and "if." The meaning here is clearly "If it happens that . . ." or "If the case arises where . . . ."

Causes a disfigurement: this expression is to be understood in a very general sense, referring to any kind of injury (see NIV, NAB, and NJB as well as TEV). The various types of possible injuries are listed in verse 20 below.

Neighbor: that is, "another person." See 6.2.

As he has done it shall be done to him: the passive form in the last part of this phrase will have to be translated actively in many languages. It may also be wise to reverse the order of the elements in the sentence by saying something like "They [indefinite] must do to him exactly what he has done to the other person."

24.20	RSV	TEV

fracture for fracture, eye for eye, tooth for tooth; as he has disfigured a man, he shall be disfigured.

If he breaks a bone, one of his bones shall be broken; if he puts out an eye, one of his eyes shall be put out; if he knocks out a tooth, one of his teeth shall be knocked out. Whatever injury he causes another person shall be done to him in return.

The wording of RSV follows very closely that of the Hebrew. TEV has chosen to render this more explicitly by making a separate sentence out of each phrase, thus describing three possible examples. The three examples are then followed by a general rule that is the same as expressed in a slightly different way in verse 19.

If the TEV model is followed, the passive structure in the last half of each of the examples may have to be rendered "they [indefinite] shall break . . . blind . . . knock out a tooth . . . ."

24.21	RSV	TEV

He who kills a beast shall make it good; and he who kills a man shall be put to death.

Whoever kills an animal shall replace it, but whoever kills a man shall be put to death.

He who kills a beast shall make it good: see verse 18.
He who kills a man shall be put to death: see verse 17.

24.22   RSV   TEV

You shall have one law for the so-   This law applies to all of you, to Isra-
journer and for the native; for I am   elites and to foreigners living among
the LORD your God."   you, because I am the LORD your
                                             God."

You shall have one law: it may be misleading in some languages to translate
literally **one law**. The meaning is that the same set of laws cover both the foreigner
(see 22.23) and the Israelite of pure descent. In many languages the collective
singular use of **law** as well as of "foreigner" and **native** will be more naturally
translated as a plural; for example, "the same laws."

For I am the LORD your God: this gives the reason behind the application of
the same law to all people. See 18.2.

24.23   RSV   TEV

So Moses spoke to the people of   When Moses had said this to
Israel; and they brought him who   the people of Israel, they took the
had cursed out of the camp, and   man outside the camp and stoned
stoned him with stones. Thus the   him to death. In this way the people
people of Israel did as the LORD   of Israel did what the LORD had com-
commanded Moses.   manded Moses.

This verse resumes the narrative of the half-Israelite who cursed God, where
it was interrupted at the end of verse 14. It may be necessary in some languages to
begin this verse by saying "After Moses had given the people of Israel these [general]
rules . . . ."

Him who had cursed: see verse 14.
Stoned him with stones: see 20.2 as well as verse 14.
Thus: or "by doing this."

Chapter 25

Chapter 25 deals with two important Israelite customs: the Rest Year, which occurred every seventh year, and the Year of Restoration, which took place on the fiftieth year. If more than one level of headings are being used in the translation, one may give a single title to the whole chapter, calling it something like "Holy Years" (as in NJB) or "Special Years." Then the second level of headings may describe the two different types of special years: "The Rest Year" or "The Seventh Year" at verse 1, and "The Year of Restoration" at verse 8, with other more specific headings at verses 18, 23, 35, and 39.

TEV Section Heading: "**The Seventh Year.**"

The Sabbath Year is so called because it is the last in a seven-year cycle. During this year, in accordance with old agricultural practice (see Exo 23.10-11), the ground was not to be cultivated. This section (verses 1-7) may equally well be called "The rest year" or "The year of rest for the earth (or, soil)."

This passage tells us nothing of the beginning of the Sabbath year, but it is quite probable that it did not correspond to the civil year which began in the spring (see the discussion of the New Year under 23.23). Like the Year of Restoration in the following section, it probably covered the period from autumn to the next summer and included the autumn seed time and the spring harvest. Compare the parallel passage in Deuteronomy 15.1-11.

25.1-2	RSV	TEV
	1 The Lord said to Moses on Mount Sinai, 2 "Say to the people of Israel, When you come into the land which I give you, the land shall keep a sabbath to the Lord.	1 The Lord spoke to Moses on Mount Sinai and commanded him 2 to give the following regulations to the people of Israel. When you enter the land that the Lord is giving you, you shall honor the Lord by not cultivating the land every seventh year.

Said to Moses: see 4.1. But note that, contrary to most other occurrences of this phrase, in this case the location is also specified (Mount Sinai). Some translators may wish to change the structure of verse 1 by saying something like "When Moses was on Mount Sinai, the LORD said . . . ."

Say to the people of Israel . . . : see 1.2.

When you come into the land . . . : see 14.34; 19.23; 23.10.

The land shall keep a sabbath to the LORD: this phrase contains several problems for the translator. The singular **sabbath** is surely intended to have a plural meaning and should be so translated in many languages. NEB has "keep sabbaths." But it is far better to translate its root meaning (seven or seventh) than to transliterate it. The construction of the sentence in Hebrew (and thus RSV) makes **the land** the subject of the verb, as if the land actually performs some action by itself. In reality it is the people of Israel that must act (or refrain from acting) in order to fulfill this rule. They must stop their usual practice of cultivating the land and so allow it to rest in order to honor the LORD. Therefore it will be necessary in many languages to restructure the sentence, making the people of Israel the subject (perhaps using the pronoun "you"). For example, "you must refrain from cultivating the land every seventh year, in order to honor the LORD."

25.3	RSV	TEV

Six years you shall sow your field, and six years you shall prune your vineyard, and gather in its fruits;	You shall plant your fields, prune your vineyards, and gather your crops for six years.

Six years . . . : it will be better in many languages to translate this phrase only once in this verse, even though the Hebrew repeats it. In some languages the repetition may even give the impression of two separate six-year periods. In other cases the repetition may simply be stylistically unacceptable. Note that TEV has shifted this information to the end of the verse for the sake of naturalness in English.

You shall sow . . . prune . . . gather: the subject of these three verbs is singular in form (the pronoun **you**), but it is collective, and the meaning is plural. See 19.9. Instead of **you shall . . .** , some languages may prefer "you may . . ." (Mft, NJV, and NEB) or "it is acceptable to . . . ."

Your field . . . your vineyard: the possessive pronouns are likewise singular in form but plural in meaning. And the singular **field** and **vineyard** are collective and should be translated as plurals, as in TEV.

25.4	RSV	TEV

but in the seventh year there shall be a sabbath of solemn rest for the land, a sabbath to the LORD; you shall not sow your field or prune your vineyard.	But the seventh year is to be a year of complete rest for the land, a year dedicated to the LORD. Do not plant your fields or prune your vineyards.

A sabbath of solemn rest: see 16.31 and 23.3.

For the land: in some languages the verb "to rest" will be inappropriate to use with **land**. So it may be more natural to say something like "a year when the land is not cultivated at all."

You: as in the previous verse, the pronouns here are singular but should be translated as plurals in most languages, since they refer to the whole people of Israel.

25.5	RSV	TEV

What grows of itself in your harvest you shall not reap, and the grapes of your undressed vine you shall not gather; it shall be a year of solemn rest for the land.	Do not even harvest the grain that grows by itself without being planted, and do not gather the grapes from your unpruned vines; it is a year of complete rest for the land.

You shall not reap . . . you shall not gather: some translators have been perplexed by the seeming inconsistency between these prohibitions and the statement in verse 7 indicating that the food produced during the rest year could be eaten. "How can you eat what you don't reap or harvest?" they ask. The solution lies in the fact that these verbs seem to refer to farming and harvesting organized by the owner of the land. But individuals—whether masters, servants or visitors—were still permitted to pick and gather whatever produce they could find.

What grows of itself: even though no new seeds were sown, some grain would be produced from seed that had fallen to the ground during the previous harvest. Both RSV and TEV may give some readers the impression of some kind of spontaneous plant life. NEB makes the meaning clearer with "the crop that grows from fallen grain."

Undressed vine: that is, a vine that has not been pruned or tended in the normal fashion. The word used here is related to the word for "Nazirite" or "consecrated one" (Num 6), since a part of the vow of a Nazirite involved not cutting the hair. NJV has "your untrimmed vines" (compare also NJB).

A year of solemn rest: or "**complete rest**." See 16.31 and 23.3 as well as verse 4 above.

25.6	RSV	TEV

The sabbath of the land shall provide food for you, for yourself and for your male and female slaves and for your hired servant and the sojourner who lives with you;	Although the land has not been cultivated during that year, it will provide food for you, your slaves, your hired men, the foreigners living with you,

For you, for yourself: this seems redundant in English because the second person singular and plural pronouns cannot be distinguished. But in Hebrew **you** is plural and refers to the people of Israel as a whole. The rest of the pronouns in this verse are singular and may indicate "each one of you, along with your slaves . . . ."

Your male and female slaves: in some languages it may be more natural simply to say "**your slaves**" as in TEV. This leaves implicit the fact that some of them may be men and others may be women.

Your hired servant and the sojourner . . . : these singular forms obviously do not imply that there would be only one servant and one foreigner. They are collective and may be translated as plurals. The term translated **sojourner** in RSV is usually understood as "foreigner" as in TEV, and NIV has "temporary resident." NJV has "the hired and bound laborers," but this is not recommended. Compare 22.10.

25.7	RSV	TEV
	for your cattle also and for the beasts that are in your land all its yield shall be for food.	your domestic animals, and the wild animals in your fields. Everything that it produces may be eaten.

Your cattle . . . the beasts: the two terms are intended to be all-inclusive in this context. The first refers to any animals that are tame and kept by human beings. The second is intended to include all other animals in the land.

This verse may be understood in two different ways: (1) The first part may be taken as a continuation of the list started in 6b, and the second part as a general conclusion picking up and amplifying the meaning of 6a (as in TEV, NIV, NEB, and NJB). Or (2) the first part of the verse may be understood as the object of the second part, which then yields the meaning "All these products will also serve as food for your domestic and wild animals." This is the interpretation chosen by RSV, NJV, JB, and NAB. This second interpretation is based on the assumption that a special construction called "chiasmus" is used here (see definition in Glossary). Translators are, however, advised to translate the first option, making a separate sentence of **all its yield shall be for food**.

TEV Section Heading: **"The Year of Restoration."**

The traditional rendering of the name for this special year is "Jubilee," which is ultimately a transliteration of a Hebrew word meaning "ram's horn." The essential element in this year was the liberation of slaves and the restoration of lands to former owners. Translators are advised not to transliterate the word Jubilee, but to look for a term in their own language that gives the idea of "liberation," "restoration," or "giving back." The word actually comes from verse 10 in this section.

Scholars have proposed more than one way in which the years of rest and the year of jubilee were to be arranged and counted. Perhaps the most simple arrangement is the one shown in the following list:

The Years of Rest and of Restoration

Years:

1-6	6 normal years	⎫
7	rest year	
8-13	6 normal years	
14	rest year	
15-20	6 normal years	
21	rest year	
22-27	6 normal years	seven series of seven
28	rest year	years each, or
29-34	6 normal years	49 intervening years
35	rest year	
36-41	6 normal years	
42	rest year	
43-48	6 normal years	
49	rest year	⎭
50		YEAR OF RESTORATION
51-56	6 normal years	

[and so on, following the same pattern]

25.8	RSV	TEV

"And you shall count seven weeks[l] of years, seven times seven years, so that the time of the seven weeks of years shall be to you forty-nine years.

Count seven times seven years, a total of forty-nine years.

[l] Or *sabbaths*

You shall count: literally, "you shall count for yourself." The two pronouns are singular in form but should be understood collectively as referring to the people of Israel as a whole. In some languages the verb here will be better translated "wait," as in the similar passage in 15.13.

Seven weeks of years: the word translated **weeks** is actually translated elsewhere as "sabbaths" and has the root meaning "seven" (see 16.31). So the phrases **seven weeks of years** (used twice) and "**seven times seven years**" have exactly the same meaning and can be translated once, if the repetition is stylistically unacceptable in the receptor language.

25.9   RSV   TEV

Then you shall send abroad the loud
trumpet on the tenth day of the
seventh month; on the day of atonement you shall send abroad the
trumpet throughout all your land.

Then, on the tenth day of the seventh month, the Day of Atonement,
send a man to blow a trumpet
throughout the whole land.

This verse repeats the same information two times in parallel structure. The
pronouns are singular in the first part of the verse and plural in the second part. The
phrase **the tenth day of seventh month** refers to "**the Day of Atonement.**" The
verse should be translated in such a way as to avoid giving the impression that it
refers to two separate events.

Send abroad the (loud) trumpet: this phrase occurs twice in this verse, but
it may be translated once in those languages where the repetition is not acceptable.
And since the trumpet cannot go around the land on its own, many languages will
prefer to say "send someone to blow a trumpet loudly" (compare TEV).

The TEV rendering "**send a man to blow a trumpet . . .**" may give the
impression that a single individual is to perform this action. But it is doubtful that
one person would have done the job alone. If TEV is taken as a model, then it will
be important to change the singular to a plural in this case.

The word for **trumpet** in Hebrew refers to the horn of a ram (see FFB, page
75), which was used as a musical instrument to give signals to large groups of people
(see Josh 6.20; Judges 3.27; 1 Sam 13.3). In those cultures where the horns of
animals are still used for such purposes, the receptor language word for this
instrument may be used in the translation.

25.10   RSV   TEV

And you shall hallow the fiftieth year,
and proclaim liberty throughout the
land to all its inhabitants; it shall be
a jubilee for you, when each of you
shall return to his property and each
of you shall return to his family.

In this way you shall set the fiftieth
year apart and proclaim freedom to
all the inhabitants of the land. During
this year all property that has been
sold shall be restored to the original
owner or his descendants, and anyone who has been sold as a slave
shall return to his family.

And: while the common conjunction is used in Hebrew, the context seems to
require a stronger transition word here in order to emphasize the connection
between this verse and the previous one. TEV has "**In this way . . . .**" NEB has "and
so . . . ."

Hallow: or "**set . . . apart**" (TEV); "declare . . . sacred" (NJB); "consecrate"
(NIV). See 11.44 and 21.8.

Proclaim liberty: if possible this should be translated by a very general term
that can be understood as referring to the release of lands which owners have had

to sell (see the end of this verse), as well as to freedom for slaves. Or, in some cases, two verbs may be required.

Jubilee: the Hebrew word originally meant "ram" (see Josh 6.5) but by extension was also applied to the "ram's horn" that was used as a musical instrument (Exo 19.13). Finally, it was also used of the celebration of the Year of Restoration which was characterized by the blowing of the ram's horn. See also the discussion above under the section heading. In this verse one may translate "It will be a time of restitution for you." Translators are advised against transliterating the English word.

Return to his property: the context indicates that what is involved here is property that has had to be sold during difficult times. The former owner was allowed during this special year to retake possession of his land. The translation should not give the impression of someone who merely pays a visit to the land he once owned. Compare the more explicit rendering of TEV. Another way of saying this is "they will give back to the man who sold it, or to his children, all land that he sold."

Return to his family: as in the case of the property, this is not a brief visit to members of the family, but a definitive release from slavery; it is a permanent return to be a part of the clan that the person had left when he became a slave. On the extended meaning of the Hebrew word translated **family**, see 20.5.

25.11   RSV   TEV

A jubilee shall that fiftieth year be to you; in it you shall neither sow, nor reap what grows of itself, nor gather the grapes from the undressed vines. | You shall not plant your fields or harvest the grain that grows by itself or gather the grapes in your un-pruned vineyards.

A jubilee shall that fiftieth year be to you: this repeats information already given in the previous verse and is awkwardly worded in RSV. It may be left implicit here, as in TEV.

The requirements for the Year of Restoration are the same as for the Rest Year (see verses 4-5).

What grows of itself: see verse 5.

25.12   RSV   TEV

For it is a jubilee; it shall be holy to you; you shall eat what it yields out of the field. | The whole year shall be sacred for you; you shall eat only what the fields produce of themselves.

For it is a jubilee: this is additional repetition of previously given information which may be better left implicit here. See verse 10. TEV, however, emphasizes the fact that the entire year is special.

Holy: see 2.3.

You shall eat what it yields out of the field: compare verse 6.

25.13

RSV	TEV
"In this year of jubilee each of you shall return to his property.	In this year all property that has been sold shall be restored to its original owner.

Verses 13-16 further develop the theme of the "restoration" of lands (see verse 10).

Return to his property: see verse 10.

25.14

RSV	TEV
And if you sell to your neighbor or buy from your neighbor, you shall not wrong one another.	So when you sell land to your fellow Israelite or buy land from him, do not deal unfairly.

Sell: literally, "sell a sale," where the noun and the verb have the same root (compare 19.17). The expression simply means "sell something," but in this context it is clearly land that is involved.

Neighbor: meaning "**fellow Israelite**" in this context. See 6.2.

You shall not wrong one another: the verb used here has the idea of exploitation (see 19.33). In this context it may be translated "take advantage of" or "deal unfairly with" (TEV). The prohibition applies to both parties, and this should be brought out in the translation. AT has "you must not cheat each other." And NEB translates "neither party shall drive a hard bargain."

25.15

RSV	TEV
According to the number of years after the jubilee, you shall buy from your neighbor, and according to the number of years for crops he shall sell to you.	The price is to be set according to the number of years the land can produce crops before the next Year of Restoration.

For the sake of clarity it will probably be necessary to restructure this entire verse. The two parts are simply different ways of saying the same thing. **According to the number of years after the jubilee** is essentially the same as **according to the number of years for crops**. Also the phrases **you shall buy . . .** and **he shall sell . . .** refer to the same business transaction. Since this whole chapter is addressed to the people of Israel in general, it may be wise in some languages to say something like "Take into account the number of years since the last [or until the next] Year of Restoration, when you buy or sell land." TEV may also provide a helpful model for some languages.

25.16   RSV   TEV

If the years are many you shall in-   If there are many years, the price
crease the price, and if the years are   shall be higher, but if there are only
few you shall diminish the price, for   a few years, the price shall be lower,
it is the number of the crops that he   because what is being sold is the
is selling to you.   number of crops the land can pro-
                                         duce.

As in the previous verse, the structure is somewhat complicated and should be
simplified in translation. One possible model is "The more time (or, years) remaining
[until the Year of Restoration], the greater the price; the less time remaining, the
smaller the price, because what you are buying is the crops that the land will
produce" (compare NEB).

25.17   RSV   TEV

You shall not wrong one another, but   Do not cheat a fellow Israelite, but
you shall fear your God; for I am the   obey the LORD your God.
LORD your God.

You shall not wrong one another: see verse 14b. Again the emphasis is on
both parties in the transaction. This seems to come out more clearly if some kind of
reciprocal form is used, as in RSV.

But: the Hebrew conjunction here is the same one that is often translated
"and," but in this case it is necessary to render it by something that shows the sharp
contrast between cheating a fellow Israelite and showing reverence for God.

You shall fear your God: the future tense has an imperative meaning, as is
often the case elsewhere in Leviticus. On the meaning of "fear God," see 19.3,14.

For I am the LORD your God: compare 18.2. The transition word **for** or
"because" indicates that it is the presence of God that should be the basis for the
Israelites not cheating each other.

TEV Section Heading: **"The Problem of the Seventh Year."**

Some other possible models for the section heading at this point may be
"Provision for the seventh year" or "God will provide food for the year of rest."

25.18   RSV   TEV

   "Therefore you shall do my   Obey all the LORD's laws and
statutes, and keep my ordinances   commands, so that you may live in
and perform them; so you will dwell   safety in the land.
in the land securely.

Therefore: the connecting word in Hebrew is the common one most often translated "and" and is sometimes left untranslated altogether. The RSV rendering gives the impression of a stronger relationship between this verse and the previous one than actually exists. Since this is the beginning of a new paragraph, it may be better to leave it untranslated here.

Do . . . keep . . . perform: the verbs translated **do** and **keep** are identical in Hebrew, although the second occurrence is accompanied by another word that reinforces the meaning. And the verb rendered **perform** has a very similar meaning. Therefore it is possible in some languages to translate the three as a single verb. Compare TEV "**Obey**."

Statutes, and . . . ordinances: see 18.4,5 and 19.37.

Securely: this indicates the absence of danger, threat or worry, whether from enemies, poor harvests, or whatever source.

25.19 RSV	TEV
The land will yield its fruit, and you will eat your fill, and dwell in it securely.	The land will produce its crops, and you will have all you want to eat and will live in safety.

The land: in Hebrew the same word may mean "earth [soil]" and "land." In other languages it will be most natural to use the word for "soil" in this context.

Yield its fruit: or "yield its harvest" (NEB), or "yield its crops" (Mft), since the term translated **fruit** is meant to be understood in its broadest possible sense.

Eat your fill: TEV conveys the meaning more clearly. Other possible models may be "be satisfied (or, filled) with the food produced," "never lack food," or "have food in abundance" (NAB).

Dwell in it securely: this is almost word-for-word the same as in verse 18. If the receptor language accepts such repetition, the translator may simply copy the previous rendering. But if variety is called for, a synonymous phrase may be used. For example, "live there without worry" or "have no problems living there."

25.20 RSV	TEV
And if you say, 'What shall we eat in the seventh year, if we may not sow or gather in our crop?'	But someone may ask what there will be to eat during the seventh year, when no fields are planted and no crops gathered.

And: since what follows is in contrast with the idea of living in the land without any worries, it is perhaps better to use a conjunction that marks this contrast, as in TEV.

If you say: this is a hypothetical situation where someone might wonder how the people would be fed during the Rest Year. It is not so much a question from one person to another, but a kind of "thinking out loud." NJB has "In case you should ask

. . . ." In many languages it will be more natural to avoid a direct quotation and to begin the verse "But if you are wondering . . . ."

25.21   RSV   TEV

I will command my blessing upon you in the sixth year, so that it will bring forth fruit for three years.

The LORD will bless the land in the sixth year so that it will produce enough food for two years.

I: this should be changed to "**The LORD**" in those languages where indirect discourse is being used. If direct discourse is used, it may be wise to remind the reader more specifically of the subject, using something like "I, the LORD."

Blessing upon you . . . so that it will bring forth fruit: the wording of RSV reflects the Hebrew but may be confusing. The pronoun **it** refers to the land. The land will produce in such abundance that the Israelites (**you**) will be blessed with plenty to eat during the Rest Year.

For three years: certain commentators think that these three years are counted in the Hebrew way:

1st year: the end of the sixth year, from the spring harvest to the autumn;

2nd year: the entire seventh year, from autumn to autumn;

3rd year: the eighth year, from autumn to the spring harvest.

If this is the case, the entire period would cover twenty-four months and should be translated "for two years" in those languages that count as in English (see TEV and GECL). But in those languages using a system of counting like that of the Israelites, it will be better translated **for three years**. Another solution is to make the whole period more explicit, with something like "for the year before the Rest Year, the Rest Year itself, and until the next harvest," although this may be a bit awkward in some languages.

Others have suggested that the period of three years is intended to cover those cases when the Rest Year and the Year of Restoration came back to back (see NJB footnote). But this is less likely.

25.22   RSV   TEV

When you sow in the eighth year, you will be eating old produce; until the ninth year, when its produce comes in, you shall eat the old.

When you plant your fields in the eighth year, you will still be eating what you harvested during the sixth year, and you will have enough to eat until the crops you plant that year are harvested.

The eighth year: that is, the year after the Rest Year or the first year in the new cycle of seven years. Sowing was permitted at the beginning of this year (in the fall), and the harvest took place in the following spring. In the meantime the people were fed by the previously harvested crop.

Old produce . . . the old: the use of the word **old** may convey the idea of staleness in some languages. But since the grain was well preserved, this idea should be avoided. TEV does so by translating "**what you harvested during the sixth year.**" It should not be necessary to repeat this a second time as in RSV.

Until the ninth year: or "until the crops you planted [in the eighth year] are harvested."

TEV Section Heading: "**Restoration of Property.**"

Other possible section headings are "How to redeem property" or "Giving back (or, Returning) land that was sold."

25.23 RSV	TEV
The land shall not be sold in perpetuity, for the land is mine; for you are strangers and sojourners with me.	Your land must not be sold on a permanent basis, because you do not own it; it belongs to God, and you are like foreigners who are allowed to make use of it.

The land: this refers to any piece of property owned by an Israelite. TEV uses the possessive pronoun "**Your**" in order to indicate the land of any Israelite.

Be sold: the passive formulation will have to be translated actively in many languages. The verse will then begin with something like "You must not sell any of your land . . . ."

In perpetuity: more literally, "for completion." But the expression really gives the idea of selling without any hope of recovering the possession. In all the Old Testament, this word is found only here and in verse 30 below. The meaning to be conveyed is something like "so that it belongs to the buyer forever" or "with no hope of getting the thing back." NJV renders the idea with the expression "beyond reclaim."

The land is mine: this gives the reason for the prohibition against selling land on a permanent basis. The people of Israel are resident aliens or passing guests in a land that does not ultimately belong to them but to the LORD, who placed them there. If indirect discourse is being used, the pronoun **mine** will have to be translated "God's" or "the LORD's."

Strangers and sojourners with me: that is, resident aliens or passing visitors. See 16.29 and 22.10. With respect to God, the owner of all things, the people of Israel are no more than guests or tenants, even if they think of themselves as proprietors of the land. In many instances it may be clearer if the Israelites are said to be "like" aliens or guests.

25.24   RSV   TEV

And in all the country you possess,   When land is sold, the right of
you shall grant a redemption of the   the original owner to buy it back
land.   must be recognized.

In all the country you possess: the word translated **country** here is the same
as translated **land** at the end of the verse and in the previous verse. The whole
phrase is intended to emphasize the general nature of the rule. It applies "throughout the whole land which you possess [as tenants]."

You shall grant a redemption of the land: this very condensed statement was
understandable to the Israelites who were familiar with the custom, but most modern
readers require a translation that is more explicit. Mft translates "you must allow the
land to be bought back." Another model can be "You must permit the person who
sold the land to buy it back." The verses that follow spell out the conditions under
which such **redemption** could take place.

25.25   RSV   TEV

   "If your brother becomes poor,   If an Israelite becomes poor and is
and sells part of his property, then   forced to sell his land, his closest
his next of kin shall come and re-   relative is to buy it back.
deem what his brother has sold.

Your brother: to whom does the pronoun **your** (singular in Hebrew) refer?
This appears to be a general rule for all Israelites and should therefore be translated
so that it is understood as such. NEB has "When one of you is reduced to poverty
. . . ." It is not advisable to translate the word **brother** literally, since this will almost
certainly be misunderstood in many languages.

Sells: TEV makes explicit the fact that the person is forced to sell against his
will by the circumstances.

Next of kin: the Hebrew term used here is closely related to the verb **redeem**
used in this same verse. It is sometimes translated "redeemer" (see Job 19.25) or
"avenger" (Num 35.19). This is because of the Israelite custom that required a close
relative to act as protector of any person in difficulty. He was required to redeem the
person if he was sold into slavery, or redeem his property if he lost it due to
circumstances beyond his control, and he was even required to avenge the death of
his relative. The term is probably best translated in this context by an expression that
brings out both the kinship and the responsibility of redeeming his relative or his
relative's property. This is done, for example, in the NEB rendering, "his next-of-kin
who has the duty of redemption." However, some have suggested that it would be
better to speak of the "right" of redemption rather than the "duty."

Come and redeem: the common Hebrew practice of using two verbs (compare
"conceives and bears" in 12.2) to convey a single main idea does not necessarily
mean that two verbs will be required in the receptor language in every such case.
Here, the verb **come** may be left implicit, since **redeem** or "buy back" is more
important. The verb **redeem** is central to the thought of the Old Testament. It

describes the giving of something in exchange for another item or for the life of a person. In some cultures the verb used to describe the ransoming of slaves may be equally appropriate for property. Compare Exodus 6.6 and 13.13.

25.26	RSV	TEV

If a man has no one to redeem it, and then himself becomes prosperous and finds sufficient means to redeem it,	A man who has no relative to buy it back may later become prosperous and have enough to buy it back himself.

If a man: commentators argue about whether this refers to the same man as in verse 25 or to a different person. But the meaning is not radically changed in either case. Probably it is better to think of it in terms of a separate case, since there is no definite article in the Hebrew. If this is true, some languages will require a transition word like "Or," "But," or "However."

No one to redeem it: the word used here is the same as in verse 25, but the translation may be shortened here, since the complete information is given in the previous verse.

Then himself becomes prosperous: in some languages one may say "earns a lot of money" or "gets rich." TEV adds the implicit information "**later**," which may be a good idea for a number of other languages.

Finds sufficient means to redeem it: literally "and his own hand reaches (or, acquires) sufficient to his redemption." That is, his new found wealth is adequate to pay his master the price required to buy back his land (see the following verse).

25.27	RSV	TEV

let him reckon the years since he sold it and pay back the overpayment to the man to whom he sold it; and he shall return to his property.	In that case he must pay to the man who bought it a sum that will make up for the years remaining until the next Year of Restoration, when he would in any event recover his land.

Since TEV begins this verse with a new sentence, it is necessary to make the relationship with the preceding verse clear. This is done by means of the words "**In that case . . . .**"

The years since he sold it: literally, "the years of its value." This may also be expressed as "the number of years that the alienation would have lasted" (NJB).

Pay back the overpayment: NJV reads "refund the difference." The word translated **overpayment** in RSV really means "balance." The man who is buying back his land must subtract the value of the crops harvested from the original price and pay the balance. Another way of saying this is that he must pay the value of the crops for the time remaining until the next Year of Restoration (compare TEV).

Return to his property: that is, take back his land. See verses 10 and 13.

25.28 RSV	TEV
But if he has not sufficient means to get it back for himself, then what he sold shall remain in the hand of him who bought it until the year of jubilee; in the jubilee it shall be released, and he shall return to his property.	But if he does not have enough money to buy the land back, it remains under the control of the man who bought it until the next Year of Restoration. In that year it will be returned to its original owner.

If he has not sufficient means: literally "if his hand does not acquire enough . . . ." Compare verse 26 above.

Remain in the hand: obviously this cannot be meant literally, since a plot of land cannot be held in the hand. The expression merely indicates that the land in question will continue to be considered the possession of the buyer until the Year of Restoration.

The second part of this verse contains two problems:

(1) **In the jubilee it shall be released**: literally "he (or, it) will go out in the jubilee." The subject of the verb may be either the buyer (who would go out of the land that is restored to the original owner) or the land (which would go out of the hands of the buyer on restitution of the land to the original owner). This latter solution is followed by RSV, TEV, and most other versions consulted.

(2) **He shall return to his property**: here also, the subject is ambiguous. It may be the buyer, who is required to return to his own property, since he has to give up the acquired land. Or it may be the original owner, who returns to the land that belonged for a time to the buyer. The second interpretation seems better adapted to this context and would have the same meaning as in verses 27 and 28.

25.29 RSV	TEV
"If a man sells a dwelling house in a walled city, he may redeem it within a whole year after its sale; for a full year he shall have the right of redemption.	If a man sells a house in a walled city, he has the right to buy it back during the first full year from the date of sale.

This verse deals with a different hypothetical case concerning a house within a city. Therefore a new paragraph is required. And the first sentence may also begin with a word like "Or" to make this clear. In some languages it may even be necessary to begin with "Another case: . . . ."

A dwelling house: in many languages the word **dwelling** will be considered redundant and may be omitted. In others it may be necessary to say "a house in which people live," in order to distinguish it from other types of buildings such as those used for animals or for the storage of grain, etc.

In a walled city: a person who lived in a fortified town was probably not a farmer. He might be deprived of his residence (see verse 30) without losing his means of livelihood. But the field (see verses 23-28) and the house (verse 31) of the farmer are considered essential to his work.

Within a whole year: in this case the right of redemption was limited to the first complete year after the sale had taken place.

For a full year: literally "for days (or, times)." The word for **year** is not specifically mentioned here, but the expression is usually taken as indicating a definite limit and referring back to the **whole year**. AT translates "throughout that time," and NJV has "throughout the ages." But other versions understand this to be an emphasis on the temporary nature of the rule. NEB has "for a time." And TOB has "is temporary." The JB rendering may be best: "is limited to a year." If the right of redemption was not exercised during that period, then it was permanently forfeited.

25.30 RSV TEV

If it is not redeemed within a full year, then the house that is in the walled city shall be made sure in perpetuity to him who bought it, throughout his generations; it shall not be released in the jubilee.

But if he does not buy it back within the year, he loses the right of repurchase, and the house becomes the permanent property of the purchaser and his descendants; it will not be returned in the Year of Restoration.

The pronoun **it** at the beginning of the verse refers to the house inside the city walls mentioned in the previous verse. Later in this verse the Hebrew text has "a house that is in a city without walls," but there is an indication in the margin that it is to be read **that is in the walled city** (see HOTTP, pages 200-201). Most versions follow the marginal reading. However, the repetition of this information (found in the previous verse) will probably be unnecessary in many languages.

Shall be made sure . . . to him who bought it: that is, after the expiration of the one year limit, the new owner will never be required by law to give it up to its former owner. This is seen by some commentators as a concession to the growing urbanization in Israel. The TEV rendering changes the point of view by stating that the former owner "loses the right of repurchase," but the meaning is essentially the same. Another way of framing the same truth may be "neither he [the new owner] nor his descendants will ever be forced to sell it back again."

In perpetuity: see verse 23.

Throughout his generations: or "for him and for his descendants."

Released: see verse 28.

The jubilee: see verse 10.

25.31 RSV TEV

But the houses of the villages which have no wall around them shall be reckoned with the fields of the country; they may be redeemed, and they shall be released in the jubilee.

But houses in unwalled villages are to be treated like fields; the original owner has the right to buy them back, and they are to be returned in the Year of Restoration.

This verse is the counterpart of verses 29 and 30 above. Since there is a contrast between the disposition of houses inside the cities and those in the countryside, this part should be introduced by a conjunction marking contrast.

Reckoned with the fields of the country: or "treated as property in the open country" (NEB), or "considered as situated in the open country" (NJB).

May be redeemed . . . shall be released: these passive verb forms will have to be rendered actively in many languages. An alternative phrasing may be "the owners can buy them back and take possession of them again in the Year of Restoration."

Jubilee: see verse 10.

25.32

RSV	TEV
Nevertheless the cities of the Levites, the houses in the cities of their possession, the Levites may redeem at any time.	However, Levites have the right to buy back at any time their property in the cities assigned to them.

The text of verses 32 and 33 is especially difficult and sometimes quite obscure. The translator must make a special effort to express the most likely meaning of the passage as clearly as possible.

Nevertheless: since this verse gives an exception to the rule concerning houses inside walled cities, it is introduced by a strong contrasting conjunction. The Levites did not own any land except that which was right around the cities that were assigned to them. Another more explicit means of indicating that these two verses constitute an exception to the general rule is to begin by saying "But the case of the Levites is different. They have the right . . . ."

Verses 32 and 33 contain the only mention of the **Levites** in the entire book of Leviticus. The word is derived from the name of Levi, one of the sons of Jacob (see Gen 29.34). Originally it designated "descendants of Levi" or "members of the tribe of Levi" (see Josh 14.3). These people were given the oversight of the religious and cultic rites of Israel. The descendants of Aaron made up the priestly class (see 1.5), while others, called "Levites" (see Num 3.6-10 and Luke 10.32), were involved in various tasks under the direction of the priests. It is not absolutely essential that this term always be translated in the same way; in its more general sense, it may be rendered "members of the tribe of Levi" or "descendants of Levi." Its more specific meaning may be rendered by a proper name based on the name of Levi (**Levites**), or by "servants of the priests," or some other term indicating their religious function. In this context it is probably best to translate it by the more specific meaning.

The cities of the Levites: see Numbers 35.1-8; Joshua 21; and 1 Chronicles 6.39-66. It may be better to translate "the cities assigned to the Levites," following TEV.

25.33   RSV   TEV

And if one of the Levites does not exercise*ᵐ* his right of redemption, then the house that was sold in a city of their possession shall be released in the jubilee; for the houses in the cities of the Levites are their possession among the people of Israel.

ᵐ Compare Vg: Heb *exercises*

If a house in one of these cities is sold by a Levite and is not bought back, it must be returned in the Year of Restoration,*ᵐ* because the houses which the Levites own in their cities are their permanent property among the people of Israel.

ᵐ Probable text If a house . . . Restoration; *Hebrew unclear.*

The Hebrew text of this verse is very confused, and most English translations as well as the ancient versions have made some changes in order to make sense of it. Two textual problems exist: (1) The Hebrew has no negative and reads "If a Levite does redeem . . . ." But the Latin adds the negation which may well have been a part of the original: "If a Levite does not redeem . . . ." So RSV has **does not exercise his right of redemption**. (2) Further in this same verse the Hebrew has ". . . a house and a town," but the Greek version reads "a house in a town." (Compare RSV **the house . . . in a city**). The copyist must have become very tired while working on this verse and therefore made some mistakes. For this reason most modern versions have acknowledged the difficulties in the Hebrew text and have made both of the corrections suggested above.

If one of the Levites does not exercise his right of redemption: this phrase, corrected according to what the original is assumed to have been, is still subject to more than one interpretation. TEV takes it to mean **"If a house . . . is sold by a Levite and is not bought back . . . ."** But it is possible that by not accepting the first of the two suggested textual changes (the addition of the negative) to understand "If a Levite buys a house . . . and its original owner buys it back from him, it returns to the Levite in the Year of Jubilee" (FRCL; see also Noth's commentary, page 191). This solution has the advantage of making less changes in the Hebrew text and follows the recommendation of HOTTP (pages 201-202).

Shall be released in the jubilee: see verse 28.

Among the people of Israel: literally, "among the sons of Israel." But this may be better translated in this context "among the other Israelites." This will avoid the danger of giving the impression to untrained readers that Levites were not Israelites.

25.34   RSV   TEV

But the fields of common land belonging to their cities may not be sold; for that is their perpetual possession.

But the pasture land around the Levite cities shall never be sold; it is their property forever.

The fields of common land belonging to their cities: this whole expression more than likely refers to the unenclosed pasture land surrounding the cities of the Levites.

Be sold: this passive will have to be translated actively in many languages. And this will require a restructuring of the verse. A possible model may be "No one can ever sell the pasture land . . . ," or "The Levites may never sell . . . ," or "No one may buy . . . from the Levites."

It is their perpetual possession: that is, they do not have the right to sell this land even for a limited period of time. This may be expressed as "it must always belong to them," or "it must remain permanently in the hands of the Levites," or "it must always belong to the priestly family." This is in contrast with their houses, which could be temporarily sold to persons outside the priestly class.

TEV Section Heading: **"Loans to the Poor."**

Some other possible models for this heading are "Help for poor people," or "Laws about poor people," or "Rules about loans." In TEV the heading covers only verses 35-38. But some versions give a more general heading intended to cover the remainder of the chapter. NEB, for example, has "The Fate of the Poor," which includes the matter of enslavement and release as well as loans to the poor.

25.35	RSV	TEV

"And if your brother becomes poor, and cannot maintain himself with you, you shall maintain him; as a stranger and a sojourner he shall live with you.

If a fellow Israelite living near you becomes poor and cannot support himself, you must provide for him as you would for a hired man, so that he can continue to live near you.

Your brother: taken in the most general sense of "fellow countryman." See verse 25 (as well as 10.4,6).

Cannot maintain himself: literally "his hand has failed." The meaning of this phrase is clearly that the person is unable to take care of himself. This may be expressed in a variety of ways in other languages. For example, "is unable to provide for himself," or "is no longer able," or "cannot feed himself."

With you: this expression occurs twice in the RSV rendering of this verse. While it may give the impression of people living together in the same house, the real meaning is rather "among you" (NJV) or **"living near you"** (TEV). Mft translates "beside you." The first occurrence of these words should probably be shifted forward in the receptor-language rendering of this verse.

You shall maintain him: literally "you will strengthen him." That is, "you must take care of him" or "you must provide for his needs."

As: following the Hebrew text literally, some versions omit this word and understand "even though he is a stranger . . ." (compare KJV). But the interpretation **as** . . . is accepted by almost all modern versions and is a legitimate reading of the text (see HOTTP, page 203). The meaning to be translated is therefore "you must help him as you would a resident alien or a passing guest." Of course this rule loses much of its force in a culture where foreigners and hired persons are not treated

390

properly. In such cases it may be necessary to reinforce the meaning of the biblical message by saying something like "you must treat him well, as you are supposed to do for aliens . . ." or "you must take adequate care of his needs, as Jews [habitually] do for foreigners . . . ."

A stranger and a sojourner: see 16.29 and 22.10.

25.36	RSV	TEV

Take no interest from him or increase, but fear your God; that your brother may live beside you.	Do not charge him any interest, but obey God and let your fellow Israelite live near you.

Interest . . . or increase: these ideas are very difficult to express in those cultures where such practices are unknown or uncommon. In the first case, according to some scholars, the interest is paid regularly and then the original loan is paid in a lump sum at the end of the period. In the second case these same scholars maintain that there is no regular payment of interest in the intervening period, but a larger amount than borrowed must be paid in the end. Exodus 22.25 deals only with the first type, and some commentators suggest that the Leviticus rule was designed to block a loophole that moneylenders had found. As to the actual translation of the meaning of these two words, one may propose a restructuring that includes both cases: "Do not make him pay back more that he [originally] borrowed . . . ." Another possibility in some languages may be "do not make him pay rent on money borrowed or pay back more than he borrowed." It should be noted, however, that there is the distinct possibility that these two terms are virtually synonymous and may be translated by a single term.

Fear your God: see 19.14. But here the idea of obedience is involved. When one stands in awe of God and respects him, the result is obedience.

Your brother: see verses 25 and 35.

Beside you: the same word translated "with you" but meaning "among you" at the end of verse 35.

25.37	RSV	TEV

You shall not lend him your money at interest, nor give him your food for profit.	Do not make him pay interest on the money you lend him, and do not make a profit on the food you sell him.

This verse further develops the thought of 36a concerning interest of any kind. It is not only money that is involved, but loans of any sort (specifically food).

Lend him your money at interest: in some languages it may be necessary to say something like "Do not give him money with the condition that he return to you more than you give him" or, as suggested above, "do not make him pay rent on money borrowed."

Give him your food for profit: as in the above case, it may be necessary to say "Do not sell him food for more than it cost you" or "Do not give him food and expect him to repay you more than you give." The latter is perhaps better, in the sense that it involves more of a friendly loan of food than a commercial transaction.

25.38	RSV	TEV

I am the LORD your God, who brought you forth out of the land of Egypt to give you the land of Canaan, and to be your God.	This is the command of the LORD your God, who brought you out of Egypt in order to give you the land of Canaan and to be your God.

I am the LORD your God: see 18.2. This verse constitutes a concluding statement and is the basis for the above requirements. This is brought out by the TEV rendering "**This is the command of the LORD your God . . . .**"

Who brought you forth out of the land of Egypt: see 19.36. This reminder of the liberation from Egypt is accompanied by the mention of the gift of **the land of Canaan**, which provides the justification for all the preceding legislation concerning land (see verse 23: "for the land is mine").

To be your God: see 11.45; 22.33.

TEV Section Heading: "**Release of Slaves.**"

The remainder of this chapter deals with the problems of those who are compelled by economic circumstances to sell themselves into slavery in order to survive. Some other possible section headings are "Laws about slavery," or "Israelite slaves must be redeemed," or "No permanent slavery for the people of Israel."

25.39	RSV	TEV

"And if your brother becomes poor beside you, and sells himself to you, you shall not make him serve as a slave:	If a fellow Israelite living near you becomes so poor that he sells himself to you as a slave, you shall not make him do the work of a slave.

Your brother: see verses 25 and 35.

Beside you: see verses 35 and 36. It may be possible in some languages to leave this information implicit in this case.

Sells himself to you: TEV makes explicit "**as a slave.**" The money paid would presumably be used to repay debts, leaving the person still as impoverished as before and therefore obliged to remain a slave.

The Hebrew word usually translated **slave** designates a "subordinate," or someone who is under the authority of a person above him in a hierarchy. It may be used of a cabinet minister serving under a king, of an army officer under his supreme commander, or of a slave serving under his master. The context must determine whether the Hebrew word corresponds to a slave, a servant, or an inferior person with respect to his superior. One must take into consideration the social status and the degree of freedom the person has. The context of this verse clearly indicates that actual slavery is indicated.

In ancient times slavery took various forms. In Israel, a person reduced to slavery never experienced a situation so terrible as in Rome, for example, where one writer described a slave as "a tool that speaks." Depending on the character of his master, a slave may have had a more or less carefree existence that was relatively pleasant. Generally speaking an Israelite slave was integrated into the family and religious life of his master. There were even cases where a slave would ask to remain in the service of his master (see Exo 21.1-11 and Deut 15.12-18).

You shall not make him serve as a slave: that is, he is not to be required to perform the duties that may be expected of a non-Israelite who had been taken as a slave. In some cases it may be necessary to translate "do not treat him like other slaves" or "do not make him work like an ordinary slave."

25.40   RSV   TEV

he shall be with you as a hired ser-   **He shall stay with you as a hired**
vant and as a sojourner. He shall   **man and serve you until the next**
serve with you until the year of the   **Year of Restoration.**
jubilee;

Depending on the translation of the previous verse, it may be advisable to begin this verse with a strong contrasting conjunction like "rather" or "but."

A hired servant: this is in contrast with the word "slave" in the previous verse. A hired servant was a person who had considerably more freedom than a slave, since he agreed to do a job and received pay for it. He did not perform tasks that involved humiliation, since these were normally left to slaves. The point of this verse is that the poor Israelite was technically a slave and received no salary, but he was to be treated like the salaried worker.

And as a sojourner: this has been omitted from TEV for some unknown reason, but should definitely be included in the receptor-language translation. The lot of the resident alien living in the house of an Israelite was even better than that of the hired servant. So this represents a further softening in the attitude toward the Israelite slave.

The year of the jubilee: see verse 10.

25.41   RSV   TEV

then he shall go out from you, he   **At that time he and his children shall**
and his children with him, and go   **leave you and return to his family**
back to his own family, and return to   **and to the property of his ancestors.**
the possession of his fathers.

Then: while the Hebrew text has only the common conjunction usually translated "and," most versions recognize that the context requires something stronger at this point. TEV has "**At that time,**" referring to the Year of Restoration.

He and his children: the children are not necessarily slaves with their father. They may be children born during the time that the father was serving as a slave.

Go back to his own family: this does not simply indicate a change of address or a moving from one house to another. It involves the liberation from slavery (however benevolent that slavery may have been) and a return to the status of a free person. Compare verse 10.

Return to the possession of his fathers: the word **fathers** is to be understood in the more general sense of all those who have gone before in the family line. Hence TEV "**ancestors.**" The **possession** refers to the family property. NEB translates the last two phrases as "he shall . . . go back to his family and to his ancestral property."

25.42	RSV	TEV

For they are my servants, whom I brought forth out of the land of Egypt; they shall not be sold as slaves.	The people of Israel are the LORD's slaves, and he brought them out of Egypt; they must not be sold into slavery.

They: the third person plural pronoun actually refers to the people of Israel, as indicated by the context that follows. The TEV rendering makes this reference clear from the beginning, and this should probably be followed in most other languages.

My servants: the Hebrew word used here is actually "slave," as in verse 39, and should be so translated so that the connection between this statement and the previous verses may be clear. The people of Israel had been slaves of the Egyptians, but when they were delivered they became the property of the one who redeemed them, the LORD himself. If indirect discourse is being used, the pronoun **my** should be changed to "**the LORD's,**" as in TEV.

I brought forth: the pronoun **I** should become "**he**" in indirect discourse.

Slaves: this is the same word as translated **servants** at the beginning of this verse. The two should be translated similarly.

The last sentence in this verse may be introduced with a more explicit "This is why they must not be sold as slaves." This will clarify the relationship between what was said previously and this statement.

25.43	RSV	TEV

You shall not rule over him with harshness, but shall fear your God.	Do not treat them harshly, but obey your God.

Rule . . . with harshness: these words are very strong and may be translated "treat with brutality" or "deal violently with."

Him: the pronoun here is singular, since it refers to any such person, that is, any Israelite that had sold himself into slavery (see verse 39). The singular, however, may be more naturally translated as a plural in some languages.

Fear your God: see 19.3,14,32; 25.17,36.

25.44   RSV   TEV

As for your male and female slaves | **If you need slaves, you may buy**
whom you may have: you may buy | **them from the nations around you.**
male and female slaves from among
the nations that are round about you.

This verse shows that the institution of slavery itself is not questioned. The practice could continue so long as the slaves were not taken from among the people of Israel.

As for . . . : literally "And . . . ." It may be better to restructure the beginning of this verse to say something like "Since you have [male and female] slaves, you should buy them from . . . ." TEV attempts to accomplish the same thing by beginning **"If you need slaves . . . ."**

Male and female slaves: in most languages it will be assumed that both males and females are concerned, if no mention is made of sex (see TEV). And the inclusion of these details may be considered stylistically unacceptable. The second occurrence in the RSV text is especially heavy.

Nations: see 18.24.

25.45   RSV   TEV

You may also buy from among the | **You may also buy the children of the**
strangers who sojourn with you and | **foreigners who are living among you.**
their families that are with you, who | **Such children born in your land may**
have been born in your land; and | **become your property,**
they may be your property.

This verse provides two additional details with regard to the foreign slaves mentioned in the previous verse. To speak of "the nations that are round about you" (verse 44) seems to exclude foreigners living within the land of Israel. But the words of this verse, **among the strangers who sojourn with you . . .** , clearly indicate that they may also be taken as slaves. And to avoid the impression that this concerned only newly-arrived foreigners, the writer also adds **and their families . . . who have been born in your land**.

There are therefore three categories of foreigners who could become slaves in Israel:

1. Those living in the surrounding countries (verse 44).
2. Those who personally immigrated into the land of Israel (45a).
3. Those whose ancestors had earlier immigrated into Israel (45b).

Buy: the RSV rendering does not provide an object for this verb, but it may be understood to be "slaves." TEV omits the preposition **from** and takes the object to be "**the children of the foreigners**" (leaving "as slaves" implicit here).

From among the strangers who sojourn with you: literally, "from the sons of the foreigners." This may be understood in its more literal sense, "**the children of the foreigners**" (TEV, NEB, and NJB), but it is also possible that "sons of" in this case merely means "members of a group" (compare 1.5 and 1.14). The emphasis is not necessarily on the age of these foreigners born in the land.

They may be your property: this phrase emphasizes the difference between the foreigner who becomes a slave, and a fellow Israelite who is required by difficult circumstances to work for a time for his countryman. An Israelite is never really the **property** of his fellow Israelite.

25.46   RSV   TEV

You may bequeath them to your sons after you, to inherit as a possession for ever; you may make slaves of them, but over your brethren the people of Israel you shall not rule, one over another, with harshness.

and you may leave them as an inheritance to your sons, whom they must serve as long as they live. But you must not treat any of your fellow Israelites harshly.

In some languages it may be advisable to introduce this verse with words like "Later on . . ." as a translation of RSV **after you**. This will show more clearly that the inheritance was to occur at a later time. But it has been left implicit in TEV.

Bequeath . . . to inherit: these two words are simply different ways of looking at a single transaction. The father "bequeathed" the slaves to his sons, and the sons "inherited" them. In languages where there are no specific words for such transactions, the first word may be rendered "pass them on to your sons," and the second as "receive them as their own."

As a possession forever: this is in contrast with the case of the Israelite, who was to be freed during the Year of Restoration. The foreigner was permanently kept as a slave of the Israelite family.

But: this may also be translated "in contrast" or "on the other hand." This is a reiteration of what has been previously stated.

Rule . . . with harshness: see verse 43.

25.47   RSV   TEV

"If a stranger or sojourner with you becomes rich, and your brother beside him becomes poor and sells himself to the stranger or sojourner with you, or to a member of the stranger's family,

Suppose a foreigner living with you becomes rich, while a fellow Israelite becomes poor and sells himself as a slave to that foreigner or to a member of his family.

This verse begins a new paragraph dealing with a prosperous foreigner living in the land of Israel. Since it is a hypothetical consideration, TEV begins with the word "**Suppose**" as a translation of **If**. Another way of saying this in some languages is "Let us say that . . . ." This formula may also serve to make more explicit the fact that this person is living among the people of Israel.

Becomes rich: this is more than the opposite of "**becomes poor**" in verse 35 and later in this same verse. In this case the foreigner has more than enough to take care of himself. He becomes sufficiently wealthy to buy slaves. It may have to be translated "earns a great deal of money."

Beside him: this probably carries the idea "in the same area" or "living near him." But in many languages this will be understood without being made explicit in the translation.

With you . . . with you: see verses 35 and 36.

Member: the corresponding Hebrew word is found only here in all the Old Testament. Consequently its meaning is not absolutely certain. It probably comes from a word meaning "root" or "origin." Both Mft and NAB take it to mean "descendant." And NJV translates it "an offshoot."

25.48 RSV TEV

then after he is sold he may be re-deemed; one of his brothers may redeem him, / After he is sold, he still has the right to be bought back. One of his broth-ers

After he is sold: this passive expression may have to be rendered "after someone (or, the rich man) has bought him . . . ." In some languages it may be possible to leave this information implicit.

He may be redeemed: transformed into an active sentence, this will be "a person can buy him back," or in other languages one may say "it is not forbidden that someone should buy him back."

One of his brothers: the Hebrew word is to be taken here in the more restricted sense of "son of the same father." See the above discussion on the right of redemption under verse 25.

25.49 RSV TEV

or his uncle, or his cousin may re-deem him, or a near kinsman belong-ing to his family may redeem him; or if he grows rich he may redeem him-self. / or his uncle or his cousin or another of his close relatives may buy him back; or if he himself earns enough, he may buy his own freedom.

His uncle: this refers to the paternal uncle of the unfortunate Israelite.

His cousin: this is the son of the paternal uncle.

A near kinsman belonging to his family: that is, "**another**" near kinsman, since the uncle and cousin are obviously near relatives. On the term **near kinsman** see 18.6. And on the word **family** see 20.5.

If he grows rich: literally "if his hand acquires," as in verses 26, 28, and 47. It is difficult to see how the TEV rendering can be correct, since a slave was not able to "earn" money. Does the text presuppose some kind of unforeseen inheritance or fortunate discovery of unknown wealth? Probably a more general expression like "if he acquires the means" (NAB) is more suitable here.

Redeem himself: or "pay for his own release (or, freedom)." Compare verse 25 above.

25.50   RSV   TEV

He shall reckon with him who bought him from the year when he sold himself to him until the year of jubilee, and the price of his release shall be according to the number of years; the time he was with his owner shall be rated as the time of a hired servant.	He must consult the one who bought him, and they must count the years from the time he sold himself until the next Year of Restoration and must set the price for his release on the basis of the wages paid a hired man.

He: this seems to refer to the slave himself, in the case where he had prospered and was able to pay for his own freedom. But it may also envision the case where one of his relatives appears with the money necessary to buy him back. In this case it will still be the unfortunate Israelite who sold himself into slavery who must now go through the accounting procedure with the man who originally bought him. In any case it may be better in some languages to translate the pronoun **he** as "the Israelite slave" or something similar.

According to the number of years: that is, according to the time remaining until the next Year of Restoration. Here the principle is the same as in other cases of redemption before the jubilee year (see, for example, verse 27). The equivalent of the wages of a hired laborer for the remaining period was to be paid. The idea behind this was that, since the Israelites were the property of the LORD, they were simply hired out to others for a limited period. This seems to indicate that a person who was heavily in debt could sell himself and then be redeemed by a relative for a lesser amount.

25.51-52   RSV   TEV

51 If there are still many years, according to them he shall refund out of the price paid for him the price for his redemption. 52 If there remain but a few years until the year of jubilee, he shall make a reckoning	51-52 He must refund a part of the purchase price according to the number of years left,

**with him; according to the years of
service due from him he shall refund
the money for his redemption.**

The wording of RSV, following the Hebrew, is long and repetitious, but the
essential meaning is captured by TEV in fewer words and a much simpler structure.

He shall refund: that is, the Israelite must pay back an amount equivalent to
the value of a hired worker for the number of years left until the next Year of
Restoration.

25.53	RSV	TEV

As a servant hired year by year shall he be with him; he shall not rule with harshness over him in your sight.	**as if he had been hired on an annual basis. His master must not treat him harshly.**

As a hired servant . . . : many see in this statement an implicit clause, "As
long as he remains with his master he shall be treated as a hired servant" (FRCL).
However, TEV sees it as a hypothetical statement linked with the previous verse. This
is also the preferred solution of NJB.

Rule with harshness: see verses 43 and 46.

In your sight: the pronoun is singular but is probably to be taken as a
collective form referring to the people of Israel as a whole. Since the handling of an
Israelite slave by a wealthy foreigner took place in the presence of other Israelites,
they were charged with the responsibility of assuring that the treatment was
benevolent. This detail seems to have been omitted by TEV and may have to be left
implicit in other languages, since its inclusion may be understood to mean that the
master could mistreat the slave as long as no one was looking.

25.54	RSV	TEV

And if he is not redeemed by these means, then he shall be released in the year of jubilee, he and his children with him.	**If he is not set free in any of these ways, he and his children must be set free in the next Year of Restoration.**

By these means: that is, by paying for his own freedom or by being redeemed
by a relative. One may also translate "**in any of these ways**" or "by any means."

Be released: this passive may be translated actively as "his master must release
him . . . ."

In the year of the jubilee: that is, the next Year of Restoration that will take
place. See verse 10.

And his children with him: see verse 41.

25.55   RSV   TEV

For to me the people of Israel are servants, they are my servants whom I brought forth out of the land of Egypt: I am the LORD your God.	An Israelite cannot be a permanent slave, because the people of Israel are the LORD's slaves. He brought them out of Egypt; he is the LORD their God.

Some versions see this verse as the conclusion to chapter 25 and make no paragraph break here (RSV, TEV, NIV, NEB, NAB, AT, and NJV). In some of these versions this verse does not even begin a new sentence. JB makes it a separate paragraph, thus treating it as a kind of transition to chapter 26, but NJB joins it with the previous verse. Both FRCL and TOB take it as the beginning of a separate section (25.55–26.2) and place a section heading at this point. There is much to be said for the unity of 25.55–26.2, even though very few English versions respect it.

For: this transition word indicates that what follows is the basis for what precedes. It is because the people of Israel belong to the LORD that they cannot be kept permanently as slaves of any person.

Me . . . my . . . I . . . : as in the rest of this chapter, the question of direct versus indirect discourse must be considered. The first person singular pronouns must be changed to third person in those languages where direct discourse is not being used.

The phrase **to me the people of Israel are servants** is identical in meaning with **they are my servants**. But in both cases the word translated **servants** should rather be "**slaves**" as in TEV. See verses 39 and following.

I am the LORD your God: see 11.44.

Chapter 26

TEV Section Heading: **"Blessings for Obedience."**

As noted under 25.55, some versions begin a new section at the end of the previous chapter rather than here. However, the majority of versions take this as the starting point for the section on blessings (1-13) and cursings (14-45). The entire chapter may be seen as a kind of summary conclusion of what is contained in the book of Leviticus. It is very similar to passages found in the book of Deuteronomy (7.12-24; 28.1-14). Other possible titles are "Rewards for obedience" (NAB) or "The results of obeying God."

26.1

RSV	TEV
"You shall make for yourselves no idols and erect no graven image or pillar, and you shall not set up a figured stone in your land, to bow down to them; for I am the LORD your God.	The LORD said, "Do not make idols or set up statues, stone pillars, or carved stones to worship. I am the LORD your God.

This verse is a further development of what is said in 19.4, and also corresponds to the commandment in Exodus 20.4.

You shall make . . . no idols: the future tense with the negative is to be understood as a negative imperative. The pronoun **you** in this case is plural in Hebrew and stands in contrast to the singular in Exodus 20. But both pronouns clearly refer to the people of Israel.

This verse contains four different words or expressions referring to false gods (or attempts to represent the deity in physical form) that are forbidden to the people of Israel. In some languages it may be difficult to find four different synonymous terms, but an effort should be made to do so if possible:

(1) **Idols**: the root of the word thus translated really means "worthless; insufficient; inadequate." NAB translates it "false gods," while Mft has "unreal gods." In some languages it may be best translated "worthless (or, useless) things [used for worship]."

(2) **Graven image**: this refers to something fashioned into the shape of an object, animal, or a person. It may be made of stone, clay, wood, or metal. According to the context here, the purpose of making such a likeness was to provide an object that could be worshiped. It may be rendered "carved out to look like something," or "made to resemble something living," or something similar.

401

(3) **Pillar**: this probably refers to a long stone that was made to stand up by itself and served as an object of worship. It is the same term used in Genesis 28.18 and Exodus 24.4, when such objects were apparently acceptable in Hebrew worship. NEB has "sacred pillars," and JB translates "standing-stone," but NJB changes this to "cultic stones."

(4) **Figured stone**: compare Numbers 33.52. It is uncertain exactly what this refers to. The root meaning of the word has to do with the verb "to look." Some commentators therefore take it to refer to some sort of remarkable stone or mosaic at which people look with adoration. However, most English versions take it to refer to a stone that has been carved or shaped by human efforts to look like an object of worship.

To bow down to them: there is a possibility that this may have been intended to mean "bow down upon" (compare NEB), but most versions take it to refer to bowing down "before" something. The specific act of bowing down before any of these concrete representations of false gods constitutes an attitude of worship. In many languages it will be clearer and more natural to use a more general and inclusive term such as "to worship." But in other languages it will be possible to show both the physical position and the attitude of worship by saying something like "prostrate yourselves to show reverence" or "bow down to worship." The object of this verb (**them**) refers not merely to the last-mentioned noun, but to all false gods no matter what form they may take.

26.2   RSV   TEV

You shall keep my sabbaths and reverence my sanctuary: I am the LORD.

Keep the religious festivals and honor the place where I am worshiped. I am the LORD.

This verse is identical with 19.30. Translators should be sure that it is rendered the same, unless there are clear contextual reasons in the receptor language for not doing so.

26.3   RSV   TEV

"If you walk in my statutes and observe my commandments and do them,

"If you live according to my laws and obey my commands,

Walk in: meaning "to live by." A literal translation of the verb "to walk" would be misleading in many languages. Compare 18.3-5; 19.37; 25.18.

Statutes . . . commandments: on the first word, see 10.11 and compare also 18.3. On the second see 22.31.

26.4   RSV   TEV

then I will give you your rains in their season, and the land shall yield its increase, and the trees of the field shall yield their fruit.	I will send you rain at the right time, so that the land will produce crops and the trees will bear fruit.

Then: showing the result of the conditions stated in verse 3.

Your rains: the possessive form may be misleading. The meaning is "the rain that you need." In some cases it may be important to assure that the word used for **rains** is one that evokes positive feelings and not one that indicates devastation or harm to crops or people. The use of the plural, **rains**, is probably intended to refer to the various kinds of rains at different times of the year (autumn, winter, and spring), which would be necessary for a good harvest.

In their season: referring to the three seasons mentioned above. Each one would come at the expected and proper time. Another way of translating the meaning here is "**at the right time**" (NJB as well as TEV).

And the land shall yield its increase: or "the land will bring forth its crops." The word introducing this clause may be better translated "in order that," showing the relationship of cause and effect between the sending of the rains and the growing of crops. The word **land** here refers to cultivated land as opposed to places where people live. In some languages one may have to change the subject and say "the crops will produce food on the land . . . ." In others it will be adequate to say simply "the land will produce."

Trees of the field: the qualification "of the fields" may be left implicit in many languages, since it adds nothing to the essential meaning of the text.

26.5   RSV   TEV

And your threshing shall last to the time of vintage, and the vintage shall last to the time for sowing; and you shall eat your bread to the full, and dwell in your land securely.	Your crops will be so plentiful that you will still be harvesting grain when it is time to pick grapes, and you will still be picking grapes when it is time to plant grain. You will have all that you want to eat, and you can live in safety in your land.

Your threshing shall last to the time of vintage, and the vintage shall last to the time for sowing: these are images of abundant harvest. The fields will produce so much grain that the people must work until the grapes are ripe in order to separate the grain from the straw. Then the grapes will be so plentiful that the task of picking them will last until it was time to plant for the next grain crop. This is not intended to give the impression that the people are overworked, but that there was more than enough to eat and drink. TEV has made this more explicit by introducing this verse with "**Your crops will be so plentiful that . . . .**" Compare Amos 9.13.

403

You shall eat your bread to the full: the word **bread** here is intended to represent foods of all kinds. In many languages it will give the wrong idea if translated literally. This is especially true where bread is not a common element in the diet. Here it is better translated as "you will receive all the food you need" or "you will have food to eat in abundance" (NAB).

Dwell in your land securely: see 25.18,19.

26.6	RSV	TEV
	And I will give peace in the land, and you shall lie down, and none shall make you afraid; and I will remove evil beasts from the land, and the sword shall not go through your land.	"I will give you peace in your land, and you can sleep without being afraid of anyone. I will get rid of the dangerous animals in the land, and there will be no more war there.

Peace: this is the well-known Hebrew word *shalom*, which indicates much more than just "calm" or the absence of war. It refers to a more general situation of tranquillity and harmonious relations between people. It is a situation in which everything is as it should be, involving the total well-being of the persons in question.

Lie down: this implies "to go to sleep," and in many languages this will have to be made explicit, as TEV has done.

None: the corresponding Hebrew word may be taken either as meaning "no one" (the solution of most English versions) or more generally "nothing" (FRCL). In view of the context, "nothing" may be better if it is indeed more general in meaning and would include the idea of "no one."

I will remove evil beasts: literally "I will cause to cease . . . evil beasts." The word translated **evil** has been variously rendered "vicious" (NJV), "savage" (NIV), "**dangerous**" (NEB, TEV), "ravenous" (NAB), "wild" (AT, Mft). A word should be sought in the receptor language that refers to animals that are greatly feared and likely to cause harm or injury to people. In some languages this idea is conveyed by "catching animals."

The sword shall not go through your land: a literal translation of this expression may be amusing if not misleading in some languages. The sword here does not mean simply a single instrument of war. Rather it represents all the dangers and problems involved in a state of war. This phrase may therefore be translated as "Your enemies will no longer make war on you" or "No one will attack your land."

26.7	RSV	TEV
	And you shall chase your enemies, and they shall fall before you by the sword.	You will be victorious over your enemies;

You shall chase your enemies: that is, "**You will be victorious over**," or "win a remarkable victory," or "defeat the enemy convincingly."

They shall fall before you by the sword: this is merely another image of victory in battle. However the focus here seems to be more on the death of the enemy. As in verse 6, the word **sword** is intended in the broader sense of offensive military activity. The phrase may be rendered "you will kill many of your enemies in war" or "your enemies will die in battle in your presence." It is probably better not to shorten and combine the two expressions of this verse into a single statement, as has been done in TEV.

26.8	RSV	TEV

Five of you shall chase a hundred, and a hundred of you shall chase ten thousand; and your enemies shall fall before you by the sword.	**five of you will be able to defeat a hundred, and a hundred will be able to defeat ten thousand.**

This verse continues the picture of military victory begun in the previous verse. The contrast between the number of victors and the number of defeated enemies may be heightened by translating "It will only take five of you to defeat a hundred of the enemy, and only a hundred of you will be triumphant over a thousand enemies in battle." Here the word **chase** means "be victorious over" (as in verse 7a), and the words **fall before you by the sword** again indicate "be defeated in battle" (see verse 7b).

26.9	RSV	TEV

And I will have regard for you and make you fruitful and multiply you, and will confirm my covenant with you.	**I will bless you and give you many children; I will keep my part of the covenant that I made with you.**

Have regard for you: literally "I will face (or, turn) toward you." The word used here is related to the word for "face." This expression may well be the opposite of "set my face against you" in 17.10. Many versions translate "look with favor upon you" (NJV, NIV, NAB). AT has "give my attention to you." NJB reads "turn towards you." Another possible model is "I will show my kindness to you."

Make you fruitful and multiply you: these are the same two verbs that constitute the blessing given to the first man and woman in Genesis 1.28. They may have to be translated by a single verb in many languages. Or one may consider "I will cause you to have many children so that the number of your group may increase."

Confirm my covenant: on the word **covenant** see 2.13, and compare also 24.8. The verb used here is taken to mean "maintain" (NJV), "uphold" (NJB), "carry out" (NAB), and "ratify" (Mft). Since the covenant or agreement was made previously, it cannot mean "establish" (AT) in the ordinary sense of the word. In some languages the idea may be expressed by the verbs "fulfill" or "honor."

26.10 RSV	TEV
And you shall eat old store long kept, and you shall clear out the old to make way for the new.	Your harvests will be so plentiful that they will last for a year, and even then you will have to throw away what is left of the old harvest to make room for the new.

This verse, like verse 5 above, concerns abundant harvest. A literal translation of the Hebrew text as seen in RSV is difficult to understand. TEV clarifies the meaning by introducing the verse with "**Your harvests will be so plentiful that . . . .**" Compare verse 5 above.

You shall eat old store long kept: the idea here may also be translated "you will be able to live a very long time on the grain stored up from one harvest." Taken literally this could indicate the eating of stale food, which is definitely not the intended meaning.

You shall clear out the old to make way for the new: following the proposal for the previous phrase, this one can be rendered "you will even have to get rid of [or throw out] what is left in order to be able to store the grain from the new harvest."

26.11 RSV	TEV
And I will make my abode among you, and my soul shall not abhor you.	I will live among you in my sacred Tent, and I will never turn away from you.

Make my abode among you: the word translated **abode** here is the same as rendered "tabernacle" in 8.10; 15.31; and 17.4. In fact, NEB translates here "establish my Tabernacle," and TEV has "**sacred Tent,**" but most versions have "dwelling [place]" or "abode." The meaning is that God will take up residence among the people of Israel. Mft approaches this idea with "I will pitch my tent among you." But one may also consider "I will make my home with you" or "I will come to live with you."

My soul: this is simply an idiomatic way of saying **I** or "I myself" that is very common in Hebrew poetry and some types of prose. A literal rendering of the word **soul** is surely misleading in many languages, but the use of this term does sometimes connote deep feelings and is stronger than a simple pronoun. See 4.2.

Abhor you: the verb here gives the idea "to despise," "reject," or "to treat with contempt." But a negative statement like "I won't hate you" is at best weak in many languages. Consequently it may be more appropriate to make a positive statement such as "I will always be with you" or "I will accept you [completely]."

26.12 RSV TEV

And I will walk among you, and will be your God, and you shall be my people. | I will be with you; I will be your God, and you will be my people.

Walk among you: the idea of "walking" is not intended literally. As in verse 3 (and 18.3) it means "to live." So NJV translates here "I will be ever present in your midst."

I . . . will be your God, and you shall be my people: these two phrases are simply two ways of looking at the same fact. The future tense here must not be taken to mean that the LORD was not their God previously. (The next verse states "I am [present tense] your God.") In some languages one may have to say "I will continue to be your God." This formula appears several times in the books of Jeremiah (7.23; 11.4; 24.7; 30.22; 31.1,33; 32.38), Ezekiel (11.20; 14.11; 36.28; 37.23,27), and Zechariah (8.8). It is also quoted in 2 Corinthians 6.16 and Revelation 21.3.

26.13 RSV TEV

I am the LORD your God, who brought you forth out of the land of Egypt, that you should not be their slaves; and I have broken the bars of your yoke and made you walk erect. | I, the LORD your God, brought you out of Egypt so that you would no longer be slaves. I broke the power that held you down and let you walk with your head held high."

I am the LORD your God, who brought you forth out of the land of Egypt: see 11.45; 22.33; 25.38. Compare also 18.2.

Their slaves: the possessive idea is not made explicit in the TEV translation. This is unfortunate, since this expression stands in contrast with "my slaves" in 25.55. In some cases this part of the verse may have to be restructured along the following lines: "I am the LORD your God, who freed you from slavery under the Egyptians and brought you out of their country."

The bars of your yoke: the figurative use of the word **yoke** in Matthew 11.29-30 is well known. The term first occurs in the Bible in Genesis 27.40. Originally a **yoke** was a wooden frame placed over the necks of two animals to harness them for work. But it was also used on human beings when they were taken captive (Jer 28.10) or made slaves. It then became a symbol of the subjection and servitude of slaves. To break the bars of a yoke would mean to liberate the person or animal held by them. TEV avoids the literal meaning and translates the figurative sense. This may also be good in many other languages. Compare Ezekiel 34.27b.

Made you walk erect: the removal of the object that holds a person in slavery allows him to walk uprightly. As the yoke is a symbol of servitude, its absence and the accompanying ability to walk with the head held high constitute a symbol of freedom and dignity. In some languages this may be rendered "let you to walk with your head up," "enabled you to live without bowing down," or "caused you not to have to submit to other people."

TEV Section Heading: **"Punishment for Disobedience."**

This section may also be called "The results of not obeying God" or "Punishment for not doing what God says." This section heading should stand in opposition to the one before the first verse of this chapter, since these two sections are in sharp contrast with each other. Compare the more lengthy passage on this same subject in Deuteronomy 28.15-68.

26.14   RSV   TEV

"But if you will not hearken to   The LORD said, "If you will not
me, and will not do all these com-   obey my commands, you will be
mandments,   punished.

This verse is the counterpart of verse 3 above. The conjunction **But** in RSV indicates the contrast between the paragraph on punishment beginning here, and the preceding one on rewards. If such a connecting word is inappropriate at the beginning of a new section like this, it may be omitted. TEV reminds the reader that it is God who is speaking, by beginning **"The LORD said . . . ."**

Hearken to me: this expression is intended to carry the meaning "listen to me in order to do what I say" or "pay attention to me." The translation should not be simply "listen to me" if this conveys no idea of subsequent obedience. NJV has simply "obey Me."

These commandments: more explicitly, "my commandments" (compare TEV), or in some languages "these commandments of mine." Compare verse 3.

Note that TEV makes a complete sentence of this by supplying the implied information **"you will be punished."** This information actually comes from the overall context, but it is supplied here because the RSV sentence (reflecting the Hebrew) is far too long and complex to be readily understood.

26.15   RSV   TEV

if you spurn my statutes, and if your   If you refuse to obey my laws and
soul abhors my ordinances, so that   commands and break the covenant I
you will not do all my com-   have made with you,
mandments, but break my covenant,

On the various synonyms for law in this verse, see verse 3 and 18.4.

Spurn my statutes: that is, "reject" (NJV and NJB) or "refuse" (JB). TEV is more explicit with **"refuse to obey . . . ."**

Your soul: the mention of the word **soul** in the receptor language translation should probably be avoided. This is simply an emphatic way of saying "you" or "you yourself," but it is good to retain the emphasis where possible. See 4.2. Compare also verse 11 above.

Abhors my ordinances: this is merely another way of saying what has already been said above. If a synonymous expression can be found, the idea may be repeated, but a repetition of the same meaning is not essential.

Break my covenant: this is the opposite of what God promises to do in the case of obedience (see verse 9). In some languages one may have to say "fail to honor," "not observe," or "show disrespect for." On the word **covenant** see 2.13 and 24.8.

26.16 RSV	TEV
I will do this to you: I will appoint over you sudden terror, consumption and fever that waste the eyes and cause life to pine away. And you shall sow your seed in vain, for your enemies shall eat it;	I will punish you. I will bring disaster on you—incurable diseases and fevers that will make you blind and cause your life to waste away. You will plant your crops, but it will do you no good, because your enemies will conquer you and eat what you have grown.

I will do this to you: the pronoun **this** looks forward to what is said in the remainder of this verse. Another way to translate this is to say "I will punish you in the following ways: . . ." or "Your punishment will be as follows: . . . ."

Appoint over you sudden terror: the use of the word **appoint** is strange in this context, because it is usually people who are appointed. It is better translated "send" or "cause to happen." The words **sudden terror** translate a single Hebrew word meaning "ruin" or "dismay." In this context it may be translated "catastrophe" or "disaster." In some languages this whole phrase may be rendered "I will ruin you" or "I will cause you to be devastated."

Consumption and fever: the words used here are found only in this verse and in similar lists of catastrophes (as Deut 28.22). The Septuagint has "scurvy and jaundice," but this is not followed by any modern English version. The exact nature of these ills is uncertain, but they are clearly terrible diseases. While **fever** (or perhaps "high fever") is probably the best rendering of the second term, the first may be translated "disease(s) that cause the body to waste away" or "incurable diseases." Both the Modern Language Bible and LB have "tuberculosis."

That waste the eyes: some versions take this to mean "cause to be blind" (TEV, GECL). But others see it as simply "making the eyes weak." Compare NEB "that dim the sight."

Cause life to pine away: literally, "draining the soul." This has been interpreted in a variety of ways, from "causing shortness of breath" (see *La Bible de la Pléiade*), to "cause the appetite to fail" (NEB), to "depressing your spirits" (AT). Probably the best way to understand it is in the sense of "eating away at your life," or "causing you to waste away," or ". . . get more and more ill."

Sow your seed in vain, for your enemies shall eat it: the counterpart of this is in verses 4-5 and 10. The final pronoun, **it**, refers not to the grain that is sown, but to the crops harvested from that grain. This may be translated "You will sow your seed for nothing, because your enemies will eat what is produced" or "There will be no point in sowing, since your enemies will gather the harvest [and eat it]."

26.17   RSV   TEV

I will set my face against you, and you shall be smitten before your enemies; those who hate you shall rule over you, and you shall flee when none pursues you.	I will turn against you, so that you will be defeated, and those who hate you will rule over you; you will be so terrified that you will run when no one is chasing you.

This is the counterpart of verses 7 and 8 above.

Set my face against you: see 17.10; 20.3,6.

You shall be smitten before your enemies: the verb "to smite" or "to strike" is often used in Scripture to mean "kill" or "defeat in battle." In some languages the passive construction may be better rendered "your enemies will defeat you."

Rule over you: the Septuagint has instead "pursue you," but this is followed only by NEB. Translators are advised to communicate the idea "dominate," "subjugate," "rule over," or "be your rulers."

You shall flee when none pursues you: TEV makes the meaning explicit by adding "**you will be so terrified . . . .**" This contrasts with verses 7 and 8, where the enemy is made to flee by a much smaller number of Israelite soldiers.

26.18   RSV   TEV

And if in spite of this you will not hearken to me, then I will chastise you again sevenfold for your sins,	"If even after all this you still do not obey me, I will increase your punishment seven times.

In spite of this: or "after all these terrible things."

Will not hearken to me: see verse 14.

I will chastise you again sevenfold: or "I will make your punishment seven times worse." The number seven used here has a symbolic value and is not intended literally. In some languages it will be better to translate "I will multiply your punishment" or "I will make your punishment much worse."

For your sins: this is left implicit in TEV, but it may be equally well translated "for your disobedience" or "because you disobeyed me."

26.19   RSV   TEV

and I will break the pride of your power, and I will make your heavens like iron and your earth like brass;	I will break your stubborn pride; there will be no rain, and your land will be dry and as hard as iron.

Break the pride of your power: this construction with **of** may be understood either as "powerful (or, strong) pride" (compare TEV and NEB "**stubborn pride**") or as "pride in your own power" (compare "proud strength" (NJB) and "the power of which you are so proud" (Mft).

Your heavens . . . your earth: these expressions with the possessive are better translated "the heavens above you" or "the heavens you look up to," and "the earth beneath you" or "the land where you live."

Like iron . . . like brass: both of these comparisons evoke the idea of "hardness." Hardness in the heavens is intended to convey the meaning "absence of rain" which results in hardness of the earth due to the lack of moisture. It will be very important in most languages to make explicit the fact that this verse is talking about the absence of rain needed for agricultural production. The entire latter half of this verse may be rendered something like "There will be no rain from the heavens above you, and so your land will dry up and become hard like metal."

26.20 RSV	TEV
and your strength shall be spent in vain, for your land shall not yield its increase, and the trees of the land shall not yield their fruit.	All your hard work will do you no good, because your land will not produce crops and the trees will not bear fruit.

Your strength shall be spent in vain: a literal rendering of this phrase may be misleading in some languages. Another way of saying this is "No matter how hard you work, it will be for nothing . . ." or "You will wear yourselves out and become exhausted, but you efforts will be worthless."

Yield its increase . . . their fruit: compare verse 4.

Of the land: some texts read "of the field," but this is of minor significance in a dynamic-equivalent translation. Several versions, including TEV, simply leave this detail implicit, since **land** has already been mentioned earlier in this same verse.

26.21 RSV	TEV
"Then if you walk contrary to me, and will not hearken to me, I will bring more plagues upon you, sevenfold as many as your sins.	"If you still continue to resist me and refuse to obey me, I will again increase your punishment seven times.

Walk contrary to me: literally, "if you walk with me in opposition." The Hebrew expression (also used in verses 23, 24, 27, 28, 40, and 41) indicates an attitude of hostility or resistance. It may be rendered "if you oppose me," or "if you remain hostile to me" (compare NJV and NIV), or "if you still defy me" (NEB).

Will not hearken to me: this may be taken as parallel to the previous expression, or as an explanation of the actual way in which they showed their opposition. In the latter case, the two may be connected as follows: "if you continue to oppose me by refusing to listen to me . . . ."

Bring more plagues upon you: the word translated **plagues** actually refers to "punishment." Since this is the second increase in their punishment (see verse 18), it may be helpful to add the word "**again**" as in TEV, or to use an expression like NJV, "I will go on smiting you . . . ."

Sevenfold as many as your sins: compare verse 18.

26.22   RSV   TEV

And I will let loose the wild beasts   I will send dangerous animals among
among you, which shall rob you of   you, and they will kill your children,
your children, and destroy your cat-   destroy your livestock, and leave so
tle, and make you few in number, so   few of you that your roads will be
that your ways shall become deso-   deserted.
late.

Let loose the wild beasts: this is the opposite of what is promised for
obedience in the previous passage. Although the words are not identical, **wild beasts**
here corresponds to "evil beasts" in verse 6.

Rob you of your children: or "make you childless." NJV has "bereave you of
your children." A literal translation of the verb **rob** may seem to hold out some hope
to the children being recovered, but the meaning is clearly "destroy" or "kill," so that
the people have no descendants.

Destroy your cattle: as in 19.19 this may be taken to refer to all domestic
animals. NAB translates "wipe out your livestock."

So that your ways shall become desolate: the result of the reduced
population will be that there will be scarcely anyone traveling on the roads. They will
be deserted.

26.23   RSV   TEV

"And if by this discipline you   "If after all of this punishment
are not turned to me, but walk con-   you still do not listen to me, but contrary to me,   tinue to defy me,

If by this discipline you are not turned to me: literally "and if after these
you are not corrected . . . ." To maintain the nuance of this passive construction, it
may be necessary to translate "if all this punishment does not cause you to return to
me," or "if all this does not make you straighten up," or ". . . change your ways."

Walk contrary to me: see verse 21. Here TEV adds the word **"continue"** in
order to show that this is not the beginning of the attitude of defiance.

26.24   RSV   TEV

then I also will walk contrary to you,   then I will turn on you and punish
and I myself will smite you sevenfold   you seven times harder than before.
for your sins.

Walk contrary to you: see verse 21.

I myself: literally, "indeed I." An emphatic form of the pronoun, underlining
the fact that God will act personally and not through an agent.

Smite you: this is not the same root verb as translated "be smitten" in verse 17. Here the meaning is more like "afflict" or "**punish**." And it is God himself who is the subject of this verb.

Sevenfold: see verse 18.

26.25 RSV	TEV
And I will bring a sword upon you, that shall execute vengeance for the covenant; and if you gather within your cities I will send pestilence among you, and you shall be delivered into the hand of the enemy.	I will bring war on you to punish you for breaking our covenant, and if you gather in your cities for safety, I will send incurable diseases among you, and you will be forced to surrender to your enemies.

Bring a sword upon you: as in verse 6, the sword here represents all the devastation of war.

Execute vengeance for the covenant: literally "avenging vengeance of covenant." The noun and the verb have the same root (compare 5.15). One way of translating the idea here is to say "I will surely punish you because you have broken my covenant." On the word for covenant, see 2.13 and 24.8.

Gather: implied here is the idea of assembling or withdrawing into the cities in order to find security. This should probably be made explicit in translation. One possibility is to say "if you take refuge in your cities . . ." or "if you assemble in the cities for protection . . . ."

Pestilence: this refers to a contagious or infectious epidemic disease that is deadly and very destructive. In some languages it may have to be translated "a terrible sickness that will kill many people."

Be delivered into the hand of the enemy: the pestilence will cause the death of many of those defending the city, and this will permit the enemy to take it over. The passive construction may be made active with God as the subject. The word translated **into the hand** means "to be subjected to." The whole phrase may be rendered "I will give you over to your enemies so that they will rule over you." The image of the **hand** may be appropriate in some languages, but in others it should be avoided.

26.26 RSV	TEV
When I break your staff of bread, ten women shall bake your bread in one oven, and shall deliver your bread again by weight; and you shall eat, and not be satisfied.	I will cut off your food supply, so that ten women will need only one oven to bake all the bread they have. They will ration it out, and when you have eaten it all, you will still be hungry.

When: the relationship between the first proposition and what follows is made clearer in TEV by using "**so that**" after the first clause, rather than introducing the verse with **When**. NEB joins the two parts with "... until ...." The result of the cutting off of the food supply will be a scarcity of flour for making bread, so that one oven will serve for ten families.

Break your staff of bread: this is a figure of speech for famine (compare Psa 105.16). There are many ways in which this may be expressed in the languages of the world. For example, "I will send great hunger," or "I will give you no food," or "I will deprive you of things to eat." TEV approaches the same meaning with "I will cut off your food supply."

Ten women shall bake your bread in one oven: instead of using the simple future tense, it may be better to say "ten women will be able to use a single oven for baking bread" or "one oven will be enough to serve ten families." This is the result of the famine. There will be so little bread that one oven would serve ten different families. Normally each family had its own oven, but the famine would reduce the need by one tenth. In some languages this may have to be made explicit by saying something like "there will be so little bread that one oven will be enough for ten women to cook in." On the word for **oven**, see 2.4.

Shall deliver your bread again by weight: the subject here is the women who were responsible for giving out the bread. There will be so little that they will have to measure out the small quantities to each recipient. Compare Ezekiel 4.16-17.

It may be difficult for translators to see why the RSV rendering includes the word **again** in this phrase. The idea is archaic English for "in return." They put the flour into a common loaf and then get it back "again." Some other languages also have special expressions for this idea, but in many languages **again** may be ignored.

Eat, and not be satisfied: this is the opposite of "eat your fill" in 25.19. It is intended to highlight the desperate situation in which the disobedient Israelites will find themselves.

26.27   RSV   TEV

"And if in spite of this you will   "If after all this you still contin-
not hearken to me, but walk contrary   ue to defy me and refuse to obey
to me,   me,

In spite of this: the Hebrew text here is the same as at the beginning of verse 23, except that the singular **this** replaces the plural "these." But since the singular may be taken as a collective, including all that God had done, the meaning is virtually the same.

Will not hearken to me: see verse 14.
Walk contrary to me: see verse 21.

26.28   RSV   TEV

then I will walk contrary to you in   then in my anger I will turn on you
fury, and chastise you myself   and again make your punishment
sevenfold for your sins.   seven times worse than before.

414

Walk contrary to you: see verse 21.

In fury: this is an addition not found in verse 24. It carries the idea of "wrath" or "**anger**."

Chastise you myself sevenfold: see verses 18, 21, and 24.

26.29 RSV	TEV
You shall eat the flesh of your sons, and you shall eat the flesh of your daughters.	Your hunger will be so great that you will eat your own children.

Eat the flesh of your sons . . . daughters: TEV makes explicit the reason for this act of cannibalism with "**Your hunger will be so great . . . .**" Another way of doing this is to add at the end of the verse ". . . because of the famine." And it also translates the separate clauses concerning **sons** and **daughters** by a single clause with "**children**." This will serve as a good model in a number of other languages.

26.30 RSV	TEV
And I will destroy your high places, and cut down your incense altars, and cast your dead bodies upon the dead bodies of your idols; and my soul will abhor you.	I will destroy your places of worship on the hills, tear down your incense altars, and throw your dead bodies on your fallen idols. In utter disgust

Your high places: this refers to the hill shrines in Canaan which were destroyed by King Josiah (2 Kgs 23.5-30). However, they were apparently once considered legitimate. In some cultures shrines and temples can still be found on hilltops. But in most cases it is probably best to make explicit that these were "**places of worship**," as TEV has done.

Incense altars: compare 2 Chronicles 34.4 and Ezekiel 6.4 and following. The meaning of the corresponding Hebrew word is not certain. It has to do with pagan ritual and possibly the worship of the sun (compare Mft's "sun-pillars"). In translation it is probably wise to distinguish it from the altar of incense in the Tent of the LORD's presence. But this may be adequately done in most cases by the possessive pronoun **you**.

The dead bodies of your idols: the word translated **idols** has as its root the meaning "logs." NEB brings this out by translating "the rotting logs that were your idols." The idolatrous nature of these objects should also be brought out in translation. And the emphasis of this expression as a whole is on the fact that these idols have no life and are therefore worthless.

My soul: or "I myself." Compare verses 11 and 15.

Abhor you: see verse 11. Some versions seem to take this last phrase in verse 30 as the conclusion of the thought of that verse, but TEV, NJV, and NAB make it the beginning of a new sentence that continues in verse 31.

And I will lay your cities waste, and will make your sanctuaries desolate, and I will not smell your pleasing odors.	**I will turn your cities into ruins, destroy your places of worship, and refuse to accept your sacrifices.**

Lay your cities waste: or "I will completely destroy your cities."

Make your sanctuaries desolate: some Hebrew manuscripts have the singular "sanctuary," which would seem to refer to the Temple in Jerusalem. But no version consulted uses the singular. The plural refers to buildings dedicated to pagan worship within the confines of the cities. They will be destroyed along with the rest of the city and will therefore no longer be visited by worshipers.

I will not smell your pleasing odors: the idea here is not that God will be unable to smell the odor; rather it indicates the rejection of sacrifices offered to him. Compare 1.9. NIV translates "I will take no delight in the pleasing aroma of your offerings."

And I will devastate the land, so that your enemies who settle in it shall be astonished at it.	**I will destroy your land so completely that the enemies who occupy it will be shocked at the destruction.**

Devastate the land: since this clearly refers to the land of the Israelites, it may be useful to translate "**your land**," as in TEV.

So that: TEV makes this clearer with "**so completely that.**"

Who settle in it: this is too neutral an expression to convey the idea of a hostile occupying force. In some languages one may say "who take it over" or "who become the masters."

And I will scatter you among the nations, and I will unsheathe the sword after you; and your land shall be a desolation, and your cities shall be a waste.	**I will bring war on you and scatter you in foreign lands. Your land will be deserted, and your cities left in ruins.**

Scatter you among the nations: the people of Israel will be separated from each other and settled in the lands of other peoples. Logically this should come after the statement that follows.

Unsheathe the sword after you: as in verses 6, 7, 8, and 25, the sword represents war as a whole. TEV has switched the positions of these first two propositions, since it is more logical to think of war occurring before the people of Israel are scattered.

26.34-35 RSV TEV

34 "Then the land shall enjoy[n] its sabbaths as long as it lies desolate, while you are in your enemies' land; then the land shall rest, and enjoy[n] its sabbaths. 35 As long as it lies desolate it shall have rest, the rest which it had not in your sabbaths when you dwelt upon it.

34-35 Then the land will enjoy the years of complete rest that you would not give it; it will lie abandoned and get its rest while you are in exile in the land of your enemies.

[n] Or *pay for*

The expression **the land shall enjoy its sabbaths** is equivalent to **the land shall rest, and enjoy its sabbaths** later in verse 34 and **it shall have rest** in verse 35. This repetition has caused TEV to combine the two verses and reduce the redundancy.

The rest which it had not in your sabbaths: this rather awkward expression emphasizes the fact that the rest years which the LORD required have not been properly observed by the people of Israel. The land will, however, be given adequate rest while the people of Israel are in exile elsewhere.

26.36 RSV TEV

And as for those of you that are left, I will send faintness into their hearts in the lands of their enemies; the sound of a driven leaf shall put them to flight, and they shall flee as one flees from the sword, and they shall fall when none pursues.

"I will make those of you who are in exile so terrified that the sound of a leaf blowing in the wind will make you run. You will run as if you were being pursued in battle, and you will fall when there is no enemy near you.

The Hebrew shifts from second person to third person plural in this verse, but TEV maintains "**you**" throughout. The same should be done in the receptor-language translation in most cases. A change in pronouns would only serve to confuse the reader.

Send faintness into their hearts: the word translated **faintness** is rendered "slavery" in the Septuagint. But its meaning is generally recognized today as "weakness" or "timidity." Other possible renderings may be "lack of courage" or "anxiety."

The sound of a driven leaf: the image here is of someone who is "afraid of his own shadow," as may be said in colloquial English. Brave men are not frightened by the sound of battle, but God will cause his people to be so fearful that a mere leaf blowing in the wind will make then run away.

This verse is in contrast with verses 7 and 8, where a handful of Israelites could cause their enemies to flee.

RSV   TEV

They shall stumble over one another, as if to escape a sword, though none pursues; and you shall have no power to stand before your enemies.	**You will stumble over one another when no one is chasing you, and you will be unable to fight against any enemy.**

This continues the image of the people of Israel, who will be so frightened that they panic and cause injury to each other even though no one is chasing them.

You: the Hebrew shifts suddenly back to the second person plural (see verse 36). But in most languages it will be better to use the second person plural pronoun consistently throughout this passage, as has been done by TEV. If this suggestion has been followed, then the abrupt shift of pronoun here will cause no problem for the receptor language.

No power to stand before your enemies: the verb used here continues the image of a people unable to maintain their footing (compare "fall" in verse 36 and **stumble** earlier in this verse). Another way of saying this is "you will be helpless to stand up to your enemies."

26.38   RSV   TEV

And you shall perish among the nations, and the land of your enemies shall eat you up.	**You will die in exile, swallowed up by the land of your enemies.**

And: in some languages it may be better to say "Finally" or "In the end . . . ," to get the right connection, since this is a kind of conclusion to the thought here.

Perish among the nations: that is, "**die in exile**" or "end your lives in a land that is not your own."

The land of your enemies shall eat you up: this probably refers to the same essential event as **perish** above. It is possible, however, that this expression refers to burial in a foreign land. It may be possible simply to add ". . . and be buried there," depending on how the preceding expression is handled. Another suggestion is that this expression may refer to the way in which the entire northern nation lost its identity and completely disappeared among its enemies.

26.39   RSV   TEV

And those of you that are left shall pine away in your enemies' lands because of their iniquity; and also because of the iniquities of their fathers they shall pine away like them.	**The few of you who survive in the land of your enemies will waste away because of your own sin and the sin of your ancestors.**

Pine away: this expression is used twice in this verse and indicates a gradual but sure deterioration. It may be rendered "decay," "rot," or **"waste away."**

In your enemies' lands: there is a minor textual problem here. Some texts have the singular "in an enemy land" (so NEB and JB), but since the meaning is virtually the same, this should have no effect on the receptor language translation.

Their fathers: that is, **"your ancestors,"** as in TEV.

Section Heading: "Hope for the Future."

According to the interpretation of some experts, verses 40-46 do not actually constitute punishments. So it has been suggested that a new section heading is needed here (FRCL, TOB, NEB). NEB entitles this brief section "Hope for the Future." Other possibilities are "God remembers his covenant," or "The possibility of conversion," or "Confession and forgiveness." Some editions of RSV have the section heading "The covenant renewed" at this point.

26.40 RSV	TEV
"But if they confess their iniquity and the iniquity of their fathers in their treachery which they committed against me, and also in walking contrary to me,	"But your descendants will confess their sins and the sins of their ancestors, who resisted me and rebelled against me,

But: contrasting the confession of a future generation with the continuation in the sins of the ancestors. However, JB has no such connecting word, since its interpretation of the passage is different. See the following discussion.

If: the grammatical relationship between verses 40 and 41 is not clear. Here at the beginning of verse 40, the conditional in RSV (as well as NIV, AT, Mft) is a simple future tense in TEV (with NJB, NJV, TOB). But this depends on the translation of the conjunction at the beginning of verse 41 (RSV **so that**). One interpretation is "Even though the (surviving) people confess . . . 41 yet I will still oppose them . . . ." The other is "The people will confess their sin and the sin of their ancestors who were unfaithful to me and who turned against me 41 so that I turned against them . . . ." This has verse 41 continuing the thought about the rebellious ancestors, while the first interpretation gives the idea that in spite of the confession of the new (future) generation, they will still suffer and be taken into exile before finally experiencing the forgiveness of God. However, it is probably better to follow the second interpretation and take verses 40-46 as a separate section with a new heading at the beginning of this verse.

They: the pronoun here refers to the descendants of those in exile. Grammatically it points back to the "survivors" mentioned in the previous verse.

Confess: this verb may also mean "declare" or, in this case, "to admit" one's guilt. Compare 5.5 and 16.21.

Treachery: this means an "unfaithful act." It is used elsewhere of (1) unfaithfulness to the marriage vows (Num 5.12, 27) and (2) betrayal of another person (see Job 21.34, where it is translated "falsehood" in RSV). Compare also 5.15,

419

where, together with the verb having the same root, this noun is translated "a breach of faith." Here the treason is clearly against God himself.

Fathers: or "ancestors." See verse 39.

Walking contrary to me: see verse 21.

26.41   RSV   TEV

so that I walked contrary to them and brought them into the land of their enemies; if then their uncircumcised heart is humbled and they make amends for their iniquity;	and caused me to turn against them and send them into exile in the land of their enemies. At last, when your descendants are humbled and they have paid the penalty for their sin and rebellion,

So that: see the above discussion on the relationship between verses 40 and 41.

I walked contrary to them: the opposite of "walking contrary to me" in the previous verse. See also verse 21.

Brought them into the land of their enemies: again, this refers to the exile of the people of Israel (see verse 39).

If then: this probably means "if at that time" or "when that time comes, if . . . ." But the exact meaning of these two words is unclear, and their interpretation is tied to the understanding of verses 40-41 as a whole. NJB has simply "Then . . ." (See HOTTP, page 205).

Their uncircumcised heart: a literal translation of this expression would be very confusing in most languages. NEB has "stubborn spirit," while TEV leaves this element implicit at this point, but it is probably better to make it explicit in the receptor language. See the discussion under 19.23. Some other possible models are "if their [descendants'] hearts are changed . . . ," or "if they stop being so stubborn . . . ," or "if they unblock their hearts . . . ."

Make amends for their iniquity: this phrase presents difficulties with regard to the understanding of both the verb, **make amends**, and the noun, rendered **iniquity** in RSV, and consequently for the interpretation of the whole. A number of versions have adopted essentially the same interpretation as RSV (NIV, NJV, and NAB). But the noun used here may mean either "guilt" or "punishment for guilt." The idea of punishment seems more probable in this context, as in 5.1,7; 10.17; and 16.22; as well as Gen 4.13. The verb translated **make amends** in RSV is sometimes used in the sense of "accept." An example of this in Leviticus is God's accepting a sacrifice in 1.4. Mft translates the whole phrase "submit to be punished for their sins," while NEB has "accept their punishment in full," leaving the idea of guilt implicit. It is especially significant that, while JB (1966) rendered the whole phrase "atone for their sins," the more recent NJB (1985) has "accept the punishment for their guilt." The latter interpretation is therefore recommended to translators.

26.42 RSV   TEV

then I will remember my covenant with Jacob, and I will remember my covenant with Isaac and my covenant with Abraham, and I will remember the land.	I will remember my covenant with Jacob and with Isaac and with Abraham, and I will renew my promise to give my people the land.

There is a great deal of repetition in this verse which may be reduced in order to make it more natural sounding in the receptor language.

Remember: a literal translation of this verb in some languages may imply that God had temporarily forgotten that he had made an agreement with the people of Israel. But the idea here is that he would keep in mind the agreement he made and would act on it. In some cases it may be wise to translate it "not forget" or "fulfill." It need not be repeated for each of the patriarchs, unless this will be more natural in the receptor language.

Covenant: the repetition of this word with each of the three patriarchs may give the impression in some languages that three completely separate agreements were made. But since God's covenant with his people is seen as unique, such an impression should be avoided. On the word **covenant**, see verses 9 and 15, as well as 2.13 and 24.8.

Jacob . . . Isaac . . . Abraham . . . : in some translations it may be well to make explicit the fact that these three men are the ancestors of the Israelites, or in this context "their ancestors."

Remember the land: this is an abbreviated way of saying "I will not forget what I promised you about the land," or something similar.

26.43 RSV   TEV

But the land shall be left by them, and enjoy[n] its sabbaths while it lies desolate without them; and they shall make amends for their iniquity, because they spurned my ordinances, and their soul abhorred my statutes.	First, however, the land must be rid of its people, so that it can enjoy its complete rest, and they must pay the full penalty for having rejected my laws and my commands.

[n] Or *pay for*

But: marking a prior condition to the granting of the land.

Be left by them: this passive formulation may be easily turned around to say "they [the people] must leave . . . ."

Enjoy its sabbaths: see verse 34.

And: some have proposed expanding this to say "during this time [away from the land], they must pay . . . ."

Make amends: see verse 41.

Spurned my ordinances . . . abhorred my statutes: these two expressions convey the same meaning: "rejected what I command." In those languages where it is difficult or unnatural to use synonymous expressions in parallel, this may be translated once.

Their soul: better "they" or "they themselves." Compare "my soul" in verse 11 and "your soul" in verse 15.

26.44	RSV	TEV

Yet for all that, when they are in the land of their enemies, I will not spurn them, neither will I abhor them so as to destroy them utterly and break my covenant with them; for I am the LORD their God;	But even then, when they are still in the land of their enemies, I will not completely abandon them or destroy them. That would put an end to my covenant with them, and I am the LORD their God.

Yet for all that: or "But in spite of this," or "**But even then.**" JB translates more dynamically as a separate sentence, "Yet this is not the end."

I will not spurn . . . abhor them: the two verbs here reflect those used in the previous verse to describe how the Israelites treated God. His treatment of them, however, would not be the same. TEV restructures in such a way as to render the two verbs **spurn** and **abhor** by the single verb "**abandon.**" And it also shifts the adverb **utterly** forward in the sentence, using "**completely**" to qualify the verb "**abandon**" instead of **destroy**. In many languages it may be preferable to follow the structure of RSV in this case. Compare also verse 11.

Break my covenant: see verse 15.

26.45	RSV	TEV

but I will for their sake remember the covenant with their forefathers, whom I brought forth out of the land of Egypt in the sight of the nations, that I might be their God: I am the LORD."	I will renew the covenant that I made with their ancestors when I showed all the nations my power by bringing my people out of Egypt, in order that I, the LORD, might be their God."

For their sake: literally "for them." But it is probably better to translate "for their good" or "for their benefit." FRCL has "for their salvation."

Remember the covenant: this repeats the affirmation given in verse 42.

Forefathers: this is the more specific word for "**ancestors**" and refers to those who were delivered from slavery in Egypt, and not to Abraham, Isaac, and Jacob. Compare verse 40.

In the sight of the nations: literally, "in the eyes of the nations." This may be more explicitly translated "to demonstrate my strength to the nations." On the word **nations** see verse 33 as well as 18.24 and 25.44.

26.46   RSV   TEV

These are the statutes and ordinances and laws which the Lord made between him and the people of Israel on Mount Sinai by Moses.	All these are the laws and commands that the Lord gave to Moses on Mount Sinai for the people of Israel.

Almost all versions make this verse a separate paragraph. It is a kind of conclusion for the entire section, from the beginning of chapter 17 to this point. It is even taken as a conclusion to the whole book by those who see chapter 27 as a later addition.

Statutes and ordinances and laws: the use of three separate terms is not essential here. Their importance lies in the intended emphasis on the totality of the various rules which God gave to the people of Israel.

The structure of this verse is awkward in RSV and should probably be changed in accordance with TEV, or in some other way that will be more natural in the receptor language. Moses is seen as the agent through whom God gave his laws to the people of Israel. The phrase **between him and the people of Israel** stresses the fact that the laws given were a matter between God and his people, even though Moses was used as an instrument.

Chapter 27

TEV Section Heading: **"Laws Concerning Gifts to the LORD."**

This chapter has no direct connection with the preceding section. Rather it is a separate, self-contained unit. It deals with the matter of the redemption of offerings, or gifts to the LORD. A single section heading as in TEV should be adequate. However, NEB also introduces a section heading at verse 14, and NJB further outlines the chapter with breaks showing that verses 1-8 deal with persons, 9-13 with animals, 14-15 with houses, 16-25 with fields, and the remainder of the chapter concerns specific rules for redemption (26-27 for the first born; 28-29 for things under a ban; and 30-33 for tithes). Other possible ways of wording an overall heading are "Redeeming what is the LORD's" (NIV), "Payment for things promised to God," or "The fulfillment of vows to the LORD."

27.1-2	RSV	TEV

RSV	TEV
1 The LORD said to Moses, 2 "Say to the people of Israel, When a man makes a special vow of persons to the LORD at your valuation,	1 The LORD gave Moses 2 the following regulations for the people of Israel. When a person has been given to the LORD in fulfillment of a special vow, that person may be set free by the payment of the following sums of money,

Said to Moses: see 4.1.

Say to the people of Israel ... : the problem of direct versus indirect discourse is the same here as in the previous passages (see 4.2). The solution should therefore probably be the same.

Makes ... vow: the Hebrew may be understood in the sense of making a promise to God or fulfilling such a promise. NJB has "discharge," but most versions take it in the sense of promising to God or making a vow rather than fulfilling the vow.

A special vow of persons: according to Judges 11.29-40 and 1 Samuel 1.11, it was possible for a person to dedicate another human being to God. At one time this apparently involved the actual sacrifice of the person involved (as in the case of the daughter of Jephthah in Judges 11). Later it was expected that the person so dedicated would serve in the sanctuary. But this passage shows that such a person could be set free by the payment of money. The following verses indicate the relative value of different types of persons for purposes of redemption.

424

Your valuation: this expression is used nineteen times in this chapter alone. Originally it referred to the estimate of the priest, but its usage in this chapter as well as the context show that the "estimate" became a more-or-less fixed amount, depending on the age and sex of the person so dedicated. TEV states directly "**by the payment of the following sums of money.**" This expression also occurs five times in verses 3-7 below, but in some languages it may be better to leave it implicit in the verses that follow, as TEV has done.

TEV also makes explicit the fact that this whole passage concerns the setting free of persons dedicated. The words "**that person may be set free . . .**" provide a good model for many other languages.

27.3-7 RSV TEV

RSV	TEV
3 then your valuation of a male from twenty years old up to sixty years old shall be fifty shekels of silver, according to the shekel of the sanctuary. 4 If the person is a female, your valuation shall be thirty shekels. 5 If the person is from five years old up to twenty years old, your valuation shall be for a male twenty shekels, and for a female ten shekels. 6 If the person is from a month old up to five years old, your valuation shall be for a male five shekels of silver, and for a female your valuation shall be three shekels of silver. 7 And if the person is sixty years old and upward, then your valuation for a male shall be fifteen shekels, and for a female ten shekels.	3-7 according to the official standard: —adult male, twenty to sixty years old: 50 pieces of silver —adult female: 30 pieces of silver —young male, five to twenty years old: 20 pieces of silver —young female: 10 pieces of silver —infant male under five: 5 pieces of silver —infant female: 3 pieces of silver —male above sixty years of age: 15 pieces of silver —female above sixty: 10 pieces of silver

The organization of this whole passage from verse 3 through verse 7 may be radically altered according to the receptor language habits regarding such lists. In some cases it may even be appropriate to number the eight different categories listed here. And in many languages, the reduction of repetition will be required. In other cases this information may be presented in table form. For example:

		MALE	FEMALE
AGE:	0-4	5	3
	5-19	20	10
	20-59	50	30
	60 and over	15	10

According to the shekel of the sanctuary: the term **shekel** itself refers to a weight or a coin weighing from 8 to 16 grams. Since there was such variety in its weight and value, it was necessary to set up some kind of official standard. Thus this whole expression refers to that standard. NEB translates "the sacred standard," and NJV says "by the sanctuary weight." In some languages it may be advisable to say something like "according to the measure decided by the priests." Compare 5.15.

Because the value of various currencies in the world is constantly changing, it is not a good idea to try to fix an amount in the local currency of the receptor language. Rather, it is preferable to use a more general term like "pieces of silver" that will convey the idea of something of considerable worth without setting a specific value. The use of different figures from 3 to 50 will then give some idea of the relative value of the different types of persons involved. If the term **shekel** is borrowed in the receptor language, it must be clearly explained in a footnote or a glossary entry. However, borrowing is not recommended.

It should be noted here that in contrast with the situation described in 25.49-52, the value of the person is not based on the number of years work he or she might be expected to do in the sanctuary. The lower amount given for the female in each case reflects the cultural attitudes of the ancient Israelites.

27.8

RSV	TEV
And if a man is too poor to pay your valuation, then he shall bring the person before the priest, and the priest shall value him; according to the ability of him who vowed the priest shall value him.	If the man who made the vow is too poor to pay the standard price, he shall bring the person to the priest, and the priest will set a lower price, according to the ability of the man to pay.

A man: this is made more explicit in TEV with **"the man who made the vow."** As elsewhere in the book of Leviticus, allowance is made for the person who is financially unable to fulfill the ordinary requirements.

He shall bring the person before the priest: literally "he shall present him before the priest." This has led some to interpret this as meaning "someone shall bring the person making the vow . . . ." While this is grammatically possible, it is very unlikely and is followed by none of the English versions consulted. The context shows that the priest is to set a price on the person dedicated and not on the one who made the vow.

And the priest shall value him: the context of this statement clearly shows that what is involved is the setting of a value lower than the fixed price stated in verses 3-7. This implicit information is made explicit in TEV's **"will set a lower price,"** and this should probably also be made clear in most other languages.

27.9

RSV	TEV
"If it is an animal such as men offer as an offering to the LORD, all of such that any man gives to the LORD is holy.	If the vow concerns an animal that is acceptable as an offering to the LORD, then every gift made to the LORD is sacred,

Verses 9-13 deal with animals that have been promised to God. Here redemption is impossible except in certain well-defined cases.

It: there is no such pronoun in the Hebrew, but what is implied is clearly stated in TEV: "**If the vow concerns . . . .**" Similarly NEB, NJV (with "[the vow concerns]" in square brackets), and JB. NAB has "If the offering vowed to the LORD is . . . ."

Such as men offer: this may be translated in some languages by the habitual form of the verb, "regularly-offer," if this also implies the acceptability of the offering. In other languages it will be better to say "an animal which is approved for sacrifice" or ". . . that can be offered," or simply "that is ritually clean." On the animals that are considered ritually pure, see chapter 11 as well as Deuteronomy 14.3-21.

All of such: or "every gift of this kind," "any such animal" (NJB), or "every such animal" (NAB). The has the character of a general statement.

Holy: see 2.3.

27.10	RSV	TEV

He shall not substitute anything for it or exchange it, a good for a bad, or a bad for a good; and if he makes any exchange of beast for beast, then both it and that for which it is exchanged shall be holy.	**and the man who made the vow may not substitute another animal for it. If he does, both animals belong to the LORD.**

He: this refers to the person who made the promise to God.

Substitute . . . exchange: these two verbs have very similar meanings but may be slightly different. According to some writers **substitute** gives the idea of replacing one animal by an exact equivalent, while **exchange** is to replace with something different. But the Septuagint translated the two by a single term. And they may be translated by a single verb in the receptor language, if synonyms cannot be found, or if it would be unnatural to use two verbs here.

A good for a bad, or a bad for a good: this information is left implicit in TEV, but it emphasizes that substitutes are forbidden under all circumstances—even when the worshiper wants to provide a better animal than originally presented. In some languages this may be stated as follows "even if a better animal is presented."

Be holy: dynamically rendered "**belong to the LORD**" in this context.

27.11	RSV	TEV

And if it is an unclean animal such as is not offered as an offering to the LORD, then the man shall bring the animal before the priest,	**But if the vow concerns a ritually unclean animal, which is not acceptable as an offering to the LORD, the man shall take the animal to the priest.**

It: see verse 9.

An unclean animal: this points up the contrast with the previously- mentioned animal, which was ritually pure.

Such as is not offered: this is the opposite of "such as men offer" in verse 9. It may be translated "that is unacceptable . . . ," or "that is ritually unclean," or something similar.

The man shall bring the animal . . . : compare verse 8, where a human being is involved.

27.12	RSV	TEV

and the priest shall value it as either good or bad; as you, the priest, value it, so it shall be.	The priest shall set a price for it, according to its good or bad qualities, and the price will be final.

Value it: compare verse 8.

As either good or bad: literally, "as good and as bad." NJV translates "whether high or low," and AT has "midway between high and low." But most commentators interpret this as meaning "taking into account its good and bad points." This may also be stated "considering both what is good and what is bad [about it]."

You, the priest: here RSV shifts from the third person to the second person singular, but some versions (Mft, for example) translate this as a sort of vocative, "O priest." In any case it would be misleading to reflect the change in pronouns in the receptor language. In almost all languages the third person singular pronoun should be maintained throughout.

So it shall be: this indicates that the decision of the priest is not negotiable. What he decides is final. Another way of saying this is "whatever the priest decides, that is what the price will be" or "and it must be just as he decides."

27.13	RSV	TEV

But if he wishes to redeem it, he shall add a fifth to the valuation.	If the man wishes to buy it back, he must pay the price plus an additional 20 percent.

But: there seems to be no reason for a strong contrasting conjunction here. In most versions this word is either translated "and" or omitted altogether.

Wishes to redeem it: or "wants to buy it back." Compare 25.25. This is intended to respond to the question of what to do in case the person offering such an animal changes his mind and decides he wants it back.

Add a fifth: see 5.16 and 22.14.

The valuation: that is, the price. See verse 2.

27.14   RSV   TEV

"When a man dedicates his   When someone dedicates his
house to be holy to the LORD, the   house to the LORD, the priest shall
priest shall value it as either good or   set the price according to its good or
bad; as the priest values it, so it   bad points, and the price will be
shall stand.   final.

Dedicates: see 22.3.

To be holy to the LORD: or "to belong to the LORD."

As either good or bad: see verse 12. In the case of a house, the value was
apparently set with a view to the state of the building at the time it was offered,
rather than the good and bad points of the original construction.

So it shall stand: although the verb ("remain" in Hebrew) differs from the
expression found at the end of verse 12 ("be"), the meaning is practically the same.
If the translator wishes to make a distinction, this one may be rendered "the price
will remain as the priest decides."

27.15   RSV   TEV

And if he who dedicates it wishes to   If the one who dedicated the house
redeem his house, he shall add a   wishes to buy it back, he must pay
fifth of the valuation in money to it,   the price plus an additional 20 per-
and it shall be his.   cent.

He who dedicates it: instead of repeating the information given in the
previous verse, it may be stylistically more appropriate to use a synonymous
expression like "the owner."

Wishes to redeem his house: see verse 13.

And it shall be his: this information is left implicit in TEV, but in many
languages there will be no harm in making it explicit. In some cases a separate
sentence may be preferable: "If he does this, it will belong to him again."

27.16   RSV   TEV

"If a man dedicates to the LORD   If a man dedicates part of his
part of the land which is his by inher-   land to the LORD, the price shall be
itance, then your valuation shall be   set according to the amount of seed
according to the seed for it; a sow-   it takes to sow it, at the rate of ten
ing of a homer of barley shall be   pieces of silver per bushel [for every
valued at fifty shekels of silver.   twenty kilograms] of barley.

Verses 16-24 deal with fields that have been promised to God by a special vow.
The first part concerns fields owned due to a family inheritance (16-21), and the
second has to do with land bought from another person.

In order to understand this paragraph properly, it is necessary to know what the usual practice would have been in such a case. If all the land dedicated to God, even during a limited period of time, had been given over to the priests, they would not have been able to take care of it. It is likely that, except in unusual cases, the land remained under the control of the owner. He would then fulfill his vow by the payment of a sum of money equivalent to the value of the land for the period of dedication. This had the important social consequence of allowing a poor person to keep on using the land and producing crops for a relatively small price (see the end of this verse). If this were not the case, he might have lost his land to a merciless creditor (compare 25.25 and following). In view of all this, it is easier to understand the existence of the "base price" (verses 16-18), the restrictions on the owner's selling the land to someone else (verse 20), and the obligation to make the payment on the very same day that the price was fixed (verse 23).

By inheritance: this is left implicit in TEV but should probably be made explicit with something like "part of his ancestral land" (NEB), or "part of his family land," or "some of the land which his ancestors gave him."

According to the seed for it: according to the majority interpretation of this expression, the value of the land would be determined by its size. But instead of measuring the field's length and width, it was measured by the amount of seed required to plant the entire area. JB, on the other hand, understands this expression to mean "according to its productivity" (NJB has ". . . its yield"). That is, according to the amount of seed (or grain) it would produce rather than the amount it would require for sowing. This latter interpretation seems to be more in keeping with what agricultural experts would expect. So translators are advised to follow the model provided by NJB, in which **seed** is understood as referring to the amount of grain produced rather than the amount planted.

Homer: according to Ezekiel 45.11 this dry measure was equal to ten "ephahs." And it is also said to be the same as the "kor." But this tells us nothing that the modern reader can relate to. Estimates of its value vary from 220 kilograms or 6 bushels (see NIV note) to 400 kilograms or about 11 bushels (see Snaith, page 117). FRCL has 300 kilograms, and GECL has 150 kilograms. The TEV rendering is based on the homer being equal to one hundred kilograms (British TEV), or five bushels (American TEV). But see the discussion below on the amount, **fifty shekels**.

Barley: a kind of grain used as food for both human beings and animals. See FFB, page 95-96. Compare also Exodus 9.31.

Fifty shekels: or "pieces of silver" (see verse 3). The dynamic restructuring of TEV has "**ten pieces of silver per bushel**" (US edition) or "ten pieces of silver for every twenty kilograms" (British edition). Given the uncertainty of the value of the homer, this may be correct, but FRCL retains the figure "fifty" for the pieces of silver while translating the homer as "three hundred kilograms." Even if we are unable to give exact equivalents for the shekel or for the homer, it seems clear that the price of fifty shekels over a period of fifty years (see verse 17), or a shekel per year, is a relatively small price to pay.

27.17   RSV   TEV

If he dedicates his field from the year of jubilee, it shall stand at your full valuation;	If he dedicates the land immediately after a Year of Restoration, the full price applies.

From: the preposition used here may be understood as meaning "in" or "during" (NJB and NIV), or "**immediately after**" (TEV). Since the cycle began again after the Year of Jubilee was over, it is probably better to translate the idea "beginning as soon as the Year of Restoration is over."

The year of jubilee: see 25.10.

It shall stand at your full valuation: the verb used here is the same as at the end of verse 14. There is no word in the Hebrew text corresponding to **full**, but it is clearly implied. On the expression **your valuation**, see verse 2.

27.18   RSV   TEV

but if he dedicates his field after the jubilee, then the priest shall compute the money-value for it according to the years that remain until the year of jubilee, and a deduction shall be made from your valuation.	If he dedicates it any time later, the priest shall estimate the cash value according to the number of years left until the next Year of Restoration, and set a reduced price.

But: since there is a clear contrast between the dedication of a field during or immediately after the Year of Restoration, and a dedication which takes place later (after the restoration year is over), it will be preferable in some languages to use a conjunction like **but**, indicating contrast here.

After the jubilee: this is clearly not immediately after the Year of Restoration but some time later in the fifty-year cycle. It may be necessary to translate it "some time later, after the end of the Year of Restoration."

Until the year of jubilee: or "**until the next Year of Restoration.**"

A deduction shall be made from your valuation: or "you must subtract the value of the years that have passed [since the last Year of Restoration] from the set price." This phrase actually repeats information already given, so that the last two phrases of this verse may be translated as one in some languages. For example, "the priest must fix a lower price, considering the number of years that are left until the next Year of Restoration."

27.19   RSV   TEV

And if he who dedicates the field wishes to redeem it, then he shall add a fifth of the valuation in money to it, and it shall remain his.	If the man who dedicated the field wishes to buy it back, he must pay the price plus an additional 20 percent,

Although the wording is slightly different, the meaning of this verse is equivalent to verse 15, where the subject is "house" in place of "land."

Add a fifth: see verse 13 and 5.16.

And it shall remain his: compare verse 15, where the same idea is expressed with the verb "to be" in place of the verb **remain**. This is the same difference noted at the end of verses 12 and 14.

27.20	RSV	TEV

But if he does not wish to redeem the field, or if he has sold the field to another man, it shall not be redeemed any more;	If he sells the field to someone else without first buying it back from the LORD, he loses the right to buy it back.

This verse is difficult to understand. There are two possible interpretations that are quite different: it is grammatically possible that the subject of the verb "sell" is not the same as the subject of "redeem." In this case the verse means "If he [the owner] does not want to buy the field back, and someone [one of the priests?] sells it, it can no longer be redeemed." But it is much more likely that the owner is the subject of both verbs. The meaning is then that the owner, after having dedicated his field to God, then sold it to someone else. This of course implies that the field was not really under the control of the priests but remained in the hands of the person who dedicated it (see verse 16). So the owner, who had failed to fulfill his agreement, would be punished by never again being able to buy the land back. This is the interpretation followed by almost all versions consulted.

But: since the description of the sale of the field, which follows, contrasts with its redemption in the previous verses, it is advisable in some languages to use a connecting word that marks this contrast.

It shall not be redeemed any more: this passive construction may be rendered actively as "they [indefinite] will never allow him to redeem it" or "he can never buy it back."

27.21	RSV	TEV

but the field, when it is released in the jubilee, shall be holy to the LORD, as a field that has been devoted; the priest shall be in possession of it.	At the next Year of Restoration the field will become the LORD's permanent property; it shall belong to the priests.

When it is released: literally "in its going out." That is, at the time when things normally revert to their original owners. But since this land cannot go back to its owner, it goes to the priests, who hold it for the LORD. Compare 25.28.

Holy to the LORD: clearly meaning "belong to the LORD" or "the LORD's possession" in this context.

Devoted: this is different from "consecrated" (in 8.15, for example) or "dedicates" (verses 14 and following). It means "set apart absolutely and irrevocably." The corresponding Hebrew word is a kind of technical term for something that must be completely withdrawn from human use. Anything that was so "devoted" to another god had to be totally destroyed (Joshua 6.18-21). But what was "devoted" to the LORD was considered so absolutely his that it could never be redeemed. The TEV rendering at this point seems weak. Others have translated "proscribed" (NJV), "under ban" (JB), "vowed unconditionally" (NJB), and "doomed" (NAB). Translators should look for as strong a term as possible to express the idea of something absolutely and forever given over to the LORD. And it should be clearly distinguished from the verb "dedicate," used elsewhere in this chapter.

The priest: the singular form here has a collective value and should therefore be translated as a plural. The land does not become the property of any individual priest but of the entire priestly family.

27.22 RSV	TEV
If he dedicates to the LORD a field which he has bought, which is not a part of his possession by inheritance,	If a man dedicates to the LORD a field that he has bought,

He: the subject pronoun here refers to the same hypothetical "man" mentioned in verse 16. But since this really means "any person," it may be better in some languages to repeat the noun in place of the pronoun here. NAB has "some man."

Dedicates: see verse 14. And the translation should be sure to make a distinction between this word and "devoted" in verse 21.

Not a part of his possession by inheritance: this has been left implicit in TEV, since the words "**which he has bought**" convey this idea. However, in many languages it will be quite acceptable to reemphasize the fact that the field in question is not inherited land.

27.23 RSV	TEV
then the priest shall compute the valuation for it up to the year of jubilee, and the man shall give the amount of the valuation on that day as a holy thing to the LORD.	the priest shall estimate its value according to the number of years until the next Year of Restoration, and the man must pay the price that very day; the money belongs to the LORD.

Compare 25.25-28.

The priest shall compute the valuation for it: this may also be understood to mean "the priest shall calculate the value for him," but this is followed only by NJV. Actually the calculation is both "of it" [the field] and "for him" [the owner]. In some languages it will be possible to make these both explicit in translation.

The man: literally "he," but the pronoun needs to be made more explicit, because there may be a danger of confusion with the priest mentioned at the beginning of the verse.

On that day: on the same day that the price was fixed by the priest, the man was expected to make the payment.

A holy thing to the LORD: or "belonging to the LORD." See 19.8.

27.24   RSV   TEV

In the year of jubilee the field shall return to him from whom it was bought, to whom the land belongs as a possession by inheritance.	At the Year of Restoration the field shall be returned to the original owner or to his descendants.

The field shall return: in some languages it may be necessary to reword this to say "they [indefinite] must return the field . . ." or "the man who bought the field must give it back . . . ." It may not be possible for the field to be the subject of the verb "return." TEV puts the verb in the passive form, but this is not a realistic solution for those languages that do not commonly use passives. Compare 25.28.

Him from whom it was bought: or "the man who sold it to him," or simply "the seller."

To whom the land belongs as a possession by inheritance: this is taken by TEV as a reference to the descendants of the man who originally sold the property. The assumption is that in some cases the original seller would have died before the land could be returned. While there are few other versions that follow this interpretation, it has much to commend it.

27.25   RSV   TEV

Every valuation shall be according to the shekel of the sanctuary: twenty gerahs shall make a shekel.	All prices shall be set according to the official standard.

The shekel of the sanctuary: that is, the official rate of value. See verse 3.

Gerahs: a unit of weight which was, according to this verse, one twentieth of a shekel. Compare also Exodus 30.13. A literal translation as in RSV is meaningless to today's reader, who is ignorant of the fact that the "gerah" was the smallest unit of measurement in the system used at that time. It was equivalent to about a half a gram. This information is, however, retained in FRCL, with "of which the basic unit weighs 10 grams." Another possible translation of this verse is "Every amount shall be decided according to the official measure, which may be divided into twenty parts."

Some versions add a section heading at this point to summarize the content of the following verses (26-34). FRCL inserts "Various offerings," while NJB has "Particular rules for redemption" and then provides the following subheadings:

(a) of the firstborn (26-27)
(b) of things vowed unconditionally (28-29)
(c) of tithes (30-34)

Such a detailed subdivision will, however, not be necessary in most languages.

27.26 RSV	TEV
"But a firstling of animals, which as a firstling belongs to the LORD, no man may dedicate; whether ox or sheep, it is the LORD's.	The first-born of an animal already belongs to the LORD, so no one may dedicate it to him as a free-will offering. A calf, a lamb, or a kid belongs to the LORD,

But: in Hebrew this verse begins with an adverb which indicates at the same time contrast and emphasis. This has been left implicit in TEV because a new paragraph begins here. It is possible in some languages to convey the essential idea of this adverb by beginning "However, ..." (AT) or "Note that . . ." (NAB). NJV has "A firstling of animals, however, ..." And JB restructures the verse somewhat, to begin the verse "No one, however, may consecrate the first-born of his cattle, for it belongs to Yahweh by right . . . ."

Firstling: this refers to the first offspring born of a female animal. If the receptor language has a special term for the first-born animal, it should be used here.

Belongs to the LORD: TEV brings out the underlying fact that the animal "**already**" belongs to God. This is why it could not be further "dedicated." Compare Exodus 13.2 and 34.19.

Whether ox or sheep: for the terminology used to refer to these animals, see 1.2,10 and 4.10. If the receptor language has specific terms for the newborn or the very young of these animals (male and female), they should be used here. Compare 7.23.

27.27 RSV	TEV
And if it is an unclean animal, then he shall buy it back at your valuation, and add a fifth to it; or, if it is not redeemed, it shall be sold at your valuation.	but the first-born of an unclean animal may be bought back at the standard price plus an additional 20 percent. If it is not bought back, it may be sold to someone else at the standard price.

It: the pronoun here refers to any first-born animal. In some cases one will have to say "If the first-born animal happens to be unclean, then . . ." or, as in TEV, the conditional may be transformed to a direct statement.

He shall buy it back: the pronoun **he** refers to the original owner. This should probably be made explicit in most languages. The verb **buy . . . back** has the same meaning as **redeemed**, so they may be translated the same, if synonyms are not available.

<u>Your valuation</u>: see verse 3.

<u>Add a fifth</u>: see verse 13 and 5.16.

<u>Be sold</u>: the passive formulation may be changed to say "they [indefinite] shall sell it," or "the priest may sell it to someone else," or simply "someone else may buy it."

27.28

RSV	TEV
"But no devoted thing that a man devotes to the LORD, of anything that he has, whether of man or beast, or of his inherited field, shall be sold or redeemed; every devoted thing is most holy to the LORD.	No one may sell or buy back what he has unconditionally dedicated[n] to the LORD, whether it is a human being, an animal, or land. It belongs permanently to the LORD.

[n] UNCONDITIONALLY DEDICATED: *Anything dedicated in this way belonged completely to the LORD and could not be used; it had to be destroyed.*

<u>Devoted thing that a man devotes</u>: the noun is the same as seen in verse 21 above. But the verb also has the same root, and the use of the two together simply reinforces the meaning. The use of the word **thing** may be misleading in some languages since, according to the context, human beings and animals are included. One way to avoid this problem is to restructure as NJV has done: "But of all that a man owns, be it man or beast or land of his holding, nothing that he has proscribed for the LORD may be sold or redeemed; every proscribed thing is totally consecrated to the LORD."

<u>Inherited field</u>: the idea of inherited is again left implicit in TEV, but since there is a clear distinction between land received by inheritance and land bought from another person, this detail should be included in the receptor language translation.

<u>Is most holy to the LORD</u>: literally "is holy of holy things to the LORD." This may be rendered "definitely (or, surely) belongs to the LORD."

27.29

RSV	TEV
No one devoted, who is to be utterly destroyed from among men, shall be ransomed; he shall be put to death.	Not even a human being who has been unconditionally dedicated may be bought back; he must be put to death.

<u>No one devoted</u>: here the reference is definitely to a human being. This should be made clear in translation. Compare verses 21 and 28 above. TEV adds the word **"even,"** to reinforce the importance of the act and stress the fact that it was absolutely final and could not be changed.

Utterly destroyed: the word used here has the same root as **devoted** above and is virtually synonymous with **be put to death** at the end of the verse. For this reason it is left implicit in TEV and NEB. Compare Exodus 22.20.

Ransomed: this is different from the word translated "redeemed" in verses 27, 28, and elsewhere, but the meaning is essentially the same.

Be put to death: literally "dying he shall die." The passive formulation of RSV may be translated "they must certainly kill him" or "he must surely die" in many languages. See 20.2.

27.30 RSV	TEV
"All the tithe of the land, whether of the seed of the land or of the fruit of the trees, is the LORD's; it is holy to the LORD.	One tenth of all the produce of the land, whether grain or fruit, belongs to the LORD.

The tithe: with the possible exception of Genesis 14.20, this is the first clear reference to a **tithe** to the Lord in the Old Testament (unless Jacob's bargaining position in Gen 28.22 is taken as a kind of tithe). In this verse it refers to that part of what the soil produces (one tenth of the total) that the Israelites dedicated to God as a sign of their gratitude to him. It provided the basic revenue of the priests and Levites serving God in the sanctuary. Compare Numbers 18. In some languages the idea of the tithe in this verse may have to be translated by an expression like "One kilogram [or whatever measure is commonly used] of grain for every ten produced, and one piece of fruit of every ten produced belongs to the LORD."

The seed of the land: most versions take this to refer to "**grain**" (TEV, NIV, NAB, AT, Mft). But the rendering of NJB is even more general, "the produce of the soil." It would probably be misleading in most languages to translate **seed** literally.

27.31 RSV	TEV
If a man wishes to redeem any of his tithe, he shall add a fifth to it.	If a man wishes to buy any of it back, he must pay the standard price plus an additional 20 per cent.

Redeem any of his tithe: since the tithe is thought of in terms of money in many cultures today, it may be better to make this more explicit, with something like "If a person wants to buy back any of the grain or fruit he has given to the LORD . . . ."

Add a fifth to it: that is, twenty percent more than the usual price. See verse 13 and 5.16.

27.32   RSV   TEV

And all the tithe of herds and flocks, every tenth animal of all that pass under the herdsman's staff, shall be holy to the LORD.	One of every ten domestic animals belongs to the LORD. When the animals are counted, every tenth one belongs to the LORD.

Herds and flocks: although the plural is used in RSV here, the words are the same as in 1.2, where they are translated as singular in form.

That pass under the herdsman's staff: according to Jewish commentators, this expression is an allusion to the way in which animals were selected for the tithe. The animals were counted as they passed single file under the staff of the herdsman. Every tenth animal was marked with a red colored stick, to show that it had been chosen for the tithe. If this image can be retained in the receptor-language translation while at the same time clearly conveying the idea of counting, then this will probably be better. But the details of the actual procedure are less important than the fact that one of every ten animals was to be designated as belonging to the LORD. One possible formulation may be "When you count your animals, cattle, sheep or goats, every tenth animal must be marked as belonging to the LORD."

27.33   RSV   TEV

A man shall not inquire whether it is good or bad, neither shall he exchange it; and if he exchanges it, then both it and that for which it is exchanged shall be holy; it shall not be redeemed."	The owner may not arrange the animals so that the poor animals are chosen, and he may not make any substitutions. If he does substitute one animal for another, then both animals will belong to the LORD and may not be bought back.

A man: more specifically "the owner of the animals" or "the man to whom the animals belong."

Shall not inquire whether it is good or bad: the temptation must have been great to examine [**inquire**] the animals and then arrange [**exchange**] them in such a way that the poorer quality sheep or goats would be selected for the tithe (compare Malachi 1.8). Such a practice is specifically forbidden in this verse.

If he exchanges it . . . : see verse 10.

It shall not be redeemed: while the pronoun **it** gives the impression of one animal, the subject here is actually the two animals—the substitute and the original. Neither could be bought back, if such an attempt was made. The passive **be redeemed** may be rendered "the owner may not buy back either one of them, because they both belong to the LORD."

27.34   RSV   TEV

These are the commandments which the LORD commanded Moses for the people of Israel on Mount Sinai.	These are the commands that the LORD gave Moses on Mount Sinai for the people of Israel.

This verse serves as a conclusion to chapter 27 and to the whole book of Leviticus as we now have it. Because of its summary character, it should be made a separate paragraph, as in most English versions. While the wording is slightly different and less detailed than 26.46, the meaning is essentially the same.

Bibliography

Lexicons

Brown, Francis; Samuel R. Driver; and Charles A. Briggs. 1907. *A Hebrew and English Lexicon of the Old Testament.* London: Oxford University Press.

Holladay, William L. 1971. *A Concise Hebrew and Aramaic Lexicon of the Old Testament.* Grand Rapids, Michigan: Eerdmans.

Books

Buttrick, George A. 1962. *The Interpreter's Dictionary of the Bible.* Four volumes. New York: Abingdon Press.

Committee on Translations. 1972, 1980. *Fauna and Flora of the Bible.* New York: United Bible Societies. (Cited as FFB.)

Crim, Keith. 1976. *The Interpreter's Dictionary of the Bible.* Supplementary volume. Nashville: Abingdon Press.

de Vaux, Roland. 1961. *Ancient Israel.* Two volumes. New York: McGraw-Hill.

Einspahr, Bruce. 1976. *Index to the Brown, Driver and Briggs Hebrew Lexicon.* Chicago: Moody.

Preliminary and Interim Report on the Hebrew Old Testament Text Project. Volume 1. 1973. Stuttgart: United Bible Societies. (Cited as HOTTP.)

Nida, Eugene, and Charles Taber. 1969. *The Theory and Practice of Translation.* Leiden: E.J. Brill.

Orlinsky, Harry M., editor. 1969. *Notes on the New Translation of the Torah.* Philadelphia: Jewish Publication Society of America.

Wolff, Hans Walter. 1974. *Anthropology of the Old Testament.* Philadelphia: Fortress Press.

Wonderly, William L. 1968. *Bible Translations for Popular Use.* New York: United Bible Societies.

Zohary, Michael. 1982. *Plants of the Bible.* New York: Cambridge University Press.

Articles

Andersen, Johs. G. 1980. "Leprosy in translations of the Bible," *The Bible Translator* 31 (April):207-212.

Arichea, Daniel. 1981. "Translating the biblical festivals," *The Bible Translator* 32 (October):413-423.

Baker, David W. 1978. "Division markers and the structure of Leviticus 1-7," *Studia Biblica* 1:9-15.

Barr, James. 1984. *"Midrash* in the Old Testament," *Journal of Semitic Studies* 29:15-31.

Ellington, John. 1978. "Translating the O.T. months into Zaïrian languages," *The Bible Translator* 29 (October):409-413.

————. 1983. "Translating Old Testament book titles," *The Bible Translator* 34 (April):225-231.

Hallaire, Jacques. 1988. "Trois problèmes de traduction," *Cahiers de traduction biblique* 10:11-14.

Hope, Edward R., and Ignatius Chidavaenzi. 1984. "Translating the divine name *YHWH* in Shona," *The Bible Translator* 35 (April):211-215.

Loewen, Jacob A. 1984. "The names of God in the New Testament," *The Bible Translator* 35 (April):208-211.

————. 1984. "The names of God in the Old Testament," *The Bible Translator* 35 (April):201-207.

Osborn, Noel D. 1990. "Tent or tabernacle? Translating two traditions," *The Bible Translator* 41 (April):214-221.

Bible Texts and Versions Cited

Die Bibel in heutigem Deutsch: Die Gute Nachricht des Alten und Neuen Testaments. 1982. Stuttgart: Deutsche Bibelgesellschaft. (Cited as GECL.)

La Bible: L'Ancien Testament. 1959. Two volumes. Translation and notes by Édouard Dhorme, Frank Michaéli, and Antoine Guillaumont. Paris: Gallimard. (Cited as *Bible de la Pléiade.*)

La Bible de Jérusalem. 1973. Paris: Éditions du Cerf. (Cited as BJ.)

La Bible du rabbinat français. 1978. Paris: Librarie Colbo.

La Bible en français courant. 1982. Paris: Société biblique française. (Cited as FRCL.)

The Bible: A New Translation. 1922. Revised Edition 1935. Translated by James Moffatt. London, New York: Harper and Row. (Cited as Mft.)

The Complete Bible: An American Translation. 1923. Translated by J.M. Powis Smith and Edgar J. Goodspeed. Chicago: University of Chicago Press. (Cited as AT.)

Good News Bible: The Bible in Today's English Version. 1976, 1979. New York: American Bible Society. (Cited as TEV.)

The Holy Bible. 1955. Ronald A. Knox, translator. London: Burns & Gates. (Cited as Knox.)

The Holy Bible (King James Version). 1611. (Cited as KJV.)

The Holy Bible: New International Version. 1973, 1978. Grand Rapids, Michigan: Zondervan. (Cited as NIV.)

The Holy Bible (Newly edited by the American Revision Committee). 1901. New York: Thomas Nelson. (Cited as American Standard Version.)

The Holy Bible (Revised Standard Version). 1952, 1971, 1973. New York: Division of Christian Education of the National Council of Churches of Christ in the USA. (Cited as RSV.)

The Jerusalem Bible. 1966. Garden City, New York: Doubleday. (Cited as JB.)

The Living Bible. 1971. Translated by Kenneth Taylor. Wheaton, Illinois: Tyndale House. (Cited as LB.)

The Modern Language Bible: The New Berkeley Version in Modern English. 1945, 1959, 1969. Revised edition. Gerrit Verkuyl, editor. Grand Rapids, Michigan: Zondervan.

The New American Bible. 1970. Paterson, New Jersey: St. Anthony Guild. (Cited as NAB.)

New American Standard Bible. 1960, 1973. Chicago: Moody Press. (Cited as NASB.)

The New English Bible. 1961, 1970. London: Oxford University Press, and Cambridge University Press. (Cited as NEB.)

The New Jerusalem Bible. 1985. Garden City, New York: Doubleday. (Cited as NJB.)

The Revised English Bible. 1989. London: Oxford University Press, and Cambridge University Press.

La Sainte Bible: Nouvelle version Segond révisée. 2me édition. 1978. Paris: Société biblique française. (Cited as Segond.)

The Torah: The Five Books of Moses. 1962. Philadelphia: The Jewish Publication Society of America. (Cited as NJV.)

Traduction œcuménique de la Bible: Ancien Testament. 1975. Paris: Éditions du Cerf. (Cited as TOB.)

Commentaries

Black, Matthew. 1962. *Peake's Commentary on the Bible.* London and Edinburgh: Thomas Nelson.

Brown, Raymond E.; Joseph A. Fitzmeyer; and Roland E. Murphy. 1968. *The Jerome Biblical Commentary.* Englewood Cliffs, New Jersey: Prentice-Hall.

Harrison, R.K. 1980. *Leviticus: An Introduction and Commentary* (Tyndale Old Testament Commentaries). Downers Grove, Illinois: Inter-Varsity.

Keil, C.F., and F. Delitzsch. 1956. *Biblical Commentary on the Old Testament: The Pentateuch* (Volume 2). Grand Rapids, Michigan: Eerdmans.

Noth, Martin. 1965. *Leviticus: A Commentary* (Old Testament Library). Philadelphia: Westminster Press.

Porter, J.R. 1976. *Leviticus* (The Cambridge Bible Commentary on the New English Bible). New York: Cambridge University Press.

Snaith, N.H. 1969. *Leviticus and Numbers* (New Century Bible). London: Oliphant's.

Wenham, G.J. 1979. *The Book of Leviticus* (New International Commentary on the Old Testament). Grand Rapids, Michigan: Eerdmans.

Glossary

This Glossary contains terms which are technical from an exegetical or a linguistic viewpoint. Other terms not defined here may be referred to in a Bible dictionary.

ACTIVE. See **VOICE.**

ADJECTIVE is a word which limits, describes, or qualifies a noun. In English, "red," "tall," "beautiful," and "important" are adjectives.

ADVERB is a word which limits, describes, or qualifies a verb, an adjective, or another adverb. In English, "quickly," "soon," "primarily," and "very" are adverbs.

AMBIGUOUS (AMBIGUITY) describes a word or phrase which in a specific context may have two or more different meanings. For example, "Bill did not leave because John came" could mean either (1) "the coming of John prevented Bill from leaving" or (2) "the coming of John was not the cause of Bill's leaving." It is often the case that what is ambiguous in written form is not ambiguous when actually spoken, since features of intonation and slight pauses usually make clear which of two or more meanings is intended. Furthermore, even in written discourse, the entire context normally serves to indicate which meaning is intended by the writer.

APPOSITION (APPOSITIONAL) is the placing of two expressions together so that they both refer to the same object, event, or concept; for example, "my friend, Mr. Smith."

ARTICLE is a grammatical class of words, often obligatory, which indicate whether the following word is definite or indefinite. In English the **DEFINITE ARTICLE** is "the," and the **INDEFINITE ARTICLE** is "a" or ("an").

BORROWED WORD refers to a foreign term that is used in another language. For example, "matador" is a Spanish word that has been borrowed by English speakers for "bullfighter."

CAUSATIVE (CAUSAL) relates to events and indicates that someone or something caused something to happen, rather than that the person or thing did it directly. In "John ran the horse," the verb "ran" is a causative, since it was not John who ran, but rather it was John who caused the horse to run.

CHIASMUS (CHIASTIC) is a reversal of the order of words or phrases in an otherwise parallel construction. For example: "I (1) / was shapen (2) / in iniquity (3) // in sin (3) / did my mother conceive (2) / me (1)."

CLAUSE is a grammatical construction, normally consisting of a subject and a predicate. An **INDEPENDENT CLAUSE** may stand alone. The **MAIN CLAUSE** is that clause in a sentence which could stand alone as a complete sentence, but which has one or more dependent or subordinate clauses related to it. A **SUBORDINATE CLAUSE** is dependent on the main clause, but it does not form a complete sentence.

COLLECTIVE refers to a number of things (or persons) considered as a whole. In English, a collective noun is considered to be singular or plural, more or less on the basis of traditional usage; for example, "The crowd is (the people are) becoming angry."

COMMON LANGUAGE TRANSLATION is one that uses only that portion of the total resources of a language that is understood and accepted by all as good usage. Excluded are features peculiar to a dialect, substandard or vulgar language, and technical or highly literary language not understood by all.

COMPLEMENT is a word or phrase which grammatically completes another word or phrase. The term is used particularly of expressions which specify time, place, manner, means, etc.

CONDITIONAL refers to a clause or phrase which expresses or implies a condition, in English usually introduced by "if."

CONJUNCTIONS are words which serve as connectors between words, phrases, clauses, and sentences. "And," "but," "if," and "because" are typical conjunctions in English.

CONNOTATION involves the emotional attitude of a speaker (or writer) to an expression he uses, and the emotional response of the hearers (or readers). Connotations may be good or bad, strong or weak, and they are often described in such terms as "colloquial," "taboo," "vulgar," "old-fashioned," and "intimate."

CONSONANTS are symbols representing those speech sounds which are produced by obstructing, blocking, or restricting the free passage of air from the lungs through the mouth. They were originally the only spoken sounds recorded in the Hebrew system of writing; **VOWELS** were added later as marks associated with the **CONSONANTS**. See also **VOWELS**.

CONSTRUCTION. See **STRUCTURE**.

CONTEXT (CONTEXTUAL) is that which precedes and/or follows any part of a discourse. For example, the context of a word or phrase in Scripture would be the other words and phrases associated with it in the sentence, paragraph, section, and even the entire book in which it occurs. The context of a term often affects its meaning, so that a word does not mean exactly the same thing in one context that it does in another context.

DEFINITE ARTICLE. See ARTICLE.

DIRECT DISCOURSE, DIRECT QUOTATION, DIRECT SPEECH. See DISCOURSE.

DISCOURSE is the connected and continuous communication of thought by means of language, whether spoken or written. The way in which the elements of a discourse are arranged is called DISCOURSE STRUCTURE. DIRECT DISCOURSE (or, DIRECT QUOTATION, DIRECT SPEECH) is the reproduction of the actual words of one person quoted and included in the discourse of another person; for example, "He declared 'I will have nothing to do with this man.' " INDIRECT DISCOURSE (or, INDIRECT QUOTATION, INDIRECT SPEECH) is the reporting of the words of one person within the discourse of another person, but in an altered grammatical form rather than as an exact quotation; for example, "He said he would have nothing to do with that man."

DYNAMIC EQUIVALENCE is a type of translation in which the message of the original text is so conveyed in the receptor language that the response of the receptors is (or, can be) essentially like that of the original receptors, or that the receptors can in large measure comprehend the response of the original receptors, if, as in certain languages, the differences between the two cultures are extremely great. In recent years the term FUNCTIONAL EQUIVALENCE has been applied to what is essentially the same kind of translation.

EMPHASIS (EMPHATIC) is the special importance given to an element in a discourse, sometimes indicated by the choice of words or by position in the sentence. For example, in "Never will I eat pork again," "Never" is given emphasis by placing it at the beginning of the sentence.

EXPLICIT refers to information which is expressed in the words of a discourse. This is in contrast to implicit information. See IMPLICIT.

FIRST PERSON. See PERSON.

FUNCTIONAL EQUIVALENCE. See DYNAMIC EQUIVALENCE.

FUTURE TENSE. See TENSE.

GENERIC has reference to a general class or kind of objects, events, or abstracts; it is the opposite of SPECIFIC. For example, the term "animal" is generic in relation to "dog," which is a specific kind of animal. However, "dog" is generic in relation to the more specific term "poodle."

IMPERATIVE refers to forms of a verb which indicate commands or requests. In "Go and do likewise," the verbs "Go" and "do" are imperatives. In most languages imperatives are confined to the grammatical second person; but some languages have corresponding forms for the first and third persons. These are usually expressed in English by the use of "must" or "let"; for example, "We must not swim here!" or "They must work harder!" or "Let them eat cake!"

IMPERSONAL VERB is a usage of the verb which denotes an action by an unspecified agent. It may involve the use of the third person singular, as in "It is raining" or "One normally prefers cake," or in some languages the use of the third person plural, as in "They say . . . ," or in still other languages the use of the first person plural, as in "We cook this way," meaning "People cook this way." Such use of a pronoun is sometimes referred to as the INDEFINITE PRONOUN.

IMPLICIT (IMPLIED) refers to information that is not formally represented in a discourse, since it is assumed that it is already known to the receptor, or evident from the meaning of the words in question. For example, the phrase "the other son" carries with it the implicit information that there is a son in addition to the one mentioned. This is in contrast to EXPLICIT information, which is expressly stated in a discourse. See EXPLICIT.

INDEFINITE PRONOUN. See IMPERSONAL VERB.

INDEPENDENT CLAUSE. See CLAUSE.

INDIRECT DISCOURSE, INDIRECT QUOTATION. See DISCOURSE.

LITERAL means the ordinary or primary meaning of a term or expression, in contrast with a figurative meaning. A LITERAL TRANSLATION is one which represents the exact words and word order of the source language; such a translation is frequently unnatural or awkward in the receptor language.

OBJECT of a verb is the goal of an event or action specified by the verb. In "John hit the ball," the object of "hit" is "ball."

PARALLEL, PARALLELISM, generally refers to some similarity in the content and/or form of a construction; for example, "The man was blind, and he could not see." The structures that correspond to each other in the two statements are said to be parallel.

PARENTHETICAL statement is a statement that interrupts a discourse by departing from its main theme. It is frequently set off by marks of parenthesis ( ).

PASSIVE. See VOICE.

PERSON, as a grammatical term, refers to the speaker, the person spoken to, or the person or thing spoken about. FIRST PERSON is the person(s) speaking (such as "I," "me," "my," "mine," "we," "us," "our," or "ours"). SECOND PERSON is the person(s) or thing(s) spoken to (such as "thou," "thee," "thy," "thine," "ye," "you," "your," or "yours"). THIRD PERSON is the person(s) or thing(s) spoken about (such as "he," "she," "it," "his," "her," "them," or "their"). The examples here given are all pronouns, but in many languages the verb forms have affixes which indicate first, second, or third person and also indicate whether they are SINGULAR or PLURAL.

PHRASE is a grammatical construction of two or more words, but less than a complete clause or a sentence. A phrase is usually given a name according to its function in a sentence, such as "noun phrase," "verb phrase," or "prepositional phrase."

PLURAL refers to the form of a word which indicates more than one. See SINGULAR.

POSSESSIVE refers to a grammatical relationship in which one noun or pronoun is said to "possess" another ("John's car," "his son," "their destruction"). POSSESSIVE PRONOUNS are pronouns such as "my," "our," "your," or "his," which indicate possession.

PREPOSITION is a word (usually a particle) whose function is to indicate the relation of a noun or pronoun to another noun, pronoun, verb, or adjective. Some English prepositions are "for," "from," "in," "to," and "with."

PRONOUNS are words which are used in place of nouns, such as "he," "him," "his," "she," "we," "them," "who," "which," "this," or "these." See also POSSESSIVE PRONOUNS.

PURPOSE CLAUSE designates a construction which states the purpose involved in some other action; for example, "John came in order to help him," or "John mentioned the problem to his colleagues, so that they would know how to help out."

QUOTATION. See under DISCOURSE.

RECEPTOR is the person(s) receiving a message. The RECEPTOR LANGUAGE is the language into which a translation is made. For example, in a translation from Hebrew into German, Hebrew is the source language and German is the receptor language.

REDUNDANT (REDUNDANCY) refers to anything which is entirely predictable from the context. For example, in "John, he did it," the pronoun "he" is redundant. A feature may be redundant and yet may be important to retain in certain languages, perhaps for stylistic or for grammatical reasons.

REFERENT is the thing(s) or person(s) referred to by a pronoun, phrase, or clause.

RELATIVE CLAUSE is a dependent clause which describes the object to which it refers. In "the man whom you saw," the clause "whom you saw" is relative because it relates to and describes "man."

RELATIVE PRONOUN is a pronoun which refers to a noun in another clause, and which serves to mark the subordination of its own clause to that noun; for example, in "This is the man who came to dinner," "who" is the relative pronoun referring to "the man" in the previous clause. The subordinated clause is also called a relative clause.

RESTRUCTURE. See **STRUCTURE.**

SECOND PERSON. See **PERSON.**

SENTENCE is a grammatical construction composed of one or more clauses and capable of standing alone.

SINGULAR refers to the form of a word which indicates one thing or person, in contrast to **PLURAL,** which indicates more than one. See **PLURAL.**

SPECIFIC refers to the opposite of **GENERIC.** See **GENERIC.**

STRUCTURE is the systematic arrangement of the elements of language, including the ways in which words combine into phrases, phrases into clauses, clauses into sentences, and sentences into larger units of discourse. Because this process may be compared to the building of a house or bridge, such words as **STRUCTURE** and **CONSTRUCTION** are used in reference to it. To separate and rearrange the various components of a sentence or other unit of discourse in the translation process is to **RESTRUCTURE** it.

SUBJECT is one of the major divisions of a clause, the other being the predicate. In "The small boy walked to school," "The small boy" is the subject. Typically the subject is a noun phrase. It should not be confused with the semantic "agent," or "actor."

SUPERLATIVE refers to the form of an adjective or adverb that indicates that the object or event described possesses a certain quality to a greater degree than does any other object or event implicitly or explicitly specified by the content. "Most happy" and "finest" are adjectives in the superlative degree.

SYNONYMS are words which are different in form but similar in meaning, such as "boy" and "lad." Expressions which have essentially the same meaning are said to be **SYNONYMOUS.** No two words are completely synonymous.

TENSE is usually a form of a verb which indicates time relative to a discourse or some event in a discourse. The most common forms of tense are past, present, and future.

THIRD PERSON. See **PERSON.**

TRANSITION in discourse involves passing from one thought-section or group of related thought-sections to another. **TRANSITIONAL** words, phrases, or longer passages mark the connections between two such sets of related sections and help the hearer to understand the connection.

TRANSLATION is the reproduction in a receptor language of the closest natural equivalent of a message in the source language, first, in terms of meaning, and second, in terms of style.

TRANSLITERATION is the representation in the receptor language of the approximate sounds or letters of words occurring in the source language, rather than the translation of their meaning; for example, "Amen" from the Hebrew, or the title "Christ" from the Greek.

VERBS are a grammatical class of words which express existence, action, or occurrence, such as "be," "become," "run," or "think."

VERBAL has two meanings. (1) It may refer to expressions consisting of words, sometimes in distinction to forms of communication which do not employ words ("sign language," for example). (2) It may refer to word forms which are derived from verbs. For example, "coming" and "engaged" may be called verbals, and participles are called verbal adjectives.

VOICE in grammar is the relation of the action expressed by a verb to the participants in the action. In English and many other languages, the **ACTIVE VOICE** indicates that the subject performs the action ("John hit the man"), while the PASSIVE **VOICE** indicates that the subject is being acted upon ("The man was hit").

VOWELS are symbols representing the sound of the vocal cords, produced by unobstructed air passing from the lungs though the mouth. They were not originally included in the Hebrew system of writing; they were added later as marks associated with the consonants. See also **CONSONANTS.**

Index

This index includes concepts, key words, and terms for which the Handbook contains a discussion useful for translators.

Aaron and his sons 27, 104
Aaron's sons 16
Aaron's sons the priests 37
abomination 99, 160, 277, 279
accepted 13
Adonay 10
adultery 305
afflict yourselves 258
altar 17
    altar of burnt offering 50
    altar of fragrant incense 49
amends
    make amends 421
anointed 85, 114
anointing oil 320
appear 130, 131
appendage of the liver 38
appointed feasts 341
ark 242
ashes 24
assembly 53, 56, 260
atonement 15, 117, 180, 250
    Day of Atonement 352, 353
augury 296
Azazel 246

baked in the oven 28
barley 430
bat 163
beasts 156
beer 147
before the Lord 16
behold 152
birds 162-163
blaspheme 367
blemish 13, 322

blessed 138
blood 267, 305
    eats any blood 266
bloodguilt 263
body 229, 230, 233
boil 189
booths 359
    feast of booths 355
bow down 402
bread 318, 404
breast 104, 123
breastpiece 113
breeches 80
brethren 143, 145
bronze vessel 89
brother 384
    brethren 143, 145
bull 13, 15, 130
    bull calf 129
burn 19
burnt offering 5, 9, 19

cakes 29, 95
calendar 351
    month 343
camel 158
caps 116
carnal
    lies carnally 293
carrion vulture 163
cast lots 245
cattle 12, 292
cedarwood 207
censer 141
cereal offering 5, 25, 348
chameleon 168

children 301
cistern 171
city
    walled city 387
clean 148, 182
cleansing 195
cloven-footed 157
coat 112
common 148
common people 59
community 260
confess 420
congregation 52, 131
consecrate 304, 319
    consecrated 115, 117, 124
    consecration 107
convocation 341, 342
    holy convocation 351
cormorant 163
covenant 34
    covenant of salt 34
creeping thing 329
cricket 165
crocodile 168
crop (of a bird) 23
crown, the holy 114
cud, chews the 157
curse 289, 367
cut off 99, 102, 263, 327

deaf 289
dedicate 327
defile 279, 280
devote 278
    devote . . . by fire 278
devoted 433, 437
discharge 228, 229, 235
door 13
    door of the tent 13
    door of the tent of meeting 37
drink offering 347
due 150
dung 52, 256

eagle 162
earthen vessel 88, 170
east 24
elders 54, 128

entrails 19, 38
ephah 69, 300, 347, 364
ephod 112
everlasting 260

falcon 162
fat 38
    fat tail 41
fathers 419
fear 283, 289
feasts
    appointed feasts 341
    feast of booths 355
    feast of unleavened bread 344
fell on their faces 139
fellowship offering 5, 36, 103
figured stone 402
fins 159
fire 18, 141
    devote . . . by fire 278
first fruits 33, 346
firstling 435
flay 17
flesh 99, 267
flock 12, 20, 78
flour 26
    fine flour 26
forefathers 423
foreign 141
    foreigner 258, 338
forever 83
fountain 309
frankincense 26
freewill offering 97

garment, garments 80, 109
gecko 168
generations 43, 147, 327
gerah 434
girdle 112
glory 131
    glorified 143
    glory of the Lord 131
goat demons 265
goats 20
gold, pure 363
grain 25
grain offering 5

grasshopper 165
graven image 401
griddle 29
guilt offering 5, 66, 67, 70, 72
guilty 53, 77

hallowed 340
hands
    lay . . . hands 54, 368
hare 158
harlot 298
    play the harlot 265
harvest festival 347
hawk 163
herd 12
heron 163
high places 415
hin 300, 347
holocaust 9, 19
holy 28, 84, 88, 148, 174, 304
    clean 148
    hallowed 340
    Holiness Code 262
    holy convocation 341, 342, 351
    holy garments 260
    holy place 213, 242, 250, 255
    holy thing, holy things 71, 286
    holy to the Lord 433
    unholy 141
homer 430
honey 32
hoof, parts the 157
hoopoe 163
horns
    horns of the altar 49
house 251
house of Israel 145
husband 316, 317
hyssop 208

ibis 163
idols 284, 401, 416
'im 12
image
    graven image 401
incense 141
    sweet incense 248
inherit 311

iniquity 421
    bear his iniquity 270
insects 164
interest 391, 392
intestines 52
Israel
    assembly 53
    common people 59
    congregation of Israel 52
    house of Israel 145
    Israelites 46
    people of Israel 46, 149
    sons of Israel 46
itch 194

Jehovah 10
Jubilee 375, 378
judgment 289

ki 12
kidneys 38
kite 162

laborious work 345
lamb 40, 60
lampstand 363
laver 115
law 79, 205, 218
lay . . . hands 54
leaven 32
leavened bread 96
leper 181, 199
leprosy 181, 183
    leprosy in a garment 200
    leprous 183
    mildew 200, 218, 219
Levites 388
linen 80, 243
liver
    appendage of the liver 38
living creatures 160
living things 156
lizard 168
loaves 95
locust 165
log 211
loins 38

Lord 10
>   *Adonay* 10
>   Jehovah 10
>   LORD 10
>   the Name 367
>   Yahweh 10
>   *YHWH* 10
lots
>   cast lots 245

make amends 421
male 13
mediums 298
memorial 352
memorial portion 27
mercy seat 242
mildew 200
milk and honey
>   land flowing with milk and honey 312
minchah 25
Molech 278, 301
molten gods 284
month
>   calendar 343
mouse 168

name 278
>   the Name 367
nations 280
neighbor 76, 288
nighthawk 163
north 21

oath 65
odor
>   pleasing odor to the Lord 19
offering 5, 9, 12, 96, 103
>   burnt offering 9, 19
>   cereal offering 25, 348
>   drink offering 347
>   fellowship offering 36, 103
>   freewill offering 97
>   grain offering 25
>   guilt offering 66, 67, 70, 72
>   holocaust 19
>   offering by fire 6, 19
>   offering of grain 25
>   peace offering 36, 103, 264
>   repayment offering 70, 72, 90
>   sin offering 53, 68, 70
>   special contribution 96
>   special gift 104
>   votive offering 97
>   wave offering 104
oil 26
>   pure oil 361
ordained 85
>   ordination 107
ordinance 68
osprey 162
ostrich 162
oven 28
>   baked in the oven 28
owl 163
ox 50, 130

pan 30
Passover 343, 344
peace 404
peace offering 5, 36, 103, 264
pelican 163
people 100
>   peoples 312
people of Israel 149
perversion 277, 279
pig 158
pillar 402
plate, the golden 114
pleasing odor to the Lord 19
portion 106
present the blood 16
priest, priests 16, 27
>   Aaron and his sons 27, 104
>   Aaron's sons the priests 37
>   anointed priest 47
>   High Priest 47, 320
>   priest who is chief 320
profane 278, 286, 298
pure gold 363
purified 117

qorban 25

rabbit 158
ram 78, 119

ransomed 437
raven 162
redeem 384
    redemption 384
remember 421
repayment offering 5, 70, 72, 90
Restoration
    Year of Restoration 375
revere 283
robe 112
rock badger 158
ruler 57

sabbath 259, 342, 373
sacrifice 9
sanctify 304
sanctuary 115, 144, 153, 260
    sanctuaries 325
sash 112
satyrs 265
scales 160
scapegoat 252
scarlet 208
seagull 163
sheaf 346
    first sheaf 346
sheep 20
shekel 72, 426
    shekel of the sanctuary 72, 426
shirt 112
sin offering 5, 53, 68, 70
sins 46
slave 331, 393
sojourner 269, 287, 331
sons 183
soul 46, 267, 406, 408
south 21
spring 171
sprinkle 48
statute 149, 257, 271
    perpetual statute 43
stork 163
strangers 258
strong drink 147
swarming creatures 64, 160
swarming things 168
swine 158

tabernacle 114, 115, 263
tail
    fat tail 41
tent 11
    tent of meeting 6-8, 11, 115,
        250
    Tent of the Lord's presence 6,
        7, 8, 11
testimony 249, 362
thank offering 5
thanksgiving 95
thigh 104
throw the blood 16
tithe 437
token 27
trumpet 377
turban 114, 116

uncircumcised heart 420
unclean 63, 148, 182
    abomination 99
    common 148
    uncleanness 327
    uncleannesses 250
unholy 141
unleavened 29
Urim and Thummim 113

veil
    veil of the sanctuary 49
    veil of the testimony 362
votive offering 97
vow 424
vulture 162
    carrion vulture 163

wafers 29, 95
walk 271, 311, 402
walled city 387
water hen 163
wave 346
    wave offering 5, 104
weasel 168
wickedness 276
wilderness 107
wine 147
witchcraft 296
wizards 298

INDEX

wool 201
work
    laborious work 345

Yahweh 10
yeast 29, 32, 96
YHWH 10
yoke 407

PRINTED IN THE UNITED STATES OF AMERICA